UNIVERSITY LIBRARY
UW-STEVENS POINT

D0216748

CHRONOLOGICAL HISTORY OF UNITED STATES FOREIGN RELATIONS 1776 TO JANUARY 20, 1981

GARLAND REFERENCE LIBRARY
OF SOCIAL SCIENCE
(VOL. 196)

CHRONOLOGICAL HISTORY OF UNITED STATES FOREIGN RELATIONS 1776 TO JANUARY 20, 1981

Lester H. Brune
Consulting editor: Donald R. Whitnah

Volume II

GARLAND PUBLISHING, INC. • NEW YORK & LONDON
1985

© 1985 Lester H. Brune
All rights reserved

Library of Congress Cataloging in Publication Data

Brune, Lester H.
  Chronological history of the United States foreign
relations, 1776 to January 20, 1981

  (Garland reference library of social science ; v. 196)
  1. United States—Foreign relations—Chronology.
I. Title. II. Series.
E183.7.B745 1985   327.73   83-48210
ISBN 0-8240-9056-X (alk. paper)

Cover design by Stan Rosinski

Printed on acid-free, 250-year-life paper
Manufactured in the United States of America

CONTENTS

Volume I

Volume II

364288

381285

ACKNOWLEDGMENTS

Arthur Stickney of Garland Publishing suggested the idea for this chronology-history. Following up on his proposal, I discovered no similar volume which included both dates and explanations of events in U.S. foreign relations; other chronologies were simply lists containing little explanation for understanding the event. Subsequently, as I prepared items for this volume, I realized as a teacher and researcher the value of Mr. Stickney's suggestion. Checking the details of many items which I previously took for granted, I gained new insights on and a deeper understanding of events outside my personal area of expertise.

Second, I am grateful for the excellent suggestions, comments, and corrections made by my consulting editor, Dr. Donald Whitnah, who read the manuscript material in preparation. Both his assistance and his encouraging words on the project are appreciated.

Third, excellent secretarial assistance was essential to the preparation of this reference volume. Most of this work was performed by Marian Phelps, our office secretary, and Patty Schramek, my work-study assistant. In addition, Jacqueline Kandyba provided valuable help. The activity of each was both vital and greatly appreciated.

Finally, but of course, not least, I acknowledge the patience and understanding of my wife, Joan. Her concession to my home work habits enabled this project to be completed expeditiously.

I dedicate this volume to Art, Don, Marian, Patty, Jackie, and Joan.

Lester H. Brune
Bradley University
Peoria, Illinois
August 1983

FOREWORD

PURPOSE OF CHRONOLOGY

This chronological history of United States foreign relations is designed as a reference for scholars, librarians, students, researchers, journalists, and citizens seeking a straightforward explanation of particular events regarding America's relations with other nations. It also cites events in foreign countries that influenced American decisions regarding a particular issue; these basically foreign events are identified in the text by italicized type.

USING THE CHRONOLOGY

Although some users of this volume may simply be fascinated by the varied and often unusual stream of events in American foreign activity, the volume is designed for searchers of information about a person, event, or subject in U.S. foreign relations. These persons are advised to use a search process as follows:

1. *Date*: Look for the month, day, and year of the event. The entire volume is organized chronologically.
2. *Index*: Use the index, which is comprehensively organized according to person, nation, and subject of event. The only nation *not* listed in the index is the United States. To assist researchers, the text capitalizes important names associated with an event.
3. *Prior and Future Events*: After finding the event being researched, review the events backwards for one year and forward for one year or more in order to place the event in its broader historical setting.
4. *Reference to Other Events*: If the explanation of any event cites other reference dates, check those references.
5. *Other Index References*: If the researched event concerns a particular nation, use the index to find other references for U.S. policy with that nation, past or future.

REQUEST FOR SUGGESTIONS TO ASSIST REVISED EDITIONS

As any scholar–author realizes, regardless of the amount of attention given to the accuracy of detail and the inclusion of items, a work of the magnitude of this volume may suffer from mistakes of omission and commission. Because I expect to update and revise this volume within the next decade, I would appreciate and duly acknowledge the aid which any user of this volume may recommend. Such comments should be addressed to me at the History Department, Bradley University, Peoria, Illinois 61625.

LIST OF MAPS

CHRONOLOGICAL HISTORY OF
UNITED STATES FOREIGN RELATIONS
1776 TO JANUARY 20, 1981

XI.   POLITICAL ISOLATION; ECONOMIC GLOBAL CONCERNS:
WASHINGTON NAVAL CONFERENCE; DAWES AND YOUNG PLAN;
DEPRESSION ERA (1921-1932)

1921

January 7, 1921   THE U.S. NAVY'S ORANGE WAR PLANS AGAINST JAPAN ARE
GIVEN TENTATIVE APPROVAL BY THE SECRETARIES OF WAR
AND THE NAVY.

In accordance with their pre-1917 naval strategy for the Pacific Ocean, U.S.
naval leaders reformulated their Orange War Plans against Japan as the most
likely future American enemy. On March 29, 1919, Captain Harold E. Yarnell,
head of the Navy War Plans Division, outlined a Pacific Ocean strategy which
became the basis for the Navy's and the Joint Board of the Army and Navy's
strategic plans until May 11, 1939.

Yarnell did not envision a U.S. conflict in Europe, where Great Britain
would be the only likely U.S. antagonist. Moreover, the United States held
strategic advantages in a war against England which would not require a large
U.S. naval force. In the Pacific, however, Japan's power had increased as a
result of World War I and the possibility of a U.S. conflict with Japan had
increased proportionately. The tensions between the United States and Japan,
Yarnell warned, were "permanent and cannot be arbitrated."

Based on Yarnell's analysis, Orange War Plans projected the need for a
U.S. Navy "second-to-none," capable of offensive action in the western Pacif-
ic, home-waters of Japan. The Navy also desired stronger fortifications in
Hawaii and Guam as well as the stationing of a large fleet in the Philippine
Islands.

These Navy plans conflicted with the State Department view of Europe as
first priority for America. Although this conflict was never obvious or debated, it became apparent during the Washington Conference preparations of
which Secretary of State Hughes took charge during the fall of 1921. The
Orange Plans also laid the basis for the Navy's opposition to the Washington
Conference treaties of 1922 which limited the Navy's battleships and placed
a *status quo* on fortifications by the United States in the western Pacific
islands.

January 25, 1921   SENATOR BORAH OFFERS A RESOLUTION TO INVESTIGATE WHAT
                       "CONSTITUTES A MODERN FIGHTING NAVY--A NAVY WITH THE
                       TYPE OF SHIPS AND WITH AIR AND SUBMARINE WEAPONS" TO
                       BE EFFECTIVE IN FUTURE WARS.

Borah followed up his proposal for a naval disarmament conference on December
14, 1920, with a January 25 resolution to determine whether U.S. defense policy should be changed.

     The modern American navy which Borah suggested would include aircraft
and submarines for coastal defense. As a nationalist, Borah did not want to
weaken America's defense forces; thus, his resolution of January 25 asked
the Senate Naval Affairs Committee to determine the influence of new weapons
on American defense forces.

     The submarine and the airplane had played vital roles during World War I.
As a result, some military observers believed these new weapons would trans-
form future warfare. In America, two notable spokesmen for the new weapons
were Brigadier General William MITCHELL of the Army Air Service and Rear Admiral William FULLAM of the U.S. Navy. Both of these men provided information
to Borah in January, 1921, which contended that better and less expensive
American coastal defense could be obtained with submarines and aircraft. Admiral Fullam argued that battleships would be useless in future wars unless
they were protected by submarines and aircraft. In addition, a sufficient
force of these new weapons would make America "perfectly safe from attack
from any other country."

     General Mitchell had even greater claims for the future abilities of
airplanes in coastal defense. Airplanes, Mitchell stated, would sink any
naval ships approaching within 100 to 200 miles of the American continent.
Mitchell also coined a slogan which appealed to Borah: "1,000 airplanes can
be bought for the price of one battleship." As Borah informed congress in
February, 1921, the nation was wasting $240 million by building battleships
rather than aircraft and submarines.

     To demonstrate the airplane's potential, Mitchell urged the Army and
Navy to test aircraft bombs against former German battleships. With the backing of Senator Borah and other congressmen, Mitchell overcame the Navy's opposition and a test was held. See July 21, 1921.

March 4, 1921   CHARLES EVANS HUGHES IS COMMISSIONED AS SECRETARY OF
                       STATE BY PRESIDENT HARDING.

Soon after his election in November, 1920, Harding wrote to Hughes, asking
him to serve as Secretary of State. Harding fully trusted Hughes's advice
on foreign relations and generally permitted him a free hand in foreign policy
decisions. Hughes served as secretary until Harding's death and for President
Coolidge until March 4, 1925.

April 27, 1921   *THE ALLIED REPARATIONS COMMISSION REPORTS THAT GERMANY*
                       MUST PAY A TOTAL OF 132 BILLION GOLD MARKS ($33 BIL-
                       LION).

The Treaty of Versailles provided for a Reparations Commission to determine
the exact amount Germany had to pay to the Allies for damages during World
War I. The meetings of the commissioners, without delegates from America,

began at Spa on July 5, 1920, and formulated a tentative plan for German pay-
ments to France, Great Britain, Italy, Belgium, and the smaller nations that
fought the Central Powers.

At the London Conference (February 21 to March 4, 1921), further discus-
sions were held with German representatives, in order to work out a payment
schedule. The final figures for total costs were not set, however, until
April 27. The Germans were also told in April that they had already fallen
behind in their payments and must pay one billion gold marks by June 1, 1921.
To do so, the Germans borrowed funds in London. This, however, was just the
beginning of European difficulties in assessing and collecting German repara-
tions. See January 11, 1923, and September 1, 1924.

May 19, 1921   CONGRESS APPROVES THE EMERGENCY QUOTA ACT RESTRICTING
                     IMMIGRATION TO THE UNITED STATES.

Disillusionment with World War I, fears that larger numbers of East Europeans
with socialist-communistic beliefs would arrive, and a general xenophobic view
held by 100% Americanists caused congress to pass a law that generally restricted immigration for the first time in the nation's history. The 1921 law limited
the number of aliens admitted to the United States from a given country in
one year to about 3% of the number of such nation's inhabitants in America
in the 1910 census.

In 1922, the Quota Act became more restrictive. Congress extended the
1921 emergency law by reducing the annual admissions to 2% of the national
residents in the United States in 1890. The purpose of this change was to
favor immigrants from northern and western Europe over those from eastern
and southern European nations. See May 15, 1924.

May 25, 1921   CONGRESS APPROVES THE BORAH RESOLUTION FOR A NAVAL
                     DISARMAMENT CONFERENCE AS AN AMENDMENT TO THE NAVAL
                     APPROPRIATIONS BILL OF 1921.

Borah's resolution of December 14, 1920, had been tacked on to the Naval Appropriations Bill on February 24. It passed congress in that form with only
four negative votes.

June 7, 1921   *THE LITTLE ENTENTE IS COMPLETED BY A TREATY BETWEEN*
                     RUMANIA AND YUGOSLAVIA.

The Little Entente was designed to protect former nations of the Austro-
Hungarian Empire and to forestall a possible restoration of Hapsburg rule.
On August 14, 1920, Czechoslovakia and Yugoslavia signed a treaty that became
the basis of the entente. On April 23, 1921, the Czechoslovakian-Rumanian
agreement linked the triad of small powers created on former Hapsburg terri-
tory.

July 2, 1921   THE U.S. CONGRESS PASSES A JOINT RESOLUTION DECLARING
                         THAT HOSTILITIES WITH THE CENTRAL POWERS HAVE CEASED;
                         PRESIDENT HARDING APPROVES THE RESOLUTION.

This resolution resembled the one President Wilson vetoed in 1920 following
the Senate's rejection of the Treaty of Versailles. The congressional resolution declared that the United States reserved all the rights and privileges
provided by the Central Powers to the Allied nations under the treaties made
during the peace conferences. The State Department used this resolution as
the basis for separate treaties with Germany, Austria, and Hungary which were
signed during August, 1921, and promptly ratified by the U.S. Senate.

July 11, 1921   HARDING'S ADMINISTRATION ANNOUNCES THAT PRELIMINARY
                         REQUESTS HAVE BEEN MADE TO INVITE THE MAJOR NATIONS
                         TO A DISARMAMENT CONFERENCE.

The State Department's preliminary messages regarding the conference were
sent on July 8 to Great Britain, France, Italy, and Japan. The public announcement of the invitations was made on July 11, in order to forestall the
announcement that Great Britain would request a conference on the Far East
to be held in London. The British Commonwealth ministers had been meeting
in London since June 20 and had agreed to seek a conference on the Far East
in order to obtain an agreement that would terminate the Anglo-Japanese Alliance. Because Secretary of State Hughes wanted the conference to be held
in Washington where Americans would be closer to the conference process, he
agreed with Great Britain to include the Far Eastern issues on the conference
agenda.
     Japan hesitated to accept conference participation because both the naval
and Far Eastern issues vitally affected Japanese policies. Tokyo could not,
however, afford to reject the British and American desire to hold a conference, and so Tokyo agreed to attend. In addition to the four large powers
invited to the meeting on July 8, Hughes also sent invitations to the Netherlands, Belgium, Portugal, and China, each of whom agreed to be represented.
See November 12, 1921.

July 21, 1921   U.S. AIR SERVICE PLANES BOMB AND SINK THE "UNSINKABLE"
                         GERMAN BATTLESHIP *OSTFRIESLAND* DURING AN ARMY-NAVY
                         TEST IN CHESAPEAKE BAY.

Since January 25, 1921, when Senator Borah requested an investigation of what
constitutes a modern navy, plans had been devised to determine whether aircraft bombs could sink a battleship, as General William Mitchell contended.
Consequently, on July 21, while the 27,000-ton displacement German battleship
the *Ostfriesland* lay at anchor 60 miles off the Virginia coast, Army Air Service bombers dropped six 1,000-pound and seven 2,000-pound bombs, most of which
scored direct hits on the ship. In 21½ minutes the *Ostfriesland* listed to
one side and plunged to its deep ocean grave.
     Although Mitchell, Borah, and others were convinced that battleships
had become obsolete, the Joint Board of the Army and Navy disagreed. Because
the conditions were not "warlike" and no battleship defensive tactics were
used, the board would admit only that there was a potential for future aircraft use in war. The battleships, however, remained as the board's choice

to be "the backbone of American defense" as long as trade and transportation
were used on the seas of the world. The air power versus sea power debate
had simply grown to larger proportions. Significantly, however, Borah believed aircraft and submarines were the best weapons for protecting the coastline of an isolated America.

August 20, 1921   RUSSIA AGREES TO ADMIT AN AMERICAN RELIEF ADMINISTRA-
                           TION (ARA) TO PROVIDE FOOD FOR ITS STARVING CITIZENS.

The ravages of World War I and the civil war between the Bolsheviks and the
various White armies left Russia in a disastrous economic situation, in which
lack of food supplies and poor distribution systems combined to cause large-
scale famine. In July, 1921, the Soviet government called for aid from the
workers of the world and Herbert Hoover's relief organization responded immediately. The Hoover-Nansen offer of food relief in April, 1919, had been
affected by political problems between the Allied powers and Lenin's regime.
In 1921, however, there were direct contacts between Hoover's ARA and Maxim
Litvinov, the Soviet's Assistant Minister of Foreign Affairs.
       On August 20, Litvinov and the ARA agreed on terms for relief supplies
to be distributed in Russia by ARA members. The ARA insisted on the right
to distribute relief to make certain that the aid reached those in need. Although granting this authority to foreign representatives was humiliating
to Soviet authorities, the need for food was so great that Litvinov had no
alternative.
       During the next year, ARA delegates brought food and medicine to dis-
tribute in Russia. Most aid went to the Volga River region where the famine
was most serious. In December, 1921, the All Russian Congress of Soviets
formally thanked the ARA for $66 billion of assistance, a greater amount than
all other sources combined gave to Russia after its July call for help. Unfortunately, the anti-communist attitude of the ARA delegates, which caused
them to treat all Russians with disdain, resulted in ill will among the Russian people despite their gratitude for the supplies.

November 12, 1921   AT THE OPENING SESSION OF THE WASHINGTON CONFERENCE,
                           THE UNITED STATES PROPOSES THAT THE NAVAL POWERS SCRAP
                           CAPITAL NAVAL SHIPS AND ACCEPT A 10-YEAR NAVAL CON-
                           STRUCTION HOLIDAY.

Secretary of State Hughes surprised the conference delegates and pleased the
public by using his opening speech as conference chairman to urge the delegates to limit all naval forces not only by scrapping old naval ships or those
under construction but also by accepting a 10-year naval construction holiday
that would stabilize the great powers' naval ratios at 5 for Great Britain
and America to 3 for Japan.
       Hughes's proposal to limit naval fleets had been carefully prepared and
was approved by President Harding and the U.S. delegation. In addition to
Hughes, the U.S. delegates were Republican Senator Henry Cabot Lodge and Democratic Senator Oscar Underwood, the leaders of their parties in the Senate
Foreign Relations Committee, and Elihu Root, a former senator and former Secretary of State.
       During the conference preparations in September and October, Hughes had
asserted State Department leadership, using the U.S. Navy officers as experts

to provide him with necessary information but rejecting the Navy's strategic plans for an offensive American naval fleet capable of operating against Japan in the western Pacific Ocean (Orange War Plans). The Navy plans had projected American needs for a battle fleet equal to the combined Anglo-Japanese fleets. After obtaining data on the existing naval fleets of the three major naval powers, Hughes proposed to freeze each nation's navy at existing ratios. This worked out to be the 5:5:3 ratio suggested on November 12.

The Secretary of State believed his concept was a realistic assessment of the existing situation in the three-power naval race. According to data from U.S. naval intelligence, if each of the three powers completed its current naval construction plans, the ratio of capital ships in 1928 would give the United States 100; Great Britain, 108; Japan, 87. Assuming that the U.S. congress appropriated all funds necessary for the Navy program, the 1928 ratio would be 10:10:8.7, leaving Japan better off than the 5:5:3 ratio. Congress did not, however, appear willing to authorize the necessary Navy funds. During the current 1921-1922 fiscal year, congress had cut $332 million from the Navy budget and Senators Lodge and Underwood believed such cuts would continue. At the same time, Japan had increased its 1921 navy budget by $61 million, consistent with Japan's recent increases of $177 million over the past four years. Furthermore, U.S. Navy plans required congressional approval for increasing fortifications in the Philippine Islands and Guam, which the Navy had unsuccessfully sought since 1907. In brief, these estimates meant that the 5:5:3 ratio would give American naval forces a better ratio than future U.S. prospects in congress anticipated.

The Navy Department did not, however, accept Hughes's proposed ratio. On October 26, Secretary of the Navy Edwin Denby countersigned a protest to Hughes by the General Board of the Navy. The board report argued that "Our superiority today lies in these ships." Japan, it contended, respected only force, and if the United States cut out 15 capital ships as planned, "the temptation of Japan to take a chance becomes very great."

According to Hughes and the State Department, however, the U.S. interests in East Asia were not sufficient to prepare for war with Japan. Diplomacy which used the support of Britain and other powers could contain Japan's aggressive intentions. Moreover, military operations should not be contemplated in the western Pacific because this region was not vital to U.S. security.

In November, 1921, Hughes's policies had widespread support, and he offered naval limitation principles which the other nations' Washington delegates generally accepted at the conclusion of the conference on February 6, 1922. The four naval limitation principles he proposed on November 12 were:

1. abandoning all capital shipbuilding programs, both actual or projected;

2. reducing the navy's size by scrapping older ships;

3. maintaining the existing 5:5:3 ratio of the three naval powers;

4. using capital ship displacement tonnage as the yardstick to measure the strength of navies with a proportionate allowance for auxiliary combatant seacraft. Capital ships were those displacing more than 10,000 tons, i.e., battleships and heavy battle cruisers.

In order to attain these limits Hughes announced the United States would agree to scrap 15 old battleships and 15 uncompleted ships on which $330 million had already been spent. In turn, Great Britain would scrap 19 old ships and 4 new Hood-class ships; Japan would lose 10 old ships, 7 capital ships under construction, and 8 being planned. Altogether, the three nations would destroy 78 capital ships which were built or being prepared, a total of 1,878,043 displaced tons.

For the long term, Hughes proposed a 10-year holiday on building capital ships. After 10 years, ships could be replaced after a vessel was 20 years old but no ship could exceed 35,000 tons.

Hughes believed his proposed agreement would stop all plans for offensive naval war. In addition, the naval competition would end and "enormous sums will be released to aid the progress of civilization." The national defense of each power would be adequate, and after 10 years the naval powers could consider a future course of further limitations.

For the conference results see February 6, 1922.

December 16, 1921   THE STATE DEPARTMENT AND THE COMMERCE DEPARTMENT AGREE
                            TO GIVE FOREIGN LOAN CONTROL TO THE STATE DEPARTMENT.

Secretary of Commerce Herbert Hoover had indicated that his Department's Bureau of Foreign Commerce should have more jurisdiction over foreign commerce and loans. Secretary of State Hughes denied this concept and wanted U.S. consular officers to retain their position in commercial affairs and the Secretary of State to retain control over foreign loans. U.S. diplomacy had become a complex of economic and political problems and Hoover believed the Commerce Department should have jurisdiction in economic affairs, including relations with foreign nations.

In spite of Hughes's authority over loans, Hoover's department expanded its overseas operations, and by the end of the decade many U.S. businessmen believed the Commerce Department could serve them better at home and abroad than the State Department. Hoover and Hughes worked cooperatively to encourage American bankers to set guidelines for judging foreign loans.

1922

February 6, 1922   THE WASHINGTON CONFERENCE ENDS AFTER AGREEMENTS ARE
SIGNED ON NAVAL LIMITATIONS AND TO FREEZE THE *STATUS
QUO* IN THE PACIFIC AND EAST ASIA.

Following the opening ceremonies on November 11, 1921, and Secretary Hughes's
dramatic opening speech, which proposed drastic naval limits, the delegates
met in both plenary and subcommittee sessions until early February. Many of
the critical decisions were made in *ad hoc* meetings of the Big Three: Britain's Foreign Minister Lord Balfour; U.S. Secretary of State Hughes; and Jap-
pan's Minister of the Navy, Admiral Baron Tomosaburo Kato. The conference
resulted in the following treaties:

1. FIVE-POWER NAVAL LIMITATION TREATY. This agreement prohibited the
construction of new capital ships for 10 years and established national ratios
for the possession of capital ships which displaced more than 10,000 tons: a
ratio of 5 for Great Britain and the United States; 3 for Japan; 1.67 for
France and Italy.

Because aircraft carriers displaced an average of about 25,000 tons,
these ships received a special status based on similar ratios. The United
States and Great Britain could construct 5 carriers (135,000 tons); Japan 3
(81,000 tons); Italy and France 2 (48,000 tons). A separate treaty clause
permitted America and Japan to convert two battle cruisers under construction
into 33,000-ton carriers. The carriers' value in naval warfare was uncertain
in 1922. The U.S. Navy's first carrier, the U.S.S. *Langley*, went into service
in March, 1922, but generally American naval officers denied that aviation
would affect the status of the battleship fleet, an estimate that did not
begin to change until the 1930's.

Agreement on the naval ratios presented fewer difficulties than might
have been expected by outside observers. In fact, England had agreed to accept naval parity with the United States in private negotiations during the
spring of 1921 when Britain's First Lord of the Admiralty, Lord Lee of Fare-
ham, corresponded with Secretary of the Navy Edwin Denby. This critical
change in British naval policy resulted from Britain's postwar belief that
by establishing better relations with the United States, England could end
the Anglo-Japanese alliance and have America assume the primary role of the
Western power that restricted Japanese expansion in the Pacific and East Asia.
This would give England primary responsibility for the defense of its empire
on a line running from Singapore to New Zealand. The United States never
accepted and may not have comprehended this shift in British foreign and defense policy after 1919. Nevertheless, Britain's change greatly influenced
U.S. global strategy during the inter-war years from 1918 to 1940.

The Anglo-American agreement on naval parity left Japan as the nation
that had to be persuaded to accept a lower naval ratio. Japan reluctantly
agreed to the ratio of 3 to 5 on the basis that the two English-speaking countries accepted the freeze on their fortifications in the western Pacific

Ocean. America agreed not to fortify bases west of Hawaii, that is, at Guam, Samoa, the Philippines, and the Aleutians; England agreed not to alter its fortifications at Hong Kong or in the Pacific east of the meridian 110° east longitude except those off the coasts of Canada, Australia, and New Zealand.

U.S. Navy strategists disliked the limits on ships and fortifications because they anticipated having to fight Japan in a future war through offensive operations in the western Pacific. In fact, there was no expectation that the Navy's Orange War Plans against Japan would be provided for by the U.S. government in 1922. As early as 1907, Theodore Roosevelt had decided the Philippines could not be defended from Japan, and while the U.S. Navy continued to seek fortifications in the Far Pacific, these plans had never been approved. Furthermore, Senator Lodge and the Republican leaders in Congress reported that the Navy could not expect to obtain appropriations for the 48-battleship fleet which its "second-to-none" program advocated or for the fortifications they desired in the Pacific. The special treaty clause which permitted two battle cruisers to be converted into carriers was recommended as the only means for the U.S. Navy to obtain carriers in the near future.

With agreement made on the freezing of fortifications in the Pacific, the three naval powers accepted Hughes's original proposal almost intact. The one significant change resulted from Japan's desire to retain the *Mutsu*, a battleship she had just completed. Hughes and Lord Balfour eventually agreed to allow Japan to retain the *Mutsu*, while America and the British could complete two new battleships to offset the *Mutsu*'s size.

The Washington Conference naval ratios applied only to capital ships. Hughes had hoped the ratios would be extended to all auxiliary naval vessels but France prevented this. Claiming that submarines, light cruisers, and torpedo boats were essential to its defenses, France demanded an exorbitant tonnage for its auxiliary ships: 330,000 tons for light cruisers and 90,000 tons for submarines. Premier Aristide Briand asserted that France sacrificed in accepting a low capital-ship ratio and could not accept the same for its other "defensive" vessels. Because of French intransigence, the aircraft carrier was the only auxiliary ship limited by the Five-Power Treaty.

2. FIVE-POWER TREATY ON SUBMARINES AND GAS WARFARE; NO AGREEMENT, HOWEVER, ON AIR WAR. By this treaty the signatory powers accepted traditional principles of maritime warfare regarding the use of submarines in future war. They also agreed to outlaw the use of asphyxiating gases in war. An attempt by the British to abolish submarine warfare was not accepted by the conferees.

The conference subcommittee on aircraft in war could not reach an agreement during the conference. Therefore, the treaty provided for a separate commission of jurists to meet at a later date in order to establish limitations on the use of aircraft and radios in warfare. For the results of this commission see February 18, 1923.

3. FOUR-POWER TREATY ON PACIFIC OCEAN POSSESSIONS. By this treaty, England, France, Japan, and the United States agreed to respect each nation's rights in the Pacific and to consult together in the event of aggression by any nation in that region. Thus, the *status quo* on existing insular possessions and dominions in the Pacific was recognized. More significant, perhaps, was the agreement for consultation if any power were threatened by the aggression of another power. In such event, the four nations would "communicate with one another fully and frankly" in order to reach an understanding. The United States and Japan concluded a separate treaty on Yap Island on February 11, 1922.

The Four Power Treaty's long-range importance was to substitute a multilateral pact for the Anglo-Japanese Alliance which those two powers abrogated.

4.   NINE-POWER TREATY TO PROTECT THE "OPEN DOOR" IN CHINA AND GIVE CHINA GREATER CUSTOMS AUTONOMY.   The Chinese delegation to the Washington Conference did not obtain its four basic objectives. These were: (1) release from the unequal treaties made during the 19th century; (2) the restoration of its sovereignty over Shantung; (3) cancellation of its Japanese treaties of 1915 and 1918; (4) equal treatment by all nations.

Almost ignoring China's desires, Secretary of State Hughes worked to secure the multilateral approval of America's open door principles. Essentially, the United States achieved this within the context of the existing situation in East Asia. The Nine-Power Treaty agreed to the following:

a.   to recognize China's sovereignty, independence, and territorial integrity;

b.   to provide an opportunity for China to maintain a stable government;

c.   to maintain the equal opportunity for commerce and industry of all nations in China;

d.   not to seek special rights or privileges in China which abridged the rights of citizens of "friendly states."

Although clauses of the Nine-Power Treaty appeared to require the powers to end the spheres of influence and special privilege, it did not do so. The French, British, and Japanese retained their existing spheres of influence in China in the minutes of sessions that reserved rights of the powers. Secretary Hughes reserved the rights of the United States to seek equal benefits in those areas, but this was rhetoric which did not influence the delegates. Like John Hay in 1899, Hughes substituted the outward appearance of an open door for the existing reality of the Japanese, French, and English spheres of influence, a tactic not suited to enlightenment of the American public which found it difficult to understand.

The Nine-Power Treaty did not bind the United States or any nation to defend the open door or Chinese territorial integrity. It was a statement of what each power would not do and depended on the good faith of each power for fulfillment.

The Nine-Power Treaty regarding Chinese customs raised Chinese tariff rates and gave China more administrative rights regarding customs duties and collections. A commission was also established to study the question of extraterritoriality in China. Any nation trading with China could sign this treaty.

5.   SINO-JAPANESE TREATY ON SHANTUNG.   Signed on February 4, this treaty general economic control in the area for at least 15 years through Japanese loans to China for the Tsinan-Tsingtao Railway. Japan did agree to withdraw its troops from Shantung.

This treaty retained Japan's special rights and privileges in Manchuria. Although Hughes wanted Japan to abrogate these rights, neither France nor England would support the American attempt to persuade Japan to relinquish these rights. Hughes could do nothing except assert the American right to pursue similar concessions in Manchuria if she desired.

6.   SIX-POWER TREATY ON CABLE RIGHTS IN FORMER GERMAN ISLANDS.   Although the United States had been the only power to challenge Japanese power on Yap Island where the cable rights were centered, the other powers with Pacific

possessions signed a treaty to provide their rights to use former German islands for cables if the need arose.

The U.S. Senate ratified each of the Washington treaties which directly involved America. The only restrictive provision of the Senate was placed on the Four-Power Treaty. The Senate added a reservation for this treaty which provided that "there is no commitment to armed forces, no alliances and no obligations to join in any defense." The provision required congressional approval before the president or State Department committed the nation to act in case of aggression in East Asia.

All nations except France had ratified the Washington treaties by July 28, 1923. The French Chamber of Deputies eventually ratified all the treaties except the Five-Power Treaty on submarines and gas warfare.

February 11, 1922   JAPAN AND AMERICA SIGN A TREATY WHICH SETTLES THE YAP ISLAND DISPUTE.

In 1920, the United States disputed Japan's control of the former German island of Yap because it was located on proposed sea cable routes between Hawaii and the Philippines (see November 9, 1920). The issue was not resolved until the American-Japanese agreement of February 11, 1922.

By this convention, American citizens received cable, radio, and residential rights and facilities on Yap on a basis of equality with the Japanese. In return, the United States recognized Japan's right to the mandated control over all former German islands north of the equator in the Pacific Ocean. This latter recognition had previously been accepted by the United States, but not in a formal treaty.

February 28, 1922   *GREAT BRITAIN ENDS ITS PROTECTORSHIP OVER EGYPT.*

An Egyptian Nationalist Party (WAFD) had grown in strength during World War I and had undertaken an insurrection on March 8, 1919. While fighting the WAFD rebels, the British also conducted an investigation of their problems in Egypt. The commissioners recommended independence for Egypt with guarantees that British interests would be protected.

Attempts to reach a compromise with the WAFD failed, and on February 28, the British unilaterally ended their protectorship in favor of King FUAD I who assumed control on March 15, 1922. The British reserved the right to negotiate with Egypt to protect communications, defense policy, and the protection of foreigners. These negotiations were carried on over a decade, and a treaty was not signed until 1936. See August 27, 1936.

September 7, 1922   SECRETARY OF STATE HUGHES HEADS THE U.S. DELEGATION TO BRAZIL WHERE THAT NATION CELEBRATES ITS CENTENNIAL ANNIVERSARY OF INDEPENDENCE. HUGHES'S SPEECHES DURING THE WEEK'S CELEBRATION URGE GREATER PAN-AMERICAN CO-OPERATION.

Hughes's most notable speech during his visit to Brazil was delivered at the dedication site for the American centennial monument. He urged the people of the Americas to understand that the United States held no imperial designs over its neighbors. The sincere desire of America was to see in "the hemi-sphere an abiding peace, the reign of justice and the diffusion of the bless-ings of a beneficent cooperation."

September 21, 1922   CONGRESS PASSES THE FORDNEY-McCUMBER TARIFF, RENEWING
                         U.S. PROTECTIONISM BUT PERMITTING THE PRESIDENT TO
                         NEGOTIATE RECIPROCITY.

The 1922 tariff reversed the downward trend of the Underwood Tariff of 1913, raising rates more than 25% higher than those of the Payne-Aldrich Tariff of 1909. While the minority of congressional progressives objected, their only success was the addition of Section 317, a clause allowing the president to raise or lower the tariff by 50% in order to obtain reciprocity tariff rates with other nations. The reciprocity provisions failed because both Britain and France wanted America to reduce its tariffs before negotiations began.

December 6, 1922   PROCLAMATION OF THE IRISH FREE STATE.

The British-Irish war which began on November 26, 1919 led to several months of serious conflict in 1920. Finally, some order was restored after the British Parliament passed The Government of Ireland Act on December 23, 1920. This act divided Ireland into Northern Ireland and Southern Ireland with a council to represent the two parts. Members of the Sinn Fein party led by Eamon DE VALERA rejected the partition, but their insurrection was defeated by the moderate Dail Eireann led by Arthur Griffith.

The Dail Convention adopted a constitution on October 25, 1922, which became effective on December 6 with William T. COSGRAVE as President.

December 29, 1922   SECRETARY OF STATE HUGHES PROPOSES THAT AMERICAN EX-
                        PERTS SHOULD PREPARE METHODS FOR GERMAN REPARATIONS
                        PAYMENTS.

Because European nations were experiencing problems regarding payment of Amer-ican debts and collecting German war reparations, Secretary of State Hughes used a speech before the convention of the American Historical Association to suggest U.S. assistance. Following the adoption of the London Schedule for Reparations on April 27, 1921, Germany found it necessary to delay or postpone its payments. On March 21, 1922, the Reparations Commission reduced Germany's cash payments for 1922 from 2 billion to 720 million marks, but when this sum could not be paid, the commission suspended German payments for six months.

During the fall of 1922, the commission had to decide if the German de-faults were "willful" or the result of monetary transfer problems. The Brit-ish accepted Germany's argument that the rebuilding of her wartime economy and the inflation of German currency relative to gold marks caused transfer problems. The French delegation argued that Germany refused to raise taxes and to make the sacrifices necessary to meet her obligations. This "willful" default, the French said, justified the Allied use of military intervention to force Germany to pay.

Although America received no German reparations, Secretary Hughes became concerned as early as September, 1922, and suggested to French Premier Raymond

POINCARÉ that a group of financiers ought to prepare Germany's payment schedule. Poincaré refused because he contended payment was a German not a French problem. Germany, he said, was obligated to pay the existing schedule.

On December 26, the Allied powers declared Germany had defaulted on its payments, opening the possibility of military action against the Germans. Hughes hoped to prevent a military conflict and, being scheduled to address the American historians on December 29, the secretary decided to publicly call on world opinion to help avoid a crisis between France and Germany. With President Harding's consent, Hughes proposed in his address that a group of "distinguished Americans" should examine the problem and prepare a German payment plan. The European problem, he argued, was a world problem and Americans "cannot escape the injurious consequences of a failure to settle [it]... There will be no permanent peace," Hughes contended, "unless economic satisfactions are enjoyed. We should view with disfavor measures which instead of producing reparations would threaten disaster." Although Hughes rejected the contention that German reparations and European debts to the United States were linked, America wanted the reparations issue settled on its merits because its outcome would enable the United States to determine the allies' capacity to pay their U.S. debts.

While many observers lauded Hughes's speech, the French did not. Poincaré became upset, claiming Hughes had condemned the military occupation planned for the Ruhr before it had begun. Thus, France ignored Hughes and proceeded with its plans. See January 11, 1923.

1923

January 2, 1923   AMERICA AND JAPAN FORMALLY CANCEL THE LANSING-ISHII
AGREEMENT.

Following the acceptance of the Nine-Power Treaty at the Washington Conference
on February 6, 1922, Secretary of State Hughes began discussions with Japan
to formally cancel the Lansing-Ishii agreement of November, 1917. The Lansing-
Ishii agreement included a clause which from the American viewpoint was crucial
but which had been kept a secret since 1917. In the secret clause Japan
agreed not to seek special rights in China that abridged the rights of citizens of friendly nations.
    On December 27, 1922, Japan's foreign minister sent Hughes a note accept-
ing the cancellation of the Lansing-Ishii agreement. On January 2, 1923,
Hughes wrote to Japanese Chargé Saburi in Washington formally responding and
acknowledging America's agreement to abrogate the 1917 understanding. Because
the Lansing-Ishii agreement was not a treaty, its cancellation required no
Senate action.

January 11, 1923   *FRENCH AND BELGIAN TROOPS OCCUPY THE RUHR DISTRICT
AFTER DECLARING GERMANY HAD DEFAULTED ON COAL DELIVER-
IES UNDER REPARATIONS AGREEMENTS.*

*The Allied Reparations Commission had debated the reparations issue and Ger-
many's ability to pay throughout 1922. At the Second London Conference, on
December 9-11, 1922, Bonar Law offered to cancel Allied debts to Britain if
changes were made regarding German payments, but French Premier Raymond
Poincaré refused. On December 26, the Reparations Commission declared Germany
at default on its debt but recommended no further action at that time.*
    *In a meeting on January 9, the Reparations Commission again discussed
the situation. The British delegation argued that the German default was
not willful and military intervention should be avoided. To bolster its case,
the British asked the U.S. observer at the commission, Roland W. Boyden, to
offer his opinion. Boyden supported the British view and stated that the
United States wished to prevent military action. This ploy failed to persuade
the French who, backed by the Belgians and Italians on the commission, voted
that Germany had defaulted and, in particular, was behind in its coal deliveries. In spite of British objections, the other three European nations
agreed to send troops to occupy the Ruhr district of Germany. They did so
on January 11, 1923. For the results of the Ruhr occupation see September 1,
1924.*

February 7, 1923   *A WASHINGTON CONFERENCE OF CENTRAL AMERICAN STATES*
                          RESULTS IN A NEUTRALITY TREATY THAT PROVES TO BE IN-
                          EFFECTIVE.

Secretary of State Hughes and the State Department's Chief of the Latin Amer-
ican Division, Sumner Welles, had proposed a conference of Central American
states to end the friction between Honduras, Nicaragua, and El Salvador. Each
of these states accused its neighbors of assisting revolutionary plots against
them.

In August, 1922, Hughes arranged a temporary settlement of a crisis in
Central America by sponsoring a meeting of the presidents of each nation on
the U.S.S. Tacoma *in Fonseca Bay. To obtain a permanent agreement, Hughes*
invited the three states to meet at Washington on December 22, 1922. During
the following sessions in December and January, the Central American delegates
established a Central American Tribunal to act as an arbitration court. Five
Latin American nations pledged not to assist or recognize a government set
up by a coup d'état, or to intervene "directly or indirectly, in the internal
affairs of any other Central American republic."

Although they composed a model treaty that was signed on February 7,
1923, the signatory nations did little to make it effective. The past anxi-
eties and problems persisted among these five states: Nicaragua, Honduras,
El Salvador, Costa Rica, and Guatemala.

February 18, 1923   A COMMISSION OF JURISTS AT THE HAGUE SIGN A TREATY TO
                          REGULATE AERIAL WARFARE: AN AGREEMENT NEVER RATIFIED.

Because the subcommittee on aircraft and radios could not reach agreement
during the Washington Conference of 1921-1922, the delegates referred the
issue to a special commission of experts. On December 11, 1922, the Special
Commission of Jurists convened at the Hague to negotiate a pact, giving their
particular attention to aerial bombing. John Bassett MOORE who headed the
American delegation also became commission chairman. Under his guidance a
treaty was signed on February 18 by delegates from France, Britain, Italy,
Japan, the Netherlands, and the United States.

Essentially, the Hague pact proposed rules of air war based on traditional naval bombardment regulations. These rules restricted bombing "within
bounds of military operations directed against combatant forces." Non-
combatant areas were not to be bombed. In addition, the Hague rules anticipated a form of aerial war that some air power advocates were considering:
terror bombing. The 1923 rules asserted that "Bombardment by aircraft for
the purpose ... of terrorizing the civilian population is forbidden."

Following the conference, the Hague Rules on Aircraft Bombing met a dis-
mal fate. The U.S. State Department tried for four years to obtain an indication that the other powers would ratify the treaty, contending America would
seek Senate ratification if the pact was accepted by other nations. Only
Japan indicated it would ratify. The European nations decided aircraft were
developing so rapidly that rules should not restrict this progress at such
an early stage. Consequently, on April 9, 1928, the State Department placed
the Hague agreement in the dead file. The attempt is notable as the first
effort to restrict air raids by heavier-than-air planes.

February 19, 1923   THE U.S. SUPREME COURT RULES THAT AMERICA CAN DENY
                        NATURALIZATION RIGHTS TO ANY IMMIGRANTS EXCEPT FREE
                        WHITE CAUCASIANS.

In the case of *U.S. v. THIND*, the Supreme Court gave general validation to
state alien land laws which had been passed in California and duplicated by
14 other states: Arizona, Arkansas, Delaware, Idaho, Kansas, Louisiana, Missouri, Montana, Nebraska, Nevada, New Mexico, Oregon, Texas, and Washington.
     The court rulings reflected the xenophobia of the 1920's which was ex-
plicit in the Emergency Quota Act of May 19, 1921, and in the various state
laws. Earlier, on November 13, 1922, the court had decided in the case of
Ozawa v. U.S. that Japanese were not eligible to be naturalized. Later, in
the cases of *Terrace v. Thompson* (November 12, 1923) and *O'Brien v. Webb* (November 19, 1923), the alien land laws of Washington and California were sustained as being constitutional and not violating the Japanese Treaty of 1911.

April 10, 1923   THE SECOND CHESTER CONCESSION IS GRANTED BY THE TURKISH
                        GOVERNMENT.

Admiral (ret.) Colby M. Chester had received but failed to fulfill an investment concession from Turkey on December 11, 1911. In May, 1920, Chester asked
the State Department to assist him in obtaining another Turkish concession
for railway and mineral rights. Although Secretary of State Hughes discounted
Chester's project, the U.S. Navy Department encouraged the plan and the U.S.
High Commissioner to Turkey, Admiral Mark Bristol, aided Chester.
     On April 10, Chester seemed to have succeeded when the Ankara government
granted Chester's Ottoman-American development company a concession to construct a railway and exploit mineral resources along its right of way.
Chester could not, however, raise the financial backing in the six months
allocated to him, and Turkey cancelled the concession in December, 1923.
Chester's default left the consortium of seven U.S. oil companies as the one
representative in the Middle East in 1923. See July 21, 1928.

May 3, 1923   THE FIFTH PAN-AMERICAN CONFERENCE ADJOURNS IN SANTIAGO,
                        CHILE.

Although Secretary of State Hughes had planned the meeting of the Fifth International Conference of American States, a lingering illness kept him home.
He appointed Ambassador to Belgium Henry P. Fletcher to head the American
delegation. Future Secretary of State Frank Kellogg was also a delegate.
     The convention met from March 25 to May 3, 1923, and agreed on two prin-
cipal measures. First, it formed a commission of jurists to codify international law. Second, it adopted the Gondra Convention, an agreement to provide a "cooling-off" period for the nations in any dispute by first referring
the issue to an inquiry committee for study and a report.

June 19, 1923   GREAT BRITAIN ACCEPTS A PLAN TO REPAY ITS U.S. WAR
                        DEBTS WHICH BECOMES THE BASIC MODEL FOR AMERICAN AGREE-
                        MENTS WITH OTHER WORLD WAR ALLIES.

The United States emerged from World War I as the Allies' major creditor nation, European nations owing nearly $11 billion to the American government. During the period immediately following the Paris Peace Conference, British and French officials discussed with America the mutual cancellation of war debts but the Wilson administration refused, a policy continued by Harding. In a message to Prime Minister Lloyd George on November 3, 1920, President Wilson made it clear that the United States would not cancel any debts nor would America allow the Allies to correlate U.S. war debts with the reparations Britain, France, and other nations assessed against Germany for their war guilt.

Although Great Britain, France, and Russia agreed in February, 1915, to unite their financial as well as military forces against the Central Powers, the United States had persistently rejected this concept and accounted for the Allied war loans on a nation-by-nation basis.

Continuing to insist that the Allies must accept plans to fund their debt payments, Harding's Secretary of the Treasury, Andrew Mellon, asked Congress in 1921 for full authority to negotiate separate debt payments with each nation. Congress rejected this request but created a World War Foreign Debt Commission, with Mellon as the chairman, to negotiate agreements. This law was signed by Harding on February 9, 1922. It instructed the eight-member commission to settle all debts on a 25-year basis, at no less than 4.25% interest. Each national agreement would be submitted by the commission for ratification by congress.

The commission's first major agreement was accepted by Great Britain on June 19, 1923, following several commission meetings with Britain's Chancellor of the Exchequer, Stanley Baldwin. Although the British first refused to accept the term of the congressional act of February 9, 1922, the commissioners worked out a method to circumvent the strict application of the 25 years at 4.25% interest and Britain agreed to its terms. The commission made the funded principal less than the total debt and recalculated the accrued interest from 1918 to 1922 at 4.25% rather than the original 5%. By also extending the payments of the funded amount over 62 years, the commission reduced the British debt in actuality while enabling congressmen and U.S. spokesmen to claim that there was no reduction or cancellation. The British debt with interest would be $11.1 billion, paying an average interest rate of 3.3%.

Similar treaties were made with 12 other nations between 1923 and May 3, 1926. Such nations as Italy and France received very low interest rates. France was charged no interest for the first five years and low rates thereafter, for a French interest rate of 1.6% on $4.025 billion; similarly, Italy's interest was 0.4% on $2,042 billion.

The commission reported to congress that its work had essentially ended on May 3, 1926, when a debt agreement was signed with Yugoslavia.

Because the debt commissioners and the congressmen who worked on the debt funding feared the consequence of being candid with the American public, they led the public to believe that the debt charges were not reduced. Herbert Hoover, for example, explained privately that the U.S. concessions were necessary during the negotiations. In public, therefore, the United States was referred to as "Uncle Shylock." In financial reality, the settlement reduced the Allied debts for 13 countries by 43.1% when calculated on the basis of the 4.25% interest supposedly required by the act of February 9, 1922, and the debt plus accrued interest of the original loans.

Nevertheless, these reductions left the European nations with large interest and principal payments to bear for a 62-year period. The cancellation of all war debts and German reparations may, ideally, have provided a sounder financial basis for Western Europe and the United States. This was not politically possible in the United States at the time. Thus, debts and reparations continued to plague the Western powers and Germany for another decade, leaving a reservoir of ill feelings among the nations concerned.

July 24, 1923   *THE TREATY OF LAUSANNE CONCLUDED ALLIED PEACE TERM*
                          WITH TURKEY'S NATIONALIST GOVERNMENT OF MUSTAPHA K.

The Turkish nationalists never accepted the Treaty of Sevres of August 10, 1920, and Kemal continued at war with the Greeks, who were aided by a British force which was sent on September 16, 1922, to save the Greeks from a complete defeat.

Following the landing of British troops, Kemal began to confer with the Allies. After several minor skirmishes, a peace conference began at Lausanne on April 23, 1923. In the Treaty of Lausanne, Turkey ceded all non-Turkish territory lost during World War I except Eastern Thrace. Greece received all the Aegean Islands except Imbros and Tenedos. The British occupied Cyprus. Turkey again gained control of Constantinople although Kemal retained the capital city at Ankara.

During the 1920-1922 war, Kemal's armies also forced Sultan Mohammed VI into exile. On October 29, 1923, Turkey was proclaimed a republic with Kemal as its first president.

August 2, 1923   PRESIDENT HARDING DIES AND IS SUCCEEDED BY VICE
                          PRESIDENT COOLIDGE.

The president died in San Francisco, while returning from a trip to Alaska. The cause of his death was listed as embolism. On August 3, Calvin Coolidge took the oath of office as president.

August 6, 1923   A U.S.-TURKISH TREATY OF AMITY AND COMMERCE IS SIGNED.

During the Lausanne Conference between the Allied powers and Turkey (see July 24, 1923), the U.S. observers at the meeting negotiated a treaty with Turkey's new government. The American observers were Ambassadors Joseph C. Grew (to Switzerland) and Richard W. Child (to Italy) and the U.S. High Commissioner to Turkey, Admiral Mark Bristol. The Turkish representative was Ismet Inonu.

The treaty of August 6 provided for the exchange of diplomatic officials; the most-favored-nation commercial treaty; the abrogation of all treaties between America and the Ottoman Empire; and the legal recognition of American educational, religious, and medical institutions in Turkey. The treaty engendered a lengthy dispute before the U.S. Senate rejected it. See January 18, 1927.

August 31, 1923   AMERICA RECOGNIZES OBREGÓN'S REGIME IN MEXICO AFTER
                          HE AGREES TO SETTLE THE OIL ISSUE OF 1918.

Following his election on September 5, 1920, Obregón attempted to settle all foreign claims against Mexico in order to gain recognition. Since the revolution, which began in 1911, Mexico had been unable to pay its foreign debts

and the bonded public debts which foreign investors held. Although the French
and British held the largest share of these debts, they delegated the negotiations to representatives of American bondholders and bankers.

The United States held claims on Mexico in addition to the loan indebt-
edness. In 1919, a congressional subcommittee of the Committee on Foreign
Relations, led by Senator Albert B. FALL, investigated all claims against
Mexico and issued a 3,000-page report which both protested Mexico's outrages
and compiled a list of claims. Among U.S. claims were those of citizens for
damages since the claims commission of 1868; claims for violence, damage,
and arbitrary decrees during the decade of revolution; land claims affected
by Mexico's land reforms; damages to American interests under Article 27 of
Mexico's 1917 constitution (see February 19, 1918); and interest and principal
on Mexican government bonds.

As a condition of recognizing Obregón's government, both Wilson and
Harding insisted that Mexico guarantee all claims. During the spring of 1923,
Secretary of State Hughes persuaded Harding to send Charles Beecher Warren,
the former Ambassador to Japan, and John B. Payne, former Secretary of the
Interior, to Mexico City to negotiate a settlement. After consulting with
Thomas Lamont, the J.P. Morgan representative who had negotiated a bankers'
agreement with Mexico on June 16, 1922, Payne and Warren began discussions
with two Mexican commissioners on May 14, 1923, at No. 85 Bucareli Street in
Mexico City. Two treaties resulted from the Bucareli Commission: a Special
Claims Convention for losses between November 10, 1910, and May 31, 1920, and
a General Claims Convention covering losses from 1868 to 1910. In addition,
the commission produced an "extra official pact" of its conference minutes in
which each side stated its policy on agrarian and subsoil issues. The result
of the commission pact was to leave the issues of oil and land uncertain.
The U.S. position reserved "all" the rights of U.S. citizens; the Mexican
statement was that Article 27 of their Constitution of 1917 was not retro-
active if the persons with prior concessions had made "some positive act"
which would manifest the intention of the owner "to use the oil under the
surface." "Positive act" was defined broadly; thus, it was not exact.

Initially in 1923, diplomatic relations appeared to have improved between
Mexico and America. The claims conventions were ratified, and when an uprising by Adolfo de la Huerta threatened Obregón, the United States supported
Obregón's government by selling him military equipment to suppress the rebellion.

In 1925, however, the Mexican congress passed new legislation regarding
petroleum and land reform, causing the United States to protest. The new
dispute again cooled U.S.-Mexican relations. See January 11, 1928.

September 27, 1923   *MUSSOLINI'S ATTEMPT TO CONQUER CORFU FROM GREECE FAILS*
                            DUE TO BRITISH INTERVENTION.

*After several Italians were assassinated along the Greek-Albanian border on
August 27, the Italians bombarded and occupied Corfu. Greece appealed to
the League of Nations, and the League together with British pressure finally
forced Italy to pull out of the island and restore Greek political rule. This
was Mussolini's first attempt at military adventurism.*

December 20, 1923   SINCLAIR OIL OBTAINS OIL CONCESSIONS IN NORTHERN ITALY;
                                THE PROJECT FAILS IN 1925.

Following World War I, the Soviet Union ended the czar's treaties with Iran
(officially Persia until March 21, 1935), and pulled out of northern Iran.
Because the Iranian nationalists held strong anti-British attitudes, they
asked W. Morgan Shuster, the American financier who had aided Iran in 1911
(see May 12 and November 29, 1911) to help them. Shuster contacted Jersey
Standard and Sinclair Oil regarding an oil concession in northern Iran. Jersey Standard withdrew, however, because of its connection with the British
oil concession in Iraq (see July 21, 1928).

     Subsequently, on December 20, 1923, Iran granted the Sinclair Oil Company
a concession. In exchange for 50-year oil rights in four of the five northern
provinces, Sinclair arranged a $10 million loan for Iran and gave Iran 20% of
the oil profits. Unlike Jersey Standard, Harry Sinclair planned to send oil
through Russian territory in order to avoid Britain's southern Iranian control. The Russians agreed to accept Sinclair's plan provided the U.S. government recognized the communist regime. The United States would not grant
recognition, however, and combined with its embroilment in the 1924 Teapot
Dome oil scandal, Sinclair's fortune fell and it withdrew from the Iranian
agreement in 1925.

     Sinclair's attempt to exploit Iranian oil was one of two U.S. failures
in Iran before 1940. In 1937, the U.S.-controlled Amiranian Oil Company received an oil concession from Iran's shah but had to surrender it within a
year because of the company's financial problems.

1924

March 10, 1924   AMERICA SENDS ADDITIONAL MARINES TO HONDURAS WHEN PRES-
                     IDENT GUTIERREZ TRIES TO ESTABLISH A DICTATORSHIP.

On September 11, 1919, the United States had sent marines to Honduras in order
to prevent a civil war by supporting President Rafael Gutierrez. Since 1919,
however, Gutierrez had moved to create dictatorial power, stimulating an insurgency led by Tiburcio CARIAS. On March 10, following the killing of
Gutierrez, the United States ordered more marines to land in Honduras to suppress the disorders. Nevertheless, Carias' forces captured the capital city,
Teguigalpa, on March 31.

     At this juncture, the State Department sent Sumner Welles to settle the
dispute. On May 3, 1924, Welles met with representatives of Honduras' neighboring states, Nicaragua, Guatemala, and El Salvador and persuaded them to
sign the Pact of Anapala. By this agreement, the neighboring states cut off
aid to the insurgent forces. In 1925, Welles conducted elections in Honduras
which prohibited revolutionary leaders from being candidates. The election
was won by Miguel Paz BARAHONA. Unfortunately, the long-term Honduran political difficulties remained, and the United States had not established permanent order in the area. In 1933, General Carias became dictator of Honduras.

May 15, 1924   CONGRESS PASSES A GENERAL IMMIGRATION LAW INCLUDING A
                   CLAUSE TO EXCLUDE ORIENTALS: JAPAN PROTESTS.

The Chinese and Japanese governments had been persistently irritated by the
unequal treatment of their people by U.S. immigration laws. Beginning on
May 19, 1921, when congress passed the Emergency Quota Act, Japan protested
the action as well as California's Alien land laws. Tokyo did not object to
control of immigration per se, but to the discriminatory treatment accorded
Asians.

     On the west coast of America, prejudices against Orientals continued
although the 1907 Gentleman's Agreement and the 1911 Commercial Treaty with
Japan virtually ended Japanese immigration. Between 1907 and 1922, the net
increase of Japanese-Americans was 16,096: those entering the United States
and Hawaii numbered 171,584; those leaving, 155,488. Many of these immigrants
were Japanese "picture-brides" sent by marriage brokers in Japan to wed
Japanese-American men, a custom most Americans did not understand. The influx
of women had increased the Americans born of Japanese ancestry from 4,502
births in 1910 to 29,672 in 1920.

     During these years, the west coast Exclusionist League also expanded.
Its membership spread to Oregon, Washington, Nevada, and Arizona; its activity
secured state laws to prohibit Orientals from owning or leasing land (see
November 2, 1920).

     By 1921, there was a crisis in American-Japanese relations because of
the land and immigration discrimination. In Tokyo, U.S. Ambassador Roland S.

Morris tried to negotiate a more restrictive gentleman's agreement with Foreign Minister Baron Shidehara. When drafts of the Morris-Shidehara proposals reached America in 1921, Senator Hiram Johnson of California and other west coast politicians strenuously objected and the project ended.

In Washington, Secretary of State Hughes and President Coolidge both urged in vain for congressional leaders to seek some compromise in 1924. Hughes wrote to Congressman Albert Johnson of the House Committee on Immigration to indicate that the exclusion of Japanese damaged U.S. relations with Japan. The Washington Treaties of 1922, Hughes stated, had improved U.S.-Japanese relations, and "fixing a stigma" on the Japanese would affront a friendly nation. Hughes pointed out that placing Japan under the European quota system would allow only 250 Japanese each year to enter America.

After the House Committee ignored Hughes's pleas, the president suggested that congress postpone the exclusion clause for two years while a treaty could be negotiated with Japan. But congress rejected this proposal.

Consequently, despite objections of the State Department and president, congress overwhelmingly passed the Immigration Bill of 1924 including the exclusion of Oriental immigrants. The House vote was 308 to 62; the Senate vote was 69 to 9. Coolidge signed the law on May 26, explaining that if the anti-Japanese measure had stood separately, he would have vetoed it. The president believed, however, that a general immigration law was necessary. For 30 years, the U.S. government had avoided a Japanese exclusion law; now it was a reality.

Although Secretary of State Hughes called Japan's Ambassador Hanihara to his office to attempt to minimize the effect of the congressional action, this was difficult to accomplish. Hanihara resigned as ambassador and returned to Japan in humiliation for failing to avert this insult. As representatives of the liberal political groups in Japan which opposed the aggressive methods of the military conservatives, Hanihara and Shidehara suffered a disastrous blow before Japanese public opinion, which turned in favor of the more aggressive militarists during the next five years.

May 23, 1924   THE SOVIET UNION ABROGATES MOST OF THE CZAR'S TREATIES
                        WITH CHINA.

Knowing that the Chinese revolutionaries had been urging the abolition of the "unequal treaties" forced on the Ch'ing dynasty between 1842 and 1914, Lenin's government announced as early as July, 1919, that the Soviet Union would repudiate those treaties. By 1924, however, the Red Army had defeated the White armies in Central Asia. Now, Moscow was less willing to end all of the czar's previous arrangements in East Asia. Therefore, while generally ending the czar's tariff and economic concessions with China, the Soviets worked out two exceptions with China: (1) Russia retained control of the Chinese Eastern Railway in order to restrain Japanese interests in Manchuria; (2) Outer Mongolia continued to be a Russian protectorate. This decision required that the Red Army intervene in Outer Mongolia to defeat refugees from Cossack and other White armies who were terrorizing the Mongolians. The Russian army suppressed these military bandits and placed a "friendly" ruler in control of Outer Mongolia under Soviet guidance.

May 24, 1924   THE ROGERS ACT UNITES THE U.S. CONSULAR SERVICE AND
DIPLOMATIC SERVICE INTO ONE BRANCH OF THE STATE DEPART-
MENT, CREATING THE FOREIGN SERVICE OF THE UNITED
STATES.

In 1919, Representative John Jacob Rogers of Massachusetts first offered legislation to unite the consular and foreign service branches. Secretary of
State Lansing had advised Rogers that conflicts of jurisdiction had frequently
taken place and necessitated the reorganization of the two branches. On May
24, 1924, the Rogers Act became law. It not only united these two parts of
the State Department's overseas functions but placed appointments to the Foreign Service on a merit basis.

On February 23, 1931, the Moses-Linthicun Act revised the Rogers Act in
order to correct deficiencies of the 1924 act regarding classification of
service officers and the appointment and promotion process. Together these
enactments became the basis of the U.S. Foreign Service.

July 1, 1924   SECRETARY OF STATE HUGHES REAFFIRMS AMERICA'S REFUSAL
TO RECOGNIZE THE UNION OF SOVIET SOCIALIST REPUBLICS.

Although Hughes, like President Wilson in 1917, said he was sympathetic toward
the Russian people, he continued to refuse to grant diplomatic recognition
to the U.S.S.R., although most European nations had done so. After Great
Britain recognized the Bolshevik government on February 1, 1924, the question
of U.S. policy on Russia arose.

Subsequently, on July 1, Hughes issued a statement to clarify America's
reasons for non-recognition. Hughes's three basic reasons for not granting
recognition were: (1) the U.S.S.R.'s refusal to accept the debts of the Russian State and its repudiation of all prior Russian debts including the $187
million loaned to the Kerensky government by the United States; (2) the attempt of Moscow to seek the overthrow of the existing social and political
order of the United States through the subversive activity of the U.S. Communist Party and the Worker's Party; (3) the U.S. claim that the new regime
had not yet been accepted by the Russian people. See October 25, 1924.

July 12, 1924   IN THE DOMINICAN REPUBLIC, HORACIO VASQUES BECOMES
PRESIDENT FOLLOWING AN AGREEMENT WITH THE UNITED STATES
FOR THE WITHDRAWAL OF AMERICAN MARINES.

Soon after taking office in 1921, Secretary Hughes endeavored to withdraw
the U.S. marines that President Wilson had sent to Santo Domingo in 1916.
He appointed Rear Admiral Samuel S. Robison as the military governor, in-
structing him to prepare for free elections and ultimate withdrawal.

Initially, the Dominican people suspected some trick by Hughes. But in
March, 1922, the secretary sent word to the island that he would welcome emis-
saries to make an agreement in Washington. General Horacio Vasques and
Federico Valasquez came to the United States and agreed on an evacuation plan.
As a result, Hughes sent Sumner Welles to Santo Domingo as a special commis-
sioner to arrange an election and the U.S. withdrawal.

The agreement for the transfer of independence to the Dominicans was
signed on June 30, 1922. Thereafter, American rule was transferred to a provisional government on October 21, 1922, and preparations for a constitution

and the election of a president were undertaken in 1923. The result was the election and inauguration of Vasques as president on July 12. The last American marines withdrew from the Dominican Republic on September 18, 1924.

September 1, 1924   THE DAWES PLAN BECOMES OPERATIVE TO SOLVE THE GERMAN
                        REPARATIONS PROBLEM AND END THE RUHR OCCUPATION.

On January 11, 1923, an international crisis began when French and Belgian troops occupied Germany's Ruhr District because Germany defaulted on its reparations payments under the Treaty of Versailles. Two consequences of this action were that Germany stopped all reparations payments and Germany's economy collapsed, depreciating the value of the German mark to nearly nothing and causing staggering inflation. One result of the German economic plight was Adolf Hitler's beer-hall putsch in Munich on November 9, 1923. The fledgling Nazi Party protested that the German Republican government could not effectively combat the communist menace within and the French invaders from without. Hitler's putsch failed but gave the Nazis a prominence from which they profited after 1930.

The Ruhr occupation caused a stalement between France and Germany. Not only did reparations cease but also the German government encouraged passive resistance by the Ruhr workers, with the result that production of the coal and metallurgical industries declined precipitously in 1923–1924. France gradually realized that a new reparations scheme was necessary and, during the fall of 1923, David Lloyd George of Britain revived Secretary Hughes's proposal of December 29, 1922, for a commission of experts. On November 30, 1923, the Reparations Commission agreed to form two committees: the first to find a method for restoring German financial stability; the second to repatriate German capital exports that had fled the country.

On the request of Louis BARTHOU, Chairman of the Reparations Commission, Secretary Hughes arranged for Barthou to invite Charles G. Dawes and Owen D. Young to the currency stabilization commission and Henry M. Robinson to the committee on foreign German funds. Hughes cooperated unofficially in the appointment of the U.S. commissioners. Dawes became chairman of his group and its recommendations became the Dawes Plan. Other nations represented were France, Great Britain, Italy, and Belgium.

The currency commission met between January 14 and April 9, 1924. It submitted its report to the Reparations Committee, which accepted it and later agreed to make it effective on September 1, 1924. During the commission's study, Secretary Hughes studiously avoided the direct involvement of the State Department. Nevertheless, Hughes influenced the British and French acceptance of the Dawes Plan by visiting the Continent as president of the American Bar Association, leading a group of U.S. and Canadian lawyers on a pilgrimage to Europe between July 12 and August 2, 1924, at the time when the commission's report was under consideration. In particular, Hughes's visits with French Premier Edouard Herriot and President Poincaré seem to have persuaded the French to accept the Dawes Plan. When Herriot complained that accepting the plan would cause his cabinet to fall, Hughes told him it would fall if the German problems were not solved. If France rejected the plan, Hughes warned, no further American aid could be expected.

Consequently, France agreed and the European powers signed the Dawes Plan on August 30, 1924. The plan, which based its findings on what Germany could pay rather than on what she should be *forced* to pay, may be summarized as follows:

1. The Dawes reparation schedule would be temporary, to be made perma-
    nent following a review in four or five years. Thus, the total
    amount of reparations would be fixed later.

2. A five-year payment schedule required one million marks the first
    year and a gradual increase to 2.5 million annually in five years.

3. Bonds from a reorganized German railroad system and industrial bonds
    would underwrite German reconstruction and provide income for the
    reparations during the five-year period.

4. A special Transfer Commission would collect German payments in marks
    and distribute the funds through the monetary exchange markets to
    preserve the stability of all national currencies including Ger-
    many's.

5. Annual payments would be flexible to adjust to changes in economic
    circumstances in Germany and the nations collecting reparations.

6. Loans of $200 million would be extended to Germany and the loan in-
    terest and amortization charges were to be included in the annual
    payments.

7. Germany's cash payments, payments in kind, payments for the occupa-
    tion forces, and other charges were unified into the one annual pay-
    ment schedule.

Following approval of the Dawes Plan, Germany, Belgium, and France made
agreements providing for the evacuation of Allied forces from the Ruhr District. At French insistence, clauses in these agreements recognized previous
German defaults and the right of the Allies to use military sanctions if Germany defaulted again.

The Dawes Plan functioned as the reparations schedule until 1928 when a
commission headed by Owen Young met to make permanent reparations arrangements. For the Young Plan see August 31, 1929.

October 25, 1924   *THE ZINOVIEV LETTER CAUSES DIPLOMATIC TENSIONS BETWEEN*
                            GREAT BRITAIN AND THE SOVIET UNION.

Within British politics, the issue of recognizing the Soviet government con-
tinued to be controversial after Ramsay MacDonald's Labour Cabinet extended
de jure recognition to Moscow on February 1, 1924. The Labour Cabinet signed
a commercial treaty on August 8, which gave the Soviets the most-favored-
nation trading status. Together, these actions by MacDonald gave the election
campaign of the fall of 1924 a major issue which Stanley Baldwin's Conserva-
tives capitalized on due to an unwise letter which Gregory Zinoviev sent on
October 25.

Speaking on behalf of the Communist Third International, whose head-
quarters were in Moscow, Zinoviev wrote a letter to leaders of the British
communists which allegedly urged British subjects to provoke a revolution in
Great Britain. The publicity about Zinoviev's message was largely responsible
for the victory of Baldwin in the elections of October 29, 1924. Immediately,
on November 21, 1924, Baldwin's ministry abrogated the August commercial trea-
ties and adopted a hard-line policy toward the Soviet Union. The hostile
British policy eventually caused a break in Anglo-Soviet relations on May 26,
1927. See October 1, 1929.

October 28, 1924   *FRANCE GRANTS* DE JURE *RECOGNITION TO THE SOVIET UNION.*

November 4, 1924   PRESIDENT COOLIDGE IS ELECTED PRESIDENT.

Although Robert LaFollette bolted the Republican Party to run as the Progressive Party candidate, Coolidge easily defeated both LaFollette and the Democratic Party nominee, John W. Davis.

1925

January 5, 1925   SECRETARY OF STATE HUGHES OFFERS HIS RESIGNATION.

In November, 1924, following the reelection of Coolidge, Hughes had notified the president of his intention to resign. The secretary had worked diligently for eight years as governor of New York and Secretary of State. But his expenses had exceeded his income during this period and he desired a better-paying job to provide for the future of his family. Hughes recommended Frank B. Kellogg to be his successor. See March 5, 1925.

March 5, 1925   FRANK B. KELLOGG BECOMES SECRETARY OF STATE.

Kellogg had been a senator from Minnesota (1917-1923) and Ambassador to Great Britain (1923-1925). He had been trained as a lawyer and once served as president of the American Bar Association. Thus, while his foreign experience was limited, he brought good credentials to the office of secretary. He served in this position until March 28, 1929.

March 13, 1925   THE U.S. SENATE RATIFIES THE ISLE OF PINES TREATY WITH
                          CUBA, ENDING ONE OF AMERICA'S PROBLEMS WITH THAT IS-
                          LAND.

During World War I, American relations with Cuba were peaceful, due largely to the profits obtained by the Cuban sugar industry during the war. In 1920-1921, however, sugar prices fell and Cuba's financial problems grew under the government of Alfredo ZAYAS. Following an election dispute in December, 1920, General Enoch Crowder had been sent to Cuba by President Wilson to prevent a civil war. In new elections on March 15, 1921, Zayas won again but Crowder remained in Havana until 1923 to try to straighten out Cuba's finances.

Shortly before leaving office as Secretary of State, Hughes revived a treaty negotiated originally in 1904 by which the United States renounced all claims to the Isle of Pines. The State Department had not requested Senate ratification because Senator Borah and others wanted to retain some interests of American citizens in the isle.

Hughes believed the issue should be ended and wrote to Senator Joseph T. Robinson to seek ratification in order to resolve an issue that harmed good relations with Cuba. With Robinson's aid, Borah's opposition was overcome and the Senate ratified the treaty on March 13, 1925.

June 27, 1925   THE GENEVA PROTOCOL IS SIGNED. IT PROHIBITS THE USE
                          OF POISONOUS GAS AND BACTERIOLOGICAL WEAPONS OF WAR.
                          ALL THE GREAT POWERS RATIFY THE PACT EXCEPT JAPAN AND
                          THE UNITED STATES.

At the 1925 Geneva Conference for the Supervision of the International Traffic
in Arms, the United States proposed that the nations prohibit the export of
gases for war use. At suggestions from France and Poland, the conference
drew up a protocol on non-use of poisonous gas and bacteriological methods
in war.

     Before World War II, many countries ratified the Geneva protocol. Japan
and the United States were the two major powers that did not ratify the pact.
In addition, some nations--including Great Britain, France, and the U.S.S.R--
declared the protocol would not be binding if their enemies did not respect
the prohibition. Although Italy signed the protocol, it used poison gas in
the Ethiopian war of 1935.

     In 1926, the Senate Foreign Relations Committee favored ratification.
The Senate never voted on the pact because there was strong lobbying against
it. See November 25, 1969, and January 22, 1975.

August 4, 1925   U.S. MARINES LEAVE NICARAGUA FOLLOWING THE ELECTION
                          OF PRESIDENT SOLORZANO.

Secretary of State Hughes desired to remove U.S. marines from their interventions in Latin American nations as quickly as possible. Nicaragua presented special difficulties because America had been its protector since 1914
without solving its political problems. In 1917, Wilson had set up a Financial High Commission to reorganize the nation's finances. Under its guidance,
British foreign debts had been satisfied and the debts due for American banking advances were paid by 1924.

     Three recent developments had convinced Secretary Hughes that the marines
should leave Nicaragua as soon as a new president was inaugurated in 1925.
First, Nicaragua's finances appeared to be in order. Second, on February 7,
1923, the Central American Court of Justice was set up to keep peace in the
region. Third, by the Pact of Anapala of May 3, 1924, the Central American
states agreed to keep insurgent bands off their bases.

     Unfortunately, the Nicaraguan election of 1924 demonstrated the diffi-
culty of the United States' "teaching" democracy to Latin Americans. From
the beginning, disputes raged between political factions. To prevent the
Chamorro faction of the Conservative Party from winning, a coalition ticket
led by the Conservative Carlos Solorzano and the Liberal Party's Dr. Juan
Sacasa united their political groups. The coalition ticket won, but Emiliano
Chamorro immediately protested election fraud, and called for a new election.

     President-elect Solorzano pleaded with Secretary Hughes not to withdraw
the marines until a trained native constabulary could maintain order. Hughes
agreed to provide six months' training, but between January, 1925, when
Solorzano was inaugurated and August, the training process lagged badly. Nevertheless, Secretary Kellogg like Hughes was anxious to withdraw U.S. troops
in order to end the inter-American accusations about American interference
in other states. Therefore, on August 4, 1925, the U.S. marines withdrew.
Solorzano soon realized his fears about a new crisis if the United States
withdrew. On October 25, a revolt led by Chamorro brought renewed political
disorder to Nicaragua. See May 12, 1927.

October 16, 1925   *THE LOCARNO CONFERENCE: SEVEN EUROPEAN NATIONS CONCLUDE*
                          A CONFERENCE WITH TREATIES TO GUARANTEE PEACE IN WEST-
                          ERN EUROPE.

*The "spirit of Locarno," which prevailed among the European delegations be-
tween October 5 and 16, 1925, appeared to herald a new era of peace and cooperation. The delegates never talked of alliances or enemies but of cooperative pacts to avoid future war. On October 16, the delegates initialed the
treaties of Locarno which were formally drawn up and signed in London on December 1, 1925.*

The principal parts of the treaties of Locarno were:

*1. a mutual guarantee of the borders between Germany and France and
Germany and Belgium;*

*2. arbitration treaties between Germany and Poland, Germany and Czech-
oslovakia, Germany and France, and Germany and Belgium;*

*3. mutual assistance treaties between France and Poland and France and
Czechoslovakia in case of attack by Germany.*

1926

January 26, 1926   THE U.S. SENATE APPROVES MEMBERSHIP IN THE WORLD COURT
BUT WITH AMENDMENTS WHICH MAKE THE AMERICAN ACCEPTANCE
UNSATISFACTORY TO THE EXISTING COURT MEMBERS.

Secretary of State Hughes had been an ardent advocate of a Permanent Court of
International Justice for many years before 1919. Hughes's friend and fellow
Republican Elihu Root had been on the jurist commission that prepared the
court protocol approved by the Assembly of the League of Nations on December
13, 1920. As designed by the commission, nations not in the League of Nations
could hold membership on the court without joining the league.

In spite of his eagerness to have the United States join the court,
Hughes delayed sending the matter to the Senate for approval until February
24, 1923. In his recommendation to the Senate, Hughes proposed that the
United States join under conditions which did not involve America with the
league but would give the United States equality in the proceedings of the
court and the selection of judges. Although Hughes had anticipated that Senator Lodge's support for the World Court would expedite its acceptance, he
had misjudged Lodge. The senator objected to features of the court which he
interpreted as requiring compulsory arbitration and as involving the United
States in enforcing court decisions. Hughes could not convince Lodge or other
Republicans on the Senate Foreign Relations Committee that their views were
incorrect. Therefore, although the House of Representatives approved court
membership by a vote of 301 to 28, Lodge stalled the act in the Senate.

When the Senate adopted the bill on January 26, 1926, it approved amendments that prohibited the court's advisory opinions in a dispute and prevented
an American case from reaching the court without a two-thirds Senate vote.
The International Court of Justice members would not accept the U.S. amendments and America dropped its application for court membership.

May 18, 1926   THE PREPARATORY COMMISSION FOR A DISARMAMENT CONFERENCE
OPENS ITS FIRST SESSIONS AT GENEVA.

Although the Treaty of Versailles of 1919 called for a general disarmament
treaty, no steps were taken to effect these treaty clauses until 1925. Following the provision for Germany's admission to the League of Nations at the
Locarno Conference, disarmament advocates persuaded the League Council to
invite 19 nations, including America, to attend a consultation meeting to
prepare for a disarmament conference. The French government wanted the consultations to work out definitions and a prospectus for success prior to a
formal conference.

The 1926 preparatory commission met until November 26, 1926, but reached
no conclusions. The principal dispute was between France's desire to obtain
guarantees of security before disarming and the Anglo-American desire to disarm first and discuss security arrangements later. During the next five

years, six more sessions of the Preparatory Commission argued this issue and a host of other general and detailed questions about arms and warfare. They achieved nothing. Finally, on December 9, 1930, the Preparatory Commission recommended that the conference on disarmament should be held in 1932. See February 2, 1932.

September 8, 1926   GERMANY IS ADMITTED TO THE LEAGUE OF NATIONS.

This action indicated the belief that Germany was willing to fulfill its obligations under the Treaty of Versailles.

December 16, 1926   GREAT BRITAIN ANNOUNCES A CHANGE IN ITS CHINA POLICY.

For some time, Great Britain had considered changing the 19th-century policy which made it the leader of foreign powers in pursuing political and economic concessions in China. As Chinese antagonisms arose against the Western imperial powers, Britain decided that its interests required Chinese good will and an end to military ventures against the Chinese.

An incident at Shanghai on May 30, 1925, stimulated Chinese nationalist antagonism to a point where the British government decided a new policy was imperative. The Shanghai incident began when a crowd of 2,000 Chinese rushed a police station in the International Settlement to protest Western mistreatment of the Chinese. A British police inspector shouted for the mob to stop or be killed. When they did not halt, police fired on the crowd, killing 12 Chinese and wounding 17.

Because no foreign authorities took steps to investigate and punish the perpetrators of these killings, the Chinese populace began a series of demonstrations, strikes, and boycotts of Western products and businesses. Clashes took place between police and demonstrators in Canton, Hankow, and Kiukiang.

Following 18 months of such troubles, Great Britain issued a decree declaring a new policy toward China, designed to gain good will. On December 16, Foreign Secretary Sir Austen Chamberlain recognized that the growth of nationalism in China aimed at giving China an equal place among nations of the world. England, he said, would meet this movement with understanding. He particularly called on the United States to join Britain in negotiating with China "as soon as the Chinese themselves have constituted a new government." This would permit China to increase its tariffs and to resolve all matters of foreign extraterritorial powers with Great Britain and other foreign nations.

December 25, 1926   JAPAN'S TAISHŌ EMPEROR DIES; THE SHOWĀ ERA BEGINS UNDER
                        THE EMPEROR HIROHITO.

In contrast to the liberal political developments in the Taishō era (see September 29, 1918), the Showā period gradually became militaristic and imperialistic, particularly after the Mukden incident of September 18, 1931. See also May 3, 1928.

1927

January 18, 1927   THE U.S. SENATE REJECTS A TREATY OF AMITY AND COMMERCE
MADE WITH TURKEY IN 1923.

During the Lausanne Conference of 1922-1923, U.S. and Turkish delegates agreed
to a treaty establishing diplomatic and commercial relations with the Turkish
Republic led by Mustapha Kemal (Ataturk). The treaty was signed on August 6,
1923, but action had been delayed in the U.S. Senate because of strong opposition from religious opponents, an Armenian-American lobby, and political
partisanship against Coolidge.

Following the Armenian massacres which occurred during the 1890's under
the Ottoman Empire (see October 1, 1895; August 26, 1896), Armenian refugees
in America formed a group that implored U.S. assistance against Turkish policy. By the 1920's, the Armenian ethnic organization had become one of many
in the United States that opposed any conciliatory policies by America toward
European nations. The Armenian-American group led by Vahan CARDASHIAN vehemently opposed the U.S. treaty with Turkey, using propaganda which presented
the "Terrible Turk" picture of all Turkish people, making no differentiation
between those governed by the sultan's empire in the 1890's or the new,
smaller Turkish nation of Ataturk following 1920. Ataturk's efforts to modernize and liberalize Turkish society were either ignored or discounted by
Cardashian's followers.

There were a few groups in the United States which by 1927 supported the
treaty with Turkey. The moderate Armenian-American Society favored the
treaty. In addition, while some U.S. missionaries opposed the treaty in 1923,
they had been convinced by 1927 that the treaty would protect their educational, religious, and hospital organizations in Turkey.

In the U.S. Senate, however, a minority led by Senator William H. King
of Utah strongly protested against the treaty. King claimed that the State
Department had forsaken the Armenians in order to support U.S. investors in
the Chester mission which had gained concessions in Turkey. Although King's
charges lacked substance, some politicians accepted them despite the State
Department's denials.

The Turkish treaty had been sent to the Senate by President Coolidge on
May 3, 1924, but the vote on it was delayed in order to gain approval by a
sufficient number of senators. The task failed, however, and in the vote on
January 18, 1927, the Turkish treaty lost, 50 to 34, six votes short of the
necessary two-thirds.

By 1927, U.S. newspapers and other groups had begun to publish more favorable reports about Ataturk's government. In order to establish relations
with Ankara, the U.S. High Commissioner to Turkey, Admiral Bristol, and Turkey's Foreign Minister, Tevfik Aras, signed a memorandum on February 15, 1927,
agreeing to restore diplomatic relations on a friendly basis. Subsequently,
on February 27, Joseph Grew was appointed U.S. Ambassador to Turkey.

January 27, 1927   SECRETARY KELLOGG INDICATES AMERICA'S WILLINGNESS TO
                            END THE CHINESE TREATIES MADE DURING THE 19TH CENTURY.

In 1927, many factors inspired Kellogg to announce the willingness of America
to alter its tariff, customs, and extraterritoriality treaties with China.
On May 31, 1924, the Soviet Union had fulfilled earlier commitments to end
the "unequal treaties" made by the czar with the Chinese. Incidents at Shanghai (May 30, 1925) and Canton (June 23, 1925) and Britain's announcement on
December 16, 1926, of a new Chinese policy indicated the Western powers' desire to adjust to Chinese nationalism. Finally, in January, 1927, the House
Committee on Foreign Affairs began congressional hearings on extraterritoriality in China, which indicated enthusiasm among religious mission societies
in favor of such changes.

    Therefore, on January 27, Kellogg asserted that the United States had
been ready since 1922 to negotiate with China on customs duties, tariffs,
and legal conditions in China. His statement concluded, "if China can agree
upon the appointment of delegates representing the authority or the people
of the country, we are prepared to negotiate such a treaty." The United
States would conduct talks with China in conjunction with Britain and other
powers or alone. The only obstacle preventing new treaties was the appointment of Chinese delegates to represent their people.

    Gaining recognition for appropriate Chinese delegates was not easy. In
1925, a special tariff conference had tried to meet in Peking but experienced
difficulty because of disputes among various political groups in China. In
1926, an extraterritorial commission had a similar problem. Until a stable
political, judicial, and military authority was established in China, a treaty
revision seemed impossible. See April 11 and 12, 1927.

April 11, 1927   THE UNITED STATES JOINS FOUR OTHER NATIONS IN PROTEST-
                            ING CHINESE ATTACKS ON FOREIGNERS AT NANKING.

The Nanking incident of March 24, 1927, took place soon after Chiang Kai-
shek's Nationalist forces captured that city from the Peking regime. For
some time, China had experienced political difficulties and civil war. In
addition to many local warlords who controlled certain provinces of China,
there were three main political factions in China: a moribund successor of
Yüan Shi-kai in Peking; and two Nationalist (Kuomintang) factions, one directed from Hankow, the other from Nanking in April, 1927.

    The anti-foreign riots in Nanking were apparently encouraged by the left-
wing elements of the Kuomintang. The demonstrators burned the American, British, and Japanese consulates and 10 Christian mission buildings; looted foreign businesses and hospitals; and pillaged the homes of missionaries. Six
foreigners were killed: one American, Frenchman, and Italian each; and three
Englishmen. British and American naval vessels on the Yangtze River helped
a group of Standard Oil Company employees to safety by throwing a barrage of
shells at the Nationalist troops while the foreigners escaped over a city
wall.

    To protest the Chinese attack, the representatives of the United States,
England, France, Italy, and Japan presented identical notes to the Nationalist
Foreign Minister, Eugene Chen. The notes of April 11 demanded the punishment
of commanders who were responsible for the attack and complete reparation
for all damages. They also requested an apology from the commander of the
Nationalist Army and his written agreement to stop all agitation and attacks

on foreign lives and property.

American consulates were closed at Chunking, Changsha, Nanking, and Kalgan. The U.S. Minister to China, John Van A. MacMurray, urged Secretary of State Kellogg to take strong action to deter further violence.

Neither Secretary Kellogg nor President Coolidge was willing to use force to carry out the April 11 demands. The War Department told Kellogg that 50,000 troops would be needed for the short route between Tientsin and Peking, but the secretary did not believe American interests were worth a war in China or the loss of any U.S. troops. As Coolidge told a press conference, the United States already had 13,200 American soldiers, sailors, and marines in China to protect 14,038 U.S. citizens. Kellogg believed the era of gunboat diplomacy in China had ended and that better relations had to be established with Peking.

April 12, 1927   *IN SHANGHAI, CHIANG KAI-SHEK LAUNCHES A WHITE TERROR*
                          AGAINST CHINA'S COMMUNISTS WHICH GIVES HIM FULL CONTROL
                          OF THE KUOMINTANG (KMT).

Following the formation of the Chinese Communist Party (CCP) in 1921, Moscow directed the CCP members to join a united front with the KMT under Sun Yat-sen for the purpose of abolishing foreign control and infiltrating the KMT.

After Sun Yat-sen died in 1925, the KMT-CCP alliance became precarious. CCP leaders such as Ch'en Tu-ksiu suspected the KMT had bourgeois tendencies; the KMT never fully trusted the communist extremists. By 1927, the policy divergences in the united front increased as Chiang Kai-shek used Russian help to create an impressive military force while the CCP organized workers and peasants to control China. Nevertheless, even after Chiang sent his Russian advisors home and purged the KMT of influential communists, Stalin advised the CCP to cooperate with Chiang. Previously, Leon Trotsky had opposed the CCP-KMT front, so Stalin had to prove its practicality to his adversary.

In 1926, therefore, Michael Borodin returned to Canton to represent the Comintern and urge the CCP to work with Chiang in forming a northern expeditionary army to capture Peking. In return for Chiang's promise to restrain the right-wing faction of the KMT, Borodin offered Soviet aid and agreed to restrict CCP opponents of the KMT. With his status secure in Canton, Chiang launched his campaign to control central and northern China. His men "liberated" Nanking on March 24, 1927. When the Nationalists conducted attacks on the Westerners in Nanking, Chiang blamed the Communists. Thus, the same day-- April 11--that the foreigners protested against the Nanking demonstrations, their representatives in Shanghai were working with Chiang to plot his bloody terrorist raids on the Communists.

On April 12, 1927, with the support of British police and Shanghai merchants who were anti-Communist, Chiang moved to eliminate the CCP and its worker allies in Shanghai. Beginning at 4 a.m., KMT forces attacked working-class headquarters throughout the city. All workers and union organizers in the buildings were either shot on the spot or marched into the streets to be executed. All CCP members were disarmed; over 700 CCP leaders were killed during the day.

The purge and disorders continued for several weeks. Eventually, the KMT forced businessmen to pay them money or be charged with treason. Chiang's dictatorship made the bourgeoisie pay a high price, but he saved them from communism. Similar purges were conducted by Chiang's men at Ningpo, Foochow, Amoy, Swatow, and Canton. Temporarily, at least, Chiang controlled the strongest political and military bloc in China.

May 12, 1927   THE PEACE OF TIPITAPA ENABLES THE UNITED STATES TO
                     END POLITICAL DISPUTES IN NICARAGUA FOLLOWING THE LAND-
                     ING OF U.S. MARINES.

During the spring of 1927, President Coolidge sent a personal representative,
Henry L. Stimson, to Nicaragua to settle a civil war which had developed and
forced the president to again dispatch marines to preserve order on May 2,
1926.

Nicaragua's problems began just three weeks after the U.S. Marines withdrew on August 4, 1925. The marines had been in Nicaragua since 1912, and
the Coolidge administration believed they could leave following the election
of President Carlos Solorzano, who took charge of the government on January
1, 1925. Two months after the marines left on August 4, 1925, Emiliano
Chamorro, a long-powerful politician in Nicaragua, staged a coup d'état which
forced Solorzano and Sacasa into exile. Chamorro claimed the election of
Solorzano in 1924 had been corrupt and therefore invalid. Subsequently, the
Nicaraguan senate selected Chamorro as president, and he took office on January 16, 1926.

The question of Chamorro's legitimacy arose because by the Central American treaty of February 7, 1923, a revolutionary leader was not permitted to
become leader of the government and new elections were required. The United
States, while not a signatory to the 1923 treaty, had agreed to respect it
and put pressure on Chamorro who resigned on October 30, 1926. The Nicaraguan
senate designated Adolfo Diaz as president on November 11.

Meanwhile, the Liberal Party in Nicaragua began an insurrection against
Chamorro and Diaz. Led by former Vice-President Juan Sacasa, whom Chamorro
had ousted in 1925, the Liberals had the support of General José M. MONCADA.
Sacasa had also obtained the backing of President Calles of Mexico who supplied the Nicaraguan Liberal insurgents with arms, ammunition, and soldiers.

Mexico's intervention became the principal reason why Secretary Kellogg
recommended the dispatch of U.S. Marines, who reached Managua on January 6,
1927. Marine contingents also landed on February 20 on the west coast of
Nicaragua to halt the influx of Mexican arms and to protect Americans who
lived there. On January 12, Kellogg sent a memorandum to the Senate Foreign
Relations Committee which used nearly hysterical terms to justify the intervention as resulting from Bolshevik plans to take over Central America under
Mexican auspices.

To avert U.S. involvement in direct war on behalf of the Diaz government,
Secretary Kellogg sent Henry L. Stimson to Nicaragua. Kellogg and President
Coolidge instructed Stimson to keep Diaz in power but to offer new elections
in 1928 in which Sacasa could be the Liberal Party nominee.

Meeting first with Diaz and later with Sacasa and General Moncada,
Stimson worked out an agreement on May 12, known as the Peace of Tipitapa.
The agreement provided for a general amnesty for the insurgents as well as
the forces of Diaz. The soldiers would receive $10 for each serviceable rifle
or machine gun. Any weapons not turned in would be forcibly taken by the
U.S. Marines. Diaz's government would be recognized while new elections were
prepared under the supervision of the United States.

During the next year, Americans worked out a peaceful election, held on
November 4, 1928. Election regulations included closing all *cantinas* on election day, stationing at least one marine at each poll, and dipping the finger
of each voter into mercurochrome to discourage repetitive voting. General
Moncada won the election and became president.

One difficulty clouded Stimson's apparent success in 1927. A general in Sacasa's Liberal Party, Augusto C. SANDINO, rejected the Peace of Tipitapa. Condemning both the Liberals and Conservatives in Nicaragua as well as the "imperialist Yankees," Sandino's small group of followers retired to the north and continued to fight. Following the election of 1928, Sandino withdrew to Mexico but in 1931 began further guerrilla warfare in northern Nicaragua. The Sandanistas were suppressed in 1933 and Sandino killed in 1934, but his followers continued sporadic fighting for many years. See September 30, 1978, and July 17, 1979.

June 20, 1927   AS THE GENEVA NAVAL LIMITATIONS CONFERENCE CONVENES
                         AN IMMEDIATE ANGLO-AMERICAN DISPUTE BEGINS.

President Coolidge invited the signatory powers of the 1922 naval treaty to a conference designed to extend the naval limits to vessels other than battle-ships and aircraft carriers. Although France and Italy refused to attend, the three major naval powers, Great Britain, Japan, and the United States, convened on June 20.
     At the first session of the conference, a dispute about cruisers arose between U.S. and British naval experts. U.S. Navy Admiral Hilary P. Jones presented the American view that cruiser tonnage should be no greater than 40,000 tons and should focus on light cruisers. Britain's leading spokesman, Lord John R. Jellicoe, described England's preference for limits on heavy cruisers with a minimum tonnage limitation of 462,000 tons. British naval strategy was to have many small cruisers to cover large areas of the ocean; the American naval planners desired fewer, heavier cruisers capable of long-range action in the western Pacific Ocean near Japan. Thus, even though U.S.-British war plans did not envision competition leading to war, their naval experts argued rather than cooperated in setting ship limits.
     The principal reason for the failure at Geneva was that naval experts, not diplomats, dominated the proceedings. The head of the U.S. delegation was Hugh Gibson, the Ambassador to Belgium. Robert Cecil, the British chief of delegation, was not in the British cabinet and was recuperating from ill-ness during the conference. Thus, Jones and Jellicoe, the naval experts, readily held control of the discussions and avoided limitations on the forces they cherished. Not surprisingly, therefore, the Geneva Conference adjourned on August 4, without any achievements.

November 11, 1927   *FRANCE AND YUGOSLAVIA SIGN A "TREATY OF FRIENDLY UNDER-*
                         STANDING," LINKING PARIS WITH THE LITTLE ENTENTE NET-
                         WORK ON GERMANY'S EASTERN BORDERS.

In order to gain greater security from future German aggression, French policy after 1919 included the attempt to gain alliances surrounding Germany. In order to by-pass Article 18 of the League of Nations regarding alliances, the French negotiated "understandings" which technically were not military alliances. France created a network of such agreements with Belgium (1920), Poland (1921), Czechoslovakia (1924), Rumania (1926), and, finally, Yugoslavia on November 11, 1927. The Little Entente had been formed by Yugoslavia, Czechoslovakia, and Rumania in 1921. See June 7, 1921.

January 11, 1928   A MEXICAN-AMERICAN DISPUTE OVER SUBSOIL RIGHTS IS RE-
SOLVED WITH THE PASSAGE OF A MEXICAN LAW WHICH WITH-
DRAWS ITS CLAIMS.

Diplomatic relations between America and Mexico deteriorated to crisis proportions between 1925 and 1928. Following the election of President Plutarco
Elias CALLES in 1925, the Mexican legislature passed two laws enacting Article
27 of its Constitution of 1917. Because Article 27 gave all oil and mineral
resources of Mexico to the state, American and other foreign oil companies
appealed to their governments to prevent the implementation of the Petroleum
Law and the alien land law passed in December, 1925, because they violated
the Bucareli Agreements of 1923.

The oil companies' appeals to Washington ran into two problems: one theoretical, one personal. The theoretical issue was Mexico's assertion of the
Calvo Doctrine, a formula offered by Argentina's Carlos Calvo during the
1880's which declared that corporations doing business in a foreign nation
should appeal only to the native government's institutions, not to their home
government. The United States had consistently opposed the Calvo Doctrine
and President Coolidge also upheld an American investor's right to appeal to
his home government. Coolidge stated his opposition to the Calvo theory in
a public speech on April 25, 1927.

For Mexico, Minister of Foreign Relations Aaron Saenz destroyed the U.S.
arguments, calling them double standards when compared with America's internal
sovereignty laws. In addition to citing American state laws regulating property rights of foreigners, Saenz quoted Chief Justice John Marshall's court
ruling that "The jurisdiction of the nation within its own territory is necessarily exclusive and absolute.... Any restriction on it, deriving validity
from an external source, would imply a diminution of its sovereignty."

The more serious problem of U.S.-Mexican relations was personal, "being
based on the conservative Secretary of State Kellogg's belief that all land
reforms were communistic, and on the prejudiced U.S. Ambassador James R.
Sheffield's intense and prejudiced disdain for all things Mexican." Kellogg
and President Coolidge believed Mexican policy was directed by Russia's Communist Third International. Kellogg informed the Senate Foreign Relations
Committee in January, 1926, that "The Bolshevist leaders have had very definite ideas with respect to the role which Mexico and Latin Americans are to
play in their program of world revolution. They have set up as one of their
fundamental tasks the destruction of what they term American imperialism...."
While these accusations held no substantive basis to support them, they fit
the continued fears of communism which began in the United States during 1919.
The *cause célèbre* of the 1920's witch hunt had climaxed on August 23, 1927,
when Nicola Sacco and Bartolomeo Vanzetti died in the electric chair in
Charlestown, Massachusetts.

Nevertheless, such fears did not justify President Coolidge's appointment
of an anti-Mexican ambassador to Mexico City. The least of Sheffield's faults

was that he spoke no Spanish. Sheffield personified all the worst aspects
of America's self-righteous, racist, and closed-minded elite. A former corporation lawyer and Yale University graduate, Sheffield complained in a letter
to Nicholas Murray Butler that "There is very little white blood in the [Mex-
ican] cabinet--that is it is wholly thin." In addition, the Mexicans "recognize no argument but force" for, as Sheffield wrote to former President Taft,
Mexico "is one of the only countries where the gun is mightier than the pen."
In brief, Sheffield detested everything Mexican from Mexico City's high altitude to what he called its greedy, mixed race and inefficient people.

Sheffield took on the "white man's burden," however. His duty was to
uphold American principles of property rights abroad. The United States had
44% of its investments in Latin America, Sheffield contended, and those rights
had to be protected from confiscation. "Any weakness in our attitude,"
Sheffield wrote to Kellogg, "is certain to be reflected almost immediately
in other foreign countries."

In view of Kellogg's and Sheffield's attitudes, the U.S. adoption of a
hard line of protests against Mexico's land laws was inevitable. By the end
of 1926, Mexico and America were on a collision course. Nevertheless, following his January, 1927, report to the Senate Foreign Relations Committee, which
explained his dispatching of marines to Nicaragua as an anti-Bolshevik measure
(see May 12, 1927), Kellogg began a gradual retreat from the hard-line policy.
Various groups in America attacked Coolidge's policies in Nicaragua and Mexico including disparate sources such as the American Federation of Labor and
the Ku Klux Klan, the *New York Times* and the Brooklyn *Eagle*. In congress,
strange bedfellows who criticized these policies were Senators Borah, La
Follette, Burton K. Wheeler, and George Norris. Religious groups and academic
interests also opposed American intervention in Mexico and Nicaragua.

Senator Borah initiated action to thwart the Kellogg-Sheffield policies
in Mexico. Although it was bad protocol, Borah sent a personal letter to
Mexico's President Calles in January, 1927, requesting him to explain Mexican
policy. On January 25, 1927, the U.S. Senate unanimously passed a resolution
recommended by the Senate Foreign Relations Committee, which asked President
Coolidge to arbitrate all issues with Mexico. At least nine similar resolutions were introduced in the House of Representatives.

Although irritated that Borah had by-passed official channels, Coolidge
decided on April 25 to placate Mexico, issuing a statement of concern to the
Mexican people which concluded that "we do not want any controversy with Mexico."

About this time, Kellogg's assistant secretary, Robert E. Olds, took
charge of Mexican affairs and assumed a more conciliatory attitude than
Kellogg. The most significant result of these shifts in Mexican policy was
the decision in September, 1927, to remove Sheffield as ambassador in favor
of Dwight W. MORROW.

Morrow's arrival in Mexico City inaugurated a complete change in U.S.-
Mexican relations. A proponent of cooperation with Mexico, Morrow left his
position at J.P. Morgan and Company and on his arrival in Mexico City demonstrated legal, social, and personal qualities that won over Mexico's president
and the Mexican people. Morrow's biographer, Sir Harold Nicolson, wrote
praisingly about his Mexican tactics:

> He applauded their food, their climate, their agriculture, their
> hats, their ancient monuments, the bamboo cages in which they kept
> their tame parrots, their peasant industries, their patriotism,
> their volcanoes, even their finances. Here at last was a North
> American who neither patronized nor sneered.

By November, 1927, Morrow was ready for interviews with President Calles to discuss Article 27, the principal point of conflict with Mexico. On November 8, Morrow suggested that the questions of Article 27 and the land laws were not diplomatic but legalistic. Morrow noted that Article 14 of the 1917 Constitution stated that no legislation should apply retroactively in Mexico. Perhaps, he said, the Mexican courts could inquire if Article 14 invalidated any law which affected oil rights contracted before 1925. Calles responded quickly, observing that perhaps a Supreme Court decree would settle the difficulty.

Calles acted almost as fast as his response to Morrow. By November 17, the Mexican court ruled the law of 1925 was not constitutional. On December 28, the Mexican legislature passed a new law which applied Article 27 only to future subsoil concessions. The bill was signed by President Calles on January 3 and became effective on January 11, 1928. The oil issue was not permanently settled because new efforts to nationalize began in Mexico in 1935. For the moment, however, Morrow and Calles had solved the most difficult problem between these neighboring nations. This solution opened the door for Morrow to assist in the settlement of church-state relations in Mexico. See June 30, 1929.

February 6, 1928   THE UNITED STATES AND FRANCE SIGN AN ARBITRATION TREATY
                            WHICH REVISES THE ROOT FORMULA OF 1908 THAT LIMITED
                            THE USE OF ARBITRATION.

Secretary of State Kellogg believed a new formula for arbitration was necessary that would no longer exclude such questions as national honor. Kellogg's formula excluded from arbitration only matters of domestic jurisdiction, third parties, the Monroe Doctrine, and the League of Nations. He signed the first of these new treaties with France on February 6. Before leaving office, 18 other nations signed new arbitration agreements with America. None of these were invoked during the next 50 years.

February 18, 1928   CHARLES E. HUGHES DEFENDS THE NECESSITY OF U.S. INTER-
                            VENTION IN DISORDERLY STATES DURING THE FINAL PLENARY
                            SESSION OF THE SIXTH PAN-AMERICAN CONFERENCE IN HAVANA.

Because of recent U.S. problems in Mexico and Nicaragua, the American delegation went to the Havana Conference, which convened on January 16, fully expecting anti-American resolutions by Argentina, El Salvador, and other delegations. Charles E. Hughes had been selected to head the U.S. delegation in order to add stature to the American group and to provide excellent statesmanship during the expected difficult sessions.

Hughes fulfilled his duties in commendable fashion. Setting a theme during his opening conference speech, Hughes said America was not an aggressor. "Nothing could be happier for the United States than that all the countries of the Caribbean region should be strong, self-sufficient, fulfilling their destiny, settling their problems, with peace at home and the fulfillment of their obligations abroad."

The anti-American tone of many discussions remained, however, until the conference's final regular session. The question of the right of intervention in a nation had been discussed in the Committee on International Public Law but no "balanced" view of the proper position had been agreed upon. The committee members agreed to delay the subject until the 1933 conference. Then, during the final session, Salvador's Foreign Minister, Gustavo GUERRERO, offered a resolution which stated, "No State has the right to intervene in the internal affairs of another."

A lengthy debate ensued because Hughes insisted that the opposition should be heard and the matter settled. For some time, Hughes listened to a variety of accusations against the "colossus of the north," as well as the efforts of some friends to defend the United States. By the time Hughes rose to speak, the potential vote on the Guerrero resolution was not certain.

Hughes convinced the delegates and the large crowd of visitors, mostly Cuban, to disapprove Guerrero's resolution. Asking the interpreter to translate each sentence, not to summarize, Hughes explained that he believed this critical decision should be delayed until 1933 so that a proper resolution could be studied. He restated his concept of U.S. policy in the Western Hemisphere. America, he asserted, yielded to none in its desire that all nations be independent and sovereign. "We do not wish to intervene in the affairs of any American republic. We simply wish peace and order and stability and recognition of honest rights properly acquired so that this hemisphere may not only be the hemisphere of peace but the hemisphere of international justice." He said U.S. citizens were in danger of their lives in Nicaragua. "Are we to stand and see them butchered in the jungle because a government ... can no longer afford reasonable protection?" The United States had a right to protect its citizens and it would not forsake that. Nations must accept duties as well as rights. If all states recognized their duties and carried them out, interventions would not be necessary. Justice as well as rights was essential.

Hughes's speech proved to be so effective that Guerrero withdrew his resolution. Notably, however, Hughes's demeanor and attitude throughout the conference had contrasted sharply with the often arrogant, superior tones which Americans such as Theodore Roosevelt used toward Latin Americans or the moralistic tone Woodrow Wilson had used. In this respect, Hughes's speech directed the evolution of U.S. policy away from American intervention toward greater sensitivity and respect for Latin Americans. See February 28, 1929.

May 3, 1928   JAPANESE AND CHINESE FORCES CLASH IN SHANTUNG BECAUSE
                       THE JAPANESE INTERVENE TO BLOCK THE NORTHWARD CONQUESTS
                       OF CHIANG KAI-SHEK'S NATIONALIST ARMY.

Japan had briefly intervened in Shantung during May-June of 1927 to stop the Nationalist Army's march toward Peking. In April, 1928, Japan again landed forces in Shantung and seized control of the railroads in that region. There were several skirmishes between Japanese and Chinese forces for a week before Japan and Chiang's representatives met to resolve the issue. On March 28, 1929, the dispute was compromised and Japan withdrew its troops on May 20, 1929.

July 21, 1928   AN AMERICAN OIL CONSORTIUM RECEIVES A SHARE OF THE
                       INTERNATIONAL OIL CONCESSIONS IN THE FORMER OTTOMAN
                       EMPIRE, ESPECIALLY IRAQ.

Because the Chester concessions had failed (see December 11, 1911, and April 10, 1923), the first successful U.S. oil concession in the Middle East was undertaken by a consortium of seven (later merged into two) U.S. oil companies.

Acting on his belief that the United States needed to secure future oil supplies, Secretary of Commerce Herbert Hoover met with oil company representatives in May, 1921, encouraging them to seek oil rights under an open door policy in Mesopotamia. In November, 1921, seven oil companies formed a consortium to negotiate with the British-owned Turkish Petroleum Company (TPC), which controlled oil concessions in Mesopotamia. The seven U.S. companies were Jersey Standard, SOCONY, Sinclair, Texas, Gulf, Mexican, and Atlantic.

Between 1922 and 1928, the oil consortium, led by W.C. Teagle of Jersey Standard, held talks with TPC while the British diplomats ironed out details of the postwar status of the former Ottoman Empire's territory. As a result, on July 21, 1928, the American group signed an agreement with TPC (later renamed the Iraq Petroleum Company) which gave the Americans a 23.75% share of oil rights in former Ottoman territory. The other oil companies with shares of the TPC concessions were the Anglo-Persia, Royal Dutch Shell, and the French Petroleum. These members agreed not to pursue independent explorations for oil within a "Red Line Agreement" region which virtually encompassed all of the old Ottoman Empire except Turkey proper. The two American corporations which because of mergers by 1928 remained in the U.S. oil consortium were Jersey Standard (Exxon) and Socony Vacuum (Mobil).

July 25, 1928 THE UNITED STATES RECOGNIZES CHIANG KAI-SHEK'S NATIONALIST GOVERNMENT OF CHINA, SIGNING A TARIFF TREATY WITH THE CHINESE.

Between 1926 and 1928, the Kuomintang had severed its communist influence (see April 12, 1927) and, on June 8 it completed the pacification of most of central China by capturing Peking. In addition, Chiang's government had negotiated a settlement of the Nanking protests of April 11, 1927, by paying reparations for damages and accepting an American apology for the U.S. naval bombardment of Nanking.

The tariff treaties of July 25 ended previous unequal treaties and awarded China tariff autonomy *as soon as the other tariff-treaty nations did likewise*. Following the concurrence of the other powers, U.S.-Chinese trade would be on a most-favored-nation basis. Between July 25 and December 22, 1928, 12 other nations approved similar treaties with China. Nevertheless, because Japan delayed a new tariff agreement until May, 1933, the U.S. treaty of 1928 did not go into effect for five years.

Sino-American attempts to end the unequal extraterritorial treaties did not succeed. The 1926 Commission on Extraterritoriality had met in Peking in 1926 but civil disorders prevented the commission's work between 1926 and 1928. In 1928, the Nationalist government unilaterally abrogated extraterritoriality treaties with Portugal, Italy, and Denmark but did not risk similar tactics against the larger foreign powers. U.S.-Chinese discussions on these legal matters lasted for another 15 years before the last unequal treaty ended in 1943.

August 27, 1928   14 NATIONS SIGN THE KELLOGG-BRIAND PACT TO OUTLAW WAR.

The signing of this treaty culminated the search for an easy solution to international problems which began after the U.S. Senate defeated the Treaty
of Versailles in 1920. A Chicago lawyer, Salmon O. Levinson, formed the American Committee for the Outlawry of War which urged nations to declare war
illegal so that they would never again go to war. Members of the committee
included Senator William Borah, Chairman of the Senate Foreign Relations Committee; philosopher John Dewey; and Charles C. Morrison, editor of the *Christian Science Monitor*. Two American officers of the Carnegie Endowment for
International Peace also claimed that in 1927 they influenced Aristide Briand,
the French Foreign Minister, to formulate a pact to renounce warfare. The
two Carnegie officers were Nicholas Murray Butler, President of Columbia University, and Dr. James T. Shotwell, professor of history at Columbia University.

     Dr. Shotwell drafted Briand's speech of April 6, 1927, which became the
basis for the peace pact. Briand believed that some sort of agreement with
the United States would assist France in avoiding a future war with Germany.
France was completing a Little Entente series of alliances with several small
European nations (see November 11, 1927), but Briand thought a negative pact
condemning an aggressor nation as an outlaw would place the United States on
the French side in a war. In this context, Briand's message of April 6 proposed to the American people and Washington officials that France was prepared
to accept a Franco-American agreement to "outlaw war."

     Even though Briand's speech was not offered through normal diplomatic
channels, Secretary of State Kellogg responded on June 11 by informing newsmen that he was ready to consider Briand's proposal.

     On June 20, 1927, Briand sent Kellogg a draft proposal by which the
French and the American people would mutually condemn the use of war and settle all disputes between their nations by "pacific means."

     Belatedly, Kellogg and his State Department advisors now planned to ig-
nore Briand's suggestion. Realizing that Briand hoped to gain some type of
U.S.-French alliance, they hoped silence would quietly bury the French proposal. Peace groups in America would not be silent, however, and they pressured the State Department to accept Briand's offer. Levinson's committee
promoted a letter-writing campaign, sending the State Department huge bags
of mail in favor of outlawing war. Feminist advocates such as Carrie Chapman
and Jane Addams also organized a pro-treaty group.

     Unable to ignore these public expressions, Kellogg consulted with Sena-
tor Borah who agreed that a multinational pact on peace would prevent a treaty
with France from being construed as a French alliance. On this basis, Kellogg
answered Briand's note of June 20 in a December 28, 1927, note which said
the United States accepted the French proposal and hoped all nations could
be invited to join the movement to outlaw war as a method for settling disputes. In reality, of course, this ploy weakened a Franco-American treaty
under the diplomatic principle that the more parties there are to an agreement, the less likely it is to be binding on any one power. Through Borah's
office as Chairman of the Senate Foreign Relations Committee, Kellogg had
that group accept his treaty proposal prior to responding to Briand.

     As drawn up by Kellogg on December 28, the peace pact proposed to abolish
all war. There would be no reservations or qualifications to the treaty permitting a nation to justify war. The treaty would simply bind all nations
to declare they were "renouncing war as an instrument of national policy."
Ideally, there would be no war, no need for alliances, no need for armies

and navies. It was a bold concept but far in advance of the capacity of na-tions to honor.

Kellogg's response placed Briand on the defensive. He did not want a multilateral treaty which sounded like Jesus Christ's Sermon on the Mount. Yet Briand could not denounce Kellogg's suggestion. Briand had received the Nobel Peace Prize for negotiating the Locarno Treaty and his reputation would not permit him to back away from a peace proposal. Kellogg rejected Briand's proposal for the United States to sign a treaty with France before calling an international peace conference. Nor would Kellogg agree to add any statements about sanctions against an aggressor who violated the treaty. Kellogg's only qualification was made in a circular note to the great powers on June 23, 1928, wherein he said America accepted the "interpretation" that it would not be illegal for a nation to defend itself against violators of the league cov-enant, the Locarno treaties, or the French alliances.

Between April 23 and August 27, 14 nations accepted the Kellogg proposal as "interpreted" by the note of June 23. Great Britain accepted with a fur-ther qualification that excluded world regions vital to British security. Partly to persuade the United States to make a cooperative pact, partly be-cause they did not desire the embarrassment of failing to accept the pact, the major powers accepted the Kellogg Pact.

Thus, on August 27, delegates of 14 nations assembled in Paris to sign the short, simple two-article agreement. The U.S. Senate ratified the treaty on January 15, 1929. The other signatory nations ratified the pact by July 24, 1929, when President Herbert Hoover proclaimed the treaty to be in effect. Other nations later joined in signing the pact, and by 1929, 64 nations had accepted the peace pact which outlawed war.

Although Kellogg received the Nobel Peace Prize in 1930 for his work on the 1928 pact, the agreement never fulfilled its promise. Before 1929 ended, Russian and Chinese troops went to war in Manchuria, and in 1931, Japan's attack on Manchuria inaugurated a decade during which the Kellogg-Briand Pact was repeatedly violated.

October 20, 1928   *CHINA'S KUOMINTANG (KMT) PROMULGATES ORGANIC LAWS CRE-ATING THE CHINESE NATIONALIST GOVERNMENT.*

By the laws of October 20, five administrative divisions of government were established under the jurisdiction of China's president and highest military authority, Chiang Kai-Shek. Only the KMT party was legal, and as leader of the KMT's executive council Chiang was both the party and government head. In brief, Chiang Kai-Shek was the military dictator of China.

Chiang's government resembled the Soviet-Communist system which Sun Yat-sen set up in 1924. China had official political unity under Chiang. Never-theless, followers of the Chinese Communist Party were busy organizing peasant support in Kiangsi province under the leadership of Mao Tse-tung.

November 6, 1928   HERBERT HOOVER IS ELECTED PRESIDENT.

The Republican Party nominated Hoover at its convention in Kansas City on June 14. The Republican platform favored a federal farm board to assist farm-ers but rejected the McNary-Haugen Act desired by the farm bloc but which Coolidge had twice vetoed. The party also favored the protective tariff and Coolidge's foreign policies.

The Democratic Convention selected Governor Alfred E. Smith of New York for its candidate. Regarding foreign policy, the Democrats wanted immediate independence for the Philippines and condemned the Coolidge policies in Central America.

Smith's loss was attributed partly to religious prejudice because he was a Roman Catholic. Together with his opposition to continued prohibition of alcohol, Smith's religion cost him the electoral votes of five southern states. Hoover won by 444 electoral votes to Smith's 85. The Republicans also retained control of congress.

December 6, 1928   *BORDER CONFLICTS BETWEEN BOLIVIA AND PARAGUAY ARE A PRELUDE TO THE CHACO WAR.*

There had been attempts to settle the Chaco territorial dispute between these two nations before World War I but their claims continued to stimulate friction. Armies of the two states clashed at the border on December 6, and war seemed imminent. The Pan-American Conference offered to mediate and drew up an arbitration treaty on August 31, 1929. Neither Bolivia nor Paraguay would arbitrate but they agreed to negotiate. On April 4, 1930, each side stated it would return to the status quo. The border skirmishes continued, however, and became full-scale war in 1932. See June 14, 1935.

December 20, 1928   *GREAT BRITAIN RECOGNIZES CHIANG KAI-SHEK'S NATIONALIST GOVERNMENT OF CHINA.*

In addition to recognition, Britain concluded a treaty with the Chinese which granted them tariff autonomy provided China abolished coastal and interior duties on English trade. This commercial treaty provided a partial release for China from the unequal treaties which the British instituted after the Opium War in 1842.

1929

January 5, 1929   A SPECIAL INTER-AMERICAN CONFERENCE ADOPTS TREATIES
FOR CONCILIATION AND ARBITRATION.

Meeting at Washington between December 10, 1928, and January 5, 1929, this
special session of delegates from 20 Pan-American states adopted two treaties:
one provided for arbitration of all juridical questions and set up a commission to handle such cases; the other provided methods to conciliate other
categories of disputes. Of the 20 states, 16 ratified the arbitration treaty,
which became effective on October 28, 1929; 18 ratified the conciliation
treaty, which went into effect on November 15, 1929.

February 28, 1929   SECRETARY OF STATE KELLOGG "REVOKES" THE ROOSEVELT
COROLLARY TO THE MONROE DOCTRINE.

Kellogg's experience in Latin American affairs increasingly steered his
thoughts to oppose U.S. intervention as a proper policy. He preferred the
tone of respect if not the entire substance of Hughes's speech of February 18,
1928, which defended the right to intervene. Yet he had expressed anti-
intervention views privately in a letter to Ambassador Robert Woods Bliss on
April 10, 1928.
    On February 28, 1929, as his term of office neared its end, he sent a
circular letter of instructions to the U.S. envoys throughout Latin America,
expressing his favor for cooperation with Latin American nations. The United
States, he said, had no right to enforce good behavior in Latin America as
Theodore Roosevelt had implied in 1905. The Monroe Doctrine, Kellogg contended, was against Europe, not Latin America. "The Doctrine is not a lance;
it is a shield."
    Evidently, Kellogg's circular letter expressed views based on a study
of the Monroe Doctrine by J. Reuben Clark, the Undersecretary of State. Clark
concluded that the Roosevelt Corollary could be justified on the basis of
self-preservation but not in terms of the Monroe Doctrine. Clark's study
was not publicized until 1930 when the Government Printing Office published
it for the State Department. It is usually referred to as the Clark Memorandum.

March 5, 1929   HENRY L. STIMSON IS COMMISSIONED AS SECRETARY OF STATE
BY PRESIDENT HOOVER.

Stimson was well qualified to serve as Secretary of State. Trained as a lawyer, he was a progressive Republican who admired Theodore Roosevelt. He
served as Secretary of War under President Taft (1911-1913); as a special
presidential representative to Nicaragua during a crisis in 1927; and as Governor General of the Philippine Islands from 1927 to 1929. During the debate

on the League of Nations in 1919, Stimson favored the Lodge reservationist
position although he believed Lodge permitted the irreconcilable Republicans
to have too much influence in the Senate. Stimson was secretary throughout
Hoover's term of office.

March 28, 1929   THE STATE DEPARTMENT ASSISTS STANDARD OIL OF CALIFORNIA
                         (SOCAL) TO ARRANGE OIL CONCESSIONS IN BAHRAIN.

Located on several islands in the Persian Gulf, the Sheikhdom of Bahrain had
been under British protection since the 1880's. On December 12, 1928, SOCAL
purchased oil rights in Bahrain from the Gulf Oil Company but discovered that
a British treaty with the sheikh required that the registration and direction
of any oil company had to be British.

To obtain Britain's consent for the concession, SOCAL sought State Department assistance, and on March 28, the U.S. Embassy in London undertook
discussions with England to resolve the issue. During 1930, the British
agreed that SOCAL could arrange a contract with Bahrain through its Canadian
subsidiary, the Bahrain Petroleum Company, which was Canadian incorporated
and British directed. This procedure complied with the British treaty requirements and permitted the American-owned company to invest in Bahrain.
By 1935, SOCAL had 16 producing oil wells in Bahrain.

June 3, 1929   *CHILE AND PERU SETTLE A LONG-LIVED BOUNDARY DISPUTE.*

*This dispute had begun during the 1870's, led to war in 1883, and eventually
to an uneasy truce and a break in diplomatic relations in 1910. (See October
20, 1883.) In 1922, Secretary of State Hughes heard that the two nations
would accept his good offices to resolve their problem and invited their representatives to Washington.*

*Hughes worked with delegates of both nations, finally persuading them
to agree to arbitration regarding a plebiscite to determine territorial ownership. After they agreed on July 20, 1922, they asked Hughes to act as the
arbitrator. The secretary sought to dissuade them, but because both sides
trusted Hughes's judgment, they insisted and Hughes accepted that duty.*

*With the assistance of William C. Dennis, Hughes examined all documents
in the dispute from both Chile and Peru and decided a plebiscite should be
held. He prescribed conditions for conducting the election, including the
selection of a Plebiscitary Commission with delegates from each nation and a
chairman named by the President of the United States.*

*President Coolidge named General John Pershing to head the commission,
but its task proved hopeless. Both sides sought to move people in and out
of the disputed land of Tacna and Arica and the election was postponed several
times. Although the election was not held, Hughes had provided for continued
negotiations by both sides until the dispute ended.*

*Finally, the two nations resolved the question on June 3, 1929. Chile
occupied Arica, Peru received Tacna. Chile agreed to allow Peru to use the
port in Arica and gave Bolivia a railway outlet to the Pacific Ocean. Chile
also aided Bolivia in its border dispute with Paraguay.*

June 30, 1929   AMBASSADOR MORROW ASSISTS IN RECONCILING CHURCH-STATE
                                RELATIONS IN MEXICO.

Following President Calles' election in 1925, controversy arose not only over
subsoil properties (see January 11, 1928) but also about enforcement of the
anti-clerical articles of the Constitution of 1917. The revolutionaries distrusted the power of the Church in both political and economic affairs. Consequently, in January, 1926, Calles issued decrees to nationalize Church property, close Church schools, and stop the teaching activity of religious orders. In response, the Mexican bishops, with approval of the papacy, suspended all Church services on July 31, 1926.

Three years of political-religious antagonism resulted in Mexico, leading
U.S. Ambassador Morrow to seek a settlement not on a diplomatic basis but on
a personal basis. The U.S. ambassador believed Mexico's social order would
be endangered until a settlement was reached with the Church. To assist this
process Morrow brought American Catholic Church representatives to Mexico for
secret meetings in April and May, 1928. These contacts inaugurated a series
of proposals for a settlement of the outstanding Mexican disputes between
Calles and the Mexican Church authorities. The government reached a compromise with the Mexican Catholic Church leaders which, after the pope approved,
became effective on June 30, 1929. On that day at Cuernavaca, Ambassador
Morrow heard the cathedral bells peal for the first time in three years. He
told his wife, "I have opened the churches of Mexico."

August 31, 1929   THE HAGUE ECONOMIC CONFERENCE COMPLETES AGREEMENTS
                               WHICH RATIFY THE YOUNG PLAN ON GERMAN REPARATIONS.

The Agent General for Reparations Payments, who was the executive officer of
the Transfer Committee set up in 1924, provided annual reports on the German
reparations under the Dawes Plan. In his fourth interim report on June 7,
1928, the agent indicated that an agreement for the final reparations schedules should be made soon. Through the foreign loans Germany had secured,
they had met the payments scheduled by the Dawes Plan in 1924 and the Transfer
Committee believed Germany now had long-term paying capacity, a view which
later historians found to be unduly optimistic.

Nevertheless, the Allied powers began discussions for a second reparations meeting, with France being especially eager to obtain a final settlement. Following negotiations, France convinced the allies to link the reparations settlement to an agreement for the allies to end their occupation of
the Rhineland, and a new commission was agreed to on September 16, 1928.
Germany objected because she wished to separate the evacuation issue but, as
usual in the 1920's, the German Republic's views were overridden. The new
commission added German and Japanese delegates to the 1924 Dawes Committee,
which included Great Britain, France, Belgium, Italy, and the United States.
The principal U.S. delegate, Owen D. Young, chaired the commission.

The Young Committee met from February 9 to June 7, formulating a series
of recommendations which became the basis of the final reparations settlement.
The committee did not settle all details of procedure, however. These agreements necessitated the approval of political representatives of all the Allied
nations of World War I. The political sessions were held at the Hague between
August 6 and 31, 1929, when the preliminary agreements were signed by 15 governments, including Germany. The United States attended the Hague meetings
only as an observer.

The Young Plan recommendations as changed slightly by the Hague delegates resulted in the following reparations agreements:

1. *Fixed total German liabilities.* The total reparations were divided into two categories: conditional and unconditional. The conditional payments gave Germany some possible relief in case of financial problems. The more critical unconditional payments could not be delayed and, as adjusted at the Hague, amounted to 673.8 million marks per year for 59 years. Payment in kind could only be made during the first 10 years.

2. *Linkage of reparations to U.S. debt requirements.* The agreement recognized that the conditional reparations could vary according to the charges the Allies had to make to pay their debts to the United States. Both Britain and France wanted the total annual payments to at least equal their debt payment to America.

3. *An end to safeguards on Germany.* Both the Transfer Committee of 1924 and other earlier organizations to oversee German payments were abolished. Germany was made solely responsible to determine that the Young Plan schedule was complied with when due.

4. *Creation of a Bank for International Settlements.* This bank acted as the intermediary between Germany and the Allies, changing all problems of payment into economic not political disputes. The bank would also serve to stimulate international trade and to exchange information on financial conditions with all parties to the agreement.

5. *Changes in earlier percentages for receipt of reparations.* In particular, Great Britain decided it needed more funds to meet its U.S. debts, and at the Hague conference asked for a higher percentage than it originally had been allocated. To provide more for the British, France agreed to reduce her total reparations in return for a larger percentage of unconditional reparations.

6. *Settlement of any dispute over the reparations payments by arbitration.*

7. *Evacuation by Great Britain, France, and Belgium of all their Rhineland Occupation forces by June 30, 1930.*

The Hague Conference agreements left certain matters open for further settlement by seven special committees which continued to work until November, 1919. A jurists' commission drafted these reports into legal agreements and, between January 3 and January 20, 1930, a second Hague Conference settled those issues. See January 20, 1930.

October 1, 1929   *GREAT BRITAIN RESUMES DIPLOMATIC RECOGNITION OF RUSSIA.*

The Zinoviev letter's alleged interference in Britain's election of October, 1924, resulted in generally bad relations with Russia and a diplomatic break between the two nations on May 26, 1927. The Labour Party's victory in the elections on May 30, 1929, returned Ramsay MacDonald as prime minister, and new British discussions began with Russia. On October 1, the MacDonald government renewed relations with the Soviet Union on an official basis.

October 29, 1929   THE WALL STREET STOCK MARKET PLUNGE IN PRICES REACHES
                            DISASTROUS PROPORTIONS: DATE USUALLY ASCRIBED TO THE
                            BEGINNING OF THE WORLDWIDE GREAT DEPRESSION.

Although there had been signs of trouble in the stock market before October
29, the trading of 16 million shares in one day heralded a four-year period
of price declines. By November 13, nearly $30 billion of market value of
listed stocks had been lost. As John Kenneth Galbraith notes, the lost sum
was greater than all the dollars in circulation in America in 1929. The international financial community of all nations suffered except for the Soviet
Union, which was isolated generally from the capitalist financial structure.
The low point of the Great Depression was reached in March, 1933.

December 2, 1929   SECRETARY STIMSON INVOKES THE KELLOGG-BRIAND PACT TO
                            PREVENT A SINO-SOVIET WAR. ALTHOUGH THE PACT IS IG-
                            NORED, WAR IS AVOIDED BECAUSE NEITHER NATION WANTS A
                            CONFLICT.

On July 10, 1929, Chinese Nationalist troops seized the Chinese Eastern Railway in Manchuria in an attempt to end the Soviet Union's control over the
railroad. Chiang Kai-shek proposed to regain the Chinese rights in Manchuria
which Russia and Japan had shared since 1896, with Russia controlling the
Chinese Eastern Railway (see May 23, 1924). The Russians opposed
the July 10 attack, and in November, 1929, Soviet forces invaded Manchuria
where several armed skirmishes resulted with China's army.
        Because the Kellogg-Briand Peace Pact had gone into effect on July 24,
1929, Secretary of State Stimson tested its strength by using the pact to
avert a Sino-Soviet conflict. On July 25, Stimson called on Great Britain,
France, Germany, Italy, and Japan to join America in a six-power commission
acting under the Peace Pact to settle the Manchuria dispute. The other nations resented Stimson's interference largely because he had not consulted
them in advance but also because they believed the request was not consonant
with the pact.
        On November 26, Stimson tried again. He sent identical notes to the
five powers, asking them to publicly urge China and Russia to observe the
Kellogg peace agreement. Although all the powers except Italy ignored Stimson's note, the secretary assumed that silence was consent, and on December
2, he wired notes to Russia (by way of France since the United States did
not recognize the Soviet regime) and China, admonishing them to follow the
Peace Pact's obligations because both nations had signed the pact in 1928.
Similar notes were sent to the antagonists by 37 other nations, but their
efforts were pointless. China denied it had violated the pact; Russia told
the other nations to mind their own business.
        By early December, aside from the Peace Pact, China and Russia undertook
discussions to avert war. Russia was too concerned about its domestic Five-
Year Plan to fight a war; China was too weak for a long struggle. On December
22, China and Russia accepted the *status quo* in Manchuria by signing the Protocol of Khabarovsk.

1930

THE SECOND HAGUE ECONOMIC CONFERENCE MAKES AGREEMENTS
WHICH RESOLVE PENDING REPARATIONS PROBLEMS.

Convening on January 3, the Hague conference finalized details of the Young
Plan recommendations of August 31, 1929. The important agreements of this
conference were:

1. A treaty between Germany and the World War I allies ended all financial questions. German accounts under the reparations clauses of
   the Versailles Treaty would be fulfilled when Germany ratified the
   Young Plan as modified by the Hague Conferences ending August 31,
   1929, and January 20, 1930. Germany agreed to implement the plan
   for the Bank for International Settlements that would receive its
   payments.

2. In a separate treaty, the United States and Germany on December 28,
   1929, disassociated American claims from other Allied claims. These
   included German payments for the occupation army and mixed claims
   of American citizens. The occupation payments would run to March 31,
   1966, ranging between 16.4 and 35.3 million marks annually. The
   mixed claims would run until March 31, 1981, at 40.8 million marks
   per year.

3. Sanctions for German default were provided for. Although the Young
   Plan recommended that German good faith should replace the sanctions
   for non-payment contained in the Dawes Plan, an incident during the
   fall of 1929 forced France to insist on the possibility of sanctions.
   In Germany, the Nationalist Party had obtained a plebiscite asking
   Germans to repudiate the war guilt clause and the financial obligations incurred by Germany in the Treaty of Versailles. The plebiscite vote of December 22, 1929, rejected the proposal by 20 million
   votes to 5.5 million, but France feared that a new German government
   might repudiate these treaty obligations. Consequently, the French
   insisted on adding a statement that expressed hope there would be
   no default but that in the event of a default, the creditor nations
   could appeal to the Permanent Court of International Justice. If
   Germany rejected the court's findings, the Allies reserved their
   "full liberty of action to force German compliance."

4. The Bank for International Settlements was set up in Basel as a Swiss
   corporation. The Swiss agreed to neutralize the bank's activity in
   both peace and war.

During the Second Hague Conference, the delegates also concluded reparations issues with the non-German members of the World War I Central Powers
Alliance. These agreements included:

1. *Austria*. Excepting a few minor claims, all reparations claims against Austria were absolved and Austrian accounts with the Allied powers were closed.

2. *Hungary*. This nation was treated more harshly because of claims by Rumania, Greece, Czechoslovakia, and Yugoslavia. A final reparations schedule was drawn up at the Hague Conference but was not finalized until April 28, 1930.

   In 1924, Hungary had been assessed 200 million gold crowns to be paid over a 20-year period. The Hague Conference altered these payments to provide compensation to Magyar landowners whose estates had been confiscated by Czechoslovakia and Yugoslavia. The 20-year schedule of 1924 remained intact to 1943, but between 1944 and 1966, Hungary would pay 13.5 million gold crowns per year to its four creditor nations, part of these payments going from the Bank for International Settlements to the landowners whose property had been confiscated.

3. *Bulgaria*. This nation's reparations were reduced from the terms of the Treaty of Neuilly. Bulgaria would pay reparations until 1966 on a varied schedule: 10 million gold francs annually between 1931 and 1940; 11.5 million from 1941 to 1950; 12.5 million from 1957 to 1966.

February 6, 1930   *AN AUSTRIAN-ITALIAN FRIENDSHIP TREATY IS SIGNED; MUSSOLINI BEGINS A PUBLIC CAMPAIGN TO REVISE THE PEACE TREATIES OF WORLD WAR I.*

Since 1927, Mussolini sought to coordinate Hungarian and other eastern European nations' proposals to revise the peace treaties in favor of the national demands of lesser powers of Europe. Austria agreed to this proposal as part of the treaty with Italy.

Mussolini's revision campaign resulted in the signing of the Rome protocol by Italy, Austria, and Hungary on March 17, 1934. These agreements provided closer trade relations and foreign policies to counteract France's organization of the Little Entente in eastern Europe.

April 22, 1930   THE LONDON NAVAL CONFERENCE DELEGATES AGREE ON A THREE-POWER TREATY LIMITING CRUISERS, DESTROYERS, AND SUBMARINES.

To assure some success for the London Conference, Great Britain and the United States had carried on discussions during 1929. Designed to extend the Washington naval treaty of 1922 by limiting ships other than battleships and aircraft carriers, the conference preparations required a rapprochement between London and Washington to avoid the failure of the Geneva Conference of 1927 and create good will between England and America. On May 9, Secretary of State Stimson and British Ambassador Sir Esme Howard agreed that high-ranking diplomatic officers would attend the conference so that naval experts would not dominate as they had at Geneva. Later, from October 4 to 10, 1929, Prime Minister Ramsay MacDonald visited America for talks with President Hoover and to speak before a joint session of congress. Although no naval agreements resulted, MacDonald's visit set the stage for closer Anglo-American cooperation during the 1930 conference.

In contrast to these positive preparations for the conference, other developments in 1929 presaged trouble. On August 12, the Japanese informed Washington and London that they would insist on a 10:7 ratio in all ship categories at the next conference. France also indicated its dissatisfaction with the 1922 ratios, contending that its long European coastline and far-flung empire required a larger French allocation of ships. Finally, U.S. and British naval experts continued to disagree about cruiser size, ratios, and whether or not tonnage was the proper method to determine naval allocations. In the United States, Allen W. DULLES, a lawyer who had attended the 1925 and 1926 Geneva Conferences, proposed the use of a naval "yardstick" that would base combat strength on gun caliber, age, and tonnage of ships (see Dulles' article in *Foreign Affairs* for January, 1929). U.S. naval leaders considered this proposal but could not agree on a satisfactory method of calculating combat strength by such a measure.

Although these preparatory events left the success of the conference in doubt, Great Britain invited the five naval powers to sessions at London which opened on January 21 and continued until April 22. During the conference, Italy and France rejected agreements beyond those of the 1922 treaties, signing only the treaty to extend battleship limits. Japan, Great Britain, and the United States signed a three-power pact which included the following important agreements:

1. The 5:5:3:1.75:1.75 limits of 1922 battleships were renewed by the five powers and extended to December 31, 1936. Italy and France accepted this treaty but none of the remainder.

2. The tonnage ratio of heavy cruisers with 8-inch guns would be 10:10:7 until December 31, 1935, after which the United States could build additional cruisers which would make the ratio 5:5:3 once again. The United States agreed to this because in 1930 the U.S. naval construction program lagged greatly behind its 1922 limits and could not reach the 1930-1935 ratio before 1936. England did not rely on heavy cruisers but preferred light cruisers.

3. The ship ratio of light cruisers and destroyers would be 10:10:7. In both these categories of ships, Japan was near treaty limits by 1930; Great Britain had built to its small cruiser limits, but not to the destroyer limits; the U.S. Navy lagged in its construction of both kinds of ship.

4. All three powers received parity in submarines.

Obviously, Japan gained most from the 1930 treaty, having received the 10:10:7 ratio or better for all ships except battleships and heavy cruisers. Realistically, the British and Americans limited Japan's naval program more than their own. The U.S. congress in particular had cut the navy budget severely between 1922 and 1929. Although congress approved a 15-cruiser program on February 13, 1929, none of these ships was well under way in April, 1930, and would not be completed until 1939 even if congress continued to fund them. In 1922, the United States had negotiated from a position of naval strength; it held a weak position in 1930.

During hearings on Senate ratification during 1930, U.S. naval leaders largely opposed the London treaties, as they had opposed the 1922 agreements. The naval officer who defended the treaties was Admiral William V. Pratt. As a younger officer in 1922 Pratt saw the advantages in the limitation of battleships. Pratt strongly advocated the rapid development of an aircraft carrier task force, a concept forward-looking naval theorists preferred to battleships and heavy cruisers. President Hoover had appointed Pratt as a delegate to the London Conference and subsequently he defended the treaties in the Senate hearings.

In contrast, Admiral Hilary P. Jones, who had led the U.S. delegation during the aborted Geneva Conference of 1927, strongly opposed the London agreements. Hoover had recalled Jones from retirement to act as a delegate at London. During February, however, Jones realized that he was in the minority because Secretary Stimson and other U.S. delegates at the London Conference held views on naval limits similar to Pratt's. Jones withdrew from the conference on the excuse that "ulcers" had resulted in illness, making it impossible for him to continue.

An interesting issue that arose during the conference was a French request for an Anglo-American security treaty. French Premier André Tardieu told MacDonald and Stimson that France could accept further naval limits provided they obtained some type of agreement to guarantee their security from future invasion. Although Secretary Stimson agreed to consider a consultative pact if one could be worked out, President Hoover rejected negotiations regarding a guarantee treaty. Hoover knew the U.S. Senate would reject such a treaty.

Despite objections from U.S. Navy officials, the Senate ratified the London treaties on July 24, 1930, by a vote of 58 to 9. The hearings on the treaty disclosed that the U.S. Navy would require an additional one billion dollars to begin to reach the 1922 treaty limits. Such expenditures were unthinkable to senators in 1930.

September 6, 1930   *IN ARGENTINA, THE DEMOCRATIC-REPUBLICAN GOVERNMENT IS SUSPENDED WHEN JOSÉ URIBURU OUSTS PRESIDENT IRIGOYEN.*

A democratic Argentine government, established in 1912, had instituted reforms such as factory acts, pensions, and regulation of workhouses. Irigoyen had been elected president from 1916 to 1922 when Marcelo Alvear won a six-year term. In 1928, Irigoyen was again elected, but after the depression began he sought greater authority to deal with the nation's problems. Uriburu's coup d'état gave the conservatives control of the government. In 1932, the Conservative Augustin JUSTO was elected president. He undertook a recovery program which was successful. Nevertheless, disorders and opposition from Liberals and Radicals continued in parts of Argentina.

November 14, 1930   *JAPAN'S PREMIER, YŪKŌ HAMAGUCHI, IS ASSASSINATED, MARKING A MOVEMENT TOWARD MILITARY CONTROL OF JAPAN'S GOVERNMENT.*

Against the wishes of Japanese naval leaders, Hamaguchi recommended that the emperor should ratify the London Naval Treaty of April 22, 1930. A military fanatic shot the premier on November 14. Although another member of Hamaguchi's party, Reijiro Wakatsuki, became premier, Japan's party leaders were gradually subordinated to the influence of naval and military groups over the next 18 months. See May 15, 1932.

1931

June 17, 1931   THE U.S. CONGRESS APPROVES THE SMOOT-HAWLEY TARIFF

This law continued the American protective tariff policy, raising agricultural raw materials rates from 38 percent under the 1922 Fordney-McCumber Act to 49 percent and other commodity rates from 31 percent to 34 percent.

June 20, 1931   PRESIDENT HOOVER OFFERS TO POSTPONE ALL DEBT PAYMENTS OWED AMERICA IF THE EUROPEANS POSTPONE PAYMENTS ON DEBTS DUE THEM.

The world-wide economic depression, which began on October 29, 1929, combined with Germany's already shaky economy of the 1920's, had brought the German Republic to severe economic problems including its inability to continue reparations payments after June 1, 1931. Since 1924, German reparations payments of about 5 billion marks had been managed largely with foreign loans, not with a surplus in the German budget or balance of trade. By the spring of 1931, as the German economy experienced greater difficulty and the Austrian Credit-Anstalt failed on May 11, gold and foreign-exchange funds began leaving Germany, many gold reserves going to the United States.

    As the crisis became apparent, Hoover's fiscal advisors recommended that he call a moratorium on U.S. debt payments provided the Europeans agreed to delay payments on German reparations. Hoover agreed but first obtained the consent of 21 senators and 18 representatives of both major parties. With their concurrence, Hoover made the American proposal for a one-year debt moratorium on June 20.

    In making his announcement, Hoover implicitly showed the necessary interrelation of war debts, reparations, and the fiscal stability of both Europe and America. He hoped the moratorium would reestablish economic confidence and provide "political peace and economic stability in the world." The debtor nations had to recover their national prosperity. "I am suggesting," he said, "to the American people that they be wise creditors in their own interest and be good neighbors."

    For the first time in America, Hoover's debt moratorium officially recognized the connection between American war credits and German reparations. Heretofore, U.S. presidential administrations, congress, and the public refused to acknowledge these complex aspects of international finance. Many Americans continued to object to this analysis and thought of national debts as personal debts. To carry out Hoover's proposal, both the European governments and the U.S. congress had to approve. See July 24, August 11, and December 23, 1931.

July 24, 1931   A SEVEN-POWER CONFERENCE IN LONDON SEEKS TO RESTORE CONFIDENCE IN GERMAN FINANCES.

In addition to the one-year debt-reparations moratorium proposed by Hoover on June 20, 1931, the Western powers needed to stop the withdrawal of foreign capital funds from German banks. The flow of gold and foreign-exchange notes from Germany continued until July, when the rate of flow began to double. As a result, the fiscal future of the other west European nations became shaky and gold funds left England as well.

To end the fund outflow of Germany, England invited six other nations to send delegates to London to resolve the problem. On July 21, the conference convened with delegates from France, Germany, Italy, Belgium, Japan, Great Britain, and the United States. Secretary of State Stimson and Secretary of the Treasury Mellon represented America, and their proposals formed the basis of the London agreements on July 24. The conference delegates asked their respective governments to use influence to maintain private and central bank credits in Germany at a stable level. They asked the Bank for International Settlements to establish a committee to study means to replace Germany's foreign capital. Finally, they recommended greater political cooperation with Germany to provide long-term German stability. See August 18, 1931.

August 11, 1931   A COMMITTEE OF FINANCIAL EXPERTS AGREES ON A PLAN TO IMPLEMENT PRESIDENT HOOVER'S MORATORIUM PROPOSAL.

Before this finance committee could be formed, a French-American agreement became necessary because the French government strongly objected to the moratorium as suggested on June 20. Subsequently, the French delayed the agreement for two weeks during which Secretary of the Treasury Andrew Mellon and U.S. Ambassador Walter Edge persuaded the French Foreign Minister to approve the moratorium.

According to the French-American agreement of July 6, the moratorium terms included the following:

1. Germany would be loaned funds for the unconditional payment schedule of the Young Plan as a form of continued payment during the moratorium.

2. The suspended payment loans would be paid in 10 years under a separate payment schedule to begin on July 1, 1933.

Although the two-week delay caused further problems for Germany, the committee of experts suggested by Hoover met in London on July 17. On August 11, the delegates accepted the one-year moratorium plan as proposed by Hoover and as qualified by the July 6 French-American understanding.

August 18, 1931   A COMMITTEE OF CENTRAL BANKS RECOMMENDS METHODS TO HELP RESTORE CONFIDENCE IN GERMANY'S ECONOMY.

This committee of banking leaders resulted from the London Conference, which had adjourned on July 24. Headed by the U.S. delegate, Albert H. Wiggin, it became known as the Wiggin Committee. This group surveyed Germany's credit status and reported the following:

1. Germany's existing foreign credits should be maintained in line with the "standstill" agreement for all short-term credits.

2. All or part of the foreign capital which left Germany should be restored. Long-term loans should be made to Germany and its external obligations should be revised.

September 1, 1931   AN INTERNATIONAL FINANCE MEETING IN LONDON ARRANGES A
                        "STANDSTILL" AGREEMENT ON GERMANY'S PRIVATE SHORT-TERM
                        CREDITS.

Following announcement of the Hoover moratorium on war debts on June 20, 1931,
a financial conference of bankers met in London to negotiate similar arrangements for private short-term credits. These credits had enlarged considerably
since 1924, totaling approximately $5 billion, of which $1.7 billion was from
U.S. banks.

On September 1, the British, French, and American financiers agreed to
a six-month standstill on German payments. The standstill agreement became
an annual affair, being extended to 1940 by U.S. banks under provisions that
allowed liquidation of some funds with losses to the creditors. In 1940,
the U.S. credit had been reduced, with losses, to $40 million.

September 18, 1931   THE "MUKDEN INCIDENT" LEADS TO JAPAN'S OCCUPATION OF
                         A LARGE PART OF EASTERN MANCHURIA.

*According to Tokyo, the Kwantung Army guarding the South Manchurian Railway
near Mukden had been startled by an explosion and had fired on Chinese soldiers fleeing from the site. This incident led the army to move on the night
of September 18-19 to defend itself from the Chinese troops at Mukden and
elsewhere. This version of the incident was fabricated by local Japanese
officers, a fact which the Lytton Report by the League of Nations implied on
October 2, 1934, and the Tokyo War Crimes Trials of 1946 to 1948 verified in
detail. The later evidence shows that the Mukden plot was devised by Colonel
Itagaki and Lieutenant Colonel Ishiwara of the Kwantung Army with the implied
consent of the Commander of the Kwantung Army, General Honjo, and General
Tatekawa of the Army General Staff. Although General Tatekawa was sent to
Manchuria by the Tokyo authorities to avert overt action by the Kwantung Army,
Tatekawa arrived in Manchuria on September 18 but went directly to a geisha
house without delivering his message. Consequently, following the explosion,
Colonel Itagaki ordered his troops to attack the Chinese forces in Mukden
and General Honjo launched a general attack by all Japanese forces in Manchuria. On September 19, the Kwantung Army seized Amt'ung, Yingh'ou, and
Changchu. On the grounds of self-defense, the army advanced throughout the
three eastern provinces of Manchuria, occupying each of them by February 5,
1932.*

*The Mukden incident resulted from a long series of Chinese-Japanese dis-
putes going back to the war of 1894-1895. Japan gained dominance in eastern
Manchuria between 1905 and 1929 while retaining the fiction of Chinese territorial integrity. The rise of Chinese nationalism challenged Japan following
Chiang Kai-shek's unification of China in 1928. Subsequently, Chinese boycotts and demonstrations threatened the Japanese. Also in 1928, Chang Tso-lin,
the Manchurian ruler who disliked Chiang Kai-shek and cooperated with Tokyo,
was replaced by Chang Hsueh-liang. The new Chang ruler was an avowed Chinese
nationalist who received an appointment from Chiang Kai-shek as the commander-
in-chief of the Northeastern Frontier Army and ruler of Manchuria, Jehol, and
part of Inner Mongolia.*

*During the late summer of 1931, the Kwantung Army leaders advocated a
more forceful policy against the Chinese but the Japanese Ministries of
Hamaguchi and Wakatsuki desired to negotiate with China to maintain Japan's
economic controls in Manchuria. Dissatisfied with the ministries' proposals,*

officers in the Kwantung Army fabricated an incident to justify their take-
over in Manchuria.

   In Tokyo, the Kwantung Army's offensive was popular with the public but
divided Prime Minister Wakatsuki's government. See December 10, 1931, and
January 7 and 28, 1932.

September 21, 1931   THE BANK OF ENGLAND IS FORCED TO ABANDON THE GOLD
                       STANDARD.

Great Britain's economic difficulties had been exacerbated by the world-wide
economic depression which disrupted the world trade on which British finances
depended. When the British loss of gold reserves grew in 1931, the Federal
Reserve Bank of New York and the Bank of France provided Britain with £25 million of credits, but these funds did not suffice to balance England's budget
and balance of payments deficits. Therefore, in September the National Coalition Ministry was formed under Prime Minister Ramsay MacDonald and its members agreed to abandon the gold standard in face of the £100,000 budget deficit for 1931.

   The devaluation of the British pound sterling caused England's currency
to depreciate from $4.86 to $3.49 on the world exchange. The British action
also affected other nations whose currency value had been based on the pound
sterling.

December 2, 1931   IN EL SALVADOR, MAXIMILIANO H. MARTINEZ CREATES A
                       RIGHT-WING DICTATORSHIP, SUPPRESSING COMMUNISM AND
                       OTHER LIBERAL MOVEMENTS.

December 9, 1931   SPAIN ADOPTS A REPUBLICAN CONSTITUTION, ABOLISHING
                       THE MONARCHY.

Spain did not participate in World War I, but its industrial developments
grew due to European demands for iron, munitions, and other goods. Liberal
uprisings against King Alfonso XIII and favoring a constituent assembly began
in 1917 but were staunchly repressed after General Miguel Primo de Rivera
established a military dictatorship with the king's consent on September 13,
1923. Although dissolved in 1925, de Rivera's dictatorial government retained
power because he became prime minister.

   In 1929-1930, the economic problems resulting from the depression caused
new liberal agitation, leading to a series of military mutinies following
de Rivera's death on March 16, 1930. The king finally agreed to hold elections during early 1931. The Republicans won an overwhelming victory in mu-
nicipal elections on April 12 and in assembly elections on June 28, 1931.
King Alfonso left Spain in April but refused to abdicate. Nevertheless, the
constituent assembly accused the king of treason, forbade his return, and
confiscated royal property on November 12, 1931.

   The Spanish constitution adopted on December 9 gave universal suffrage,
a single-house assembly, and a ministry responsible to the parliament (cor-
tes). On December 10, the Republican leader Alcala Zamora was elected president of Spain; Manuel Azana was elected prime minister.

December 10, 1931   THE LEAGUE OF NATIONS COUNCIL APPROVES A COMMISSION
                        (THE LYTTON COMMISSION) TO INVESTIGATE THE MUKDEN IN-
                        CIDENT OF SEPTEMBER 18-19, 1931; A U.S. DELEGATE JOINS
                        THE COMMISSION.

Immediately after Japan's army occupied many Manchurian towns on September
19, Secretary of State Stimson and the European diplomats hoped the conflict
would be localized and settled quietly by Tokyo and Peking just as the Sino-
Russian dispute had been in 1929. By November, however, talks had not begun
between the antagonists and the conflict spread when Japanese airplanes bombed
Chinchow on November 9.
    Stimson and President Hoover agreed to work independently but in concert
with the League of Nations Council which considered the conflict at Geneva.
The council sessions, which convened on October 17, were momentous because a
U.S. representative, Prentiss Gilbert, sat at the council table to consult
with the league's members. The October meetings reached no solution to the
dispute but urged China and Japan to negotiate and asked Japan to withdraw
its occupation forces by November 16.
    The council met again on November 16, but Japan had not complied with
the request to withdraw. Therefore, at the suggestion of Tokyo's representative, Tsuneo Matsudaira, the council agreed to appoint an investigatory commission to visit Manchuria. China reluctantly agreed to the proposal because
Japan's forces stayed in place, but Peking could secure no other assistance
from the League of Nations.
    When the commission was being organized in December, Secretary of State
Stimson approved, with Hoover's concurrence, the appointment of General Frank
Ross McCoy to serve as a commission member. The Earl of Lytton, a British
delegate, became chairman of the league's investigation committee. For its
report see February 24, 1933.

December 23, 1931   A U.S. CONGRESSIONAL RESOLUTION APPROVES HOOVER'S DEBT
                        MORATORIUM AFTER AMENDING THE LAW TO DECLARE THAT THE
                        AMERICAN POLICY WAS NOT TO REDUCE OR CANCEL WAR DEBTS.

When Hoover proposed a one-year moratorium on June 20, 1931, his consultation
with 39 congressmen from both parties indicated that they sanctioned his proposal. By the time congress convened for its next session in December, 1931,
the doubts and complaints of many politicians became evident. In particular,
the popular feeling that the Europeans must fully pay their debts caused Americans who did not comprehend international finances to fear that the moratorium was a ploy eventually to abolish all debts.
    Consequently, when the moratorium resolution was introduced to congress
on December 10, the opposition insisted on amendments saying: (1) the one-
year delay did not imply that the debts would be abolished, and (2) the postponed payments on the debts would be funded separately for future repayment
at 3 to 4% interest, depending on the prevailing U.S. bond interest rate.
Congress approved the amended resolution and President Hoover signed the legislation on December 23, 1931.

1932

January 7, 1932   SECRETARY OF STATE STIMSON ANNOUNCES THE "HOOVER-
STIMSON NON-RECOGNITION DOCTRINE" TO PROTEST JAPAN'S
AGGRESSION IN MANCHURIA SINCE SEPTEMBER 19, 1931.

Heretofore, the only step taken against Japan by the League of Nations, England, and France was the league council's request that China and Japan negotiate and Japan withdraw. The investigation commission established by the
league on December 10 only delayed possible action.

The possibility of economic sanctions against Japan had been discussed
but avoided by the Europeans and the league. The Europeans had asked if the
United States would join an embargo or other sanctions to punish Japan.
Stimson informed them that America could not join cooperatively in an embargo
because President Hoover opposed it. On November 19, however, Stimson notified the league council that the United States would not oppose an embargo
or interfere with the league's attempt to employ such action. This was the
closest the United States came to committing itself to cooperation.

Throughout December, 1931, Japan stepped up its attacks in Manchuria and
on January 2, 1932, it captured Chincow, bringing its armies to the border of
China's Great Wall in Jehol. The fall of Chincow persuaded Stimson immediately to issue a proposal which he and President Hoover had discussed as early
as November 9, 1931. Stimson sent non-recognition notes to Peking and Tokyo
on January 7, 1932. The same day he informed the ambassadors of all the
signatory nations of the Nine-Power Pact of 1922 about the American action.

Stimson's non-recognition policy was based on Japan's violation of the
Nine-Power Treaty and the Kellogg-Briand Peace Pact. Although he did not
solicit other nations to follow the American policy, he hoped others might
make similar protests against Japanese aggression. The basic clause of the
non-recognition statement was that the United States "cannot admit the legality of any situation *de facto*" or any agreement between China and Japan which
impaired the treaty rights of Americans. In addition, Stimson asserted, the
United States "does not intend to recognize any situation, treaty, or agreement which may be brought about by means contrary to the covenants and obligations of the Pact of Paris of August 27, 1928...."

The Hoover-Stimson policy was moralistic in tone but had no constructive
results beyond putting the United States on record. Japan's reply to Stimson
on January 16 employed diplomatic politesse to cloak its derisive repudiation
of non-recognition. Moreover, by the end of January, Japan's new military
offensive prepared to be extended south of the Great Wall into China proper,
a region where European and American interests exceeded those in Manchuria.
See January 28 and 31 and March 11, 1932.

January 28, 1932   *JAPANESE TROOPS LAND AT SHANGHAI TO COMPEL CHINA TO*
                       STOP ITS JAPANESE BOYCOTT.

The Japanese landed 70,000 soldiers at the international settlement in Shanghai, driving the 19th Route Chinese Army out of the region. Japan's forces controlled Shanghai until March 4 when China agreed to fulfill Japan's surrender terms. In an agreement signed on May 5, a demilitarized zone was set up in Shanghai and the Chinese ended their Japanese boycott. Because of British and American protest, Japan withdrew its forces from Shanghai by the end of May.

The Shanghai attack rallied world opinion against the Japanese even though no one proposed effective action to stop them. The Japanese air forces bombed civilian urban targets, terrorizing and killing thousands of men, women, and children. Most U.S. newspapers condemned the attacks as uncivilized or "insane imperialism." Few, however, supported proposals to boycott Japanese goods.

January 31, 1932   PRESIDENT HOOVER AND SECRETARY STIMSON PROVIDE MILITARY
                       PREPARATIONS TO PROTECT AMERICANS IN THE PACIFIC AND
                       CHINA.

On January 31, three days after Japan landed forces at Shanghai, Hoover ordered the American Asiatic Squadron to move from Manila to Shanghai. This action paralleled a British decision to follow its protest of Japan's attack by sending two cruisers and a reinforcement of marines to Shanghai.

About two weeks later (February 13), the American fleet arrived in Hawaii as part of the U.S. Navy's winter fleet exercises conducted between California and Hawaii. Because these exercises occurred during the time Japan's military aggression expanded in China, Stimson and Hoover decided to keep the U.S. fleet based at Pearl Harbor rather than return to the Atlantic Ocean when their maneuvers ended.

Although the U.S. fleet movements were designed to demonstrate U.S. purpose in the Pacific, this was a hollow threat. During discussions about American army or navy capabilities in 1932, Secretary of the Navy Charles Francis Adams informed Hoover that U.S. naval experts advised against challenging Japan because the navy was not prepared to engage the Japanese navy if war began. This should not have been news to Hoover because he made the largest budget cuts in U.S. naval history when he approved the 1931-1932 budget. Disarmament on a unilateral basis could be rationally defended for isolated America provided the president and Secretary of State did not risk war in the western Pacific. Of course, Hoover constantly restrained Secretary Stimson during the Manchurian crisis because the president never intended to risk war; Stimson may have.

February 2, 1932   A DISARMAMENT CONFERENCE CONVENES AT GENEVA.

In accordance with a proposal of the Preparatory Commission on Disarmament's recommendation of December 9, 1930 (see May 18, 1926), 60 nations met at Geneva to negotiate a general disarmament agreement. From the outset, the conference's success was doubtful. The draft treaty, which the Preparatory Commission had taken five years to draw up, did not resolve the basic disputes between French and German officials. The Germans desired equality of armaments and the French continued to insist on security guarantees prior to any disarmament.

In an attempt to get the conference to agree, the U.S. delegation, led by Secretary of State Stimson, offered a proposal on June 22, 1932, by which all nations would cut their armaments by one-third. This proposal was not successful. During debates on the concept, the delegates became aware that any military arms limit had to be correlated with political guarantees for the security of all nations from aggression. As France asserted, military cuts could not be accepted unless there were compensatory security pledges. The United States was not willing to make such a commitment. Therefore, the conference adjourned in July and the delegates decided to convene another session on February 2, 1933. During the interim, a special group tried to compromise the German and French demands. See December 11, 1932.

February 18, 1932   *UNDER JAPANESE PROTECTION, THE INDEPENDENCE OF MAN-*
                             CHUKUO (MANCHURIA) IS PROCLAIMED.

Initially, the state of Manchukuo included the three eastern provinces of Manchuria and the province of Jehol, areas the Japanese army occupied between September 19, 1931, and February 1, 1932. Local Manchu officers proclaimed their independence of China on February 18. Three weeks later (March 9) the Japanese installed Henry P'u-i to replace the pro-Chinese Nationalist Manchu-rian ruler Chang Tso-lin. P'u-i, who had abdicated the Chinese throne in 1912, became the emperor of the K'ang Te region in Manchukuo.

February 24, 1932   SECRETARY STIMSON WRITES A LETTER TO SENATOR BORAH
                             STATING THAT IF ANY NATION VIOLATES THE 1922 TREATIES,
                             IT WILL NO LONGER BE COVERED BY OTHER 1922 TREATY PRO-
                             VISIONS.

Searching for a way to show clearly American discontent with Japan's aggres-sion in Manchuria and Shanghai and to warn Tokyo that it risked the abrogation of all the 1922 treaty agreements, including limits on U.S. fortifications in the western Pacific islands, Secretary Stimson wrote a letter that Senator Borah agreed to publicize. The secretary's letter showed America's moral and psychological objections to Japan's action in East Asia but had no other immediate consequences. Stimson also hoped, apparently, to encourage Great Britain to undertake action to forestall Japan, but the British government took no effective action against Japan during 1931-1932.

Following Japan's attack on Shanghai on January 28, Stimson had frequent transatlantic telephone conversations with Sir John Simon, Britain's Foreign Secretary. Stimson urged Simon to obtain league sanctions against Japan in which the United States could cooperate under the Nine-Power Pact of 1922. The British did not wish to act directly, however, contending that they could function only with the League of Nations' agreements and recommendations. For this reason, Stimson's letter to Borah provided a forum for the public American expression of protest against Japan and the application of pressure to get the Europeans to do something. Of course, the letter tactic offered no official American commitment to restrain Japan's aggression.

February 29, 1932   GREAT BRITAIN ENACTS PROTECTIVE TARIFF LEGISLATION,
                         ENDING THE FREE TRADE POLICY BEGUN DURING THE 1840's.

The protective tariff laws included a "corn law" guaranteeing British farmers
about $1 per bushel for specified quantities of home-grown wheat.
    In order to correlate the protective tariff acts with its imperial obli-
gations, the British met with the commonwealth countries from July 21 to August 20. During this Ottawa Imperial Economic Conference, agreements were
made for certain imperial preferential tariffs.

March 11, 1932   THE LEAGUE OF NATIONS ASSEMBLY ADOPTS STIMSON'S NON-
                         RECOGNITION STATEMENT IN ORDER TO AVOID THE INVOCATION
                         OF SANCTIONS AGAINST JAPAN.

This league action was interpreted by some observers as support for the U.S.
position in China. Actually, it was a British-French maneuver to forestall
a league vote for sanctions against Japan which the smaller nations of the
league advocated. Britain's Foreign Minister, Sir John Simon, proposed non-
recognition as a substitute for sanctions and the league assembly adopted
his resolution. For further league action on the Manchurian crisis see February 24, 1933.

May 15, 1932   THE ASSASSINATION OF JAPAN'S PREMIER KI INUKAI ENDS
                         PARTY GOVERNMENT IN TOKYO; MILITARY REACTIONARY GROUPS
                         GAIN POLITICAL CONTROL.

The political leaders in Japan had been blamed by Japanese nationalist spokesmen for a weak foreign policy and for the economic difficulties created in
Japan by the world depression which began in 1929. Following the Mukden incident of September 19, 1931, military groups in Japan issued nationalistic
propaganda favoring a strong Japanese policy abroad to solve the country's
domestic economic problems.
    Following Inukai's assassination, the new ministry consisted entirely
of non-party members in Japan, with the Viscount Makoto Saito as premier.
Patterned on the German constitution of 1871, the ministry was responsible
to the emperor, not to the legislature (the Diet). From 1919 to 1932, party
leaders such as Hamaguchi, Wakatsuki, and Inukai governed with majorities in
the Diet and favored the adoption of this system. Japan's nationalistic and
military officers generally opposed the party policy, asserting that the divine Japanese emperor must wield all power. In 1931-1932, the nationalist-
military factions gained the backing of Emperor Hirohito and disregarded the
party structure in the Diet. This arrangement was opposed by Japan's liberal
politicians, but they did not regain power until Japan surrendered in August,
1945, ending World War II.

July 9, 1932   AT THE LAUSANNE CONFERENCE THE WESTERN EUROPEAN POWERS
                         AND JAPAN PROPOSE THE REORGANIZATION OF GERMANY'S REP-
                         ARATIONS DEBT.

The Lausanne Conference of 1932 became necessary because within a month after
the seven-power agreement on Hoover's one-year moratorium, it became obvious

that Germany's attempt to restore its economic stability would require more than one year.

During the fall of 1931, French Premier Pierre LAVAL met with President Hoover in Washington to discuss a longer period of moratorium. On October 25, Hoover and Laval issued a statement indicating that a longer moratorium would probably be necessary and asking the debtor nation, Germany, to request modifications in the Young Plan.

At Germany's request, a special Advisory Committee of the seven powers met in Basel to review the German debt status. On December 8 that group, which was chaired by Italian delegate Professor Alberto Beneduce, reported:

1. *Germany would not be financially able to resume payments in July, 1932.*

2. *There was a need to adjust all world debts because the Young Plan did not provide for the extreme change in world finances that occurred after 1929.*

Following the Advisory Committee's report, Great Britain invited the signatory nations of the Hague agreements of January 20, 1930, to meet at Lausanne on June 6, 1932, to discuss the debt-reparations problem. No American delegate attended the Lausanne Conference.

On July 9, the 13 governments represented at Lausanne signed an agreement which included the following:

1. *The Young Plan of 1929 and the Hague agreements of 1929-1930 were terminated regarding reparations payments.*

2. *To replace the Young Plan, Germany would deliver bonds worth 3 billion gold marks (approximately 715 million dollars) to the Bank for International Settlements. The bonds would bear 5% annual interest. Following a three-year delay, the bonds would be sold, provided that no issue was below 90% par. Bonds not sold in 15 years would be cancelled and the minimum price would be charged to Germany, assuming its credit was restored. In effect, this plan eliminated nine-tenths of Germany's reparations liability because if all the bonds were sold, German costs would have been $2 billion compared to the $25 billion due under the Young Plan.*

3. *The signatory creditor nations agreed to suspend all war debts payments among themselves.*

4. *RATIFICATION OF THE LAUSANNE TREATY. This clause provided that the agreements would become effective only after a satisfactory settlement was concluded between the signatory nations and their creditor nation (America). If the signatories could not settle with their creditor, the reparations would revert to their status before the Hoover moratorium of 1931. The ratification clause meant the Lausanne pact was effective only if America renegotiated or cancelled its war debts with the Europeans. The United States refused to do this. America was in the middle of the 1932 presidential election campaign and both candidates stated they would not recommend America's compliance with the Lausanne Agreements. See December 15, 1932.*

September 20, 1932   THE MUNRO-BLANCHET TREATY PROPOSES AMERICA'S GRADUAL
                         WITHDRAWAL FROM HAITI; ALTHOUGH HAITI'S ASSEMBLY RE-
                         JECTS THE TREATY, PRESIDENT HOOVER CONTINUES TO RELIN-
                         QUISH U.S. CONTROL.

The United States had taken effective control over Haiti's political and eco-
nomic affairs on July 29, 1915. Although Secretary of State Hughes reviewed
U.S. policy toward Haiti in 1922, President Harding appointed General John H.
Russell as High Commissioner of Haiti, and American control continued to be
dictated by Washington for another eight years. Under Russell's guidance,
Louis Borno became President of Haiti and followed U.S. directions until his
resignation in 1930.
    Between 1926 and 1929, several American investigations of conditions in
Haiti publicized unfavorable circumstances regarding the U.S. occupation.
Emily Greene Balch's *Occupied Haiti* (1927) contained a moderate but sound
criticism of U.S. failings in Haiti. In 1929, both the Council on Foreign
Relations and the Foreign Policy Association issued derogatory reports on
American policy in Haiti. Finally, a series of strikes in Haiti during the
fall of 1929 led President Hoover to ask congress to appropriate funds for a
commission to recommend procedures for American withdrawal from Haiti.
    The resulting commission, chaired by W. Cameron Forbes, recommended a
process that Hoover implemented over the next two years. Following the Forbes
plan, Borno resigned as president on May 15, 1930, and Eugene Roy became interim president during a period when a new Chamber of Deputies was elected.
In accordance with Haiti's Constitution of 1918, which Borno had violated,
the new chamber selected Stenio Vincent as president in November, 1930. About
the same time (November 1, 1930), General Russell resigned as the U.S. High
Commissioner and Hoover appointed Dana G. Munro as U.S. Minister to Haiti.
    Munro continued to follow the Cameron process, granting more training
and more responsibility to Haitians so that by October 1, 1931, Haitians controlled all domestic offices except fiscal and military positions. One year
later, Munro negotiated a treaty with Haiti's Foreign Minister, Señor
Blanchet. The treaty provided that Haiti's Garde National would gradually
replace the U.S. Marines, who would withdraw completely, except for a "training mission," by December 31, 1934. Fiscal operations would, however, continue to be under U.S. supervision until Haiti's loans had been fully liquidated.
    On September 20, 1930, Haiti's National Assembly rejected the Munro-
Blanchet Treaty. The Haitian representatives disliked the remaining U.S.
strings on military and financial policies, desiring the complete withdrawal
of all U.S. officials.
    Despite the defeat of the treaty, President Hoover followed its basic
provisions by relaxing U.S. controls. Franklin D. Roosevelt accepted Hoover's
decision, and during his administration the U.S. Marines withdrew in 1934;
the U.S. fiscal officials left in 1941.

November 8, 1932   FRANKLIN DELANO ROOSEVELT IS ELECTED PRESIDENT.

On June 19 at Chicago, the Republican Party Convention renominated Herbert
Hoover for president. Its platform advocated a balanced budget, the protective tariff, U.S. participation in an international monetary conference, preservation of the gold standard, and revision of the prohibition amendment.
    The Democratic Convention selected Franklin D. Roosevelt, governor of

New York, as its nominee. Flying to Chicago to personally address the convention, Roosevelt told the delegates: "I pledge you, I pledge myself to a
new deal for the American people." The Democratic platform called for a balanced budget, a competitive tariff, a sound currency, repeal of prohibition,
banking reform and aid to farmers.

In the November balloting, Roosevelt secured 472 electoral votes to
Hoover's 59. Roosevelt carried 42 of the 48 states.

December 11, 1932   THE FIVE-POWER DECLARATION RETAINS GERMAN COOPERATION
                           IN THE GENEVA DISARMAMENT CONFERENCE.

In July, 1932, the Geneva Conference suspended its sessions and agreed to
reconvene on February 3, 1933. During the interim, a Bureau of the General
Disarmament Conference was set up to explore issues raised during the sessions
held from February 2 to July, 1932. This bureau met from September 21 to
December 13, during which the disputes between France and Germany became so
difficult that Germany's delegate, Baron von Neurath, asserted that his nation
would not attend the 1933 sessions. The Germans wanted to be treated as an
equal power rather than a "defeated" power.

The French-German dispute resulted in extensive negotiations leading to
the five-power declaration of December 11 by Germany, France, Great Britain,
Italy, and the United States. The declaration stated that the five nations
resolved not to settle "future differences by a resort to force." It also
asserted that at the disarmament conference the principle must be followed
that Germany and the other nations which had been forced to disarm by the
post-World War I treaties should be given "equality of rights in a system
which would provide security for all nations." Under the terms of this declaration, Germany agreed to attend the February 3, 1933, meeting at Geneva.

December 15, 1932   FRANCE REFUSES TO PAY ITS U.S. WAR DEBTS; BRITAIN MAKES
                           A CONDITIONAL FINAL PAYMENT: THE VIRTUAL END OF THE
                           ALLIED WAR DEBT PAYMENTS TO THE UNITED STATES.

Because America refused to cancel the war debts requested by the Lausanne
Treaty (see July 9, 1932), the December 15 installments came due on the war
debts that European nations owed to America. The U.S. moratorium of June 20,
1932, had not been extended again by Hoover's administration. Hoover and
Stimson realized few debtor nations could pay but they hoped the majority
would do so.

In December, 1932, the British made a full payment of $95 million in
gold but also sent the United States a note which effectively wrote off future
payments. France defaulted on its payment of $20 million. Poland, Belgium,
Estonia, Yugoslavia, and Hungary also defaulted. Greece made a partial payment on a blocked account. Full payments were made by Italy, Czechoslovakia,
Finland, Latvia, and Lithuania. Nevertheless, the default of the major powers
in future years led all nations but Finland to default. The incoming Roosevelt administration could do nothing to change the situation.

XII. FRANKLIN D. ROOSEVELT: NEUTRALITY FAILURE AND WORLD WAR II (1933-1944)

1933

January 30, 1933   *ADOLF HITLER, LEADER OF THE NAZI PARTY, IS APPOINTED CHANCELLOR OF THE GERMAN GOVERNMENT.*

In Germany, the Great Depression resulted in grave dangers for the fledgling Weimar Republic's government. Both the National Socialist (NAZI) Party and the Communist Party attacked the republic's policies as well as each other. The republican leaders were attempting to fulfill the cooperative policies represented by the League of Nations and other international conferences of the 1920's. The radical left and reactionary right groups advocated the abandonment of the Treaty of Versailles and all the horrible consequences which they blamed on the allies' unjust punishment of Germany since 1919.

When the economic collapse in America ended the illusion of German prosperity based on U.S. loans, the plight of the republic multiplied. During the Reichstag elections of September 14, 1930, the National Socialists emerged as a major party, increasing their previous 12 seats to 107. On the left, the Socialists retained their 143 seats. The moderate center parties, the mainstay of the republic, lost nearly 100 seats. In presidential elections on March 13, 1932, Hitler received 11,300,000 votes and the Communist Ernst Thalmann, 4,983,341. President Paul von Hindenburg was eventually reelected but only after a runoff election against Hitler on April 10. In the March election, Hindenburg received 18,651,497 votes, which was short of a majority. In the April election, Hindenburg's majority over Hitler was 6 million out of 36 million votes.

The loss of Reichstag votes in 1930 handicapped the center coalition government. On July 31, 1932, new Reichstag elections made the moderates' situation more precarious because they became a minority in the legislature. The Nazis held 230 seats, the Socialists and Communists 222 seats, but neither would join a coalition ministry. A second Reichstag election on November 24 resulted in a similar deadlock with no group able to form a viable coalition. On December 2, General Kurt von Schleicher tried but failed to form a center-left coalition cabinet.

On January 28, Schleicher resigned and President von Hindenburg offered Adolf Hitler the opportunity to form a center-right coalition. Hitler agreed, provided he was made chancellor. Hindenburg accepted and named Hitler to head a ministry on January 30 which joined the Nazis with the Nationalist Party. Hitler's coalition required a few Center Party votes to receive a majority and when the Center Party leader, Ludwig Kass, rejected Hitler's demands, the Reichstag dissolved. Chancellor Hitler called new elections in

*which he controlled key lines of authority in Germany's government. For the
results see March 5, 1933.*

*February 22, 1933   OLIVEIRA SALAZAR BECOMES THE FASCIST DICTATOR OF POR-
                         TUGAL, CREATING A NEW CONSTITUTION WITH HIMSELF AS
                         PRESIDENT, A CABINET RESPONSIBLE TO HIM ALONE, AND A
                         TWO-CHAMBER LEGISLATURE RESEMBLING ITALY'S CORPORATE
                         ASSEMBLY UNDER MUSSOLINI.*

*Throughout the 1920's, Portugal's politics were a struggle between liberal
republican forces and military dictatorships. On August 27, 1928, Salazar
became minister of finance. In this post, he became a dominant leader by
solving Portugal's financial problems through strict economic action and a
tight budget. After becoming premier on July 5, 1932, Salazar moved to reorganize the government to legally grant himself full power, a task accomplished on February 22, 1933, when a new Constitution was promulgated by
Salazar.*

*February 24, 1933   THE LEAGUE OF NATIONS ASSEMBLY ADOPTS THE LYTTON REPORT
                         ON THE MUKDEN INCIDENT OF 1931. JAPAN DENOUNCES THE
                         LEAGUE, WALKS OUT OF THE ASSEMBLY, AND QUITS THE LEAGUE
                         ON MAY 27, 1933.*

*Following its establishment by the league on December 10, 1931, the Commission
to Investigate the Manchurian Affair was organized under the chairmanship of
the Earl of Lytton. After visiting Manchuria and obtaining evidence from
Chinese and Japanese officials, the Lytton Report was presented to the league
on October 2, 1932. At Japan's request, the league provided time to study
the 139-page report and set up a Committee of Nineteen to deal with the matter
for later league action.*
*   Although the Lytton Report was conciliatory, the Japanese rejected it.
The report laid blame for the Mukden incident on both sides but did not believe Japan's response was self-defense. Nor, said the report, did the creation of Manchukuo come from a "genuine and spontaneous independence movement."
It recommended the establishment of an autonomous Manchurian government under
Chinese sovereignty. It also recognized Japan's economic interests in the
area and believed these should be protected.*
*   In Japan, the growing ultra-nationalist sentiments opposed the compromises implied in the Lytton Report. The cabinet of Premier Wakatsuki was
divided on what action to take and resigned in December. The new cabinet of
Premier Inukai accepted the conquest of Manchuria but opposed any army expansion in China. Thus, the cabinet opposed the recommendation that Japan should
leave Manchuria. When the Assembly of the League of Nations approved the
Lytton Report, the Japanese, who had denounced the report, left the assembly.*
*   Japan's decision to quit the League of Nations was taken following the
assassination of Premier Inukai on May 15, 1932. Inukai was the second moderate premier to be killed in two years by a nationalistic fanatic, and his
death marked the shift to power of the ultra-right wing nationalist-militarist
group in Japan.*

March 4, 1933   CORDELL HULL IS COMMISSIONED AS SECRETARY OF STATE BY
                         PRESIDENT ROOSEVELT.

Hull held the high respect of Democratic Party regulars, having served as a
Tennessee congressman (1907–1921 and 1923–1931) and senator (1931–1933) for
23 years. Roosevelt chose Hull largely because he was well known as an economic internationalist who opposed protective tariffs and desired reciprocal
agreements. Hull served as secretary until November 30, 1944.

March 5, 1933   *THE REICHSTAG ELECTIONS GIVE THE NAZIS A 44% VOTE BUT
                         THE OUTLAWED COMMUNIST PARTY OBTAINS ONLY 81 SEATS.*

*The election campaign during February led to further violent street fights
between the Nazis and Communists. On February 27, a fire destroyed part of
the Reichstag building and Hitler denounced the incident as a communist plot.
On that basis, President Hindenburg issued emergency decrees to suspend free
speech and the free press. The Nazi storm troops were now free to intimidate
the opposition Communists with impunity.*
    *The resulting election gave the Nazis 288 seats, the Nationalists 52.
The Socialist-Communist seats fell from 222 the previous November to 201.
With some Catholic Center votes, the Nazi-Nationalist coalition outlawed the
Communist Party and on March 23, 1933, voted dictatorial powers to Hitler
until April 1, 1937. A Nazi "legal" revolution occurred during the next two
years. The Nazi Party became the only party on July 14, 1933, and Germany
became a nation (the Third Reich) rather than a federal state on January 30,
1934. Judicial, racial, religious, economic, and military legislation gave
Hitler and his party complete control of Germany.*

March 18, 1933   THE UNITED STATES AGREES TO COOPERATE WITH A LEAGUE
                         OF NATIONS COMMISSION TO AVERT WAR BETWEEN PERU AND
                         COLOMBIA OVER LETICIA.

Because of a border dispute between Peru and Colombia, the Peruvian army had
invaded and occupied the small village of Leticia on September 1, 1933. At
first, the Lima government agreed to withdraw its army, but it changed its
policy and by March, 1933, a large-scale war appeared imminent. The League
of Nations Advisory Commission offered to mediate the issue, and after Peru
agreed, the league's Secretary General asked the United States to cooperate
because he did not wish to infringe on the Monroe Doctrine. Secretary Hull
and Roosevelt agreed to participate in the league's commission of mediation
although not as a voting member.
    The league's mediation averted the conflict. The commissioners, includ-
ing the non-voting U.S. delegate, went to Leticia and supervised the withdrawal of troops by both nations. A final settlement was made under league
auspices on November 2, 1934.

April 19, 1933   THE UNITED STATES OFFICIALLY ABANDONS THE GOLD STAN-
                         DARD.

This action caused a decline in the dollar value abroad and increased the
price of commodities, silver, and stocks on the U.S. exchanges.

May 29, 1933   STANDARD OIL OF CALIFORNIA (SOCAL) RECEIVES OIL RIGHTS
                         IN SAUDI ARABIA WITHOUT THE NEED FOR STATE DEPARTMENT
                         ASSISTANCE.

SOCAL obtained oil concessions from King Ibn Saud because of two favorable
circumstances. First, the British Treaty of 1927 with Saudi Arabia cancelled
Britain's right to veto the Saudis' oil concessions included in the Anglo-
Arabian Treaty of 1915. Second, an American philanthropist, Charles Crane,
had a genuine interest in Arabian culture and gained the friendship of King
Ibn Saud who distrusted the British.

      Under Crane's guidance, the king invited Karl S. Twitchell to conduct a
geological survey of Arabia which indicated potential oil in that nation.
Twitchell and Crane favored SOCAL's proposal for an oil concession and encouraged SOCAL to apply for a grant in 1932.

      On May 29, King Ibn Saud chose SOCAL's oil bid in preference to an offer
from Britain's Iraq Petroleum Company. To handle its Saudi concession, SOCAL
established a subsidiary, the California-Arabian Standard Oil Company, which
began oil production just before World War II interfered with its further
output.

May 31, 1933   *THE T'ANG-KU TRUCE ENDS THE CONFLICT BETWEEN CHINA*
                         AND JAPAN THAT BEGAN ON THE NIGHT OF SEPTEMBER 18-19,
                         1931.

By March, 1933, Japanese forces occupied all of Jehol province just north of
the Great Wall. In April, their forces made further advances south of the
wall into China. At this juncture, Tokyo agreed to sign a truce with China
by which Chinese troops evacuated the Tientsin area. The neutralization of
the area between Tientsin and Peking eventually became Japan's first move
toward the conquest of China in 1937.

July 3, 1933   PRESIDENT ROOSEVELT DISRUPTS THE LONDON ECONOMIC CON-
                         FERENCE BY REPUDIATING ALL TEMPORARY CURRENCY STABILI-
                         ZATION PROPOSALS.

The London conference met in order to resolve the chaos of international economic difficulties. Factors which caused the crisis included: America's rejection of the Lausanne Conference of 1932 proposal to repudiate all war
debts; the default by most Europeans on their December 15, 1932, war debt
payments; Great Britain's leaving the gold standard; Roosevelt's calling of
a U.S. bank holiday on March 5 in order to stop bank failures. The London
Conference hoped to create a degree of fiscal certainty to offer businessmen
and investors a more optimistic future.

      Exactly where the new American president stood on these issues did not
become clear until July 3. As early as November 22, 1932, the president-elect
met with President Hoover to discuss the problems of debts, reparations, and
disarmament, but Roosevelt hesitated to commit himself. He desired to retain
the full support of congress and the nation when he assumed office on March
4, 1933. In subsequent talks before his inauguration, Roosevelt indicated
that an international conference would be acceptable, but he did not make it
clear whether or not the war debts problem would be negotiable with other
economic problems. Evidently Roosevelt desired to improve the American

economy by short-term nationalistic economic measures while seeking better world economic cooperation through long-term international action. In 1933, however, these two goals came into conflict.

Shortly before meeting with British Prime Minister Ramsay MacDonald and French Premier Edouard Herriot on April 21, Roosevelt urged action in congress to give him authority to devalue the dollar (see April 19, 1933). Roosevelt's action angered and confused the European leaders but the president calmed their anxiety by discussing proposals for a truce on tariff competition and the possibility of relief for their June 15 debt payments. The three national leaders agreed to convene an economic conference in London on June 12, before the due date for the debt payments. Herriot and MacDonald could not, however, agree with Roosevelt's proposal to wait until each nation settled its domestic economic problems before trying to stabilize international problems. The British and French wanted a temporary stabilization of the dollar value as a basic necessity for their economic reconstruction.

Indeed, while debts and reparations appeared to be the primary question during the London Conference, which began on June 12, the most critical question was international currency value because this directly affected every specific economic issue. The resolution of the U.S. banking crisis by passage of the Glass-Steagall Acts and the Emergency Banking Relief Act in March-April, 1933, strengthened the dollar on the world currency exchange but weakened the European currencies. Between May and July, 1933, the dollar value relative to the British pound sterling increased from $4.02 to a high of $4.40, fluctuating on the speculative market between these figures but generally being between $4.15 and $4.30.

During the first week of the London Conference, Roosevelt appointed three special negotiators to discuss currency stabilization with Britain and France. As a result of these tripartite meetings, James P. Warburg, Oliver W. Sprague, and George L. Harrison, the U.S. negotiators, recommended on June 16 that Roosevelt agree to stabilize the dollar at about $4 to the pound sterling and not to inflate the dollar further. The president rejected their proposal, a decision which presaged Roosevelt's statement of July 3, which, because it was made publicly and in definite terms, destroyed the London Conference's chance for success.

In mid-June, however, Roosevelt had not yet closed the door on the stabilization of the dollar. Rumors of stabilization encouraged speculators to increase the dollar value, which reached $4.18 on June 12. The president, therefore, could not accept the $4 proposal of the tripartite committee, and its sessions ceased to be effective after June 17.

On June 21, Roosevelt dispatched Raymond Moley, one of his chief economic advisors, to London to convince the Europeans to accept the American terms. Moley and Roosevelt appeared to have agreed that controlling a limited fluctuation of the dollar value between $4.15 and $4.25 to the pound sterling should satisfy the Europeans. Thus, Moley's arrival in London on June 28 raised hopes that an agreement would result from the London Conference.

On July 3, however, Roosevelt's message to Secretary of State Hull, who headed the U.S. conference delegation, abolished the limited stabilization compromise which Moley had presented and asserted the president's commitment to national recovery preceding an international currency stabilization. By July, the president realized that America's recovery would not come as fast as he had expected in March. In addition, he sensed that the majority of congress placed American recovery ahead of international, especially European, recovery. Americans generally did not comprehend that their economic status correlated closely with international economic health, some blaming European debt defaults and European lassitude for the American problems.

Thus, the July 3 note to Hull stated that the president could not agree to the recent suggestion by Moley that the U.S. Federal Reserve Board should cooperate in limiting the dollar currency fluctuations at about $4.15. The sound internal economy of the nation was, the president said, "a greater factor in its well being than the price of its currency in changing terms of other nations." The concept of stable currencies was, Roosevelt stated, an "old fetish of so-called international bankers...." In contrast, he said, stabilization could be attained only after the majority of nations balanced their budgets and reached economic health.

The European delegates at London were astounded by the president's July 3 message. Since April 21, MacDonald and Herriot had believed Roosevelt was ready to reach some compromise on currency values, debts, and other financial matters. It was evident on July 3 that the president's request for general not specific cooperation at the London Conference was designed to promote U.S. recovery, if necessary, at the expense of Europe's general recovery. Indeed, Roosevelt's peculiarly American attitude about international cooperation had been succinctly stated in his instructions to Moley before Moley left for London on June 21. The president declared: "If other nations will go along and work in our direction, as they said they would ... then we can cooperate. If they won't, then there's nothing to cooperate about."

In order to avoid a complete display of disunity between England, France, and America, Roosevelt urged Secretary Hull to keep the conference alive for a while by proposing that the nations work together to raise their domestic prices. In spite of the Europeans' desire to end the conference, Hull kept the sessions going for three weeks, until July 27. No agreements were made, however. Roosevelt's concept of the U.S. national interest prevented a cooperative effort at an international economic settlement in 1933.

July 15, 1933   *THE FOUR-POWER PACT ATTEMPTS TO ALIGN EUROPE'S FOUR*
                         BIG POWERS TO MAINTAIN PEACE.

A favorable idea of Benito Mussolini, this pact was signed by Italy, Germany, France, and England. Mussolini disliked the influence of the small nations in the League of Nations and proposed this pact to unite the larger nations to dominate the league. In practice, this agreement had no significance.

August 12, 1933   GENERAL MACHADO LEAVES CUBA: U.S. AMBASSADOR SUMNER
                        WELLES EARNS "WARM CONGRATULATIONS" FROM PRESIDENT
                        ROOSEVELT.

On May 1, 1933, Welles was sent as Ambassador to Havana with instructions to mediate an end to the civil disorders which opposed the military dictatorship of President Gerardo Machado. The uprising against Machado had begun in 1929. Machado had generally suppressed it in 1930, but underground resistance continued especially among university students and liberal intellectuals in Cuba. Both sides used terroristic tactics, inflicting hazards and death on many innocent Cubans. In addition, the Cuban economy suffered because the Hawley-Smoot Tariff of 1930 levied high duties on sugar, disrupting sales of the export product which yielded 85% of Cuba's income.

Throughout four years of Cuban disorders, President Hoover and Secretary Stimson remained aloof, arguing that their policy was non-intervention in another nation. Although the Platt Amendment permitted U.S. action in Cuba, Hoover and Stimson claimed no Americans, only Cubans, were suffering, and that the Cubans must settle their own problems.

In 1933, Roosevelt and Secretary of State Hull also preferred not to intervene in Cuba, but they believed something should be done to end the increasing disorder and terror in the nearby island. They agreed to send Assistant Secretary of State Sumner Welles as Ambassador to Cuba with instructions to negotiate a trade treaty that would ease Cuba's poor economic condition; to urge Machado to stop his terrorist methods; and to negotiate a truce that would bring free elections to Cuba. Welles had been a State Department troubleshooter in both Santo Domingo and Honduras during the 1920's and believed he could end the Cuban problems.

Between May and August, Welles discovered that Machado would not cooperate effectively in following his proposals. Therefore, Welles contacted Cuban army officials and undertook confidential discussions with the Secretary of War, General Alberto Herrera. Although Welles's precise role is not documented, he encouraged army officers collectively to oppose Machado. On August 12, 1933, Machado took a "leave of absence" and fled Cuba by airplane. Before Machado left, however, Welles approved the commissioning of General Carlos Manuel de Cespedes as Cuba's Secretary of State, the officer in line for constitutional succession to the presidency when Machado "retired." Because Cespedes' rule followed constitutional provisions, it was an "orderly" change of government not requiring any diplomats to raise questions about recognition.

Although Welles received Roosevelt's and Secretary Hull's "warm congratulations" for maneuvering Machado's overthrow, their praise proved to be premature. Welles, of course, was ecstatic in describing Cespedes' government as a "new deal for Cuba" and one which "commands" the confidence of the Cuban people. History, however, has a cynical way of turning on a politician's words. In a second "bloodless" coup, Cespedes' rule ended in less than one month. See September 5, 1933.

September 5, 1933   A CUBAN COUP D'ÉTAT OVERTHROWS CARLOS CESPEDES, BRINGING TO POWER A REGIME WHICH ROOSEVELT REFUSES TO RECOGNIZE.

Following the U.S. optimism that greeted Machado's departure from Cuba on August 12, 1933, Roosevelt's "good neighbor" policy experienced a severe and eventually a tarnished test when the man whom Ambassador Welles supported was overthrown on September 5.

Cespedes' overthrow was led by a group of army sergeants led by Sergeant Fulgencio BATISTA. Cuba's non-commissioned officers had joined with the university students and liberal intellectuals in the belief that General Machado's regime had implicated all the army's generals in the terroristic suppression between 1929 and 1933. Although Batista and his army colleagues shared few ideas with the liberals and students, they united on September 5 in the successful overthrow of Cespedes and the military junta which had backed his government.

Unfortunately, Ambassador Welles had staked his prestige on Cespedes. During the next six months, Welles's prejudices prevented him from seeing anything but "evil" communism and disorder in the new government. Moreover, Welles was a personal friend of President Roosevelt, a relationship which often resulted in the president's failure to look objectively at a problem.

As a result, when the leaders of the coup established a civilian junta and installed Dr. Ramon Grau San Martin as provisional president, Roosevelt accepted Welles's opinion that Grau's government should not be recognized. According to Welles, Grau's supporters were radicals and communists who lacked the support of the Cuban people. Although Welles's poor judgment about the Cespedes regime should have cautioned Roosevelt about his evaluation of Cuban support, the president did not recognize the new government. This action handicapped Grau's efforts to reform Cuba and became a major factor in his subsequent loss of power to Batista's military faction.

Subsequently, Roosevelt tried a dual policy to give the impression he was a "good neighbor" helping developments in Cuba. He conducted discussions with representatives of Argentina, Brazil, Chile, and Mexico, emphasizing to them that the United States wished to avoid intervention in Cuba even though the situation was dangerous. On the same day, September 6, he sent 20 to 30 ships to Cuban waters to "protect" Americans from disorders. While Welles maneuvered against Grau's government, he was backed not only by Roosevelt but by the American warships in Havana and Santiago harbor. For the consequences of indirect U.S. intervention see January 15, 1934.

October 14, 1933   GERMANY WITHDRAWS FROM THE GENEVA DISARMAMENT CONFER-
                            ENCE AND THE LEAGUE OF NATIONS.

Although the Five-Power Declaration of December 11, 1932, brought Germany to the Geneva Disarmament Conference in February, the divergence between German and French demands grew greater after the Nazis gained power in Germany on January 30, 1933. Although there were intermittent full and subcommittee sessions of the conference during the next eight months, the German withdrawal on October 14 appeared to William DODD, the American Ambassador to Germany, to have been a premeditated act correlated with Hitler's having gained full power in Germany by September (see March 5, 1933).

President Roosevelt named Norman Davis to head the U.S. delegation at the Geneva Conference, but the only commitment the president seemed politically able to make was to support Ramsay MacDonald's March 16 proposal to combine a partial reduction of all armies by half a million with an agreement of the powers to consult if an aggressor attacked another nation. In a speech on May 16, Roosevelt went one step further to placate France by agreeing that the United States would relinquish its traditional neutral rights and refrain from any activity that might damage the attempt of a collective action to punish an aggressor. Of course, Roosevelt made this offer in the context of a disarmament reduction's having been agreed to by the European states. The Germans prevented an agreement on MacDonald's plan, demanding their right to begin rearming because the other European nations had taken no steps to disarm during the 14 years after the 1919 peace treaties.

During the last weeks leading to Germany's withdrawal from both the conference and the League of Nations, Norman Davis realized the discussions were fruitless. All that he and Roosevelt could do was to put the United States on record as being concerned about the need for European disarmament. The failure of this conference, which had been in preparation since 1926 and was publicized as the real hope for peace in Europe, resulted in an increase of American isolation. The national hatreds among European states seemed impossible to resolve. Thus, the U.S. public thought the Europeans should be left to suffer for their irrational shortcomings and national hatreds.

November 17, 1933 PRESIDENT ROOSEVELT AND THE SOVIET UNION'S FOREIGN MINISTER SIGN AN AGREEMENT TO NORMALIZE RELATIONS BETWEEN THE UNITED STATES AND THE U.S.S.R.

Following the Bolshevik revolution of November, 1917, the United States had refused to recognize the Soviet government. In 1933, however, Roosevelt discerned that American public opinion no longer strongly opposed recognition of the Communist regime. Some businessmen believed diplomatic relations would stimulate trade with Russia, and some internationalists thought U.S.-Soviet diplomacy could restrain Japanese ventures in Manchuria. In April, 1933, Roosevelt urged Senator Claude Swanson to promote a national discussion about the benefits of recognition.

Roosevelt's principal concerns in Russian relations were the opposition of religious groups who opposed recognition of the atheist Communist government and American nationalists who disliked the propaganda and possible subversive activity of the Communist Party through the Third Communist International (Comintern). To forestall criticism, Roosevelt met in October with Father Edmund A. Walsh of Georgetown University, who was the nation's leading Catholic spokesman against Russian recognition. Roosevelt persuaded Walsh to trust his ability as "a good horse dealer" to require the Russians to grant Americans religious rights in the U.S.S.R. and to obtain guarantees against Communist subversive activity in America. Walsh's backing assisted the president.

Having secured some acceptance from public leaders, Roosevelt arranged through Boris Skvirsky, Moscow's trade representative in New York, to issue an invitation to the Russian government to send a representative to discuss American-Soviet relations. Because Joseph Stalin's international policy had just entered a stage where he desired cooperation against the rising threat of fascism, the Russians responded positively and appointed their Foreign Minister, Maxim LITVINOV, to come to Washington for talks.

Litvinov's negotiations took place from November 8 to 16, 1933. Initially, in his formal discussions at the State Department, Litvinov showed little interest in meeting American conditions for recognition. On November 10, however, he began direct discussions with the president, and agreements were reached which resulted in the normalization of Russian-American relations. The Russians agreed to extend religious freedom to American citizens in the Soviet Union and to negotiate an agreement to provide fair trials for Americans accused of crime in Russia. The Russian government also agreed not to engage in subversive activities, although the wording of this clause did not include the action of the Communist Party as distinct from the government. Finally, details regarding the Russian debts and U.S. financial claims were delegated to future discussions, the Soviets agreeing to pay between $75 million and $150 million dollars in claims. The debt issue raised less suspicion than it had previously because most European nations defaulted on their U.S. debts after 1931.

Although the 1933 agreements restored U.S.-Soviet diplomatic recognition, the trade and international stability which advocates of recognition predicted did not result. No immediate consequences may be attributed to recognition. However, the critical issue had been resolved and later permitted the "strange alliance" of 1941 to 1945 to proceed without difficulty after Hitler invaded Russia in June, 1941.

December 26, 1933   THE UNITED STATES AGREES TO A NON-INTERVENTION PACT
                             DURING THE SEVENTH PAN-AMERICAN CONFERENCE AT MONTE-
                             VIDEO.

Although the Hoover administration had taken steps toward a "good neighbor"
policy in the Western Hemisphere, President Roosevelt more strongly forwarded
a cooperative policy with Latin American nations. Both in his March 4 inaugural address and during a speech on April 12, 1933, to the Board of the Pan-
American Union, the president expressed his determination to be a good neighbor and respect the rights of other nations.

     Consequently, when the State Department prepared for the Montevideo Con-
ference during October, 1933, Roosevelt and Secretary of State Hull, who
headed the American delegation to the Uruguay meeting, agreed to focus on
promoting Pan-American cooperation. Although Hull experienced the anti-Yankee
posters and demonstrations in Latin America as soon as he arrived at Montevideo, he was determined to overcome their animosity.

     On December 26, Hull cast the American vote favoring a convention on
the rights and duties of states. Article 8 of this agreement included a
clause stating: "No state has the right to intervene in the internal or external affairs of another state." Hull accepted this pact with the reservation that a state may "protect lives and property where government has broken
down and anarchy exists." He urged the signatories to codify a clear definition of the non-intervention terms in the 1933 treaty and announced that
Roosevelt's administration would not intervene in another state's affairs.
Somewhat ironically, Hull made this statement at the same time the U.S. warships in Havana harbor protected indirect American political interference
in Cuba. Many U.S. critics in Latin America did not overlook this anomaly.

1934

January 15, 1934   INDIRECT AMERICAN INTERVENTION IN CUBA RESULTS IN PRES-
IDENT GRAU'S RESIGNATION; A REGIME CONTROLLED BY
BATISTA GAINS POWER AND U.S. RECOGNITION.

Due largely to the influence of U.S. Ambassador Sumner Welles, the Roosevelt
administration refused to recognize the provisional presidency of Grau San
Martin who created a civilian junta following Cepedes' overthrow on September
5, 1933. Without U.S. recognition, Grau could arrange no trade agreement
with the United States or obtain help in reforming the Cuban economy.

By November, Grau's regime became disgusted with Sumner Welles's political maneuvering in Cuba and asked Roosevelt to recall the ambassador. Welles
had earned the antagonism of most Cuban newspapers and become the symbol of
U.S. interference in Cuba. Because Secretary Hull was attending the Inter-
American Conference at Montevideo, Welles and Roosevelt decided to keep Cuba's
request for Welles's recall secret and to wait several weeks before Welles
returned to Washington as Assistant Secretary of State. On November 24,
Roosevelt issued a news release that expressed his confidence in Welles but
indicated that the ambassador would be replaced in December by Jefferson
Caffery. This did not mean there would be a policy change, Roosevelt asserted, because Caffery's appointment would not bring recognition to Grau's
regime. Roosevelt argued that Grau did not have the support of the Cuban
people.

Welles returned to Cuba and remained until December 13, hoping he could
obtain Grau's resignation on behalf of a candidate approved by Welles. On
December 12, Welles reported to Washington that he expected Grau to resign
and Carlos Mendieta to become provisional president. To arrange this, Welles
held discussions with Colonel (formerly Sergeant) Batista urging the new Chief
of Staff of the Cuban Army to withdraw his support from Grau. At the last
minute, however, Welles's plans fell through. Grau remained in office for
another month and Welles could not return to the State Department with the
prestigious victory he hoped for: the fall of Grau San Martin.

Welles had, however, paved the way for the change in Cuba's government
on January 15. When Caffery arrived in Cuba, Grau's followers hoped the new
ambassador would be conciliatory, providing an opening for Grau's recognition
and American economic aid. Caffery disappointed them, however. Having participated in the Welles-Roosevelt decisions on Cuba during November, Caffery
knew that the success of his job required the resignation of Grau. More important, Colonel Batista, too, realized that his success depended on American
backing which, above all, required a stronger law-and-order regime in Havana.

In early January, Batista informed Grau that the army could no longer
support the existing government. Consequently, Grau resigned on January 15
and Carlos Mendieta, head of the Nationalist Party and the person whom Welles
had approved for the job in December, became president of Cuba. Mendieta
was the first of a series of presidents who fronted for Batista's control in
Cuba. In 1940, a Cuban convention prepared a new constitution organized on

the lines of a fascist corporate state. On July 14, 1940, Batista assumed direct control over Cuba, a position he held until December 31, 1958.

In January, 1934, Roosevelt moved quickly to grant Mendieta the recognition he withheld from Grau. With Welles's support (Hull returned from Uruguay on January 21), Roosevelt decided on January 18 to recognize the new government soon after Mendieta officially became provisional president. Roosevelt concluded the Mendieta government would bring order to Cuba and had the support of the Cuban people. How Mendieta's good qualities as ruler were determined so quickly remains a mystery, other than that Mendieta had the approval of Welles in Washington and Batista in Havana. On January 24, the United States recognized Mendieta's government. For U.S. support of the new regime see May 29, 1934.

January 30, 1934   CONGRESS PASSES THE GOLD RESERVE ACT, ENDING ROOSE-
VELT'S EXPERIMENT WITH DEVALUATION AS A METHOD TO IN-
CREASE COMMODITY PRICES IN AMERICA'S FAVOR.

During the fall of 1933, Professors George Warren, Irving Fisher, and James Harvey Rogers persuaded the president to purchase gold at rates higher than the world market prices as a means for increasing the price of gold and reducing the dollar's value. Therefore, on October 19, Roosevelt ordered the Reconstruction Finance Corporation to purchase newly mined gold because, the president said, "The United States must take firmly in its own hands the control of the gold value of our dollar" in order to gain "the continued recovery of our commodity prices...."

Foreign nations strongly opposed Roosevelt's action. The Governor of the Bank of England claimed, "The whole world will be put into bankruptcy." This complaint was not accurate, but neither were the expectations of Roosevelt and his three economics professors. Commodity prices did not rise. The United States had, however, profited from the devaluation by adding dollars to monetary circulation. The president added these gains to a monetary stabilization fund that could limit British fluctuations of the pound sterling in international exchanges.

Roosevelt also asked congress on January 15 to pass a Gold Reserve Act. This act permitted the president to stabilize the dollar value at 50 to 60% of its former value. On January 31, the day after congress approved the Gold Reserve Act, Roosevelt fixed the dollar at 59.06% of its pre-1933 gold value. The effect of this act permitted the treasury to print about $4 additional for each ounce of gold.

February 2, 1934   PRESIDENT ROOSEVELT ESTABLISHES THE EXPORT-IMPORT BANK
TO ENCOURAGE OVERSEAS COMMERCE.

Acting under provisions of the Reconstruction Finance Corporation and the National Recovery Act, the president established this bank to finance foreign trade with short-term credits for exporting agricultural commodities; longer-term credits for U.S. firms exporting industrial manufacturing; and loans to U.S. exporters where foreign governments did not provide sufficient exchange credit to meet their dollar obligations. Originally two banks were set up: one for trade credits to the Soviet Union; the other for credit facilities with Cuba and other foreign nations. In 1936, these two banks were merged.

March 24, 1934   THE TYDINGS-McDUFFIE ACT PROVIDES INDEPENDENCE TO THE
                          PHILIPPINE ISLANDS IN 1946.

In 1932, congress passed legislation over President Hoover's veto which
granted independence to the Philippines. In May, 1933, however, the Philippine legislature refused to ratify the bill because Manuel QUEZON opposed it.
The bill had passed congress while Quezon was out of Washington and, his opponents said, that was his reason for rejecting the bill.

     As passed on March 24, the Tydings-McDuffie Act of 1934 provided for
establishing the Philippines as a self-governing commonwealth by 1936. Following 10 years under this government and U.S. supervision, the Philippines
would receive independence on July 4, 1946. The Philippine legislature ratified the bill on May 1, 1934.

March 27, 1934   THE VINSON NAVAL PARITY ACT AUTHORIZES A U.S. NAVY
                          PROGRAM TO REACH TREATY STRENGTH.

President Roosevelt designed the Vinson Act as part of the New Deal unemploy-
ment relief program. Sometimes referred to as the Vinson-Trammel Act, this
bill authorized a treaty-sized navy.

     In 1928, with the completion of the two aircraft carriers U.S.S. *Lexing-
ton* and U.S.S. *Saratoga*, the U.S. Navy nearly achieved its 1922 Five-Power
Treaty strength of 5:5:3. The Hoover administration, partly due to the Depression, drastically cut the navy's budget for the next four years; these
cuts weakened the navy. In 1933, Roosevelt set aside $238 million of public
works funds for the construction of 32 ships which totaled 120,000 tons. Not
until the Vinson Act of 1938 did congress authorize a navy program designed
to reach treaty strength in five years. To attain this goal, 100 warships
and 1,000 aircraft would be built. Congress did not, however, allocate sufficient funds for the program, and until 1938, the navy was able only to replace obsolete ships.

     Although some scholars view the Vinson Act as a hard-line policy against
Japan, a policy to achieve the treaty strength of 1922 was insufficient to
carry out the U.S. Navy's Orange War Plans against Japan. A treaty-size navy
was only a navy for defense. A hard-line navy to oppose Japan required a
superior U.S. fleet capable of offensive action in the western Pacific region
of Japan's home islands, a navy whose size exceeded the 1922 treaties.

April 12, 1934   NYE MUNITIONS INVESTIGATIONS ARE APPROVED: THE SENATE
                          ESTABLISHES A COMMITTEE TO INVESTIGATE THE ARMS MANU-
                          FACTURERS AND THE SALE OF MUNITIONS AS A CAUSE OF WAR.
                          THIS COMMITTEE'S WORK LASTED TWO YEARS AND STIMULATED
                          ISOLATIONIST SENTIMENT IN AMERICA.

Advocates of peace and disarmament between 1919 and 1933 had generated several
studies about the causes of war which connected the "merchants of death" (arms
manufacturers) to warfare. Allegedly, these arms salesmen published extensive
propaganda to stimulate international hatred and antagonisms which made defense departments able to purchase their armament products.

     An isolationist senator from North Dakota, Gerald P. Nye, used these
allegations to request a Senate investigation of the activity of arms manufacturers before, during, and after 1914. The Senate approved the resolution

and Senator Nye became chairman of the investigation committee. The hearings
of the committee began in September, 1934, and received vast publicity from
the witnesses' testimony and the charges of Nye and other committee members.
The large profits of the munitions industry were conclusively shown. The
ability of these war profiteers to exert covert pressure on governments to
declare war could not be demonstrated. Nevertheless, many Americans believed
there was a connection between war manufacturers and governments which, in
oversimplified fashion, resulted in war.

The Nye investigations were one influence in the growing isolationist
sentiments in the United States at the time when the fascist powers became
aggressive in Europe and the Far East. The Neutrality Acts passed between
1935 and 1937 were partly a consequence of this committee's allegations. See
August 31, 1935.

April 13, 1934   THE JOHNSON DEBT DEFAULT ACT PROHIBITS LOANS TO GOV-
                          ERNMENTS WHICH DEFAULTED ON THEIR DEBTS TO THE UNITED
                          STATES.

President Roosevelt decided to support Senator Hiram Johnson's loan default
act because the major European powers, especially Great Britain, offered ri-
diculous terms to settle the debt issue. During the fall of 1933, England
said it would pay $460 million to settle all its debts of $8 billion, a sum
Roosevelt rejected. On December 15, France defaulted for the third successive
time, while England and Italy made only token payments.

Therefore, Roosevelt agreed to support Johnson's bill provided the senator dropped the clause referring to debts of private citizens. Roosevelt was
willing to make the U.S. government directly responsible only for default on
government bonds and loans. Johnson accepted this change, and the bill passed
congress on April 4. The president signed it on April 13.

The default bill did not produce its intended results. The European
nations did not pay their debts or agree to negotiate better terms for cancellation. Furthermore, during the early days of World War II in Europe,
Roosevelt had another obstacle to overcome before he could lend money to Great
Britain to buy arms in America.

April 24, 1934   THE UNITED STATES AND MEXICO SIGN A CLAIMS CONVENTION
                          ENDING A POINT OF DISAGREEMENT EXISTING SINCE 1923.

On August 31, 1923, Mexico had agreed to arbitrate the settlement of indemnity
claims incurred between Mexico and America since the claims convention of
1868. A special claims commission worked on the claims cases from 1924 to
1932 but could not reach agreement except on two out of 3,617 claims. In
total, Americans held a half billion dollars of claims, the Mexicans held a
quarter billion dollars. Many of these claims were exaggerated, however.
As Roosevelt's new ambassador to Mexico, Jonathan DANIELS, discovered, one
claim was by an American inventor who demanded $42 million for anticipated
profits on a patent used in Mexico; another was by a group of Mexicans claiming title to a sizable chunk of land in Los Angeles.

Ambassador Daniels determined that the "good neighbor" policy required
a sympathetic settlement with Mexico. He found that Mexico's foreign minister, Puig Casauranc, was willing to reach a compromise but that old-time bureaucrats of the State Department were slow to adjust the issue with Mexico.

Daniels decided to seek a lump sum payment based on the proportion of
claim awards six European nations had settled with Mexico in recent years.
The Europeans had scaled down 382 million pesos of claims to about 10 million
pesos. The percentage varied from country to country but the foreign returns
averaged 2.65%. On this basis, Daniels and Dr. Puig agreed on an amount of
2.65% for memorialized claims accepted previously by any claims commission
and 1.25% for unmemorialized claims of dubious authenticity. Mexico would
pay these claims in 15 years (the Europeans used 30 years) and in dollars
(the Europeans used pesos).

Between February and April, 1934, Daniels' main obstacle was the Washington bureaucracy in charge of the Mexican claims. These officials argued
for another 0.5% payment. Dr. Puig refused this concept, and negotiations
nearly ended. Finally, Daniels held discussions by phone with the State Department and gained its reluctant agreement on the originally proposed percentages. The convention with Mexico was signed on April 24, 1934.

April 28, 1934   SECRETARY OF STATE HULL PROTESTS THE "AMAU STATEMENT"
                          OF A JAPANESE FOREIGN OFFICE SPOKESMAN. SOON AFTER,
                          HULL REJECTS A JAPANESE SUGGESTION FOR A SPHERES OF
                          INFLUENCE ARRANGEMENT IN THE PACIFIC OCEAN.

On April 17, 1934, Eiji Amau, a Japanese foreign office spokesman, told a press
conference in Tokyo that Japan's geographic position and world mission gave
it a duty "to keep peace and order in East Asia." For this reason, the Japanese objected to joint operations by outside groups such as the League of
Nations in China.

Amau's statement alarmed both London and Washington because it appeared
to be a new statement of Japanese policy. In Tokyo, U.S. Ambassador Joseph
C. Grew learned from Foreign Minister Hirota that Amau gave reporters the
wrong impression. Hirota said Japan observed the Nine-Power Treaty of 1922
and would not interfere with the bona fide trade of other nations.

Nevertheless, Hull believed Hirota's explanation was vague, and he protested to the Japanese foreign office on April 28. Japan, Hull wrote, had
multilateral treaties with other nations regarding China and could not assert
its will in areas where others had legitimate interests. Great Britain joined
Hull in filing a similar protest to Tokyo. As a follow-up to the Amau statement, Hull disclosed his rejection of "realistic" power balance politics with
Japan. In May, 1934, Hull spoke with the Japanese Ambassador to Washington,
Hiroshi Saito, who suggested that the United States and Japan might consider
the recognition of their mutual interests in the Pacific Ocean. His concept
envisioned that America would accept Japan's sphere of influence in the western Pacific and Japan would recognize American interests in defined areas of
the eastern Pacific. Hull objected to the concept, lecturing Saito on the
obligations of "highly civilized countries" to have many duties in international behavior. In addition, Hull said, any special agreement with Japan
was contrary to American traditions against any political alliance.

Generally, Hull's protest to the Amau statement and his conversation
with Saito indicated the Roosevelt administration's opposition to Japan's
recent actions in Manchuria, although in 1934, Secretary Hull played down
American differences with Japan. From 1934 to 1937, Roosevelt hoped to avoid
provocation of Japan, but the naval conference of 1935 failed in spite of
the president's efforts.

May 29, 1934   THE UNITED STATES ABROGATES THE PLATT AMENDMENT, ENDING
                         THE LIMITS ON CUBAN SOVEREIGNTY BUT RETAINING GUANTA-
                         NAMO NAVAL BASE.

Although the Roosevelt administration had fulfilled only the non-military
pacts of the "good neighbor" test in Cuba between May, 1933, and January,
1934, the abrogation of the Platt Amendment became another indication of the
United States' desire to avoid direct intervention in Latin America. Sumner
Welles's interference in Cuban politics between May and December, 1933, and
Roosevelt's refusal to recognize the Grau regime between September, 1933, and
January, 1934 did not disclose the equally effective American capacity to
influence Latin American affairs without the use of the army or marines. Only
certain scholars, Latin American nationalists, and anti-Yankee Latin Americans
connoted indirect interference with the failings of the "good neighbor."
     Following the rise to power of the Mendieta-Batista junta in 1934, the
Roosevelt administration demonstrated its ability to provide positive assistance to a "friendly" regime in Cuba. In February, the State Department undertook trade negotiations with Cuba which reduced the tariff on Cuban sugar and
expanded U.S.-Cuban trade. In March, Roosevelt approved a $4 million loan
to help Cuba revive its ailing economy. In June, when "conditions of domestic
violence" indicated that some Cubans disliked the new regime, Roosevelt limited arms sales to Cuba except to the Mendieta government or those it authorized.
     Most dramatic and publicized, however, was the treaty abrogating
the Platt Amendment, by which the United States had assumed the right to intervene in Cuban affairs following the Spanish War of 1898.
     The treaty ending the Platt Amendment was signed by Hull, the Cuban Am-
bassador, and, at his special request, Sumner Welles. By this treaty, the
United States retained Guantanamo naval base until it might be surrendered
by mutual consent in the future. The U.S. Senate ratified the Cuban Treaty
on June 9, 1934.

June 12, 1934   THE RECIPROCAL TRADE AGREEMENTS ACT OF 1934 IS SIGNED
                         INTO LAW, APPROVING THE PRESIDENT'S AUTHORITY TO NE-
                         GOTIATE THE REDUCTION OF TARIFF AND OTHER TRADE BAR-
                         RIERS.

One of Secretary of State Hull's favorite ideas and the one for which Roosevelt agreed to appoint Hull as secretary in 1933, was the belief in the need
for all nations to end their discriminatory trade barriers.
     Although Roosevelt informed Hull during the spring of 1933 that he wanted
to postpone the Reciprocal Trade Act until 1934, the president appointed an
Executive Committee on Commercial Policy on November 11, 1933, and the process
of drafting a trade bill began. The committee included Francis B. SAYRE of
the State Department as chairman, representatives from the departments of
the Treasury, Commerce, and Agriculture; the Tariff Commission; the Agricultural Adjustment Act Commission; and the National Recovery Act administrator.
     The bill was offered to congress on March 2, 1934, and after the neces-
sary committee hearings was passed by the House on March 29 and the Senate
on June 4. As approved with three amendments added by congress the Reciprocal
Trade Act provided:

1. Congress delegated power to the president to raise or lower tariffs by 50% or to freeze existing agreements made with separate nations. The delegation of the power to permit the president to make executive agreements on trade relieved the president of having to present each agreement to the U.S. Senate for the two-thirds ratification vote required of a treaty. This would expedite the conclusion of new trade agreements.

2. The State Department would negotiate bilateral trade agreements with separate nations by amending the circumstances existing under the Hawley-Smoot Tariff Act of 1930. As Hull pointed out, however, the most-favored-nation clauses of existing treaties would generally apply any reductions on a product to the same product on existing treaties with all other nations.

3. In addition to tariff reductions, new trade agreements could be made regarding trade quotas, prohibitions, exchange controls, barter agreements, and other trade provisions.

4. A Senate amendment required public hearings to be held on an agreement before it was signed by the president.

5. Cuba's preferred trade status was retained.

6. The president's authority was limited to three years but could be extended.

June 19, 1934   CONGRESS PASSES A SILVER PURCHASE ACT WHICH BENEFITED
                             U.S. SILVER PRODUCERS BUT DESTROYED CHINA'S SILVER
                             MONETARY STANDARD.

Senator Key Pittman of Nevada, who was Chairman of the Senate Foreign Relations Committee, had a strong interest in making it government policy to buy silver until it was raised in price to one-third the value of gold. The congressional approval of this measure resulted in the presidential order of August 9 to the Treasury to buy all U.S. silver at 50 cents an ounce and all newly minted silver at 64.64 cents. The Treasury would pay for these purchases with silver certificates at the rate of $1.29 an ounce. A 50% profits tax precluded a windfall for silver speculators.

The Silver Purchase Act aided U.S. silver producers but disrupted China's monetary system during a difficult political and economic period for the Nationalist Chinese government. The increased silver price produced an increased market in China for American products but drained off China's silver reserves. China's silver exports increased sevenfold, and by November 3, 1935, China had to go off the silver standard.

China appealed to Washington for help in solving its problem, but Roosevelt initially refused to consider the silver purchase as the real cause of China's problem. Not until the Chinese abandoned the silver standard in November did Roosevelt approve some aid. At China's request, the United States bought 173 million ounces of silver on November 13. China agreed to use the funds to stabilize its currency, not to add to its military power against Japan. The Chinese economic situation was partly repaired, but the Japanese had been antagonized by Roosevelt's somewhat erratic behavior toward China.

July 16, 1934   THE STATE DEPARTMENT PRESENTS A VIGOROUS, LENGTHY *AIDE*
                        MEMOIRE TO THE GERMAN GOVERNMENT, COMPLAINING OF GERMAN
                        DEBT PAYMENT POLICIES TO AMERICANS SINCE MAY, 1933.

Although the State Department received frequent complaints about the persecution of Jews and treatment of American citizens in Germany in 1933-1934, these
were considered internal German matters which the United States could orally
protest to the Nazi officials but for which they could not strongly contend.
Regarding Hitler's policy on the payment of U.S. debts on loans, however,
Secretary of State Hull indicated his outrage in talks with German representatives in Washington and urged the U.S. Ambassador to Berlin, William DODD,
to protest strongly to Germany.

The German-American debt disagreement occurred in May, 1933, but grew
larger by July, 1934. On May 8, the German President of the Reichsbank,
Dr. Hjalmar Schacht, followed visits with Hull and President Roosevelt by
making the surprise announcement that the German government would cease payments on its external debts including $2 billion held by Americans. Hull
objected strongly, and during the London Economic Conference in July, Schacht
agreed to modify his May 8 declaration. Between August, 1933, and June, 1934,
the Germans again made unilateral alterations in their debt policy. The
Germans announced that the American debts would be paid 50% in cash, 50% in
scrip redeemable at the German Reichsbank for 75% of the value. The remaining
25% of the scrips value would subsidize German exports. According to Secretary
of State Hull, this partial devaluation of U.S. bonds also allowed the Germans
to repurchase the bonds at depreciated market prices.

In Berlin, Ambassador Dodd had presented several ineffective protests to
German Foreign Minister Konstantin von Neurath, leading the State Department
to file a final, more vigorous protest on July 16, 1934. Dodd, a former University of Chicago history professor with a dislike for "Wall Street" bankers,
had not offered effective protests on the debt issue even though he intensely
disliked Hitler's government. Therefore, Hull instructed him to present the
entire text of the July 16 memorandum to von Neurath. As a result, the Germans knew of Hull's displeasure even though they assumed no responsibility
to change the partial repudiation policy. From the Nazi view, because the
Western Allied powers defaulted on their debts, anything Germany did to repay
American bondholders was sufficient.

July 25, 1934   *A NAZI PUTSCH IN VIENNA FAILS; ITALY AND YUGOSLAVIA*
                        AID AUSTRIA.

A band of Nazis seized the radio station in Vienna and announced the resigna-
tion of Chancellor Engelburt DOLLFUSS. The Nazis then invaded the chancellery
and unintentionally killed Dollfuss, who had established a Fascist dictator-
ship in Austria during 1933. Dollfuss had destroyed the Socialist opposition
by political raids on February 11-15, 1934. However, he also rejected the
proposed dominance of the Nazis who wished to merge with Germany. His anti-
Nazi policy caused the coup attempt on July 25. Because Italy and Yugoslavia
supported the Austrians, Hitler decided in 1934 not to take over this "German
territory."

One result of the putsch of 1934 was Mussolini's temporary willingness
to work with France and England against German expansion. Not until 1936
did Hitler and Mussolini agree to work together. See October 25, 1936.

October 9, 1934   KING ALEXANDER OF YUGOSLAVIA AND FRENCH FOREIGN MIN-
                         ISTER LOUIS BARTHOU ARE ASSASSINATED.

*King Alexander and Barthou were in Marseilles following a European tour during
which they tried to build an alliance system against Nazi Germany. The assas-
sin was a Macedonian revolutionary who opposed the Yugoslavian state that included Croatia and Macedonia. Because the revolutionists' headquarters were
in Hungary, a crisis arose in which war was narrowly averted between Yugoslavia and Hungary.*

December 23, 1934   THE AMERICAN GULF OIL COMPANY JOINS THE ANGLO-PERSIAN
                        COMPANY IN OBTAINING OIL CONCESSIONS IN KUWAIT.

In 1931, the Gulf Oil Company requested State Department assistance in gaining Great Britain's approval to apply for oil rights in Kuwait. Gulf had
purchased concession rights from the Eastern and General Syndicate in 1925,
but the British Colonial Office refused to approve Gulf's application. Under
a treaty of 1899, the Sheikh of Kuwait agreed to reject any application unless
Great Britain approved.
      Secretary of State Stimson protested to the British government, and
after two years of discussion, London offered to commend both Gulf and the
British-owned Anglo-Persian Company to the sheikh. Because Kuwait's government declined to award two concessions, Gulf and Anglo-Persian agreed to form
the Kuwait Oil Company as an equally owned corporation to apply for the concession. Following the formation of this company, the sheikh awarded it the
oil rights on December 23, 1934. The company began oil drilling operations
in 1936.

December 29, 1934   JAPAN GIVES THE NECESSARY TWO-YEAR'S NOTICE THAT SHE
                        WILL TERMINATE THE WASHINGTON NAVAL LIMITATION TREATY
                        OF 1922, EFFECTIVE DECEMBER 31, 1936.

Throughout 1934, American, British, and Japanese delegates had informal discussions preparatory to the anticipated naval limitation conference of 1935.
The London Treaty of 1930 expired at the end of 1936 and a change in the
limits was being considered.
      Throughout the discussions of 1934, Japan sought some method to achieve
naval parity with Britain and America. Following the London Treaty of 1930,
two political assassinations resulted in Japan, and the military-naval faction which gained power in Tokyo in 1931 would countenance nothing except
parity. Great Britain wanted, as during the 1920's, to increase the number
of light cruisers in contrast to the American desire for more heavy cruisers.
The U.S. delegates were firmly controlled by Roosevelt, however, and the president preferred to continue the existing treaty limits or to reduce the current naval allocations.
      By the end of 1934, the forthcoming London Conference appeared to be
doomed. Each of the three nations refused to compromise. While Britain was
ready to consider a Japanese increase of ratios in exchange for more cruisers,
the United States rejected both suggestions. As a result, Japan's announcement on December 29 surprised neither President Roosevelt nor Prime Minister
Ramsay MacDonald. They decided nevertheless to proceed with the London Conference, although it was delayed until December 9, 1935, in order to attempt

to find a solution which would permit further limits on naval ships. See
January 15, 1936.

1935

January 7, 1935   *FRANCE AND ITALY SIGN AN AGREEMENT REGARDING NORTH AFRICA.*

France agreed to concesssions with Mussolini regarding Italian rights both in Tunisia and Ethiopia. The French Foreign Office hoped this would promote Italy's good will against Germany.

January 13, 1935   *A PLEBISCITE IN THE SAAR BASIN APPROVES REUNION WITH GERMANY.*

In accordance with the Treaty of Versailles, the League of Nations conducted this vote in the Saar. 90% of the people voted to join Germany in preference to union with France or their continued administration by the League of Nations. On March 1, the Saar again became part of the German Reich.

January 29, 1935   THE U.S. SENATE FAILS TO OBTAIN A TWO-THIRDS VOTE AND DENIES AMERICAN MEMBERSHIP IN THE WORLD COURT.

Although the Senate had rejected membership in the World Court when Presidents Harding, Coolidge, and Hoover recommended approval, President Roosevelt and Secretary Hull believed there was vast support for it in the Senate in 1934. Subsequently, the State Department prepared a draft treaty for U.S. membership and Senator Joseph T. Robinson of Arkansas offered a resolution for approval on January 16, 1935. A careful Senate poll indicated that more than two-thirds of the senators approved membership.

Over one weekend, however, anti-World Court spokesmen protested sufficiently to change the votes of several senators. The Hearst chain of newspapers opposed the court vehemently. On the radio, Father Charles Coughlin, a popular, right-wing Detroit priest, urged his listeners to write letters opposing the court to senators. Between Friday, January 25, when the Senate vote was delayed to Tuesday, January 29, Senate opposition grew from 10 to 36 members. Hearst lobbyists and messengers who carted wheelbarrows of telegrams from Coughlin's audience startled the politicians into shifting their votes. The resolution failed on January 29 by a vote of 52 to 36, 7 votes short of the necessary two-thirds.

Roosevelt was angered by the defeat of the World Court. Historian Robert Dallek contends this experience made Roosevelt and the State Department especially sensitive to isolationist views during the next several years.

February 2, 1935   A COMMERCIAL AGREEMENT WITH BRAZIL IS THE FIRST UNDER
                            THE RECIPROCAL TRADE ACT OF 1934.

Although a special and preferential pact was concluded with Cuba on August
24, 1934, the Brazilian agreement was the first one fully to apply the provisions of the Reciprocal Agreements Act.
     Following passage of the new trade bill on June 12, 1934, the president
set up a Committee on Trade Agreements headed by Assistant Secretary of State
Sayre who worked with the Trade Agreements Division of the State Department
to prepare tentative rate schedules on a country-by-country basis and to negotiate tariff relations with each nation.
     The basic principles that Sayre and the Trade Agreements Division fol-
lowed were:

   1. An item should be negotiated with the nation that was America's chief
       supplier of the product being lowered in rates.

   2. As far as possible, the commodity should be noncompetitive with a
       domestic product.

   3. The other nation must also reduce its quota restrictions on the prod-
       uct.

     In negotiating the Brazilian agreement, the principal opposition in Amer-
ica was from the manganese lobby. This opposition delayed the signing of
the agreement, but eventually that lobby's interests were satisfied and the
agreement was signed on February 2. The experience with Brazil caused Secretary Hull to realize that the State Department would have to work slowly
and cautiously to guarantee that the basic approach of tariff reductions would
not be jeopardized. Nevertheless, by the end of 1936, agreements had been
signed with 14 countries: Brazil, Belgium, Haiti, Sweden, Colombia, Canada,
Honduras, the Netherlands, Switzerland, Nicaragua, Guatemala, France, Finland,
and Costa Rica.
     The most difficult negotiations on trade reciprocity were with Great
Britain. The British agreement was not concluded until January 6, 1939. According to some observers, the shock of the Munich crisis with Hitler during
September and October, 1938, persuaded the British to make concessions to
American treaty demands. By that time, congress had extended the trade agree-
ment act on March 1, 1937 for another three years.

March 16, 1935   *HITLER DENOUNCES THE DISARMAMENT CLAUSES OF THE VER-*
                          SAILLES TREATY, ANNOUNCING THAT THE GERMAN ARMY WILL
                          BE INCREASED TO 36 DIVISIONS.

According to the German Foreign Office, the Western powers had failed to dis-
arm as provided by the 1919 peace treaty. This justified German rearmament.
     Although France, Italy, and Great Britain protested Hitler's action,
they did little else. On April 11, at the Stresa Conference, the three powers
organized a common front to oppose Germany, but the agreement proved inef-
fective.

March 23, 1935   UNDER PRESSURE FROM JAPAN, RUSSIA SELLS ITS INTERESTS
                           IN THE CHINESE EASTERN RAILWAY TO MANCHUKUO.

*This railway had been under constant dispute between Japan and Russia because
it gave Russia a direct route between Irkutsk and Vladivostok. After the
Soviet Union renounced other czarist treaties with China on May 31, 1924, it
had retained joint management with China of the railroad through Manchuria.
By the act of March 23, the Soviets yielded their control to Japan's puppet
government in Manchukuo.*

May 2, 1935   FRANCE AND RUSSIA FORM AN ALLIANCE IN CASE OF UNPRO-
                           VOKED AGGRESSION.

*Following Germany's rearmament decree on March 16, France and the Soviet Union
undertook discussions to make a defensive alliance by which an attack on one
would result in a two-front war for Germany. Stalin had entered into a phase
of Soviet policy that promoted anti-Fascist popular-front movements outside
Russia and was eager to sign. In France, however, the political divisions
between right-wing and left-wing groups deepened because of this alliance.
The rightist conservatives in France denounced any form of agreement with
the communists. This division in French politics persistently weakened French
foreign policy between 1935 and 1940. The struggle between proto-fascists
and socialists caused the deterioration of the centrist advocates of the Third
Republic.*

May 16, 1935   RUSSIA AND CZECHOSLOVAKIA CONCLUDE AN ALLIANCE BY WHICH
                           RUSSIA WOULD AID PRAGUE IN CASE OF AN ATTACK ON THE
                           CZECHS PROVIDED FRANCE ALSO ACTED.

*During the years preceding the Munich crisis of September, 1938, the Soviet
Union frequently requested united action with France and England in opposing
Nazi expansion. The appeasement policy followed by London and Paris was anti-
Communist, however. Chamberlain, Daladier, and other "appeasers" considered
the Soviets a greater menace than the Nazis. See September 29, 1938.*

June 14, 1935   THE CHACO WAR ENDS BETWEEN BOLIVIA AND PARAGUAY.

*This war broke out in 1932 after four years of peace attempts failed (see
December 6, 1928). The truce was settled by the mediation efforts of the
United States and five South American governments, which provided for peace
talks to be held at Buenos Aires. The peace conferees finally agreed on July
21, 1938, to submit the dispute to arbitration by the presidents of six American countries. The arbitrators awarded most of the Chaco territory to Paraguay but gave Bolivia an outlet to the sea by way of the Paraguay River.*

June 18, 1935   GREAT BRITAIN AND GERMANY SIGN A NAVAL AGREEMENT.

*Attempting to cause friction between France and England and to reassure Great
Britain, Hitler's government promised not to expand its navy beyond 35% of
the British navy. This, of course, permitted a build-up of the previously*

defunct German fleet but left the British navy dominant among European powers.

August 2, 1935   *THE BRITISH PARLIAMENT APPROVES THE GOVERNMENT OF INDIA*
                        ACT.

*This legislation provided a greater degree of political independence for In-
dia. Eleven provincial governments obtained legislatures with appointed gov-
ernors and received wide local autonomy. A central legislature was established at Delhi, but the British governor-general retained control of India's
national defense and foreign affairs.*

August 31, 1935   THE FIRST NEUTRALITY ACT: CONGRESS AUTHORIZES THE PRES-
                        IDENT TO EMBARGO ARMS IMPARTIALLY TO BELLIGERENTS AND
                        TO FORBID U.S. CITIZENS TO TRAVEL ON BELLIGERENT SHIPS
                        EXCEPT AT THEIR OWN RISK.

Since 1933 there had been discussion but no congressional action on an arms
embargo to warring nations. In May, 1933, President Roosevelt asked congress
for authority to embargo arms to an aggressor nation. This resolution had
been amended by the Senate Foreign Relations Committee to apply an embargo
to both warring nations. As a result, the State Department withdrew support
from the resolution and it never passed. This incident indicated, however,
a distinct divergence of attitude. President Roosevelt and Secretary Hull
wanted the president to have discretionary authority to help the victim-nation
and to punish the aggressor. Senator Key PITTMAN of Nevada, the chairman of
the Senate Foreign Relations Committee, disagreed and persistently advocated
that the United States should help neither nation because this was the only
effective way to be isolationist and not become involved in war.

     By the spring of 1935, at least three factors resulted in new congres-
sional bills to embargo armaments. First, the Geneva Disarmament Conference
had failed and, in Europe, Germany had taken steps to rebuild its navy and
army while both Japan and Italy pursued aggressive action. Second, the Italian demands escalated against Ethiopia and by August, 1935, had reached the
crisis proportions that led to war in October. American isolationists wanted
to remain out of the conflict in Ethiopia. Third, recent publications regarding America's economic and neutrality violations between 1914 and 1917
caused many Americans to believe that the United States needed new laws to
stay away from Europe's perennial problems. Chief among these publications
were news reports of the Nye Committee hearings (see April 12, 1934) and a
popular book published in April, 1934, Walter Mills's *The Road to War*, which
described how loans to the Allies and the use of neutrality favored England
and brought America into war with Germany. Other studies enumerated reasons
why the United States became involved in Europe in 1917 and implied that America could avoid war by strictly impartial neutrality.

     In the context of the failure of disarmament in Europe, the rising ag-
gression of the Axis powers, especially in Ethiopia in 1935, and the general
atmosphere promoting a need to avoid the mistakes of the period 1914 to 1917,
the neutrality resolution of 1935 became the first of a series of congressional bills to keep America neutral and isolated. These three factors also
favored Senator Pittman's desire to treat all belligerents the same, even
though President Roosevelt preferred discretionary power to identify and embargo arms only to aggressor nations.

    In July, 1935, after several congressmen introduced bills to embargo
arms to belligerents, the State Department drafted a bill for congress which
granted the president the discretionary power he desired. Senator Pittman
disliked this bill and the Senate Foreign Relations Committee rejected both
it and a second draft that would have limited the embargo to an Italian-
Ethiopian war. Because the Senate committee wanted an impartial arms embargo,
Roosevelt tried to block all arms and neutrality acts until the next session
of congress, but he failed. In mid-August, all signs indicated that Italy
would begin war against Ethiopia in the near future. Thus, the mood of congress was to pass some type of neutrality act. On August 20, a group of isolationist senators led by Senators Nye and Arthur Vandenberg began a filibuster, vowing to block several domestic New Deal bills until a mandatory
neutrality law passed. The president relented and supported Senator Pittman
who offered an impartial arms embargo limited to six months. Pittman presented his bill on August 20. By August 24, it passed both houses of congress, and on August 31 the president signed it.
    The August 31 act required a mandatory embargo on "arms, ammunition and
implements of war" to all belligerents. The president would define "implements of war" and determine when the embargo would begin. The president had
discretionary power to withhold protection from Americans traveling on belligerent ships. The law also prohibited U.S. ships from carrying munitions
to belligerents and established a Munitions Control Board to regulate arms
shipments. The bill was valid for six months on the assumption that permanent
legislation would be made at the next session of congress.

October 3, 1935   THE ITALIAN INVASION OF ETHIOPIA BEGINS.

*Difficulties between Ethiopia and Italy began on December 5, 1934, when an
Ethiopian-Somaliland border clash occurred between troops of the two nations.
Soon after, France recognized Italian concessions in Africa (see January 7,
1935). Attempts by the League of Nations and Great Britain to limit Italy's
action against Ethiopia did not succeed. Italy wished to avenge its defeat
at the Battle of Adua in 1896 and to annex all of Ethiopia.*

    *On October 7, the League of Nations declared that Italy was the aggres-
sor, but attempts to use sanctions against Italy did not succeed. The nations
disagreed on using effective oil sanctions. In addition, Hitler used the war
crisis to send German troops into the Rhineland in March, 1936. The German
action was more serious to Europeans and diverted attention from Ethiopia.
On May 5, 1936, Italy proclaimed the annexation of Ethiopia.*

October 5, 1935   PRESIDENT ROOSEVELT PROCLAIMS AN ARMS EMBARGO IN THE
                         ITALIAN-ETHIOPIAN WAR, THE FIRST OF SEVERAL U.S. AC-
                         TIONS OPPOSING ITALY'S AGGRESSION.

Although Italy attacked Ethiopia without a declaration of war, Roosevelt issued the embargo proclamation before the League of Nations acted on October
7, 1935. Applying the Neutrality Act of August 31, Roosevelt embargoed munitions to both belligerents even though Italy was the clear aggressor. His
proclamation also warned Americans who dealt with either belligerent that
they did so at their own risk.
    Between October 5 and November 15, the United States took other actions
to protect its neutrality. On October 6, Roosevelt warned Americans not to

travel on belligerent ships, a warning applying to Italian vessels because
Ethiopia had none. On October 30, the president appealed to Americans to
forego commercial or other profits made with warring nations. On November
15, Secretary Hull enlarged this "moral embargo" of October 30, urging Americans to halt exports for "war purposes" of such materials as oil, copper,
trucks, tractors, scrap steel, and scrap iron. Although not technically "implements of war," Hull said, the sale of these products violated the spirit
of neutrality. Prewar sales could be carried out but any increased sales of
these commodities would not be "morally" correct.

Unfortunately, neither U.S. action nor the League of Nations sanctions
prevented Italy's superior strength from defeating Ethiopia. See June 20,
1936.

October 11, 1935   *THE LEAGUE OF NATIONS IMPOSES SANCTIONS ON ITALY AS*
                            THE AGGRESSOR AGAINST ETHIOPIA.

*Following the Italian invasion of Ethiopia on October 3, the league council
declared Italy had "resorted to war in disregard of her obligations under
Article XII of the League covenant." On October 7, the council declared that
Italy was the aggressor nation and that the 51 members of the assembly would
be justified in imposing sanctions on Italy after October 11.*

*The action of October 11 was not implemented until November 18 when the
league applied sanctions. They prohibited the importation of Italian goods
and embargoed arms, loans, and other raw materials. Significantly, the embargo did not include oil, the product which might have injured Italy the
most. In addition, because of French-British objections, the League of Nations did not establish a naval blockade of Italy or close the Suez Canal to
Italian ships. These measures would have forced Italy to end the war quickly.
The failure of league members to block Italy's aggression indicated once again
the ineffectiveness of collective security during the 1930's.*

1936

January 15, 1936   JAPAN WITHDRAWS FROM THE LONDON NAVAL CONFERENCE BE-
CAUSE THE UNITED STATES AND BRITAIN REFUSE TO RECOGNIZE
JAPAN'S RIGHT TO NAVAL PARITY.

Following Japan's December 29, 1934, announcement that she would terminate
the Washington Naval Treaty limits in two years, preparations for the London
Naval Conference of 1935 went slowly because the United States and Britain
disagreed on how best to handle Japan. Great Britain's most vital concern
had increasingly turned to its European problems. Therefore, London's government agreed to follow Washington's lead on the naval treaty with Japan.
Roosevelt believed that if he could make Japan the nation which renounced
naval disarmament, the American defense and foreign policy program would be
assisted. In addition, Roosevelt would become the champion of disarmament
who reluctantly requested a U.S. navy program because Japan would accept no
limitations.

When the London Conference opened on December 9, 1935, the chief of the
U.S. delegation, Norman Davis, presented Roosevelt's plan for a 10-year renewal of the Washington treaty and a 20% reduction in each country's overall
naval tonnage. Japan, of course, would never accept these concepts. Tokyo's
delegate, Ambassador to the U.S. Hiroshi Saito, proposed parity for Japan with
Britain and America and the elimination of all aircraft carriers and battleships.

The conference breakdown came on January 15, 1936. Japan denounced the
fact that she was treated as an inferior power by the existing treaties. Then
Saito and his fellow delegates left London. Because Japan had previously
announced that its termination of existing limits would be in effect on December 31, 1936, the two remaining naval powers met with a French representative. Before concluding the London Conference, France, Britain, and America
signed a naval treaty on March 25, 1936. The three-power agreement committed
the United States and Britain to maintaining parity in their fleets' size
and type. The three nations also agreed to exchange information on their
fleets and to retain their treaty limits in line with whatever increase Japan
made in its fleet. One consequence of the Japanese withdrawal from the treaty
was the U.S. congressional agreement to appropriate funds for naval construction.

February 29, 1936   THE SECOND NEUTRALITY ACT: A CONGRESSIONAL JOINT RES-
OLUTION EXTENDS THE ACT OF AUGUST 31, 1935, WITH THREE
AMENDMENTS AND ONE SIGNIFICANT CHANGE IN WORDING.

On the day the Neutrality Act of 1935 was scheduled to expire, congress renewed the basic law with the following changes:

1. The law was extended to May 1, 1937.

2. Loans to belligerents were forbidden in accordance with a State Department request.

3. The president was directed to extend the arms embargo to any new belligerent entering the war. This change indicated a desire to extend the action to any collective action taken against a belligerent.

4. The president could exempt from an arms embargo any American republic at war with a non-American state, provided the American republic was not cooperating with a non-American state.

5. An inadvertent change in wording stated that "whenever the President shall find that there exists a state of war...." This phrase replaced the original, which said the president would institute the embargo "upon the outbreak or during the progress of war...."

Although the new law did not add clauses to include commodities other than "arms, ammunition or other implements of war," Roosevelt asked the nation to respect the "moral embargo" requested in the Italian-Ethiopian war. See October 5, 1935.

March 2, 1936   THE UNITED STATES AND PANAMA SIGN A TREATY ABOLISHING
                             THE AMERICAN PROTECTORATE OF PANAMA.

Intended to foster "good neighbor" relations, the 1936 Panama treaty limited the U.S. purposes in Panama to the "effectual maintenance, operation, sanitation and protection of the Canal and its auxiliary works." The United States also promised to strictly control the commissary business available to American military personnel in the Canal Zone at low prices.

Panama ratified the treaty on December 24, 1936. The U.S. Senate delayed ratification, however. Concerned about the relationship of the canal's security to America's continental defense measures, the senators demanded clarification of Article X, which required consultation between the two governments in the event of threats of aggression. The Senate wanted assurances that if necessary, the United States could act first and consult afterward. When this was clarified, the Senate ratified the treaty on July 25, 1939.

In addition to agreeing not to intervene in Panamanian affairs, the United States increased its annual payments to Panama and pledged to provide for mutual defense of the Canal Zone.

March 7, 1936   *GERMANY DENOUNCES THE LOCARNO PACTS OF 1925 AND MOVES*
                             SOLDIERS INTO THE RHINELAND.

Because of French protests against Hitler's occupation of the Rhineland, war between Germany and France appeared imminent. Although Great Britain and Italy joined France in protests, they would not invoke sanctions or take other action against Hitler. Italy was involved in Ethiopia; the British Conservative government of Stanley Baldwin was moving toward an era of appeasement toward Fascist policy which became the firm policy when Neville Chamberlain was promoted from the office of Chancellor of the Exchequer to Prime Minister on May 28, 1937.

May 5, 1936   THE ITALIAN ARMY OCCUPIES ADDIS ABABA, AND MUSSOLINI
                      PROCLAIMS THE CONQUEST OF ETHIOPIA.

*The Italian victory resulted in the collapse of the League of Nations as a
collective security agency. Ethiopia had been abandoned and the league's
economic sanctions against Italy failed to be effectively implemented.*

June 4, 1936   TREASURY SECRETARY MORGENTHAU ISSUES COUNTERVAILING
                      CUSTOMS DUTIES ON A LIST OF IMPORTS SUBSIDIZED BY THE
                      GERMAN GOVERNMENT.

In what Secretary of State Hull described as Morgenthau's "personal war
against Germany," the Secretary of the Treasury levied special duties on German imports that the Nazi government had been subsidizing. The Tariff Act
of 1930 permitted the Treasury Department to do this. With the approval of
President Roosevelt and the Attorney General, Morgenthau issued the duty list
on June 4.
    In spite of Hull's disagreement, Morgenthau succeeded. At first, Reichs-
bank President Hjalmar Schacht protested the new duties. But when the United
States stood firm, Germany backed down and removed all the subsidies it had
granted to German companies for such exports. By September, the United States
removed the special duties. Morgenthau could boast that he had checked "Germany's career of economic conquest."

June 5, 1936   *IN FRANCE, THE LEFT-WING POPULAR-FRONT COALITION OF
                      LEON BLUM GAINS CONTROL OF THE MINISTRY.*

*The parliamentary elections of May 3 had given the Socialists and Radical
Socialists a majority in the Chamber of Deputies. The Communist Party did
not join the ministry but cooperated with the Popular Front. The Blum government tried to install an extensive program of economic and social reforms
which caused financial difficulties for the French government and led many
Frenchmen to gravitate to the right wing.*

June 20, 1936   THE UNITED STATES ENDS ITS EMBARGO ACTION FOLLOWING
                      THE ITALIAN CONQUEST OF ETHIOPIA; AMERICA ALSO APPLIES
                      THE NON-RECOGNITION DOCTRINE TO ITALIAN CONTROL OF
                      ETHIOPIA.

Although President Roosevelt had considered stronger measures against Italy
between October 5, when he proclaimed the arms embargo on both belligerents,
and December, 1935, the unwillingness of England and France to agree to
stronger League of Nations measures (see October 11, 1935) and the opposition
of isolationists such as Senator Hiram Johnson led the president to drop any
thoughts of strong action against Italy. Although some observers believed
that Washington's willingness to replace European oil losses resulting from
an Italian embargo would have encouraged the league states to sanction oil,
the uncertainty of league action and the opposition of Johnson kept the United
States from such a commitment. Johnson told Roosevelt he must do nothing
which might imply that the United States was supporting the League of Nations
or Great Britain because the isolationists opposed any hint of such policy
coordination.

With no effective international opposition, Italy captured Addis Ababa
and took over Ethiopia on May 5, 1936. With the war finished, Roosevelt an-
nounced on June 20 that the arms embargo, as well as the moral embargo on
Italy, did not apply any longer. About the same time, Secretary of State
Hull declared the United States would not recognize the Italian conquest of
Ethiopia, just as Secretary Stimson had not recognized Japan's victory over
Manchuria in 1931-1932. America's official correspondence was addressed only
to the King of Italy, not to Italy's preferred title of King of Italy and
Emperor of Ethiopia.

July 17, 1936   *THE SPANISH CIVIL WAR BEGINS AS INSURGENTS LED BY GEN-*
                       ERAL FRANCISCO FRANCO AND OTHER ARMY CHIEFS REVOLT IN
                       SPANISH MOROCCO.

The Spanish Republic, which was established on December 9, 1931, experienced
difficulties with separatist movements in Catalonia and with political dis-
putes between Republican and Socialist left-wing factions. In addition, the
army and the Roman Catholic Church opposed the anti-clerical legislation
against education and the property of religious orders. During October, 1934,
the Catholic Popular Action Party gained seats in the cabinet of Prime Min-
ister Alejandro Lerroux and blocked his attempts in 1935 to solve Spanish
problems.

To offset the growth of the Catholic party and other right-wing groups,
the left united in a Popular Front; forced the Lerroux cabinet to call new
elections; and on February 16 won a decisive victory over the Conservative,
Republican, Catholic, and Monarchist parties.

The Popular Front victory precipitated General Franco's decision to rally
the rightists against the republic. Clerics and army and air force leaders
joined Franco who appealed to the German Nazis and Italian Fascists for aid.
Thus, "volunteers" from Germany and Italy joined the insurgents, and soon
Russia aided the Republican government with military equipment and advisors.

The civil war ended in a victory for Franco's forces on March 28, 1939.

August 9, 1936   *THE FRENCH PREMIER, LEON BLUM, FOLLOWS BRITISH ADVICE*
                       AND CALLS FOR A MEETING OF ALL EUROPEAN NATIONS TO
                       ADOPT NON-INTERVENTION POLICIES IN THE SPANISH CIVIL
                       WAR.

As the leader of the French Popular Front government of left-wing liberal and
Socialist parties in France, Blum's first reaction to the Fascist civil war
against the Spanish republic was to aid the Loyalist republicans in Madrid.
Great Britain's Conservative Party ministry did not support this policy, and
Foreign Secretary Anthony Eden warned Blum that if Germany attacked France
over the Spanish issue, England would not aid the French.

At Britain's suggestion, Blum called for a general European conference
to adopt a non-intervention policy in Spain. Also on August 9, Blum suspended
all French war exports to Spain. For the International Non-Intervention Com-
mittee see October 8, 1936.

August 11, 1936   SECRETARY OF STATE HULL ANNOUNCES A "MORAL EMBARGO"
                           AGAINST BOTH BELLIGERENTS IN THE SPANISH CIVIL WAR.

Following General Franco's Fascist-inspired attack on the Loyalist Republican
government of Spain on July 17, 1936, Britain and France urged a general European neutrality in the civil war. Secretary Hull and President Roosevelt
found this course of action acceptable, and on August 11, Hull publicly announced the American desire not to assist either side in the war.
        Although the Neutrality Act of 1936 did not apply to a civil war, Hull
stated he hoped all Americans would apply the spirit of that law to the Spanish conflict. The United States, he said, would "scrupulously refrain from
any interference whatsoever in the unfortunate Spanish situation."
        During the fall of 1936, the Spanish crisis had not yet acquired the
ideological dimensions that appeared clearly during the spring of 1937. While
some rumors of German and Italian aid to Franco surfaced in August and September, no overt evidence had appeared. Britain and France organized a collective neutrality system in Europe. The policy of neutrality also served
Roosevelt well during the presidential campaign of 1936. Although domestic
issues predominated in the election, Roosevelt's neutrality in Spain pleased
both the isolationists and the European-oriented internationalists during
the fall and winter of 1936. See October 8, 1936, and January 8, 1937.

August 19, 1936   *THE RUSSIAN PURGE TRIAL OF THE OLD BOLSHEVIKS OPENS.*

*In 1935, Stalin's initial purge of the Communist Party accused several of the
old-time Bolsheviks, whom he arrested, tried for treason, and imprisoned.
Beginning on August 19, Stalin again tried many of these former leaders, accused them of plotting revolution as Trotskyists, and had them executed. In
quick succession, 16 of these old Bolsheviks confessed and were executed.
Chief among these were Leo Kamenev and Gregory E. Zinoviev. Periodic purges
of large numbers of "disloyal" Russians continued throughout the next three
years.*

August 27, 1936   *EGYPT AND GREAT BRITAIN CONCLUDE A TREATY GIVING EGYPT
                           GREATER LOCAL AUTONOMY.*

*According to this agreement, the only British forces in Egypt would be in
the Suez Canal zone. Egypt would be independent and join the League of Nations as well as being able to move troops into the Sudan. Finally, Britain
and Egypt formed a 20-year alliance which would be reexamined at the end of
that period.*

September 25, 1936   THE UNITED STATES, GREAT BRITAIN, AND FRANCE AGREE TO
                           COOPERATE IN MAINTAINING CURRENCY STABILIZATION.

For over a year, British and French representatives had suggested to the U.S.
State and Treasury departments that they desired to cooperate in giving stability to the value of the dollar, franc, and pound. Since the London Economic Conference of 1933, Roosevelt and Secretary of the Treasury Morgenthau
had rejected such cooperation. By June, 1936, Morgenthau convinced Roosevelt
that currency stability would aid American trade programs. As a result,

Morgenthau conducted talks with Britain's Chancellor of the Exchequer Neville Chamberlain during the summer of 1936. France joined the discussions, and on September 25, the three nations exchanged statements agreeing to cooperate in stabilizing the value ratios of their currencies. Belgium, Switzerland, and Holland joined this cooperative effort by the end of 1936.

October 8, 1936   AT THE INTERNATIONAL NON-INTERVENTION COMMITTEE MEET-
ING, RUSSIA OBJECTS TO FASCIST VIOLATIONS OF THE AGREE-
MENTS, BUT BRITAIN AND FRANCE DO NOT ACT.

The accusations made by the Soviet delegate at the London non-intervention conference illustrate the general double-dealing policy of Germany, Italy, and the Soviet Union in proclaiming non-intervention in Spain while providing a variety of aid to either Franco's Nationalist forces or the Loyalist Republican forces in Spain. The first meeting of the Non-Intervention Committee which Leon Blum proposed on August 9, 1936, had been held in London on September 9. Subsequently, throughout the civil war, the Non-Intervention Committee gave the appearance of advocating no aid to either belligerent although each of the 24 nations working on the Non-Intervention Committee provided varying degrees of aid to either the Fascist or Republican cause. The historian Hugh Thomas describes the committee's existence after September 9 as moving "from equivocation to hypocrisy and humiliation" but enduring until Franco's Fascist forces triumphed.

The Non-Intervention Committee served each nation's interest in different ways. For the British, the conservative ministry appeared to be acting impartially while following covert practices that aided Franco's forces of "law and order." For France, the Popular Front government placated its liberal and left wings by providing small amounts of secret aid to the republic but appearing to be impartial. For Germany and Italy, their larger amount of aid to Franco was masked sufficiently to greatly assist Franco while the Spanish republicans received little aid even though they represented the legitimate Spanish government when the right-wing uprising began. Russia provided some help to the Spanish republic but was generally dismayed by the Fascist aid to Franco. The Soviets stayed on the committee in order to retain British-French good-will.

On October 15, following its complaint at the committee session about Fascist intervention, the Soviet Union rapidly increased its military aid to the Loyalists. The smaller nations which joined the Non-Intervention Committee simply followed the five larger powers: some aided the Fascists; some aided the republicans in Spain.

In retrospect, the Non-Intervention Committee's duplicity assisted Franco's forces more than the Loyalists. It did, however, provide a curious method for avoiding a general European war. In this respect, the French-British policy was a progenitor of appeasement. In each European country, the general public feared the communist revolutionary threat represented by the Spanish Republic more than the Nazi-Fascist ideology represented by Franco. The possible continuation of a liberal republican government in Spain was sacrificed to Franco's Fascist dictatorship, determining Spain's totalitarian society for the next 40 years.

October 25, 1936   THE BERLIN-ROME ANTI-COMINTERN PACT IS FORMED.

Hitler and Count Ciano of Italy signed an agreement to cooperate in seeking revision of the World War I peace treaties. In 1934-1935, Mussolini had often consulted with England and France because Italy's interests in the Danube region had differed from Hitler's. These conflicts were overlooked in 1936 and the two Fascist dictators agreed to work together against both the democratic governments and communism. In November, Japan negotiated with Germany and Italy to join the Axis alliance. See November 25, 1936.

Both Britain and France were deceived by the anti-Comintern rhetoric of the Fascist powers. As Italian Foreign Minister Count Galeazzo CIANO asserted, the anti-Comintern pact was "unmistakably anti-British" in Europe, the Mediterranean, and the Far East, not anti-communist. For Fascists, of course, anti-communism included the center liberal republican and democratic parties as well as the Soviet Union. During the 1930's, however, many who favored parliamentary government in England and France held an exaggerated and unrealistic fear of communism which led them to embrace the "law and order" speeches of the extreme right. Lacking sufficient devotion to the basic concepts of human rights, the appeasers were weak apostles of democracy for whom the watchword slogan was "better Hitler than Stalin." Americans were not immune to this disease. Sumner Welles's opposition to the Cuban regime of Grau San Martin showed similar difficulties. See September 5, 1933, and January 15, 1934.

*November 3, 1936   ROOSEVELT WINS AN OVERWHELMING VICTORY IN THE PRESI-
                         DENTIAL CONTEST.*

The election campaign was a bitter contest because the Republicans vigorously condemned the New Deal. The Republican nominee was Alfred LANDON of Kansas, and the Republican platform charged that Roosevelt had usurped great power, passed unconstitutional laws, and displaced free enterprise. No specific New Deal laws were attacked except for the desire to revise personal and corporate income taxes downward.

At their Philadelphia convention, the Democrats renominated Roosevelt. The president's acceptance speech attacked "economic royalists" who created despotisms cloaked in legality. The party platform stood on the four-year record that had ended the severest aspects of the 1929-1933 Depression.

On November 3, as one pundit said, nobody was for Roosevelt but the people. Although 80% of the press opposed the president, predictions of a close election did not materialize. Roosevelt won the biggest electoral majority since Monroe in 1820: Landon, 8, Roosevelt, 523. The Democratic majority in the Senate was 77-19; in the House, 328-107.

*November 18, 1936   GERMANY AND ITALY RECOGNIZE FRANCO'S INSURGENT GOV-
                         ERNMENT IN SPAIN.*

Although they joined the London Non-Intervention Committee on September 9, 1936, Hitler and Mussolini sympathized with General Franco by supplying arms, technical experts, and some troops. On October 1, Franco named himself head of the Spanish state. In order to overtly aid Franco in blockading the Loyalist supply routes, Germany and Italy formally recognized his regime on November 18.

Although Britain's conservative government's "appeasement" policy caused the British to prefer Franco, London withheld recognition to retain the co-operation of French Premiers Leon Blum and Daldier until their Popular Front governments fell on October 4, 1938.

November 25, 1936   GERMANY AND JAPAN SIGN AN ANTI-COMINTERN PACT.

Ostensibly, the pact between Hitler's Nazi government and Japan's military-dominated government emphasized their agreement to defeat communism as identified by the Communist Third International (Comintern), which Russia controlled. Of course, far right-wing extremists, liberal democrats, socialists, and other center and left-of-center groups were all "communist."

Japan and Italy also negotiated an agreement, completed on November 6, 1937, which joined the three extreme rightist governments as ideological allies.

December 23, 1936   CONCLUSION OF A SPECIAL PAN-AMERICAN PEACE CONFERENCE AT BUENOS AIRES.

The conference delegates drew up a common neutrality policy in the event of a war in the Americas and established principles of consultation if the peace of the hemisphere should be threatened.

Because the next regular meeting of the Inter-American Conference was not scheduled until 1938, President Roosevelt suggested in 1935 that a special meeting be held on maintaining peace in the Western Hemisphere. The Italian-Ethiopian War and the increased aggressiveness of Nazi Germany and Fascist Italy, not only in Europe but also in Latin American trade, caused the president to believe a peace conference in the Americas would be beneficial. After sounding out representatives of the American republics, Secretary Hull agreed to call a conference. On January 30, 1936, Roosevelt proposed a meeting to be held at Buenos Aires for the purpose of determining how peace in the Americas "may best be safeguarded."

In order to emphasize the importance of the meeting, President Roosevelt went by ship to Argentina and addressed the opening-day session of the meeting. Contrasting the peace of the Western Hemisphere with the rise of violence in Europe, the president urged the delegates to effect a united front for peace so that the American republics would consult together "for our mutual safety and our mutual good."

Before adjourning on December 23, the conference made a series of agreements, the most important being:

1. A Convention for the Maintenance, Preservation, and Reestablishment of Peace provided for consultation not only in case of the threat of war between American nations but if a war outside America menaced the peace of the Western Hemisphere.

2. A Declaration of Principles of Inter-American Solidarity and Cooperation "continentalized" the Monroe Doctrine; that is, the American nations would consult whenever an "act susceptible of disturbing the peace of America should be threatened or committed."

3. An Additional Protocol Relative to Non-Intervention stated that the signatories "declare inadmissable the intervention of any one of

them, directly or indirectly, and for whatever reason, in the internal or external affairs of any other of the parties." When the United States accepted and ratified this agreement without the reservations of the 1933 Montevideo meeting, it committed itself to non-intervention.

1937

PRESIDENT ROOSEVELT SIGNS CONGRESSIONAL LEGISLATION
WHICH SPECIFICALLY APPLIES THE IMPARTIAL NEUTRALITY
EMBARGO TO THE SPANISH CIVIL WAR.

From August 11 to December 28, America's "moral embargo" against the shipment of arms to either side in Spain had been generally effective. On December 26, however, the first organized group of 26 American volunteers left New York for Spain. Because these and later U.S. volunteers, all of whom fought for the Loyalist Republicans, officially volunteered when they reached France, the U.S. government could not prosecute them. After January 11, 1937, the passport office stamped all passports as "Not Valid for Spain," but after reaching France, passports became unnecessary for the volunteers.

On December 28, the moral embargo was circumvented by Robert Cruse who applied for a license to ship $2,775,000 worth of aircraft engines to the Spanish government. Cruse received his license because the State Department had no legal means to reject it. Subsequently, Cruse's cargo left New York the day before the congressional embargo was passed on January 8. Carried on board the Spanish ship *Mar Cantabrico*, the cargo was captured by the Spanish Nationalists in the Bay of Biscay and was used by the Fascists rather than the Republican forces in Spain.

Cruse's license application prompted President Roosevelt to urge congress to make such sales illegal as soon as it reassembled on January 6, 1937. The law as passed on January 6 and signed by the president on January 8 embargoed all sales of arms, ammunition, and implements of war to Spain. Neither belligerent could obtain U.S. arms.

Roosevelt's principal reason for requesting the arms embargo appears to have been his desire to align his policy to what he perceived to be the British-French policy. Whether or not Roosevelt or other Americans understood the short-sighted and duplicitous role which the British Conservatives and France were using in Europe is not certain (see October 8, 1936). Although the U.S. consul at Seville made frequent reports to the State Department on the large amount of German and Italian material and the "volunteers" entering Spain, the president may have been too concerned with the opening stages of his Supreme Court struggle to give great attention to Europe. Aroused at the court's rulings against several New Deal laws, Roosevelt prepared to seek the resignation of the elderly judges or to enlarge the court by adding new appointees. This court battle took much time in 1937 and proved to be one of Roosevelt's greatest political miscalculations.

Whatever the reason for Roosevelt's decision to act "impartially" in Spain, the net result of the U.S. embargo was, as in the case of the British-French embargoes, favorable to the Spanish Fascists. Realizing this, Franco announced in January that the president acted as a "true gentleman" in approving the Embargo Act. The Germans also praised Roosevelt. Increasingly, however, U.S. liberals, socialists, and communists condemned the embargo and supplied volunteers to assist the Spanish Republicans.

January 30, 1937   STALIN COMPLETES ANOTHER WEEK OF PURGE TRIALS AGAINST
                       COMMUNIST PARTY LEADERS.

*From January 23 to 30, Georgei Piatakov and Karl Radek were the most prominent
of 13 leaders tried and sentenced to death. Purges continued on a sporadic
basis throughout 1937 until March 15, 1938. The victims of the trials and
executions included leading military men such as Marshal Ian Gamarnik (May 31)
and Marshal Michael Tukhachevski (June 12). According to the account of the
head of Britain's code-breaking intelligence unit, William Stephenson (Intrepid), which was published in 1974, the head of Nazi Intelligence, Reinhard
HEYDRICH, engineered Stalin's decision to purge the Red Army by forging 32
documents that he allowed the Russian Secret Service to "capture," implicating
the Soviet army officers in a German plot. These documents raised Stalin's
suspicions, convincing him to execute or banish half of Russia's officer
corps, about 35,000 men.*

May 1, 1937   THE THIRD NEUTRALITY ACT: THIS ACT RENEWED THE ACT OF
                       1936 BUT ADDED SEVERAL AMENDMENTS INCLUDING "CASH AND
                       CARRY" PROVISIONS.

Although continuing the mandatory and impartial arms embargo provisions of
the 1936 act, the 1937 act had no time limit and contained three new clauses.
These additions:

1. extended the mandatory embargo to civil strife whenever the president
    should find arms exports "would threaten or endanger the peace of
    the United States";

2. stated U.S. citizens could not travel on belligerent ships except
    at their own risk;

3. provided "cash and carry" sales of other goods and empowered the
    president to forbid the export of commodities other than arms in
    U.S. ships. The belligerent nation purchasing these goods must use
    its own ships and have title transferred to the foreign government
    or agency before leaving America. In brief, non-arms commodities
    had to be paid for in cash, their title transferred from the U.S.
    seller to the foreign buyer, and the product carried away in foreign
    ships. Roosevelt liked this provision because in the event of war,
    England and France were the European nations most likely to benefit
    from U.S. purchases.

May 28, 1937   NEVILLE CHAMBERLAIN REPLACES STANLEY BALDWIN AS PRIME
                       MINISTER OF THE NATIONAL COALITION CABINET.

*Baldwin's ministry had been uncertain about the proper policy to follow re-
garding Germany and Italy. Chamberlain advocated negotiating with Hitler
and Mussolini in order to maintain peace, even if concessions were essential.
Generally, Chamberlain and the British conservatives feared the rise of
socialism-communism more than the Fascist threat. They were willing to "appease" the right wing in order to oppose such groups as Leon Blum's left-wing
Popular Front in France.*
    One of the first steps of Chamberlain's appeasement of the right wing

was taken on November 17, 1937, when Lord Halifax visited Adolf Hitler at Berchtesgaden in southern Germany. Halifax became Foreign Secretary of Britain after Anthony Eden resigned on February 20, 1938, in protest against the appeasement policy. See September 29, 1938.

July 7, 1937   *AN INCIDENT BETWEEN CHINESE AND JAPANESE TROOPS AT THE MARCO POLO BRIDGE NEAR PEKING SOON DEVELOPS INTO AN UNDECLARED WAR.*

Although Japan's war plans in 1937 were based on a war with the Soviet Union in Manchuria or Mongolia, Tokyo had nearly 7,000 troops for its "legation guard" in Peking and vicinity, many more than any other power. During 1935 and 1936, Japan had negotiated with China to gain Peking's recognition of the Japanese-supported state of Manchukuo but the Chinese nationalists would not recognize these Japanese "rights." Consequently, there was frequent friction between Chinese and Japanese in the Peking region, and on July 7, Japanese troops on maneuvers near the Marco Polo bridge, 13 kilometers outside Peking, clashed with Chinese troops.

    Exactly what happened on July 7 is a mystery. The Chinese claimed the Japanese demanded entrance to the city of Wanping to search for a missing soldier. When the Chinese refused, the Japanese fired artillery which killed or wounded 200 Chinese in Wanping. The Japanese contended that soldiers from China's 29th Army fired without provocation on Japanese troops. When the Japanese asked for negotiations to settle the dispute, the Chinese would not withdraw their troops, and further attacks began on both sides. The incident probably was not planned but it sparked a larger conflict during the next six weeks. Tokyo ordered an attack on Nanking, and following its conquest in December, attempts to localize the war ended. Fighting continued although war was not declared.

July 16, 1937   SECRETARY OF STATE HULL INFORMS THE PRESS THAT THE UNITED STATES MUST WAIT TO DECIDE ON A POLICY TOWARD THE CHINESE-JAPANESE CONFLICT. THE POWERS HOPE TO LOCALIZE THE WAR, AND HULL ISSUES A PEACE CIRCULAR TO ALL NATIONS URGING THEM TO ADOPT AND PRACTICE THE AMERICAN PRINCIPLES OF INTERNATIONAL GOOD CONDUCT.

When the "China incident" began on July 7, 1937, the United States and other Western powers hoped to resolve the crisis quickly. Both China and Japan expressed a willingness to seek peace terms, but during the next six months no mediation was accepted. The war gained a momentum that did not cease until 1945 in China.

    The United States had two principal decisions to make. First, would Japan be held to its obligations under the Nine-Power Pact of 1922? If so, what could be done to require her to follow that treaty? Second, should Roosevelt proclaim the Neutrality Act of May 1, 1937, to be in effect? Because neither side had declared war, there was a rationale for withholding the neutrality decree, which would harm China more than Japan.

    During the summer of 1937, Roosevelt and Hull chose to wait and see what developed in China. As Hull told newsmen on July 16, to invoke the Nine-Power Pact while both sides protested peaceful desires would make the concluding of peace more difficult. Therefore, Hull hoped to mobilize world opinion to bring moral pressure to bear on both Peking and Tokyo. He communicated a message to all governments of the world, urging such virtues as self-restraint, abstinence from the use of force, peaceful negotiations, sanctity of treaties, promotion of stability among nations, reduction of arms, and the use of orderly processes to resolve international problems.

On September 14, the president issued a decree that stopped government ships from carrying armaments to either China or Japan and warned private shippers that they carried arms at their own risk. Four days later, however, the watchful-waiting policy still applied. A State Department news release said that Hull and Roosevelt were acting on a 24-hour basis toward the Sino-Japanese conflict.

October 5, 1937   ROOSEVELT'S "QUARANTINE SPEECH": THE PRESIDENT STATES
                         THAT WHEN THERE IS INTERNATIONAL LAWLESSNESS THE AMER-
                         ICAS TOO COULD BE ATTACKED; THE INTERNATIONAL COMMUNITY
                         MUST JOIN "IN A QUARANTINE OF THE PATIENTS" TO KEEP
                         LAWLESSNESS FROM SPREADING.

Roosevelt's Chicago speech of October 5 attempted to counteract the isolationist trend in America because both Roosevelt and Secretary of State Hull agreed that American inaction indirectly encouraged the three Axis powers to increase their aggressive acts.

By early September, Hull believed Japan had clearly decided on all-out war in China. Violent fighting began in the area of Shanghai in August, and Japan declared a blockade of the Chinese coast. Following a bombing by Chinese planes in which 1,700 civilians including two Americans died, Roosevelt sent 1,200 U.S. marines to Shanghai on August 17, in order to protect U.S. lives and property. Finally, speeches by Premier Konoye and Foreign Minister Hirota on September 5 indicated Japan's commitment to the Chinese war.

At the League of Nations, China appealed for aid, and a special subcommittee investigated the events in China since July 7. A U.S. delegate, Minister to Switzerland Leland Harrison, joined the subcommittee as a non-voting member. Harrison kept Hull informed on the committee's progress. Hull refused, however, to make a commitment to Britain or France with regard to Japan. The United States would take parallel action with the league or other powers with whom the United States agreed, but could make no advance multilateral commitments of any kind.

The Quarantine Speech was Roosevelt's attempt to alert the American people against complete isolation from external conflicts and to highlight the need for non-belligerent cooperation to punish aggression so disorder would not spread. After describing the recent "reign of terror and international lawlessness," the president stated that the "very foundations of civilization are seriously threatened." To prevent the "spread of this international anarchy," he warned, "peace-loving nations must make a concerted effort" against aggressors. The opposition might be a "quarantine" of the "epidemic of world lawlessness" in order to secure "the health of the community against the spread of the disease...." Because America hates war, "America actively engages in the search for peace."

Although historians using the Roosevelt archives realize the president had no specific idea in mind at this time and wished only to search for peace, contemporaries in Europe and America read many hopes or fears into the speech. European leaders who sought U.S. backing for positive action against Germany, Italy, and Japan interpreted the speech as a sign that Roosevelt would approve sanctions against Japan and other aggressors. American isolationists recoiled in horror and denunciation of Roosevelt's speech, envisioning it as a collective security action that would lead the nation to war. In Secretary Hull's view, the speech failed of its intention because isolationist editors and politicians attacked the administration's desire to promote greater international cooperation.

Dorothy Borg has compiled a summary of the variety of U.S. opinion after the Quarantine Speech which shows greater support for Roosevelt than he, Hull, and others in Washington perceived. Most editors, religious groups, labor groups, and others favored action short of war to counteract the aggressors. Borg believes the administration was too sensitive to the Hearst press, business newspapers such as the *Wall Street Journal*, and vociferous isolationist senators such as Borah, Vandenberg, and Hiram Johnson. Nevertheless, the negative perceptions of the speech registered by Secretary Hull and others caused the administration to proceed more cautiously during the next two years. As William Langer and S. Everett Gleason's study indicates, the president's policies often followed, rather than led, public opinion in foreign affairs from 1937 to 1941.

October 6, 1937   *THE LEAGUE OF NATIONS ASSEMBLY CONDEMNS JAPAN FOR VIO-*
                           LATING THE NINE-POWER AND PARIS PEACE PACTS, CALLING
                           ON THE NATIONS TO GIVE MORAL SUPPORT TO CHINA.

The League of Nations acted on recommendations of a special subcommittee on the Sino-Japanese dispute. This group reported on October 5 that Japan's action was not justified by the Marco Polo Bridge incident of July 7, 1937. The League of Nations Assembly suggested that the signatory members of the Nine-Power Treaty of 1922 should consult regarding the Japanese violations. See November 24, 1937.

In the United States, isolationists believed that the assembly's condemnation of Japan voted the day after Roosevelt's "Quarantine Speech" demonstrated the president's intention to tie U.S. policy to that of other nations. There is no documentary evidence to prove this isolationist assertion except the State Department's reports from Leland Harrison on the progress of the league subcommittee.

October 27, 1937   MEXICO'S PRESIDENT CARDENAS DECREES A LAND REFORM
                           COMPENSATION SCHEME IN THE YAQUI VALLEY BECAUSE THE
                           UNITED STATES REFUSES AN OFFERED COMPROMISE.

The land reform measures undertaken on a gradual basis by the Mexican government during the 1920's increased more rapidly under President Cardenas after 1934. While 8 million hectares (20 million acres) of land were distributed from 1917 to 1933, Cardenas distributed nearly 20 million hectares during his six years in office. Because the Mexican government agreed to compensate both foreign and native landowners for the expropriation, the issuance of Mexican land bonds or other long-term obligations had to be devised to pay the former owners.

On April 24, 1934, the U.S.-Mexican claims treaty had set up a General Claims Commission to determine proper claims payments, but it allowed the land claims questions to be settled by appointed experts from the State Department and Mexico's Foreign Office. For nearly a year these experts held discussions but could not agree on a settlement. On February 1, 1936, the land compensation claims were returned to be considered by the General Claims Commission. The disputed land issue was Mexico's desire to make one lump sum payment for all land claims; the U.S. delegates refused this method, demanding that land reform must stop until Mexico could pay for the land as each section was expropriated. This U.S. position could not be accepted by Mexico because it required lengthy delays before Mexico could pay directly for the land.

Shortly after the earlier land claims negotiations failed and went back to the General Claims group, Cardenas inaugurated a land reform program in the Yaqui Valley of Northwest Mexico. The Yaqui land had a special status in Mexico. During Dictator Diaz's last years of office, a group of about 50 U.S. citizens received sizable tracts of unimproved land in the Yaqui River area. The Americans used extensive irrigation methods to develop prosperous winter wheat and rice farms.

In 1936, Mexican natives petitioned Cardenas to expropriate the irrigated lands, and the Mexican government began steps to fulfill their requests. The president understood the views of the U.S. farmers as well as his own people and took special interest in the Yaqui settlement. After visiting the region, Cardenas told Ambassador Daniels that U.S. owners had profited from their investment but he would permit them to keep a share of their land.

Throughout 1937, negotiations for a just settlement took place but were fruitless. Finally, on October 27, Cardenas instituted the guidelines he would follow for the Yaqui Valley. Each American farmer could keep 100 hectares (250 acres) of land with water rights. For their loss, they would receive nonirrigated land near the unfinished Angostura Dam. When the dam was completed in 1939, the owners would have sufficient water rights to sell the land in small parcels and make a profit. Cardenas said that negotiation of his proposal was useless. The Yaqui farmers made out well from this pact because after 1939, the land near the new dam had an excellent selling price.

The other land claims of Americans in Mexico became part of the oil expropriation settlement of November 19, 1941.

November 24, 1937   THE BRUSSELS CONFERENCE OF THE NINE-POWER SIGNATORIES
                          ENDS WITH A WEAK APPEAL TO CHINA AND JAPAN TO CEASE
                          HOSTILITIES.

Acting in accordance with the League of Nations Assembly resolution of October 6, 1937, Belgium invited all nations that had accepted the 1922 Nine-Power Treaty plus Germany, China, and the Soviet Union to attend a meeting to consult on the Sino-Japanese conflict. The treaty signatories included the United States, Great Britain, France, Italy, Japan, Bolivia, Mexico, Denmark, Norway, and Sweden.

The conference appeared to be doomed from the outset. State Department delegate Jay Pierrepont Moffat wrote on November 1 that "even before we meet people are discussing ways to end" the conference. Although pre-conference discussions indicated nothing would result, Roosevelt told Norman Davis, chief of the U.S. delegation, to prolong it as long as possible to obtain a good effect on public opinion. Germany refused to attend the meeting, and Italy came only to defend Japan. The Japanese denounced the sessions, rejecting the conference's necessity, claiming its members had already condemned Japan and asserting that the Japanese fought China only in self-defense.

The disarray among the democracies caused the conference to fail. It probably should not have convened at all because the democratic "peace-loving" powers were not willing to back their words with any other type of action. Great Britain and France wanted the United States to provide leadership; they would follow Roosevelt, and Hull willingly sent U.S. delegates to the meetings, but Britain and France did not want to be associated with the calling of the sessions or with being the leader in any decision. On November 17, Hull sent the U.S. delegation a list of items for a final conference report but informed Davis not to "assume a position of special leadership in regard thereto." Roosevelt and Hull wanted to pressure but not provoke Japan. However, their emphasis in 1937 appeared to be on "not provoke."

The U.S. State Department had generally acted since 1920 on the assumption that the United States had no interests in China which were worth a war. This dictum continued to apply in 1937 because oral protests against Japan had always been permitted while any threat to support the statements was avoided.

The Brussels report of November 24 asked China and Japan to cease hostilities and consult about ending the fighting. No threats or possible sanctions were mentioned. If Japan persisted in aggression, the report said, the Nine-Power signatories would consult again about further action. There was, however, no follow-up to the Brussels Conference.

December 12, 1937   THE U.S. GUNBOAT *PANAY* IS SUNK BY JAPANESE AIRPLANES; A BRITISH SHIP, H.M.S. *LADYBIRD,* IS FIRED UPON ON THE SAME DAY.

The *Panay* had sailed up the Yangtze River to Nanking in November, 1937, to assist Ambassador Nelson JOHNSON in evacuating the embassy and fleeing to Hankow to escape the approaching Japanese army. On December 9, the *Panay*'s officers saw Japan's shells hitting nearby and they moved the boat 28 miles above the city to avoid danger to the few embassy officials already on board. The *Panay* also convoyed three Standard Oil Company tankers.

During the day of December 12, Ambassador Johnson heard that *H.M.S. Ladybird* had been fired on by the Japanese, killing one seaman and wounding seven others. About midnight, Johnson learned that the Japanese had sunk the *Panay* as well as the three tankers, but he received no details. About the same time, Ambassador Grew in Tokyo received Foreign Minister Hirota who told Grew that Japanese planes following the Chinese Army had mistakenly attacked the *Panay*. Hirota apologized, saying poor visibility led the Japanese to believe the ships were Chinese. The same thing, he told Grew, had happened to the British ship *Ladybird*.

Not until December 15 did eyewitnesses of the attack on the *Panay* tell their stories in Shanghai. Their reports were uniformly similar and contradicted Japan's official version.

1. There was no poor visibility when the four ships were attacked.

2. All ships had U.S. flags and other markings to distinguish them. In addition, U.S. authorities kept the Japanese informed of the *Panay*'s movement on December 9.

3. Although the first Japanese planes bombed from considerable height, six planes dive-bombed the ships and machine-gunned the area for 20 minutes.

4. When the *Panay* sank, the survivors fled to the tall reeds in the marshland near shore. As Japanese planes searched and machine-gunned the area, the survivors hid until dark, when they went ashore to a nearby Chinese village for aid.

5. During the attack, two Americans died and 30 were wounded.

American public opinion was surprisingly moderate in light of the Japanese attack. Moreover, news reports in Shanghai concerned testimony from the *Panay*'s survivors and accounts of the Japanese atrocities in Nanking when they captured the city. Desiring to avoid war or at least not to fight over an incident in the Far East, many American editors blamed the United States for having ships and citizens in China and urged all Americans to evacuate the war zones. In this atmosphere the Roosevelt administration accepted Japan's apologies. Japan promised to pay indemnities and agreed to investigate and punish the guilty parties. Although Secretary of State Hull did not believe Tokyo's account of the raid, he accepted its apology on December 24 and took no further action.

During the *Panay* crisis, the British government offered to make its protests about the *Ladybird* attack a joint venture with possible punitive action against Japan. Roosevelt and Hull rejected these British advances and followed an independent course of protest to Tokyo. Nevertheless, to prepare for better future coordination of U.S.-British naval action, Roosevelt decided to send a naval liaison person to London. See December 23, 1937.

December 23, 1937   PRESIDENT ROOSEVELT ORDERS CAPTAIN ROYAL E.
                         INGERSOLL OF THE NAVY'S WAR PLANS DIVISION TO LONDON
                         TO CONDUCT STAFF TALKS WITH BRITISH NAVAL OFFICERS.

Although not directly concerned with the policy to be followed in the *Panay* crisis of December 12, 1937, Ingersoll's appointment reflected Roosevelt's growing concern for the revision of the U.S. Navy's Orange War Plans, which were based on an offensive war in the western Pacific Ocean. During the winter of 1936-1937, the president had reviewed the Orange Plans, which had been the navy's persistent war strategy since 1921. On January 9, 1937, Roosevelt requested new war plans but received only a lengthy, detailed report which repeated the old Orange Plans. The Navy War Plans Division apparently could discern no change in U.S. policy since 1922.

Neither the State Department nor President Roosevelt gave the Far East the greatest concern in their world strategy. Both were more concerned with European events. On November 10, soon after his Quarantine Speech, Roosevelt asked Chief of Naval Operations Admiral William D. Leahy to prepare new war plan contingencies based on a Western Hemispheric Defense and a two-ocean war against the Axis powers with Great Britain as an ally.

It was not easy to persuade the navy to change its old, faithful Orange Plans which required a large, offensive navy. Roosevelt seems to have hoped that direct contact between the British and Ingersoll of the Navy War Plans Division would broaden the naval officer's perspective from antagonism toward Britain to cooperation.

Roosevelt's naval ideas matched his 1938 navy appropriations request to congress as well. The president sought a two-ocean navy bill during the early months of 1938 (see May 17, 1938). Ingersoll's mission to London became the first in a series of cooperative talks between the British and American navy,

army, and air force officers.   For the change in war plans from Orange as
number one priority of the Joint Board of the Army and Navy to the five contingencies of the Rainbow War Plans, see May 11, 1939.

1938

January 10, 1938   THE LUDLOW RESOLUTION REQUIRING A NATIONAL REFERENDUM
TO DECLARE WAR FAILS IN A CLOSE VOTE BY THE HOUSE OF
REPRESENTATIVES.

Representative Louis Ludlow of Indiana tried on several occasions between
1935 and 1937 to have the House approve a resolution which would require a
nationwide vote before war could be declared. Following the *Panay* crisis of
December 12, 1937, many congressmen and news editors joined to approve Ludlow's proposal as the best way to stay out of war. Therefore, when congress
convened in January, Ludlow again introduced his bill.

Probably only President Roosevelt's ardent opposition to the Ludlow concept prevented the House from passing the measure. The president wrote a
special letter to House Speaker William B. Bankhead which asserted that Ludlow's bill would "cripple any President in his conduct of foreign relations,"
encouraging foreign nations to "violate American rights with impunity." The
House voted to return Ludlow's bill to committee by 209 to 188.

March 13, 1938   *GERMANY INVADES AND ANNEXES AUSTRIA.*

*One of Adolf Hitler's objectives was to annex German-speaking Austria as an
integral part of the Third Reich. Following the aborted Nazi Putsch in Vienna
on July 25, 1934, Hitler realized he must obtain Italy's support before moving
forcefully against Austria. Following the assassination of the Fascist dictator Dollfuss on July 25, 1934, Kurt SCHUSCHNIGG gained control in Vienna
but followed his predecessor's anti-Nazi program.*

*On July 11, 1936, Schuschnigg and Hitler agreed to stop their feud and
Germany agreed to recognize Austria's independence. This agreement pleased
Mussolini who formed an Axis alliance with Hitler on October 25, 1936.
Schuschnigg, however, interpreted the pact as a proclamation of Austrian independence and, in conflict with Hitler's wishes, announced he would decide
the right to restore the Hapsburg throne. Schuschnigg also began discussions
for an alliance with Czechoslovakia, which became a second point of Austrian
conflict with Hitler.*

*Early in 1938, however, Hitler moved to end Schuschnigg's independent
policies. During a February 12 meeting with the Austrian chancellor, Hitler
persuaded Schuschnigg to grant amnesty to Nazi prisoners and to admit Nazis
to his Austrian Fatherland Front Party. Soon after, Schuschnigg's attempts
to break free from the Nazi position resulted in Nazi riots in Austria.
Hitler demanded Schuschnigg's capitulation, and Schuschnigg resigned on March
11. The next day, Hitler's army crossed the border and without any Austrian
resistance occupied Vienna. On March 13, Arthur Seyss-Inquart, a Nazi who
was Austria's Minister of the Interior, proclaimed union with Germany, and
on March 14, Hitler took possession of Vienna.*

March 18, 1938   MEXICO'S PRESIDENT LAZAO CARDENAS ANNOUNCES THAT HIS
                          GOVERNMENT WILL EXPROPRIATE PROPERTIES OF THE AMERICAN
                          AND BRITISH OIL COMPANIES.

Cardenas' expropriation decree did not result from Article 27 subsoil clauses
of the Constitution of 1917, which had troubled U.S. oilmen during the 1920's
and resulted in the Morrow-Calles agreement of 1927 (see January 11, 1928).
The March 18, 1938, decree grew out of a labor dispute between the oil companies and the Syndicate of Petroleum Workers who used Article 123 of the
Constitution, which contained labor rights for workers.

The petroleum workers' union had organized an industry-wide union which,
on November 3, 1936, made extensive wage and fringe benefit demands on the
oil companies, threatening an industry-wide strike. When the companies refused to consider the exorbitant demands, President Cardenas called for a
120-day "cooling off" period to avoid the strike and permit further negotiations. These discussions did not succeed and, on May 28, 1937, a nationwide
oil industry strike began.

Ten days after the strike began, the petroleum workers' union applied
its labor rights under Article 123 of Mexico's Constitution, requesting proceedings by the Federal Board of Conciliation and Arbitration. This procedure
included the appointment of a commission of experts to study the case and
required the commission to audit the companies' records as a method for deciding the companies' ability to pay the workers' demands. Although the U.S.
companies protested the procedures (they never had to submit their open books
in U.S. labor proceedings), they had to comply or forfeit their properties
automatically. Meanwhile, the workers returned to work while the conciliation
board pursued its investigation.

During this period of 1937 the U.S. companies appealed to the State Department for aid. Secretary Hull asserted that until Mexico had treated them
unjustly, the State Department could not intervene. The companies were told
to use the Mexican legal process to the greatest possible extent.

On December 18, 1937, the Mexican Board of Conciliation and Arbitration
handed down its ruling. Based on the report of the commission of experts
and rebuttals by both the oil companies and the petroleum workers' union,
the board generally followed the findings of the experts' commission which
had initially been released on August 3, 1937. The report favored most of
the union demands. These included an 8-hour day, a 40-hour week, plus vaca-
tion, health, and pension beneftis. It also recommended a minimum wage for
oil workers of 5.40 pesos ($1.50) per day whereas the company offered a daily
minimum wage of 2 pesos ($0.56). The experts' report also claimed that the
oil companies' interests opposed the Mexican national interest, describing
ways by which the oil companies evaded paying full taxes on their Mexican
income by selling oil to a foreign subsidiary at a price lower than market
prices.

The oil companies, who were represented by their leading spokesman,
Thomas R. Armstrong of Jersey Standard, strongly objected to Mexico's ruling.
They convinced Secretary of State Hull that they were unfairly treated because
the Mexican government sided with the labor unions. Nevertheless, at Hull's
urging they appealed the ruling to the Mexican Supreme Court. President
Cardenas agreed to suspend the wage decision of the conciliation board until
the court had issued its ruling.

On February 28, the Mexican Supreme Court ruled that the conciliation
board ruling was correct and within the legal guidelines of the Constitution
of 1917. The U.S. oilmen opposed the court decision, contending that, as

they had always suspected, Mexico wanted to confiscate their property by economic strangulation. Contrary to the finding of the experts' audit of their books, the companies claimed the labor ruling would destroy their industry.

Nevertheless, because the British oil interests held two-thirds of the foreign oil production in Mexico and they preferred to negotiate a compromise, the U.S. companies agreed to see what could be done. When the Board of Conciliation ruled on March 15 that the oil companies were guilty of *rebeldia* (defiance) against their decision, the British and American oil representatives met with President Cardenas. Cardenas was willing to compromise with the companies on all other points of the December, 1937 labor award if they agreed to a wage increase to 96 cents an hour, an annual cost of 26 million pesos. Cardenas offered to give his promise to guarantee agreement on the other labor terms, but the oil spokesman told him, "That is hardly sufficient."

On March 18, Cardenas responded to the oil companies' adamant stand. He applied the Expropriation Act which the law called for against companies which defied the conciliation board's and the Supreme Court's rulings. Because the "paralysis of the oil industry is imminent" and damage would be suffered by the "general economy of the country," Mexico asserted its sovereign right to compel respect for the nation's legal process. The property of the oil companies was irrevocably expropriated by Mexico.

For the outcome of the dispute resulting from Cardenas' decree see March 27, 1938, and November 19, 1941.

March 27, 1938   THE U.S. TREASURY DEPARTMENT HALTS ITS SPECIAL PURCHASES OF MEXICAN SILVER, A MEASURE THE STATE DEPARTMENT URGED IN ORDER TO PRESSURE MEXICO TO CHANGE ITS OIL POLICY.

During the fall of 1937, when the dispute between the oil companies and the petroleum workers was under conciliation procedures (see March 18, 1938), a Mexican economic mission under Eduardo Suarez visited Washington seeking financial aid because of the depression and the oil companies' October decision to remove their surplus funds from Mexico. The Mexican peso's value had fallen on the world exchange market and the Mexicans wanted the United States to purchase Mexican silver to keep its value higher.

Although some Washington officials wanted Secretary of the Treasury Morgenthau to deny the Mexican request in retaliation for the oil dispute, Morgenthau preferred to separate the two questions. He wanted to support Cardenas in order to avoid any possibility that Mexico would have to seek aid from Germany, Italy, or Japan. Therefore, Morgenthau received President Roosevelt's approval to make special Mexican silver purchases. The Treasury Department agreed to monthly purchases of Mexican silver and to the immediate purchase of 35 million ounces of silver on deposit in America. Subsequently, in January and February, the U.S. Treasury purchased Mexican silver.

Following the announcement on March 18 that Mexico would expropriate the oil properties, the State Department asked Morgenthau to suspend the silver purchases. The Treasury Department agreed, and on March 27, 1938, the special monthly purchases were ended. This action did not seriously hurt Mexico because Morgenthau did not strictly enforce the act. The Treasury Department continued to buy all Mexican silver on the open spot market, and U.S. silver purchases remained high. One reason that Morgenthau's actions were not strongly opposed in the United States was that most of the silver

came from the mines of the American Smelting and Refining Company, the largest
U.S. mining interest in Mexico. Three U.S. investors suffered more than Mexico from the March 27 suspension of silver purchases. But Morgenthau's le-
neint enforcement permitted the U.S. silver investors to continue to profit.

March 28, 1938   *THE JAPANESE INSTALL A REFORMED GOVERNMENT OF THE RE-*
                          PUBLIC OF CHINA AT NANKING.

*Following the capture of Nanking on December 13, 1937, Tokyo copied the method
it used earlier in Manchukuo, establishing a Chinese government with whom it
could conduct China's business on an "official" basis. Subsequently, Japan's
armies became successful at controlling China's large cities, but the rural
areas remained under the control of Chinese guerrillas both from the Chinese
Nationalist and Communist factions.*

April 4, 1938   ROOSEVELT APPROVES SECRETARY OF STATE HULL'S RECOM-
                          MENDATION TO ESTABLISH A LIAISON COMMITTEE REPRESENTING
                          THE DEPARTMENTS OF STATE, WAR, AND THE NAVY.

The president and Hull had become aware of the lack of coordination between
State Department foreign policy decisions and the activity and policy making
of U.S. Army and Navy officials. In an attempt to repair this deficiency, a
Standing Liaison Committee was set up in the spring of 1938 to coordinate
diplomatic and military relations. The committee members were Undersecretary
of State Sumner Welles, the Chief of Naval Operations (first Admiral Leahy;
later, Admiral Stark), and the Army Chief of Staff (General Marshall).
    This committee was the first step toward the National Security Agency,
created after World War II. In the years before the Pearl Harbor attack, it
did not fulfill the original purpose. Its principal achievements between
1938 and 1941 were to coordinate cooperation of the military and diplomats
in Latin American relations. The duties Hull foresaw for the committee de-
volved to the president's War Council in 1941.
    The War Council was never an official group. It consisted of President
Roosevelt meeting informally with the Secretaries of War, Navy, and State.
By the fall of 1941, as problems with Japan increased, these men met on call
of the president to coordinate diplomatic and military activity.

April 16, 1938   *AN ANGLO-ITALIAN TREATY ON THE MEDITERRANEAN RESOLVES*
                          PROBLEMS BETWEEN THOSE TWO NATIONS.

*Great Britain recognized Italian rule over Ethiopia while Italy agreed to
respect Spanish territory and to withdraw her "volunteers" at the end of the
civil war. The two nations agreed to maintain the status quo in the Red Sea.*

May 13, 1938   THE SENATE FOREIGN RELATIONS COMMITTEE BLOCKS SENATOR
                          NYE'S RESOLUTION TO EXTEND CASH AND CARRY PROVISIONS
                          FOR ARMS TO SPAIN'S LOYALIST GOVERNMENT.

The difficulties which threatened the defeat of the Spanish Republicans by
Franco's Fascists and the terrorist attacks by German and Italian aircraft in

Spain led many Americans to advocate some action against the Fascist forces in Spain. By 1938 there were many examples of German and Italian military units fighting with Franco's armies. The bombing of Guernica on April 26, 1937, became the most dramatic evidence. Waves of German planes bombed and strafed the city for three hours, killing 1,654 people and wounding 889 in an indiscriminate attack on the civilian population. Both German and Italian soldiers and naval units fought against Republican Spain's forces.

Although some Catholic groups in America, led by Cardinal Mundelein of Chicago, supported Franco, many other liberal groups pressured Roosevelt to act to aid the Republicans. Nye's resolution of May 3 authorized the president to end the Spanish arms embargo of January 8, 1937, and permit the Spanish Loyalists to obtain arms on the "cash and carry" basis of the Third Neutrality Act of May 1, 1937.

President Roosevelt wanted to consider ways to aid the anti-Fascist forces, but he agreed with Secretary of State Hull that Nye's resolution was not suitable. Subsequently, Hull sent the Senate Foreign Relations Committee a message on May 12, opposing the Nye Resolution. Hull argued that there was danger in Europe that the Spanish war could become a wider international conflict. Therefore, he said, he feared the complications likely to arise from "a reversal of our policy of strict neutrality." The committee concurred, rejecting Nye's proposal by a vote of 17 to 1.

In November, 1938, there were renewed attempts to remove the Spanish embargo in favor of the Republicans in Barcelona. Again, Hull contended that only congress could repeal the arms legislation, and prospects for such action were nil. By the winter of 1938–1939, the Spanish embargo became part of the larger Roosevelt attempt to change the entire Neutrality Act of 1937.

May 17, 1938   A NAVAL CONSTRUCTION BILL INCREASING THE U.S. NAVY BY
                        20% IS APPROVED BY CONGRESS.

Because the Vinson Bill of 1934 had run its course of construction by replacing obsolete ships, the second Vinson bill, in 1938, authorized a total of 18 battleships which would be 20% above the treaty limits of 1922. The 1938 naval bill was promoted as a navy to provide defenses for the two oceans on either side of the United States. This force was not, however, sufficient in size to defend the western Pacific as the Navy's Orange War Plans intended. The president had, nevertheless, begun on a course to persuade the Navy to revise the Orange Plans (see May 11, 1939).

May 20, 1938   *THE FIRST CZECH CRISIS ENDS WHEN ENGLAND AND FRANCE*
                        TAKE A STRONG STAND TO BACK THE CZECH GOVERNMENT
                        AGAINST THE DEMANDS OF THE NAZI KONRAD HENLEIN.

Acting in conjunction with Henlein, the leader of the Sudete German Party in the Sudeten province of Czechoslovakia, Hitler, on February 20, 1938, promised to protect all German minorities outside the Reich. This fostered a clash between Henlein's demand for autonomy for the German Sudetens and the determination of Czech Premier Milan Hodža to reject outside interference in Czechoslovakia. The Czechs refused to grant concessions to Henlein as suggested by France and England, but Hodža retained their support. On May 20, Henlein agreed to negotiate with Hodža and the crisis temporarily ended. By September, a further crisis developed. See September 29, 1938.

August 10, 1938   *FOLLOWING NEARLY FOUR WEEKS OF FIGHTING AT CHANGKUFENG*
                          HILL, JAPANESE AND RUSSIAN FORCES ARRANGE A TRUCE WHICH
                          REASSERTS THE STATUS QUO.

The fighting took place on the borders of Siberia, Manchukuo, and Korea. This
was one of several border incidents between Japan and the Soviet Union which
recurred until the signing of the Soviet-Japanese neutrality pact of April
13, 1941.

September 27, 1938   PRESIDENT ROOSEVELT APPEALS TO HITLER TO NEGOTIATE
                          THE CZECHOSLOVAKIAN CRISIS.

A second Czech crisis regarding the German-inhabited Sudetenland began on
September 12 when Hitler told a Nazi Party Congress that the "tortured and
oppressed" Germans in the Sudetenland must be freed. Konrad Henlein, the
Sudete German leader, declared that union with Germany was the only solution
to his followers' problem, inspiring anti-Czech demonstrations in the area.
(For the first Czech crisis see May 20, 1938.)
    During the May crisis, President Roosevelt and Secretary Hull remained
aloof from the issue. Between June and September, however, Roosevelt privately urged Britain and France to take a strong stand against Hitler's demands. He could not and would not back these efforts, however. Although
Roosevelt realized that the United States had become a vital factor in world
decisions, his political fears of isolationist sentiments kept him from committing the United States.
    As the crisis grew in September and Hitler gave the Czechs an ultimatum
to meet his demands by October 1, Roosevelt sent appeals for peace to the
European powers. On September 26, he sent a humanitarian plea to Prague,
Berlin, London, and Paris, urging the governments not to break off negotiations and to find a constructive settlement. Hitler rejected the U.S. appeal,
but on September 27 the president made a second attempt. First, he asked
Mussolini to assist in persuading Hitler to continue to negotiate. Later
that day, he made a direct appeal to Hitler to find a peaceful solution to
the problem. The president suggested that a conference of all nations be
called, to deal not only with the Sudeten issue but also with "correlated"
questions.
    Significantly, Roosevelt's September 27 appeal to Hitler for a wider
international conference included a caveat reflecting the president's concern
about isolationist criticism. The president's note said that the United
States was not willing to pass judgment on the merits of Hitler's demands
and that America could not accept any responsibility in the negotiations.
    Although some commentators in 1938 and later believed the president's
appeal of September 27 influenced the calling of the Munich Conference of
September 29, the U.S. notes had little or no influence on Hitler or Prime
Minister Chamberlain. Behind the scenes in Europe, French and British officials had informed Hitler that if he agreed to another meeting, they would
accept most of his demands. Hitler attended the Munich sessions in order to
obtain his demands without going to war.

*September 29, 1938   THE MUNICH CONFERENCE SOLVES THE CZECH CRISIS BECAUSE
FRANCE AND ENGLAND "APPEASE" HITLER: THE APPEASEMENT
POLICY.*

*Since Hitler's September 12 speech demanding self-determination for the Su-
deten Germans in Czechoslovakia, the crisis had reached the level of partial
or full mobilization of forces among the European states; war appeared to be
imminent.*

*On September 15, Prime Minister Chamberlain and Hitler met at Hitler's
retreat in Berchtesgaden. Hitler demanded the annexation of the German areas
of Czechoslovakia which had been given to the Czechs for security reasons by
the Treaty of Versailles. He told Chamberlain he would risk war if necessary
to obtain these "just" demands of self-determination.*

*Before meeting with Hitler again at Godesberg on September 22, Chamber-
lain persuaded the Czech leaders to offer a suitable compromise for Hitler
to accept. Although Premier Daladier of France and the Russians wanted to
present strong opposition to the Nazi leader, Chamberlain's "appeasement"
policy rejected their suggestion. Instead, Chamberlain convinced the Czechs
to offer Hitler all areas where one-half of the population was German in exchange for guarantees of their new, less-defensible frontiers. At Godesberg,
Chamberlain proposed but Hitler refused this compromise. The Germans, Hitler
said, would identify what Czech territory belonged to the Reich. Furthermore,
Hitler wanted plebiscites only in areas with large German minorities. Czechoslovakia must accept these demands by October 1 or the Nazi armies would
occupy the German "territory."*

*Between September 24 and 29, an acute crisis resulted in western Europe.
War appeared to be certain and the Czech government ordered full mobilization.
Nazi armies prepared on the frontiers of both France and Czechoslovakia.
Chamberlain, however, believed he could avert a conflict by a rational method
to gain Hitler's agreement. Using Mussolini's "good offices" and writing a
personal letter to the Führer, Chamberlain arranged the Munich Conference
with Hitler. On September 29, the leaders of the big-four Western powers
met to decide the fate of Czechoslovakia: Hitler, Mussolini, Daladier, and
Chamberlain.*

*At Munich, Hitler received almost everything he had demanded. The Czechs
would evacuate areas designated by Hitler. An international commission would
determine what areas of Czechoslovakia should be German, Polish, or Hungarian
because these latter two governments had demanded "justice" for their people.
Britain and France would guarantee the new Czech frontier.*

*By November 28, when the international commission completed its work,
Czechoslovakia was greatly reduced in size and unable to offer any future
defense to its neighbor's demands. The basic results of the Munich agreements were:*

1. *Germany acquired 10,000 square miles with a population of 3,500,000,
   of whom 700,000 were Czech. There were no plebiscites.*

2. *Poland gained 400 square miles (Teschen region) with 240,000 inhabitants, less than 100,000 of whom were Polish.*

3. *Hungary obtained 5,000 square miles and 1,000,000 people.*

*Because Chamberlain's policy made "appeasement" a frequently used word
in the United States after 1945, the British leader's concepts and practice*

*should be understood. When Chamberlain began using the term "appeasement"
after becoming Prime Minister in 1937, he conceived it as a strong and definite policy in contrast to the uncertainty which Prime Minister Stanley
Baldwin employed in dealing with Hitler and Mussolini.*

*The most important assumptions of Chamberlain were the danger of Russian
Bolshevism and the belief that no satisfactory diplomacy could be conducted
with Stalin. A conservative in both party affiliation and attitude, Chamberlain thought the Fascists appreciated capitalism and that therefore one could
do business with them--business both in the sense of trade and of adjusting
their grievances at the bargaining table. Chamberlain believed law and order
"dictators can be extremely beneficial" if one dealt with them properly. To
do so, he ridded his cabinet of those individuals, including Anthony Eden,
whom he thought to be Germanophobes.*

*For Chamberlain, the larger diplomatic objective was the formation of a
Four-Power Pact in western Europe to protect the Continent from the Soviet
menace. In this context, the German-Italian alliance was a pillar of peace
to which Chamberlain wished to add Paris and London. He did not value the
League of Nations or the concept of collective security. Old-style diplomacy
and top-level meetings with Hitler and Mussolini would convince them of British and French friendliness in creating a generation of peace in Europe. As
one of Chamberlain's close advisors, Lord Halifax, said, a war between England
and Germany would be the "end of civilization."*

*Appeasement required concessions to Germany, for Chamberlain felt the
Germans had been treated too severely by the Treaty of Versailles. He hoped
to grant them overseas colonies as well as recognizing their predominant role
in central Europe. This should, however, be accomplished by negotiation,
not by violence. And in this final respect, Chamberlain's appeasement showed
its failure to understand the forces impelling the Fascist dictators. As
Margaret George indicates in* The Warped Vision *(1965), Chamberlain's concep-
tual frame did not comprehend the dynamics of Hitler's nationalism and master-
race emotions.*

*In the context of appeasement, Chamberlain accepted Italy's conquest of
Ethiopia and his demands in Fiume and the Dalmatian coast as well as Hitler's
annexation of Austria, dominance of Czechoslovakia, and occupation of Danzig.*

*On his return from Munich, Chamberlain's policy of appeasement reached
its apogee. The British public lauded his statement that he had brought
"peace in our time." The war preparations ended. Gas-mask drills stopped
in London. Chamberlain urged British trade unions and industrial leaders to
visit Germany and make trade agreements with Berlin. Not until March 15,
1939, did appeasement's house of cards tumble down. For the results of appeasement in 1939 see March 15, 1939.*

October 4, 1938   THE END OF FRANCE'S LEFT-WING POPULAR FRONT MINISTRY.

*From June 5, 1936, to October 4, 1938, Leon Blum and Edouard Daladier had
kept together a coalition of left-of-center Popular Front parties. The French
senate could not overthrow the ministry, but the conservatives and extreme
rightists in the senate effectively blocked the leftists from making significant economic or social changes.*

*The Munich Conference definitely broke up the Popular Front. The social-
ists were disapproved by the agreement with Hitler; the Communist Party, which
voted with but never joined the ministry, now withdrew its support. Daladier
obtained center and right-of-center support in the Chamber of Deputies, continuing to govern as premier until March 20, 1940.*

October 6, 1938   *CZECHOSLOVAKIA IS WEAKENED FURTHER AS SLOVAK LEADERS RECEIVE THE FULL AUTONOMY THEY DEMANDED; ON OCTOBER 8, RUTHENIA GAINS FULL AUTONOMY AS CARPATHO-UKRAINE.*

October 11, 1938   PRESIDENT ROOSEVELT CALLS FOR A $300 MILLION DEFENSE BUILD UP EMPHASIZING THE NEED FOR 20,000 AIRPLANES.

Fears and trepidations about a European war and aerial bombing raids which arose before and after the September 29, 1938, Munich Conference led the president to announce plans for a large defense build up in the 1939 budget. He dramatized his concerns in October and November by proposing an airplane production goal of 20,000 per year. These forces would defend the Western Hemisphere from potential attacks. According to some air theorists, Germany was becoming capable of building a 2,000-plane bomber force that could cross the 3,300 miles between West Africa near Dakar and the Americas.

Roosevelt's 20,000-airplane schedule for aircraft production did not represent the war plan theories evolved at that time by the Joint Board of the Army and Navy (see May 11, 1939). The president's plan did, however, give U.S. air power proponents their first sign that Roosevelt was aware of aviation's potential in a future war. While U.S. Army leaders persuaded Roosevelt to cut his airplane request back to 6,000 planes in January, 1939, so that other parts of the army could be funded as a "balanced force," the Army Air Corps discovered a new and high-ranking champion. By 1941, the president would order greater autonomy for the Air Force with plans for offensive bomber operations on July 3, 1941.

November 3, 1938   JAPAN'S PREMIER, PRINCE KONOYE, ANNOUNCES JAPAN'S "NEW ORDER" IN EAST ASIA.

Prior to November 3, Tokyo had persistently assured the U.S. State Department that it never intended to violate U.S. open door rights in China and that the "China incident" was atypical. On November 3, Konoye informed all other nations that they should revise their policies to adjust to the fact that Japan was overseer of a new, stable order in East Asia. The prosperity of this region would be based on mutual aid under the coordination of policies by Japan, Manchukuo, and China. As Foreign Minister Hachiro Arita later explained to Secretary Hull, Japan had freed itself from the Nine-Power Treaty and other bygone documents. Thus, former policies in East Asia were no longer applicable.

The United States protested Japan's methods of changing treaties. On December 30, 1938, U.S. Ambassador Joseph Grew told Arita that changes due to conditions were valid but should be made by the orderly methods of negotiation and agreement, not by fist.

November 8, 1938   THE MID-TERM ELECTIONS FOR CONGRESS ARE SIGNIFICANT BECAUSE REPUBLICANS AND CONSERVATIVE DEMOCRATS MAKE GAINS.

Roosevelt blundered in 1938 by speaking out against Democratic candidates who opposed New Deal reforms. Although the Democrats continued to hold over two-thirds of the Senate seats and a majority in the House, the Republicans

won 81 House seats and eight senatorial posts. Especially in the House, conservative Democrats and Republicans could block Roosevelt's legislation if
they chose to cooperate.

November 15, 1938   REACTING TO GERMANY'S ATTACKS OF VENGEANCE ON JEWS,
                          PRESIDENT ROOSEVELT RECALLS U.S. AMBASSADOR WILSON
                          FROM BERLIN. SOON AFTER, GERMANY RECALLS ITS AMBAS-
                          SADOR, LEAVING NEITHER GOVERNMENT WITH FULL DIPLOMATIC
                          REPRESENTATION UNTIL THE END OF WORLD WAR II.

Early in November, a Polish-Jewish refugee assassinated a German Embassy official in Paris. To revenge this incident, German Nazi Party personnel began
assaults on Jews in Germany. They looted synagogues, burned Jewish property,
and forbade Jews such ordinary civil liberties as attending schools and driving a car. The German government levied a fine of one billion marks on the
Jewish community and there was a determined effort to drive all Jews out of
Germany.
    The anti-Semitic ideology of the German Nazis had been evident since
April 1, 1933, when a national boycott of Jewish businesses began. Jewish
lawyers and doctors were barred from practice and many Jewish businesses were
liquidated. On September 15, 1935, the NURNBERG LAWS deprived Jews of citizenship and forbade their intermarriage with other "races." When Austria
was annexed, these laws were extended to that region as well.
    The Nazi attacks of November, 1938, were the first violent, terroristic
depredations against the German Jews. As a result, Jewish immigration increased rapidly from already large proportions between 1933 and 1938. Because the Nazis would not permit the emigres to take money or property with
them, Jewish immigration became difficult because other nations were reluctant
to admit immigrants with no sponsor, job opportunities, or money to help them
adjust. An international refugee committee was set up in western Europe but
it experienced problems because other nations were still reluctant to admit
the propertyless Jews. In addition, British policy in Palestine required that
they limit Jewish immigration because of Arab opposition (see May 17, 1939).
    On November 15, Roosevelt expressed the American outrage at the Nazis
by recalling American Ambassador Hugh Wilson from Berlin. Announcing this
action, the president stated in a press release: "I myself could scarcely
believe that such things could occur in a twentieth century civilization."
The German response to Roosevelt's action was to call Ambassador Hans-
Dieckhoff back to Berlin.

November 17, 1938   GREAT BRITAIN, CANADA, AND THE UNITED STATES SIGN A
                          TRADE AGREEMENTS PACT.

Secretary of State Hull considered the conclusion of this commercial treaty
especially significant because Great Britain took the first step away from
its imperial preference tariff system. Since the passage of the 1934 U.S.
Reciprocal Trade Act, Hull had looked forward to getting London to accept
principles of reciprocal, mutually beneficial trade adjustments.
    Until the Munich Conference era of September, 1938, Hull had enlisted
the support of MacKenzie King of Canada in his trade pact, but King had not
yet convinced London to make the necessary trade-offs in lowering tariffs.
Until October 25, 1938, the British had not offered any concessions. Once

they did, the conclusion of a reciprocal trade pact did not take long. Generally, the United States agreed to concessions on textiles, Britain agreed to concessions on agricultural commodities and products. The tripartite agreement was signed on November 17, 1938.

December 14, 1938   PRESIDENT ROOSEVELT ANNOUNCES A $25 MILLION LOAN TO CHINA.

As Japanese attacks on China intensified in 1938, Roosevelt and Secretary of the Treasury Morgenthau sought some means to assist the Chinese. Because war had not been declared nor the U.S. Neutrality Acts invoked, Morgenthau recommended a $25 million loan based on the Chinese delivery of tung oil during the next three years. Although Secretary of State Hull warned that the loan would create further Japanese antagonism, the Chinese government accepted the loan terms and Roosevelt announced the transaction on December 14.

December 24, 1938   THE LIMA DECLARATION OF THE EIGHTH CONFERENCE OF AMERICAN STATES ASSERTS THAT THE AMERICAN GOVERNMENTS WILL DEFEND AGAINST ALL FOREIGN INTERVENTION.

The Lima declaration of intent, as distinct from a treaty, pledged the 21 nations at the Inter-Americas Conference to unite and consult together in case of an outside threat to any of them. This agreement essentially provided for the unity of the Americas, which had been described at the Buenos Aires Conference on December 23, 1936. President Roosevelt had begun to prepare a national defense program for the Western Hemisphere and the Lima declaration supported this concept.

1939

January 23, 1939   NEWS IS RECEIVED IN WASHINGTON THAT A FRENCH MILITARY
OFFICER WAS INJURED WHEN AN AMERICAN DOUGLAS BOMBER
CRASHED IN CALIFORNIA.

The French officer was Captain Paul Chemidlin, a participant in a French war
mission that sought orders for U.S. military equipment. News of the bomber
crash incensed isolationist senators such as Arthur Vandenberg and William
Borah because it provided evidence for their belief that Roosevelt cooperated
with France and England by giving them the most advanced U.S. military secrets. These senators, and newspaper editors who supported them, asserted
that Roosevelt was leading the country to war through secret alliances.

   Under the cash and carry provisions of the U.S. neutrality laws, Jean
Monnet of France arrived in America as early as March, 1938, seeking U.S.
aircraft to help France's defense. Subsequently, Roosevelt skirted the edges
of legality in the Neutrality Acts by attempting to meet French aviation
needs. Despite opposition from Army Chief of Staff General Marshall and Secretary of War Woodring, the president and Secretary of the Treasury Morgenthau
expedited French aviation and other war purchases. Although France fell to
the Germans in June, 1940, before a substantial number of U.S. plane orders
reached Europe, the French invested over $13 million in the U.S. aircraft
industry in 1939, an investment which greatly assisted the rapid build up of
U.S. aircraft production capacities.

   In 1939, however, news of the Douglas bomber crash caused severe criticism of Roosevelt. It became one factor in Roosevelt's unwillingness to encourage congress to repeal the arms embargo clauses of the neutrality laws,
which congress refused to do in early 1939.

March 9, 1939   PRESIDENT VARGAS OF BRAZIL AND THE UNITED STATES CON-
CLUDE A SERIES OF AGREEMENTS TO AID BRAZIL'S ECONOMIC
GROWTH: THE HULL–ARANHA AGREEMENTS.

Since becoming President of Brazil on October 26, 1930, Getulio Vargas had
sponsored a right-of-center political program that successfully fought off
both Communist and Fascist movements. In November, 1935, a Communist uprising
in Pernambuco and Rio de Janeiro forced Vargas to use martial law and to prepare a new constitution which on November 10, 1937, gave Vargas dictatorial
powers that he said were not Fascist. To prove this claim, Vargas on March
11, 1938, suppressed a Nazi-inspired "green shirt" (*Integralista*) revolt.
He also appealed to the United States to provide economic aid.

   Brazil needed economic assistance because the decline in coffee prices
during the 1930's prevented Brazilian payments on foreign loans, a situation
Vargas wished to resolve. In November, 1937, Brazil had defaulted on its
loans, and in 1938 Vargas froze all foreign balances because the state had
insufficient exchange funds. When Foreign Minister Osvaldo ARANHA came to

749

Washington in January, 1939, to negotiate with Secretary Hull, coffee prices
were 7.5 cents per pound. They had been 21.7 cents in 1929 and 9.8 cents in
1937. Thus, Brazil greatly required U.S. aid to enable Vargas to end his
economic problems.

Although the March 9 U.S. aid package helped Brazil, it was not sufficient to satisfy the shortfall of the Brazilian budget. Brazil agreed to
renew payments on its foreign loans on July 1, 1939. In return, the United
States arranged an Export-Import Bank loan of $19.2 million and agreed to
help Brazil purchase ships and railway equipment from the Lloyd Brasileiri
Shipping Company. Hull also agreed to ask congress for $50 million of gold
to establish a Brazil Central Reserve Bank, but the U.S. congress never approved this act.

One long-term result of the March 9 agreement was the exchange of military plans and assistance to enhance the Western Hemispheric defense against
the Axis powers. General George C. Marshall visited Brazil for discussions
with Brazil's military leaders. When Marshall returned to America in April,
1939, Brazil's Army Chief of Staff, Pedro Aurelio de GOIS Monteiro, came with
him aboard the U.S.S. *Nashville*.

From this military exchange, the United States received permission to
build air and naval bases in northeastern Brazil. The United States provided
Brazil's army with technological and financial aid as well as surplus U.S.
weapons. Thus, on the eve of the European war, American defenses in the Western Hemisphere had begun to be secured.

March 15, 1939   HITLER TAKES CONTROL OVER ALL NON-GERMAN AREAS OF
                          CZECHOSLOVAKIA. HUNGARY OCCUPIES THE CARPATHO-UKRAINE
                          SECTION OF CZECHOSLOVAKIA.

Following the creation of the autonomous regions of Slovakia and Carpatho-
Ukraine on October 6 and 8, 1938, pro-Fascist leaders in those areas appealed
to Hitler for support. On March 15, Hitler fulfilled these requests. He
declared a German protectorship over Bohemia and Moravia, as well as Slovakia.
The Nazi aggressor had moved beyond his claim for justice to minorities and
advocated Germany's need for lebensraum.

On February 24, Hungary joined the anti-Comintern pact and was rewarded
on March 15. Although Hungarian forces had to fight local resistance, they
completed the conquest of the Carpatho-Ukraine on March 15.

March 17, 1939   SECRETARY OF STATE HULL STATES THAT THE UNITED STATES
                         WILL NOT RECOGNIZE HITLER'S CONQUEST OF CZECHOSLOVAKIA.

The secretary condemned Germany's aggressive action on occupying the state
it had promised to guarantee during the Munich Conference of September 29,
1938. Hull declared the United States would continue to recognize the Czech
minister to Washington as the rightful representative of the Czech people.

March 28, 1939   THE SPANISH CIVIL WAR ENDS WHEN MADRID SURRENDERS TO
                          GENERAL FRANCO'S FORCES.

The final struggle which began in Spain on July 18, 1938, had been bitter
and bloody as Franco's insurgents received vast assistance from Germany and
Italy, who had recognized his government on November 18, 1936.

*Madrid was under siege from November 6, 1936, to March 28, 1939. The
Loyalist Republican government had fled from Madrid to Valencia, and later
to Barcelona. Franco's capture of Barcelona on January 26, 1939, effectively
ended Loyalist resistance. Madrid held out, however, because General José
Miaja sought lenient terms of surrender, but Franco demanded unconditional
surrender. Following a Communist uprising in Madrid which Miaja defeated in
March, the defenders of the city decided to surrender to Franco with no conditions.*

*March 31, 1939   BRITISH AND FRENCH PLEDGES TO AID POLAND IN THE EVENT
                         OF AGGRESSION END THE BRITISH APPEASEMENT POLICY.*

These pledges were expanded into a mutual assistance pact on April 6.
    *Following his takeover of Czechoslovakia on March 15, Hitler submitted
demands to Warsaw to cede Danzig to Germany and to construct an extraterritorial railway and highway across Pomorze (the Polish "corridor" to the
sea), in return for Germany's guarantee of Poland's frontiers and a non-
aggression pact. Warsaw rejected these demands and, on appeal to Paris and
London, obtained the British-French pledges of March 31.*
    *At this juncture in European politics, Prime Minister Chamberlain's ap-
peasement policy fell into disarray (see September 29, 1938). Seeking to
deter Germany, Chamberlain did not understand Hitler's methods.*
    *Chamberlain's final mistakes in appeasement occurred between March and
September, 1939. They resulted because of appeasement's basic shortcoming:
placing the ideological fear of communism before balance-of-power diplomatic
strategy. Chamberlain and other conservatives feared the communist theory
and rejected realistic strategy for combatting the anti-democratic and totalitarian Fascists who aggressively upset law-and-order in their own states
and in the world. Chamberlain not only rejected the Soviets' offer of an
alliance in 1938 and 1939 but made the grave strategic mistake of promising
to protect Poland when there was no practical method for British and French
forces to protect Poland's weak and ineffective armed forces and nation unless
they secured Russian assistance.*
    *To be sure, Chamberlain was not the only mistaken politician in 1939.
Polish politicians during the interwar years never discovered a method to
unify and strengthen their government. From 1926 until his death on May 12,
1935, Marshal Joseph Pilsudski ruled as a military dictator with presidential
titles but met sufficient opposition to prevent him from establishing a
strong, unified state. In 1935, Poland abolished its democratic, parliamentary system, but the military leaders could not effectively end the opposition
of Socialist and Peasant Parties or the Ukrainian nationalists. On March 1,
1937, Colonel Adam Koc organized the Camp of National Unity to secure greater
government support. Koc's program emphasized army control, anti-communism,
land reform, Polonization of minorities, and violent anti-Semitism. Koc was
overthrown on January 11, 1938, by General Stanislaus Skwarczynski whose conciliatory policy loosened the government's control of society.*
    *In 1939, the Polish military exaggerated their capacity to defend the
nation from Germany. The Polish nationalists disliked the Russians and were
anti-communists as well. As a result, during discussions in 1939 about a
possible Russian alliance against Germany, the government of General
Skwarczynski added their dislike of Stalin to Chamberlain's reluctance to
trust the communists.*
    Given the political circumstances of 1939 and the ideological and

*nationalistic attitudes of Chamberlain and the Polish government, the outcome
in August, 1939, is understandable but instructive. Unlike the British and
Polish leaders, Hitler and Stalin could abandon their ideology when the circumstances required it. The Nazi-Soviet Pact of August 23, 1939, resulted.*

April 3, 1939   THE UNITED STATES RECOGNIZES GENERAL FRANCO'S GOVERN-
                        MENT IN SPAIN.

A final offensive by Franco's forces between December, 1938, and February,
1939, had devastated the Loyalist armies in Catalonia and central Spain. Following the fall of Madrid on April 3, President Roosevelt recognized Franco's
government. He had withdrawn the arms embargo from Spain on April 1 because
the Fascist Nationalist victory was certain. France and Great Britain had
recognized the Franco regime on February 27, 1939.

During the summer and fall of 1938, when a stalemate appeared to have
developed in Spain, Roosevelt had considered various means for aiding the
Spanish Republicans. Following the Munich Conference of September, 1938,
Roosevelt proposed using the Vatican offices to obtain a three-man commission
to mediate the Spanish conflict. This idea was not carried out, but an attempt to relieve starvation conditions of the besieged cities of Barcelona
and Madrid was undertaken. The president appointed a Committee for Impartial
Civilian Relief in Spain which worked with the Red Cross and the American
Friends Service Committee to deliver surplus U.S. wheat to the Spanish people.
Because this relief principally benefited the Loyalists, American Catholics
opposed the committee work. Consequently, the committee provided some assistance to Spain but raised only $50,000 in a fund drive aimed at collecting
$500,000.

In his January 4, 1939, State-of-the-Union message, Roosevelt spoke
sharply against the indifference to lawlessness which resulted in the overthrow of democracies and encouraged aggressors. Yet the president's attempt
to have congress consider a revision of the Neutrality Acts to aid Spain was
not successful. The Senate Foreign Relations Committee began a review of
the neutrality legislation, but on January 19, the committee suspended all
consideration of these bills because of the avalanche of telegrams it received
from pro-Loyalist and pro-Franco supporters in America. The suspension of
the committee's work on neutrality revision influenced not only the Spanish
situation but also Roosevelt's desire to change U.S. neutrality laws generally
in the wake of Hitler's aggression in Czechoslovakia between September, 1938,
and his takeover of that state on March 15, 1939.

Before accepting the fate of the fallen Spanish republic, Roosevelt realized that the democratic powers including America had made a grave mistake
in their Spanish policy. He told his cabinet on January 27 that America
should have simply forbidden the shipping of munitions in U.S. ships. Then
Loyalist Spain could have obtained other vessels to carry what she needed
"to fight for her life and the lives of some of the rest of us as well, as
events will very likely prove." But also, as events proved, neither congress
nor the American public had learned this lesson between 1937 and 1939. The
spirit of isolationism died slowly in the United States during the late
1930's. Congress remained reluctant to provide firm backing for the democratic forces in western Europe. But then, too, so did many British and
French statesmen.

April 7, 1939   ITALY INVADES AND CONQUERS ALBANIA.

King Zog of Albania fled to Greece, and a Fascist government was established in Albania.

April 13, 1939   BRITAIN AND FRANCE GUARANTEE GREEK INDEPENDENCE FOLLOW-
                          ING ITALY'S CONQUEST OF ALBANIA.

Since 1919, Greece came increasingly under the control of the military. In 1923, King George II became a puppet of the military. Political disputes in 1924 led George II to resign, and the proclamation of a republic on May 1 raised Admiral Paul Kondouriottis to power as a provisional president. The republic lasted less than a year before first General Theodore Pangalos (June 25, 1925) and later General George Kondylis ruled as dictators. This politi- cal chaos continued until August 4, 1936, when General John METAXAS undertook a dictatorship which rigorously suppressed all opponents. Metaxas remained in power as premier for life and on April 13 he received British-French pro- tection from the Italian threat.

April 15, 1939   ROOSEVELT ORDERS THE U.S. FLEET TO RETURN TO ITS REG-
                          ULAR STATION AT PEARL HARBOR.

The naval fleet had been on maneuvers in the Caribbean and at the New York World's Fair during the winter and early spring of 1938-1939. After Japan occupied the Spratly Islands and Hainan in February and March, 1939, the pres- ident ordered the fleet back to its Pacific base as a symbol of U.S. displea- sure with Tokyo.

Japan had made further advances down the entire coast of China by early 1939. It captured Canton on October 21, and Hankow on October 25, 1938. Chiang Kai-shek's government moved to the city of Chungking on October 25. Because Hainan was located off the southwest coast of China, it could be a vital base on the sea lanes from Japan to Singapore.

April 15, 1939   PRESIDENT ROOSEVELT APPEALS TO HITLER AND MUSSOLINI
                          TO GUARANTEE PEACE BY PLEDGING THAT THEY WILL NOT AT-
                          TACK ANY OF 31 LISTED NATIONS FOR THE NEXT 10 YEARS.

Alarmed by Hitler's aggression in Czechoslovakia during March, 1939, and It- aly's conquest of Albania on April 7, President Roosevelt sent a personal communication to the two dictators to proscribe further aggression. Indi- cating that one African and three European nations had lost their independence recently, Roosevelt listed 31 nations for which he asked a German and Italian pledge of security. Once peace was assured, the president said, the United States would join other nations to negotiate disarmament and the expansion of trade.

As Roosevelt and Hull expected, the dictators' reaction to the message demonstrated their aggressive plans to conquer other European states. Neither dictator replied directly to the president. Mussolini's comments disclosed his personal reaction as part of an exchange with the Nazi leader Hermann GOERING, who was visiting Rome. The two Fascists thought Roosevelt suffered either the side effects of infantile paralysis or "an incipient mental

disease." In a speech on April 20, Mussolini flippantly showed his contempt
for Roosevelt.

Hitler replied to Roosevelt in a Major Reichstag speech on April 28.
Using deadpan sarcasm, he delivered a humorous response which had the delegates rolling in the aisles--most tellingly, however, Hitler rehearsed all
the American isolationist reasons why the president should stay home and mind
his own business. He denied Germany wanted to go to war, saying all the Germans desired was to correct the unjust deeds inflicted on Germany in 1919.
This, he said, was no more than American intervention in neighboring states
of Latin America and other parts of the world. In ending his harangue, Hitler
stated that he had canvassed each of the governments listed by Roosevelt and
none of them feared a German attack (Hitler's listing of the states pointedly
omitted Poland). If any of these nations requested Hitler's assurances, Germany would gladly give them.

In April, 1939, the humor of the dictators pleased isolationists in the
United States who accepted their saying that they intended no future aggression and that Roosevelt should tend to his own hemispheric problems. As Senator Hiram Johnson, California's foremost isolationist, asserted: "Roosevelt
put his chin out and got a resounding whack. I have reached the conclusion,"
Johnson said, "that there will be no war.... Roosevelt wants to fight for
little things."

April 28, 1939   *HITLER DENOUNCES THE ANGLO-GERMAN NAVAL PACT OF 1935.*

May 11, 1939   THE JOINT BOARD OF THE ARMY AND NAVY APPROVES THE FIVE
                         CONTINGENCY STRATEGIES OF RAINBOW WAR PLANS, REPLACING
                         THE OUTMODED PRIMACY OF ORANGE WAR PLANS AGAINST JAPAN.

Since 1937, President Roosevelt had been reviewing and seeking to change the
Joint Board's emphasis on Orange War Plans for a war against Japan (see December 12, 1937). Although the Joint Board had other contingency war plans,
including a Red War Plan against England and a Black War Plan against Germany,
its most probable enemy since 1919 had been Japan. While this accorded with
Alfred Mahan's Pacific dominance strategy, it never agreed with the State
Department's belief that, except for the Western Hemisphere, Europe was most
vital to the United States.

In November, 1937, Roosevelt made it clear that he preferred a strategy
for a two-ocean navy with a war in Europe against the Axis as most likely.
Subsequently, between February, 1938, when Captain Royal Ingersoll returned
from discussions with England and March 11, the Navy and Army War Plans Divisions and finally the Joint Board considered new strategies which became
the basis for five Rainbow Plans between 1939 and May, 1941.

The Rainbow Plan contingencies designed the following basic estimates:

1. *Rainbow One* - The defense of the Western Hemisphere without any al-
    lies was a given factor for all the Rainbow plans. This was largely
    a coastal defense plan which concentrated U.S. forces north of 10°
    latitude south in the Atlantic and east of longitude 180° in the
    Pacific. The Pacific Ocean defense line extended from the Aleutians
    through Hawaii to the Panama Canal.

2. *Rainbow Two* - The conjecture was that the United States with England
    and France as allies would fight the Axis alliance. America's

European allies would defend in the Atlantic; the United States would mount offensive action in the Pacific. The cooperation of U.S. allies would be crucial in the Atlantic in order to give America the predominant role in the Pacific.

3. *Rainbow Three* - This was essentially the old Orange War Plan based on a U.S. war against Japan with no allies. The United States would take offensive action against Japan in the western Pacific. This plan did not become operative between 1939 and December 7, 1941.

4. *Rainbow Four* - This concept predicted the worst possible situation for America: defending the Western Hemisphere against an Axis alliance that had defeated both France and England. The United States would have full responsibility for a two-ocean war. Rainbow Four became operative when France fell to the Germans in June, 1940. Roosevelt, however, amended it by assuming that England would be assisted in surviving against Germany.

5. *Rainbow Five* - This plan assumed an alliance with England against the Axis powers. Europe and "Germany First" were given top priority. In the Pacific, defense would be emphasized, including U.S. responsibility for southeast Asia between the Philippines and Singapore. This became the basic plan in 1941. See January 27, 1941, for ABC-1.

May 17, 1939   FOLLOWING THE FAILURE OF A JEWISH-ARAB CONFERENCE ON PALESTINE, GREAT BRITAIN PUBLISHES ITS PROPOSAL FOR AN INDEPENDENT PALESTINE.

Since the British armies had occupied Jerusalem on December 9, 1917, and undertaken the League of Nations-mandated control of Palestine on April 25, 1920, the Arab-Jewish problem had created vast difficulty for England. Part of the trouble could be traced back to British duplicity during World War I when the British had made contradictory promises in the Sykes-Picot Agreement of May 9, 1916, and the Balfour Declaration of November 2, 1917. As the influx of Zionist-inspired Jews sought a homeland in Palestine, the Arab inhabitants protested and began attacks on the Jews as early as May 1, 1921. As these attacks increased, the incoming Jews organized to retaliate and Jewish riots and protests replicated Arab activity by 1932. In 1936, the Arab High Commission united Arabs in a virtual war against the Jews, forcing Great Britain to search for a compromise acceptable to both sides.

Between 1936 and 1939, British attempts at compromise failed. A partition plan (the Peel Commission Report) of July 8, 1937, seemed sensible to outsiders and was approved by the League of Nations Assembly. Although the World Zionist Congress accepted partition, Jewish non-Zionist groups rejected the Peel plan. So did the Pan-Arab Congress on September 8, 1937.

In February, 1939, Britain held a Palestine Conference in London with Jews and Palestinian Arabs, but the conference ended on March 17 with no solution. Therefore, on May 17, the British announced a plan which Britain's Parliament approved on May 23, 1939. The proposal indicated that over a 10-year period, Arabs and Jews would have to share in a Palestinian government while it made a transition to independence. Jewish emigration for the next five years would be 75,000; it would then cease unless the Arabs agreed to a new plan.

    Yet the British plan failed to solve the disputes in Palestine. Both Jews and Arabs rejected the proposal and the British could not implement it. The issue remained to be solved after World War II.

June 28, 1939   THE FIRST REGULARLY SCHEDULED COMMERCIAL TRANSATLANTIC FLIGHT IS MADE BETWEEN NEW YORK AND LISBON, PORTUGAL, BY PAN AMERICAN WORLD AIRWAYS.

July 18, 1939   ROOSEVELT'S ATTEMPT TO REVISE THE NEUTRALITY ACTS ENDS FOLLOWING THE FAILURE OF A WHITE HOUSE CONFERENCE BETWEEN THE PRESIDENT AND SENATE LEADERS OF BOTH PARTIES.

Since his State-of-the-Union message to congress on January 4, 1939, the president had endeavored to obtain some type of revision or the repeal of the U.S. Neutrality Acts. His January speech had been directed toward General Franco's impending victory over the Spanish republicans. In the January message, Roosevelt deplored the threats of aggression in the world which destroyed other democratic governments. He advocated some methods "short of war" by which America could let dictators know American opposition to their military tactics. The Neutrality Acts, he said, had aided the aggressors and damaged the victims. Therefore, these laws needed to be revised or repealed.

    During the months from January to July, isolationist strength in congress and especially on the Senate Foreign Relations Committee prevented any significant action by congress. Although Czechoslovakia and Albania fell and Hitler demanded concessions from Poland, the efforts of Hull and Roosevelt to obtain congressional unity on change in the Neutrality Acts did not succeed.

    There were many proposals to revise the neutrality laws but the only bill approved was a weak House of Representatives measure. On June 29, this House bill passed by a vote of 200-188. The resolution, presented to the House by Representative Solomon Bloom's Committee on Foreign Affairs, repealed the arms embargo and gave the president discretionary power to say when, where, and how the law would apply. Before the bill passed, however, Representative John M. Vorys of Ohio added an amendment which virtually killed the bill's effect by embargoing "arms and ammunition" but not "implements of war." According to Vorys, "implements" were airplanes and items with potential civilian use. He referred especially to the president's desire to sell aircraft to France and England. Roosevelt believed the House measure as passed did more harm than good. He wrote to a friend that "I honestly believe that the [House] vote last night was a stimulus to war and that if the vote had been different it would have been a definite encouragement to peace."

    The Senate did not pass even a weak measure in the effort to revise the Neutrality Acts. On July 11, the Senate Foreign Relations Committee rejected Senator Key Pittman's "Peace Bill" by a vote of 12-11. Although this committee action virtually killed any neutrality resolution, the president prepared an attempt to have the full Senate override the committee recommendation. On July 14, Secretary Hull sent a message to congress urging congress to join with the Chief Executive in promoting peace. Hull's message reviewed the problems and results of neutrality laws, stressing that world peace required American cooperation as an effective voice in influencing the course of action.

    To further assure congressional action, Roosevelt called a meeting of

senators from both parties at the White House on July 18. The president told
them the news of problems developing in Europe, and Secretary Hull offered
to let the senators read the confidential dispatches which the State Department had regarding imminent war. The isolationist senators were firm, however. They opposed the repeal of the arms embargo and did not believe war
was likely in the near future. Senator Borah refused to examine Hull's reports from Europe and made the most memorable remark of the meeting: "No one
can foretell what may happen. But my feeling and belief is that we are not
going to have a war. Germany isn't ready for it." On September 1, 1939,
Borah's words became famous for their inaccuracy.

July 24, 1939   *BRITAIN APPROVES THE CRAIGIE-ARITA DECLARATION WHICH
                          RECOGNIZES JAPAN'S NEW STATUS AS "ENFORCER" OF LAW
                          AND ORDER IN CHINA.*

*Japanese aggression continued in 1939 as Japan's forces occupied Hainan Island
and the Spratly Islands in February and March. In June, the Japanese sought
to pressure the English to vacate Tientsin and the foreign settlements in
Shanghai so that Japan's "new order in East Asia" could get firmer control
of China.*
     *Because Chamberlain feared Hitler's demands in Europe more than Japan's
ventures in China, the British Ambassador to Tokyo, Sir Robert Craigie, negotiated an agreement with Japan's Foreign Minister, Hachiro Arita. In their
understanding, the British recognized that Japan's army was responsible for
security in the Chinese areas they occupied. Britain's consular officers
would not impede measures taken by Japanese military authorities in China.
Clearly, Britain had retreated from its former strong position in central
China, retaining Hong Kong as its one center of economic influence in East
Asia.*

July 26, 1939   THE UNITED STATES GIVES THE REQUIRED SIX MONTHS' NO-
                         TICE THAT IT WILL TERMINATE ITS COMMERCIAL TREATY OF
                         1911 WITH JAPAN ON JANUARY 1, 1940.

Although isolationists in congress blocked neutrality changes against Germany
during the spring of 1939, they were willing to consider an arms embargo to
combat Japan's aggression in East Asia. The issue arose whether an arms embargo on Japan would violate the treaty of 1911. On July 18, Senator Vandenberg, a leading Republican isolationist, introduced a resolution to abrogate
the 1911 commercial treaty.
     Vandenberg's action led Roosevelt and Hull to take immediate action that
would supersede Vandenberg's resolution. They also claimed that the Senate
action might not be completed before congress adjourned. As a result, Roosevelt declared on July 26 that the United States would end its commercial
treaty on January 26, 1940.

August 23, 1939   *A NAZI-SOVIET PACT IS SIGNED AT MOSCOW BY WHICH EACH
                         NATION AGREES NOT TO ATTACK THE OTHER AND TO BE NEUTRAL
                         IF THE OTHER IS ATTACKED BY A THIRD POWER.*

The conclusion of the German-Soviet pact resulted from nearly six months of multi-national discussion during which Germany and Russia and England and Russia pursued separate discussions to determine Moscow's alignment in the event that Hitler's demands on Poland caused a German-Polish conflict. Britain and France conducted talks with the Soviets, but they were fruitless. Mutual distrust was the chief obstacle between London and Moscow. Prime Minister Chamberlain had reluctantly given up most of his "appeasement" policy, but because that policy was based to a great degree on strong anti-communist fears, Chamberlain found it difficult to satisfy Stalin's requests. The Polish leaders proved to be equally short-sighted, insisting that Russian troops could not enter their territory to engage the German army. The Poles had no sound military suggestion for otherwise preventing the Germans from conquering their nation. Colonel Joseph BECK, Poland's Foreign Minister, was so far on the political right wing that some considered him a Fascist. He definitely opposed concessions of any type to the Soviet Union. Beck and Chamberlain were congenial bed-partners. As the prime minister stated: "I very much agree with him [Beck], for I regard Russia as a very unreliable friend ... with an enormous irritative power on others." (On Chamberlain, see the description of "Appeasement" under September 29, 1938.)

Russia continued talks with the British and French. On July 24, 1939, Foreign Minister Vyacheslav MOLOTOV agreed to proceed to military talks with British and French leaders. Molotov's seeming satisfaction with the Western powers' proposals appears to have been another move in a complex diplomatic game. While talking with Russia, Chamberlain's confidential advisor, Horace Wilson, pursued separate and secret discussions in London with a member of Goering's economic staff, Dr. Helmut Wohlstat. Wilson asked Wohlstat if a British-German non-aggression pact could be discussed along with a trade agreement. If such discussions had been successful, Chamberlain's appeasement might have revived. The discussions failed; appeasement died.

Molotov and Stalin's indication on July 24 that a British-Soviet pact was nearing success aroused Hitler to more serious talks with Moscow. On May 5, 1939, Molotov had instructed the Soviet chargé in Berlin to discuss a possible trade agreement with Germany. This Soviet overture had little effect until July 26, when the German Foreign Office showed interest in having negotiations with Russia. By August 11, the British-French military mission reached Moscow at the same time the German-Soviet talks entered a crucial stage. The British-French military talks got nowhere, stumbling on the Polish desire for supplies from Russia but no troops. Beck insisted that if Russian troops entered Poland, they would never leave. The British and French had never resolved this issue but tended to back the Polish view because they believed the Polish army could resist a Nazi invasion. By the time the French persuaded Beck to accept certain corridors for the passage of Russian troops, the Western game had been lost.

On August 20, Berlin and Moscow announced a trade agreement. On August 22, Foreign Minister Joachim von Ribbentrop left for Moscow to finalize the non-aggression pact which he signed on August 23, 1939 (it was actually signed on August 24 at 1 a.m.). In addition to the publicly announced non-aggression pact, the Nazi-Soviet pact had a secret protocol which partitioned Poland and divided the Baltic States. Poland was divided along lines defined by the Pisia, Narew, Vistula, and San rivers. Russia would control Finland, Estonia, and Latvia as well as Bessarabia in southeast Europe. Germany received jurisdiction over Lithuania.

The British-French military mission remained in Moscow until August 26. Some hope was seen in the possibility of an additional Russian agreement with the Western powers. There was no hope, however. Hitler had an agreement that permitted him to attack Poland with little risk of defeat because of a two-front war.

August 25, 1939   PRESIDENT ROOSEVELT NOTIFIES HITLER THAT POLAND IS
                         WILLING TO NEGOTIATE, ASKING GERMANY TO ACCEPT PEACEFUL
                         MEANS TO AVERT WAR. ROOSEVELT DOES NOT EXPECT HITLER
                         TO AGREE, BUT WISHES TO MAKE GERMANY'S AGGRESSION CLEAR
                         TO THE U.S. PEOPLE.

Because a European war seemed certain at any moment after the August 23 Nazi-Soviet Pact, Roosevelt had immediately sent a message on the same day to King Victor Emmanuel of Italy to assert his influence for peace. On the 24th, he appealed to Hitler and President Ignace Moscicki of Poland, offering to act as mediator in the process of arbitration or conciliation of the dispute. Moscicki agreed; Hitler never responded.

On August 25, Roosevelt asked Hitler to accept the Polish mediation offer. The president told his advisors he wanted to "put the bee on Germany—which nobody had done in 1914." It is necessary, he said, "that history should not record ... that the first act of aggression of a military character was brought about by Poland." As expected, the Nazi leader ignored the president's second appeal. German preparations were underway for the German attack on Poland.

September 1, 1939   *NAZI GERMANY'S ARMIES LAUNCH AN INVASION OF POLAND.*

Hitler informed his generals to prepare for war on August 22, the day Ribbentrop left for Moscow. The Germans did not believe England and France would intervene because Hitler would give a good propaganda reason to justify war, "whether plausible or not." "The victor," Hitler told his generals, will not be asked "whether he told the truth or not. In starting and making war it is not right, but victory, that matters."

The alleged reason for Hitler's invasion was Danzig's demand for the right to be annexed to Germany. Danzig, a free city after the Treaty of Versailles, had come under Nazi control in 1933. In March, 1939, Hitler demanded that Warsaw permit Danzig to unite with Germany and allow the Germans to construct a railway and highway across Polish territory to Danzig. Thus, the Danzig problem was from the start Hitler's ploy to justify Germany's dominance of Poland.

On August 20, the government of Danzig again demanded to become part of Germany, and on August 29, Hitler supported Danzig's request. Hitler refused further discussions with Poland, France, or England until the Danzig demands were met. Hitler enumerated all the demands for Poland to meet in a 16-point list given to British Ambassador Sir Nevile Henderson on August 30.

In the context of Poland's refusal to comply with Germany and Danzig's just demands, the German armies launched their blitzkrieg attack on September 1, 1939. World War II began in Europe.

September 3, 1939   *BRITISH AND FRENCH ULTIMATUMS TO GERMANY ON SEPTEMBER*
                       2 HAVING BEEN REJECTED, THE TWO WESTERN POWERS DECLARE
                       WAR ON GERMANY.

*For a brief period after Hitler's attack on Poland, England and France hoped
the Nazis might localize the conflict and negotiate. Hitler had made an effort to prevent British-French intervention, sending them false signs from
August 25 to 30 that he was ready to negotiate regarding Poland and blaming
Colonel Beck of Poland for not agreeing to the proper atmosphere for discussion. Goering sent a Swedish businessman, Birger Dahlerus, to London to see
if a Munich-type conference could be undertaken on the basis that Chamberlain
would make a prior commitment to support Hitler's demands.*

*Because of these prewar diversions, England and France took 48 hours to
seek a final peaceful diplomatic solution with Hitler. It did not succeed
and London and Paris declared war on September 3.*

September 4, 1939   SECRETARY OF STATE HULL MEETS WITH BRITISH AMBASSADOR
                       LORD LOTHIAN TO ARRANGE TO MINIMIZE U.S.-BRITISH CON-
                       FLICTS ABOUT NEUTRAL RIGHTS.

During the next year, a variety of disputes arose about British action against
neutral American ships, U.S. mail, and cables. These matters never became
more than irritations, however, because Hull and Lothian equally desired to
avoid the antagonisms that developed between 1914 and 1917.

September 5, 1939   PRESIDENT ROOSEVELT ANNOUNCES U.S. NEUTRALITY IN THE
                       EUROPEAN WAR, APPLYING THE NEUTRALITY ACTS WHICH EM-
                       BARGOED ARMS TO ALL BELLIGERENTS.

The declaration of war by France and England left Roosevelt no choice but to
issue the neutrality decree. Roosevelt did not, however, ask Americans to
be neutral in thought as well as deed. In addition, the president began preparations to call a special session of congress to revise the U.S. neutrality
legislation. See November 4, 1939.

September 17, 1939   *RUSSIAN FORCES INVADE EASTERN POLAND, OCCUPYING AREAS*
                       HITLER HAD DESIGNATED FOR RUSSIA IN THE SECRET PROTOCOL
                       OF THE AUGUST 23 NAZI-SOVIET PACT.

*Soon after occupying eastern Poland, Stalin forced the Baltic states of Es-
tonia, Latvia, and Lithuania to permit the Russian army to establish military
bases on their territory. Soon after, 20,000 Russian soldiers entered these
states and the U.S.S.R. absorbed these small countries into its nation.*

*Although the original Nazi-Soviet pact gave Lithuania to Germany, a new
agreement was concluded on September 28. Stalin proposed to give Germany
additional Polish territory as far east as the Bug River (east from the Narew
River). In return, the Soviet Union occupied Lithuania.*

October 3, 1939   THE FOREIGN MINISTERS OF THE PAN-AMERICAN STATES MEET
                         AT PANAMA AND ADOPT A GENERAL DECLARATION OF CONTINEN-
                         TAL NEUTRALITY WHICH PAN-AMERICANIZED ROOSEVELT'S NEU-
                         TRALITY POLICY.

The Declaration of Panama provided for the neutral solidarity of the New World
Republics, slanting the neutrality in favor of the Western democracies much
as Roosevelt's revised Fourth Neutrality Act of November 4, 1939, would do.
The declaration said the American nations would prevent their inhabitants
from activity affecting neutrality, would recognize the transfer of a merchant
vessel flag to another American republic, and would exclude belligerent submarines from their territorial waters in a large war zone surrounding the
Western Hemisphere.

    While some observers criticized the legal implications of the large 300-
mile-wide security zone that the Panama Declaration drew up for security reasons, not the legal but the practical problems of the decree were the difficult questions. Because this zone exceeded the normal coastal limits recognized by international law, it could not be effective unless the belligerent
powers accepted it. They did not. Both the British and the French rejected
this security zone.

October 11, 1939   ALBERT EINSTEIN AND OTHER SCIENTISTS INFORM PRESIDENT
                         ROOSEVELT THAT AN ATOMIC BOMB COULD POSSIBLY BE DE-
                         VELOPED.

Einstein's letter was inspired by Leo SZILARD who, unlike Einstein, was involved in nuclear fission reserach. Einstein's letter warned that Germany
seemed to be moving to control uranium supplies that were used in nuclear
fission. From the suggestion of this message, Roosevelt eventually organized
the top-secret Manhattan Project, which produced the world's first nuclear
weapon in 1945. See August 31, 1942.

November 4, 1939   ROOSEVELT SIGNS A NEUTRALITY ACT REVISED TO END THE
                         ARMS EMBARGO AND PERMIT CASH AND CARRY SALES OF ARMS.

On September 13, the president called a special session of congress to revise
U.S. neutrality legislation. The meetings began on September 21, and in spite
of strong isolationist opposition, congress amended the neutrality laws in
about five weeks.

    During the period of debate, Roosevelt's theme was that a cash and carry
program would allow France and England to purchase arms in the United States
and keep America out of war by preventing the Nazi conquest of those two Western European democracies. The president argued that the United States would
not be severely threatened unless Germany defeated England and France. While
he avoided specifically stating that America should directly help the Western
democracies, the obvious consequence of the end of the arms embargo and cash
and carry arms sales would benefit England and France because the British
navy controlled the Atlantic Ocean. The cash and carry provisions would permit the allies to purchase all types of goods but would keep U.S. ships out
of the war zones.

    To support neutrality revision, Roosevelt encouraged bipartisan backing.
Leading Republicans such as Henry Stimson, Colonel Frank Knox, who owned the

Chicago Daily News, and Alfred Landon, the 1936 Republican presidential candidate, spoke in favor of neutrality revision.

Nevertheless, Senate isolationists continued to oppose any changes in the neutrality laws and accused the president of seeking to enhance his personal power to involve America in Europe's war. Senators Borah, Nye, and Vandenberg used a national radio campaign to promote a mail-in campaign by people who opposed any chance of involving America in war.

The mood in congress had, however, changed since the July defeat of Roosevelt's attempt to revise the Neutrality Acts. On October 27, the Senate approved the neutrality revision bill by a vote of 63 to 30; the House adopted its measure on November 2 by a vote of 243 to 18; a conference bill to settle the final wording of the law passed on November 3.

On November 4, Roosevelt signed the new bill, issued a proclamation lifting the arms embargo, and defined the combat areas where U.S. ships and citizens were excluded. The combat zone included only the waters adjacent to the British Isles and France and the North and Baltic Seas. A major handicap of the Fourth Neutrality Act was to prohibit U.S. ships with cargo other than arms from entering British and French ports. All purchases by the Europeans would be cash and carry.

In addition, the act of November 4 continued all the provisions of the Neutrality Act of 1937 except the change of the arms embargo which permitted arms to be sold on a cash and carry basis. The United States did not return to the defense of its neutral rights, which it had followed from 1914 to 1917 and prior to 1935. U.S. ships could not carry freight or passengers to belligerent ports; U.S. ships could not be armed; American citizens could not travel on belligerent ships; loans to belligerents were prohibited except for short-term 90-day credits. These provisions of the 1939 Neutrality Act restricted aid that America might have given to the European democracies.

November 29, 1939   ROOSEVELT'S ATTEMPT TO MEDIATE BETWEEN RUSSIA AND FINLAND FAILS; RUSSIAN PLANES AND TROOPS ATTACK FINLAND.

Early in October, 1939, Moscow demanded military bases in Finland similar to agreements given by the governments of Estonia, Latvia, and Lithuania on September 28. Finland refused, however, and asked Washington to assist in persuading Russia to withdraw its unreasonable requirements. On October 11, Roosevelt sent a telegram to Mikhail KALININ, titular President of the Soviet Union, asking the U.S.S.R. to limit its demands on Finnish independence.

The October 11 message, as well as a similar appeal by Roosevelt on November 29, was rebuffed by the U.S.S.R. On November 29, the Russian armies invaded Finland to impose Russia's demands but met stiff resistance from the Finnish armies.

Because Russia did not officially declare war on Finland, Roosevelt and Hull acted as they had in the Sino-Japanese conflict of 1937. They called for a "moral embargo" on airplane sales to Russia but did not apply the Neutrality Acts. Finland would have suffered from the neutrality laws more than the U.S.S.R. In addition, diplomatic relations were maintained in Moscow because the Roosevelt administration believed that sooner or later Russia would forsake its Nazi pact and join the Western Allies.

During the winter of 1939-1940, the restrictions of neutrality prevented Roosevelt from aiding Finland, much as he desired to do so. Although the president arranged an Export-Import Bank loan of $10 million, the funds could not to be used for arms. Finnish ambassador Hjalmar Procopé desired $60 million which would include arms and planes.

In January, 1940, Senator Prentiss M. Brown of Michigan presented a Senate bill to provide Finland an unrestricted loan. Although the United States had great sympathy for the gallant Finnish defenders, isolationists opposed this measure as another example of Roosevelt's desire for "dictatorial power." Therefore, the president did not strongly support Brown's resolution. On March 2, 1940, a congressional act raised the capital of the Export-Import Bank to $200 million but limited any one loan to $20 million, which could not be used for armaments. See March 12, 1940.

December 24, 1939   PRESIDENT ROOSEVELT APPOINTS A PERSONAL REPRESENTATIVE
                             TO THE VATICAN.

During the fall of 1939, President Roosevelt, Secretary Hull, and others in the State Department discussed the value of having a U.S. representative at the Vatican who could obtain data regarding such issues as the Jewish problem and internal affairs in Spain, Italy, and Germany. Inquiries through U.S. Ambassador William Phillips in Rome indicated that Pope Pius XII would look favorably on such an arrangement. Thus, on Christmas Eve, Roosevelt made public a letter he had written to the pope regarding peace at the same time that he announced that Myron C. TAYLOR had been appointed as the president's personal representative to the Vatican.

1940

January 17, 1940   PRESIDENT ROOSEVELT HOLDS AN INTERDEPARTMENTAL CON-
FERENCE TO EXPEDITE AIRCRAFT SALES TO FRANCE AND EN-
GLAND.

Although French and British orders for U.S. munitions did not materialize as
rapidly as Roosevelt had expected during the fall of 1939, by January 1,
France ordered 2,095 airplanes and 7,372 aircraft engines; Britain ordered
1,450 airplanes. During December, however, Britain and France projected an
aircraft order for 1940 of 10,000 planes and 20,000 engines provided they
could get the best type available such as the fighter P-40.

In the War, Navy, and State departments, British and French order and
their desire for the most improved aircraft models caused dissension. Secretary of War Woodring and several high military leaders opposed giving these
countries the latest U.S. planes and wanted all American needs to be filled
before offering them to France and Britain. The president, however, agreed
with Louis Johnson, the Assistant Secretary of War, who headed the industrial
mobilization office. Johnson believed the Allied orders enabled U.S. aircraft
manufacturers to expand rapidly and, in the long term, would assist U.S. defense preparations.

Although the president attempted to conciliate Woodring and the Army
generals at the January 17 meeting, he urged them to expedite the Allied
orders, which were needed immediately. It was finally agreed that a percentage of all aircraft could be sold to France and Britain and that these would
be the improved models because those were the models the U.S. industries had
to gear up to manufacture.

The conference of January 17 did not resolve all conflicts between Louis
Johnson and Secretary Woodring. In March, 1940, Roosevelt learned that Army
Air Force General Arnold and Woodring refused to let the Allies have secret
devices necessary to the planes they had ordered. Roosevelt believed this
was nonsense. He instructed Arnold to stop resisting aid to France and Britain and told all three men that their leaks of information to Republicans
and isolationists must cease. He told Woodring to accept his views or resign.
He told Arnold that any uncooperative officers would be sent to "exile" at
Guam. Temporarily, Woodring and Arnold accepted Roosevelt's lead, not challenging him again until June, 1940, after the fall of France.

January 26, 1940   THE UNITED STATES OFFICIALLY ENDS ITS 1911 COMMERCIAL
TREATY WITH JAPAN.

The American intention to end the commercial arrangements had been made in
July, 1939, to meet the necessary six-month notice before termination.

In Tokyo, Foreign Minister Nomura asked Ambassador Grew if a new treaty
would be negotiated. Following Hull's advice in December, 1939, Grew told
Nomura that at present U.S. trade with Japan was on a 24-hour basis and would

depend on Japan's further violation of U.S. rights in East Asia. Thus, no U.S. treaty negotiations were begun.

March 12, 1940   *FINLAND ACCEPTS RUSSIA'S PEACE TERMS, RETAINING INDE-PENDENCE BUT SURRENDERING TERRITORY AND MAKING ECONOMIC AND MILITARY CONCESSIONS TO MOSCOW.*

March 28, 1940   THE CONCLUSION OF SUMNER WELLES'S MISSION TO EUROPE TO EXPLORE THE CHANCES FOR PEACE.

Although opposed by Secretary of State Hull, Roosevelt on February 9 dispatched Undersecretary of State Welles to Rome, Berlin, Paris, and London where he explored the possibilities of peace and gained information on existing conditions in Europe. Since September, neither the Axis powers nor the Western democracies had pursued active military campaigns, causing the reference to this six-month period as the "phony war." Exactly what purpose Roosevelt intended for Welles is unclear. Welles said he was told to offer guarantees of disarmament, security, and trade if the four powers would attend a conference to resolve their difficulties. Since Poland had been quickly overrun by German and Russian troops, the fate of Poland could not be considered, but other issues could be identified and resolved in order to bring peace.

Therefore, Welles visited Rome, Berlin, Paris, and London and interviewed the head of each government. The mission accomplished nothing. There was, said Welles, no chance for peace based on territorial or economic changes. Each belligerent wanted to enhance its own future security; a practical plan acceptable to all four nations did not seem possible.

April 9, 1940   *GERMANY INVADES NORWAY WITH SEA AND AIRBORNE TROOPS. AT THE SAME TIME, GERMAN TROOPS OCCUPY DENMARK WITH LITTLE DANISH RESISTANCE.*

Although Norway offered some resistance and Anglo-French forces landed in southern Norway on April 16, Hitler rapidly reinforced the German army, and by April 30, effective Allied resistance ended. The English and French withdrew, and after June 10 only underground activity against Germany remained in Norway.

May 10, 1940   *WITHOUT WARNING, GERMANY ATTACKS THE NETHERLANDS, BEL-GIUM, AND LUXEMBURG. TWO DAYS LATER THE NAZIS ATTACK FRANCE, CROSSING THE MEUSE RIVER AT SEDAN.*

May 10, 1940   *WINSTON CHURCHILL BECOMES BRITAIN'S PRIME MINISTER, REPLACING NEVILLE CHAMBERLAIN.*

Churchill headed a coalition cabinet which included both Conservative and Labour Party members. Churchill's rhetoric and dogged persistence rallied the British to resist the Fascist forces and symbolized his nation's determination eventually to defeat its enemies. Churchill had previously

*established correspondence with President Roosevelt, and the Anglo-Saxon lead-
ers generally got along well in cooperating throughout the war years.*

May 16, 1940   PRESIDENT ROOSEVELT ASKS CONGRESS FOR $1.18 BILLION
                              IN ADDITIONAL DEFENSE APPROPRIATIONS.

The renewed aggression of Germany during April and May resulted in the president's request for funds to meet the nation's defense needs. Although the
president had reduced the army budget request in January, 1940, he now told
congress that the United States needed larger army preparations. In addition,
he asked for funding to build the nation's aircraft production up to 50,000
planes per year. He told congress that planes flying as fast as 300 miles
an hour eliminated the oceans as "adequate defensive barriers" to the Americas. Within two weeks, congress approved more than Roosevelt requested, voting $1.3 billion for defense purposes.
     By May 31, Roosevelt requested another increased defense funding bill.
Within one month, congress voted for another $1.7 billion dollars, expanded
the regular army from 280,000 to 375,000 men, and authorized the president
to call the National Guard into service. Hitler's rapid victories in western
Europe startled the American public and motivated congress to act quickly to
repair the strength of the armed forces, which had suffered from neglect for
nearly 20 years.

May 28, 1940   CONGRESS APPROVES LEGISLATION PERMITTING THE PRESIDENT
                              TO RELEASE ARMY AND NAVY STOCK TO LATIN AMERICAN COUN-
                              TRIES TO ASSIST WESTERN HEMISPHERIC DEFENSE.

For over a year, the War, Navy, and State departments had requested congressional approval to permit them to supply Latin American countries with ammunition, coast defense and anti-aircraft equipment, and warships. The House
passed the legislation early in 1940, but the proposal was delayed by various
Senate committees until May 28. Passage of this act permitted the American
naval and military officials to send essential equipment other than the out-
dated and obsolete surplus materials sent to the South Americans previously.

June 3, 1940   SEEKING A METHOD TO DEFEND AMERICA BY EXTENDED AID TO
                              BRITAIN AND FRANCE, ROOSEVELT DISCOVERS A TECHNIQUE
                              TO GET "SURPLUS" U.S. EQUIPMENT TO THE ALLIES.

On May 22, Roosevelt had ordered the sale of World War I equipment to the
allies although the Neutrality Act of 1939 did not permit the U.S. government
to do this. Both Premier Reynaud and Prime Minister Churchill urged the president to send whatever he could because the Germans' swift victories had not
been anticipated.
     On June 3, Roosevelt's legal advisors ruled that the government could
sell "surplus" military supplies to private parties who could resell them to
England and France. In three weeks, the first shipment reached England:
500,000 rifles, 80,000 machine guns, 900 75 mm. field guns, and 130 million
rounds of ammunition.

June 10, 1940   ROOSEVELT'S SPEECH AT THE UNIVERSITY OF VIRGINIA (CHAR-
LOTTESVILLE) DENOUNCES BOTH ISOLATIONISTS AND ITALY,
AND INDICATES THE UNITED STATES MUST AID ENGLAND AND
FRANCE.

The president said isolationists dreamed that America could be "a lone island
in a world dominated by force." Such delusions, he said, would create a
"nightmare" for people "handcuffed, hungry, and fed through the bars" by "un-
pitying masters of other continents." Only an Allied victory, he said, could
prevent such imprisonment.

Regarding Italy, the president had appealed on two occasions for Mussolini to strive for peace and to limit the war. Now, June 10, news had come
of Italy's attack on France. In Roosevelt's descriptive words, "the hand
that held the dagger has struck it into the back of its neighbor."

Finally, the president asserted, in unity America must pursue two objectives: one, to "extend to the opponents of force the material resources of
this nation"; and, two, to speed U.S. defense preparations so that "the Americas may have equipment and training to the task of any emergency and every
defense."

The president's message abandoned any pretense of neutrality. The United
States unofficially became a non-belligerent aiding England and France.

June 17, 1940   *FRANCE SURRENDERS, ASKING GERMANY FOR AN ARMISTICE.*

*The Nazi blitzkrieg moved swiftly through the Low Countries and deep into
northern France by May 21, outflanking France's defensive masterwork, the
Maginot Line. The Belgian armies surrendered on May 26 and, left in an ex-
posed condition, the British expeditionary forces of 250,000 men staged a
hasty and gallant retreat by sea at Dunkirk on May 28.*

*On June 20, Italy declared war against France and Great Britain and in-
vaded southern France. The Italian "stab in the back" served Mussolini's
moment of glory but was not essential to the Germans. After evacuating Paris
without a fight on June 13, the French government of Paul Reynaud resigned.
Marshal Henri-Philippe PÉTAIN became premier and asked the Germans for an
armistice on June 17.*

*The French signed the German armistice demands at Compiegne on June 22.
French forces were disarmed and three-fifths of France came completely under
German control. The Pétain administration set up headquarters at Vichy on
July 2. In London on June 23, General Charles DE GAULLE headed a French Na-
tional Committee, pledged to continue resistance to Germany.*

On June 24, Pétain's government and Italy signed an armistice.

June 18, 1940   CONGRESS APPROVES THE PITTMAN-BLOOM RESOLUTION WHICH
OPPOSES THE TRANSFER OF TERRITORY IN THE WESTERN HEMI-
SPHERE FROM ONE NON-AMERICAN POWER TO ANOTHER NON-
AMERICAN POWER.

The Nazi conquest of western European nations with colonies in the Americas
such as the Netherlands, Denmark, and France concerned the State Department.
Thus, Secretary Hull drafted a resolution which was sent to the Foreign Relations Committee on June 3. The bill was approved unanimously by the Senate
on June 17, and by a vote of 380-8 in the House on June 18.

June 19, 1940   ROOSEVELT APPOINTS TWO PRO-ALLIED REPUBLICANS TO HIS
                         CABINET: HENRY STIMSON AS SECRETARY OF WAR AND FRANK
                         KNOX AS SECRETARY OF THE NAVY.

By these two appointments, the president not only established a bipartisan
consensus for aid to the British but also replaced two isolationist cabinet
members. Secretary of War Harry Woodring had especially irritated the president by opposing sales of "surplus" goods to England, claiming the old equipment was useful for training the U.S. Army.

   Both Stimson and Knox were prominent Republican leaders. Stimson had
been Secretary of War under William H. Taft and Secretary of State under
Herbert Hoover. Knox was the Republicans' vice-presidential candidate in
1936.

June 27, 1940   ROOSEVELT REQUIRES THE JOINT BOARD OF THE ARMY AND
                         NAVY TO OPERATE CONTINGENCY PLANS UNDER RAINBOW FOUR
                         WAR PLANS REVISED TO ASSUME BRITISH SURVIVAL THROUGH
                         THE WINTER OF 1940-1941.

The conquest of France by the Nazis caused the Joint Board of the Army and
Navy to shift its contingency war preparations from Rainbow TWO to Rainbow
FOUR (see May 11, 1939). Rainbow Two plans assumed a British-French alliance
to control the Atlantic while the United States defended in the Pacific.
Rainbow Four was a worst-case plan: the United States against the victorious
Axis powers with no allies. Under Rainbow Four, all U.S. preparations had
to focus on immediate American defense preparations.

   Roosevelt disliked the implications of Rainbow Four because he accepted
Prime Minister Churchill's promise that Great Britain would survive regardless
of the sacrifice. In order to provide priority aid in arms and aircraft for
sale to Britain, Roosevelt rejected the opinion of Army Chief of Staff
Marshall and the Chief of Naval Operations, Harold Stark, that sending war
materials to Britain was assistance to a lost cause. Roosevelt wanted one-
half of all U.S. aircraft and munitions production for Britain.

   Of course, the Commander-in-Chief won the dispute. On June 27, Rainbow
Four was amended to reflect the president's desire to aid England. Although
the Joint Board did not fully accept Roosevelt's "Germany First" strategy
until December, 1940, Roosevelt virtually adopted it on June 27, 1940. See
November 12, 1940.

June 28, 1940   THE ALIEN REGISTRATION ACT (SMITH ACT) ATTEMPTS TO
                         CHECK SUBVERSIVE ACTIVITY IN THE UNITED STATES.

This act governed the admission and deportation of aliens, and required all
aliens to be fingerprinted. The act made it unlawful to teach or advocate
the overthrow of the U.S. government by force or violence or to organize or
become a member of any group advancing such doctrines.

July 3, 1940   *THE BRITISH NAVY ARRIVES AT ORAN TO TAKE OVER FRENCH
                         SHIPS. THE FRENCH CREWS RESIST AND THE BRITISH SINK
                         OR CAPTURE THE MAJOR PORTION OF THE FRENCH FLEET AN-
                         CHORED OFF ALGERIA'S COAST.*

July 14, 1940   BRITAIN'S SECRET AGENT IN NEW YORK--"INTREPID"--INFORMS
                        BRITISH INTELLIGENCE THAT COLONEL WILLIAM J. DONOVAN
                        HAS BEEN CHOSEN AS PRESIDENT ROOSEVELT'S PERSONAL REP-
                        RESENTATIVE.

"Intrepid" was Sir William Stephenson, a British intelligence officer and
friend of Churchill, who set up New York headquarters for British secret communications and deciphering activity. Stephenson and his colleagues had sto-
len the Germans' secret coding machine, Enigma, on August 22, 1939, and
learned how to break the German code Ultra. The first successes of Enigma
were to discover German plans which led to the British disaster at Dunkirk
in May, 1940. The interception of German messages corresponded with the
events preceding Dunkirk. When these were made known to Roosevelt, the president was sufficiently impressed to appoint Colonel Donovan as his liaison
with Stephenson. Later Donovan headed the U.S. Office of Strategic Services
(O.S.S.), working closely with Stephenson until 1945.

    News of Intrepid's activity in breaking the German Ultra code and in
frustrating German efforts to develop atomic weapons was not disclosed until
1974 when a record of the "secret war" was published in a volume titled *A Man
Called Intrepid* written by a Canadian journalist, William Stevenson.

July 15, 1940   THE DEMOCRATIC CONVENTION AT CHICAGO NOMINATES PRESI-
                        DENT ROOSEVELT FOR AN UNPRECEDENTED THIRD TERM.

The Democratic platform continued, however, to reflect an isolationist attitude, stating that the United States "will not participate in foreign wars"
or send U.S. armed forces to "fight in foreign lands outside the Americas,
except in case of attack." Although Secretary of State Hull disliked this
statement, Roosevelt told him "there would be no change in our foreign policy."

    On June 28, the Republican Convention nominated a presidential candidate,
Wendell Willkie, whose foreign policy views were similar to Roosevelt's.
Willkie opposed participation in "foreign wars" but advocated aid to Britain,
strong U.S. defenses, and hemispheric cooperation.

July 20, 1940   A NAVAL CONSTRUCTION BILL FOR $4 BILLION IS SIGNED BY
                        PRESIDENT ROOSEVELT.

This bill, combined with a bill passed on June 14, 1940, authorized the construction of a "two-ocean navy" capable of defensive action in one ocean and
freedom of action in the other. More than 1,325,000 tons of naval construction were authorized by these two bills, providing for 250 warships. The
new fleet included 7 battleships, 6 battle cruisers, 19 carriers, 60 cruisers,
150 destroyers, and 140 submarines.

July 25-26, 1940   PRESIDENT ROOSEVELT LIMITS BUT THEN QUALIFIES U.S.
                        EXPORTS OF OIL AND SCRAP METAL TO JAPAN.

The president faced a difficult decision regarding Japanese policy during
the summer of 1940. Following the Allied losses in Western Europe between
April and June, 1940, the status of the Far East became less certain. Great

Britain wanted the United States either to appease Japan or take strong action such as economic sanctions. In Washington, Morgenthau and Stimson urged sanctions while Sumner Welles and Hull feared that economic pressure would lead Japan to take over the oil supplies of the Dutch East Indies islands that British forces had occupied after the Netherlands fell to the Germans.

Roosevelt's desire to avoid a Japanese war but to take some action against Tokyo's continued conquest of southern China became a middle-course policy lacking the clarity of other extremes. Consequently, when Secretary of the Treasury Morgenthau asked the president to forbid the export of petroleum, petroleum products, and scrap metal to Japan, Roosevelt agreed and signed a bill to that effect on July 25.

Upon hearing of the Treasury Department order, Hull and Undersecretary of State Welles objected. As written, the order seemed to embargo all U.S. oil and scrap metal shipments to Japan. During a cabinet meeting that day, Roosevelt told Welles and Morgenthau to write a proper order indicating that the United States was not embargoing these products. With Welles's help, Morgenthau issued a revised order on July 26 which narrowly restricted the embargo to aviation motor fuel and high-grade smelting scrap. In this way, Roosevelt took limited action against Japan but not effective action that would lead to a crisis with Japan at that time. The State Department interpreted the July 26 order more liberally in Japan's favor. By interpreting aviation fuel to mean high-octane aviation fuel, Japan could still obtain middle-octane fuel needed for its airplanes.

On September 24, however, Roosevelt established an embargo of scrap iron and steel to all countries outside the Western Hemisphere except Great Britain.

July 30, 1940   A SPECIAL PAN-AMERICAN CONFERENCE AT HAVANA AGREES ON
                         A METHOD TO PREVENT THE TRANSFER OF NON-AMERICAN TER-
                         RITORY TO ANOTHER NON-AMERICAN POWER.

While urging congress to approve the Pittman-Bloom "no-transfer" resolution on June 18, Secretary Hull also invited the Pan-American nations to a meeting in Havana to obtain their cooperation in keeping German control from extending to possessions of the European nations conquered by the Nazis.

There had been frequent reports of Nazi activity in the Western Hemisphere and several events appeared to confirm those suspicions. On July 7, the Argentine police uncovered plans for an insurrection to establish a Nazi *Stützpunkt*. Ten days later, the Nacista Party of Chile failed in an effort to overthrow Chile's left-of-center Popular Front government. In addition, Hull feared that Vichy France's control of Martinique, Guadeloupe, and the Caribbean islands might bring German influence into the Western Hemisphere (see June 18, 1940).

At the Havana Conference, which convened on July 21, Argentina's attitude became the chief stumbling block to approval of the U.S. resolution on "no-transfer." The Argentines exported many commodities to Germany and Italy and did not wish to offend these nations. In addition, since 1833 Argentina had claimed the right to take the Falkland Islands from Britain and advocated that, perhaps, the American republics should individually occupy European possessions in the Western Hemisphere.

Eventually, however, Secretary Hull sent a personal appeal to Argentina's President Roberto Ortiz who had strongly supported the 1938 Declaration of Lima. Ortiz responded positively and Argentina ceased its opposition to the U.S. resolution while reserving the right not to ratify the Havana pact. The

Havana agreement not only opposed the transfer of non-American territory but set up a committee to administer any European territory attacked or under threat of being transferred. A collective trusteeship of the signatory American states would take over such territory pending its return to the original power once the war ended in Europe.

August 8, 1940   *THE BATTLE OF BRITAIN BEGINS AS GERMAN AIRCRAFT LAUNCH*
                          ATTACKS ON BRITISH AIRFIELDS AND VITAL INDUSTRIES.

Between August 8 and November 10, 1940, German bombing raids attacked British targets on a frequent but irregular basis. British casualties became as high as 600 per day in September. Finally, after an intensive attack which destroyed the industrial city of Coventry on November 10, German attacks became more sporadic. British defensive efforts resulted in the loss of 2,375 German airplanes to 800 British planes.

British bombers retaliated against Germany to some degree. Beginning on August 15, the Royal Air Force raided Berlin, Essen and other German cities. Britain's air attacks never achieved the size of Germany's in 1940, but they helped the morale of British citizens who valiantly endured the German attacks on England.

August 16, 1940   TO ASSIST THE LATIN AMERICAN NATIONS IN THEIR ECONOMIC
                           PROBLEMS, ROOSEVELT APPOINTS NELSON A. ROCKEFELLER AS
                           COORDINATOR OF COMMERCIAL AND CULTURAL RELATIONS AMONG
                           THE AMERICAN REPUBLICS.

During the Havana Conference (see July 30, 1940), the United States had little time to consider the economic problems and the methods for financing the defense projects of Latin American states. Therefore, on August 16, Roosevelt created an American Republics office under the Advisory Commission to the Council of National Defense. Rockefeller would centralize the U.S. efforts to assist the Pan-American nations to relieve their economic concerns. Roosevelt also aided Rockefeller in securing Export-Import Bank funds for the South American nations.

August 18, 1940   PRESIDENT ROOSEVELT AND CANADA'S PRIME MINISTER
                           MACKENZIE KING ANNOUNCE THE CREATION OF A PERMANENT
                           JOINT BOARD OF DEFENSE: THE OGDENSBURG AGREEMENT.

Although Canada was a belligerent at war against Germany, Roosevelt readily agreed that American defenses required close collaboration with Canada. Meeting with Prime Minister King in the president's railway car near Ogdensburg, New York, the two leaders adopted a plan for the joint defense of their nations. As announced on August 18, the agreement established a Joint Board of Defense consisting of four or five representatives of each nation. The board would consider the defense of the north half of the Western Hemisphere from possible attacks by sea, air, or land.

The Joint Board of Defense began meetings on August 24 and provided close cooperation between Canada and the United States throughout World War II.

September 3, 1940   GREAT BRITAIN AND AMERICA ANNOUNCE A DESTROYER-FOR-
                          BASES DEFENSE AGREEMENT.

In this agreement, President Roosevelt transferred 50 overage U.S. destroyers
to England, and Prime Minister Churchill gave the United States the right to
a 99-year lease on naval and air bases in Newfoundland, Bermuda, the Bahamas,
Jamaica, St. Lucia, Trinidad, Antigua, and British Guiana. This arrangement
originated from Churchill's June 18 request for destroyers which the British
navy needed to defend itself from German and Italian submarine attacks.

Roosevelt did not oppose the idea but required time to make certain that
the destroyer deal did not meet with strong, political opposition in America.
In August, Roosevelt offered Churchill the bases-destroyer barter plan, and
after some discussion, the British agreed. Roosevelt then sought congressional and public support in America. On several occasions in August,
Roosevelt commented on the defense advantages to America of having bases away
from the North American continent. When the response from various groups in
America appeared congenial, the president continued to work out the details
of the plan, and on September 3, Washington and London announced the joint
approval of the proposal. Although the deal was worked out without congressional sanction, the American public generally approved of the exchange. In
substance, however, this agreement moved American and British cooperation to
an even closer basis.

September 16, 1940   ROOSEVELT SIGNS THE SELECTIVE SERVICE AND TRAINING
                          ACT AS PASSED BY CONGRESS: THE FIRST PEACETIME PROGRAM
                          OF COMPULSORY MILITARY SERVICE FOR THE UNITED STATES.

This act provided for the registration of all men between 21 and 35 years of
age. As chosen in a draft lottery, the army would train 1,200,000 troops
and 800,000 reserves for one year.

On October 1, registration began and listed 16,400,000 men. The first
draft numbers were selected on October 29.

Passing this legislation presented some difficulty because of protests
by isolationist senators such as Nye and Wheeler. On August 2, 1940, Roosevelt informally and reluctantly expressed his approval of the legislation.
On August 17, Republican presidential candidate Willkie also approved the
measure. The bill passed both houses of congress on September 14.

September 27, 1940   JAPAN SIGNS A TRIPARTITE PACT WITH ITALY AND GERMANY,
                          MAKING THE ANTI-COMINTERN PACT A POLITICAL AND MILITARY
                          ALLIANCE.

Japan had been uncertain about its alliance with Rome and Berlin because it
could not comprehend the Nazi-Soviet pact of August 23, 1939, as reflecting
only Hitler's temporary policy. By July 27, 1940, however, the Konoye government pledged itself to take stronger measures to assure Japan's dominance
in East Asia. It decided to end the China Incident successfully and force
concessions from Britain in Shanghai and Burma, from the French in Indochina,
and from the Dutch East Indies. In August and September, the British withdrew from Shanghai, having previously agreed to close the Burma Road as a
supply route for Chiang Kai-shek's Chinese government. In addition, France
agreed to recognize Japan's predominant rights in Indochina, while the Dutch

undertook negotiations to supply Japan with oil for five years.

In the context of these Japanese policies toward Southeast Asia, the Japanese wanted German and Italian aid against the United States. Thus, the major part of the Axis military pact of September 27 was the three-power agreement to help each other if any were attacked by a power not currently involved in either the European or Sino-Japanese fighting. Obviously, this other power was the United States, which strongly objected to Japan's aggressive action in south and southeast Asia.

October 8, 1940   GERMAN TROOPS OCCUPY RUMANIA, BEGINNING A BALKAN CAMPAIGN BY THE AXIS POWERS. ITALY INVADES GREECE ON OCTOBER 28.

In the Balkans, only Greece offered stiff resistance to the Italian and German armies, holding out with British aid until April 23, 1941. Hungary joined the Axis alliance on November 20, Rumania on November 23, Bulgaria on March 1, 1941, and Yugoslavia on March 25. In Yugoslavia, a political coup on March 28 denied the Axis alliance and announced a neutral policy. As a result, Nazi troops moved into Yugoslavia, forcing the opposition into resistance by underground guerrilla warfare.

November 5, 1940   ROOSEVELT WINS THE PRESIDENTIAL ELECTION WITH A DECISIVE MARGIN OVER WILLKIE.

Although the character of Roosevelt's continued economic reform program was a factor in the 1940 election, the issue of war or peace became a vital element of the campaign by October, 1940. Willkie's claims that Roosevelt would lead the nation to war won the Republicans many ethnic votes. On October 30, at Boston, Roosevelt made unqualified assurances of his desire for peace. His famous words at Boston were: "I have said this before, but I shall say it again and again and again: Your boys are not going to be sent into any foreign wars."

Later, Roosevelt's critics complained of the deceit in the president's words, "be sent into any foreign wars." Post-election polls showed, however, that the possibility of war caused some people to vote for Roosevelt as the best leader in case of war (11%); only 2% favored Willkie because he would keep the nation out of war.

Although Willkie won 5 million more votes than Landon had in 1936, he won in only 10 states. The electoral count in 1940 was Roosevelt, 449; Willkie, 82.

November 12, 1940   THE "GERMANY FIRST" GRAND STRATEGY IS RECOMMENDED BY CHIEF OF NAVAL OPERATIONS HAROLD STARK.

Since 1937, the U.S. Navy had been reluctant to divorce itself from the "Japan First" strategy of its traditional Orange War Plans. Although President Roosevelt's influence had established a "Germany First" strategy under an amended Rainbow Four plan on June 27, 1940, CNO Stark and other naval officers continued to focus on the Pacific Ocean for their principal war effort. On November 12, Admiral Stark prepared an extensive analysis of global war strategy which assumed that Plan D (dog) was the best assumption for U.S.

policy. Plan Dog had three essential principles of action: (1) preserving
the integrity of the Western Hemisphere; (2) preparing offensive action in
the Atlantic to save Britain from Germany; and (3) avoiding war with Japan
by making U.S. proposals so specific that Japan would accept them or, if Japan
attacked, using defensive action in the Pacific.

On November 12, Stark presented his recommendations to the Joint Board,
General Marshall, Secretary of State Hull, and the president. The other offi-
cials ratified Stark's study and it became the basis for discussions with
Great Britain and Canada in 1941. See January 27, 1941.

December 29, 1940   PRESIDENT ROOSEVELT'S "FIRESIDE CHAT" OVER NATIONAL
                          RADIO NETWORKS EMPHASIZES THE AXIS POWERS' THREAT TO
                          AMERICA AND URGES AN AMERICAN PRODUCTION BUILD UP TO
                          BE THE "GREAT ARSENAL OF DEMOCRACY."

During the fall of 1940, Great Britain experienced financial problems in attempting to continue its war supplies purchases in America. On December 9,
Winston Churchill wrote a personal appeal to Roosevelt, outlining Britain's
need for more war implements and ships as well as its cash requirements to
pay for these materials. Although the potential for a German invasion of
the British Isles had diminished, England needed funds and arms to defeat
the Fascists, and asked Roosevelt to find "ways and means" to continue the
flow of supplies to Britain.

By December 12, Roosevelt had conceived the Lend-Lease program to aid
Britain (see January 6, 1941), but he decided to prepare the way for the favorable U.S. reception of this program. On December 20, he established the
Office of Production Management under William D. KNUDSEN to coordinate defense
production and to speed all aid "short of war" to Great Britain and other
anti-Axis nations.

In this context, Roosevelt's speech of December 29 further stimulated
American opinion to provide aid to the democracies. Emphasizing that events
abroad affected America, Roosevelt said that democracy and the United States
faced their most serious challenge since Jamestown was founded in 1607. If
Great Britain fell, the president said, all the world would be threatened by
Fascist militarism. To meet this threat, the United States would send all
possible aid to opponents of aggression. There would be less likelihood of
the United States' facing war if the United States supported other nations
than if the United States waited for others to be defeated. While any course
of action was risky, providing aid to the people of Europe fighting aggression
would save America from the agony of war. "We," he said, "must be the great
arsenal of democracy. For us this is an emergency as serious as war itself."

Roosevelt's speech proved one of his most popular and effective. Of
those who heard the speech, a poll showed that 80% agreed with and only 12%
opposed his argument. Moreover, 76% of the public heard the speech, the largest number recorded for a presidential speech.

1941

January 6, 1941   THE PRESIDENT'S STATE-OF-THE-UNION MESSAGE INFORMS THE
                   NATION OF HIS PROPOSAL FOR A LEND-LEASE PROGRAM AND
                   ENUNCIATES THE "FOUR FREEDOMS."

Having prepared the way for a lend-lease bill during his December 29, 1940,
speech, the president in his annual message to congress indicated his intention to send congress a bill to support peoples who were resisting aggression.
This, he said, was the best means to keep "war from our Hemisphere" and to
oppose aggressors. Indicating the common objectives of the democratic powers
in their fight against totalitarian fascism, Roosevelt declared that victory
over the aggressors would mean a world "founded upon four essential human
freedoms": the freedom of speech, of religion, from want, and from fear. For
passage of the Lend-Lease Act see March 11, 1941.

January 27, 1941   HIGH-RANKING MILITARY OFFICERS OF THE UNITED STATES,
                   BRITAIN, AND CANADA CONVENE MEETINGS IN WASHINGTON TO
                   COORDINATE CONTINGENCY WAR PLANS.

These staff talks were to coordinate American and British activity in the
Atlantic and Pacific Oceans. American and British cooperative discussion
had been informally pursued since December 23, 1937, when Captain Ingersoll
was sent to London by the president. During the summer of 1940, American
officers visited London to observe firsthand British experiences in the Battle
of Britain.
    The meetings from January 27 to March 29 were conducted in secret. The
British officers arrived as members of a British purchasing mission. By March
29, the staff officers formulated ABC-1, a coordinated war plan that emphasized a strategy to defeat Germany first, an analysis similar to Admiral
Stark's Plan Dog of November 12, 1940. Although President Roosevelt did not
technically approve ABC-1, it was the basis for Rainbow Five war plan of the
U.S. Joint Board of the Army and Navy and of a November, 1941, revision of
Rainbow Five drawn up to reflect Japan's aggression in southeast Asia during
the summer of 1941.
    According to ABC-1 (and Rainbow Five), a war with Japan should be delayed
or avoided as long as possible. If Japan attacked, the U.S. fleet would fight
defensively in the Pacific until the German defeat was certain. Any American
offensive action in the Pacific would be designed to weaken Japan's economy
or protect Singapore, the strategic point Churchill considered vital to the
British Commonwealth.

March 5, 1941   AN AMERICAN AGREEMENT WITH PANAMA PERMITS THE UNITED
                            STATES TO EXTEND AIR DEFENSES FOR THE CANAL BEYOND
                            THE CANAL ZONE.

Roosevelt and the Republic of Panama informally agreed that the threat of
war in Europe required additional air bases to protect the canal for the duration of the war crisis. This agreement became the basis for a formal treaty
signed with Panama on May 18, 1942.

March 11, 1941   CONGRESS APPROVES THE LEND-LEASE ACT.

On January 10, Democratic leaders introduced H.R. 1776 as the Lend-Lease Bill
entitled "An Act to Further Promote the Defense of the United States, and
for Other Purposes." The legislation authorized the president to "sell,
transfer title to, exchange, lease, lend, or otherwise dispose of ... any
defense article" to countries whose defense was deemed "vital to the defense
of the United States." The president would decide if repayment would be "in
kind or property, or any other direct or indirect benefit" he thought satisfactory.
    Although the Lend-Lease Bill had safe majorities in both houses of con-
gress, the isolationists attacked the measure and required several amendments,
none of which seriously hurt the measure. The most extreme isolationist assertion about the proposal was a remark by Senator Burton Wheeler. The senator called the act the "New Deal's Triple A foreign policy; it will plow
under every fourth American boy." The amendments which Roosevelt agreed to
placed a time limit on his authority, required periodic reports and consultation with the army and navy on defense equipment, and prevented use of the
U.S. Navy to transfer Lend-Lease goods.
    On March 11, the amended bill passed the Senate by a vote of 60 to 31;
the House by 317 to 17. The initial Lend-Lease Bill authorized expenditures
of $7 billion. From 1941 to 1945, Lend-Lease aid amounted to $50,226,845,387.

April 3, 1941   GERMAN TROOPS COMMANDED BY GENERAL ROMMEL REINFORCE
                            THE ITALIANS IN LIBYA AND BEGIN A COUNTERATTACK TO
                            DEFEAT THE BRITISH.

The North African fighting began on September 13, 1940, when Italian armies
invaded Egypt from Libya. By December 8, a British offensive drove the Italians out of Egypt and captured Tobruk. In addition, British Imperial forces
defeated the Italians in the Somaliland and Ethiopia, liberating Addis Ababa
on April 6, 1941.
    To regain the offensive, Hitler sent General Erwin Rommel to North Africa
with a German army. Rommel's ability and the fact that the British sent
60,000 troops to assist Greece forced the British to retreat in Libya, returning to the Egyptian frontier on May 29, 1941.

April 9, 1941   THE UNITED STATES AND DENMARK MAKE AN AGREEMENT WHICH
                            PROVIDES RIGHTS FOR U.S. DEFENSE BASES IN GREENLAND.

Secretary of State Hull and Danish Minister Henrik de Kauffmann signed this
pact, which effectively permitted the U.S. occupation of Greenland for the

duration of the war. Greenland had normally been considered part of the Western Hemisphere, and following the Nazi conquest of Denmark, both England and
the United States feared that the Germans might occupy that large Atlantic
island.

Although the Hitler-controlled government in Copenhagen rejected this
agreement and recalled Kauffmann from his post, the United States did not recognize the recall and continued to accept Kaufmann as the representative of
the Danish people.

April 11, 1941   ROOSEVELT INFORMS CHURCHILL THAT THE U.S. NAVY WILL
                          PATROL A U.S. SECURITY ZONE WHICH INCLUDES GREENLAND
                          AND THE AZORES ISLANDS.

In accordance with the Lend-Lease Act, Roosevelt began to aid British convoys
in what became known as the "BATTLE OF THE ATLANTIC" or the "UNDECLARED WAR."
With America committed to offer $7 billion of goods to the Allies (mostly to
Britain), the British ships required aid to assure their safety. German submarine war had previously sunk 688,000 gross tons between September 3, 1939,
and April 9, 1940, and another 2,314,000 gross tons by March 17, 1941.

Initially, U.S. escorts of British ships had been considered the best
method, but for political reasons, Roosevelt decided the air and navy patrol
of a security zone would involve less risk and be acceptable to the majority
of Americans. To patrol this zone, Roosevelt eventually brought 25% of the
Pacific fleet to the Atlantic. He decided, however, not to publicly acknowledge this move. He and Hull desired to retain the naval base at Pearl Harbor
as a continued symbol of U.S. concern for Japanese aggression.

April 13, 1941   JAPAN AND RUSSIA SIGN A MUTUAL NON-AGGRESSION PACT.

Until the conclusion of this neutrality pact between Tokyo and Russia, Roosevelt and Hull considered the possibility that Japan would move north against
Russia rather than south against Singapore and the Dutch East Indies. Hitler,
however, encouraged Tokyo to move to attack Singapore. By obtaining Russian
neutrality in the north, the Japanese could begin action in Indochina during
June and July, 1941.

April 15, 1941   PRESIDENT ROOSEVELT ISSUES AN EXECUTIVE ORDER AUTHO-
                          RIZING RESERVE OFFICERS AND ENLISTED MEN TO JOIN GEN-
                          ERAL CHENNAULT'S AMERICAN VOLUNTEER GROUP ("FLYING
                          TIGERS") IN CHINA.

Although General of the Army Air Force Arnold opposed Claire Chennault's attempt to recruit pilots to fly for the Chinese, Roosevelt and Secretary of
the Treasury Morgenthau backed Chennault's suggestion. The Chinese had bought
P-40 fighter planes and needed pilots and mechanics to fly and maintain them.

Following the president's approval, Chennault's followers recruited about
one hundred men who left for China on July 10, 1941. A second contingent
left for China in November, 1941. These volunteers became famous as the "flying tigers" because of the emblem painted on the nose of their planes.
Throughout the war, Chennault's pilots bombed, strafed, harassed, and shot
down Japanese aircraft, but contrary to Chennault's expectation, these planes

were not sufficient to make up for Chinese military shortcomings.

April 27, 1941   AMERICAN, BRITISH, AND DUTCH NAVAL OFFICERS CONCLUDE
                          HIGH-LEVEL STAFF PLANNING SESSIONS AT SINGAPORE.

These sessions at Singapore were announced publicly when they began on April
21. Roosevelt hoped they would provide a symbol of American concern for potential Japanese action in southeast Asia. British naval officers sought
American assistance in defending that region because the Royal Navy had been
largely shifted to the Atlantic and Mediterranean regions. In coordination
with ABC-1 war plans formulated at Washington between January 27 and March 29,
the Singapore conference prepared ABCD-1 as coordinated efforts to defend
the region between Singapore, the Dutch East Indies, and Australia. One consequence of this and other discussions was Roosevelt's decision on July 26
to reinforce the Philippine Islands as a defensive base. See July 26, 1941.

May 6, 1941   PRESIDENT ROOSEVELT DESIGNATES THAT CHINA IS ELIGIBLE
                          FOR LEND-LEASE ASSISTANCE.

This executive action inaugurated a direct U.S. aid program to the Chinese
Nationalist government of Chiang Kai-shek. Over the next five years, Chiang's
government received $1.5 billion from America. China received only about 3%
of the total Lend-Lease aid given during World War II, because Anglo-American
war plans gave China a low military priority and because Japan's occupation
of China's coastline required all goods to be airlifted to China's interior
from India or Burma. Most Lend-Lease aid went to Great Britain and Russia
to fight against Germany. American forces performed the largest share of
the fighting that defeated Japan in the Pacific theater of war.

May 12, 1941   DISCUSSIONS BETWEEN SECRETARY OF STATE HULL AND JAPAN'S
                          AMBASSADOR KICHISABURO NOMURA REACH A COMPLICATED MIS-
                          UNDERSTANDING.

Following Nomura's arrival as ambassador in February, 1941, Hull undertook
frequent meetings with him to explore possible solutions to U.S.-Japanese
disputes in east Asia. The talks had been inspired in part by a White House
visit of two Roman Catholic clerics on January 23. Bishop James E. Walsh
and Father James M. Drought of the Catholic Mission Society of Maryknoll had
been in Tokyo and met Japanese Foreign Minister Yosuke MATSUOKA. They gave
Roosevelt a memorandum containing their understanding of a Japanese offer to
settle disagreements with Washington. Although Hull and Roosevelt were skep-
tical, they pursued any possible avenue to peace as long as no U.S. principles
were sacrificed.
    Although Nomura told Hull he did not know about the Drought-Walsh talks
with Matsuoka, this gap was soon filled when two other Japanese emissaries
arrived in Washington: Tadao Wikawa, a banker, and Colonel Hideo Iwakuro, an
army spokesman. They knew Drought and Walsh and the four men collaborated
in drawing up a proposal for a U.S.-Japanese agreement which Iwakuro and
Drought composed and sent to Hull on April 9.
    Many points in the April 9 memorandum appeared acceptable to Hull, but
those regarding China's status were not. Because these latter points could

be negotiated, Hull met Nomura on April 14 and 16, telling the ambassador
that if Tokyo officially offered the Iwakuro-Drought memo, it could be the
basis of negotiation. Hull also enumerated four basic U.S. principles that
Japan had to respect: (1) territorial integrity, (2) non-interference in another country, (3) equality of commercial opportunity, and (4) changes in
the status quo to be made only by peaceful means.

Nomura sent the April 9 Iwakuro-Drought draft to Tokyo, together with
Hull's four principles and Hull's statements about the April 9 draft.
Nomura's message became garbled in the trans-Pacific communications. Because
Foreign Minister Matsuoka never recognized Wikawa and Iwakuro as official
representatives or as Nomura's "associates," Tokyo's officials believed the
April 9 draft originated with Hull. Many sections of the proposal favored
Japan. Therefore, the Japanese Foreign Office accepted it as a basis of dis-
cussion, adding other requirements to benefit Tokyo.

In fact, Hull not only did not originate the proposal, he generally disliked it. The important parts of the April 9 proposal were:

1. Japan would join the Axis in the war only if a nation not presently
    at war should aggressively attack Germany or Italy. Japan would
    decide who was aggressive.

2. The United States would request that Chiang Kai-shek negotiate with
    Japan on the following basis:

    (a) Japan would gradually withdraw its troops;

    (b) no territorial acquisitions except that Japan would possess
        Manchukuo (Manchuria);

    (c) no indemnities;

    (d) return to the "open door" as the United States and Japan would
        interpret;

    (e) Chiang to form a coalition with the Nanking government of Wang
        Ching-wei;

    (f) economic cooperation between China and Japan;

    (g) a joint Chinese-Japanese defense against communism.

3. If Chiang Kai-shek refused to negotiate, the United States would
    discontinue aid to China.

4. The United States would resume normal trade with Japan and would
    assist Tokyo in obtaining oil, rubber, tin, and nickel.

Acting under the misunderstanding that the April 9 proposal was Hull's,
Tokyo enlarged the demands that were already unsatisfactory to Hull. In the
"Confidential Memorandum" given to Hull on May 12, Tokyo accepted the proposed
basis for the Chinese peace talks. However, Matsuoka altered other parts of
the April 9 proposal as follows:

1. Japan joined the Axis to prevent other nations (i.e., America) from
    joining the European war. The United States must agree not to take
    aggressive measures or assist one nation against another in Europe.
    Furthermore, the United States and Japan would act "speedily to re-
    store peace in Europe."

2. The United States should sign a secret protocol or make a pledge to stop aid to Chiang if he did not negotiate.

3. In addition to normal trade, the Philippines' independence should be guaranteed by the United States and Japan.

4. The United States should end discrimination against Japanese immigration.

Because Hull believed the April 9 memo was Japan's first proposal (not Hull's as Tokyo thought), the Secretary of State thought Japan had enlarged its earlier requests. To the contrary, when Hull offered a response to Nomura on May 16, Tokyo thought the United States was demanding more concessions than on April 19.

In responding to the May 12 memo, Hull's note to Nomura on May 16 included the following points:

1. Hitler, not the United States or Great Britain, was the aggressor in Europe. Other nations reacted in self-defense. Hitler must withdraw from his conquests and stop aggression, not the anti-Fascist nations.

2. The U.S. attitude toward Europe was self-defense. Japan must declare that its Axis alliance did not affect its negotiations on the Far East.

3. Japanese and Chinese peace talks should be on the basis of friendship, respect for sovereignty, a scheduled Japanese withdrawal, equal commercial opportunity, and negotiations about Manchuria's future.

4. There could be no provisions for the United States to halt its aid to China.

As historian Robert J.C. Butow's detailed study of the early Hull-Nomura talks indicates, this original misconception of proposals between Hull and Tokyo continually plagued the 1941 negotiations. The efforts of Father Drought and his colleagues were well intended but did not bring salutary results.

In order to continue the talks, Hull accepted the May 12 Japanese memo as the basis of discussion, hoping to persuade Nomura to modify his country's extreme demands. There were other conversations between Hull and Nomura on June 15 and June 21. Hull received new suggestions from Nomura and offered the American objections to the continued unacceptable demands of Tokyo. At this juncture, Japanese aggression in Indochina caused President Roosevelt to take firm action against Japan. See July 26, 1941.

May 27, 1941   PRESIDENT ROOSEVELT ANNOUNCES AN UNLIMITED NATIONAL
                         EMERGENCY.

In proclaiming this emergency, Roosevelt made an address to congress which described the threat to the Western Hemisphere resulting from the Nazi occupation of French possessions in Africa which reached to Dakar on the western extremity of Africa across from Brazil. The Battle of the Atlantic, he said, required a victory for the British fleet. To assist, the United States needed to build more ships and to help Britain cut its losses from submarine attacks.

Roosevelt's speech did not outline specific measures to meet the emergency. Yet the positive public reaction to the speech enabled the president to take some action in June. On June 14, he froze all German and Italian assets in the United States, and on June 16, he ordered all German and Italian consulates to be closed.

June 22, 1941   GERMANY LAUNCHES AN INVASION OF THE SOVIET UNION.

The German attack did not surprise Washington. Earlier, England and the United States had learned about the German preparations and had warned Stalin of the Nazi plans. As soon as the war began on the eastern front, Winston Churchill, who had since 1917 been an ardent anti-communist, welcomed the Soviets as a British ally. In Churchill's view, "any man or state who fights on against Nazidom will have our aid." Within two days, Roosevelt agreed (see June 23, 1941).

The Nazi invasion of Russia penetrated along a 2,000-mile front from Finland (which had allied with the Axis) to Rumania. The Germans overran the Ukraine and reached Leningrad by early September. Nazi armies reached the outskirts of Moscow before Russia undertook a counteroffensive in December, 1941.

June 23, 1941   PRESIDENT ROOSEVELT ANNOUNCES THE UNITED STATES WILL
                              AID THE SOVIET UNION'S WAR AGAINST GERMANY; HE DOES
                              NOT YET OFFER LEND-LEASE AID TO RUSSIA.

Following the announcement of the 1939 Nazi-Soviet pact, American relations with Russia had cooled considerably. When Russia attacked Poland and Finland, the United States requested a moral embargo on airplane and aviation supplies to Russia and tried to prevent all war exports to Russia. The Neutrality Act had not been invoked, because Roosevelt wished to aid Finland and not push Russia further into Germany's alliance.

Friendlier American overtures to the Soviet Union began after Japan signed the Tripartite Pact with the Axis on September 27, 1940. Undersecretary of State Welles began regular conversations with Soviet Ambassador Constantin Oumansky between September, 1940, and the spring of 1941, but he had no success in wooing Russia from the German alliance.

Prior to the German attack on June 22, the State Department seemed reluctant to assist Russia against the Nazis. The attack, however, caused a fast change in Hull's views. He immediately told Roosevelt and Welles, "We must give Russia all aid to the hilt." Subsequently, Welles told a press conference on June 23 that aid to Russia in some form would be vital to the defense of America. Welles reported that the president said that "Hitler's armies are today the chief dangers of the Americas."

Between July and November, U.S. aid to Russia was minimal. The president was seeking additional Lend-Lease aid for Britain and did not wish to bring the communist situation into the political arena in congress. The additional Lend-Lease funds passed congress on October 28, 1941, and on November 6, Roosevelt ordered a credit of $1 billion for Soviet aid, informing the Lend-Lease administrator that the U.S.S.R.'s defense was "vital to the defense of the United States." The United States and Russia signed a master Lend-Lease agreement on June 11, 1942.

July 3, 1941   ROOSEVELT REORGANIZES THE ARMY AIR FORCE TO GIVE IT
                       GREATER AUTONOMY AND AN AIR WAR PLANS DIVISION.

Since October 11, 1938, President Roosevelt had shown his interest in air-
bombing operations. To give greater effect to this in 1941, he worked with
Army Chief of Staff General George MARSHALL to organize the Army Air Forces
under General Henry H. ARNOLD as Commanding General with an Air Staff similar
to the Army General Staff. Lieutenant Colonel Harold L. GEORGE was selected
to head the Air War Plans Division, and by September, Air War Plan-1 had been
prepared, giving the Air Force's bombers four tasks: a Western Hemispheric
air defense, an air offensive against Germany, tactical air operations for
an invasion of Europe, and other air operations to defeat the Axis powers.

July 7, 1941   THE PRESIDENT ANNOUNCES THAT U.S. MARINES HAVE LANDED
                       AND OCCUPIED ICELAND.

In 1940, the British occupied Iceland after the fall of Denmark. In March,
1941, reports of German air and submarine activity in the area alarmed
Churchill and Roosevelt. A U.S. destroyer sent to the area had become involved in an incident with a German U-boat.
     As a result of this incident, Harry HOPKINS and Sumner Welles spoke with
Iceland's prime minister. On July 1, Iceland accepted U.S. protection and
the landing of the marines began on July 6. Because these marines had to be
supplied, the U.S. Navy convoyed vessels into Icelandic waters with British
and Canadian ships joining these convoys for protection.

July 26, 1941   ROOSEVELT FREEZES JAPANESE ASSETS AND REQUIRES LICENSES
                       FOR OIL SHIPMENTS TO JAPAN FOLLOWING JAPAN'S OCCUPATION
                       OF INDOCHINA. THE SAME DAY HE INCREASES THE DEFENSES
                       OF THE PHILIPPINE ISLANDS BY NAMING GENERAL MacARTHUR
                       AS COMMANDER OF JOINT U.S.-PHILIPPINE DEFENSE UNITS
                       AND ORDERING U.S. AIRCRAFT TO THOSE ISLANDS.

Japan's aggressive moves in southeast Asia in June and July, 1941, nearly
resulted in a complete break in American relations with Tokyo. Because American cryptanalysts had broken the Japanese diplomatic code in the spring of
1941, Hull and Roosevelt learned about Japan's planned action in Indochina,
but because of Nomura's negotiations in Washington, they hoped Tokyo would
delay such acts. The Japanese did not delay.
     On July 2, Japan's cabinet decided to move into Indochina toward Singa-
pore and the East Indies. On July 18, the Japanese demanded that France permit them to occupy eight air and two naval bases in southern Indochina. On
July 24, they began moving their armed forces into these bases. The previous
day, Undersecretary of State Welles warned Tokyo not to advance its forces
into threatening positions against the British and Dutch in southeast Asia,
but Ambassador Nomura could not change the decisions made in Tokyo.
     Desiring to delay a break in Japanese relations but to act more force-
fully to pressure Tokyo, Roosevelt took two actions between July 24 and 26,
1941. First, to attempt to placate Japan, he offered to neutralize southeast
Asia and guarantee equal access to all resources of the region (that is, Dutch
East Indies oil) if Japan withdrew from Indochina. At the same time, he announced that Japan's assets in the United States would be frozen and more

severe trade restrictions would be applied. Oil and gasoline might still be
shipped to Japan but an export license would be required before such shipments
took place.

Actually, Roosevelt's licensing order became a *de facto* oil embargo on
Japan between August and December 7, 1941. The president's policy was applied
vigorously by the government agencies processing the license applications.
Secretary of State Hull drew up licensing guidelines that were ambiguous.
As a result, the agents reviewing oil license applications found a reason to
reject all of them. When Roosevelt learned about the *de facto* oil embargo
in September, he let it stand rather than show weakness to Tokyo.

The decision on July 26 to increase the defense capacity of the Philippine Islands was a significant change in traditional U.S. policy. From 1922
to 1935, the Nine-Power Pact prevented the construction of fortifications in
the Philippines. After 1935, U.S. war plans continued to assume that the
Philippines could not be defended. When the Joint Board of the Army and Navy
prepared Rainbow Five War Plans in May, 1941, it included these prior decisions on the Philippines.

In July, however, Germany's attack on Russia relieved the Nazi threat
to the British Isles while Japan's aggression in southeast Asia threatened
the British and Dutch. Moreover, Britain had urged the U.S. Joint Board to
provide some tangible assistance to the British Commonwealth defenses in the
south Pacific. By reinforcing the Philippines, the United States could aid
Britain and, perhaps, deter further Japanese aggression. Strong defenses in
the Philippines, once established, would block the sea route between Japan
and the East Indies.

The attempt to build the Philippine defense was two-fold. First, General
Douglas MacArthur was recalled to active duty as the commander of American
and Philippine army units. MacArthur had helped the Philippine army to be
organized during the mid-1930's and was most sympathetic to the concept of
strongly defending that area. Second, at the suggestion of Air Force General
Arnold, Roosevelt ordered four groups of long-range B-17 bombers to be sent
to the Philippines as fast as possible. These bombers, once established at
Philippine bases, might sink Japanese ships or bomb Japan's bases in Formosa.

After the war plans were changed to defend the Philippines, military
estimates indicated that eight months would be the minimum time required before the Philippines would be adequately prepared. When Japan attacked on
December 7, 1941, MacArthur had only a few of the coastal defense preparations
completed. The air force preparations had barely begun. One group of B-17's
arrived in September, 1941; another group was en route and had reached Hawaii
on December 7.

In a continued attempt to delay further Japanese aggression, Secretary
Hull renewed his negotiations with Nomura on August 6. Hull preferred not
to continue these talks because of Tokyo's duplicity in acting aggressively
at the same time that Hull and Nomura negotiated between May and June 21.
He agreed to try again because, as he remarked, "From now on our major objective with regard to Japan was to give ourselves more time to prepare our
defenses."

August 12, 1941   SECRET MEETINGS BETWEEN ROOSEVELT AND CHURCHILL, DURING
                          WHICH THE ATLANTIC CHARTER IS PREPARED, COME TO AN END.

Since December, 1940, Roosevelt had sought an occasion to meet with Prime
Minister Churchill in order to dramatize for U.S. and world opinion the

principles at stake in the fight against the Nazis. Arrangements were made in July, and on August 9, 1941, British naval ships brought Churchill to Placentia Bay off Newfoundland where the two leaders held their first meeting on board the president's ship, *Augusta*, a heavy cruiser. The major U.S. participants in the talks were General Marshall and Admiral Stark, Undersecretary of State Welles, Lend-Lease Administrator W. Averell Harriman, and Harry Hopkins.

In addition to the Atlantic Charter, the Roosevelt-Churchill meeting resulted in the president's commitment to a larger U.S. Navy role in the Atlantic. Churchill pleaded with Roosevelt to obtain a declaration of war from congress. The president refused because he feared a congressional debate on the issue would divide the nation seriously. To offset Churchill's pleas, Roosevelt agreed to occupy the Azores Islands and to escort British convoys. The Azores project was dropped in September by mutual agreement between Churchill and Roosevelt. The naval escort was undertaken almost immediately (see September 6, 1941).

The Atlantic Charter was the historic document formulated by Roosevelt and Churchill between August 9 and 12. The charter was a joint declaration of principles issued by Washington and London on August 14. It was not an alliance but became the basis for Allied war objectives after December 7, 1941. The important points in the charter were:

1. Both nations renounced the desire for territorial or other aggrandizement at the expense of other peoples.

2. The people concerned must decide territorial changes for themselves.

3. People have a right to choose their own government.

4. With due respect to existing obligations (i.e., Britain's Commonwealth preference duties), trade restrictions would be eased and equal access given to raw materials.

5. Cooperation would aid the economic security of all peoples of the world.

6. There must be freedom from want and fear.

7. There must be freedom of the seas.

8. There would be disarmament of aggressors after the war, pending creation of a permanent peace structure.

By September 15, 1941, the Soviet Union and 14 other non-Axis nations had endorsed the Atlantic Charter.

August 12, 1941   WITH ONLY A ONE-VOTE DIFFERENCE, THE HOUSE OF REPRESENTATIVES APPROVES LEGISLATION TO EXTEND THE DUTY OF SELECTIVE SERVICE DRAFTEES FOR ANOTHER 18 MONTHS.

The House vote was 203 to 202. The Senate had approved the measure by a vote of 46 to 30 with 21 senators not voting.

Congressional opposition to an amended Selective Service measure built up in June when Roosevelt approved a War Department recommendation to extend the service of army draftees and National Guardsmen for the duration of the emergency and to have congress eliminate the Selective Service Act provision that limited the number of draftees to 900,000 and prevented them from serving outside the Western Hemisphere.

On July 21, Roosevelt sent a strongly worded message to congress, saying "We ... cannot afford to speculate with the security of America." If the extension were rejected, he said, our "small" army would disintegrate in two months. "The responsibility rests solely with Congress." Roosevelt had already agreed to drop the amendments regarding the use of draftees outside the hemisphere and increasing the size of the army. Yet, as the House vote indicated, the nation was divided on this issue. A public-opinion poll at that time indicated that only 51% of the nation favored the extension of U.S. military service.

August 17, 1941   ROOSEVELT AND HULL MEET WITH AMBASSADOR NOMURA TO WARN JAPAN AGAINST ANY FURTHER AGGRESSION IN EAST ASIA.

The August 17 meeting resulted from a decision by Roosevelt and Churchill at the Atlantic Conference to warn Japan that future Japanese "encroachments" in the southwest Pacific "might lead to an American-Japanese war." Before informing Nomura of this warning, however, the State Department deleted "war" and added that the United States might "take any and all steps" to safeguard its legitimate rights. In addition, Roosevelt told Nomura that this statement was simply an informal informational memo, not a formal warning.

During the August 17 meeting, Nomura proposed that Roosevelt consider a possible meeting with Premier Konoye in order that the two leaders could resolve all outstanding disputes. The president agreed to consider this suggestion, and on August 28, Hull told Nomura that a high-level meeting could take place if there were a prior agreement in principle on what points would be ratified by the leaders. Any high-level meeting that was inconclusive, Hull said, would do more harm than good. Nomura accepted this suggestion, and the possible Konoye-Roosevelt meeting highlighted U.S.-Japanese discussions in September and October, 1941. See October 16, 1941.

August 25, 1941   BRITISH AND SOVIET FORCES BEGIN THE OCCUPATION OF IRAN.

In a fashion similar to the British-Russian agreement before World War I, the Russian forces took over Azerbaijan and provinces in the north of Iran; the British occupied the southern region and protected the Persian Gulf.

September 6, 1941   PRESIDENT ROOSEVELT ANNOUNCES HIS "SHOOT-ON-SIGHT" ORDERS TO U.S. NAVAL PATROLS IN THE ATLANTIC DEFENSIVE ZONES.

Although it was not publicly known on September 6, Roosevelt had promised Churchill at the Atlantic Conference (see August 12, 1941) to escort British convoys in waters as far east as Iceland and the Azores and to attack any U-boat showing itself. These escort duties began on September 1, and on September 4, a U.S. destroyer, the *Greer*, was shot at by a German submarine. On September 6, Roosevelt referred to the attack on the *Greer* in announcing to the nation that, henceforth, American naval vessels "will no longer wait until Axis submarines lurking under the water ... strike their deadly blow first."

"We have sought no shooting war with Hitler," Roosevelt said. "We do not seek it now.... But when you see a rattlesnake poised to strike, you do not wait until he has struck before you crush him." Roosevelt realized, he told the national radio audience, that he took a grave step and he had thought and prayed about it. But, he asserted, "In the protection of your Nation and mine it cannot be avoided."

The president's announcement of a virtual "undeclared war" on German ships had been revealed in a misleading fashion. He had not accurately described the circumstances of the attack on the *Greer* or the fact that the *Greer* instigated the attack by cooperating with British aircraft in seeking to destroy the U-boat.

Because newsman in Washington heard rumors about the *Greer* incident which differed from Roosevelt's implied version of the German attack, the Senate Naval Affairs Committee prepared hearings on the incident. By early October, opposition senators revealed a letter from Admiral Stark dated September 20, 1941, which described the *Greer* incident in a different fashion than the president's words had done.

Stark's memorandum to Senator David I. Walsh of the Senate Naval Affairs Committee described the attack as follows: (1) a British airplane spotted the German sub and informed the captain of the *Greer*, which was on escort duty in Icelandic waters. The plane and the U.S. destroyer chased the sub for three hours and the plane dropped four depth charges; (2) the sub fired a torpedo at the *Greer* which crossed about 100 yards astern; (3) the *Greer* dropped eight depth charges and the sub fired another torpedo; (4) the *Greer* lost the sub but after a two-hour search discovered it again and dropped 11 more depth charges; (5) after another three-hour search, the *Greer* proceeded to Iceland.

The October news reports of Stark's letter did not result in a loud cry of outrage in the United States. Although historian Charles Beard and other revisionist writers criticized Roosevelt for his deviousness, the U.S. public in October, 1941, apparently wished to attack Germany as much as possible without going to war. Historian Robert Dallek admits Roosevelt's deviousness in a "good cause" but contends that the public did not oppose the president because Americans did not want to have to choose between war and no action. Opinion polls indicated 70% of the public wanted to stay out of war but 70% also wanted to do everything possible to defeat Hitler. Roosevelt was, however, setting a precedent used by later presidents to manipulate public opinion in a "good cause" which could also be used in a "bad cause."

October 16, 1941   PREMIER KONOYE RESIGNS; GENERAL TOJO BECOMES PREMIER TWO DAYS LATER. DISCUSSIONS ABOUT A ROOSEVELT-KONOYE SUMMIT CONFERENCE END.

Although the prospects for a Konoye-Roosevelt meeting were never good, the end of Konoye's cabinet and the rise of General Tojo as premier signified the victory of Japan's military hard-liners. On September 6, Japan's Imperial Conference had come the closest ever to seeking a compromise with Britain and America. The conference agreed to use diplomatic means to secure certain minimum demands from London and Washington. Although Japan would agree not to use Indochina as a base of operations to the south and would suspend military activity in the Far East, the Japanese would not leave occupied areas or permit interference in China. Unless drastically revised in negotiations, these Japanese terms would never have been accepted by the Western powers.

Thus, Japan's minimum demands were not acceptable to the United States.

In September and early October both Hull in Washington and Grew in Tokyo searched for a method to obtain agreement. Nevertheless, on October 2, Hull's note to Nomura indicated that basic disagreements precluded a Roosevelt-Konoye meeting. Neither Konoye nor the less moderate members of the Japanese Imperial Conference would accept terms that included the withdrawal of Japanese forces from any area under their control by conquest or force. On October 12, Tojo, Japan's Minister of War, rejected any withdrawal even as a point of principle on which details would be worked out at a future date.

Tojo now insisted that Konoye stop all discussions of a meeting with Roosevelt. To effect this, Tojo proposed that Konoye's cabinet resign and a new ministry be formed. Konoye complied by resigning on October 16. Two days later Tojo formed a new government. Although Tojo agreed to continue talks with America and sent Saburo KURUSU to aid Nomura in Washington, an Imperial Conference of November 5 adopted a more restricted timetable for concluding discussions with the United States. (See November 26, 1941.)

October 17, 1941   ELEVEN U.S. SEAMEN DIE WHEN A GERMAN SUBMARINE ATTACKS
THE DESTROYER *KEARNY*.

As in the case of the *Greer* (see September 6, 1941), the *Kearny* was fired on by a German submarine in Icelandic waters. The Germans fired three torpedoes, with one hitting on the ship's starboard side near the forward fire room. The destroyer was knocked out of action and went to its port in Iceland for repairs.

Although the Navy Department announced the attack and Secretary of State Hull denounced the Germans for an act of piracy, Roosevelt did not refer to the attack until he made a Navy Day Address on October 27, 1941. In that message, he misled the public into believing the Germans shot first. He said: "We have wished to avoid shooting. But the shooting has started. And history has recorded who has fired the first shot.... America has been attacked."

In contrast to Roosevelt's words, Secretary of the Navy Knox issued a report on October 29 which said that the *Kearny* had gone to the aid of a convoy of merchant ships which were being attacked by German submarines. Knox continued: "On arriving at the scene of the attack the U.S.S. *Kearny* dropped depth bombs when she sighted a merchant ship under attack by a submarine. Some time afterward three torpedo tracks were observed approaching the U.S.S. *Kearny*." One of the three torpedoes hit the U.S. destroyer. Thus, while the convoy of ships was under attack first, the *Kearny* fired first at the German submarine. For further comments on Roosevelt's incomplete statements about such attacks, see September 6, 1941.

October 30, 1941   A U.S. DESTROYER, THE *REUBEN JAMES*, IS ATTACKED AND
SUNK BY A GERMAN SUBMARINE; 115 AMERICANS DIE.

The *Reuben James* was on convoy escort duty near Iceland when the German submarine attacked. The incident aided Roosevelt in convincing some congressmen that the U.S. neutrality laws should be repealed.

November 5, 1941   JAPAN'S IMPERIAL CONFERENCE MAKES THE DECISION THAT
                          WILL LEAD TO WAR. IF WASHINGTON HAS NOT AGREED TO
                          COMPROMISE BY NOVEMBER 25, JAPAN WILL LAUNCH MILITARY
                          ACTION IN SOUTHEAST ASIA AND HAWAII.

Outside the Japanese political groups, more extreme military factions pushed
for a firm solution to the dispute with America. On November 2, a Liaison
Conference of extremist Japanese civilian and military officials sent recommendations to the Imperial Conference which the latter group adopted on November 5.

The Japanese decided to submit a set of demands for the United States
to accept (Plan A). If Washington rejected Japan's proposal, a second proposal (Plan B) would be issued as an ultimatum. Thus, the Japanese had set
a series of deadlines for shifting from negotiations to war.

Ambassador Nomura presented Plan A to Hull on November 7, 1941. From
that time until December 7, the United States faced the alternative of accepting Japan's demands or expecting further Japanese aggression. See November
26, 1941.

November 6, 1941   ROOSEVELT IDENTIFIES THE SOVIET UNION AS BEING ELIGIBLE
                          FOR LEND-LEASE.

On June 23, when the president announced that the United States would aid the
Soviet Union in its war with the Nazis, he did not indicate what that aid
would be and hesitated to apply the Lend-Lease Act. On June 24, he released
$39 million of frozen Russian assets and the next day decided not to invoke
the Neutrality Act, which would have prohibited U.S. ships from carrying goods
to Russia. Then, on July 23, he sent $22 million of war materials to Russia.

The president's most significant decision in July was to send his close
advisor Harry Hopkins on a mission to Moscow. Hopkins talked with Stalin
late in July and returned to report to Roosevelt just before the Atlantic
Conference of August 9. Hopkins said Stalin was confident that the Soviet
armies would eventually triumph, although a long war was expected. Stalin
wanted the United States to send anti-aircraft guns, aluminum for planes,
50-caliber machine guns, and 30-caliber rifles. Both Roosevelt and Churchill
agreed that they should provide all possible aid to Russia.

Washington planners worked on a Victory Program during the summer of
1941 to increase U.S. production which would supply Britain, Russia, and the
American armed forces. In September, Lend-Lease Administrator Harriman visited Moscow with Britain's Lord Beaverbrook to discuss Russia's military
needs. Because the Russians had 280 army divisions (2 million men) engaging
over 3 million German and Axis-power troops, the eastern front was crucial
to the Allied effort.

Prior to the announcement of Lend-Lease aid to Russia, Roosevelt undertook methods to convince possible American opponents of Russia to accept such
aid. He encouraged American Catholics to accept Russian aid as a necessity
and obtained a petition of 100 Protestants who supported help for Russia.
Nevertheless, little opposition appeared to the idea of providing Lend-Lease
to Russia. After congress approved $6 billion additional Lend-Lease funding
on October 24, the president allocated part of it for Russia. His decision
was formalized on November 6 when he declared that assistance for Russia under
the Lend-Lease Act was approved because its fight was "vital to the defense
of the United States."

November 17, 1941   THE PRESIDENT SIGNS LEGISLATION THAT EFFECTIVELY RE-
PEALS THE NEUTRALITY LAWS PASSED BETWEEN 1935 AND 1939.

The restricted portions of the neutrality laws were section 2, excluding U.S.
ships from belligerent ports; section 3, excluding ships from combat areas;
and section 6, forbidding the arming of U.S. merchant ships. Planning to
repeal each section separately, Roosevelt asked congress to repeal section 6
on October 6, 1941. When the Senate Foreign Relations Committee recommended
changes on October 25, it added sections 2 and 3, which Secretary Hull told
them needed to be abolished eventually.

By the time congress voted on the bill in November, German submarines
had damaged the destroyer *Kearny* (see October 17, 1941) which the president
said had been Germany's first shots on America. The Senate passed the bill
easily on November 7, but the House vote was close. Largely on a partisan
vote, the House approved the repeal of sections 2, 3, and 6 by a vote of 212
to 194. The president signed the measure on November 17.

November 19, 1941   THE UNITED STATES AND MEXICO ANNOUNCE THE SETTLEMENT
OF AN OIL AND AGRARIAN EXPROPRIATION COMPENSATION
AGREEMENT.

Following Mexico's decision on March 18, 1938, to expropriate American and
British oil companies property, President Cardenas asserted his desire to compensate the oil companies for their property. Until 1941, however, the oil
companies avoided serious negotiations of the settlement because they hoped
to pressure Mexico into abrogating the expropriation act. The company's attempts failed, however, because of the desire of President Roosevelt and U.S.
Ambassador to Mexico Josephus Daniels to deal sympathetically with Mexico
and to make the Good Neighbor Policy work.

Daniels played a central role in averting strong State Department pressure in cooperating with the oil companies. Daniels was an old-time Democratic
progressive. As President Woodrow Wilson's Secretary of the Navy, Daniels
knew firsthand about the 1913 conflict between Mexican nationalists seeking
a better life for their people and the attempt of leaders such as Huerta to
return to the Diaz policy of benefiting foreign investors in Mexico. Consequently, Daniels took a strong stand against State Department bureaucrats
who supported the oil companies' viewpoint and knew little of the desires of
the Mexican populace and their backing for Cardenas' policies. Even Secretary
of State Hull succumbed to the oil lobbyist contention that Cardenas was a
communist who wished to create a Mexican Soviet as part of Moscow's world
revolution.

Daniels knew the oil lobbyists' propaganda was a lie and desired to back
Mexican leaders seeking a legal but Mexican solution to the issue. Thus,
while Hull catered to the oil companies by forbidding the U.S. Navy to purchase Mexican oil between 1938 and 1942, Daniels, with Roosevelt's approval,
urged the oil companies to negotiate a settlement with Mexico. Although the
oil managers sent Donald Richberg to discuss a settlement between March, 1939,
and January, 1940, they required Richberg to present such large demands that
Mexico could not accept them.

Two events finally led the oil companies and Hull to begin serious negotiations with Mexico. First, Harry Sinclair's oil company sent Patrick
Hurley to Mexico to conclude a settlement separate from that of the other
oil holders. Formerly Secretary of War under Herbert Hoover, Hurley achieved

a Mexican settlement in January, 1940, by which Sinclair Oil received nearly
$14 million.   Second, the oilmen's hope did not materialize that a conserva-
tive candidate for Mexico's presidency would win the election of 1940 or stage
a counterrevolution such as General Franco had done in Spain. The conservative candidate was General Juan Andreu Almazan. In the July 7, 1940, elections, Almazan lost to General Manuel Avita CAMACHO who was Cardenas' nominee
to succeed him. Although Almazan's followers predicted a revolution because
of a "corrupt election," no uprising occurred. Later, Almazan claimed the
oil companies did not give him the $200,000 they promised, but historians
have no evidence to corroborate the general's assertion.

Both Roosevelt and Daniels hailed Camacho's victory and Sinclair's independent agreement. Thus, in 1941 serious negotiations began in Washington.
The principal dispute was over the value of the U.S. oil properties that were
to be compensated. The oil companies demanded payment for their investment,
improvements, and, most significantly, the existing subsoil oil to which they
claimed title. Their estimated value was $450 to $500 million. Mexico
claimed the companies should be paid for investments and improvements less
depreciation. As Hull and his advisors examined the record they found that
the oilmen greatly exaggerated their claims. U.S. tax records of Jersey Standard, the largest U.S. holder, and a U.S. Interior Department study both indicated that the estimated property value was between $13.5 and $20 million.

Secretary Hull reached an agreement that satisfied him in September,
1941. The oilmen objected, however, continuing to claim compensation for
subsoil rights. When Jersey Standard again rejected Hull's agreement on November 13, Daniels and Roosevelt intervened to convince Hull that he should
sign the agreement without the oil companies' approval. Hull obliged and on
November 19, he and Mexican Ambassador Castillo Najera signed an exchange of
notes outlining the agreement.

The agreement finalized both the oil and agrarian claims of the United
States. Mexico promised to pay a total of $40 million over a 14-year period
to settle all oil and agrarian claims. Each government appointed an expert
to determine the amount owed to American oil companies. Mexico made an immediate down payment of $9 million. The United States agreed to spend up to
$40 million to stabilize the Mexican peso by purchasing 6 million ounces of
Mexican silver a month. The U.S. Export-Import Bank loaned Mexico $30 million
for road construction, in particular, for Mexico's section of the Pan-American
highway.

The U.S. oilmen were bitter, and rejected the settlement. Yet, after
some hesitation, they cooperated in supplying data for the U.S. expert, Morris
L. Cooke, to reach an exact estimate of their oil values without subsoil
rights for the future. Cooke, too, found that the oilmen's estimated values
were nowhere near $400 million. On April 18, 1942, Cooke and the Mexican
expert, Manuela J. Zevada, issued their report that the oil properties' value
was $23,995,991 plus interest since 1938 of $5 million. Jersey Standard's
holdings were $18,391,641, a figure corresponding to that made by State De-
partment geologists. These oil estimates did not, of course, include the
anticipated future oil profits which the oil companies included in their valuation.

November 26, 1941   ROOSEVELT AND HULL DECIDE NOT TO SEEK A *MODUS VIVENDI*
                            WITH JAPAN BUT REAFFIRM THAT JAPAN ACCEPT AMERICAN
                            PRINCIPLES TO SECURE PEACE IN EAST ASIA.

On November 5, Japan's Imperial Conference set a timetable for Japan's conclusion of negotiations. If the United States did not appease Japan by accepting the demands, Japan would wage war in the Pacific.

On November 7, Ambassador Nomura gave Hull a portion of Japan's Plan A
proposal for peace in east Asia; the remainder of the proposal was communi-
cated to Hull and Roosevelt on November 10. Plan A proposed Japanese requests
that were less satisfactory than those of May 12, 1941. Japan wanted the
"open door" principles to apply all over the world. Japan would withdraw
from China after peace was firmly established. This might take 25 years,
Nomura stated. Nomura's aide, Kurusu, brought no new proposals as Hull had
hoped. Consequently, Plan A could not be accepted by the United States. On
November 18, it was obvious that Hull's talks with Nomura and Kurusu could
not proceed on the basis of Plan A.

On November 20, Nomura presented Plan B to Hull. Essentially, Plan B
proposed a *modus vivendi*. Both sides would cease armed advances in southeast
Asia and the south Pacific, and commercial relations would be restored on the
basis existing before July 26, 1941. America would supply oil to Japan and
obtain Dutch cooperation in the East Indies. Finally, the United States was
to stop aiding Chiang Kai-shek's government in China.

As Hull and his staff began considering a response to Plan B, an ominous
warning arrived in the decoded messages of the Japanese foreign office. Exactly how much it meant to Hull at that time is uncertain, but Nomura and
Kurusu must have realized the implication of Tokyo's note. As translated by
America's "Magic" cryptanalysis, Tokyo's secret instructions to Nomura extended to November 29 the deadline for U.S. acceptance of Plan B. This extension was final, however. "This time we mean it that the deadline absolutely
cannot be changed. After that, things are automatically going to happen."
Tokyo had continued its preparations for war against Britain, the East Indies,
and the United States. After November 29, the momentum of those preparations
could not be cancelled by Japan.

In the State Department, U.S. officials first agreed on seeking the 90-
day *modus vivendi*. American Army and Navy officers believed 90 days' time
would just about complete preparations for defending the Philippines (see
July 26, 1941). If the United States offered Japan some "chicken feed" concessions for three months, Hull believed Nomura might accept them.

The *modus vivendi* was not, however, approved by some U.S. allies. Between November 20 and 26, Hull consulted with other diplomats concerned with
southeast Asia. The Netherlands agreed to the *modus vivendi* but Britain,
Australia, and China did not. Churchill approved part of the concept, but
Chiang Kai-shek vigorously opposed a *modus vivendi*.

On November 26, Hull and Roosevelt made a final decision on answering
Plan B, deciding not to offer a 90-day or any other *modus vivendi*. On November 25, Hull and Roosevelt met with Army Chief of Staff General Marshall,
Chief of Naval Operations Admiral Stark, and the Secretaries of War and the
Navy, Stimson and Knox. This war council approved the *modus vivendi* for 90
days as the best way to enable the Philippine defenses to be completed. Although Secretary of State Hull cautioned them that Japan might not agree, he
accepted the decision until sometime early the next day.

In a final conversation with Roosevelt on the morning of November 26,
Hull opposed the *modus vivendi*, largely on the basis of two reports he

received that morning. First, Winston Churchill wired Hull to complain of the *modus vivendi* and asserted that China was getting a "very thin diet." Second, Hull received a military report indicating Japanese troop movement in the area of Thailand and Burma, while five Japanese army divisions had steamed south out of Shanghai. Roosevelt also "blew up" at the news of Japan's clandestine activity in southeast Asia, actions that anticipated Japanese aggression in that region.

Hull's reports added to Roosevelt's dismay and the two agreed to drop the *modus vivendi* without again consulting the Navy or War departments. Hull recommended a hard line that would reassert America's basic principles.

Following the conversation with Roosevelt, Hull met in his office at 4:45 p.m. with Ambassador Nomura and his aide, Kurusu. He told them that if Tokyo accepted U.S. principles, financial cooperation could be worked out immediately. Proposal B was rejected by Hull and the *modus vivendi* of 90 days was not mentioned.

In addition to stating the principles that the United States wanted Japan to accept, Hull's November 26 note listed 10 points that Tokyo should approve. These points stated the maximum demands of the United States, including Japan's withdrawal from China and Indochina, recognition of the Nationalist government of China at Chungking (Chiang Kai-shek's government), and the abolition of extraterritorial rights of all powers in China. In return, the United States would conclude a new commercial treaty with Japan and cooperate in stabilizing the values of the dollar and the Japanese yen.

Because Hull must have known that Nomura could not accept most of the 10 points, the November 26 memo was referred to by some writers as an ultimatum. It was not. Only Tokyo's deadline, which Hull knew of only through the secret decoding of Japan's code, made the rejection of Plan B the last significant discussion between Hull and Nomura. The Japanese representatives told Hull they were not prepared to respond to his notice. They asked for a delay while they consulted their home government. See December 6 and December 7, 1941.

November 27, 1941   A WAR WARNING IS SENT TO ALL COMMANDERS OF THE ASIATIC
                        AND PACIFIC FLEETS AND TO GENERAL MacARTHUR IN THE
                        PHILIPPINES.

The Roosevelt-Hull decision of November 26 to drop the *modus vivendi* and affirm U.S. principles led Washington officials to believe that Japan would attack in the near future. When he told Secretary of War Stimson of the decision on the morning of November 27, Hull said: "I have washed my hands of it and it is now in the hands of you and Knox--the Army and the Navy." Although the military leaders, General Marshall and Admiral Stark, asked Roosevelt to reconsider the November 26 decision, it was too late.

Therefore, although a war warning had been sent to all Pacific commanders on November 24, Stimson, Knox, Marshall, and Stark decided to send another, more direct warning on November 27. This message said:

> This dispatch is to be considered a war warning. Negotiations with Japan ... have ceased and aggressive move by Japan is expected within the next few days. The number and equipment of Japanese troops and organization of naval task forces indicates an amphibious expedition against either the Philippines, Thailand or Kra Peninsula or possibly Borneo.

December 1, 1941   THE EMPEROR AND PRIVY COUNCIL OF JAPAN APPROVE WAR
                         WITH THE UNITED STATES AND BRITAIN.

Although the final action of the Emperor of Japan was a simple formality,
the Liaison Committee of the Imperial Conference recommended war. The committee reported that all steps of the November 5 timetable had ended with
the United States unwilling to accept Japan's demands. Therefore, the committee recommended that the war preparations that had been underway since
November 5 should be followed. The emperor approved.

December 6, 1941   PRESIDENT ROOSEVELT APPEALS TO THE JAPANESE EMPEROR
                         TO MAINTAIN PEACE WITH THE UNITED STATES BY WITHDRAWING
                         JAPANESE TROOPS FROM SOUTHEAST ASIA.

Roosevelt's appeal was a last-ditch attempt to prevent an imminent Japanese
attack against Singapore, Burma, and the Dutch East Indies. Following news
of Japanese troop build ups in southeast Asia since November 26, Roosevelt
requested an explanation from Tokyo and discussed possible U.S.-British action
in the event of such an attack. Japan had responded to Roosevelt's inquiry
by saying the troops were responding to Chinese activities on the frontier
of Indochina and Burma.
     At the same time, the president's conversations with British Ambassador
Lord Halifax indicated that he wished to take parallel not united action with
Britain in their protests to Japan. He also implied to Halifax that if Japan
attacked Britain and Dutch territory in southeast Asia, the United States
would help Britain, possibly by air attacks from the Philippines or a naval
blockade of Japan.
     On December 6, as Japanese troop ships entered the Gulf of Siam, the
president sent his peace message to Emperor Hirohito. Roosevelt said the
only certain means to maintain peace and to dispel the "dark clouds" of war
was for Japan to withdraw its troops from southeast Asia. Roosevelt's reply
came the next day, not from the emperor but at Pearl Harbor.

December 7, 1941   JAPANESE PLANES ATTACK U.S. MILITARY INSTALLATIONS IN
                         AND AROUND PEARL HARBOR AT 7:55 A.M. (1:55 P.M. IN
                         WASHINGTON). JAPAN'S REPRESENTATIVES ARE DELAYED AND
                         DO NOT ARRIVE TO INFORM HULL OF THE DECLARATION OF
                         WAR UNTIL 2:05 P.M.

Soon after November 29, Japan's final preparations for attacks on southeast
Asia, the Philippine Islands, and Pearl Harbor received imperial approval to
go forward. News of preliminary Japanese troop movements in southeast Asia
reached Washington on November 26, and Japan's forces were expected to attack
there. The Japanese air and naval attacks on Hawaii by a specially trained
carrier fleet had not been expected. The Japanese planned to cripple the
U.S. Navy so seriously that America would have to surrender. This was Japan's
biggest mistake. Not only did the attack not cripple the fleet because U.S.
aircraft carriers were at sea that morning, but the attack rallied the U.S.
populace to become nearly unanimous in its determination to win the war.
Although Roosevelt had indicated he would help Britain if their bases in
southeast Asia were attacked, the president would have had difficulty getting
congressional consent to declare war based on Japan's attacks on Malaya,

Thailand, and the Dutch East Indies. Certainly he would not have received the strong backing of the U.S. people which resulted from the direct Japanese attack on Hawaii and the Philippine Islands.

At Pearl Harbor, the Japanese attack lasted from 7:55 to 9:45 a.m. All eight U.S. battleships in port were either sunk (the *Arizona*, *California*, and *Utah*); grounded (the *Nevada*); capsized (the *Oklahoma*); or damaged (the *Pennsylvania*, *West Virginia*, and *Tennessee*). A total of 19 U.S. ships were sunk or disabled. In addition, 177 U.S. planes were destroyed; 2,335 soldiers and sailors and 68 civilians were killed.

Americans often overlook Japan's simultaneous attacks on December 7-8 in the Philippines and against British forces in Hong Kong and Malaya. Because of the international date-line these attacks were on December 8 but occurred the same day as the Pearl Harbor raid. The first unofficial word of the Japanese attack in Hawaii reached the Philippines at 3:00 a.m. General MacArthur received confirmation of this at 3:55 a.m. Although MacArthur's staff began meetings at 5:00 a.m., Japan made a successful "surprise" attack on Clark Field at 12:35 p.m. Japan's bombing and strafing attack continued until 1:37 p.m., reducing the U.S. Far Eastern Air Force by 50%. Of 35 B-17's, 18 were destroyed at Clark Field. Also destroyed were 53 pursuit planes and 25 aircraft of other types. The airfield was extensively damaged and 80 servicemen were killed.

Blame for the Clark Field disaster belongs to MacArthur and Air Force Major General Lewis H. Brereton, although MacArthur's hesitancy in permitting an immediate air attack on Formosa gives him a larger share of blame. At 5 a.m. Brereton went to MacArthur's headquarters to request permission for an air offensive against Formosa. Because MacArthur was in conference, his Chief of Staff, Major General Richard K. Sutherland, told Brereton to prepare for an attack but not to launch it until MacArthur approved. At 10:10 a.m. Sutherland told Brereton that MacArthur approved a reconnaissance mission to Formosa. At 11 a.m. Sutherland called Clark Field and approved a bombing mission.

Events at Clark Field between 5 a.m. and 11 a.m. complicated matters. At dawn, Japanese planes bombed the Philippine ports at Davao in Mindanao and Aparri on Luzon. At 8:30 Brereton ordered all B-17's to become airborne because Japanese planes had been reported north of Clark Field. Brereton again requested that Sutherland give him authority to attack Formosa. When MacArthur's approval came at 10:10 for a reconnaissance flight, Brereton recalled the B-17's to Clark Field to be refueled and readied for an afternoon attack on Formosa. At 12:35, while the pilots were being briefed or at lunch and the bombers were being checked and fueled for their long flights, Japanese bombers and fighters attacked Clark Field. Brereton had not provided air cover for the planes, which were bunched together in preparation for the bombing mission. Exactly why MacArthur delayed ordering the attack on Formosa has never been clarified. Three and a half hours passed between Brereton's first request and the time the B-17's went aloft at 8:30; between 8:30 and 10:10, the B-17's could have been sent but were wasting fuel while airborne as an evasive measure. In Washington, news of Japan's attack on Pearl Harbor was a surprise because the first attacks were expected to begin in southeast Asia or, perhaps, the Philippines. On December 6, reports of Japanese ships in the Gulf of Siam and the Indochina area had inspired Roosevelt's last-minute appeal to Emperor Hirohito. At 9:30 on the evening of December 6, Roosevelt received the decoded "Magic" translations of 13 out of 14 parts of Japan's response to Hull's November 26 demands to Nomura and Kurusu. On reading the "Magic" reports, Roosevelt realized they meant war, but

conjectured that the attacks would be in southeast Asia. The 14th part of
the Japanese message did not come through and was not decoded until Sunday
morning. This message told Nomura to meet at 1 p.m. with Hull and to announce
the break in relations with the United States. The message did not say where
and when the attack would be, nor did it tell Nomura to declare war.

Although the "Magic" decoding gave Hull advance notice that Nomura
planned to announce the break in relations, the Secretary of State did not
learn about the Japanese attack on Pearl Harbor until 2:05 p.m. Nomura had
called to delay his 1 p.m. appointment with Hull because the clerks in the
Japanese embassy had not yet translated and prepared the official notes to
break relations with the United States. Nomura apparently did not know the
full significance of making his appointment at 1 p.m.

Thus, almost at the same time (2:05) that Roosevelt called Hull to inform
him of the attack on Pearl Harbor, Nomura and Kurusu arrived in Hull's outer
office. Hull did not receive the Japanese until 2:20 p.m. Hull then read
the Japanese response to his November 26 message. The Japanese had denounced
all of Hull's requests and told Hull that Tokyo had to break diplomatic relations with America. After reading Japan's note, Hull told the Japanese that
"In all my fifty years of public service I have never seen a document that
was more crowded with infamous falsehoods and distortions." He dismissed
the Japanese from his office without giving them an opportunity to respond.

December 8, 1941   CONGRESS FORMALLY DECLARES WAR ON JAPAN.

President Roosevelt's message to congress asking for war on December 8 emphasized Japan's treachery in already causing a state of war to exist. His famous opening words were: "Yesterday, December 7, 1941--a day which will live
in infamy--the United States was suddenly and deliberately attacked by naval
and air forces of the Empire of Japan." Congress promptly voted for war with
only one dissenting vote. Japan's attack united U.S. politicians as nothing
else could have, except a similar attack by the Germans. On December 8,
Roosevelt did not ask for a declaration of war against Germany and Italy,
waiting until they declared war.

December 10, 1941   JAPANESE FORCES MAKE AMPHIBIOUS LANDINGS TO ATTACK
                           THE PHILIPPINE ISLANDS.

Although Japanese air raids on the Philippines began soon after the attack
on Pearl Harbor, their forces did not land until two days later. General
MacArthur and his defense forces held out on Luzon Island longer than many
expected. Manila fell on January 2, 1942, but the defenders retired to Bataan Peninsula while MacArthur established headquarters on Corregidor in
Manila Bay. Although MacArthur left Bataan on March 17 to go to Australia
as Commander of Allied Forces in the southwest Pacific, Filipinos and Americans under General Jonathan A. WAINWRIGHT held out on Corregidor until their
surrender on May 6, 1942.

In December, 1941, Japanese forces also occupied Guam (December 13),
Wake Island (December 22), and Hong Kong (December 25).

December 11, 1941   GERMANY AND ITALY DECLARE WAR ON THE UNITED STATES.

Acting under their agreements as Axis allies of Japan, Rome and Berlin declared war. In response the same day, the U.S. congress issued a declaration of war against Germany and Italy.

1942

January 1, 1942   THE UNITED NATIONS DECLARATION IS SIGNED AT WASHINGTON
                       BY 26 NATIONS FIGHTING THE AXIS POWERS.

By this declaration the 26 nations affirmed the Atlantic Charter, pledged
not to make a separate peace with the Fascist enemies, and agreed to use all
of their military and economic resources to defeat the Axis. The four major
nations signing were Great Britain, the Soviet Union, China, and the United
States. By the spring of 1945, 47 nations signed the Declaration of the
United Nations.
        Unlike its position in World War I when the United States was an "associ-
ated power" rather than an ally, this declaration was a virtual alliance made
without Senate approval. Roosevelt's legal advisors checked the documents
to be certain the language was a declaration and not a treaty.

January 14, 1942   ARCADIA CONFERENCE: WINSTON CHURCHILL CONCLUDES A VISIT
                       TO WASHINGTON IN WHICH, SINCE DECEMBER 22, HE AND
                       ROOSEVELT HAD BEEN PLANNING COOPERATIVE ANGLO-AMERICAN
                       GROUPS TO FIGHT THE WAR.

During this series of sessions, the president and prime minister set up an
Anglo-American Combined Chiefs of Staff to conduct the war. Then, soon after,
they established the Combined Boards for Raw Materials, Munitions Assignments,
Shipping Adjustments, Production and Resources, and Food. Together these
boards and the Combined Chiefs formed a Supreme War Council, but they did
not include representatives of China or the Soviet Union. The latter two
had been considered for membership, but Roosevelt and Churchill decided that
their inclusion caused too many problems.
        Strategy for the conduct of the war was also discussed by Churchill and
Roosevelt. Basically, ABC-1 became the grand strategy for the conduct of
the war. Germany and the defeat of the Axis powers in Europe received first
priority of the Anglo-American alliance. Second priority went to defensive
action against Japan in the Pacific until Germany's defeat was assured. Some
offensive action would be permitted in the Pacific provided it did not damage
the Allied plans for Europe. Finally, third priority was given to the China-
Burma-India theater (CBI). Because the basic strategy was that eventually
sea power would conquer the chain of islands leading toward Japan, the China
theater would entail defensive holding action unless Chiang Kai-shek could
be persuaded to prepare and mount a large land-offensive action with Chinese
forces. The story of Chiang's lack of desire to fight such an action is a
separate matter. See February 9, 1942.
        During the January meetings, Roosevelt and Churchill also considered
the matter of a second front in Europe, deciding that an Allied landing in
North Africa would cut German expansion in western Africa and assist the
British campaigns in Libya. Before the conference ended, however, Roosevelt

agreed to table the question of a North African attack because General
Marshall opposed it. In addition, the British army in Libya suffered rever-
sals. Thus, for the time being the African venture was laid aside for future
reconsideration.

January 28, 1942   AT THE RIO DE JANEIRO CONFERENCE OF AMERICAN FOREIGN
                          MINISTERS, 21 AMERICAN REPUBLICS VOTE TO RECOMMEND
                          THAT THEIR GOVERNMENTS BREAK RELATIONS WITH THE AXIS
                          POWERS.

For the United States the important action desired by the Rio meeting of foreign ministers from January 15 to 28, 1942, was to have each republic break
relations if not declare war against the Axis powers. In this respect, Undersecretary of State Welles, who headed the U.S. delegation, had yielded a significant point to Argentina's delegate by changing the conference resolution
from "declaring" to read "recommending" that each government should break
relations. Secretary of State Hull strongly admonished Welles for giving in
to Argentina, but the consequences of the wording probably did not change
the circumstances much. Argentina did not sever relations until January 26,
1944, but the pro-Fascist government of President Castillo would not have
acted otherwise regardless of the word used. Chile was the only other government at the Rio conference which did not immediately sever relations, waiting
until January 20, 1943, to do so.
    Other decisions made at the Rio Conference included: (1) condemning Japan
for the Pearl Harbor attack; (2) endorsing the Atlantic Charter; (3) creating
an inter-American defense board; (4) severing commercial and financial relations with the Axis nations.

February 2, 1942   THE AFFAIR OF ST. PIERRE AND MIQUELON ENDS WITH THE
                          ISLANDS OCCUPIED BY THE FREE FRENCH BUT WITH SECRETARY
                          OF STATE HULL READY TO RESIGN.

This issue arose in December, 1941, when General de Gaulle proposed that the
Free French should replace the Vichy government's administration of these
islands situated off the coast of Newfoundland. Without obtaining permission
from the United States and Canada, whose governments preferred to keep the
situation as it existed in the islands, General de Gaulle ordered Admiral
Emile Muselier to occupy the islands on December 24 "without saying anything
to the foreigners (Canada and America)." Secretary Hull feared this act would
damage U.S. relations with the Vichy government, but Roosevelt would not
strongly back the secretary and Winston Churchill thought it a minor issue.
Consequently, the Free French stayed in control and on February 2, Hull decided not to contest the matter. Hull was, however, left consistently re-
sentful of de Gaulle's high-handed action. Hull considered resigning but
Norman Davis persuaded him not to do so over this issue.

February 4, 1942   SECRETARY OF STATE HULL AND ROOSEVELT REJECT RUSSIAN
                        DEMANDS FOR RECOGNITION OF ITS WESTERN BOUNDARY AS
                        BEING THAT WHICH THE SOVIETS OCCUPIED WHEN HITLER AT-
                        TACKED IN JUNE, 1941.

The Russians told Britain's Foreign Secretary, Anthony Eden, during a visit
late in December, 1941, that they wanted their legitimate western boundary
line to be that of June, 1941. This recognition would have included Russian
possession of Estonia, Latvia, Lithuania, part of eastern Poland, and Bessarabia in Rumania. Eden referred this issue to Churchill and Roosevelt in
January, 1942, but the Anglo-American leaders rejected Stalin's request as
violating the Atlantic Charter.
     Because Stalin continued to pursue his request to Eden and to the Ameri-
can Ambassador at London, John G. WINANT, Hull sent the president an extended
memorandum on this issue on February 4, 1942. Hull indicated that Stalin's
demand for a boundary settlement generated mutual suspicions because the small
nations which signed the United Nations Declaration would be alarmed at such
agreements. He told Roosevelt that Stalin's test of our "good faith" should
not be an agreement to accept new boundaries but to provide the promised military supplies to the Soviet Union.
     Roosevelt agreed with Hull and inaugurated a general boundary policy
for the United States that all boundary questions should wait until the war
ended. During the next several months, Churchill nearly agreed to give in
to Russia but Roosevelt and Hull prevented this. See May 26, 1942.

February 9, 1942   PRESIDENT ROOSEVELT MEETS WITH GENERAL STILWELL, WHO
                        IS BEING SENT TO CHINA AS CHIEF OF STAFF TO CHIANG
                        KAI-SHEK; ROOSEVELT IS ATTEMPTING TO BOLSTER CHINA'S
                        IMPORTANCE AS MUCH AS POSSIBLE.

During the January meetings between Churchill and Roosevelt, the Allied leaders endeavored to agree on China's precise role in the war effort against
Japan. Churchill thought the president overestimated the importance of China's contribution, finding that Roosevelt adopted "a wholly unreal standard
of values" regarding China. The president, however, appreciated the fact
that U.S. public opinion had, for some curious reason, made China its favorite
ally. Roosevelt had to placate this "curious" attitude of Americans toward
the Chinese. According to a 1942 public opinion poll, 80 to 86% of Americans
believed China could be depended on to cooperate with the United States during
and after the war.
     On January 5, with Churchill's reluctant consent, Roosevelt offered and
Chiang accepted the post of Supreme Commander of the China Theater of War.
This title implied more than it meant. Chiang had requested a joint Far East
command with headquarters at Chungking, and although the British rejected
this concept, they agreed to the title offered Chiang because it gave him
control only of Allied forces in China. A separate Southwest Pacific Command
under Supreme Commander General Sir Archibald WAVELL was established for south
and southeast Asia. Equally significant was the fact that China was not included on the Combined Chiefs of Staff of the Anglo-American command.
     On February 9, Roosevelt met with General Joseph W. STILWELL, who had
been selected to go to Chungking to serve as Chief of Staff to Generalissimo
Chiang Kai-shek and as Commander of the United States forces in China, Burma,
and India. Both Roosevelt and General Marshall had difficulty telling

Stilwell exactly what his responsibilities would be in China. Officially, Stilwell was to "increase the effectiveness" of U.S. aid to China and "to improve the combat efficiency of the Chinese army." He was to accept any staff or command position "tendered" to him by Chiang.

The basic problem for Roosevelt to convey to Stilwell was that while Chiang Kai-shek had visions of China's and Chiang's vast importance to the Allied war effort, the president and Churchill gave the China theater a low priority in terms of strategic need and, therefore, of the men, materials, and war equipment to be supplied to China. The United States decided to emphasize its aviation effort in China and to maintain and improve air transport service to Chungking. With respect to the latter, the president agreed to replace the Burma Road transport link to China, which Japanese forces had captured, with an air route from India across the Himalayan Mountains to China.

Because American aid to China had low priority, Roosevelt hoped to keep Chiang happy by emphasizing China's status as one of the Big Four powers and the long-term gains China would receive by continuing to fight Japan. Although Churchill found these views of the president "strangely out of proportion," Roosevelt substituted the rhetoric about Chiang Kai-shek's importance for the practical assistance Chiang desired. Like Churchill, Stilwell was not impressed by the president's banter. "Just a lot of wind," Stilwell wrote after his talk with Roosevelt on February 9.

Over the next three years, Stilwell repaid the scorn of Chiang's dissatisfaction because he confronted the Chinese daily with the reality of their low strategic priority. Roosevelt appeared to be China's friend because his words belied the realistic fact that the president and Churchill could not and did not believe they should give Chiang all the men, equipment, and monetary aid he wished. See June 29, 1942.

February 19, 1942   JAPANESE AMERICANS LIVING ON THE WEST COAST CAN BE
                           RELOCATED BY THE WAR DEPARTMENT UNDER AN ORDER AUTHO-
                           RIZED BY PRESIDENT ROOSEVELT.

Following the Japanese attack on Pearl Harbor and the victories of the Japanese in the southwest and central Pacific, the long-standing racial antagonism against Orientals in the western United States aroused false reports of Japanese espionage. In addition, a government report on Pearl Harbor blamed Japanese spies in Hawaii for assisting the success of the attack. (For anti-Japanese attitude in the western states see November 2, 1920 and May 15, 1924.

Never a strong civil libertarian, Roosevelt reacted to U.S. Army reports of Japanese disloyalty by authorizing the War Department to prescribe restricted military areas in the United States from which persons could be excluded. Thus, Roosevelt represented as a "military necessity" the forcible relocation of 110,000 Japanese-Americans. These citizens were sent to concentration camps in the interior of the United States where many of them remained until their release on January 2, 1945.

April 17, 1942   THE UNITED STATES RECALLS AMBASSADOR LEAHY FROM THE
                           FRENCH VICHY GOVERNMENT TO PROTEST GERMANY'S PRESSURE
                           TO REINSTATE PIERRE LAVAL AS FRENCH PREMIER.

Prior to Marshal Pétain's resignation as premier on April 15, the State

Department informed the Vichy government that if Laval returned to power the United States would "discontinue its existing relation of confidence." Therefore, when Laval assumed office, Washington recalled Ambassador William Leahy.

The United States retained diplomatic relations with France and the U.S. Chargé d'Affaires acted *ad interim* as the U.S. representative. Secretary Hull desired to retain relations with Vichy because U.S. consuls remained in southern France and North Africa. The U.S. agents distributed supplies of petroleum and food in North Africa and, under the direction of Robert D. MURPHY, served as sources of information with anti-German groups among the French. After the decision of June, 1942, to invade North Africa, these U.S. agents provided more direct assistance to the American effort in French North Africa. See November 8, 1942.

April 18, 1942   AMERICAN ARMY PLANES BOMB TOKYO AND OTHER JAPANESE
                          CITIES, A PROJECT URGED BY PRESIDENT ROOSEVELT TO RAISE
                          THE NATION'S MORALE AFTER JAPAN'S MANY VICTORIES IN
                          THE WESTERN PACIFIC.

One of President Roosevelt's major concerns during the spring of 1942 was to counteract U.S. critics who wanted some action to offset Japan's victories in the Pacific. As the president noted, many of the same isolationists who deplored defense preparations before December 7, 1941, now expected miracles to be performed.

Many of Roosevelt's critics advocated an all-out effort against Japan in contrast to the "Germany first" strategy agreed to with the British. The fall of Singapore on February 15 led some leading Anglophobe newspapers in America to renounce the British as only fighting "to the last American."

Disdaining this opposition, Roosevelt made a radio speech on Washington's birthday to recall the hard times at Valley Forge during the early days of the Revolutionary War. He warned the American people not to listen to those who would "divide and conquer" the members of the United Nations by destroying "our confidence in our own allies." Britain, Russia, and China, he said, have endured in the war longer than the Americans and we, too, must adopt their "conquering spirit" and the spirit of Washington to resist the enemy. On the United Nations, see January 1, 1942.

Roosevelt knew, however, that tangible evidence such as the bombing of Tokyo would help build U.S. morale. Therefore, he encouraged a suggestion for 16 B-25 bombers to fly from an aircraft carrier to bomb Japan. With less than one month's training in flying a bomber from a carrier deck, Colonel James H. DOOLITTLE led a squadron of 16 planes to attack Japan. Although all the planes dropped their bombs and escaped Japan's anti-aircraft guns, none of the planes made it to their destined Chinese airfields. All the B-25's were crash-landed or abandoned when they ran out of fuel. Nevertheless, only 5 of the 80 crew members died in the attack. The raid was praised in America; Colonel Doolittle became a war hero.

May 7, 1942   BATTLE OF THE CORAL SEA REPELS A JAPANESE FORCE HEADED
                         FOR NEW CALEDONIA AND NEW HEBRIDES, STOPPING JAPANESE
                         ADVANCES TOWARD AUSTRALIA.

From December 10 to early May, Japan had advanced swiftly in southeast Asia. Japan occupied the Netherlands East Indies by January 31; Rangoon, Burma, on

March 9; and parts of New Guinea on March 8. The conflict in the Coral Sea
was fought entirely by planes from aircraft carriers.

May 20, 1942   THE PRESIDENT REVERSES AN EXECUTIVE ORDER OF APRIL 13
                        WHICH GAVE THE BOARD OF ECONOMIC WARFARE (BEW) THE
                        POWER TO NEGOTIATE ECONOMIC MATTERS WITH FOREIGN GOV-
                        ERNMENTS.

Vice President Henry A. WALLACE, who chaired the Board of Economic Warfare,
had convinced the president that the BEW required authority to deal with export and import controls of commodities other than weapons and munitions.
On April 13, the president issued an order giving Wallace this authority in
spite of the protests of Undersecretary of State Welles who said this order
interfered with State Department jurisdiction over trade relations.
     Late in April, Secretary Hull returned from a sick leave and immediately
urged the president to rescind the new power of the BEW. He told Roosevelt
that Wallace misled him by saying that the Secretary of State did not disapprove of the order of April 13. Wallace admitted his lack of candor and
Roosevelt drew up a new order on May 20, placing all BEW actions and agents
under the State Department and foreign diplomatic offices. Nevertheless,
Wallace often interfered in diplomatic matters during the next three years.

May 26, 1942   ENGLAND AND RUSSIA SIGN A 20-YEAR ALLIANCE TREATY WHICH
                        DOES NOT MENTION THE SOVIETS' WESTERN BOUNDARY, AN
                        OMISSION DUE TO AMERICAN OPPOSITION.

Between January and May, 1942, Anthony Eden and Russian Commissar for Foreign
Affairs MOLOTOV negotiated a formal treaty of alliance. The principal issue
in the discussions was Molotov's insistence that England recognize Russia's
western borders as of June 22, 1941 (see February 4, 1942). Secretary of
State Hull and President Roosevelt objected strongly to the Russian demand,
and the result was the initial dispute between the Big Three allies.
     On March 7, 1942, Churchill cabled Roosevelt that he wanted to accept
Russia's border request. In the "deadly struggle" with the Nazis, Churchill
said, we cannot "deny Russia the frontiers she occupied when Germany attacked
her." Although Roosevelt searched for some compromise, Hull opposed the Russian position and Roosevelt eventually agreed with the secretary. The United
States informed the British that any boundary agreement would be a "terrible
blow" to the "whole cause of the United Nations." In addition, Roosevelt
asked Russia to send Molotov to Washington to discuss a second front (see
June 1, 1942).
     Consequently, Eden asked Molotov to accept an alliance with England
which did not mention boundaries. Although Molotov had not changed Russian
policy, he agreed. The Anglo-Russian treaty of May 26 was signed on the basis
that neither nation sought "territorial aggrandizement" in the war. From
Russia's view, of course, her boundary of June 22, 1941, did not mean that
"territorial aggrandizement" by the Soviets between 1939 and 1941 was included.

June 1, 1942   ROOSEVELT PROMISES RUSSIA THERE WILL BE A SECOND FRONT
                           IN EUROPE BY THE END OF 1942.

During April, 1942, when Britain and Russia discussed an alliance and the
Soviets' future boundaries (see May 26, 1942), Roosevelt heard about and accepted a U.S. Army plan to have coastal raids on Europe by August, 1942, preceding a major assault in France by April 1, 1943. To entice the Russians
to forego their boundary issues in favor of the advantages of a second front
against Germany, Roosevelt asked Stalin on April 20 to send Soviet Foreign
Minister Molotov to America to discuss a second front. Although Churchill
and British officers opposed the plan to attack France in 1942, they permitted
Roosevelt to explore the possibility of a second front with Russia.

On May 29, Molotov arrived in Washington to discuss with the president
and America's military leaders future supplies to Russia and a second front.
Stalin greatly desired a second front as the best means to relieve German
activity on the eastern front. On June 1, Roosevelt, Hopkins, Marshall, and
the new CNO, Admiral Ernest S. King, met with Molotov to discuss a second
front. Marshall and his aide, General Dwight D. EISENHOWER, had, in April,
1942, planned attacks on western Europe. They calculated that the western
allies could begin diversionary air and coastal raids on Europe beginning in
August, 1942, so that by April 1, 1943, 48 divisions and 5,800 planes would
be ready to attack the Continent. On this basis, the president told Molotov
to inform Stalin "that we expect the formation of a second front this year."
Marshall told the president to qualify this statement because there were many
difficulties to overcome. Therefore, the president said the attack would be
"sometime in 1942."

Nevertheless, Churchill and the British continued to oppose a cross-
channel invasion in 1942. To assuage Roosevelt, the prime minister decided
to emphasize the significance of a North African attack as a better preliminary attack on German troops. See July 27, 1942.

June 6, 1942   BATTLE OF MIDWAY ENDS JAPAN'S ADVANCE IN THE CENTRAL
                           PACIFIC OCEAN WITH A MAJOR NAVAL DEFEAT OF JAPAN.

This naval and air battle prevented Japan from seizing Midway Island and eliminated the threat to Hawaii. Japan lost four aircraft carriers and 275
planes, restoring the balance of naval power in the Pacific. The U.S. Navy
lost one carrier and one destroyer in the battle.

June 13, 1942   THE OFFICE OF STRATEGIC SERVICES (O.S.S.) IS ESTAB-
                           LISHED.

By executive order, President Roosevelt created the O.S.S. for intelligence
operations abroad and the analysis of strategic information. William J.
DONOVAN become the director of the O.S.S.

June 29, 1942   CHIANG KAI-SHEK COMPLAINS TO ROOSEVELT AND THREATENS
                           TO "LIQUIDATE" THE CHINESE THEATER OF WAR AGAINST
                           JAPAN.

Tensions and personality conflicts between General Stilwell and Chiang

Kai-shek began to be serious soon after the miserable performance of Chinese troops in the Burma campaign of April, 1942.

When Stilwell arrived in China in February, 1942, he found that Chiang blamed the British Command in India and General Wavell for China's difficulties. When Chiang first offered up to 80,000 Chinese troops to Wavell, he had refused. Wavell disliked Chiang's demand that the Chinese should operate in a selected area as an independent unit. Wavell also preferred to rely on British Commonwealth forces from India and Australia to defend Burma. Only through Stilwell's mediation and Australia's reluctance to send forces to Burma did Wavell agree that China should supply three divisions under Stilwell's command in Burma.

The Burma campaign was a disaster. Although American newspapers printed uncritical accounts of Chiang's gallant forces fighting the Japanese in Burma, Generals Wavell and Stilwell knew the Chinese had not performed well. The Chinese did not move when and where they were ordered. In addition, officers to whom Stilwell gave orders appealed to Chiang or acted as they thought Chiang desired. At other times they simply objected to what Stilwell asked them to do. In his diary, Stilwell complained, "I can't shoot them; I can't relieve them." This situation, combined with poor British attitudes and ineptness and swift moves by the efficient Japanese, led to the closing of the Burma Road when Lashio fell to Japan on April 29, 1942.

Historian Herbert Feis says of the Burma defeat: "What a trail of harm this debacle left behind." Cut off from their main supply route, Chiang's government became isolated in its mountain capital of Chungking. Chiang could not or would not act aggressively to improve his situation. He blamed everyone except himself for his problems: the small amount of U.S. Lend-Lease aid, British opposition, and Stilwell, who had "rashly risked" China's armies in Burma. Stilwell blamed Chiang and his inept and corrupt military affiliates for China's problems because their weakness demoralized the entire Chinese army.

Against this background, Chiang presented a formal ultimatum to Washington on June 29. He made three demands: the United States should send three divisions to Burma to reopen the Burma Road, should begin operating 500 combat planes in China by August, and should deliver 5,000 tons of supplies per month over the main route from India to China. If these demands were not fulfilled, the generalissimo said, there would be a "liquidation" of the Chinese war against Japan.

Although Roosevelt never fulfilled Chiang's demands, the Chungking government depended too much on the United States to do more than threaten or act independently as often as possible. Roosevelt told Chiang that he had to consider the problems of the Middle East and the Pacific as well as China. He agreed to send Lauchlin Currie as a personal representative to Chungking. Finally, although no U.S. divisions could be spared for Burma, the Tenth American Air Force of 265 planes would be built to full capacity for use in China by October 11. In addition, Roosevelt hoped to be able to fly 5,000 tons of supplies per month from India by 1943.

Stilwell recognized that Roosevelt's promised aid was not much more than China already had from the United States. Ever able to provide a cryptic and descriptive summation, Stilwell wrote to his wife: "Peanut [his name for Chiang] and I are on a raft, with one sandwich between us, and the rescue ship is heading away from the scene."

July 1, 1942   A FORMAL LEND-LEASE AGREEMENT BETWEEN RUSSIA AND AMER-
                           ICA GOES INTO EFFECT.

This agreement was formally approved when Molotov visited Washington on May
29-June 1, 1942. The pact provided that materials received from the United
States would not be transferred by Russia to other parties and that at the
end of the war any materials still available would be returned to the United
States.

July 27, 1942   AN ANGLO-AMERICAN DECISION TO INVADE NORTH AFRICA IN
                           THE FALL OF 1942 (TORCH) IS SEEN BY PRESIDENT ROOSEVELT
                           AS A "TURNING POINT" IN THE WAR.

Since April, 1942, American and British leaders had discussed the question
of where a second-front attack on German forces could best be implemented in
1942. Initially, General Marshall and U.S. Army leaders preferred to work
immediately for a cross-channel invasion of France in 1943. Churchill and
his advisors recommended action against either Norway or North Africa, preferring to delay the attack on France in order to make certain that once
begun, the cross-channel landings would be followed through to the defeat of
Germany. These matters were fully explored in meetings in Washington between
June 18 and 27, but no conclusion was finalized.
     On July 18, General Marshall and Admiral King visited London for staff
talks with Churchill and the British Chiefs of Staff. The British convinced
Marshall that an attack on France (coded SLEDGEHAMMER) could not succeed.
Marshall referred the issue to Roosevelt for a decision. Because the president wanted some type of ground operations against Germany in 1942, he opted
for an invasion of North Africa as soon as possible. The British concurred,
and as preparations began for this TORCH operation, Roosevelt cabled Churchill
that he believed TORCH would be a "turning point" in defeating the Axis for
"we are on our way shoulder to shoulder." See November 8, 1942.

August 7, 1942   U.S. FORCES IN THE PACIFIC MAKE THEIR FIRST MAJOR OF-
                           FENSIVE ATTACK AT GUADALCANAL IN THE SOLOMON ISLANDS.

Action in Guadalcanal lasted until February 9, 1943, when the Japanese withdrew. Although Allied war strategy called for defensive action only in the
Pacific, the entreaties of Admiral King and General MacArthur caused the president to send more men and aircraft to assist in the attack on Guadalcanal.
By the end of 1942, 9 of 17 U.S. army divisions and 19 of 66 air groups sent
overseas went to the Pacific.

August 13, 1942   THE MANHATTAN PROJECT TO DEVELOP THE ATOMIC BOMB IS
                           TO BE COMMANDED BY GENERAL LESLIE R. GROVES.

Under Groves's direction, construction began by the end of 1942 on the three
basic installations of the Manhattan District: the Oak Ridge, Tennessee,
U-235 separation plant; the Los Alamos, New Mexico bomb development laboratory; and the Hanford, Washington, plutonium production works.
     At the University of Chicago, scientists on the Argonne Project succeeded
in effecting the first self-sustaining nuclear reactor on December 2, 1942.

August 15, 1942   THE FIRST MOSCOW CONFERENCE ENDS: CHURCHILL INFORMS
                         STALIN THAT THE SECOND FRONT WILL BE IN NORTH AFRICA,
                         NOT EUROPE.

At Churchill's request, Stalin invited the prime minister to visit Moscow in
order to discuss the two major issues facing Russia and the Western Allies:
the second front and the difficulties of Allied convoys bringing supplies to
Russia through Archangel. At Churchill's meetings with Stalin, W. Averell
Harriman, the Lend-Lease administrator, represented Roosevelt.

   After describing the British air force plans for large bombing attacks
on Germany, the prime minister informed Stalin that the second front would
be North Africa, not west Europe. Using his charm and enthusiasm on Stalin,
Churchill said Anglo-American strategy depicted Germany as a giant crocodile.
By going through North Africa and into southern Europe, Churchill said, the
Allies would attack both the "soft underbelly" and the hard snoot of Hitler's
empire. Stalin was intrigued at first but later turned surly and objected
that insufficient German divisions would be diverted by the North African
campaign. Hitler would only shift large numbers of his forces from the eastern front if France were attacked directly. Thus, the second-front dispute
with Stalin continued.

   Regarding the supply routes to Russia, Stalin showed greater concern
about Russia's need for more war material. In mid-July, German submarines
sank 23 out of 34 merchant ships being convoyed to Archangel. The Allied
losses in the North Atlantic reached 400,000 tons in one week, more than twice
the Allies' weekly construction ability. As a result, the northern convoys
to Russia were suspended for the summer because the long daylight hours in
the area of the North Cape of Norway made them easy targets. To supplement
the convoy, the Allies made plans for a trans-Caucasian air transport service
which they hoped to begin in October. Following the Moscow sessions, Roosevelt and Churchill also decided to try some smaller convoys, and ten ships
were sent to Archangel in October. Meanwhile, German army attacks were pene-
trating deep into southern Russia. Stalin needed planes in particular to
help launch his counteroffensive against the Germans, which began in November,
1942.

November 8, 1942   THE INVASION OF NORTH AFRICA BY AN ANGLO-AMERICAN FORCE
                         COMMANDED BY GENERAL DWIGHT D. EISENHOWER.

The Allied troops made amphibious landings in French Morocco and Algeria.
Aided by Admiral Jean-François Darlan of the French Vichy government, Allied
forces overran the French garrison and an armistice was made on November 11.

   One consequence of this invasion was the German occupation of all parts
of France on November 11, 1941. This action caused many French in North Africa to end their former allegiance to the French Vichy government.

   Nevertheless, the so-called Darlan Deal caused extensive criticism in
Britain and America because Admiral Darlan had been a Vichy collaborator with
the Germans. When the North Africa campaign was planned, Robert Murphy, the
U.S. representative in North Africa, recommended that Eisenhower bring General Henri Honoré Giraud with him. Giraud, it was hoped, would obtain the
cooperation of French officers in North Africa because he was a veteran of
both wars and had escaped from a German war camp. When Eisenhower and Giraud
reached North Africa, however, Eisenhower discovered that French officers
loyal to Marshal Pétain considered both Giraud and General de Gaulle to be

disloyal traitors who violated their oaths to the French army.

    Luckily, Eisenhower and Murphy learned on November 14 that Admiral Darlan was in Algiers to visit a critically ill son. Although Darlan had continued to work with the Vichy government, he had let Murphy know in October that he could be persuaded to join the Allied cause. In October, Murphy had ignored this suggestion, but when Giraud failed to obtain support from the French officials, Murphy and General Mark Clark visited Darlan, who agreed to stop French resistance in Algeria and Morocco and to cooperate with the Allies. Believing this would save American lives and enable the conquest of these two African states to be easily concluded, Eisenhower agreed to let Darlan be in political charge in Algeria and Roosevelt accepted this action.

    Although Darlan's compliance achieved excellent military results, General de Gaulle's Free French headquarters objected vigorously, loosing a propaganda barrage against Darlan's deal as a "nullification of the United Nations." Until Darlan's assassination on December 24 by a French monarchist, Roosevelt and Secretary Hull, who backed Robert Murphy's proposals, suffered extensive criticism even though Roosevelt on December 16 persuaded Darlan to end Vichy's discriminatory laws against the Jews and other French personnel. By this time, the French in North Africa had turned strongly against Vichy because the Germans had occupied all of France.

November 19, 1942   RUSSIA'S COUNTEROFFENSIVE AGAINST GERMANY BEGINS AT
                             STALINGRAD.

German armies drove deeply into the southern part of the Soviet Union during the summer of 1942, capturing Sevastopol on July 1, Rostov on July 24, and beginning the siege of Stalingrad on September 13. On September 21, the Russians began thrusts against the German lines, first to the northeast, later to the southeast of Stalingrad. On November 19, a full-scale offensive began against Germany. The Soviets' successes temporarily ended Germany's offensive activity on the southern front. At Stalingrad, Russia's pincer movements surrounded and cut off 22 army divisions, and 80,000 Germans capitulated on February 2, 1943.

1943

January 11, 1943   EXTRATERRITORIALITY RIGHTS IN CHINA ARE ENDED BY TREA-
TIES SIGNED BETWEEN CHINA AND AMERICA IN WASHINGTON
AND BY CHINA AND BRITAIN IN CHUNGKING.

For some time Secretary Hull had been aware of the need to end the extraterritorial "unequal treaties" forced on China after the Opium War of 1839-1842.
Shortly before Japan invaded China in 1937, Washington and London had undertaken discussions to join in parallel action to end these treaties. The Japanese war delayed these talks until 1942 when the British and Americans again
considered action to abolish these treaties with their wartime ally China.
     On October 10, 1942, London and Washington simultaneously announced that
they were offering treaties to the Nationalist government of China to end
these extraterritoriality rights, and negotiations began in November, 1942.
Because China's principal desire since 1919 had been to be treated on an equal
basis with other powers, a clause indicating this was included in the treaty.
On January 11, treaties were signed between both China and the United States
and China and Britain. Both extraterritoriality and the special privileges
granted after the Boxer Rebellion were abolished. The British treaty also
ended its special concessions in Tientsin and Canton. Only the immigration
issue remained as a disturbing part of U.S.-Chinese historic relations. See
December 17, 1943.

January 24, 1943   THE CASABLANCA CONFERENCE RESULTS IN TWO SIGNIFICANT
DECISIONS: THE PLAN TO INVADE SICILY AND ITALY AND AN
AGREEMENT ON REQUIRING THE AXIS TO SURRENDER UNCON-
DITIONALLY.

Roosevelt and Churchill began plans for their meeting at Casablanca in December even though Stalin said he could not attend. Roosevelt wanted to plan
campaigns for 1943 and to get Churchill's agreement for unconditional surrender.
     The 1943 campaign issue arose because of basic disagreements between
U.S. and British military leaders. General Marshall and his staff preferred
giving full attention to the cross-channel attack. American military doctrine
centered on the concentration of forces to attack the major enemy fortress
at its strongest and most destructive point. This would defeat the enemy
quickly and decisively, and in Europe the best way to achieve this goal was
to attack through Cherbourg, France, to Berlin. Roosevelt, however, saw immediate advantages in the British plan to hit the soft underbelly of southern
Europe, especially Italy and southern France.
     Because pre-conference discussions indicated the president's preference,
Marshall went to Casablanca in order to obtain Britain's commitment to build
up the Allied base in England for a 1944 assault on western France. Marshall
received these commitments at Casablanca, and the British also accepted a

combined planning staff for the 1944 assault. In 1943, however, the Allied attacks would be on Sicily and Italy.

In the Pacific, Admiral King and the U.S. Joint Chiefs received some support for following up their Guadalcanal victory by additional attacks on Japanese-held islands. These operations were limited, however, because they were not to endanger the plans for the continued action against Germany in 1943-1944.

Regarding unconditional surrender, Roosevelt had begun to discuss such a policy as early as May, 1942. Saying he desired to avoid Wilson's "mistake" in 1918, Roosevelt also wanted not only to disarm the Axis nations but also to compel them to abandon their Fascist philosophy. Significantly, Roosevelt did not discuss this policy with the Joint Chiefs of Staff. He had discussed it with Secretary of State Hull who opposed the announcement of unconditional surrender. Hull, like later critics of the policy, contended that such a public announcement would end the possibility of any flexibility in later decisions and would force Germans and Japanese who disliked the Fascists to fight for their nations' honor rather than the overthrow of their distasteful military dictators.

On this issue, however, Roosevelt developed a closed mind. Telling Averell Harriman that Secretary Hull had "rigid ideas" and was stubborn, Roosevelt did not permit Hull to come to Casablanca. The president's excuse was Hull's implication in the "Darlan Deal" in North Africa.

At Casablanca the unconditional surrender decision was discussed but not made part of the official final communique by Churchill and Roosevelt. Exactly why is not clear. The only dispute about the doctrine had been whether or not to include Italy in the statement because there were signs that an Italian group hoped to overthrow Mussolini and appeal to the Western powers for an armistice. Later, on January 24, Roosevelt made an oral declaration to newsmen that he and the prime minister had agreed to demand the unconditional surrender of Germany, Italy, and Japan as the only way to assure future peace in the world. Although Roosevelt and Churchill claimed the statement of January 24 was a spontaneous act by the president, historic records do not substantiate this account. Churchill did not want to include Italy in the formula, which probably led the two leaders to avoid further debate on that question by agreement on an oral statement.

One final aspect of the Casablanca Conference was the attempt to get General de Gaulle to agree on plans for France's future role with the United States and Britain. Initially, de Gaulle refused to come to Casablanca. When he finally came on January 12, he generally complained about such incidentals as being surrounded by American bayonets on French territory. De Gaulle had refused to accept Giraud as the head of the North African government following Darlan's assassination, but he consented to be photographed with Giraud for the sake of Allied unity. Generally, de Gaulle proved objectionable to Roosevelt because he claimed authority with no semblance of democratic backing in France. Churchill, however, had become committed to the Free French leader who came to symbolize for the British the better side of France's fighting ability. On the last day of the conference and without Churchill's knowledge, the president signed the Anfa agreements which bound the United States to support Giraud in uniting French opponents of Germany. Churchill later insisted that de Gaulle must be included in these agreements.

March 8, 1943   ROOSEVELT AGAIN APPEARS TO YIELD TO CHIANG KAI-SHEK'S
                         DEMANDS AS A CONDITION FOR KEEPING CHINA IN THE WAR.

During the winter of 1942-1943, Britain, China, and the United States argued
over a campaign in Burma and General Chennault's plan for a strong air offensive against Japan. Although Generals Marshall and Stilwell argued that effective aid to build ground forces against Japan should be obtained by opening
the Burma Road, the British and Chiang, although for different reasons, were
reluctant to pursue a war in the jungles of Burma and used the air attacks
advocated by Chennault.

     In February, 1943, General Arnold visited Chungking where Chiang pre-
sented conditions for the United States to meet in order that China would
remain in the war. First Chiang wanted Chennault to head an independent air
force for China to lead attacks on Japan. Between March and May, 1943,
Roosevelt agreed to assist intensive air operations in China although
Chennault remained under Stilwell's jurisdiction. This decision was, however,
not finalized until Chennault and Stilwell visited Washington in April, 1943,
to argue their case. In addition, the Burma campaign would be delayed although Chiang agreed to work with the British on a future battle to liberate
Burma. This decision was backed by Roosevelt and accepted by Churchill during
the Trident Conference (see May 25, 1943). Finally, Roosevelt agreed to send
about 500 aircraft to China by November and to increase the air transport
supplies to Chiang from India to 10,000 tons per month.

     Although Roosevelt seems to have realized that Chiang's forces were cor-
rupt and inefficient because all U.S. and British estimates agreed on this
fact, he told Churchill that he had to placate Chiang for political reasons.
Madame Chiang Kai-shek had "invaded" Washington and New York society and ex-
uded a pro-Chinese propaganda that made her the most popular hero in America
since Charles Lindbergh in 1927. Churchill could not fathom this mysterious
American attraction for Madame Chiang and the Chinese, but after witnessing
the emotional attachment of pro-Chinese U.S. politicians and the pro-Chiang
publicity of the *Time-Life* magazine chain of Henry Luce, the prime minister
was politically astute enough to appreciate the president's problem. Thus,
when Roosevelt spoke to congress of Chiang as a great democratic leader of
China, Churchill and others knew the president's rhetoric was to drum up backing for U.S. ventures overseas. Because Roosevelt seemed to support Chiang,
his rhetoric aided Madame Chiang and the China Lobby in creating an unrealistic evaluation of the Chinese Nationalists which caused vast problems for
General Marshall and President Truman in 1949.

     Some of Roosevelt's backing of Chiang also lay in the strategic hope
that during the postwar era a strong China would become a counterweight to
Russia in Asia. This was a geopolitically astute perception but Roosevelt
refused to force Chiang to adopt any measures that would strengthen his army
and gain the support of the Chinese people. Because Roosevelt attached no
strings to Chinese aid requiring reforms such as Stilwell recommended, he
did nothing to guide the Nationalist government out of its ironically Fascist
channels.

April 27, 1943   THE SOVIET UNION SUSPENDS RELATIONS WITH POLAND'S
                         LONDON GOVERNMENT-IN-EXILE FOLLOWING A DISPUTE OVER
                         THE KATYN MASSACRES.

In April, 1943, the Germans announced that a mass grave containing 10,000

Polish officers had been found near Smolensk in the Katyn Forest. The Germans
alleged that the Soviets had massacred these men in the spring of 1940. Although Churchill cautioned the leader of the London Polish exiles, General
Wladyslaw Sikorski, to beware of the German attempt to sow discord among the
Allies, Sikorski asked the International Red Cross to investigate the allegation, which Stalin had denied in a message of April 18.

The Polish request for an investigation became the proclaimed reason
for Stalin to break relations with the London exile government, which he had
recognized since June, 1941. Later investigations confirmed the German allegations of the Soviet massacre of the Polish officers. Probably, however,
Stalin had been looking for a suitable reason to break relations with Sikorski
because the Soviets sponsored a communist Polish group, the Union of Polish
Patriots. The 1943 Polish split began the Allied dispute over the postwar
status of Poland.

May 13, 1943   THE NORTH AFRICA CAMPAIGN ENDS WHEN 250,000 AXIS TROOPS
                           SURRENDER IN CAPE BON, TUNISIA.

As the U.S. forces under General Eisenhower moved into Morocco, Algiers, and
Oran after November 8, 1942, British troops in the east forced General
Rommel's armies to retreat from Egypt and regained Tobruk on November 13.
On March 19, American troops captured El Guettar in Tunisia and joined with
British forces from Libya on April 7 near Gafsa. The final action against
the Germans in Cape Bon ended on May 13.

May 22, 1943   MOSCOW ANNOUNCES THE DISSOLUTION OF THE THIRD INTER-
                           NATIONAL (COMINTERN).

Since 1933, the United States had repeatedly asked the Soviet Union to abandon
the subversive activity of the Comintern. Stalin officially did so on May 22.
Although this was a gesture of friendship to the United States, the Russians
did not end their attempts to influence activity of communist parties in the
world, including the Communist Party of the United States, which Earl Browder
led in 1943.

May 25, 1943   THE TRIDENT CONFERENCE ENDS: ROOSEVELT, CHURCHILL,
                           AND THEIR ADVISORS CONCLUDE A SERIES OF STRATEGIC
                           MEETINGS IN WASHINGTON.

In addition to decisions about the China-Burma theater (see March 8, 1943),
the Trident Conference worked out further plans for an Allied attack on Sicily
and a build up of forces for the 1944 cross-channel attack. Although British
military leaders continued to push for greater efforts in the Mediterranean,
General Marshall secured further commitments for the Allies to prepare for
the cross-channel attack. The invasion of Sicily in 1943 and perhaps of Italy
would be designed as preludes to help the major attack on western France.
It was also agreed that the full-scale attack on France (ROUNDUP) would be
ready by May 1, 1944. A final decision approved an Italian invasion after
the Sicilian attack ended.

June 3, 1943   THE FOOD AND AGRICULTURAL ORGANIZATION OF THE UNITED
                       NATIONS IS ESTABLISHED AT A MEETING IN HOT SPRINGS,
                       VIRGINIA.

July 10, 1943   ANGLO-AMERICAN FORCES LAUNCH AN INVASION OF SICILY--
                       OPERATION HUSKY.

The capture of Sicily, which provided the necessary springboard to the invasion of Italy, was completed by August 17.

July 25, 1943   *THE RESIGNATION OF PREMIER MUSSOLINI AND HIS CABINET*
                       IS ANNOUNCED BY KING VICTOR EMMANUEL II OF ITALY.

Mussolini was replaced by Marshal Pietro Badoglio who dissolved the Fascist
Party on July 28.) After German troops rescued him from a prison in Rome on
September 12, Mussolini proclaimed a Fascist Republic in Italian areas under
German control. Badoglio's government surrendered to Eisenhower on Septem-
ber 3 and declared war on Germany on October 13.

August 24, 1943   THE CONCLUSION OF THE FIRST QUEBEC CONFERENCE (QUAD-
                       RANT) OF ROOSEVELT, CHURCHILL, AND THEIR MILITARY
                       ADVISORS.

These meetings from August 11 to 24 confirmed and finalized military decisions
made or begun at the Trident Conference, which ended on May 25. The Normandy
invasion (OVERLORD) was reaffirmed for May 1, 1944, and supplemental landings
in southern France were added (ANVIA, later DRAGOON). An attempt to step up
military operations in Burma was agreed to and Lord Louis MOUNTBATTEN was
named Supreme Commander in southeast Asia.
     A decision was also made at Trident to drop the British plans for an
Allied attack through the Balkans into central Europe. The Joint Chiefs of
Staff opposed this project so strongly that Roosevelt backed them against
the British. Although Churchill argued that a Balkan attack would have postwar political advantages against the Soviet Union, General Marshall believed
that if the Allied forces became bogged down in the mountainous areas of
southeastern Europe, the Russian armies would capture all of Germany and the
Rhineland. Thus, with the president's support, the invasion of the Balkans
was not undertaken.
     Finally, at Quebec, Roosevelt agreed to the full exchange with Britain
of U.S. data on atomic energy. In 1942, U.S. and British scientists undertook
a joint research effort on the atomic bomb. By 1943, however, U.S. facilities
under the Manhattan Project worked on development and manufacturing of the
weapon and restricted the exchange of this data. Churchill wanted full cooperation on this project, and to keep the prime minister happy, Roosevelt
agreed to resume the unrestricted exchange of data. In a document signed on
August 19, the British and Americans agreed not to use this data against each
other or communicate it to third parties. Because the United States had the
basic production role, the U.S. president had the power to determine what
postwar commercial advantages Britain might receive.

September 3, 1943   THE ITALIAN CAMPAIGN BEGINS WHEN BRITISH FORCES ATTACK
                       FROM SICILY ACROSS THE STRAITS OF MESSINA. ON SEPTEM-
                       BER 9, AMERICAN FORCES MAKE AMPHIBIOUS LANDINGS AT
                       SALERNO.

The day before the major Allied operations against Italy began (September 8),
the surrender of Italy's government under General Badoglio was announced.
Although there was some German resistance in the southern part of Italy, the
initial Allied landings were comparatively easy. Salerno was captured by
September 18, and by October 14, the Allies crossed the Volturno River north
of Naples.
     On September 10, German forces took Rome. After Mussolini escaped on
September 12 and proclaimed a Fascist republic, German-dominated forces made
the central and northern Italian campaign very difficult for the Allies.

September 10, 1943   THE ALLIES ESTABLISH A MILITARY-POLITICAL COMMISSION
                       FOR NEGOTIATING WITH GERMAN ALLIES BECAUSE STALIN DIS-
                       LIKES THE ANGLO-AMERICAN SETTLEMENT WITH ITALY WITHOUT
                       RUSSIAN INVOLVEMENT.

When British and U.S. authorities began talks with the new Italian ministry
of Badoglio in July, 1943 (see October 13, 1943), Stalin complained that the
Soviet Union was not represented on the negotiating team. The Western powers
agreed to keep Stalin informed of their discussions, but in August Stalin
insisted on forming a special commission to negotiate with "Governments dis-
associating themselves from Germany."
     On September 10, Churchill and Roosevelt agreed to establish a commission
at Algiers to deal with Axis negotiations except those with Germany and Japan.
Roosevelt, however, instructed General Eisenhower that the commission was
subordinate to the Allied Commander in Chief. Although Stalin protested,
Roosevelt stood firm.
     The president realized at this time that the occupation of Italy would
set a precedent because it was the first "liberated" European state. He realized also that east Europe would fall under Russian domination when the
Soviet armies "liberated" those areas. In Italy, however, Roosevelt preferred
to minimize Russia's role and this set that precedent. When Russian armies
took over Rumania early in 1944, both Secretary of State Hull and the Joint
Chiefs of Staff assumed the Russians would have prime responsibility there.
They did.

September 25, 1943   UNDERSECRETARY OF STATE WELLES RESIGNS DUE TO LONG-
                       STANDING DIFFICULTIES WITH SECRETARY OF STATE HULL.

Roosevelt disliked losing Welles because they were close friends and the president got along with Welles better than with anyone else at the State Department. That relationship often led Hull to believe Welles usurped his authority. In addition, by the summer of 1943 Washington circles buzzed about
Welles's alleged homosexual activity. Thus, when Hull told Roosevelt that
the president would have to choose between the two, the president realized
that Welles had become a political liability and accepted his resignation.

October 13, 1943   BRITAIN AND THE UNITED STATES RECOGNIZE BADOGLIO'S
                        GOVERNMENT IN ITALY.

General Badoglio replaced Mussolini as premier of Italy on July 25 and soon
contacted the Western Allies about surrender terms. Although the British
favored recognizing a monarchy under King Victor Emmanuel II, the Americans
hesitated to do this, preferring a more liberal government in Italy. The
issue was not yet settled on September 3, when Badoglio agreed to military
terms of Italy's surrender.
    Somewhat reluctantly, and because Churchill said the only alternatives
in Italy were a monarchy, Fascism, or communism, Roosevelt agreed to accept
Badoglio's regime if he declared war on Germany and expressed his interest
in holding democratic elections in the future. On October 13, Badoglio fulfilled these conditions and Roosevelt and Churchill recognized the Italian
government.

October 30, 1943   THE MOSCOW CONFERENCE OF FOREIGN MINISTERS ENDS.

Sessions in Moscow between October 19 and 30 were the first three-power meetings of the war. The participants were Secretary of State Hull, Foreign Minister Anthony Eden, and Foreign Minister V.M. Molotov, with their military
advisors. The important decisions at this conference were:

1. Russia was assured that plans for a second front in west Europe were
   underway.

2. Stalin refused to renew the relations with the Polish London
   government-in-exile which he had ended on April 27, 1943.

3. A European Advisory Commission was created to formulate a postwar
   policy for Germany. An Advisory Council for Italy was also set up.

4. Stalin promised to enter the war against Japan as soon as Germany
   was defeated. This was an informal oral commitment made to Secretary
   Hull.

5. The Four-Nation Declaration stated that a general international organization to maintain peace and security was a necessity. The Four-
   Nation Declaration was signed for China by the Chinese Ambassador
   to Moscow, Foo Ping-sheung.

6. The Declaration of German Atrocities stated that German war criminals
   would be apprehended and sent for trial to countries where their
   crimes had been committed. The Allied governments would jointly
   punish the "major criminals."

7. Not approved was a proposal by Secretary Hull which was a declaration
   against colonialism. Molotov approved this idea but the British
   prevented its passage.

8. Austria's annexation by Germany on March 15, 1938, was declared null
   and void. Although Austria held responsibility for participating
   in the war on the side of Germany, the final war settlement would
   consider Austria's contribution to its own liberation.

November 5, 1943   THE SENATE APPROVES THE CONNALLY RESOLUTION WHICH FA-
                           VORS AN INTERNATIONAL PEACE ORGANIZATION AFTER WORLD
                           WAR II; PREVIOUSLY THE HOUSE HAD APPROVED (SEPTEMBER
                           21) A SIMILAR RESOLUTION OF J. WILLIAM FULBRIGHT.

Early in 1943 a group of senators began a bipartisan movement to commit the
United States to a postwar international peace-keeping organization. On September 21, the House adopted the Fulbright Resolution to create international
machinery with power adequate to establish and to maintain a just and lasting
peace. The resolution of Senator Tom Connally was worded similarly and approved by the Senate. The Connally Resolution said any treaty to carry out
the bill would require a two-thirds Senate vote. It passed the Senate by
85-5.

November 7, 1943   SOVIET FORCES RECAPTURE KIEV IN THE UKRAINE.

Following the Russian successes at Stalingrad on February 2, 1943, the Germans
launched a counterattack on July 5, but they made few advances. The Russian
armies repelled them and undertook a new offensive in August which recaptured
Smolensk on September 25 and won Kiev by November 7.
     The capture of Kiev opened the path toward Polish territory, which the
Russian armies entered on January 3, 1944.

November 9, 1943   THE UNITED NATIONS RELIEF AND REHABILITATION ADMINIS-
                           TRATION (UNRRA) IS ESTABLISHED BY A MEETING OF 44 NA-
                           TIONS IN WASHINGTON.

UNRRA would provide aid to liberated populations of Europe and the Far East.
Former New York Governor Herbert H. Lehman was named as the first Director
General of UNRRA.

November 26, 1943   THE FIRST CAIRO CONFERENCE RESULTS IN BRITISH AND AMER-
                           ICAN AGREEMENTS ON CHINA AND THE FAR EAST.

At Roosevelt's insistence American and British military advisors met with
Churchill, Chiang Kai-shek, and China's military leaders. Beginning with a
November 22 session on a possible Burmese invasion plan, the delegates considered east Asia's future. While Chiang agreed with the U.S. Army that
there should be an attack against Japan in Burma, the British could not commit
any amphibious troops to attack by crossing the Bay of Bengal. As a result,
the Burmese attack was delayed for another year.
     Roosevelt particularly pleased Madame and Generalissimo Chiang by agree-
ing to strip Japan of all its Pacific possessions. Formosa, Manchuria, and
all areas taken from China would be returned to China. In turn, Chiang agreed
that Russia would receive all of Sakhalin and the Kurile Islands as well as
the use of Darien as a free port. Russia would cooperate with Chiang in
China and agree not to impair China's territorial integrity. In addition,
Roosevelt promoted the idea that China was one of the Big Four powers that
would have a vital role in Asia after the war. After the sessions ended in
Cairo on November 26, Roosevelt and Churchill went to Teheran for discussion
with Stalin and Soviet military experts. During informal sessions at Teheran,

Roosevelt and Churchill obtained Stalin's oral affirmation of the territorial
changes agreed to with Chiang Kai-shek at Cairo. See December 1, 1943.

December 1, 1943   THE BIG THREE CONFERENCE ENDS AT TEHERAN, IRAN.

For the first time, Roosevelt, Churchill, and Stalin met to discuss a variety
of strategic war issues and postwar plans. Regarding the military situation,
the three leaders discussed the coordination of Soviet attacks on Germany
with the D-day landings in France in 1944. Once again, Stalin agreed to enter
the war against Japan as soon as Germany was defeated.

Three key postwar matters were discussed but not finalized at Teheran.
First, Roosevelt tried to convince Stalin to use American methods to insure
the future security of Russia in eastern Europe. Rather than simply annexing
the Baltic states or Poland, Roosevelt urged Stalin to use "referendums" and
to allow for "self-determination." Churchill indicated that since England
had gone to war in 1939 to protect Poland, the British were particularly concerned about the future of Poland. Churchill wanted Stalin to recognize the
London Polish government or to give it a vital role in Poland's future government. Neither Roosevelt nor Churchill was concerned about the exact borders
of Poland, for these could be adjusted. They desired, however, that some
semblance of self-determination should be used in all areas liberated by the
Big Four powers.

Regarding Poland's government, Stalin expressed his willingness to grant
some representation to the London exiles. He wanted them first to accept
the Curzon Line as Poland's eastern border, to renounce Nazism, and to sever
all connections with German agents in Poland. They should also give support
to the partisans fighting underground in Poland. No final decisions on Poland
were made, however.

A variety of ideas were considered by the Big Three concerning postwar
Germany. Roosevelt suggested dividing Germany into three parts for political
purposes. Churchill conjectured that Prussia, Bavaria, and other states could
be separated while Austria and other sections should be formed into a Danu-
bian Confederation. These and other ideas were given to the European Advisory
Commission for detailed consideration on Germany.

Finally, Roosevelt requested that the other two leaders join the United
States and China in sponsoring an international peace organization after the
war. Although Churchill and Stalin both preferred regional peace blocs, the
president argued that these seemed to be too much like spheres-of-influence
pacts. Stalin eventually agreed that some sort of world organization should
be established after the war.

December 6, 1943   THE SECOND CAIRO CONFERENCE CONCLUDES.

Following the Teheran Conference, Roosevelt and Churchill returned to Cairo
for further discussions between their military chiefs and with Ismer Inönü,
president of Turkey. Great Britain reaffirmed its alliance with Turkey, and
the "firm friendship" between Turkey, the United States, and the Soviet Union
was recognized. The most significant military decision at the Cairo Conference was the appointment of Dwight D. Eisenhower as Commander of Allied Forces
for the invasion of western Europe.

In personal conversations with Churchill at Cairo, the president indicated his suspicions about Stalin's keeping his word regarding intervention

in China or in the postwar peace organization. The president also believed that realistic solutions to European problems would be difficult because of the American public's insistence on idealistic standards with other nations.

December 17, 1943   THE IMMIGRATION LAW EXCLUDING CHINESE FROM IMMIGRATING TO THE UNITED STATES IS ABROGATED.

In 1943, a New York group headed by Richard Walsh, editor of *Asia and the Americans*, formed a Citizens Committee to Repeal Exclusion. Subsequently, several repeal bills were introduced in congress, and by September, House Speaker Sam Rayburn informed the State Department that a bill being considered by the Immigration Committee appeared likely to be approved. Both the president and Undersecretary of State Edward Stettinius for the State Department sent letters recommending this act. As a result, both the House (October 21) and the Senate (November 26) passed the repeal bill, which the president signed on December 17.

The bill applied only to Chinese, not all Orientals as the Oriental Exclusion Bill had stated. In addition to repealing Chinese exclusion, the law admitted Chinese under the quota basis of the general Immigration Law. The quota for Chinese immigrants was 105 per year. The bill also permitted Chinese to become naturalized American citizens.

December 21, 1943   GENERAL STILWELL BEGINS A CAMPAIGN TO OPEN A ROAD FROM LEDO THROUGH NORTHERN BURMA TO CHINA.

At the Cairo Conference (see November 26, 1943), the south Burma campaign was cancelled. Nevertheless, General Stilwell opened the campaign from Ledo, India, because he wanted a supply road to Yunnan province of China and he wished to demonstrate that the Chinese soldiers he trained in India were good fighters. In addition to assistance from the Chinese under Stilwell, the Ledo Campaign was aided by American air-borne troops known as Merrill's Marauders, named after General Frank Merrill, and British air-borne troops under General Orde Wingate.

Throughout the winter of 1943-1944, Stilwell tried to persuade Chiang Kai-shek to use the Chinese forces in Yunnan to attack from the east toward Ledo, but Chiang refused. Finally, on April 3, 1944, President Roosevelt made a strong appeal to Chiang to use the Yunnan forces which the United States had armed and trained. Chiang finally yielded, and on May 10, the Yunnan Chinese army of 40,000 began an attack across the Salween River into northern Burma.

Nevertheless, the 1944 Burma campaign to open the Ledo Road was extremely long and difficult. The Japanese brought reinforcements and fought strongly. The monsoon rains from May to October made the struggle wet and brought disease to Merrill's Marauders. Supplies from America through Ledo had a 15,000-mile journey to reach the 31,000 U.S. forces along the route. Finally, the Japanese in China began an offensive toward Chungking during the spring of 1944 and frightened Chiang into reducing aid to the Yunnan forces in Burma. The Ledo Road was not opened until January 26, 1945, when the Yunnan forces linked up with Stilwell's forces from India.

1944

January 11, 1944　　　AN EXTENSIVE AIR BOMBING CAMPAIGN BEGINS AGAINST GER-
MANY.

Although there had been Allied air raids against the European continent from
England since 1939, the 1944 effort had the objective of preparing the way
for the Allied attack with amphibious forces against Germany. The air action
accelerated, reaching its peak in May, 1944. One notable air attack was made
by 800 U.S. planes against Berlin on March 6, 1944.

　　Air Force General Arnold called the week of February 20-26, 1944, "probably the most decisive of the war." During that week, Allied bombers inflicted severe damage on German installations, including the machine plants
in Essen and Schweinfurt.

　　The Anglo-American bombing of Germany intensified from 1943 until the
end of the war in May, 1945, as the Allies gained air control over the Luft-
waffe. Most analysis of the bombing effort indicates that the strategic objectives of the air attacks were not met. Until the Allied armies invaded
Germany late in 1945, the bombings did not materially reduce Germany's productive capacity nor did they break the morale of Germany's civilians. Attacks on German cities caused great damage but did not affect production.
By the end of 1944 and in early 1945, the Allied raids became "terrorist,"
hitting anything on the ground whether it was a target or not. The smallest
villages became a "military objective." See February 14, 1945.

January 16, 1944　　　A REPORT FROM HENRY MORGENTHAU ON THE NAZI JEWISH PRO-
GRAM RESULTS IN ROOSEVELT'S ESTABLISHMENT OF A WAR
REFUGEE BOARD.

Reports since 1942 had indicated that the Nazis had become committed to a
policy of the total destruction of the Jews. Governments of the Western powers engaged in the war effort against Germany had found no effective method
to rescue or aid the Jewish population. On January 16, Secretary of the Treasury Morgenthau prepared a report on the "Acquiescence of this Government in
the Murder of the Jews" which charged that the State Department procrastinated
in helping to rescue European Jews.

　　As a result of this report, Roosevelt created a special agency, the War
Refugee Board, to assist the immediate rescue of Jews or other minorities
threatened with extermination. Consisting of the Secretaries of State, Treasury, and War, this board helped Jews in Europe secure visas and funds to
emigrate to safety in North Africa, Italy, and America. To avoid immigration quotas, it set up an "Emergency Rescue Shelter" in America as a temporary
haven.

January 22, 1944   IN ITALY, LANDINGS AT ANZIO BEACHHEAD NEAR ROME BEGIN
                          AN ASSAULT AGAINST STRONG GERMAN POSITIONS IN CENTRAL
                          ITALY.

The Italian fighting was difficult because of the mountainous terrain and the
key German defenses at the Gustave Line. Cassino was overrun on May 18, and
on June 4, Rome was liberated by the U.S. Fifth Army.
     The Italian campaign did have a salutary effect on preparations for the
June attack on Normandy. The Germans committed nearly 39 divisions to Italy,
which subtracted from Hitler's strength in France and eastern Europe.

March 26, 1944   AS RUSSIAN TROOPS BEGIN TO INVADE RUMANIA, CHURCHILL
                          OBTAINS STALIN'S APPROVAL TO GIVE BRITAIN PRIMARY RE-
                          SPONSIBILITY FOR GREECE.

Russia's successful drive through the Ukraine after the capture of Kiev (November 6, 1943) brought the Soviet army to the borders of Rumania by late
March. In Greece, Communist-inspired uprisings began, causing Great Britain
to be concerned about its traditional control in the Aegean and Mediterranean
seas. As a result, Churchill requested and Stalin agreed that while the Soviets would have responsibility in Rumania, Britain could have the same in
Greece.
     When Churchill asked Roosevelt to accept this, the president hesitated
to give approval because he feared that Americans would understand such an
arrangement as a "sphere-of-influence." Nevertheless, Roosevelt agreed to
try it for three months, after which the matter could be reviewed. The
Stalin-Churchill agreement became the first of several attempts to reach a
settlement on eastern Europe's future.

June 2, 1944   THE FRENCH PROVISIONAL GOVERNMENT-IN-EXILE IS FORMED
                          IN FRENCH ALGIERS.

This government developed as a joint venture of Giraud and de Gaulle who had
compromised their differences on May 31, 1943, by forming the French Committee
of National Liberation (see January 24, 1943, on the Casablanca Conference).
On June 2, the French Provisional Government proposed its full support in
the war against the Axis powers. On October 23, 1944, the United States,
Great Britain, and Russia recognized this government.

June 6, 1944   D-DAY: OPERATION OVERLORD BEGINS AN ALLIED INVASION
                          60 MILES WIDE ALONG THE NORMANDY COAST OF WESTERN
                          FRANCE.

Preceded by parachute and glider forces, a spearhead assault of 176,000 troops
aided by 4,000 invasion craft, 600 warships, and 11,000 airplanes invaded
France. The large-scale landings succeeded and by June 27, Cherbourg was
captured. By July 2, the Allies had landed 1 million troops plus 566,648
tons of supplies and 171,532 vehicles. By August 10, Normandy was secured
and the Allied armies advanced into France, liberating Paris on August 25,
Belgium on September 4, and Luxembourg on September 11.

June 12, 1944   GERMANY LAUNCHES V-1 PILOTLESS AIRCRAFT TO BOMB SOUTH-
                       ERN ENGLAND.

These jet-propelled aircraft were launched from special sites in France and
Belgium, most of them being targeted for London. Later, on September 7, the
Germans fired 3,400-mile V-2 rockets at London. These attacks were terror-
type raids because rocket developments had not yet advanced sufficiently to
have a substantial effect on the war.

June 21, 1944   VICE-PRESIDENT WALLACE VISITS CHINA IN AN EFFORT TO
                       ASSIST THE FORMATION OF A COALITION CHINESE GOVERNMENT
                       OF THE COMMUNISTS AND NATIONALISTS.

Throughout the war against Japan, Chiang Kai-shek had preserved his armies
by avoiding conflict with the Japanese in order to blockade the Chinese Communist forces in north China and to have troops to fight the communists after
the United States and Great Britain defeated Japan. Nearly 500,000 Nationalist forces were in constant use to block any Communist advances.
     In 1944, Roosevelt and his advisors decided to strive for a Nationalist
Communist Party coalition government so that all of China's efforts could be
directed against the Japanese enemy. When neither Stilwell nor U.S. Ambassador Clarence Gauss could persuade Chiang to talk with the communists,
Roosevelt sent Vice-President Henry Wallace to China to obtain Chiang's cooperation.
     Wallace received only a few small concessions from Chiang. He allowed
U.S. observers to visit Communist-controlled areas and accepted Roosevelt's
offer to attempt a mediation with Moscow. Chiang would not open discussions
with Mao Tse-tung and strongly opposed cooperation with the Chinese communists. According to Chiang, Mao was both subject to the "orders of the Third
International" and "more communistic than the Russian Communists." Too many
Americans, he said, were fooled by the communists. The United States could
best remain aloof and cool toward Mao's bandits.
     Chiang told Wallace he agreed with Roosevelt's efforts to gain better
relations for the Nationalists with Moscow. He wanted to reach an understanding with the Soviet Union that would cut off aid to Mao. He also asked the
vice-president to get rid of Ambassador Gauss and General Stilwell and asked
the president to appoint a personal representative so that Chiang could deal
directly with Roosevelt. For the results of Chiang's requests see October 21,
1944.

June 22, 1944   THE UNITED STATES SEVERS DIPLOMATIC RELATIONS WITH
                       ARGENTINA AND URGES OTHER AMERICAN REPUBLICS TO DO
                       LIKEWISE.

Following Argentina's failure to uphold the Declaration of the Rio Conference
(see January 28, 1942), Secretary of State Hull became increasingly upset
with the pro-Fascist sympathies of Argentina. First Argentine President
Castillo and, after February 15, 1944, the new, Peron-backed President Edel-
miro Farrell refused to take effective action against the Axis although Argentina broke relations with Germany on January 26, 1944.
     When Farrell's government did not implement its break with the Axis
announced in January, 1944, Hull decided to pressure the government to change

its policy. Therefore, on June 22, 1944, Hull recalled U.S. Ambassador Norman
Armour from Buenos Aires and sent memos to Britain and other Latin American
republics to do the same. Britain and all but three of the other American
republics did so, virtually isolating Argentina from hemispheric politics.
Later Hull froze Argentina's assets in America and called for a boycott of
Argentina's products. Great Britain's refusal to join the boycott caused
this action to fail. Many Americans believed Secretary Hull was being too
harsh with Argentina. After Hull resigned in November, 1944, steps were taken
to repair U.S. relations with Argentina.

July 11, 1944   ROOSEVELT RECOGNIZES GENERAL DE GAULLE'S FRENCH COM-
                            MITTEE ON NATIONAL LIBERATION AS THE TEMPORARY *DE FACTO*
                            AUTHORITY FOR FRANCE.

From the outset, Roosevelt and Secretary Hull had disliked the arrogance of
de Gaulle's claim to represent the French people. At the Casablanca Conference in January, 1943, de Gaulle reluctantly agreed to become a co-president
with General Giraud in North Africa. In November, 1943, however, de Gaulle
forced Giraud off the National Committee to give himself sole authority. On
November 11, 1943, he dismissed Lebanese demands for independence by suspending the Lebanese constitution, imprisoning Lebanon's ministers, and abolishing
Lebanon's parliament.
    In early 1944, de Gaulle refused to cooperate with the Allied invasion
of France unless the Allies recognized his provisional government as indis-
pensable for a successful liberation battle. Roosevelt rejected this concept,
arguing that the French people, not de Gaulle, needed to determine their future. Consequently, de Gaulle refused to endorse Allied military francs as
legitimate currency or to broadcast his support for the invasion on June 6,
1944. He sent only a few liaison officers to join the invaders on D-day.
    In June, however, Roosevelt decided to compromise with de Gaulle because
of military necessity. He hoped the French general would obtain greater assistance from the French resistance and would aid in the southern invasion
of France in August, 1944. Thus, he invited de Gaulle to visit Washington,
where a recognition agreement was approved. On July 11, Roosevelt announced
that the United States recognized the French Committee of National Liberation
as France's political authority. Recognition was conditional because
de Gaulle agreed that Eisenhower held complete military authority and that
the French people retained the right to choose their own government.

July 22, 1944   THE UNITED NATIONS MONETARY AND FINANCIAL CONFERENCE
                            ENDS AT BRETTON WOODS.

The Bretton Woods Conference achieved cooperative agreements by 44 nations
to stabilize national currency and stimulate world trade. The principal results of the conference were:

    (1) establishment of the International Monetary Fund (IMF) of $8.8 bil-
        lion to be used to stabilize national currency exchanges. The United
        States contributed about 25% of this fund;

    (2) creation of the International Bank for Reconstruction and Develop-
        ment. Capitalized at $9.1 billion, this bank made loans to nations

for postwar economic reconstruction. The United States supplied 35% of these funds.

Significantly, the Soviet Union refused to be part of these financial arrangements by which "capitalists" sought to continue to control the world economy.

August 1, 1944   POLISH UNDERGROUND FORCES IN WARSAW ATTACK THE GERMAN OCCUPATION TROOPS WHILE THE SOVIETS REFUSE ASSISTANCE.

The Warsaw uprising occurred about the same time that Stalin and Prime Minister Mikolajczyk of the London exile government met in Moscow to settle their difference of opinion.
   The uprising began because the Polish underground, led by the London exiles, hoped to demonstrate its power by assisting the Soviet troops, which were six miles from Warsaw. Moscow radio appealed for an insurrection to aid the liberation of Warsaw, but when a German thrust halted the Soviet army, Stalin refused to assist Warsaw's underground effort.
   In Moscow, Stalin conducted talks with Mikolajczyk and an agreement seemed imminent on August 9. The Soviet leader told Mikolajczyk he would aid the insurgents, but he did not. Stalin seemed content to destroy his principal adversaries for control of Poland. The Poles, Churchill, and Roosevelt all pleaded with Stalin at least to airlift supplies and arms to the underground. Stalin refused, saying the underground acted recklessly without his authorization. The Russians would not even agree to let U.S. planes drop supplies and land for refueling in Russia.
   After repeated requests throughout August for Soviet help, Stalin finally began an offensive on September 18. He also now allowed 104 U.S. planes to drop supplies to Warsaw, but only once. As the supplies ran out, a request for a second airlift was made, but was rejected by Moscow.
   By October 4, 1944, the Germans suppressed the Warsaw rebellion. One-fourth of Warsaw's population died. Any hope of creating an anti-Soviet regime in Poland vanished. The Soviet army captured Warsaw on January 17, 1945.

August 15, 1944   ALLIED FORCES LAND IN SOUTHERN FRANCE, LAUNCHING ANOTHER INVASION AGAINST GERMAN FORCES.

This attack, Operation DRAGOON, was made on the coast between Nice and Marseilles. After securing a beachhead, the U.S. Seventh Army continued an offensive up the Rhine River Valley.

September 10, 1944   AMBASSADOR TO THE SOVIET UNION AVERELL HARRIMAN REPORTS THAT RUSSIA HAS BECOME UNCOOPERATIVE IN THE PAST TWO MONTHS.

Harriman sent a message to President Roosevelt through Harry Hopkins, indicating his concern that relations with the Soviets "have taken a startling turn" since July. The Soviets had become indifferent to U.S. requests and to discussion of vital problems. Specific American requests had been ignored, such as those for air-shuttles by U.S. bombers between Britain and Russia to

bomb or make air reconnaissance of Germany; for the transport of trucks
through Russia to China; to allow U.S. air officers to appraise their bombing
raids on Ploesti in Rumania; and to plan for later aid against Japan.

The Soviets, Harriman contended, were now "unbending" toward Poland and
acted as a "bully" where their interests were involved. Harriman told Roosevelt he would like to return home to report more precisely on these matters.
The United States, he said, must be "firm but friendly" and should use a "quid
pro quo attitude" in Russian discussions.

September 12, 1944   U.S. FORCES BEGIN THE INVASION OF GERMANY NEAR TRIER.

This advance force was the first to reach German territory. The first large
German city captured by the Allies was Aachen on October 21. The Germans
had built secure defenses, known as Westwall, which offered strong resistance
to the Allies.

September 16, 1944   AT THE SECOND QUEBEC CONFERENCE, ROOSEVELT AND
                         CHURCHILL MAKE FINAL PLANS FOR VICTORY OVER GERMANY
                         AND JAPAN.

The chief topic of the conference was the German issue. The Anglo-American
leaders decided to create occupation zones in Germany. In addition, the
Morgenthau plan for Germany was accepted tentatively. This plan wanted to
reduce Germany to an agrarian economy by destroying its industrial and war-
making capacity and assuring its future weakness in the postwar world.

This decision on Germany did not last long, however. Following the conference, Britain changed its mind about the Morgenthau plan because it wanted
industrial reparations from Germany. In addition, reports of the concept in
U.S. newspapers forced Roosevelt to reconsider his approval of the plan. By
September 29, the president told newsmen that "no one wants to make Germany
a wholly agricultural nation again." Privately, he said that Morgenthau had
"pulled a boner."

To some degree, the Morgenthau plan had been a reaction to a State Department postwar-planning document and a War Department report that were considered to be "soft" on Germany. Roosevelt told Secretary of War Stimson on
August 24 that he had the impression that "Germany is to be restored just as
much as the Netherlands or Belgium." The president believed the German people
had to realize they were a defeated nation, and Morgenthau's plan seemed to
clarify this.

By October, 1944, Roosevelt had been embarrassed by the severity of
Morgenthau's plan. He still wanted to be "tough with Germany," however, and
at Yalta the president took a firm stand in trying to limit German reparations
for the war. It took some time for U.S. officials to know whether they preferred to repress or rehabilitate postwar Germany.

October 7, 1944   THE DUMBARTON OAKS CONFERENCE PREPARES A BASIC DRAFT
                         FOR THE UNITED NATIONS ORGANIZATION.

Representatives of the United States, Great Britain, the Soviet Union, and
China met to draw up plans for the postwar international organization that
had been agreed on at the Moscow and Teheran Conference of 1943.

Held in a suburban area of Washington, D.C., the conference agreed on the form of a General Assembly and Secretariate for the United Nations. It could not decide on the veto issue for the Security Council. This and other questions were considered at Yalta by the Big Three in February, 1945. The Dumbarton Oaks draft was finalized at the San Francisco Conference, which convened on April 25, 1945.

October 18, 1944   THE SECOND MOSCOW CONFERENCE ENDS. DURING THE SESSIONS CHURCHILL AND STALIN DECIDE ON EAST EUROPEAN "SPHERES-OF-INFLUENCE" WITH WHICH ROOSEVELT LATER CONCURS.

During the sessions at Moscow between October 9 and 18, Churchill and Stalin conducted detailed negotiations regarding eastern Europe while Ambassador Harriman represented President Roosevelt.

The most dramatic decision of the conference took place on October 9 when Stalin and Churchill arranged a temporary sphere-of-influence agreement for eastern Europe. Russia received 90% predominance in Rumania, 75% in Bulgaria, and equal influence with Britain in Yugoslavia and Hungary. Britain and America would have 90% influence in Greece. During and after the Quebec conference in September, 1944, Roosevelt and Churchill had discussed the need to check Russian influence in the Balkans. Churchill was especially concerned about controlling Greece and limiting Russian influence in Yugoslavia. Roosevelt supported Churchill's ideas and told the U.S. Joint Chiefs to assist the British plans to send forces to Greece and the Istrian Peninsula of Yugoslavia. Therefore, Roosevelt concurred with the October 9 agreement after he was informed of it on October 10.

Churchill did not include Poland in these agreements. At the Moscow meetings, Churchill tried to convince Stalin to accept the London Polish government for some role in Poland and to compromise on the boundary lines Russia desired. Decisions on Poland were delayed until the February, 1945, Yalta Conference.

The final major result of the Moscow meetings was that Churchill and Harriman obtained Russia's plans to attack Japan in Manchuria as soon as the German war ended. This pleased both Britain and the United States because it relieved the Anglo-American army of the need to send large ground armies to China.

October 20, 1944   THE PHILIPPINE CAMPAIGN BEGINS AS GENERAL MacARTHUR'S FORCES INVADE LEYTE.

Throughout 1943 and early 1944, preparations leading to the return to the Philippines required a series of Allied campaigns such as landings at the islands of Arawe and New Britain in the Solomon Islands in December, 1943, and the Admiralty Islands and Dutch New Guinea during the spring of 1944. The naval and air battle of the Philippine Sea on June 19-20 sank 3 Japanese carriers and 200 planes as well as crippling several battleships and cruisers. Later, on October 23-25, the Battle of Leyte Gulf was the last great naval action of the war. It decisively destroyed Japan's sea power and gave the United States control of the Philippine waters. The land battle for the Philippines continued for four months. See February 5, 1945.

October 21, 1944   GENERAL STILWELL LEAVES CHINA AFTER BEING RECALLED AT
                        CHIANG KAI-SHEK'S INSISTENCE. CHIANG SUCCESSFULLY
                        RESISTS ROOSEVELT'S ATTEMPT TO GET CHINESE FORCES TO
                        UNITE IN A CAMPAIGN AGAINST THE JAPANESE.

As a result of Vice-President Wallace's visit with Chiang (see June 21, 1944),
President Roosevelt decided in July to make a strong demand that Chiang agree
to undertake a vigorous campaign against Japan, which he had delayed since
1941. Roosevelt lost the struggle, however. By October 21, Chiang's ability
to avoid Roosevelt's demands that China attack Japanese troops demonstrated how
a military ruler of a lesser, dependent nation can ignore with impunity the
requests of a greater power. The tragedy of Chiang's persistent resistance
in refusing to engage Japanese forces in China is that military historians can
never know how the Japanese war would have ended if the Chinese had fought
against Japan with the determination that the Americans did in their Pacific
campaigns.

In July, 1944, Roosevelt tried for the first time to pressure Chiang
into accepting conditions that might have resulted in an effective Chinese
war against Japan. Telling Chiang that the "future of Asia is at stake,"
Roosevelt proposed drastic measures to stem Japanese advances in China and
to save both the American and Chinese interests. Roosevelt wanted General
Stilwell to command all Chinese resources in China, including the Communist
armies. He also told Chiang that "air power alone cannot stop" Japan, a tactic for which Chiang and General Chennault had been contending since 1942
with no apparent results. Both of these measures reversed Roosevelt's earlier
policy of placating Chiang by avoiding any strings on U.S. aid to obtain a
more effective Chinese military effort.

Although in theory Roosevelt held all the high cards to make Chiang comply and fight Japan actively, Chiang had survived since 1927 under great odds
and he survived again. Initially Chiang wrote Roosevelt that he agreed in
principle with all his requests. However, it would take "preparatory time"
to effect a change of command to General Stilwell. On July 13, the President
walked into Chiang's "time-trap." Seeing only a difference in timing between
immediate and "preparatory," Roosevelt urged "speed" on Chiang and in August
accepted Chiang's request to send a personal representative to China. The
president sent Patrick Hurley and Donald Nelson to persuade Chiang to comply.
Before Hurley and Nelson arrived at Chungking on September 7, Chiang informed
Roosevelt that certain limits would have to be placed on the changes the president proposed in July. These limits, if accepted, would have the practical
effects of nullifying Roosevelt's intentions. Chiang's requests were:
(1) the Communist forces must accept the Nationalist government of Chiang;
(2) clearer relations must be defined between Chiang and Stilwell; (3) the
Chinese Nationalists must control all Lend-Lease aid; (4) Stilwell would command only those Chinese forces *already* fighting Japan. In particular, the
first and fourth of these demands would preclude both a settlement with the
communists and Stilwell's effective uniting of all Chinese troops to fight
the foreign enemy. For Chiang, Mao was the major enemy, not Japan. As
Stilwell wrote to General Marshall, Chiang simply did not want to risk a fight
with Japan. He wanted the United States to defeat the Japanese so he could
retain all of his strength to fight the Chinese Communist Party. Ironically,
Henry Luce's *Time* and *Life* magazines edited out Theodore White's accurate
reporting on Chiang's unwillingness to fight Japan, so Americans who read
these popular magazines believed that Chiang had been a democratic freedom-
fighter against Japan since 1937.

President Roosevelt knew that Luce's pro-Chiang publications were not correct, but he found no method to counteract these stories. Roosevelt himself subscribed to Chiang's administration as the only political group the United States could accept in China. If Roosevelt forced Chiang to comply or caused his replacement by another Chinese leader, he feared the U.S. public would not understand.

On September 16, Roosevelt made one final effort to convince Chiang to take stronger action against Japan. In a message which General Stilwell believed had "a firecracker in every sentence," Roosevelt told Chiang that the United States was faced with losses both in Burma and eastern China. He feared that China would be lost if Chiang did not act immediately. He concluded that it appeared evident that all "our efforts to save China are to be lost by further delays."

Chiang did not accept Roosevelt's analysis or demands for action. Smug in his contentment to compromise with Japan by living in Chungking while the Japanese controlled all of the major cities and strategic areas of China, Chiang could wait for the United States to defeat Japan with American lives. Then Chiang could control China. The Chinese leader won the battle with Roosevelt. However, he lost the long-term struggle with Mao because he failed to realize that corruption and moral decay rotted armies and their officers that remained at ease for almost 10 years.

Rather than respond directly to the president's September 16 message, Chiang demanded Stilwell's recall. Chiang told Roosevelt that the only way the centralized command which Roosevelt desired could be effective would be if the American commander was someone acceptable to Chiang; Stilwell was not. Furthermore, Chiang said, Roosevelt cannot question the Supreme Commander on China's right to request the recall of Stilwell in whom Chiang held no confidence.

Roosevelt gave in. Having learned from Russia in September and October that it planned to invade Manchuria to fight Japan as soon as the war in Europe ended, Roosevelt decided that a campaign by the Chinese would be unnecessary. This decision meant Roosevelt would not have to face the domestic political risk of precipitating Chiang Kai-shek's loss.

On October 21, Roosevelt recalled Stilwell, who left for India immediately. On October 28, Major General Albert L. Wedemeyer replaced Stilwell as commander of U.S. forces in China. Roosevelt also withdrew his July suggestion that all Chinese forces should be united under one command. Henceforth, Roosevelt did not expect to have any effective Nationalist army operations against Japan. The president's policy in China shifted toward finding a method to have Russia cooperate in preventing a civil war in China between Mao and Chiang.

November 7, 1944   ROOSEVELT IS ELECTED PRESIDENT FOR A FOURTH TERM.

The Republican National Convention nominated Thomas E. DEWEY, governor of New York, on June 27. At Chicago on July 20, the Democrats selected President Roosevelt for reelection. Both parties backed U.S. participation in a postwar international organization and agreed in September not to debate the merits of various forms of organization. Roosevelt's age and ability to survive another four years became a major campaign issue. Roosevelt frequently looked gaunt during the campaign, but he also made some notable campaign speeches recalling the fighting, reformist days of the 1936 campaign.

While the popular vote results were the closest since the Wilson-Hughes campaign of 1916, Roosevelt won a huge electoral victory, 432 to 99. His popular majority was 3.6 million votes.

November 30, 1944   EDWARD R. STETTINIUS, JR., REPLACES CORDELL HULL AS SECRETARY OF STATE.

Secretary Hull had held the secretaryship longer than any other person, having served since March, 1933. Hull's illness made it increasingly difficult for him to continue to serve, leading to his resignation.

Roosevelt selected Stettinius as secretary because he had served usefully as Undersecretary of State. The president wanted an uncontroversial person who would encourage bipartisan support for a sound postwar foreign policy. Stettinius agreed later to serve President Truman until the end of the San Francisco Conference, resigning on July 2, 1945, to become a representative to the United Nations Organization.

Part D. *Global Relations in the Nuclear Age: Overview, 1945 to 1980*

The United States accepted the responsibility of being the global leader
of the "free world" soon after 1945. President Franklin D. Roosevelt's death
in April, 1945, just prior to the chartering of the United Nations Organization and the German surrender, brought Harry Truman to office. Although he
had not been closely initiated into Roosevelt's wartime plans for the postwar
world, Truman proved to be a decisive, strong-willed president who established
a new pattern for U.S. global foreign policy. Truman had to be decisive because the end of World War II resulted in increased tensions between the Soviet
Union and the United States.

Whether Truman or Stalin was more responsible for the decline of World
War II cooperation and the rise of the cold war diplomatic confrontation between the two super-powers is an historiographic question that academics continue to debate. From the broad historical perspective, the Communist-
capitalist clash began in November, 1917, when Lenin denounced the imperial
capitalist war and the English, French, American, and Japanese allies intervened in the Russian civil war. In addition, the suspicions of the capitalist
powers toward the Soviet Union and the Third International Communist Organization created further antagonism over the next 24 years. Although these fric-
tions had been temporarily hidden after Hitler invaded Russia in June, 1941,
they were not forgotten. The four years of Communist-capitalist alliance
against the Fascists generated some cooperation. Suspicion continued, however, being evident during the war in such disagreements as those over the
long-delayed second front against Germany and the proper Polish exile regime.
Thus, President Roosevelt's hopes for postwar cooperation with Stalin had
always been shaky, making the possibility of continued agreements after the
war a long-shot.

Within five years of the Japanese surrender in August, 1945, cold war
tensions increased as the United States perceived and acted against Communist
threats in both Europe and the Far East. Fearing Americans might return to
political isolationism, Truman and Winston Churchill used their best rhetoric
to define the divisions between the "free" capitalist world and the commun-
nists' plans to create world tyranny. First in Greece and Turkey, soon after
in western Europe in 1947, Truman formulated a "doctrine" that rallied Americans to support a cold war program that would protect "free" nations from
communism by strengthening the free world's economy. Backed by U.S. funding
and NATO's defensive military alliances, America's European allies would re-
construct their domestic economy to discourage Communist gains outside East
Germany.

In the Far East, Chiang Kai-shek's loss of China in 1949 to the peasant
armies of Mao's Communist regime focused American attention on the threat to
east Asia. Sooner than anticipated, North Korea's Communist regime invaded
South Korea in June, 1950. Deciding that communism must be contained in North
Korea, President Truman committed U.S. forces to help Seoul and gained United
Nations support against North Korea's aggression.

Truman's decision to globalize the cold war in 1950 encouraged Senator

Joseph McCarthy's campaign to criticize the president's limited containment policies as an ineffective response to communism. McCarthy blamed Truman for the loss of China, claiming that communism, like Fascism, should be destroyed in a crusade fought as vigorously as World War II. For U.S. policymakers, McCarthyism generated a new challenge. A vocal minority of Americans agreed with McCarthy that communism should not be simply contained by defensive alliances and U.S. economic aid, it should be defeated as totally as the Axis alliance had been. Although McCarthy's proposals never became operative, his ideas had sufficient appeal among Americans that for the next 30 years, American leaders could not ignore the potential growth of the crusading spirit embodied in McCarthyism from 1950 to 1954.

From 1952 to the end of 1980, American foreign policy experienced periods of lessened or greater cold war confrontations with communism. Under Presidents Dwight Eisenhower (1953 to 1960) and Richard Nixon (1969 to 1974), tensions relaxed as consultations with the Soviet leaders brought periods of peaceful coexistence and détente. Under Presidents John F. Kennedy and Lyndon Johnson and after 1979 under Jimmy Carter, cold war tensions increased as stronger U.S. measures appeared necessary to stop the spread of Communist influence.

More specifically, after 1953 the cold war focused on the Third World, not on Europe where containment, peaceful coexistence, and détente worked successfully. In the Third World areas where Western imperialism had dominated, Soviet communism held an advantage because Russia had not been classified as an imperial power. The Soviets had nothing to lose if Third World nations struggled to gain national liberation.

Until 1954, Great Britain and France endeavored to retain their colonial influence. After fighting a colonial war in Indochina from 1946 to 1954, France decided to change its policy and joined England in yielding to nationalist demands in Africa and Southeast Asia. When the French withdrew from Vietnam in 1954-1955, President Eisenhower assumed a U.S. obligation to contain communism in Southeast Asia. The Geneva Conference of 1954 ended French jurisdiction in Indochina by creating three states: Laos, Cambodia, and Vietnam. While former princely rulers were given authority in Laos and Cambodia, Vietnam was divided. South Vietnam came under control of the Emperor Bao Dai, whom France had previously recognized; North Vietnam came under the Communist rule of Ho Chi Minh, who had led the fight against France. Eisenhower committed the United States to backing Bao Dai and South Vietnam's premier, Ngo Dinh Diem, thereby linking the United States to the regime France had supported.

Although Eisenhower wanted to limit the U.S. commitment to South Vietnam, he established a pattern for American policy in former colonial regions. This policy supported rulers willing to accept American aid for an anti-Communist regime regardless of the local popularity or the commitment to democratic "freedom" of the American-backed regime. To further implement this policy, the United States formed two new alliances in Third World areas. In the middle East, the Baghdad Pact (later CENTO) was formed; in Southeast Asia, the Southeast Asia Treaty Organization (SEATO) was established. These alliances, added to the NATO alliance in Europe and the Japanese, National Chinese, and South Korean alliances in east Asia, provided a network of "defensive" anti-Communist alliances that nearly encircled all of the U.S.S.R.

While creating this alliance network, Eisenhower endeavored to relax the policy of confrontation with the Soviet Union that Truman had begun. After Stalin died in 1953, his successor, Nikita Khrushchev, and Eisenhower encouraged negotiations for a nuclear test ban and the settlement of the Berlin issue, but their efforts failed in 1960. The Eisenhower-Khrushchev summit conference planned for May, 1960, ended in disarray because an American spy plane (U-2) was shot down over Russia several days before the conference began.

The U-2 affair contributed greatly to John F. Kennedy's presidential campaign of 1960. Since 1957, Democratic presidential contenders had criticized Eisenhower for not acting vigorously in the cold war and for allowing an "alleged missile-gap" to endanger American nuclear superiority over the Soviet Union. The U-2 incident, for which Eisenhower apologized to Khrushchev, dramatized the effects of "peaceful coexistence," according to the president's critics.

Having rallied opposition to the Republicans on a foreign policy platform which favored the vigorous prosecution of the cold war, the Kennedy and Johnson administrations (1961-1969) urged Americans to sacrifice in the "greatest hour of danger to the free world." First at Cuba's Bay of Pigs (April, 1961), later in West Berlin, the Congo, the Dominican Republic, Vietnam, and elsewhere, the two Democratic presidents instituted an era of vigorous competition along the periphery of the communists' iron and bamboo curtains. Their tactics varied from indirect aid at the Bay of Pigs in Cuba, to the Peace Corps everywhere, from rhetoric in West Berlin to the intensive bombings of North Vietnam, from the space race and moon shot to the rapid build up of U.S. missile superiority. By 1968, however, the vigorous prosecution of the cold war resulted in a vast amount of dissent, Johnson's resignation from the race for a second term, and the election of a Republican, Richard Nixon.

From 1969 to 1974, President Nixon and his erstwhile alter ego, Henry Kissinger, tried unsuccessfully to institute a radical shift in U.S. foreign policy. First as National Security Advisor, later as Secretary of State, Henry Kissinger joined President Nixon in pursuing a more "realistic" program of U.S. power politics. Eschewing the ideological fervor of Truman's cold war attitudes, Nixon undertook "realistic" negotiations with Moscow, Peking, and other Communist nations willing to exchange benefit for benefit with Washington. Calling their program "détente" they demonstrated how practical results could be gained by consulting with the communists. The major consequences of détente were the gradual withdrawal of U.S. troops from Vietnam, dramatic presidential visits to Peking and Moscow, and Strategic Arms Limitation agreements with the Soviet Union in 1972. Lesser but no less significant agreements were concluded on Berlin, trade relations between the capitalist and the Communist nations, cultural exchanges, and a joint U.S.-Soviet space rendezvous in 1975.

Détente floundered, however, on Nixon's Watergate imbroglio and the American public's inability to perceive the Soviets as a conciliatory adversary. Following Nixon's resignation in August, 1974, President Ford adopted Kissinger as his Secretary of State but could not subdue the complaints of right-wing Republicans and Democrats against the treachery-behind-the-smile which they saw as détente with the Kremlin's leaders. Russia's limits on Jewish immigration, its interference in the Middle East, and its activity in Angola and the Horn of Northeast Africa in 1975 and 1976 caused Ford to drop détente as a viable concept.

Ford's loss to Jimmy Carter in the 1976 presidential race hastened the decline of détente. Although Carter continued Nixon's China policy by granting full recognition to Peking in 1979, Carter's emphasis on human rights led almost inevitably to a "second" cold war era. Although Carter's "human rights" issue gained some admiration from liberal Americans who disliked

linking the "free world" to Fascist-style military rulers in many Third World
areas, the "human rights" issue also renewed the ideological overtones of
Truman's cold war concepts. By the end of 1979, Carter shifted to a hard
line of confrontation with the Soviet Union. He dropped efforts to ratify
SALT II, described Russia's Afghanistan venture as Communist aggression, embargoed U.S. grain sales to Russia, and boycotted the Moscow Olympics. Carter
set the stage for the even more vigorous cold war methods of President Ronald
Reagan who defeated Carter for the presidency in 1980. Reagan had consistently opposed détente and was prepared in 1981 to rectify the Soviet advantage
gained by Moscow during the détente appeasement era of the 1970's. Renewed
cold war tensions appeared likely to become the characteristic U.S. policy
for the 1980's.

XIII. ORIGINS OF THE COLD WAR: YALTA, POTSDAM, AND THE ATOMIC
BOMB; TRUMAN DOCTRINE, MARSHALL PLAN, AND NATO; THE KOREAN WAR (1945–1952)

1945

January 21, 1945   WESTERN FRONT: THE ALLIED ARMIES RESTORE THE LINES
                          WHICH THE GERMANS DISRUPTED DURING THE "BATTLE OF THE
                          BULGE."

Between December 16 and 26, 1944, a German counteroffensive dislodged Allied
armies near the Ardennes Forest. A portion of the Allied lines gave way as
the German tanks tried to strike toward Antwerp. Although the German offensive was checked on December 26, the Allies required nearly four weeks to
regain the territory they had lost. The "battle of the bulge" cost 77,000
U.S. casualties with 8,000 deaths. In addition, 21,000 men were captured.
The Germans sacrificed 600 tanks and over 100,000 men in the offensive.

January 23, 1945   *EASTERN FRONT: A RUSSIAN OFFENSIVE COMPLETES THE "LIB-*
                          ERATION" OF POLAND.

Beginning on January 12 from the eastern outskirts of Warsaw, the Soviet ar-
mies captured Warsaw on January 17 and carried forward to the Oder River by
January 23. There the Russians regrouped preparatory to an assault on Germany
and Berlin.

February 5, 1945   THE INVASION OF LUZON BY U.S. FORCES BEGINS.

On this day, General MacArthur achieved his promise to return to the Philippines, from which he had fled in 1942. Manila was liberated on February 23,
1945.

February 11, 1945   YALTA CONFERENCE CONCLUDES, HAVING BEEN IN SESSION
                          SINCE FEBRUARY 4.

This summit conference of the Big Three--WINSTON CHURCHILL, JOSEPH STALIN,
and FRANKLIN D. ROOSEVELT--planned for the postwar status of Europe and for
establishing the United Nations. The important conference decisions were:

   1. *EASTERN EUROPE*: The spheres-of-influence of the U.S.S.R. and Great
Britain remained as agreed to at the Moscow Conference of October 9, 1944.

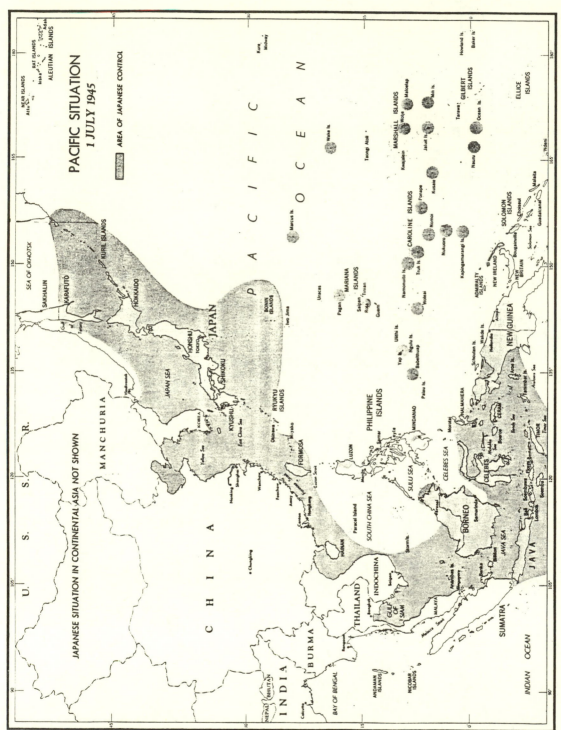

The Far East in World War II, 1941–45.

However, a "DECLARATION ON LIBERATED EUROPE" asserted the "right of all peoples to choose the form of government under which they will live."

2. *POLAND*: The Soviet-backed Polish Provisional Government (LUBLIN GOVERNMENT) was accepted, but Stalin agreed to expand its personnel to include "democratic leaders" both from Poland itself and from the Polish government-in-exile in London.

It was agreed that, with a few digressions, the Curzon Line of 1919 would be the eastern boundary. This line gave Russia Vilna and other territory gained by Poland in the Treaty of Riga (March 18, 1921) ending the Russo-Polish War of 1920. To compensate Poland, the western Polish border took territory from Germany by being extended to the Oder-Neisse line.

3. *GERMANY*: In order to give "future peace and security" in Europe, Germany would be required to disarm, and be demilitarized and dismembered. Germany would be divided into three zones for occupation purposes, with a fourth zone given to France from portions of the British and American zones. Stalin did not recognize France as a fourth "big power" but Churchill and Roosevelt wished to reward the French.

The Big Three also agreed that Germany should pay REPARATIONS, a proposal strongly advocated by Stalin. Specific details on reparations would be prepared by an Allied Reparations Commission consisting of representatives of each of the Big Three powers. Although Churchill objected, a special clause of the Yalta agreements stated that the commission should consider as one proposal that reparations would be $20 billion dollars with 50% to go to the Soviet Union.

4. *THE FAR EAST*: The SOVIET UNION AGREED TO DECLARE WAR ON JAPAN within two or three months after Germany surrendered. In return for fighting Japan, Russia would "regain rights" lost in the 1904-1905 Russo-Japanese war: rights to the southern part of SAKHALIN ISLAND, to Port Darien and Port Arthur in China, to the MANCHURIAN RAILWAY, and to the KURILE ISLANDS.

To ratify these Russian rights, Stalin would make a TREATY OF FRIENDSHIP AND ALLIANCE with CHIANG KAI-SHEK'S Nationalist government, and gain CHIANG'S concurrent approval of the YALTA agreements.

5. *UNITED NATIONS*: Stalin's wish to give separate membership in the United Nations to Byleorussia and the Ukraine was approved; the argument used was that this was similar to separate membership for nations in the British Commonwealth.

The veto power of the Big Five powers in the Security Council was also discussed. The agreement was that substantive action could be vetoed but that discussion of a topic could not be prevented by veto. Thus, topics involving the Big Five could be discussed and might assist the peaceful settlement of a dispute.

February 14, 1945   U.S. AND BRITISH AIR FORCES BOMB DRESDEN, AN ATTACK THAT WAS EXAGGERATED INTO A SYMBOL OF ALLIED TERROR BOMBING.

The bombing of Dresden on the night of February 14 caused widespread damage that led to inflammatory reports of the bombing of innocent, culturally important cities. The bombing raid of February 14 plus two later raids in March actually killed only about 35,000 persons, according to research by David Irving in 1966. In 1945, exaggerated reports estimated deaths at as low as 135,000 and as high as 250,000.

Dresden's fame as a terror target probably arose because of a mistaken statement by a briefing officer at Eisenhower's headquarters. The officer said the attack was a new terror-raid policy of the Allies. A check with General Arnold in Washington led Eisenhower's office to announce that the officer's statement was not correct. The Allies had not begun a terror-raid policy. As often happens, the press retraction was not highly publicized, nor was the air force explanation that Dresden was a communication and transportation center for eastern Germany.

March 9-10, 1945   MASS FIRE BOMB AIR RAID ON TOKYO IS MADE BY 334
                       U.S.A.F. B-29's FLYING FROM BASES IN THE MARIANAS.

One-fourth of Tokyo's buildings were destroyed and over one million persons became homeless. Casualties were 83,793 killed and 40,918 injured. Frequent air raids continued and by June, more than 3,100,000 Japanese were homeless in Tokyo.

April 1, 1945   INVASION OF OKINAWA BEGINS.

After fierce fighting, American troops secured the island by June 21, giving American planes a base only 325 miles from Japanese cities.

April 4, 1945   THE BERNE INCIDENT: THE UNITED STATES AND BRITAIN DO
                       NOT ALLOW THE RUSSIANS TO PARTICIPATE IN DISCUSSIONS
                       ABOUT THE GERMAN SURRENDER OF NORTHERN ITALY.

As in the case of the Anglo-American talks with Badoglio's representatives (see September 10, 1943), the United States and Britain had undertaken discussion with Germany's General Karl Wolff to surrender his Italian forces. Wolff came to Berne, Switzerland, early in March, 1945, to discuss surrender terms and Roosevelt told the Joint Chiefs of Staff to handle it as a military matter even though it contained political implications.

When Stalin protested on March 15, Ambassador Harriman told him that his delegates could sit as observers during the formal negotiations but that the Berne talks with Wolff were only preliminary discussions. On March 29, Stalin again protested, claiming that the Germans had shifted three divisions from Italy to the Russian front. He believed the Anglo-Americans were plotting with Germany to let the Western Allies take over Germany while the Germans increased their fight against Russia. On April 4, Roosevelt responded to Stalin's accusations by saying that they were "vile misrepresentations of my actions" and were bitterly resented.

The increased antagonism between Russia and the Western powers indicated that the "strange alliance" of World War II had rapidly deteriorated between September, 1944, and April, 1945. The Berne incident ended because the German surrender in Italy became part of the Anglo-American effort to cooperate with Stalin in the German surrender during April-May, 1945. The Western powers desired to work with Russia in defeating Germany and assuring four-power allied control in Germany and Berlin as agreed to at Yalta.

In accordance with Eisenhower's decision, the U.S. forces reached the Elbe River on April 11, and Russian forces began fighting their way into Berlin on April 20 where they met strong German resistance until May 1. U.S.

and Soviet armies joined at Torgau on the Elbe River on April 25, 1945.

April 7, 1945   GENERAL EISENHOWER INFORMS GENERAL MARSHALL THAT WHILE
                        IT IS MILITARILY UNSOUND TO "MAKE BERLIN A MAJOR OB-
                        JECTIVE," HE WOULD ADJUST PLANS IF THE COMBINED CHIEFS
                        OF STAFF GAVE HIM A DIRECTIVE TO PLACE POLITICAL CON-
                        SIDERATIONS FIRST. THE CHIEFS DO NOT RESPOND.

My mid-March, 1945, the Anglo-American forces had captured Trier (March 2),
Cologne (March 5), and Remagen (March 7). The Russian armies had forced the
Germans to abandon their whole Vistula River defense line, and by February
20, Russia's mechanized units spearheading the armies were within 30 to 35
miles of Berlin. Consequently, in order to establish contact with the Russians for an agreement on the hook-up of Soviet and Allied troops, Eisenhower
telegraphed Stalin late in March and insisted on a clear demarcation line,
suggesting the Elbe-Mulde River line, about 53 miles west of Berlin. Churchill objected to Eisenhower's contact with Stalin, telling Marshall that the
Anglo-Americans should proceed to Berlin to reach there first. But Marshall
and President Roosevelt believed that the field commander had to make the
best military decisions on such issues and supported Eisenhower. Eisenhower
wanted to stop his advance at the Elbe-Mulde River as the most definite dividing line. He did not believe his army could reach Berlin first. He also
wanted to send his armies north to the Baltic near Lubeck and south to prevent
the Germans from setting up defenses at the National Redoubt.
    Later, looking back from the perspective of the Berlin crisis of 1948,
the March-April, 1945, decision was interpreted as a mistake by Eisenhower,
Marshall, and Roosevelt. Militarily, the decision in 1945 was the best possible. It also saved an estimated 100,000 American lives.

April 12, 1945   PRESIDENT FRANKLIN D. ROOSEVELT DIES AND HARRY S.
                        TRUMAN IS SWORN IN AS THE 32ND PRESIDENT.

Roosevelt died of a cerebral hemorrhage at Warm Springs, Georgia. President
Truman had seldom been consulted about foreign policy decisions, and he did
not share Roosevelt's inclination to formulate an understanding with the Russians. Although there were indications before his death that Roosevelt, too,
had become convinced that a stronger stand needed to be taken toward Stalin,
Truman came to symbolize the concept of resistance to the Soviet Communists.

April 21, 1945   THE SOVIET UNION AND POLAND SIGN A 20-YEAR MUTUAL AS-
                        SISTANCE PACT.

Stalin signed this treaty with the Polish Provisional Government which the
Soviets had established under the Lublin Polish leaders. They had not enlarged the government to include members of the London exile government as
Stalin had promised At Yalta. Later, at the San Francisco Conference, which
opened on April 25, the Russians nearly destroyed the conference work by attempting to have Poland represented.

April 25, 1945   THE SAN FRANCISCO CONFERENCE ON THE UNITED NATIONS
                         CONVENES.

During the early weeks of the conference, the seating of the Polish delegation
and the veto procedure in the Security Council caused much debate. See June
6 and June 26, 1945.

May 1, 1945   ADOLF HITLER DIES IN A BERLIN BUNKER.

Hitler's death was announced in Berlin by Admiral Karl Doenitz. On April 28,
Benito Mussolini was killed in a village near Lake Como, Italy.

May 7, 1945   GERMANY'S UNCONDITIONAL SURRENDER IS SIGNED BY FIELD
                         MARSHALL ALFRED JODL AT 2:41 A.M. FRENCH TIME.

President Truman and Winston Churchill announced the end of the war in Europe
on May 8.

May 11, 1945   PRESIDENT TRUMAN ORDERS AN END TO UNCONDITIONAL AID
                         TO RUSSIA AND MAKES CUTBACKS IN THE SOVIETS' LEND-LEASE
                         AID, LIMITING SUCH AID TO THE SOVIET UNION'S MILITARY
                         NEEDS FOR WAR AGAINST JAPAN.

LEO CROWLEY, the Foreign Economic Administrator, interpreted Truman's orders
strictly so that ships bound for Russia were recalled and prior orders being
filled were halted immediately. When he discovered this practice, Truman
rescinded Crowley's action on May 12, but not before the Soviet Union complained about this unilateral action.
    Actually, Truman's policy on cutbacks in Lend-Lease as soon as the war
ended hurt the British and French more than the Russians. Truman knew that
some leading congressmen wished to stop Lend-Lease early so that this aid
would be used only to fight the war, not for postwar reconstruction.

May 14, 1945   THE DEMOCRATIC REPUBLIC OF AUSTRIA IS ESTABLISHED
                         WITH SOCIALIST KARL RENNER AS CHANCELLOR.

Austria was still occupied and divided into four zones but the Four Powers
agreed to recognize the republic within its 1937 frontiers. Attempts to make
a final peace treaty with AUSTRIA were unsuccessful until 1955.

June 5, 1945   THE EUROPEAN ADVISORY COMMISSION DECIDES ON THE DIVI-
                         SION OF GERMANY AND BERLIN.

Consisting of representatives of Britain, France, Russia, and America, the
European Advisory Commission had been studying the best means of dividing
Germany for postwar occupation. Because of decisions by the Big Three at
the Teheran and Yalta Conferences, France received a portion of the U.S. and
British zones but none of the Soviet zone. As agreed on June 5, the Soviets
controlled the east zone, Great Britain the north, and the United States and

France divided the southern zone of Germany. Berlin was also divided into four parts under the administration of a four-power military command. Berlin was surrounded entirely by Russia's eastern zone.

June 6, 1945   HARRY HOPKINS REPORTS FROM MOSCOW THAT STALIN HAS COM-
PROMISED ON THE U.N. VETO AND POLISH QUESTIONS.

President Truman sent Hopkins to Moscow to confer on issues that were handicapping decisions at the San Francisco Conference. Truman selected Hopkins for this job because as Roosevelt's former confidant, Hopkins wanted to obtain Russian cooperation.

Regarding Poland, Hopkins stated the U.S. viewpoint, which accepted the concept of having a government friendly to Russia in Poland. The U.S. public had been outraged by Stalin's unilateral recognition of Poland's Provisional government. Some of the London Polish government members, Hopkins said, should be accommodated by Russia as Polish officials.

After explaining that Russian security required a non-hostile government in Poland, Stalin agreed that the present Warsaw regime could be enlarged by adding four or five members of other friendly Polish groups to the 18- or 20-member Polish cabinet. Although the London exiles did not like this compromise, Hopkins accepted it and Truman concurred. Truman hoped Stalin would later accept a free election in Poland.

Stalin also agreed to the U.N. Security Council proposal that any member of the Big Five powers could veto substantive issues but could not veto discussion of any item to be put on the agenda of the council.

June 21, 1945   U.S. FORCES WITHDRAW FROM PARTS OF EAST GERMANY IN
THE RUSSIAN ZONE, PARTS OF CZECHOSLOVAKIA, AND MOST
OF AUSTRIA.

Truman ordered the withdrawal in compliance with the Yalta agreement. The Soviet Union also followed the Yalta pact by permitting American and British troops to move into their Berlin zones on July 4, 1945, and French troops to enter its Berlin zone on August 12, 1945.

Winston Churchill had, since April, urged Truman not to withdraw unless the Soviets met certain requirements regarding Allied arms in east Europe. Truman rejected this advice, although he delayed the withdrawal by about six weeks.

June 26, 1945   THE UNITED NATIONS CHARTER IS SIGNED BY DELEGATES OF
50 NATIONS MEETING IN SAN FRANCISCO.

The charter had been unanimously approved on June 25. During the convention, the principal disputes were about Polish representation; the admission of Argentina's delegation because Argentina had not declared war on Germany and Japan until March 27, 1945; and voting procedures in the Security Council.

The United Nations organization consisted of four groups: (1) a General Assembly in which all members were represented and had one vote; (2) a Security Council to supervise military and political problems and to approve any substantive action by the United Nations, with veto powers for the Big Five (China, France, Great Britain, the United States, and the U.S.S.R.); (3) an

Economic and Social Council; and (4) an International Court of Justice. The
United Nations would be administered by a Secretary General elected by the
General Assembly.

On July 28, the U.S. Senate ratified the United Nations Charter by a
vote of 89 to 2 after six days of debate.

July 3, 1945   JAMES F. BYRNES BECOMES SECRETARY OF STATE.

Although Byrnes had little diplomatic experience, he had served in both houses
of congress, on the Supreme Court, and as director of the Office of War Mobilization and Reconversion. In July, 1945, both Byrnes and Truman hoped to
end U.S. military and economic responsibilities in Europe as quickly as possible. They believed the U.S. public desired a retreat to its pre-1941
status. Byrnes served as secretary until January 21, 1947.

July 16, 1945   TRUMAN, CHURCHILL, AND STALIN BEGIN DISCUSSIONS AT
                             POTSDAM, NEAR BERLIN.

During the conference, Truman learned that the United States had successfully
detonated the atomic bomb. Thus, he made several significant decisions at
Potsdam while he was also negotiating with Stalin and Churchill. On July 26,
Clement Attlee replaced Churchill as Britain's prime minister and representative at Potsdam.

July 16, 1945   ATOMIC BOMB IS SUCCESSFULLY EXPLODED AT ALAMAGORDO,
                             NEW MEXICO.

Until this experiment, scientists working on the MANHATTAN PROJECT did not
know exactly when their effort would succeed.

Anticipating the success of the A-BOMB, discussions about using the bomb
had begun on May 9, 1945, when an Interim Committee was charged with advising
the president on the use of the atomic weapon. The committee consisted of
men who wanted the bomb to be used to end the war: Secretary of War Henry
Stimson (Chairman); George L. Harrison, Deputy Secretary of War; Vannevar
Bush, Director of the Office of Scientific Research and Development; Karl T.
Compton of the Manhattan Project; Navy Undersecretary Ralph Bard; Assistant
Secretary of State Will Clayton; and James Byrnes, who would replace Stettin-
ius after the end of the San Francisco Conference.

On June 16, the Interim Committee reported that there was no "acceptable
alternative to direct military use of the bomb." The bomb should be used
against Japan as soon as it was operational. A war plant or military instal-
lation in Japan should be the target and Japan should not be warned in advance
of the A-Bomb.

There were scientists aware of the Manhattan Project who disagreed with
the Interim Committee. Seven members of the University of Chicago group,
headed by James O. Franck, proposed holding a public demonstration of the
bomb in a deserted place, followed by a warning to Japan to surrender or suffer the consequences of an A-Bomb attack. The Interim Committee opposed such
a test.

On June 18, Truman met with his War Council (the Joint Chiefs of Staff
and the Secretaries of War and the Navy) to consider future plans against

Japan. The A-Bomb was mentioned but only briefly, because the test had not yet been made in New Mexico. The Joint Chiefs presented plans for Operation Olympic, an invasion of Kyushu Island on November 1, 1945; and for Operation Coronet, an invasion of Honshu, on or about March 1, 1946. General Marshall believed the invasion would cause at least 250,000 U.S. deaths plus a million Japanese deaths. This invasion was preferred, however, to an offensive against Japan in China and Manchuria.

Truman ordered plans for the invasion of Kyushu to proceed, but delayed a decision on the Honshu invasion. These plans were again reviewed on July 16, when Truman had to consider the use of the A-Bomb against Japan.

July 24, 1945   TRUMAN ORDERS USE OF THE ATOMIC BOMB ON ANY OF FOUR POSSIBLE MILITARY TARGETS IN JAPAN.

The identified targets were in the cities of HIROSHIMA, KOKURA, NIIGATA, and NAGASAKI. The precise target would be determined by weather conditions permitting a daylight visual-bombing attack.

July 26, 1945   THE UNITED STATES AND GREAT BRITAIN, IN CONCURRENCE WITH CHINA, ISSUE AN ULTIMATUM TO JAPAN, ASKING FOR AN UNCONDITIONAL SURRENDER AND WARNING THAT REJECTION WILL LEAD TO THE USE OF VAST, DESTRUCTIVE FORCE AGAINST JAPAN.

July 28, 1945   U.S. PLANES DROP 27 MILLION LEAFLETS OVER JAPANESE CITIES TO EXPLAIN THE JULY ULTIMATUM AND LISTING 11 CITIES OF WHICH 4 WOULD BE DESTROYED FROM THE AIR IF JAPAN DID NOT SURRENDER.

However, the A-Bomb was not mentioned, nor was there any mention of a compromise to permit the Emperor Hirohito to remain on the throne.

August 2, 1945   THE POTSDAM CONFERENCE ADJOURNS.

The Big Three talks considered the details of the German occupation and other European problems. The principal decisions were:

1. *German reparations* - The Soviet Union dropped the $20 billion proposal made at Yalta, agreeing to base reparations on useful materials in the Eastern zone and capital equipment available in the three Western zones of Germany.

2. *Transfer of Germans* - More than 6.5 million Germans would be transferred to Germany from previously disputed territory in Hungary, Czechoslovakia, and Poland.

3. *War crimes* - It was agreed to try leading Nazis for war crimes; an International Military Tribunal was to be set up soon after the conference ended.

4. *German economy* - Proposals accepted would convert the German economy to become principally agricultural. Powerful industrial cartels

Occupation zones in Germany and Austria. From Robert H. Ferrell,
American Diplomacy, New York: W.W. Norton, revised edition, 1969.
Used with permission.

would be abolished and only peaceful products would be manufactured by German industry.

5. *Other peace treaties* – A Council of Foreign Ministers representing each of the Big Five powers was directed to prepare peace treaties for Austria, Hungary, Bulgaria, Rumania, and Finland. Once Germany regained a central government, the council would draft a peace treaty for Germany.

August 6, 1945   FIRST ATOMIC BOMB USED IN THE WAR IS DROPPED ON HIRO-
                            SHIMA, JAPAN.

Flying from an airfield on Tinian Island, a U.S. Air Force plane, named ENOLA GAY for pilot PAUL TIBBETS' mother, dropped a uranium nuclear bomb code-named "Little Boy" at 8:16 a.m. Some of the initial consequences for Hiroshima, a town with 320,000 inhabitants at the time, were: 160,000 killed or seriously injured; 62,000 of 90,000 buildings destroyed; 70,000 water-main breaks; 52 of 55 hospitals and clinics destroyed; 180 of 200 doctors and 1,654 of 1,780 nurses killed or injured. The bomb had a yield of 13 kilotons, equal to the explosive power of 13,000 tons of TNT. The largest conventional bomb used in World War II yielded the power of 10 tons of TNT.

August 8, 1945   *RUSSIA DECLARES WAR ON JAPAN; SOVIET ARMIES INVADE*
                            MANCHURIA.

August 9, 1945   SECOND ATOMIC BOMB IS DROPPED ON NAGASAKI.

Although scheduled originally to be dropped on August 11 if Japan had not surrendered, "Fat Boy," a plutonium bomb, was dropped within 75 hours of the first bomb because of predictions of bad weather over Japan on August 10 and 11. Although the plutonium bomb was more powerful than "Little Boy," damage and casualties were less extensive because of Nagasaki's terrain; approximately 100,000 were killed or seriously wounded.

August 14, 1945   *CHINA AND THE U.S.S.R. SIGN A TREATY OF FRIENDSHIP*
                            AND ALLIANCE.

Stalin recognizes Chiang Kai-shek's Nationalist regime as the central government of China. Chiang accepts the Yalta Conference decisions which gave Russia the 30-year control of the Manchurian Railway, the use of Darien, and the right to join with China in the exclusive use of Port Arthur as a naval base.

August 15, 1945   JAPAN SURRENDERS UNCONDITIONALLY, BUT WITH THE UNDER-
                            STANDING THAT THE JAPANESE CAN CHOOSE LATER IF THEY
                            WISH TO KEEP THE EMPEROR HIROHITO.

Initially, the Emperor would be subject to the Allies' commander. On August 10, the Japanese had requested that the Emperor retain his throne. The United

States did not permit this, but made the compromise understanding that the emperor might later be chosen. The Japanese cabinet accepted this agreement.

U.S. occupation forces began to land in Japan on August 26. On September 2, 1945, Japanese delegates signed the formal surrender terms with General Douglas MacArthur on board the U.S.S. *Missouri* in Tokyo Bay.

August 21, 1945   LEND-LEASE AID IS TERMINATED BY THE UNITED STATES.

From its beginning in March, 1941, until its final orders were filled in September, 1946, Lend-Lease aid amounted to $50.6 billion, minus reverse Lend-Lease of $7.8 billion received by the United States from its allies.

September 2, 1945   *IN HANOI, HO CHI MINH PROCLAIMS THE INDEPENDENCE OF VIETNAM.*

Following the Japanese surrender, Ho Chi Minh and his Viet Minh forces entered Hanoi to replace the Japanese and proclaim his nation's independence from France as well as Japan.

The Viet Minh (Vietnamese Independence League) was a national coalition organization formed in May, 1941, in order to attract all Vietnamese patriots to fight the occupation by Japan as well as the French. It was based on the Indochinese Communist Party, largely because the French had suppressed all the moderate nationalist groups during the 1930's while the smaller Communist group went underground. By 1945, however, the Viet Minh included nationalists from various political groups who united against France and Japan.

During World War II, the Viet Minh aided Americans on missions against the Japanese in Indochina. They rescued downed pilots, committed sabotage at Japanese military bases, and gave intelligence information to the American Office of Strategic Services (OSS). Many OSS officers admired the Viet Minh's capabilities, urging them to seek U.S. support in their independence struggle.

Not surprisingly, therefore, when Ho Chi Minh declared independence in 1945, his decree began: "All men are created equal. They are endowed by their creator with certain inalienable rights, among these are life, liberty, and the pursuit of happiness."

Within four weeks, however, the Viet Minh's elections turned sour. Although President Roosevelt had once spoken on behalf of the end of French colonial power in Indochina, British forces "liberated" that area and brought French colonial officials with them. The French regained Saigon in September and moved to end Vietnamese independence. President Truman ignored Ho Chi Minh's appeals for assistance. Even the Communist leaders in Paris and Moscow counseled Ho to compromise with France. See November 23, 1946.

September 9, 1945   *JAPAN SIGNS CAPITULATION TERMS WITH THE NATIONALIST GOVERNMENT OF CHINA AT NANKING AND WITH THE BRITISH AT SINGAPORE (SEPTEMBER 12).*

China regained control of Inner Mongolia, Manchuria, Formosa, and the Hainan Islands. The British reoccupied Hong Kong.

October 20, 1945   COUNCIL OF FOREIGN MINISTERS ADJOURNS ITS FIRST MEETING IN LONDON.

Since beginning on September 20, 1945, the sessions demonstrated serious disagreement of U.S.-BRITISH delegates with RUSSIA's representatives. While intended to consider peace treaties with former belligerents, the council spent most of its time disputing the participation of the Chinese and French delegates in the council decisions. Other disagreements arose over control of Japan, the Italian peace treaty, and Russian failure to have "free elections" in Rumania and Bulgaria.

October 21, 1945   *LEFT-WING PARTIES WIN THE FRENCH ELECTIONS FOR A CONSTITUENT ASSEMBLY.*

In the elections the Communists won 152 seats; the Socialists 151, and the Moderates (Mouvement Républicain Populaire--*MRP), 138. Nevertheless, on November 16, 1945, General Charles de Gaulle was elected as president of the Provisional Government.*

November 15, 1945   AMERICA, CANADA, AND BRITAIN AGREE ON AN ATOMIC ENERGY CONTROL PLAN TO SUPPORT IN THE UNITED NATIONS.

As Truman remarked in the fall of 1945, the control of atomic weapons would become mankind's major problem. Neither he, Secretary Byrnes, nor others had any precedent on which to proceed. Therefore, a variety of proposals had appeared from advocates of ideas ranging from the free exchange of all secrets with Russia to American use of the bomb to compel all nations to adopt our policies. Neither of these extremes held the attention of serious American leaders who searched for a viable means to prevent a nuclear arms race and promote peaceful uses of atomic power.

    On November 15, Truman, Attlee, and MacKenzie King agreed on a basic step-by-step proposal to be established under the auspices of a United Nations Atomic Energy Commission. Dr. Vannevar BUSH of the Office of Scientific Research had suggested the steps in the proposal, which were:

1.   extending the international exchange of all scientific information as a first test of Russia's good intentions;

2.   establishing a U.S. Committee of Inspection to inspect science laboratories of all nations engaged in atomic research. This would be done on a gradual basis so that the United States would not disclose any "secrets" immediately;

3.   stockpiling by all nations capable of atomic fission of such materials, which would be used only for peaceful purposes; the Committee of Inspection would oversee their use.

The U.N. commission would also work to eliminate atomic weapons and to provide safeguards for nations which cooperated with the U.N. commission. Each stage of the commission's work would be completed only when the confidence of the world had been secured to proceed to the next step.

    Once this plan was announced in November, 1945, its supporters, critics, and adversaries began to discuss and dissect the plan. The problems of

establishing possible international control increased as suspicions between
the Western nations and the Soviet Union grew after August, 1945.

November 27, 1945   PATRICK J. HURLEY RESIGNS AS U.S. AMBASSADOR TO CHINA;
                             HIS EFFORTS TO MEDIATE BETWEEN CHIANG KAI-SHEK AND
                             MAO TSE-TUNG FAIL.

In announcing his resignation, Hurley leveled charges against State Department
officers and Truman's China policy that provided ammunition for attacks during
the next decade on Truman, the Democratic Party, the U.S. Foreign Service,
and the State Department. Hurley blamed the failure of his efforts and
Chiang's weakness on "career diplomats in the Embassy at Chungking and Far
Eastern Division of the State Department." These officials, he asserted, did
not implement the "principles of the Atlantic Charter" but supported both
Chinese Communists and British Imperialists against Chiang Kai-shek.
     President Roosevelt had sent Hurley to China on August 18, 1944. As
the president's special representative, Hurley was charged with resolving
the lengthy dispute between U.S. General Stilwell and Chiang Kai-shek and
establishing unity between the Chinese Nationalist and Communist forces so
that they would fight the Japanese. Hurley interpreted his mission as maintaining the Nationalist government by supporting Chiang.
     Hurley's year in China caused much controversy. He oversaw the removal
of General Stilwell; replaced Clarence Gauss as Ambassador to China on December 12, 1944; demanded the removal of two career Foreign Service China
experts, George Atcheson and John Service, because they disputed his analysis
of Chinese developments; and became a friend and admirer of Chiang Kai-shek.
     In addition, visiting Moscow on his way to China in August, 1944, he
became convinced that the Soviet Union differed with Mao Tse-tung's regime
and would cooperate with the Nationalist government. Finally, as an old-time
Irish-Anglophobe, Hurley was equally convinced that Winston Churchill had
usurped Roosevelt's anti-colonial policy because he wanted Hong Kong returned
and planned to restore Anglo-French control in East Asia. Thus, he blamed
U.S. diplomats both for aiding Mao's communist growth and for supporting British attempts to renew their imperial regime in Asia.
     Because he accepted Moscow's good faith and Chiang's power, Hurley lauded
the August, 1945, pact between China and Russia. He also was pleased that
Truman extended Lend-Lease to Chiang for six months after the war's end and
that the U.S. Navy aided Chiang by carrying Nationalist troops to northern
China. Thus, on September 26, 1945, Hurley returned home ready to resign
because he believed everything was calm in China.
     During the next month, the State Department kept Hurley informed of the
deteriorating relations between the two Chinese factions. Truman and Secretary Byrnes urged him to return to Chungking. Contrary to Hurley's expectation, the Soviet Union did not keep its promises to cooperate with Chiang.
The Soviets helped the communists gain control in Manchuria and refused to
allow Nationalist troops to disembark from U.S. ships at Darien or other ports
near Manchuria. Hurley also learned that the truce arrangements between Mao
and Chiang had been postponed, and the two sides were as far apart as ever
by November, 1945. Finally, Hurley was dismayed to discover that against
his advice, both George Atcheson and John Service had been posted to Tokyo
as consultants on General MacArthur's staff.
     Russell Buhite, Hurley's biographer, is not certain what caused Hurley's
actions in November, 1945. First, he agreed to return to China, but later

surprised both Byrnes and Truman by calling a press conference to announce his resignation. Moreover, Buhite cannot explain why Hurley, in his resignation and his testimony to the Senate Foreign Relations Committee, blamed China's problems on the Foreign Service and State Department rather than on the Soviet Union's failure to cooperate and the intransigent policies of both Mao and Chiang. Hurley's Senate testimony exaggerated the blame of career officers who disagreed with him or "favored" the British and Chinese Communists.

Subsequent to Hurley's charges, Secretary of State Byrnes defended Service and Atcheson, stating that these experts had to be free to give their honest judgments on policy. They were not, Byrnes said, disloyal to Hurley, but their long years of experience in China gave them different perspectives. Byrnes's support for the Foreign Service officers in 1946 contrasts with the treatment accorded to these experts during the McCarthy era from 1950 to 1954.

November 27, 1945   THE MARSHALL MISSION TO CHINA BEGINS.

Immediately after learning of Patrick Hurley's resignation, President Truman called George Marshall, asking him to act as the president's personal representative to China. Truman, Marshall, and Secretary of State Byrnes agreed on December 9, 1945, that U.S. policy was (1) to seek a united and democratic China and (2) to retain Chinese sovereignty over Manchuria. To do this, Marshall would seek a truce between Mao and Chiang in north China and assist the Nationalist government in replacing the Japanese and Soviet troops that had evacuated northern China.

Marshall's most perplexing problem was how to mediate between the two Chinese groups while the United States continued to support Chiang Kai-shek. He was told that he should pressure Chiang as much as possible, but that the United States would not cease support of the Nationalists. This, of course, made real pressure impossible and, as under Stilwell, Chiang thought he could do as he wished by appealing to either the White House or to the friends of the China-Chiang lobby in congress.

Although Marshall secured a temporary truce in February, 1946, by the summer of 1946 he realized that neither Mao nor Chiang wanted a genuine truce. Chiang wanted to control all Manchuria and seemed successful in June, 1946. A new truce from June 7 to 30 was broken by the communists and by July 1, 1946, all-out civil war began. (See October 10, 1946.)

December 3, 1945   THE HEAD OF THE MANHATTAN PROJECT, GENERAL LESLIE GROVES, DISCLOSES THE "REAL ATOMIC SECRET" TO THE COMBINED POLICY COMMITTEE AND REPRESENTATIVES OF THE TRUMAN ADMINISTRATION.

The "real secret" was NOT AMERICA'S SPECIAL TECHNOLOGICAL KNOWLEDGE BUT AN ASSUMED U.S. MONOPOLY ON URANIUM ORE.

Knowing that the Soviet Union had the scientific and technological ability to build the bomb eventually, GROVES DECIDED IN 1943 TO SECURE AMERICAN CONTROL OF THE SUPPLY OF FISSIONABLE MATERIAL, uranium and thorium. At the Quebec Conference of 1943, the COMBINED POLICY COMMITTEE was set up to obtain British and Canadian cooperation, and to enlist the aid of the Belgian government in exile in obtaining uranium from the BELGIAN CONGO.

GROVES WORKED IN HIGHLY SECRET FASHION to reach his goal, which he

thought he had achieved by December 3, 1945. On that day, he reported that
America and its allies controlled 97% of the world's high-grade uranium ore.
In addition, it had 35% of the low-grade deposits even though these deposits
were expensive to use for the atomic bomb. The rest of the low-grade ore
was controlled by Sweden, Britain, Russia, and the South American nations.

Because Groves believed America controlled uranium and because he underestimated Russia's scientific ability, he predicted the Soviet Union would
need up to 20 years to build an atomic weapon.

If Groves had shared his "secret" with scientists on the Manhattan Project, he might have realized his mistake. The scientists knew, but apparently
Groves did not, that Russia could and did get high-grade uranium from the
East Saxony region of Germany. Soviet armies "liberated" Saxony and quickly
began mining uranium in 1945.

The scientists could also have informed Groves that even if uranium were
monopolized, the Russians would soon have a bomb. By 1945, American scientists such as LEO SZILARD, VANNEVAR BUSH, and JAMES CONANT discarded the idea
that the control of uranium would protect the proliferation of the bomb. In
1944, Conant told Secretary of War Henry Stimson that a hydrogen bomb would
soon be developed and a monopoly of raw materials was unpractical "for the
supply of heavy hydrogen is essentially unlimited." Thus, scientists predicted RUSSIA WOULD HAVE THE BOMB IN FOUR OR FIVE YEARS, a major contrast
with Groves's estimate.

By keeping the "real secret" quiet, GROVES CREATED THE MYTH that a U.S.
MONOPOLY of SCIENTIFIC-TECHNOLOGICAL BRAIN-POWER PREVENTED RUSSIA from getting
a bomb. As Vannevar Bush noted, even such a sophisticate as Admiral William
Leahy believed the secret of the bomb was "written perhaps on a single sheet
of paper." If the United States guarded its secret carefully, no one else
would be able to duplicate the bomb. Thus, the myth given the U.S. public
was that a network of disloyal Americans who spied for Russia gave the secret
data to Russia. THIS MYTH OF U.S. TECHNOLOGICAL SUPERIORITY AIDED THE SPY
SCANDALS and caused Americans continually to be suspicious whenever Russian
technology made innovative breakthroughs.

December 13, 1945   *FRANCE AND BRITAIN AGREE TO EVACUATE SYRIA AND GRANT*
                         INDEPENDENCE.

*French forces sought to reoccupy Syria and Lebanon in May, 1945. After six
months of rioting and warfare in Syria, the two Western powers agreed to
leave Syria by August 31, 1946.*

December 20, 1945   THE TRUMAN ADMINISTRATION BACKS LEGISLATION FOR CIVIL-
                         IAN CONTROL OF AMERICA'S ATOMIC ENERGY.

Although General Leslie Groves and others desired military control of atomic
developments, Senator Brien McMahon's bill provided for civilian control.
The McMAHON BILL passed congress and became law on August 1, 1946.

December 26, 1945   MOSCOW CONFERENCE OF THE COUNCIL OF FOREIGN MINISTERS
                         IS HELD.

Disagreement was again the hallmark of this conference. Issues discussed included control of atomic energy, control of Japan, a trusteeship plan for Korea, and a peace conference to draft treaties with former governments associated with the Nazis.

Generally, the two 1945 meetings of foreign ministers indicated a growing tension between Russia and the Western powers.

1946

January 1, 1946   THE EMPEROR HIROHITO DISCLAIMS HIS DIVINITY.

Although General Douglas MacArthur, commander of the U.S. occupation of Japan, refused suggestions that the emperor be tried as a war criminal, he retained him in office but instructed him to renounce his divine ancestry, thereby giving him the status of a monarch such as the king of England.

The emperor's disclaimed divinity was one of a series of reforms instituted by General MacArthur as Supreme Commander for the Allied Powers (SCAP). During the fall of 1945, MacArthur issued decrees which restored civil liberties, freed political prisoners, dissolved the secret police, liberalized educational curricula, granted the franchise to all adults, encouraged labor unions, abolished feudal land tenure, and ended compulsory Shintoism.

January 10, 1946   *FIRST SESSION OF UNITED NATIONS OPENS IN LONDON.*

January 19, 1946   *U.N. SECURITY COUNCIL HEARS ITS FIRST COMPLAINT.*

IRAN contended that the SOVIET UNION was interfering in its internal affairs and refused to leave territory in northern Iran occupied as a World War II measure. For the result of Iran's complaint see March 27, 1946.

January 27, 1946   IN THE U.S. ZONE OF GERMANY, LOCAL ELECTIONS ARE HELD.

The Christian Democratic party won the greatest number of local offices; the Social Democrats ranked second. Soon after, similar elections in the British and French zones were also won by the Christian Democrats. The Christian Democrats were a middle-of-the-road party whose principal strength was with business interests and Catholics. The Social Democrats were a slightly left-of-center, evolutionary Socialist party.

The Soviet Union conducted elections in its zone on April 21, 1946. In East Germany, the Social Democrats merged with the Communist Party to form the SOCIALIST UNITY PARTY (S.E.D.), the party which dominated subsequent elections in East Germany.

February 3, 1946   SOVIET SPY RING IN CANADA IS DISCLOSED ON DREW
                        PEARSON'S RADIO PROGRAM.

Two weeks later, Canada arrested 22 men accused of spying. According to Prime Minister MacKenzie King, the Canadian authorities moved earlier than their investigation of the spies required, because of Pearson's report.

A WAVE OF SPY SCANDALS AND ACCUSATIONS began in the United States as a

result of these actions. Soon after, Washington columnist Frank McNaughton
said a "confidential source" claimed that the Canadian spies sought data on
U.S. atomic secrets and that a Russian spy ring also operated in America.
This second ring, McNaughton reported, had not been broken by the FBI, because
certain "State Department men" believed it "would upset our relations with
Russia."

McNaughton's source was later found to be General Leslie Groves, head
of the Manhattan Project. Groves and the army were then involved in a dispute
about civilian or military control of U.S. atomic energy policy. Senator
Brien McMahon led a group seeking civilian control. Thus, the spy accusations
led congress to amend prior McMahon legislation so that the military could
defend against "spies."

Notably, at this time the American public believed there existed some
single secret of the atomic bomb which only spies could communicate to the
Russians. Atomic scientists and experts such as Groves knew this was not the
case. The only "secrets" were who had supplies of uranium and what were the
precise technological methods used in the United States to efficiently enrich
uranium as the source of atomic power. Groves incorrectly believed he had
secured a monopoly of uranium supplies for America--incorrectly because the
Russians already had a supply in Czechoslovakia.

When the Canadian government issued its report on the spy cases in the
summer of 1946, it indicated the Russians obtained little from their spy ring.
The alleged master spy, British physicist Alan Nunn May, gave them samples
of enriched uranium ore that General Groves had presented to the Canadian
scientists in 1944. As Groves later admitted, May had only general knowledge
about the atomic bomb and the Soviets did not gain details about building
this bomb.

Nevertheless, Russian spy stories and allegations became recurrent in
America after February, 1946. This "scare" influenced congress and the public
to refuse to share nuclear "secrets" with allies as well as to accept a larger
degree of military control over atomic energy.

February 9, 1946   A SPEECH BY JOSEPH STALIN IS "THE DECLARATION OF WORLD
                        WAR III," IN THE WORDS OF SUPREME COURT JUSTICE WILLIAM
                        DOUGLAS.

Stalin asserted that capitalistic developments led inevitably to war and he
called on the Soviet people to sacrifice as they had during the 1930's.

February 24, 1946   COLONEL JUAN D. PERON IS ELECTED PRESIDENT OF ARGEN-
                        TINA.

As the leading military official in Argentina, Juan Peron had effective control of Argentina during most of World War II when Argentina remained neutral
and became a haven for Fascist and Nazi sympathizers including Adolf Eichmann.
When Peron decided to run for the presidency, the U.S. State Department issued a "Blue Book," based on captured German documents, which accused Peron
of collaboration with the Nazis.

The U.S. report was inspired by former U.S. Ambassador to Argentina
Sprulle BRADEN, who had an intense dislike for Peron and had often spoken
against him while he was ambassador in Buenos Aires. The attempt to damage
Peron backfired. Peron accused the United States of intervention in his

country's internal affairs, and he won the election with no difficulty.

March 4, 1946   AMERICA, BRITAIN, AND FRANCE ISSUE AN UNUSUAL APPEAL,
                         ASKING THE SPANISH PEOPLE TO OVERTHROW FRANCO'S FASCIST
                         REGIME.

Partly because President Truman had a hatred for General Franco's government,
the United States joined Paris and London in this appeal. The three Western
powers searched for some means to give Spain an anti-Communist but democratic
order. Spain had been excluded from the United Nations at the San Francisco
Conference. Later, on December 11, 1946, the U.N. General Assembly voted to
prohibit Spain from participation in any U.N. activities and urged its members
to sever diplomatic relations with Madrid. The appeal of March 4 did not
succeed. Franco's hold on the Spanish government was too great for outsiders
to overthrow by moralistic appeals.

March 5, 1946   WINSTON CHURCHILL DELIVERS HIS "IRON CURTAIN" SPEECH
                         AT FULTON, MISSOURI.

Churchill's speech delineated the growing chasm between the Soviet regions
of eastern Europe and the western "free states." President Truman evidently
knew in advance of Churchill's intent. Not only did Churchill contend that
"police states" ruled eastern Europe, he also emphasized that the Soviets
desired "the indefinite expansion of their power and doctrines." The Anglo-
Americans, he said, must work with the aid of atomic weapons to create unity
in Europe to protect the free nations.

March 6, 1946   *FRENCH FOREIGN OFFICE SEEKS PEACE IN INDOCHINA BY THE*
                         ACCORDS OF MARCH 6.

Vietnam, Laos, and Cambodia were recognized as "free" (not independent) states
in the FRENCH UNION. These accords proved to be only a temporary armistice.

March 27, 1946   THE IRANIAN CRISIS MOVES TOWARD A RESOLUTION ALTHOUGH
                         THE SOVIETS REFUSE TO DISCUSS THE PROBLEM IN THE U.N.
                         SECURITY COUNCIL.

A crisis to get the Soviet Union to withdraw its troops from northern Iran
had been pending in the Security Council since January 19, 1946. Great Britain and Russia had moved into the southern and northern sections of Iran in
1942, but in 1945 they agreed to withdraw by the end of 1946.
     When the Russian troops made no effort to leave the province of Azer-
baijan by January 1, 1946, the Iranians took the issue to the Security Council. On January 30, a Security Council resolution asked the two parties to
conduct negotiations, which began in February. These talks were still in
progress when, on March 6, the United States received reports that Russian
forces were moving toward Turkey, Iraq, and Teheran. After Russia did not
respond to an American request for an explanation of the troop maneuvers,
Secretary Byrnes urged Iran to take this issue to the opening session of the
Security Council on March 25.

On the day of the council meeting, the Russian news service TASS announced that the U.S.S.R. promised to pull out of Azerbaijan in five or six weeks. Nevertheless, Byrnes insisted that the issue should be left on the council agenda for discussion. The Russian delegate Andrei Gromyko protested angrily at Byrnes's request and walked out of the session.

The dispute ended, however, within one week. The TASS report was correct, and in early May, the Soviet troops evacuated northern Iran. Part of the Soviet-Iranian agreement for withdrawal would have given the Russians 51% of the shares in a joint Iranian-Soviet Oil Company. The Iranian parliament refused to approve this action and the Soviets lost all control over Iranian oil.

Byrnes insisted on acting "tough" toward Russia on March 27 in order to demonstrate that the Truman administration was not being conciliatory toward the Soviet Union, as some Republican Party critics averred.

April 14, 1946   CHINESE CIVIL WAR IS RENEWED ONLY THREE MONTHS (SINCE JANUARY 10) AFTER GENERAL MARSHALL THOUGHT A TRUCE HAD BEEN REACHED.

The conflict arose in Manchuria because the Russian troop withdrawal was timed to benefit a take-over by the Chinese communists. Chiang Kai-shek objected to this procedure and fighting broke out between the Nationalists and Mao's forces. Marshall reestablished a truce from May 12 to June 30, but an all-out civil war began again in July.

April 20, 1946   U.S.-SOVIET DISCUSSIONS REGARDING AN AMERICAN LOAN TO THE U.S.S.R. CONCLUDE WITH NO RESULTS.

Stalin referred to a possible loan on January 23, 1946, in a discussion with U.S. Ambassador Averell Harriman. He alluded to the recent British loan and wondered if the United States would consider such a Soviet request.

After the Iranian crisis abated in April, 1946, the United States agreed on discussions with the Soviets about a loan. The negotiations collapsed, however, because the Russians rejected the Americans' desire to link talks about the loan with agreements on trade with the Balkans and various peace treaties.

The U.S. refusal to formulate a loan for Russia was one of many factors indicating less cooperative policies between the two governments after April, 1945.

May 3, 1946   THE HEAD OF THE AMERICAN MILITARY GOVERNMENT IN GERMANY, GENERAL LUCIUS D. CLAY, ANNOUNCES THAT RUSSIA CAN MOVE NO MORE REPARATIONS MATERIAL OUT OF THE THREE WESTERN ZONES OF GERMANY.

Disagreement on Germany increased in 1946 after the Soviet Union refused Secretary of State Byrnes's offer to permit German reunification if she agreed to be demilitarized. In March, the Soviets changed their reparations policy in East Germany. Rather than continue to remove machinery to Russia, the communists decided to use East German labor and resources to produce goods for shipment to Russia. Coupled with Clay's announcement of May 3, Soviet-

American decisions made it nearly impossible to negotiate a treaty for a united Germany.

May 25, 1946   *THE KINGDOM OF TRANSJORDAN IS PROCLAIMED UNDER KING EMIR ABDULLAH.*

Great Britain relinquished its protectorship and recognized the independence of Transjordan on May 25, 1946.
     The nation was renamed THE HASHEMITE KINGDOM OF JORDAN on June 2, 1949.

June 2, 1946   *IN A PLEBISCITE, THE ITALIANS VOTE FOR A REPUBLIC, REJECTING THE RESTORATION OF A MONARCHY.*

June 3, 1946   JAPANESE WAR CRIME TRIALS BEGIN IN TOKYO UNDER AMERICAN JURISDICTION.

Similar trials were held in Southeast Asia and the South Pacific by British and Australian Tribunals.

June 14, 1946   BERNARD BARUCH PRESENTS TO THE UNITED NATIONS THE AMERICAN PLAN (BARUCH PLAN) FOR THE INTERNATIONAL CONTROL OF ATOMIC ENERGY.

In accepting this plan, President Truman opted for a "hard-line" policy on international control. The United States would accept agreements on atomic disclosure and disarmament *after* safeguard and inspection procedures had been adopted which would protect American national security. Previously, the Dean Acheson-David Lilienthal plan would have permitted partial disclosure of information as a good faith gesture prior to acceptance by all nations (including Russia) of inspection agreements.
     Key parts of the Baruch Plan were:

1. *PUNISHMENT* - Penalties for violating the control agreements would be made in the U.N. Security Council by action which would allow NO VETO by one of the Big Five powers.

2. *SCIENTIFIC DISCLOSURES* - These would initially be provided in published data only. If any nation desired some data, its request would be approved and filled only if national security was not impaired by its release.

3. *INSPECTION* - MUTUAL INSPECTION OF ANY NATION'S ATOMIC FACILITIES would be permitted and AGREED TO BEFORE detailed disclosure took place.

     The Russian U.N. delegate, Andrei Gromyko, wanted prior agreement on disclosure and disarmament with inspection and controls to come later. His views diverged from Baruch's to such a degree that an international control plan was not possible. See December 31, 1946.

July 1, 1946   THE UNITED STATES TESTS ATOMIC BOMBS NEAR BIKINI ATOLL
                                  IN THE SOUTH PACIFIC.

These July tests used an advanced Nagasaki-type implosion device. Their purpose was to demonstrate the bomb's use in naval warfare, an experiment advocated by the Navy Department.
     Directed by Vice Admiral William H. Blandy, two tests resulted from the
project code-named "CROSSROADS." On July 1, bomb "Able" dropped from an airplane and landed two miles from its target, a flotilla of 75 obsolete ("moth-
balled") or captured enemy ships of World War II. The results were unimpres-
sive. The bomb exploded in shallow water, sinking few of the ships but making
most of them radioactive. On July 25, the second bomb, "Baker," was suspended
in 90 feet of water and exploded electrically. It caused spectacular damage
in destroying the naval vessels and reinforced the U.S. Navy's desire to have
a larger role in nuclear development.

July 4, 1946   THE PHILIPPINE ISLANDS ARE GRANTED INDEPENDENCE BY
                                  THE UNITED STATES.

The Philippines created a republic, having elected MANUEL A. ROXAS, head of
the Liberal Party, as president on April 23. The U.S. congress also passed
the REHABILITATION ACT and the BELL ACT to assist in the economic development
of the islands. In return for this aid, a national referendum in the Philippines on March 11, 1947, passed a constitutional amendment to enable U.S.
citizens to exploit the island's national resources on a basis of equality
with the Filipinos.
     One problem in 1946, which was destined to persist for many years, was
insistent guerrilla war with a communist-led group, the HUKBALAHAPS ("HUKS"),
who demanded land reform and whose party was strong in central Luzon.

July 15, 1946   TRUMAN SIGNS LEGISLATION GRANTING GREAT BRITAIN CREDITS
                                  OF $3.75 BILLION.

After the cut-off of Lend-Lease aid in August, 1945, the British government
experienced increased difficulty in financing the rebuilding of its economy.
At Truman's request, Congress approved credits to the British to assist them
in purchasing American goods.

August 1, 1946   THE McMAHON BILL ON ATOMIC ENERGY IS SIGNED INTO LAW
                                  BY PRESIDENT TRUMAN.

Against McMahon's wishes, the committee bill had transformed his desire for
civilian control into a U.S. military veto on decisions by civilians on the
Atomic Energy Commission (AEC). In addition, the bill emphasized restrictions
on atomic energy information. The bill even restricted information which
the United States could share with Britain and Canada as it had done during
World War II. Finally, the War Department retained control of two essential
duties: responsibility for stockpiling uranium and thorium and for monitoring
foreign progress on the atomic bomb.
     The revised McMahon Bill, which gave the military a large measure of
control over the AEC, fit the "hard-line" character of the Baruch Plan for
control of atomic energy.

August 1, 1946   THE FULBRIGHT ACT TO FINANCE FOREIGN STUDY BECOMES
                          LAW.

By act of congress, U.S. surplus property in foreign countries would be sold
and the funds used in that nation to finance scholarships for research, and
academic exchanges of faculty members. Its purpose was to enhance American
information about the peoples of foreign nations.

August 15, 1946   THE DISPUTE BETWEEN RUSSIA AND TURKEY PROMPTS PRESIDENT
                          TRUMAN TO APPROVE A MEMO STATING THAT THE UNITED STATES
                          WOULD RESIST ANY SOVIET AGGRESSION AGAINST TURKEY.

The Soviet Union wanted to share control of the Straits of Dardanelles and a
naval base in Turkey, objectives that were opposed by the Turkish government
and the United States.

September 1, 1946   *A GREEK PLEBISCITE VOTES 69% IN FAVOR OF RESTORING
                          ITS MONARCH, KING GEORGE II.*

*After British forces liberated Greece on October 13, 1944, a civil war broke
out between leftist factions (including the EAM Communists) and the Royalist
Popular Party. The British arranged a truce on January 11, 1945, with a re-
gency government under Archbishop Damaskinos.*
     *Political instability continued, however, and no leader appeared who
could capably mediate between republicans, royalists, and the left-wing. The
civil war began again in 1946, with the EAM gaining covert aid from Albania,
Yugoslavia, and Bulgaria. The September election of George II took place
during the guerrilla struggle, with the left-wing parties boycotting the election.*

September 20, 1946   SECRETARY OF COMMERCE HENRY A. WALLACE IS FORCED TO
                          RESIGN BECAUSE TRUMAN OBJECTS TO HIS MADISON SQUARE
                          GARDEN SPEECH ON SEPTEMBER 12 IN WHICH HE CRITICIZED
                          THE PRESIDENT'S "HARD-LINE" AGAINST RUSSIA AND CALLED
                          FOR COOPERATION WITH THE SOVIETS.

This incident disclosed disagreement within Franklin Roosevelt's New Deal
coalition about Truman's postwar policies. Harold Ickes and Henry Morgenthau,
Jr., two of Roosevelt's stalwarts, joined Wallace, who had been Roosevelt's
vice-president from 1941 to 1945, in opposition to Truman's unwillingness to
emphasize international cooperation as the means to peace.

September 30, 1946   THE NUREMBURG WAR CRIMES TRIBUNAL ANNOUNCES ITS DE-
                          CISIONS.

Of the 22 persons tried, 3 were acquitted, 7 received prison terms, and 12
were sentenced to death. Of the latter 12, Herman Goering committed suicide
before his execution, and Martin Borman was sentenced *in absentia* because he
was never apprehended.

October 10, 1946   AMBASSADOR GEORGE MARSHALL'S MISSION TO CHINA IS AT
                            AN IMPASSE AFTER CHIANG KAI-SHEK VIOLATES A PROMISE
                            AND CAPTURES KALGAN.

Marshall instructed Chiang not to continue his offensive by capturing Kalgan
because the Chinese Communists had agreed to negotiations if the Nationalist
army stopped its offensive. In addition, Marshall warned Chiang that the
front lines of his armies had been overextended, giving the Communist armies
a tactical advantage of supply and attack if the civil war continued. In
order to strengthen his warning, Marshall told Chiang that the United States
would cut its economic aid and withdraw the American Marines stationed in
China unless Chiang stopped outside Kalgan and accepted peace talks with Mao.
     Since the renewal of fighting in June, 1946, Marshall had continued ef-
forts to secure negotiations between the Nationalist and Communist leaders.
Meanwhile, Chiang's armies had been well supplied by the United States, and
the American navy had moved Nationalist troops to strategic places. As a
result, the Nationalist offensive had great success between July and October.
     Although he originally promised Marshall he would stop his offensive
and not capture Kalgan, Chiang changed his mind early in October and announced
an offensive against Kalgan. Consequently, Marshall believed his mission's
attempt to end the civil war through mediation was no longer possible. He
wrote to President Truman that his recall would be appropriate. Both Marshall
and the U.S. Ambassador to China, J. Leighton STUART, believed that Marshall
could no longer be impartial between the two warring factions in China.
     Despite Marshall's forebodings in October, he remained in China because
other methods to achieve a truce seemed possible. Not until December 28 did
President Truman and Marshall finally agree that the peace mission was doomed
to failure. On January 3, Truman formally recalled Marshall to Washington.

November 5, 1946   THE REPUBLICAN PARTY GAINS CONTROL OF BOTH HOUSES OF
                            CONGRESS IN NATIONAL ELECTIONS.

This was the first national Republican Party victory since 1930. Although
President Truman had previously sought bipartisan support for his international policies, the results of this election necessitated even closer cooperation of the president and the opposing party for the next two years.

November 10, 1946   *FRANCE'S FOURTH REPUBLIC BEGINS WITH ELECTIONS FOR*
                            THE NATIONAL ASSEMBLY.

*After a referendum on May 5 rejected the first draft constitution, a second
constituent assembly revised the document and the electorate adopted it on
October 13. The new constitution closely resembled that of the Third Republic.*
     *The Assembly election resulted in a deadlock between the Communists with
186 seats and the MOUVEMENT RÉPUBLICAIN POPULAIRE (M.R.P.) with 166 delegates.
Consequently, the Socialists with 103 seats formed a coalition cabinet under
Leon Blum. As in the Third Republic, the coalition governments in France
found it difficult to formulate stable policy and French political divisions
continued to plague the nation.*

November 19, 1946   *IN RUMANIA, A GENERAL ELECTION IS WON BY THE COMMU-*
                         NISTS, CONFIRMING THE RULE OF THE COMMUNIST-CONTROLLED
                         NATIONAL DEMOCRATIC FRONT WHICH GAINED POWER AFTER
                         SOVIET TROOPS OCCUPIED BUCHAREST ON AUGUST 31, 1944.

On January 7, 1946, British and American complaints caused the National Demo-
cratic Front to give several cabinet posts to members of opposition groups.
The opposition parties were restricted, however, and violent attacks on non-
Communists took place before and during the elections of November 19. The
United States protested that the Russians violated the YALTA AGREEMENTS by
not permitting free elections, but little could be done except protest. With-
in a year, the non-Communists in the cabinet resigned and on July 28, 1947,
the opposition National Peasant Party was dissolved. The Communists had con-
trol of Rumania.

November 23, 1946   *FRENCH FORCES BOMBARD HAIPHONG PORT IN VIETNAM, AN*
                         EVENT LEADING TO RENEWAL OF VIETNAM'S WAR OF INDEPEN-
                         DENCE.

The March 6, 1946, accords had led to further discussions between Ho Chi Minh
and the French Colonial Office, but an agreement was never reached which would
give a permanent basis for Vietnam as part of the FRENCH Union.
     The French attack on Haiphong resulted from disagreements between French
customs officers and the Viet Minh commanders. On December 19, 1946, Viet-
namese guerrillas attacked the French troops in Hanoi and war began again.
The French were determined to hold their position in Indochina.

December 2, 1946   THE UNITED STATES AND GREAT BRITAIN AGREE TO PROVIDE
                         AN ECONOMIC FUSION OF THEIR GERMAN ZONES.

This fusion, known as BIZONIA, hoped to strengthen West Germany's economy.
The Anglo-American governments invited France and the Soviet Union to join
them, but they refused.
     As early as September 6, Secretary of State James Byrnes announced in
Stuttgart that the United States would follow a more lenient policy toward
Germany and desired to unify the German economy.

December 12, 1946   PEACE TREATIES ARE COMPLETED WITH SMALLER AXIS ALLIES
                         OF WORLD WAR II.

Beginning in Paris on April 25, 1946, a series of conferences among foreign
ministers of 21 nations who fought the Axis prepared drafts of these treaties.
On December 12, at a meeting in New York City, the treaties were finalized
for Italy, Rumania, Hungary, Bulgaria, and Finland. The treaties were signed
on February 10, 1947.
     The U.S. role in obtaining a relatively lenient peace treaty for Italy
is of interest. Discussions on the terms of the Italian treaty had begun
during the Council of Foreign Ministers meeting in April, 1946. By that time,
Italy was treated by the United States and Britain as a friendly power more
than a former enemy. Therefore, the Anglo-Americans persuaded Russia to cut
its reparations demands from $300 million to $100 million which could be paid

from Italian assets in the Balkans or Italian goods over a period of years. Together with the claims of small countries against Italy, the total Italian reparations payment was $360 million in the treaty of December 12.

On the Italian colonies and the Italy-Yugoslav border there was greater dispute. According to Foreign Minister Molotov, the Russians held rights to Italian colonies in Africa because the Soviet navy needed bases in the area. The British and Americans opposed this claim and it was decided to leave the colonial issue until after a peace treaty was made.

On the border issue, the old problem of Trieste and Dalmatia appeared once again. In April, the Russians agreed to accept less territory for Yugoslavia but Marshal Tito objected, and during the December sessions in Paris, Molotov insisted on changes in the Italian border. Finally, the delegates agreed that the April, 1946, territorial border favoring Italy would stand but Italy would pay another $35 million of reparations to Yugoslavia. The peace treaty with Italy was signed with only the colonial issue remaining to be settled. See February 10, 1947.

December 31, 1946   THE U.N. SECURITY COUNCIL VOTES TO ACCEPT THE BARUCH
                             PLAN FOR CONTROL OF ATOMIC ENERGY.

The U.N. Atomic Energy Committee had debated the Baruch proposal since July. A Russian plan offered by Andrei Gromyko had been rejected on July 24. Baruch believed that with effort the committee's approval could overcome Russian efforts to delay his plan. Despite criticism from such opponents as Henry Wallace, Baruch refused to compromise on his plan's basic terms.

By mid-December, Truman, Secretary Byrnes, and Baruch decided to force a U.N. vote by the year's end. Thus, on December 31, Baruch called for a vote. Ten nations approved; Russia and Poland abstained.

In effect, the Baruch Plan left the United States with a rigid, exclusive monopoly of atomic power until the Russians could develop their own bomb. No effective international control of nuclear power was attained.

1947

January 8, 1947   GEORGE C. MARSHALL BECOMES SECRETARY OF STATE.

Secretary Byrnes resigned from office because he was tired and in poor health.
General Marshall had just returned from China, and the president had decided
earlier to appoint Marshall as secretary. Although he was a military man,
Marshall's aura of integrity made him a readily acceptable choice. Marshall
served as secretary until January 20, 1949.

January 19, 1947   *ELECTIONS IN POLAND ARE WON BY SOCIALIST PREMIER EDUARD
                          OSOBKA-MORAWSK'S PARTY, WHICH WINS 394 SEATS TO 28
                          SEATS FOR THE PEASANT PARTY.*

*Deputy Premier STANISLAW MIKOLAJCZYK's Peasant Party suffered from repressive
measures by the government. This election ended the Provisional Government
which OSOBKA-MORAWSK's former Lublin government dominated. MIKOLAJCZYK, who
had represented the London exile government, was soon subject to intense criticism. He fled to exile in London on October 24, 1947.*
    *Both Great Britain and the United States charged that the January 19
elections violated the Yalta Agreement for "free and honest" elections, but
their protests were unavailing as the Communists, with Soviet backing, gained
control of Poland's government.*

January 29, 1947   THE UNITED STATES ABANDONS MEDIATION EFFORTS IN CHINA.

In his final report on the Chinese mission, George Marshall said compromise
failed because reactionaries in the Kuomintang of Chiang Kai-shek as well as
extremists in the Communist Party of China did not want peace. U.S. aid continued to Chiang Kai-shek, reaching over $2 billion between August, 1945,
and December 31, 1947.

February 10, 1947   PEACE TREATIES ARE SIGNED IN PARIS WITH STATES ASSOCI-
                           ATED WITH GERMANY IN WORLD WAR II.

Italy lost four border areas to France, her Adriatic Islands and Venezia
Giulia to Yugoslavia, and the Dodecanese Islands to Greece. Trieste became
a Free Territory although boundary disputes continued between Italy and Yugo-
slavia.
    Italy and Austria also had persisting boundary disputes in the Tyrol.
By a 1946 agreement between Austria and Italy, the Italians regained South
Tyrol as the autonomous province of Trentino-Alto-Adige (formerly Bolzano).
Italy agreed to adopt both German and Italian as official languages. Problems
continued, however, between the German and Italian population groups.

In eastern Europe, Rumania lost Bessarabia and northern Bukovina to Russia but added Transylvania to her nation. Hungary regained her 1930 borders except for a few minor changes favoring Czechoslovakia. Bulgaria retained southern Dobrudja; Finland lost the port of Petsamo to Russia.

March 10-April 24, 1947   THE BIG FOUR FOREIGN MINISTERS CONTINUE TO DISAGREE ON GERMANY.

The Soviets wanted $10 billion in reparations, which conflicted with the British and American policy of making West Germany self-supporting.

The Council of Foreign Ministers met in London later in 1947 (November 25-December 15) to consider the German treaty but, again, could not resolve their differences.

March 12, 1947   THE TRUMAN DOCTRINE IS INITIATED BY THE PRESIDENT IN A SPEECH TO CONGRESS.

The immediate occasion for the DOCTRINE was a request to congress for $400 million aid to GREECE and TURKEY. Both of these countries experienced either internal or external Communist threats, which the Truman administration evaluated as evidence of Russia's plot to expand its control wherever possible.

During the winter of 1946-1947, economic problems in Great Britain caused Prime Minister Attlee's government to decide that the expenses of British naval power in the Mediterranean and economic aid for the Greek government could no longer be met by London. During 1946, the U.S. Navy had gradually enlarged its Mediterranean activity by adding the battleship *Missouri* and the aircraft carrier *Franklin D. Roosevelt* to cruise the area.

In January, 1947, the British government informed the White House that it had to withdraw from the Aegean-Mediterranean region, and appealed to the U.S. to take over its duties. Truman, Marshall, and Dean Acheson consulted with congressional leaders including Senator Arthur Vandenberg, the ranking Republican on the Foreign Relations Committee, and with bipartisan political support, the president proposed to seek congressional aid for Greece and Turkey.

Acting on suggestions by some advisors to "scare the hell out of the American people," Truman did the job in this speech. To justify economic and military aid to Greece and Turkey, the president envisioned a world struggle between the "free world" and the tyrannical world of communism. Only America, he said, could defend the free world against "attempted subjugation by armed minorities or by outside pressure." Using a version of a "domino theory," first suggested by Undersecretary of State Acheson during a White House session with congressmen, Truman claimed that if Greece fell, Turkey would fall, and "confusion and disorder might well spread throughout the entire Middle East."

Truman's rhetoric earned the support of congress and his doctrine became the guideline for world-wide American commitments after March, 1947. Although the doctrine was originally planned only for Europe and the Mediterranean, Truman's critics used the implications of his speech to charge him with failure to apply his beliefs in Asia and other parts of the world when communists threatened.

On May 27, Truman signed the congressional bill providing economic and military aid to Greece and Turkey.

April 2, 1947   THE U.N. SECURITY COUNCIL AWARDS FORMER JAPANESE IS-
                        LANDS IN THE PACIFIC TO THE UNITED STATES UNDER A
                        TRUSTEESHIP.

The United States had occupied these islands during World War II and President
Truman had bluntly said the United States would retain them regardless of
the U.N. action. These small but strategic islands were the Marianas, Mar-
shalls, and Carolinas.

May 3, 1947   *JAPAN'S NEW CONSTITUTION BECOMES EFFECTIVE.*

*The constitution recognized the sovereignty of the people, making the emperor
only a symbolic figure. It also protected individual rights and provided
large measures of local self-government. The central government would consist
of a two-house parliament (DIET) and a ministry whose term of office required
a majority approval of the Diet.*
      *In the April, 1947, elections, a right-wing majority gained control of
the upper house of councillors while the Social Democratic Party won the
greatest plurality of seats in the House of Representatives. On May 23, the
Socialist leader TETSU KATAYAMA formed a coalition government approved by
the Diet.*

May 5, 1947   POLICY-PLANNING STAFF IS ESTABLISHED IN THE STATE DE-
                        PARTMENT WITH GEORGE KENNAN AS DIRECTOR.

The purpose of the planning group was to assure long-range policy, to provide
a framework for program planning, and to guide current policy decisions and
operations.

June 5, 1947   SECRETARY OF STATE MARSHALL PROPOSES ECONOMIC AID TO
                        ENABLE EUROPEAN NATIONS TO REHABILITATE THEIR ECONO-
                        MIES.

Two years after the German surrender, the nations of western Europe continued
to suffer from the destruction of industry and economic dislocation of war.
Although the United States had provided refugee relief and some loans to Britain and France since 1945, the standard of living of these and other European
nations had not recovered from the war.
      At the time when Truman offered aid to Greece and Turkey in March, 1947,
a committee of the State-War-Navy Coordinating Committee prepared estimates
of European needs and presented a report to Marshall and Undersecretary of
State Dean Acheson in the middle of April. It was soon decided that Marshall
should propose an aid program for Europe in a Harvard University commencement
address on June 5.
      Marshall told the Harvard audience that the United States would do what-
ever was necessary to assist in "the return of normal economic health ...
without which there could be no political stability." The United States
wished to fight "hunger, poverty, desperation and chaos." He asked the Europeans to indicate their desire to cooperate with America. If they would
draft a program of their needs, the United States would help them. See June
27, 1947.

June 25, 1947   RUSSIA VETOES A UNITED NATIONS REPORT THAT FOREIGN
                       NEIGHBORS ARE INTERFERING IN THE GREEK CIVIL WAR.

Responding to a request of the Greek government, a U.N. Commission investigated the charges of foreign intervention in the Greek civil war. The Greek
Communist rebels, the report said, received aid from Albania, Bulgaria, and
Yugoslavia. In a vote on the report, the Security Council rejected the commission's action because of a Soviet veto. The official vote had been nine
for and two against.

June 27, 1947   FOREIGN MINISTERS OF THE THREE MAJOR EUROPEAN POWERS
                       MEET TO CONSIDER SECRETARY MARSHALL'S AID PROPOSAL.

Immediately after Marshall's Harvard University speech, British Foreign Minister Ernest BEVIN rushed to arrange a British-French-Russian meeting in Paris
and began talks with Georges BIDAULT of France. Although Bevin and Bidault
hoped the Russians would not attend, they did. Foreign Minister Molotov arrived in Paris on June 27, with 140 "technical advisers."
     During the formal talks, Bevin and Bidault united in preventing Molotov
from using delay tactics or seeking a "blank check" from America. Following
a session on July 2, there was a clear break with Russia. Molotov would not
budge from his views; Bevin and Bidault told him they would proceed without
him.
     On July 3, the British and French governments invited all European states
to meet in Paris on July 12 to draw up a coordinated plan for the U.S. government to describe their economic needs. The Russians still could have attended but did not. Because the United States told Moscow it would have to
share information on its financial conditions as did all other participants,
Stalin refused to participate. If Stalin had joined, Truman and Marshall
would have had greater problems in getting congress to accept the Marshall
Plan. For the results of the Paris meeting see September 22, 1947.

July 26, 1947   NATIONAL SECURITY ACT CREATES A UNIFIED ORGANIZATION
                       OF THE AMERICAN ARMED FORCES.

Although suggestions for a united organization of the nation's defense program had recurred since the 1920's, the serious study of such a plan did not
begin until April, 1944, when a House Select Committee on Postwar Military
Policy held hearings on a War Department unification plan. Additional studies
continued throughout 1945, with the War Department generally favoring a *consolidation* of the armed forces and the Navy Department generally preferring
closer inter-service *coordination*. The army plan was prepared by General
J. LAWTON COLLINS; the navy plan appeared in the EBERSTADT COMMITTEE REPORT
OF SEPTEMBER, 1945.
     Eventually, on December 19, 1945, PRESIDENT TRUMAN sent a message to
congress on military reorganization, indicating that he favored consolidation
of the armed forces. As a result, throughout 1946 there was extensive debate
and a number of congressional hearings on military organization. Truman's
consolidation view prevailed, however, and the 1947 legislation reflected
his ideas, modified to secure the support of army, navy, and air force leaders.
     The 1947 act established the army, navy, and air force as equal

departments with civilian administrators, supervised by a single, civilian
SECRETARY OF DEFENSE. The act also reorganized the various agencies and departments of government concerned with national security.

Three groups separated from the military were established by Title I of
the 1947 Act: (1) National Security Council; (2) Central Intelligence Agency;
(3) National Security Resources Board.

The National Security Council (NSC) would coordinate the foreign and
military policies of the nation and advise the president on integrating those
policies. Its members were the president; the Secretaries of Defense, State,
Army, Navy, and Air Force; the Chairman of the Resources Board; and other
government officers the president might designate.

The Central Intelligence Agency (CIA) was under the NSC. It would coordinate the intelligence-gathering activity of all government departments,
evaluate the data obtained, and report its findings to officials with a "need
to know."

The National Security Resources Board (NSRB) would coordinate all military, civilian, and industrial capacities of the nation needed for an emergency mobilization. Chaired by a civilian, the board drew its members from
government departments and agencies designated by the president.

Title II of the 1947 Act established the National Military Establishment
(NME), led by a civilian Secretary of Defense with cabinet status. The NME,
which on August 10, 1949, was renamed the DEPARTMENT OF DEFENSE, consisted
of the Departments of the Army, Navy, and Air Force; the Joint Chiefs of Staff;
the War Council; the Munitions Board; and the Research and Development Board.

The Secretary of Defense had authority over all parts of the NME. He
was directed to eliminate unnecessary duplication or overlapping in defense
procurement, supply, transport, health, research, and storage; and to coordinate the budget preparation of the parts of the NME.

Within the NME (Defense Department) the Joint Chiefs held a prominent
role. They formulated strategy, issued military directives, and recommended
defense policy to the NSC and president. James FORRESTAL became the Secretary
of Defense on September 17, 1947.

August 15, 1947   *THE DOMINION OF PAKISTAN IS ESTABLISHED WITH LIAQAT*
                          ALI KHAN AS PRIME MINISTER AND MOHAMMED ALI JINNAH AS
                          GOVERNOR-GENERAL.

This state was the Muslim section of partitioned India.

August 15, 1947   *INDIA GAINS INDEPENDENCE FROM GREAT BRITAIN.*

*The activity of the Indian Nationalist movement since 1920 resulted in Brit-
ain's decision to gradually give India self-government. The internal religious divisions in India were finally resolved in 1947, and the English Parliament passed an Independence Bill (July 5) to partition the country between
the Hindus of India and the Muslims of Pakistan. Soon after, on January 30,
1948, India's national leader, Mahatma Gandhi, was assassinated.*

September 2, 1947   NATIONS OF THE WESTERN HEMISPHERE SIGN THE RIO PACT.
                            THIS INTER-AMERICAN MUTUAL ASSISTANCE TREATY INTENDED
                            TO COUNTERACT ANY AGGRESSOR ATTACKING A DEFENSE ZONE
                            THAT EXTENDED FROM GREENLAND TO ARGENTINA.

This was the forerunner of the Organization of American States formed in 1948.

September 19, 1947   GENERAL ALBERT WEDEMEYER REPORTS TO TRUMAN ON HIS VISIT
                            TO CHINA.

The president sent Wedemeyer to China on July 9 to conduct a fact-finding
mission on events since Marshall's mission ended in December, 1946. In particular, Truman wanted to know if Chiang Kai-shek had instituted any of the
reforms Marshall recommended. Since 1946, the U.S. Marines had evacuated
China and a limited arms embargo was used to pressure Chiang to change. Nevertheless, the Marines left 6,000 tons of ammunition for Chiang as they evacuated.
     Truman wanted data because the China lobby and Chiang's friends in con-
gress had become ardent critics of Truman's China policy. They demanded that
the Nationalist Chinese should be given whatever Chiang needed.
     Wedemeyer's visit ended on August 24, and he took several weeks to write
his analysis. Much like Marshall, Wedemeyer believed both sides in the civil
war shared blame for the disunity. Nevertheless, he recommended that the
United States should provide greater military aid if Chiang agreed to "sweep-
ing changes" in his administration and army.
     Truman and Marshall disliked Wedemeyer's emphasis on greater aid because
Chiang had had 20 years to reform the government and vitalize the army and
had continually failed to do so. Because of their dissatisfaction, Truman
sought to keep Wedemeyer's report secret. In doing so, however, he caused
greater suspicion among his critics and the general public. Only after the
China lobby had successfully depicted Chiang as a loyal warrior whose aid
was unceremoniously cut by Truman did the administration, in August, 1949,
issue a full explanation of all reports on China. We cannot know whether
providing better information at an early date would have avoided the criticism
about China, which greatly influenced U.S. policy after 1949.

September 22, 1947   SIXTEEN EUROPEAN NATIONS REPORT TO THE UNITED STATES
                            ON THEIR NEEDS UNDER THE MARSHALL PLAN.

The delegates who convened at Paris on July 12 set up an interim Committee
of European Economic Cooperation (CEEC) to prepare a report for the United
States. The CEEC estimated that the 16 European nations would need between
$16.4 and $22.4 billion over the next four years. Truman presented to congress his request for funding of the CEEC program on December 17, 1947.

October 5, 1947   *THE COMMUNIST INFORMATION BUREAU (COMINFORM) IS CREATED
                            IN A CONFERENCE AT WARSAW.*

*While officially designed to coordinate activity of Europe's Communist par-
ties, Western observers believed it replaced the COMINTERN as the mechanism
for the Kremlin to control all local communist organizations. This propaganda*

agency was open to nations with Communist governments or to the Communist Parties of non-Communist nations.

October 21, 1947   CHILE'S GOVERNMENT BREAKS RELATIONS WITH THE SOVIET
                       UNION AFTER A SERIES OF COMMUNIST-LED STRIKES RESULTS
                       IN THE ARREST OF 200 COMMUNIST LEADERS.

October 30, 1947   THE GENERAL AGREEMENT ON TARIFFS AND TRADE (GATT) IS
                       SIGNED.

Following a six-month conference in Geneva, 23 nations approved an effort to lower trade barriers. The GATT had three essential features: a multilateral schedule of tariff concessions; a code of principles governing imports and exports; and periodic meetings which provided an international forum for discussing trade problems. Tariffs were first negotiated on a bilateral basis before there were multinational discussions to form a schedule of tariff concessions. The agreement was initiated at Geneva by 23 nations whose commerce covered three-fourths of the world's trade. The countries were: Australia, Belgium, Brazil, the Netherlands, Luxembourg, Canada, Chile, the Republic of China, Cuba, Czechoslovakia, France, India, Pakistan, Ceylon, Burma, Lebanon, Syria, New Zealand, Norway, the Union of South Africa, the United Kingdom, Southern Rhodesia, and the United States.

The 1947 Geneva Conference resulted in significant lowering of tariff barriers among the participating nations. About 54% of U.S. dutiable imports were affected by the Geneva reductions. The average of reductions was 18.9%, a sum which was calculated on lower levels which the United States had previously negotiated in bilateral agreements under the Reciprocity Act of 1934.

November 14, 1947   *THE U.N. GENERAL ASSEMBLY VOTES TO RECOGNIZE KOREA'S*
                       INDEPENDENCE.

In September, the United States had referred the issue of the future status of Korea to the United Nations because America and the Soviet Union could not agree on the establishment of a provisional government for all of Korea. A U.N. study recommended plans for the withdrawal of both U.S. and Russian forces and the creation of a Korean government, a proposal approved on November 14, 1947.

November 29, 1947   *THE U.N. GENERAL ASSEMBLY APPROVES A PARTITION PLAN*
                       TO DIVIDE PALESTINE BETWEEN ARABS AND JEWS.

During World War II (May, 1942), the Conference of American Zionists had rejected the British Plan of 1939 to give Palestine independence under joint administration. In August, 1945, President Truman asked Britain to admit at least 100,000 displaced Jews to Palestine after the World Zionist Congress demanded that one million Jews should be admitted. Although an Anglo-American committee advised against the partition of Palestine on August 29, 1946, the Zionists rejected any state without full Jewish autonomy.

By early 1947, the British announced they would withdraw from Palestine as they had from Greece. On April 2, the British referred the Palestinian problem to the United Nations. A commission studied the issue and on November 29 recommended that Palestine should be divided into Arab and Jewish states. Jerusalem would be under a U.N. Trusteeship. The Jews accepted the U.N. plan but the Arab League rejected it.

On December 17, the council of the Arab League announced it would use force to stop partition and began raids on Jewish communities in Palestine. For the Jews, a terrorist group, the Irgun ("Stern Gang"), retaliated by war-like attacks on Arabs.

December 17, 1947   CONGRESS PASSES THE FOREIGN AID ACT OF 1947.

This act provided $540 million of interim relief to France, Italy, Austria, and China. The legislation was designed to carry the European nations through the winter, pending final enactment of the Marshall Plan aid in 1948.

China was added to the list of those receiving aid because of the pro-China views of such leading Republicans as Senators Vandenberg and Styles Bridges. While Marshall, the Joint Chiefs of Staff, and Truman believed aid to China was a poor risk expense, the China lobby vociferously complained that Chiang Kai-shek should be aided as well as Europe.

President Truman also requested funds for the European Recovery Program (Marshall Plan). On March 31, 1948, Congress authorized $5.3 billion for this program. Truman appointed Paul G. Hoffman as chief of the European Cooperation Administration on April 6.

December 17, 1947   THE TRUMAN ADMINISTRATION PLANS TO CONTROL EXPORTS TO
                          COMMUNIST STATES: NSC-17.

The National Security Council prepared a report titled "Control of Exports to the USSR and Eastern Europe" which described means for combatting the cold war by economic action. NSC-17 recommended limited shipment of all goods which were "critically short" in America or which would "contribute to Soviet military potential." This policy was based on a recommendation of the Commerce Department, approved by the State Department.

In order to operate as quietly as possible and avoid breaking existing commercial treaties with east European nations, Secretary of Commerce Averell Harriman suggested an "R" export-control procedure. The "R" procedure named all Europe as a "recovery area." To assist economic recovery, America would issue EXPORT LICENSES for commodities to Europe, granting a license to an area found to have the "greatest need."

This "R" policy, but not its purpose, was announced by the Commerce Department in a press release of January 15, 1948. As described publicly, goods were not embargoed to any nation; they were simply sent where they were most required. The Department of Commerce, of course, would decide what nation had the "greatest need."

1948

January 21, 1948   THE STATE DEPARTMENT PUBLISHES CAPTURED GERMAN DOCU-
MENTS ON THE 1939 NAZI-SOVIET PACT.

These documents on the temporary alliance of Hitler's Germany with Stalin's
Russia seemed to reinforce the growing American belief that German Nazi totalitarianism and Russian Communist totalitarianism were synonymous. Although
Secretary of State Marshall denied it, some American reporters believed the
publication of these documents in 1948 supported the U.S. desire to implicate
Stalin in using the same tactics that Hitler used in seeking world domination.
Because the documents showed only the Berlin events and Russian dispatches
to Germany, the impression grew that Stalin sought the alliance with Germany
in 1939 because Germany and Russia shared political goals. Therefore, Americans such as President Truman could assert that there was no difference between the totalitarianism of Nazi Germany and Communist Russia.
     Although this analysis had some validity in terms of the Soviet Union's
methods of deceit and ruthlessness during the purges of the 1930's, it blurred
the ideological distinctions between communism and fascism. Marxian theory
adhered to humanistic goals which the Soviet Union failed to implement; the
Nazis' antihumanistic and destructive ideology had been vigorously carried
out by Hitler by aggressive warfare and by an attempt to exterminate the Jewish people. In addition, this analysis considered Russian armies in eastern
Europe as aggressors, whereas, in fact, they had liberated east European nations from Nazi conquests just as the Anglo-American offensive liberated west
Europe.

January 27, 1948   TRUMAN SIGNS LEGISLATION FINALIZING THE U.S. INFORMA-
TION AND EDUCATION EXCHANGE ACT OF 1948.

Under the law, America would prepare and distribute information to promote
understanding between the people of the UNITED STATES and other peoples of
the world.

February 2, 1948   THE UNITED STATES AND ITALY SIGN A TREATY OF FRIEND-
SHIP, COMMERCE, AND NAVIGATION.

February 4, 1948   *CEYLON BECOMES A SELF-GOVERNING DOMINION IN THE BRITISH
COMMONWEALTH.*

February 25, 1948   *A COMMUNIST COUP OCCURS IN CZECHOSLOVAKIA.*

In the 1946 elections for a constituent assembly, the Communists won 114 of

300 seats, gaining a plurality which permitted the Communist Klement Gottwald to form a coalition government. Now Gottwald threatened a coup unless President Eduard Benes agreed to a predominantly Communist ministry. The Communists then proceeded to purge the country of anti-Communist groups; one instance of this plan included the mysterious death of Foreign Minister JAN MASARYK, who reportedly committed suicide by falling from his office window. New elections on May 30 had only a single list of Communist candidates, which assured that party's victory. On June 7, President Benes resigned and Klement Gottwald became president of the Communist government.

March 4, 1948   *ARGENTINA AND CHILE AGREE TO DEFEND JOINTLY THEIR RIGHTS IN ANTARCTICA AND THE FALKLAND (MALVINAS) ISLANDS AGAINST THE BRITISH.*

March 17, 1948   *THE BRUSSELS TREATY IS SIGNED AS A STEP TO EUROPEAN COOPERATION.*

The 50-year defensive alliance was approved by delegates of Great Britain, France, Belgium, the Netherlands, and Luxembourg. They also pledged cooperation in economic, social, and military affairs.

The Brussels Treaty broadened a previous French-British defensive alliance against Germany into a pact to coordinate military policies of the five nations against any power that might attack one of them. It was clearly directed against the Soviet Union and ended the traditional neutrality policy of the Benelux nations. It also indicated that both Great Britain under the Labour Party government and France, whose centrist parties had placated the French Communists previously, had become alarmed at Stalin's policies in Europe. France and Britain therefore began a united western European action to indicate their willingness to confront the Soviet Union if necessary.

March 20, 1948   THE SOVIET UNION'S DELEGATES WALK OUT OF THE ALLIED CONTROL COUNCIL, CHARGING THAT THE THREE WESTERN POWERS SOUGHT TO UNDERMINE THE FOUR-POWER CONTROL OF BERLIN.

Early in 1948, previous rifts between the Russian delegate to the Four-Power Control Council for Germany, Vasile D. SOKOLOVSKY, and the three Western delegates began to increase because Sokolovsky vigorously denounced the Allied moves to unify their three zones of West Germany. Russia hoped to use its veto power in the Control Council to block the Allies' actions, but the three Allied nations became determined not to be deadlocked by the Russians.

Subsequently, the conflicts at the Four-Power Control Council meetings became what historian Herbert Feis called "brawls." The Western delegates, led by General Lucius Clay of the United States, strongly argued with Sokolovsky and protested Russian actions in East Germany which violated the Control Council decisions.

Finally, on March 20, the Four-Power Council's sessions broke up and never again were conducted. The final split took place when the Russians asked the council to consider an attack by Poland and Yugoslavia against Western policy in West Germany. Clay refused, saying those complaints contained false and distorted facts. Sokolovsky read a long statement to repeat all of Russia's charges against the Western powers in Germany. Then the Russian, who was the March council chairman, adjourned the meeting and left. No new meeting date was set and General Clay decided not to ask Russia for another session. See June 24, 1948.

March 28, 1948   THE CHARTER OF THE INTERNATIONAL TRADE ORGANIZATION
                        (ITO) IS FINALIZED AT THE HAVANA WORLD CONFERENCE ON
                        TRADE AND EMPLOYMENT.

Sixty nations participated in this conference sponsored by the United Nations, convened on November 21, 1947. The ITO developed from a suggestion made by the United States in December, 1945. Its purpose was to create an organization for consultation on trade issues and to formulate a fair practices code for international commerce.

April 6, 1948   *FINLAND AND THE SOVIET UNION SIGN A MILITARY ASSISTANCE
                        AGREEMENT.*

Earlier in 1948 (February and March), the Soviets also signed treaties of friendship and military assistance with RUMANIA, HUNGARY and BULGARIA.

April 16, 1948   SIXTEEN EUROPEAN NATIONS FORM THE ORGANIZATION FOR
                        EUROPEAN ECONOMIC COOPERATION (OEEC).

This agreement provided for the non-Communist European nations to work together in using aid under the EUROPEAN RECOVERY PROGRAM (THE MARSHALL PLAN).

May 2, 1948   ORGANIZATION OF AMERICAN STATES (OAS) IS ESTABLISHED
                        AT BOGOTA, COLOMBIA.

Following up on the Rio Pact of August, 1947, the Ninth International Conference of American Republics formed the OAS as an anti-Communist pact for the Western Hemisphere. During the conference deliberations at Bogota, the meetings had to be suspended for several days because of a local Communist-led revolt which wrecked the city and took hundreds of lives.
        The OAS formed a hemispheric defense council and created a process to call sessions of the defense council in case of aggression against any member nation. It also adopted at Bogota an anti-Communist resolution.
        Not all was harmonious in the Western Hemisphere, however. Many of the Latin American delegates wanted the United States to provide "little Marshall Plan" aid to solve their economic problems. President Truman disappointed them by offering only a half-billion dollars of Export-Import Bank funds.

May 7, 1948   *THE CONGRESS OF EUROPE MEETS AT THE HAGUE TO DISCUSS
                        PLANS FOR ESTABLISHING A EUROPEAN UNION.*

The honorary chairman was Winston Churchill. The dream of such European statesmen as JEAN MONNET, the congress was intended to create a political means to unite Europe.

May 14, 1948   *THE STATE OF ISRAEL IS PROCLAIMED UNDER A PROVISIONAL GOVERNMENT HEADED BY DAVID BEN GURION.*

After the British mandate ended and British troops withdrew, the U.N. partition plan went into effect, but war between Arabs and Jews broke out almost immediately. Both the United States and the Soviet Union recognized Israel by May 16, 1948.

June 1, 1948   BRITAIN, FRANCE, THE UNITED STATES, BELGIUM, LUXEMBOURG, AND THE NETHERLANDS AGREE ON (1) THE INTERNATIONAL CONTROL OF THE RUHR, (2) GERMAN REPRESENTATION IN THE EUROPEAN RECOVERY PROGRAM, (3) INTEGRATING THE THREE WESTERN ZONES OF GERMANY, AND (4) DRAFTING A FEDERAL CONSTITUTION FOR WEST GERMANY.

June 11, 1948   THE VANDENBERG RESOLUTION IS APPROVED BY THE U.S. SENATE.

Sponsored by Republican Senator ARTHUR H. VANDENBERG, this resolution affirmed American support for regional security pacts such as the Brussels Pact. This resolution was meant to support the State Department's efforts to negotiate U.S. membership in a European defense pact.

Senate approval of the Vandenberg Resolution marked a significant point in the final shifting of U.S. policy from isolationism to international responsibility. As Herbert Feis has remarked, Hitler could not change the Republican Party's isolationism; Stalin did. Beginning on April 11, Senator Vandenberg worked with Undersecretary of State Robert Lovett in drafting a resolution that would commit America to the collective defense of western Europe against any acts of aggression.

On May 19, Vandenberg introduced his resolution as recommended by the Senate Foreign Relations Committee. As approved by the Senate on June 11, the resolution gave Senate favor to any "regional and other collective security arrangements for individual and collective self-defense." The Senate approved the resolution by a vote of 64 to 4. See April 4, 1949.

June 24, 1948   THE BERLIN BLOCKADE BEGINS, RESULTING IN U.S. AIRLIFT.

Dismayed by the success of the French, British, and Americans in uniting their zones of Germany, the Russians retaliated by shutting down all land, rail, and water traffic through their zone to Berlin. Apparently the Russians hoped the Western Allies would abandon Berlin and permit it to become the capital city to rally Germans to communism.

After the Russians sidetracked two trains sent to test the blockade, President Truman determined, with British support, to stay in West Berlin and use an airlift to supply the 2.5 million Berliners in their zones. The Western Allies also hurt the Russian-East German economy by a counterblockade of their zone.

The airlift, code-named "Operation Vittles," continued to supply West Berlin for over a year. Up to 4,500 tons of supplies, including coal, were flown in each day. Although at times these planes had incidents with Soviet fighter planes, the Russians did not want a war and finally agreed in 1949 to end the blockade. See May 11, 1949.

Truman's action in challenging the Russians gave the United States and its allies much support in Europe and reacted strongly against the Russians. It also seemed to demonstrate the validity of the president's "get tough" policy toward communism.

June 28, 1948   TRUMAN ORDERS 60 B-29 BOMBERS SENT TO BRITISH BASES
                         AND A SMALLER NUMBER TO GERMAN BASES.

Although this action had been under consideration for some time, the Berlin blockade underscored the need for U.S. bombers in advance European bases as part of the "Forward Strategy" of defending Europe.

Some news sources implied these bombers were "atomic-capable" but, in fact, the B-29's sent to Europe had not been modified to carry the atomic bombs being used at that time.

June 28, 1948   *YUGOSLAVIA IS EXPELLED FROM THE COMINFORM FOR IDEOLOG-
                         ICAL ERRORS AND HOSTILITY TO THE SOVIET UNION.*

MARSHAL TITO (JOSIP BROZ), the wartime resistance leader who was elected to rule Yugoslavia on November 11, 1945, rejected the charges and SEPARATED HIS NATION FROM RUSSIAN CONTROL.

During the next 12 months, efforts to heal the breach between Moscow and Belgrade did not succeed. See September 27, 1949.

July 30, 1948   WHITTAKER CHAMBERS AND ELIZABETH BENTLEY TELL THE HOUSE
                         UN-AMERICAN ACTIVITIES COMMITTEE (HUAC) THAT COMMUNISTS
                         INFILTRATED THE STATE DEPARTMENT IN THE 1930's.

Chambers and Bentley were self-confessed former Communist Party members whose testimony became the highlight of the HUAC hearings in the late 1940's.

Chambers soon identified ALGER HISS, who had worked in several executive departments after 1933, including the State Department in 1944, as a Communist Party agent. Hiss denied Chambers' testimony and the long-lived HISS-CHAMBERS AFFAIR had begun, an affair which would, among other things, propel Richard Nixon into the national limelight when Nixon backed Chambers.

August 18, 1948   A SOVIET-DOMINATED CONFERENCE ON NAVIGATION OF THE
                         DANUBE RIVER ENDS WITH THE UNITED STATES, BRITAIN,
                         FRANCE, AND AUSTRIA REJECTING THE DANUBE CONVENTION
                         AS SIGNED BY SEVEN COMMUNIST NATIONS.

The Conference on the Danube opened on July 30, 1948, at Belgrade, after Moscow's refusal to delay the sessions until December. The three Western powers reluctantly attended, arguing Austria could have no official role because the Austrian peace treaty was pending. The seven Communist states represented were the U.S.S.R., Bulgaria, Czechoslovakia, Hungary, Rumania, Yugoslavia, and the Ukraine.

Rather than negotiate a new treaty to supersede the Convention of 1921, Russia insisted, and its allies agreed, on using the Soviet draft treaty as the basis for debate and voting. The three Western powers claimed the Soviet draft violated the free navigation of the river by giving the Soviets a "monopoly control" of the Danube. The Western powers offered amendments to the draft but were consistently out-voted by 7 to 3.

The agreement signed on August 18 was essentially a Soviet convention. It passed 7 to 1, with the United States voting no. France and Britain believed that abstaining was the best method for objecting to the "railroading" tactics used by Andrei Vishinsky of Russia. At the final session, the French delegation spoke harshly of the convention which "one power issued and a docile majority" accepted.

Following the sessions, France, Great Britain, and the United States issued statements that rejected the document as "Soviet imperialism," and claimed that the non-riparian nations which used the Danube but were not invited to the meeting RETAINED THE RIGHTS OF THE 1921 CONVENTION. Austria's delegate stated he could not accept the convention because Austria had not had a vote at the conference.

October 29, 1948   *IN A MILITARY COUP IN PERU, GENERAL MANUEL ODRÍA OVER-*
                            THROWS PRESIDENT JOSE LUIS BUSTAMENTE'S GOVERNMENT.

The new government outlawed both Peru's Communist Party and the peasant-worker-supported APRA party.

November 2, 1948   HARRY S. TRUMAN IS REELECTED PRESIDENT, WINNING A SUR-
                            PRISE VICTORY OVER THOMAS E. DEWEY.

Truman received 303 electoral votes to Dewey's 189. The Democrats also gained control of both houses of congress.

The election campaign included a bitter foreign policy struggle between the Democrats and Henry Wallace's PROGRESSIVE PARTY. Wallace blamed Truman for the COLD WAR AGAINST RUSSIA because he stopped Roosevelt's cooperative policies with the Soviet Union.

Yet despite the defection of Wallace and left-wing New Dealers as well as the right-wing DIXIECRATS whose candidate was STROM THURMOND, TRUMAN AND THE DEMOCRATIC PARTY CENTER POLITICIANS defeated Dewey, Wallace, and Thurmond.

November 12, 1948   THE JAPANESE WAR CRIME TRIALS END.

The Military Tribunal sentenced General Hidiki Tojo and 6 other Japanese leaders to death for major war crimes; 16 others received sentences of life imprisonment.

November 20, 1948   THE AMERICAN CONSUL GENERAL AT MUKDEN, CHINA, IS CON-
                            FINED TO HIS QUARTERS BY THE CHINESE COMMUNISTS, BE-
                            GINNING A YEAR OF HIS "HOSTAGE"-STYLE CONFINEMENT
                            WITH 21 OTHER STAFF MEMBERS CAPTURED AT THE CONSULATE.

Mukden, Manchuria, became the first urban center with foreign diplomatic representation to be captured by Mao Tse-tung's Communist armies. The Communists gained control of the city on October 31 and initially seemed willing to discuss trade agreements with the American, English, and French consuls in Mukden.

On November 14, a problem arose because the three foreign consuls were requested to turn their radio transmitters over to the government within 48 hours. The French and British had no independent transmitters and the U.S. Consul, Angus J. WARD, refused to do so until he could receive permission from Washington. He offered, however, to stop transmitting radio messages.

Ward's offer was rejected by the Communists without further consultation. On November 20, Communist soldiers cordoned off the office and residence compounds of the American consulate. The Chinese officials informed Ward that no one could leave the compound or communicate with the outside. The troops cut the consulate's telephone and electrical lines and shut off the water supply. Ward's radio transmitters and generators were also seized. During the next 30 hours, the guards gave the 22 persons only one bucket of water and no food. Although the consulate's electricity was restored in December, Ward did not get to communicate with the outside world until June 7, 1949. The plight of the 22 "hostages" continued for more than a year, causing President Truman to consider military measures to free the "prisoner." See November 24, 1949.

December 9-10, 1948   THE U.N. GENERAL ASSEMBLY ADOPTS THE UNIVERSAL DECLA-
                          RATION OF HUMAN RIGHTS AND THE CONVENTION ON THE PRE-
                          VENTION AND PUNISHMENT OF GENOCIDE.

1949

January 20, 1949   PRESIDENT TRUMAN'S SECOND INAUGURAL ADDRESS PROPOSES
                          THE POINT FOUR POLICY.

The Point Four program was a "bold new program of aid to economically underdeveloped areas." Although Point Four received much publicity, the Truman
administration did not give it much attention. Congress finally authorized
funds for Point Four in May, 1950, but appropriations were meager--far below
the standards used in the Marshall Plan.

     During Truman's address to congress his other three points were: encour-
aging European recovery, fully supporting the United Nations, and pledging
aid to those nations defending themselves. These three points were not new;
Point Four was injected into Truman's speech for dramatic effect.

January 21, 1949   DEAN ACHESON REPLACES GEORGE MARSHALL AS SECRETARY OF
                          STATE.

Acheson had been Undersecretary of State from 1945 to 1947, resigning in the
spring of 1947 to return to private legal practice. Nevertheless, when
Marshall's health required him to resign in December, 1948, Truman immediately
asked Acheson to become secretary and the appointment was announced on January
7, 1949.

     Concerning later false accusations about Acheson by Senator Joseph
McCarthy, the basis of those charges is evident in the Senate hearings on
Acheson's appointment. The unproven allegations had been raised by former
U.S. Ambassador to Poland Arthur Lane Bliss and a former State Department
associate, Adolf Berle. Bliss wrote a book titled *I Saw Poland Betrayed*
(1948) which accused Acheson of appeasing the Soviet Union by giving loans
and credits to the Polish government from 1945 to 1947. Berle in August,
1948, told the House Un-American Affairs Committee that Alger Hiss was one
of the "Acheson-group" in the State Department which had a "pro-Russian point
of view." This latter charge was disproven by Acheson during the Senate hearings in January, 1949. Not Alger Hiss but his brother, Donald Hiss, had
worked with Acheson. This testimony did not, however, receive the widespread
attention that Berle's charges obtained in 1948.

     Acheson's nomination as secretary was endorsed by a large variety of
people who knew and had worked with him, including Herbert Hoover and John
Foster Dulles. Senator Vandenberg, the leading Republican on the Senate Foreign Relations Committee, also supported Acheson, knowing that far from being
"soft" on communism, Acheson had strongly urged measures to combat the Soviet
Union between 1945 and 1947.

April 4, 1949   THE NORTH ATLANTIC TREATY ORGANIZATION (NATO) IS CHAR-
                         TERED BY 12 NATIONS, INCLUDING THE UNITED STATES.

The other 11 charter members were Great Britain, France, Belgium, the Netherlands, Luxembourg, Italy, Portugal, Denmark, Iceland, Norway, and Canada.
    The ratification of the North Atlantic Treaty by the U.S. Senate on July
21, 1949 (a vote of 82 to 13), committed the United States to a peace-time
political-military alliance with Europe for the first time since the abrogation of the French Alliance in 1800.
    The treaty signatories agreed to consult together if any one's security
were threatened. Article 5 was a key clause, because it stated that "an armed
attack against one or more of them ... shall be considered an attack against
them all." Thus, they would join together with whatever action was necessary
"including the use of armed force" to restore the security of the North Atlantic area.
    The clause "such action as it deems necessary" limited the pledges of
each nation and made the alliance uncertain. The United States believed that
the clause was essential because the American constitution required congressional approval to go to war. But other signatories could also use this
clause to limit their military commitment.
    The NATO charter was more than a military alliance because it permitted
continuous cooperation in political, economic, and non-military fields. Cooperation among the NATO allies was through the Treaty Organization. Each
member sent delegates to the NATO Council which could "meet promptly at any
time." The council appointed a secretary-general and various committees to
assist in its work. Committees included such groups as: Defense Planning
Committee, the Nuclear Defense Affairs Committee, the Economic Affairs Committee, and others. A Military Committee had special responsibilities for
guidance and recommendations on military matters.
    ALL MEMBERS RATIFIED THE NATO CHARTER, WHICH BECAME EFFECTIVE ON AUGUST
24, 1949.

May 8, 1949   *THE FEDERAL REPUBLIC OF GERMANY (FGR) IS FORMED AT*
                        BONN.

The Germans adopted the Basic Laws of the Federal Republic in meetings at
Bonn. On August 14, 1949, Bundestag elections resulted in a victory for
Konrad ADENAUER's Christian Democratic Party, which won a plurality of 31%
of the vote compared to the Social Democrats' 29.2%. Theodore HEUSS became
president of the republic and Adenauer became Chancellor.

May 11, 1949   THE BERLIN BLOCKADE ENDS AFTER A FOUR-POWER ACCORD ON
                        BERLIN.

As early as January 30, 1949, Stalin told an American journalist, Kingsbury
Smith, that he was willing to end the blockade. Serious discussions on an
agreement to end the crisis did not begin until April. Russia realized that
the blockade had not been successful but that it had drawn the Western powers
closer together rather than dividing them. Finally, the Western counter-
measures hurt the economic life of East Germany and the Soviet satellites of
east Europe.
    On May 5, the four powers announced in Berlin that accords had been

achieved to end the Soviet blockade as well as the Western nations' counter-measures since the summer of 1948.

The U.S. airlift continued to send supplies to West Berlin until September 30. During the airlift from July 24, 1948, to September 30, 1949, the Western Allies flew 277,264 flights to Berlin. When the airlift reached its peak between February and June, 1949, an average of one plane landed in Berlin every two minutes; 7,000 to 8,000 tons of food and fuel were airlifted each day.

May 12, 1949   THE FAR EASTERN COMMISSION ANNOUNCES THE TERMINATION
                        OF REPARATIONS TO AID JAPAN'S ECONOMIC RECOVERY.

The 11-nation Far Eastern Commission had been established in Washington in 1945 to oversee the Allied control council in Tokyo. By 1947, the commission began to change its policy from punishing the Japanese to strengthening them as much as possible.

The initial change in policy took place in 1948 when the Allies abandoned the policy of dissolving the *zaibatsu* -the economic empires of 10 Japanese families which controlled 75% of Japan's financial, industrial, and commercial business. In March, 1948, George Kennan visited with MacArthur in Tokyo to explain the necessity for promoting the interests of those upper-class Japanese who were friends of America. This required not economic reform but recovery. American business and banking officials also visited Tokyo to emphasize the same thing to MacArthur.

MacArthur quickly got the message. Previous decrees for the dissolution of 325 Japanese corporations which were under *zaibatsu* control ended after only nine had been broken up. MacArthur also had the Japanese government alter its labor laws to deny government workers the right to strike or to engage in collective bargaining. In June, 1950, MacArthur purged 23 leaders of the Japanese Communist Party and other radical leaders.

The May 12, 1949, order to end the removal of Japanese goods as reparations effectively ended all reparations for Japan. Reparations based on industrial equipment had stopped in 1948. The policy after 1948 was to build a strong Japan as a U.S. friend because China's collapse appeared certain in 1949.

May 15, 1949   *COMMUNISTS GAIN CONTROL OF THE HUNGARIAN GOVERNMENT.*

In the first postwar elections on November 3, 1945, the anti-Communist SMALL-HOLDERS' PARTY won an absolute majority and Ferenc Nagy became premier. With Soviet backing, however, the Communists began a gradual purge of the Smallholders' leaders, accusing them of conspiracy. By early 1949, the Communists' NATIONAL INDEPENDENCE front had purged Nagy and other Smallholders. Joseph Cardinal MINDSZENTY had been sentenced to life in prison but fled to asylum in the American Embassy.

On May 15, 1949, a general election resulted in a complete Communist victory with Istuan DOBI as premier and the real Communist boss, Matyas RAKOSI, as deputy premier.

May 17, 1949   *THE BRITISH HOUSE OF COMMONS ADOPTS THE IRELAND BILL,*
                        GIVING FULL INDEPENDENCE TO IRELAND BUT AFFIRMING THAT
                        NORTHERN IRELAND IS WITHIN THE UNITED KINGDOM.

The issue of the partition of Ireland had been disputed since 1945 when North-
ern Ireland voted for partition and the British government supported its
wishes.
    On December 21, 1948, the Irish parliament passed and President SEAN T.
O'KELLY signed the Republic of Ireland bill. On February 10, Northern Ireland
again voted for union with Great Britain. The British reorganized both the
Ireland Bill and the partition on May 17, 1949.

June 14, 1949   *THE FRENCH GOVERNMENT RETURNS THE EMPEROR BAO DAI TO*
                        RULE VIETNAM.

In the Elysée Agreement of March 8, 1949, French President Vincent AURIOL and
BAO DAI agreed on the establishment of the Independent State of Vietnam within
the French Union. Paris continued to control matters of finance, trade, de-
fense, foreign affairs, and internal security in Vietnam, but agreed to re-
organize the southern province of Cochin China as part of a United Vietnam.
    Because Ho Chi Minh's forces continued to fight French forces, Paris
hoped Bao Dai would provide a political solution to the war by symbolizing
Vietnamese independence under French authority.
    Bao had few followers in Vietnam and further alienated himself by taking
the title of "Emperor" as well as chief of state. Bao said the people could
prepare a constitution in the future, after order was restored.

July 16, 1949   *CHIANG KAI-SHEK PREPARES RETREAT TO FORMOSA.*

Chiang formed a reorganized supreme council of the NATIONALISTS. When the
civil war renewed in 1946, Chiang's forces seemed to make notable advances,
but throughout 1948, his corrupt and ineffective officers were not able to
withstand the large popular support rallying to the Communists. On January
21, 1949, Chiang resigned as president and retreated to the southwest while
Vice President Li Tsungjen tried to persuade Mao to negotiate a truce. By
July, the Communists' eventual victory appeared certain. Thus, Chiang Kai-
shek prepared to move to Formosa, claiming his followers would reconquer the
mainland of China in the future. See October 1, 1949.

August 5, 1949   TO EXPLAIN AMERICAN POLICY RELATING TO CHIANG KAI-
                        SHEK'S LOSS OF CHINA, THE STATE DEPARTMENT ISSUES A
                        "WHITE PAPER."

Consisting of 1,054 pages of documents and a lengthy introduction by Secretary
of State ACHESON, the volume's thesis was that the loss of China "was beyond
the control of the government of the United States." The consequences of
the Chinese civil war resulted from "internal Chinese forces" and the inade-
quate policies of Chiang Kai-shek.
    The "White Paper" marked a break in the bipartisan foreign policy fos-
tered by Senator Vandenberg and the Roosevelt-Truman administrations. Many
conservative Republicans followed an "Asia-first" policy based strongly on

support of Chiang Kai-shek's policies as rationalized by the so-called China Lobby, whose leading proponent was the charming Madame Chiang.

The Republican China bloc claimed the "White Paper" was a "whitewash of a wishful, do-nothing policy" which placed all of Asia in danger of Russian conquest. Its emphasis on Moscow's monolithic control of Communists envisioned Mao's victory as a Soviet triumph, downplaying or denying that Chinese nationalism made Mao strongly suspicious of all Soviet moves.

Others reacted differently to the White Paper. Walter Lippmann, a well-known news columnist, said the White Paper failed to explain "Chiang's stronghold in American policy" for so long. John K. Fairbank, an expert on Chinese history who taught at Harvard, declared the volume was a frank admission that the United States "made the wrong approach to the problem of revolution in Asia."

Nevertheless, the strongly partisan debate over the "loss of China" affected the rise of McCarthyism and extreme anti-Communist emotions throughout the 1950's and, for some Americans, for the rest of the century.

August 10, 1949   THE DEPARTMENT OF DEFENSE IS ESTABLISHED

President Truman signed congressional legislation which renamed the National Military Establishment as the Department of Defense. This act gave broader and more definite powers to the Secretary of Defense.

August 22, 1949   THE FIRST USE OF ATOMIC WEAPONS BY U.S. FORCES IS SANCTIONED IN A RECOMMENDATION OF THE JOINT CHIEFS OF STAFF (JCS).

Approved two weeks later by the National Security Council (NSC-57), the "first use" principle was part of a NATO defense plan integrating the use of atomic weapons into the war plan. Although the contingency war plan hoped the American nuclear umbrella would deter a Soviet attack on western Europe, the plan permitted use of the atomic bomb if the Communists invaded. This JCS plan both promoted and required the May, 1949, JCS request for additional funds to EXPAND THE PRODUCTION OF ATOMIC BOMBS.

From a strategic viewpoint, the JCS action backed the AIR FORCE AIR-ATOMIC METHODS, AND REJECTED THE NAVY'S CARRIER PLANE ATTACK METHOD. The Air Force plan code-named "OFFTACKLE" was prepared during the summer of 1949. It proposed that aircraft, particularly the new B-36, would carry atomic bombs against the Soviet Union, the bomber being the nation's primary weapon. The U.S. Navy advocated that "super-carriers" capable of launching planes with atomic bombs should be the first line of U.S. defense.

During the fall of 1949, the navy was losing the status it had before 1941. The JCS war plan denigrated the navy carrier-attack program, and Secretary of Defense Louis Johnson stopped construction of the super-carrier, the U.S.S. *United States*, which Johnson claimed was too costly.

In October, 1949, U.S. Navy officers, led by Chief of Naval Operations Admiral Louis Denfeld, staged a last-ditch "Admirals Revolt" to PROTEST AGAINST JOHNSON AND THE JCS PLAN. Taking their case to the congress, high-ranking naval leaders testified in opposition to the "air-atomic" strategy at hearings of the House Armed Services Committee. The Navy claimed Air Force bombers would not be able to penetrate Soviet defenses sufficiently. They also pointed out that if the bombers got through, the Air Force doctrine

of saturation bombing would, as in World War II, not make the victims surrender but would create in them a stronger "will to survive and resist." By
using carrier-based bombers, the Navy proposed to hit only military targets
and Russian forces in order to defeat the enemy.

The October "Admirals revolt" lost. Both Truman and Secretary of Defense
Johnson favored the air-atomic strategy, and the coming of the H-Bomb between
1950 and 1952 seemed to them to confirm that view. Soon after the conclusion
of the October hearings, Truman removed Denfeld and other participants in
the revolt from their high-level positions.

September 2, 1949   *THE UNITED NATIONS COMMISSION ON KOREA ANNOUNCES FROM*
                         SEOUL THAT MEDIATION HAS FAILED.

Since the United States referred the Korean problem to the United Nations in
September, 1947, the commission had sought some means to unify the country
and hold national elections. The commission was not, however, permitted by
the Communists to operate north of the 38° latitude. In 1948, the Republic
of Korea was set up in South Korea (August 15), and the Korean People's Dem-
ocratic Republic in North Korea (September 9).

In respect of the U.N. Commission findings, both the Soviet Union (by
December 25, 1948) and the United States (by June 29, 1949) withdrew their
occupation forces. Nevertheless, the U.N. Commission could not persuade KIM
IL SUNG, the northern leader, and SYNGMAN RHEE, the south's president, to
work together to try to reach a satisfactory compromise.

September 15, 1949   THE RECIPROCAL TRADE AGREEMENT ACT IS EXTENDED FOR
                         TWO YEARS.

This act renewed the Hull program of 1934 although Hull's original hope of
lowering tariffs had been damaged since 1945 because the Republican congress inserted "escape" clauses to allow certain American producers to get
higher tariffs and to set an export control program designed to discriminate
against the Communist bloc, but which could also be used in trade with the
"free" world.

September 23, 1949   A WHITE HOUSE PRESS RELEASE ANNOUNCES THAT THE SOVIET
                         UNION HAS DETONATED AN ATOMIC BOMB.

The exact date of the Soviets' successful explosion is not known. U.S. in-
telligence estimates are that the explosion occurred late in August, 1949.
On September 9, the AEC monitors detected excessive radioactivity coming from
central Asia, and on September 14, samples of rainwater clouds confirmed this.
American intelligence estimated the samples were one month old and that the
Soviets used a Nagasaki-type plutonium bomb.

President Truman learned of this success on September 12. He and General Groves doubted the accuracy of the data, however; Groves believed that
there was a nuclear accident in Russia. The intelligence and scientific experts were certain and convinced Truman that the data should be released.
It was, on September 23.

*September 27, 1949   THE U.S.S.R. REPUDIATES ITS 1945 TREATY OF FRIENDSHIP
                        WITH YUGOSLAVIA.*

*This announcement from Moscow resulted from a lengthy dispute with Yugoslav-
ia's ruler, MARSHAL TITO. While Tito claimed to follow Communist doctrine,
he was a Yugoslavian nationalist who rejected Moscow's attempt to centrally
control all Communist parties. This intraparty split persisted and "TITOISM"
became synonymous for NATIONALISTIC COMMUNISTS who followed policies in the
best interests of their own nations and were often ANTI-SOVIET COMMUNISTS.*

*October 1, 1949   MAO TSE-TUNG PROCLAIMS THE CREATION OF THE PEOPLE'S
                        REPUBLIC OF CHINA.*

*Mao was head of the central people's administrative council.
      Chiang Kai-shek continued to claim to be the legitimate head of the Chi-
nese government as he and his Nationalist followers moved their government
to the Island of Formosa.*

*October 7, 1949   THE SOVIET ZONE OF GERMANY IS ESTABLISHED AS THE GERMAN
                        DEMOCRATIC REPUBLIC (GDR).*

*The Communist Party dominated the new government with Wilhelm PIECK as Presi-
dent and Otto GROTEWOHL as Minister President.*

November 18, 1949   THE SOVIET UNION AND OTHER COMMUNIST DELEGATES CHAL-
                        LENGE THE NATIONALISTIC GOVERNMENT OF CHINA'S RIGHT
                        TO REPRESENT CHINA IN THE UNITED NATIONS AND ON THE
                        SECURITY COUNCIL.

France, Great Britain, and other nations had recognized the new Chinese government, but the United States had not. America continued to recognize the
Chinese government on Formosa until, as Acheson stated on October 12, the
new Peking government "met traditional American conditions." The United
States did not finally recognize the People's Republic of China until 1979.
      The issue of China's status was first considered by the Security Council
in September, 1949, when the Nationalist government charged that Russia had
interfered in Chinese affairs, asking the United Nations to condemn China
and to recommend that no U.N. member should assist the Communist regime in
Peking. This caused the People's Republic to inform the Secretary General
that the Nationalists had no right to continue to represent the Chinese people
in the United Nations. The Nationalist Chinese retained their U.N. membership
until October 25, 1971.

November 24, 1949   THE U.S. CONSUL AT MUKDEN AND 21 OTHERS ARE RELEASED
                        BY THE CHINESE AUTHORITIES AFTER A YEAR'S CONFINEMENT.

Angus Ward, the U.S. consul at Mukden in Manchuria, China, had been held in-
communicado by the Chinese Communists since November 20, 1948. During this
time, the U.S. State Department possessed little knowledge of the exact situation at Mukden, although American diplomats in other Chinese cities hoped
the problem would end as soon as the civil war ended in China. Mukden had

been the first city with foreign consulates captured by the Communists. The
offensive advances of Mao's armies had proceeded rapidly during the next nine
months and on October 1, the Communists controlled all of China.

During this time, the U.S. State Department and President Truman considered a variety of measures designed to free Ward and the other 21 persons
held at the Mukden consulate. On April 26, Secretary Acheson instructed
Oliver CLUBB, the U.S. Consul General in Peking, to inform the communist government that unless it removed the arbitrary restrictions on the Mukden consulate, the United States would close the Mukden office and withdraw its
staff. Mao's government did not respond, and on May 17, Acheson notified
Clubb that the Mukden consulate should be closed.

Somehow, Acheson's May 17 order to close the Mukden consulate was delivered to Ward on June 7. On June 10, Ward sent a telegram to Clubb in Peking,
saying he was trying to evacuate his staff.

Ward's hopes proved to be premature in June, 1949. On June 19, the Chinese Communist press reported that its Mukden consulate was discovered to
contain a major U.S. spy operation against the Chinese people. Both Ward in
Mukden and the U.S. Embassy in Nanking refuted the spy charges. Nevertheless,
Ward's plan to evacuate the consulate at Mukden was delayed by the Communist
authorities.

Ward's continued detention led President Truman to consider harsher measures in October, 1949, when two events raised questions in Washington.
First, on October 1, China's Foreign Office asked all foreign representatives
in China to recognize the Communist government. Concerned about Hong Kong,
Great Britain wanted to recognize the new regime as soon as possible. Concerned about its war in Indochina, France preferred to delay recognition.
The United States believed it could not establish relations with Mao's regime
until the Ward-Mukden affair was settled. These considerations enabled the
U.S. State Department to begin a diplomatic "offensive," asking all foreign
representatives to withhold recognition until the Mukden affair ended. China,
Acheson said, must demonstrate it can protect diplomatic officials.

The second event in China in October seemed to be the most serious. On
October 24, Ward and four members of his staff were arrested by the Chinese
for allegedly directing a mob which beat up a Chinese worker. As Ward later
explained, the trumped-up assault charges resulted from his attempt to escort
from the consulate a Chinese messenger, JI YUTTENG, who had been fired from
the consulate staff. Because Ji refused to leave, there was a scuffle in
which Ji and his brother were injured.

Ward's arrest caused an angry reaction in America where Truman's administration was already under political attack for not supporting Chiang Kai-
shek against the Communists. As a result, between October 31 and November
18, Truman explored the possibility of either a blockade of China or military
action to liberate Ward and his staff. The Joint Chiefs of Staff and General
Omar Bradley, its Chairman, advised Truman that military action would be difficult and might lead to a global war. A blockade, they advised, would not
be effective. Secretary Acheson's diplomatic offensive seemed to be the best
option. At a news conference on November 16, Acheson stated that the United
States could not consider recognition until the Americans at Mukden were released.

China's desire for diplomatic recognition by foreign governments may
have been the reason that the Mukden affair suddenly ended on November 24.
The precise reasons for China's action on November 20, 1948, and on November
24, 1949, are not known. On the latter date, Ward called Clubb in Peking,
reporting that he and his four co-defendants had been found guilty of the

charges against them. They were to be deported, however, in lieu of imprisonment. Within a month, on December 12, Ward and the others who had been confined at Mukden left China on the liner *Lakeland Victory*.

Exactly why the Mukden incident arose is not certain. The best evaluation seems to be that of William N. Stokes who, as the Vice-Consul at Mukden,
had been confined with Ward. Stokes believed that because Mao's civil-war
propaganda had denounced the United States and the Western powers for aiding
Chiang Kai-shek, and because Mukden was the first contact that Communist authorities and troops had with Western representatives, the hostility of the
red armies against the West caused the Mukden affair. A year later, the Chinese Communists desired Western recognition; hence the change in China's attitude at Mukden on November 24, 1949.

One consequence of the Mukden affair may have been the U.S. non-recognition of the People's Republic of China for the next thirty years. Indications
are that in 1948-49, the United States was ready to join the English in accepting the new Chinese government. The Mukden crisis delayed recognition by
Washington. Furthermore, the arrest of Ward in October 1949 inflamed U.S.
feelings against China, making it difficult for Truman to grant recognition.

December 1, 1949   THE U.N. GENERAL ASSEMBLY ADOPTS A U.S.-BRITISH-
                           SPONSORED "ESSENTIALS OF PEACE" RESOLUTION.

The "Essentials of Peace" proposal was the U.S.-British answer to a Soviet-
sponsored U.N. resolution against the North Atlantic Treaty Alliance. On
September 29, the General Assembly agreed to consider a U.S.S.R. resolution
titled "Condemnation of the preparations for a new war and conclusion of a
five-power pact for the strengthening of peace." Without specifically citing
the Atlantic pact, the Russians claimed that the Anglo-American bloc followed
an aggressive policy to isolate Russia from European politics. They stated
this was contrary to the U.N. Charter and that the Big Five powers should
handle basic issues of world peace.

The American delegation decided to submit the "Essentials of Peace" resolution as a substitute motion which eventually passed the General Assembly
on December 1 by a vote of 53 to 5. The "peace" resolution affirmed the principles of the U.N. Charter and asked all members to cooperate to ease world
tensions. The key clause stated the U.S.-British contention that peace was
endangered by the Soviet Union's frequent use of the veto power in the Security Council. This clause called on the five powers to show cooperation and
"to exercise restraint in the use of the veto" so that the Security Council
could act effectively to maintain peace.

December 27, 1949   *INDONESIA IS GRANTED SOVEREIGNTY BY THE NETHERLANDS.*

*Since the Japanese evacuation of the East Indies in 1945, the Republic of
Indonesia, which declared independence on August 17, and the Netherlands,
which desired to reclaim its colonial ownership, had clashed in war and endeavored to negotiate. After intermittent periods of war, the Netherlands,
on the urging of the United States, agreed to a settlement concluded with
the aid of the United Nations Good Offices Committee. The Indonesian leader
in the independence movement was ACHMED SUKARNO.*

December 28, 1949   NATIONAL SECURITY COUNCIL DOCUMENT NSC 48/1 INDICATES
                         SOUTHEAST ASIA IS A VITAL AREA FOR THE UNITED STATES.

This document, which was classified secret until the *Pentagon Papers* were
published in 1971, indicates that important personnel of the State and Defense
departments, probably Paul Nitze and Dean Acheson, believed even before the
Korean War that U.S. interests in Indochina needed to be protected from communism.

NSC 48/1 read in part:

> The extension of communist authority in China represents a grievous political defeat for us. If southeast Asia also is swept by communism we shall have suffered a major political rout the repercussions of which will be felt throughout the rest of the world....

Thus, Mao's victory in China caused the NSC to believe Indochina was the next objective of communism. Notably, no one in the NSC seems to have realized the historic tradition of antagonism between China and Vietnam, a fact on which all academic scholars of Vietnam agreed.

1950

January 12, 1950   IN A SPEECH TO THE NATIONAL PRESS CLUB, SECRETARY OF
                      STATE DEAN ACHESON DESCRIBES THE U.S. "PERIMETER STRAT-
                      EGY" BEING USED IN EAST ASIA.

Based on sea power theories of Alfred Mahan, the "perimeter strategy" intended
to control large land areas, such as mainland China, by controlling the surrounding sea. In the Far East, the American defense line ran on the perimeter
of Asia from the Aleutian Islands through Japan and the Ryukyus Island to
the Philippines.
    In addition, Acheson asserted that American policy did not foresee a
lengthy Sino-Soviet alliance. Mao Tse-tung would not permit Moscow to dominate China because Chinese nationalism was a stronger force than communism
and, unlike eastern Europe, China was not occupied by Russia. Eventually,
Acheson argued, Peking would find the United States to be the best friend of
"national independence for China."
    Although recognizing Washington's special economic responsibilities in
Korea and Japan, America's major East Asian concern would be a Communist attack west of the defense perimeter.
    Finally, the secretary told the Press Club, he did not believe the Com-
munists would use military aggression in East Asia. The Communists could be
expected to use "subversion and penetration" to extend their influence in
Asia; these tactics would be more difficult for politicians in Washington,
London, or Paris to counteract. But they were methods more adaptable to the
anti-colonial movement in Asia.
    In retrospect, Acheson's speech contained many insights regarding future
Sino-Soviet disputes. It became best known, however, for its "failure to
predict" the North Korean attack across the 38th parallel on June 25, 1950.
Acheson's critics would argue that his enunciation of the perimeter strategy
led the Communists to believe they could attack South Korea without fear of
American retaliation.

January 13, 1950   THE DELEGATE OF THE SOVIET UNION, JACOB MALIK, WALKS
                      OUT OF THE SECURITY COUNCIL SESSION, BEGINNING A SEVEN-
                      MONTH SOVIET BOYCOTT OF U.N. MEETINGS.

Russia's decision to walk out of the Security Council followed the FAILURE
of a motion to EXPEL THE CHINESE NATIONALISTS FROM THE UNITED NATIONS. The
vote was 6 to 3 against the motion (Great Britain and Norway abstained). Although the Russians appeared adamantly in favor of the Peking government,
U.N. observers such as British delegate Sir Alexander Colgan believed the
Soviet Union preferred to impede admission of Mao's government to the United
Nations in order more effectively to dominate the People's Republic. By preventing further debate on the China issue after the first vote, the Russian
boycott kept China out of the United Nations.
    The Soviet Union's boycott continued until August 1, 1950.

January 21, 1950   ALGER HISS IS CONVICTED OF PERJURY ON TWO COUNTS OF
                       FALSE TESTIMONY BEFORE A GRAND JURY OF NEW YORK WHEN
                       HE STATES:

(1) he had not turned over any secret, confidential, or restricted documents
to Whittaker Chambers in 1938, and (2) he definitely said he had not seen
Chambers after January 1, 1937, whereas he had seen and conversed with
Chambers in February and March, 1938.

Hiss had been an active New Dealer who worked for the Nye Investigation
Committee in the early 1930's and for the State Department. During World
War II, he helped plan the foundation of the United Nations and in this ca-
pacity had been present at the Yalta Conference of February, 1945.

Chambers first called attention to Hiss in 1948, during hearings of the
House Un-American Activities Committee where, as an ex-Communist, Chambers
became a star witness. Chambers claimed he had known Hiss from 1934 to 1938
as a member of a special underground group in the Communist Party.

Before HUAC and later the grand jury, Hiss denied having been a member
of such a Communist group. He also denied having given Chambers any confidential State Department data. The chief interrogator of Hiss during the
HUAC hearings was Congressman Richard Nixon.

Two trials became necessary to convict Hiss. In the first trial, the
jury could not reach a verdict (July 8, 1949). The second trial began on
November 17, 1949; the jury found him guilty on both counts on January 21.

The precise nature of Hiss's trial and conviction was generally lost on
the public, who conceived of Hiss as a Communist spy whose influence aided
the Soviet Union during and after World War II. When friends of Hiss, such
as Dean Acheson, refused to believe Chambers' testimony and accepted the evidence that contradicted Chambers, the critics of Truman and Acheson alleged
this was further evidence of Communist infiltration of the State Department.

Although Hiss appealed his conviction to various channels up to the Supreme Court, his petitions for review were denied. On March 22, 1950, he
surrendered to a U.S. marshal and was imprisoned until November, 1954.

January 24, 1950   *BRITISH ATOMIC PHYSICIST KLAUS FUCHS CONFESSES TO BEING
                       A SOVIET SPY.*

*Fuchs was a division chief of theoretical physics in the British atomic pro-
gram at Harwell. He confessed to giving the Russians data about American
activity at Oak Ridge, Tennessee, and Los Alamos, New Mexico. On March 1,
1950, English courts convicted him of espionage, sentencing him to 14 years
in prison. Fuchs's confession led to charges against Harry Gold and, subsequently, Julius and Ethel Rosenberg.*

January 30, 1950   *THE SOVIET UNION RECOGNIZES HO CHI MINH'S COMMUNIST
                       REGIME AS THE LEGITIMATE VIETNAMESE GOVERNMENT.*

January 31, 1950   THE DECISION TO HASTEN DEVELOPMENT OF THE HYDROGEN
                       BOMB IS ANNOUNCED BY PRESIDENT TRUMAN.

This decision ended intensive debate within the administration about building
the super-bomb. David Lilienthal and George Kennan wanted the United States

to renounce the first use of any atomic bomb and to strongly seek international control. Advocates of the H-Bomb included General Omar Bradley, the chairman of the Joint Chiefs, and the physicist Edward Teller.

Surprised by news of the Soviet atomic test in 1949 and believing in the unqualified threat of the Russians' desire to expand, President Truman gave little thought to abandoning the development of the H-bomb. Clearly, by 1950 the nuclear weapon had become a winning, therefore necessary, weapon for America to possess in its most advanced form.

February 7, 1950   THE UNITED STATES RECOGNIZES BAO DAI'S GOVERNMENT OF
                            VIETNAM.

At the same time, the United States recognized the governments of VIETNAM, LAOS, AND CAMBODIA as "ASSOCIATED STATES WITHIN THE FRENCH UNION."

Laos had been made a free state in the French Union in 1946 under KING NORODOM SIHANOUK. In the fall of 1949, France gave *de jure* independence to Cambodia but, as in the case of Vietnam, controlled its defense, foreign affairs, and internal security.

Bao Dai's government had been established with French help in 1949, with the hope that Bao could gain a following to counteract Vietminh influence in Vietnam. See June 14, 1949.

February 9, 1950   SENATOR JOSEPH McCARTHY CHARGES THAT MANY COMMUNIST
                            SPIES HAVE INFILTRATED THE STATE DEPARTMENT.

McCarthy's first accusations came during a speech at Wheeling, West Virginia, when he said 205 Communists held high, influential positions in the State Department. He continued to make such charges in other speeches, giving the number of spies variously as 57, 81, 205, or 11.

Apparently, McCarthy's charges were intended to help his 1950 senatorial campaign in Wisconsin, but they also became a simple way for friends of Chiang Kai-shek's government to blame the Chinese Nationalist loss on "reds" in the State Department who had allegedly "sold China down the river."

Regardless of how vague, incorrect, or false, McCarthy's charges found a receptive audience--an audience conceived in Truman's March, 1947, "scare the hell out of them" speech and nourished with the evidence of Russian expansion in "East Europe and China," and the Soviet explosion of an atomic bomb in 1949.

The years from 1950 to 1954 may be called the ERA OF McCARTHYISM to denote the near-hysterical anti-Communist emotions affecting U.S. society and foreign policy. Politicians feared to deny or denounce the Wisconsin senator, lest they be pointed to as Communists. Even President Truman and Dean Acheson, in spite of their efforts to initiate America's anti-Communist containment program, fell victim to McCarthyism. Their denials of McCarthy's charges were often not accepted by many Americans.

February 14, 1950   *THE U.S.S.R. AND THE PEOPLE'S REPUBLIC OF CHINA SIGN*
                            A THIRTY-YEAR TREATY OF ALLIANCE.

April 14, 1950   NSC-68 IS PRESENTED TO THE NATIONAL SECURITY COUNCIL.

This secret document later achieved notoriety as a candid plea for a greatly enlarged U.S. military establishment and an activist containment policy against the Soviet Union. Depicting Russian communism as aggressively seeking world conquest, NSC-68 advocated a build up of all branches of the U.S. armed forces to counter any Soviet move and make America less dependent on nuclear weapons alone. This, of course, would greatly enlarge the American defense budget. Such balanced forces would, however, enable the United States to resist Communist tactics of infiltration and intimidation to subvert non-Communist nations. Finally, NSC-68 described urgency in establishing a greater American defense force because it projected 1954 as the time when Russia would be capable of launching a surprise atomic attack, which the United States must be able to counter.

NSC-68 also called for a diplomatic and psychological offensive to roll back prior Soviet expansionism. These methods should strive to discredit the Communist regime and give America a positive image of leadership in the non-Communist world.

Although President Truman never explicitly approved NSC-68, the statement as drawn up by the Secretaries of State and Defense reflected the world policy and rearmament program desired by the Truman administration. Whether or not the huge defense build up would have been enacted by congress became an academic question because the outbreak of the Korean War in June, 1950, necessitated a large increase in the Army, Navy, and Air Force.

NSC-68 was declassified on February 27, 1975. Before that time, however, much of its content had been leaked to reporters and became an "open secret," except for some details, to the public and scholars interested in such knowledge.

June 5, 1950   PRESIDENT TRUMAN SIGNS THE THIRD FOREIGN AID BILL,
                         GRANTING NEARLY $3 BILLION FOR THE EUROPEAN RECOVERY
                         PLAN AND POINT FOUR PROGRAM.

June 25, 1950   NORTH KOREAN FORCES ATTACK SOUTH KOREA.

Because a U.N. commission was present in South Korea, North Korea was readily identified as the aggressor in crossing the 38th parallel. In the Security Council, the Soviet boycott facilitated action because Russia could not veto council measures (see January 13, 1950). Consequently, after North Korea rejected a Security Council order to withdraw, President Truman ordered U.S. forces in Japan to support South Korean forces (June 26). The next day, the Security Council asked U.N. members to assist South Korea in defeating the aggressor (June 27). On June 30, Truman ordered U.S. ground troops into the fighting in South Korea and on July 7, the Security Council agreed that U.N. troops would fight under a commander designated by the United States. President Truman appointed General Douglas MacArthur as the commanding general of UNITED NATIONS FORCES IN KOREA.

Despite his U.N. designation, MacArthur took orders from Washington, not from the United Nations. Truman and the State Department favored the concept of a unified war effort, but they acted unilaterally in directing military and diplomatic policies in Korea. Sixteen nations sent troops to assist in Korea, with the United States providing 50% of the ground force (South Korea provided most of the other 50%), 86% of the naval power, and 93% of the air power.

July 20, 1950 SENATOR McCARTHY'S CHARGES THAT COMMUNISTS HAVE IN-
FILTRATED THE STATE DEPARTMENT ARE FOUND TO BE UNTRUE
BY A SPECIAL SENATE SUBCOMMITTEE CHAIRED BY SENATOR
MILLARD TYDINGS.

McCarthy did not, however, stop his speeches but continued to level accusations against the Truman administration. Soon after the committee report,
McCarthy named OWEN LATTIMORE as the "top Russian espionage agent" in the
United States. Lattimore was a professor at Johns Hopkins University who
frequently served as a consultant to the State Department on affairs of China
and Mongolia. When asked to verify his charges against Lattimore, McCarthy
said President Truman kept his evidence locked up in the loyalty files. The
Tydings Committee then conducted investigations and cleared Lattimore of
McCarthy's charges.
    Nevertheless, the Tydings Committee received less attention than Senator
McCarthy. Fear and suspicion came to infect many avenues of American life,
an emotional atmosphere suited to the irrational accusations of the senator,
not to reasoned efforts at response from his critics.

August 30, 1950 THE UNITED STATES AND THE PHILIPPINES SIGN A MUTUAL
ASSISTANCE PACT.

This treaty extended and implemented legislation of 1946. Its three major
clauses were: (1) a Trading Act to continue free trade until 1954 before a
gradual imposition of U.S. tariffs; (2) a Rehabilitation Act to give economic
aid to the Philippines; and (3) a military assistance act, which included
U.S. bases in the Philippines as well as equipment for the Filipino armed
forces.

September 15, 1950 A DARING ATTACK AT INCHON BY MacARTHUR'S FORCES FI-
NALLY HALTS NORTH KOREA'S OFFENSIVE BY OUTFLANKING
THE INVADERS AND TRAPPING NORTH KOREAN FORCES IN A
PINCER MOVEMENT.

The U.N. offensive soon drove the North Koreans back across the 38th parallel,
raising new questions: (1) Should North Korea be liberated from communist
control? (2) Should the U.N. objective be only to contain North Korea at
the 38th parallel. See October 7, 1950 and April 10-11, 1951.

September 23, 1950 OVER PRESIDENT TRUMAN'S VETO, CONGRESS ADOPTS THE
McCARRAN INTERNAL SECURITY BILL.

This law required members of the COMMUNIST PARTY and Communist "front" organizations to register with the Attorney General. Indirectly, such registration would self-incriminate a person because the Smith Act of 1940 made it a
crime to belong to any group advocating the violent overthrow of the government.
    The McCarran Act also allowed deportation of aliens who were Communists
and gave broad jurisdiction for the government to detain persons in time of
war.
    Truman vetoed the bill on September 20, arguing it was a confused measure

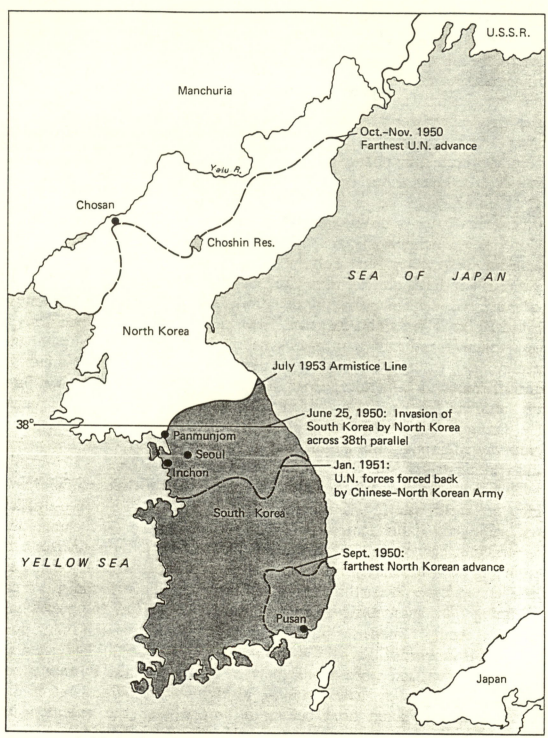

Korea: Divided Since 1945. Adapted from Armin Rappaport, A History of American Diplomacy, New York: Macmillan, 1975. Used with permission.

and would not work properly. But the nation's hysterical anti-Communist mood made it necessary for congressmen to vote for the bill. In the House, whose members faced an election in November, the president's veto was overridden after only one hour of discussion. In the Senate, Hubert Humphrey and Paul Douglas conducted a 22-hour filibuster, but failed to convince their colleagues to uphold Truman's veto.

October 7, 1950   A U.N. GENERAL ASSEMBLY RESOLUTION AGREES THAT THE OBJECTIVE IN KOREA IS TO "ENSURE CONDITIONS OF STABILITY THROUGHOUT KOREA," AND CALLS FOR A "UNIFIED, INDEPENDENT AND DEMOCRATIC GOVERNMENT OF KOREA."

Both in the Truman administration and at the United Nations, controversy had developed about the waging of the Korean War. Some nations wished to be lenient to Kim Il Sung's government and simply return to the *status quo ante bellum*. Others, including Truman, wished to move across the 38th parallel, overthrow Sung's government, and stage "free elections" for a united Korea. The October 7 U.N. resolution was somewhat ambiguous but appeared to favor unification of Korea. At least, Truman first interpreted it in this fashion.

October 15, 1950   PRESIDENT TRUMAN AND GENERAL MacARTHUR MEET AT WAKE ISLAND.

Since July, 1950, Truman and MacArthur had disagreed about using Chiang Kai-shek's forces against either North Korea or mainland China. MacArthur especially irritated the president by sending a message to the Veterans of Foreign Wars convention, in which he called the efforts to restrain Chiang's forces an "appeasement" of communism.
     At Wake Island, Truman reviewed American policy for MacArthur, including the desire to protect Formosa but not to use Nationalist armed forces against the People's Republic of China.

November 1, 1950   AN ASSASSINATION ATTEMPT IS MADE AGAINST PRESIDENT TRUMAN BY TWO PUERTO RICAN NATIONALISTS.

The attempt on Truman's life occurred outside Blair House in Washington, D.C., where the president lived while parts of the White House were being rebuilt. Truman's Secret Service killed one of the assassins, Griselio Torresola. The second, Oscar Collazo, killed a Secret Service agent, a crime for which Collazo was arrested, tried, and sentenced to death. Truman, however, commuted his sentence to life imprisonment.
     The two Puerto Ricans were members of a minority radical group which advocated complete independence for their homeland. There was, in fact, a division among Puerto Ricans regarding their future status. Many desired to retain their special commonwealth status with the United States; others wished to get statehood; finally, the most radical group desired full independence. In the years after World War II, the radicals often committed terrorist acts in the United States in an attempt to dramatize their program. The attempt on Truman's life was one such terrorist act.

November 3, 1950   A "UNITING FOR PEACE" RESOLUTION IS PASSED BY THE GEN-
                          ERAL ASSEMBLY OF THE UNITED NATIONS.

This action gave the assembly the right to recommend collective security measures to U.N. members if the use of the veto in the Security Council prevented
U.N. action. In effect, this resolution weakened the Big Powers veto, not
only for the Soviets but also for the United States. At the time, however,
the American delegation believed that its influence dominated in the votes
of the assembly and that some method for collective action was needed to by-
pass the U.S.S.R.'s frequent use of the veto power.

November 4, 1950   THE UNITED NATIONS RESCINDS A 1946 RESOLUTION CONDEMN-
                          ING SPAIN'S FASCIST GOVERNMENT.

This action reversed not only past U.N. policy but also U.S. policy. In 1945,
America, Britain, and France opposed Spain's membership in the United Nations,
and in 1946 they appealed to the Spanish people to end Francisco Franco's
dictatorship. See March 4, 1946.
    By 1950, AMERICAN EFFORTS TO UNITE ALL NON-COMMUNISTS AGAINST THE SOVIET
UNION caused a shift in policy. This first became evident when congress approved $62.5 million Marshall Plan loans to Spain on September 6, 1950.
    The U.N. action on November 4, 1950, prepared the way for Spain's admis-
sion to the Western anti-Communist camp. It removed a U.N. resolution of
December 11, 1946, which had excluded Spain from all U.N. activity. Several
Latin American countries sponsored the resolution to rescind previous action
against Spain. The action permitted Spain to participate in special agencies
of the United Nations; full U.N. membership for Spain was approved on October
14, 1955.

November 7, 1950   CONGRESSIONAL ELECTIONS REDUCE THE DEMOCRATIC MAJORITY
                          IN BOTH HOUSES OF CONGRESS.

Senator McCarthy's activity played a role in this election, with his proponents helping Republicans to win at least three Senate seats: John M. Butler
defeated McCarthy's nemesis Millard Tydings of Maryland; Everett Dirksen won
over Majority Leader Scott Lucas of Illinois; and Richard Nixon defeated Helen
Gahagan Douglas in California. Altogether, the Democrats lost five Senate
seats and 28 House seats.

November 26, 1950   CHINESE COMMUNIST FORCES LAUNCH A MASSIVE COUNTER-
                          OFFENSIVE AGAINST U.N. TROOPS IN THE YALU RIVER VALLEY.

Since the U.N. resolution of October 7 to unify Korea, the Chinese government
had denounced U.N. activity north of the 38th parallel. After October 21,
when U.N. troops captured PYONGYANG and moved toward the Manchurian border,
there were reports of Chinese troops aiding North Korea.
    Finally, on November 26, after MacArthur ordered an "end-the-war" offen-
sive, the Chinese sent large numbers of troops into Korea to attack U.N.
forces.
    The Chinese offensive caused U.N. armies to retreat south of the 38th
parallel until Seoul was again captured by the Communists on January 4, 1951.

November 28, 1950   *COLOMBO PLAN IS APPROVED BY BRITISH COMMONWEALTH PAR-*
                          LIAMENT.

For six years, this program would provide £8 billion of economic aid to India,
Pakistan, Ceylon, Sarawak, and Borneo.

December 18, 1950   BRUSSELS CONFERENCE OF NATO'S FOREIGN MINISTERS AP-
                          PROVES PLANS FOR THE DEFENSE OF WESTERN EUROPE.

The next day, the ministers named GENERAL DWIGHT D. EISENHOWER AS SUPREME
COMMANDER OF THE NORTH ATLANTIC FORCES.

The foreign ministers' action finalized NATO plans under preparation
since October, 1949. The military plan's important sections were: (1) the
United States had responsibility to use atomic weapons if necessary to defend
NATO nations; (2) a "FORWARD STRATEGY" provided for the defense of Germany
as far east as possible; (3) sea control would be the duty of the U.S., British, and French fleets; (4) western European aircraft would have defensive
and short-range bombing responsibilities.

Adoption of the plan raised two vital questions: (1) How would the NATO
ground forces be increased? and (2) How would Germany be rearmed? The first
question caused problems in America because congressional critics opposed
Truman's plan to send from four to six U.S. divisions to augment NATO forces.
The second question raised problems in France because French opinion opposed
the rearmament of Germany. To increase NATO's forces, the United States proposed forming 10 divisions of German troops as part of the defense effort.

On September 9, 1950, Truman had announced that America would send four
new divisions to Europe. In congress, opponents of this Europe plan challenged Truman's decision. Such spokesmen as former President HERBERT HOOVER,
Senator ROBERT TAFT, and Senator KENNETH WHERRY disliked the European orien-
tation of this policy. Generally, they desired greater American activity in
the Pacific region, arguing that Europe could defend itself.

Other Republicans backed Truman, however. After New York's Republican
Governor THOMAS DEWEY AND GENERAL EISENHOWER DEFENDED THE VALUE OF TRUMAN'S
PROGRAM, the Senate passed a series of resolutions on April 4, 1951, which
accepted Truman's NATO policy. The Senate agreed that the four U.S. Army
divisions could go to Europe but requested that the president consult with
congress before sending additional troops.

In contrast to the American difficulty, the German rearmament question
caused a lengthier dispute because of French opposition. In October, the
French Assembly adopted Prime Minister RENE PLEVEN's plan to include German
troops in NATO only at the lowest (the regiment) level, under a European political authority. Generally, however, the NATO foreign ministers disliked
the PLEVEN PLAN. At the December, 1950, meeting a satisfactory solution could
not be reached. The foreign ministers finally accepted, in principle, German
troop participation, but left the details of the plan for later discussion.

December 23, 1950   THE UNITED STATES, FRANCE, AND THE ASSOCIATED STATES
                          OF INDOCHINA (VIETNAM, LAOS, AND CAMBODIA) SIGN A MU-
                          TUAL DEFENSE AGREEMENT FOR MILITARY AID IN COMBATING
                          COMMUNIST FORCES UNDER HO CHI MINH.

This agreement finalized prior American agreements on May 8, 1950, to give aid to France for use in Indochina and to send 35 U.S. military advisors to Indochina.

Although Washington wanted the funds for Indochina to go directly to Saigon, the French insisted that all aid must go through the Paris office. By December, 1950, the United States committed $50 million for arms, ammunition, naval vessels, military vehicles, and aircraft.

December 28, 1950   O. EDWARD CLUBB, A HIGH-RANKING U.S. FOREIGN SERVICE OFFICER AND EXPERT ON CHINA, IS ORDERED TO ANSWER ALLEGATIONS BEFORE THE STATE DEPARTMENT'S LOYALTY SECURITY BOARD (LSB).

A Foreign Service Officer since 1928, Clubb served principally as a consul in China. He had been the last official closing the American consular office in Peking on April 12, 1950, when he returned to Washington to be the Director of the Office of Chinese Affairs of the State Department.

The allegations made against Clubb on December 28 were anonymous and largely indefinite. Such charges as "viewed some aspects of Communism favorably, 1932–1934," or "friendly toward the U.S.S.R. and Communism, 1935–37," made up all but one of the charges. The one specific allegation was that he "delivered a sealed envelope to the office of the editor of the *New Masses* ... for transmittal to GRACE HUTCHINS," a reputed Communist. This event took place in 1932. Later, Clubb learned that Whittaker Chambers, an editor of *New Masses* in 1933, was the accuser and that the "sealed envelope" was his letter of introduction to WALT CAMERON, the 1932 editor of *New Masses*.

Following many lengthy interrogations, Clubb received clearance from the LSB on February 8, 1952. He decided, however, to retire from the Foreign Service, dismayed at the shabby treatment accorded someone who had worked for the government for over 20 years.

Clubb's experience was repeated frequently enough to DEMORALIZE PROFESSIONAL, OBJECTIVE FOREIGN SERVICE OFFICERS. Clubb and others had committed the offense of expertly analyzing the events where they served even when their superiors and political appointees in Washington wanted to hear reports that confirmed their prejudices in favor of Chiang Kai-shek. In addition to Clubb, other State Department experts on China who suffered similar rebuffs were John Carter Vincent, John S. Service, and John Paton Davies.

The reality of demoralization in the State Department was reviewed and concurred in by a special State Department Committee on Personnel. In 1954, this committee reported to Secretary of State John Foster Dulles: "The morale of the [Foreign] Service today stands in need of repair."

1951

February 26, 1951   THE 22ND AMENDMENT TO THE U.S. CONSTITUTION IS RATI-
FIED.

This amendment LIMITED THE PRESIDENT of the United States to serving not more
than two terms of office. If a vice-president became president to serve for
more than two years of his predecessor's term, he could have only one other
four-year term of office. The amendment did not apply to President Truman,
the incumbent.

April 5, 1951   JULIUS AND ETHEL ROSENBERG ARE SENTENCED TO DEATH,
HAVING BEEN CONVICTED OF CONSPIRING WITH OTHERS TO
TRANSMIT SECRET INFORMATION ON ATOMIC FISSION TO THE
SOVIET UNION.

The Rosenbergs had been arrested in July, 1950, consequent to the confession of the British spy KLAUS FUCHS. His testimony led first to the arrest
of HARRY GOLD AND DAVID GREENGLASS, who implicated the Rosenbergs and MORTON
SOBELL. Allegedly, the Rosenbergs were the Russian contacts for Greenglass
who worked at the Los Alamos project.

The Rosenbergs persistently claimed their innocence, and their trial
bore a remarkable resemblance to the political trial of Sacco and Vanzetti
during the 1920's. The Rosenbergs were not accused of any specific overt
act of espionage, but of conspiracy to transfer secret materials. Nevertheless, the American press as well as the court treated the conspirators as
traitors who endangered all of American society. The trial judge, Irving
Kaufman, declared that "All our democratic institutions are ... involved in
this great conflict.... The punishment to be meted out in this case must
therefore serve the maximum interest for the preservation of our society
against these traitors in our midst."

The government's case depended largely on the confessions of David
Greenglass and Harry Gold. Judge Kaufman also allowed wide latitude for the
prosecutor to question the Rosenbergs about their political beliefs. This
enabled the government to convince the jury that their motivation to spy depended on their Communist sympathies.

Following their conviction, the Rosenberg case followed normal appeal
procedures for the next two years. The appeals were based on procedures,
not evidence, and were not successful. After the Supreme Court rejected a
further review, the possibility arose that President Eisenhower would commute
the death sentence provided the Rosenbergs confessed. They did not because
they said they were innocent and they could not confess a lie. Consequently,
they were electrocuted at Sing Sing Prison, New York, on June 19, 1953.

The co-conspirators in the Rosenberg case received prison terms. Morton
Sobell and Harry Gold each were given 30-year sentences; David Greenglass was
sentenced to 15 years.

The political overtones and uncertain evidence in the Rosenberg's case
and execution led later to a number of dramatizations of the event. These
included a documentary film, "The Unquiet Death of Julius and Ethel Rosenberg"; a play, Donald Freed's *Inquest*; and three novels: Robert Coover's *The
Public Burning*; E.L. Doctorow's *The Book of Daniel*; and Helen Yglesias' *How
She Died*.

April 10-11, 1951   PRESIDENT TRUMAN DISMISSES GENERAL MacARTHUR FROM ALL
                             HIS COMMAND POSITIONS.

Truman signed the order to relieve the general for insubordination late in
the evening of April 10, announcing the decision in a White House press release at 1 a.m. on April 11, 1951. Although Truman's "firing" of the popular
general brought criticism from conservatives, Republicans, and Asia-firsters,
the president had the unanimous backing of the Joint Chiefs of Staff, who
realized that MacArthur had frequently undermined Truman's policy and failed
to follow proper procedures in the past six months.
    The dispute between the general and the president centered on the ad-
ministration's decision to use limited-war concepts to fulfill specific political objectives as the best means of national security policy in the nuclear age. MacArthur preferred to continue the traditional American military
policies of permitting the armed forces to take whatever action was necessary
to win a "total victory" over the enemy. Thus, the Truman-MacArthur controversy represented a major conflict in policy perceptions prevalent in America
during the last half of the 20th century.
    One policy recognized that wars were, at best, fought for limited polit-
ical objectives and that containment of Communist expansion was a major goal
of U.S. policy. The second attempted to attain a total triumph not just over
a political foe but also over an ideologically different way of life that
appeared to threaten capitalist democracy.
    Specifically, in 1950-1951, the Truman-MacArthur conflict translated
into the methods for fighting in Korea after the Chinese intervened in November, 1950. MacArthur claimed his military restrictions had prevented him
from responding effectively to the Chinese attack. He had been directed to
use only Korean forces north of the 38th parallel and, even worse, was instructed not to conduct air raids along the Manchurian border. In December,
MacArthur publicly objected to these restrictions, telling newsmen that the
limits imposed from Washington were "an enormous handicap, without precedent
in military history." He could not retaliate effectively against the Chinese.
    Initially, Truman sought to silence MacArthur by issuing directives that
required that all public statements should first be cleared with the White
House. MacArthur remained quiet only until February, 1951. By that time the
opposing Korean forces had fought to stabilized positions near the 38th parallel. Then, on February 6, a news "leak" from MacArthur's headquarters disclosed the general's impatience to eliminate the restrictions on his activities. He wanted to bomb the Manchurian sanctuaries of Chinese supplies and
to defeat communism not just in Korea but throughout the Orient, a total victory over communism.
    In contrast, Truman, in consultation with allies from the United Nations,
decided after the Chinese intervention that neither an atomic war nor a Russian attack on Western Europe could be risked over Korea. The prevailing
decision was to contain the communists in Asia at the 38th parallel.
MacArthur opposed this policy, claiming it was an "appeasement" of communism.

Until March, Truman continued to be patient with the general. On March 20, he and the Joint Chiefs agreed to approach Korea and China to seek a truce in Korea that would restore the 38th parallel. MacArthur responded to this effort by issuing a statement on March 24 in which he offered a military settlement with the Communist commanders. He added a thin threat, however, a threat that if they refused a truce, the United Nations might extend military operations to coastal areas and interior bases of China.

MacArthur's uncalled for statement convinced Truman to find the right time to dismiss the general. The general's statement undermined the negotiating proposals being laid out. Furthermore, the general went further, sending a letter to the House Minority Leader and a MacArthur favorite, Republican Joseph W. Martin. The letter of April 5, which Martin read to congress, reiterated the general's former proposals: to end limits on military operations, to use Chiang Kai-shek's forces in Korea, and to recognize that Asia not Europe was the place to defeat the Communist threat.

The letter to Martin was not the cause but the occasion for Truman to remove MacArthur. After consulting with the State Department and the Joint Chiefs of Staff and receiving their unanimous agreement that the general should be dismissed, Truman signed the orders on April 10, appointing General Matthew Ridgeway to replace MacArthur.

The large public outpouring of sympathy for MacArthur on his return to the United States and his speech to a joint session of congress on April 19 symbolized the split in American understanding of the differences between limited and total war in the nuclear age. Unable to comprehend or uncaring about the implications of a total war against Communist China and, perhaps, the U.S.S.R., American demonstrators and many news editors issued startling accusations against the president. The state legislatures of Illinois, Michigan, Florida, and California passed resolutions condemning Truman. Senator Richard Nixon called the dismissal "rank appeasement," asking the Senate to insist on MacArthur's reinstatement and to censure the president. The most extreme criticism came, of course, from Senator McCarthy who said the president was a "son of a bitch who ought to be impeached."

On May 3, a Senate investigating committee began hearings on the reasons for MacArthur's dismissal, hearing 13 witnesses and recording 3,691 pages of testimony in 42 days. At its finish, the report generally concurred with Truman. General Marshall's statement to the committee summarizes the essence of the group's conclusions. According to Marshall, it was not new for a military commander to be required to act in disagreement with the directives given to him. "What is new and what has brought about the necessity for General MacArthur's removal," he stated, "is the wholly unprecedented situation of a local theater commander *publicly expressing* his displeasure and his disagreement with the foreign and military policy of the United States" (italics added). In such a case, Marshall concluded, "there was no other recourse but to relieve him."

For Truman, not just policy but principle was involved: the principle that the American constitution guaranteed the superiority of the president, a civil and elected official, over military officers.

In 1951, MacArthur was replaced and, after a brief effort to seek the Republican presidential nomination in 1952, he "faded away." The Senate did not seek to impeach, censure, or override the president's decision. A truce with North Korea was delayed for over two years. The political objective of containment at the 38th parallel was sustained over the concept of total war. Yet the supporters of MacArthur and his attitudes lingered on into future decades.

May 2, 1951   THE WEST GERMAN FEDERAL REPUBLIC BECOMES A FULL MEMBER
                          OF THE COUNCIL OF EUROPE.

*This was one step toward the American objective of having the Germans rearmed
and integrated into the NATO forces, a process which France was reluctant to
approve.*

May 2, 1951   IRAN'S MAJLIS (PARLIAMENT) AND SENATE VOTE TO NATIONAL-
                          IZE IRAN'S OIL INDUSTRY.

*This action followed an Iranian effort in 1950 to secure a larger share of
the oil profits from the British controlled Anglo-Iranian Oil Company. On
April 29, an extremist nationalist leader, MOHAMMED MOSSADEGH, was named premier, and he quickly pushed the oil nationalization decree through both legislative bodies.*
     *The British objected to the decree, appealing to the International Court
of Justice to require Iran to arbitrate the dispute. Mossadegh refused to
recognize the court's jurisdiction and an impasse ensued. For the next two
years, Britain and the Iranian govenrment engaged in a diplomatic conflict.
Britain demanded compensation for its oil holdings; Iran objected because it
claimed the right to abrogate the 1933 oil concession treaty between the two
countries. See August 19, 1953.*

May 4, 1951   THE UNITED STATES AND ICELAND AGREE ON A TREATY TO
                          USE ICELAND'S DEFENSE FACILITIES FOR NATO FORCES.

May 18, 1951   THE U.N. GENERAL ASSEMBLY APPROVES AN ARMS EMBARGO
                          AGAINST COMMUNIST CHINA.

*This action followed an assembly declaration on February 1, 1950, that Com-
munist China was an aggressor in the Korean War.*

June 19, 1951   THE U.S. DRAFT OF MEN FOR MILITARY SERVICE IS EXTENDED
                          TO JULY 1, 1955.

President Truman signed legislation which lowered the draft age to 18½ years
and authorized universal military training (UMT) for all American young men
at some unspecified future date. Truman had requested UMT for several years
but congress opposed it. Although this bill approved UMT in principle, congress did not provide the necessary details to make it effective.

July 8, 1951   TRUCE NEGOTIATIONS BEGIN IN KOREA.

Arrangements for the talks originated on June 23, 1951, when Jacob A. Malik
called for cease-fire and armistice talks. Truman announced that the United
States was ready for such discussions, and by July 8 talks began at KAESONG.
In August, the negotiations stopped, first over American objections to Communist violation of agreed regulations and later because the communists
claimed U.N. planes bombed Kaesong.

On October 8, talks began again at PANMUNJOM near the 38th parallel, where they continued over the next two years. During this time, heavy fighting by both sides frequently interrupted the discussions. Each time, however, the talks began again. During 1952, the principal issue became the repatriation of prisoners of war. After reports that nearly half of the 130,000 prisoners held by the United Nations did not wish to return to Communist tyranny, the North Koreans and Chinese refused to accept such claims and insisted on the full exchange of all prisoners.

Not until the election of President Eisenhower in 1952 did the truce negotiations move toward a successful cease-fire in Korea. Meanwhile, there was a stalemated war during which talking and fighting occurred at different times. See July 26-27, 1953.

July 20, 1951   *KING ABDULLAH OF JORDAN IS ASSASSINATED IN JERUSALEM.*

Abdullah incurred the wrath of many Arabs by proclaiming on December 1, 1948, that he was sovereign and that Jordan would unite all Arab Palestinians.

Abdullah's immediate successor was EMIR TALAL, but on August 11, 1952, the parliament declared Talal unfit to rule, naming 17-year-old Prince HUSSEIN AS KING, a position he assumed on his 18th birthday.

August 30, 1951   THE UNITED STATES AND THE PHILIPPINES SIGN A TREATY
                         OF MUTUAL DEFENSE.

An armed attack on either of the parties in the Pacific would be dangerous "to its own peace and safety" and each party would act against the common danger "in accordance with its own constitutional processes."

September 1, 1951   THE ANZUS TRIPARTITE SECURITY TREATY IS SIGNED.

This was a mutual assistance agreement between AUSTRALIA, NEW ZEALAND, AND THE UNITED STATES.

September 6, 1951   A U.S.-PORTUGUESE PACT INTEGRATES THE MILITARILY STRA-
                         TEGIC AZORES INTO NATO'S DEFENSE STRUCTURE.

September 8, 1951   A PEACE TREATY IS SIGNED WITH JAPAN AT SAN FRANCISCO.

The treaty had been negotiated by John Foster Dulles of the United States and Premier SHIGERU YOSHIDA of Japan. At the treaty conference, the Soviet Union objected to the proceedings and its delegate boycotted the final session, refusing to sign the treaty. Because of the relative leniency of the final treaty and the Anglo-American desire to make Japan a strong capitalist nation in East Asia, the treaty is referred to as "the Treaty of Reconciliation." Japan's Diet ratified the treaty on November 18, 1951, the U.S. Senate on March 20, 1952.

September 8, 1951   JAPAN AND THE UNITED STATES SIGN A MUTUAL SECURITY
                          TREATY.

Under terms of the treaty, American troops and naval and air bases would remain in Japan indefinitely; Japan would not permit any other nation to have
bases or military authority within its boundaries without America's consent.

September 20, 1951   GREECE AND TURKEY BECOME NATO MEMBERS.

A meeting of the NATO COUNCIL in Ottawa, Canada, recommended the admission
of these two states. The formal admission took place in Lisbon on February
20, 1952.

October 16, 1951   *LIAQAT AL KHAN, THE PRIME MINISTER OF PAKISTAN, IS
                          ASSASSINATED.*

He was replaced by KWAJA NAZIMUDDIN.

October 19, 1951   THE WAR BETWEEN GERMANY AND THE UNITED STATES ENDS
                          FORMALLY.

President Truman signed a joint congressional resolution declaring an end to
the conflict of 1941-1945. Earlier, on July 9, 1951, Great Britain and France
signed a formal agreement with Germany which ended the war. On September 10,
the foreign ministers of Great Britain, France, and the United States agreed
to replace the West German occupation statute and to use West German troops
in a European army.

October 25, 1951   *WINSTON CHURCHILL AND THE CONSERVATIVE PARTY WIN THE
                          BRITISH ELECTIONS.*

*Churchill replaced Attlee's Socialist government, which had been in power
since July, 1945. Anthony Eden became Minister of Foreign Affairs.*

October 27, 1951   *EGYPT ABROGATES THE ANGLO-EGYPTIAN TREATY OF 1936.*

*Under the 1936 treaty, the last vestiges of British protectorship, including
control of the SUEZ CANAL to 1956, had been approved. Thus, by 1956, the
British would no longer have a political protectorship over Egypt.*

November 14, 1951   AN AID AGREEMENT IS SIGNED BY THE UNITED STATES AND
                          YUGOSLAVIA.

By this pact, the United States supplied military equipment, materials, and
services to the armed forces of Tito's government. See September 27, 1949.

December 31, 1951   MARSHALL PLAN AID ENDS; THE MUTUAL SECURITY AGENCY
*   REPLACES THE OEEC.*

Not all of western Europe's economic problems had been solved by the Marshall
Plan, but most of the nations had recovered sufficiently from World War II
to permit the restoration of an economic pattern resembling that of the Eu-
ropean countries in 1938. Moreover, the new Mutual Security program provided
$7.428 billion for economic, military, and technical aid to Europe.

1952

January 5, 1952 INDIA AND THE UNITED STATES SIGN A FIVE-YEAR "POINT FOUR" AGREEMENT.

Each country would contribute equal funds to develop the Indian economy. Later, on March 1, 1952, PRIME MINISTER PANDIT NEHRU'S CONGRESS PARTY won India's first national elections under the federal republican constitution adopted on November 26, 1949.

Although Nehru agreed to this program of economic aid, he refused to accept any political agreements tied to it because he desired to follow a strict neutral policy between the United States and Russia.

January 11, 1952 THE GENERAL ASSEMBLY OF THE UNITED NATIONS CREATES A 12-NATION DISARMAMENT COMMISSION TO WORK TO REGULATE, LIMIT, AND ACHIEVE A "BALANCED REDUCTION" OF ARMED FORCES AND ARMAMENTS.

The members of the commission were the 11 Security Council nations and Canada. Frequent disarmament discussion resulted from this commission but no significant treaties resulted from its work in the next 10 years.

U.S. policy, as stated early in the commission discussions, was not to accept any disarmament or other limitations on military affairs without strict international control and inspection mechanisms to prevent cheating.

February 2, 1952 *GREAT BRITAIN ANNOUNCES IT HAS SUCCESSFULLY EXPLODED AN ATOMIC BOMB AT TESTS IN THE MONTE BELLO ISLANDS NEAR AUSTRALIA.*

February 6, 1952 *KING GEORGE VI OF ENGLAND DIES; QUEEN ELIZABETH II BECOMES THE RULER OF THE UNITED KINGDOM.*

March 10, 1952 *IN CUBA GENERAL FULGENCIO BATISTA OVERTHROWS PRESIDENT PRIO SOCARRAS AND MAKES HIMSELF CHIEF OF STATE AND PREMIER.*

Socarras had been elected president for a four-year term on June 1, 1948, but proved to be an ineffective leader.

Batista had been military ruler of Cuba from 1933 to 1944, when he permitted elections to be held while he retired from politics. During the next eight years, however, the predominant AUTENTICO Party failed to carry out necessary reforms and increased corruption and economic instability. Therefore, just before elections were to be held in 1952, Batista again took

control in order, he said, to save Cuba from economic chaos and left-wing
radicals who opposed the existing regime.

April 28, 1952   GENERAL MATTHEW B. RIDGEWAY REPLACES EISENHOWER AS
                          SUPREME ALLIED COMMANDER IN EUROPE.

Eisenhower resigned on April 12 in order to campaign for the Republican nomination for president.
     In KOREA, GENERAL MARK W. CLARK replaced Ridgeway as the U.N. Far Eastern
Commander.

May 26, 1952   WEST GERMANY'S INTERNAL INDEPENDENCE IS AGREED TO BY
                          BRITAIN, FRANCE, AND THE UNITED STATES.

In four so-called peace conventions signed at Bonn, West Germany, the three
Allies ended their occupation of Germany and gave West Germany virtually complete sovereignty.

May 27, 1952   THE EUROPEAN DEFENSE COMMUNITY (EDC) IS CREATED TO
                          UNIFY WESTERN EUROPEAN DEFENSE PLANS AND TO BIND WEST
                          GERMANY TO THIS DEFENSE.

In meetings at Paris, a series of documents were signed: (1) the EDC charter
signed by France, West Germany, Italy, Belgium, the Netherlands, and Luxembourg; (2) an EDC treaty with Britain to join together if any nation were
attacked; (3) a NATO protocol with West Germany to extend NATO guarantees to
that nation; and (4) a declaration in which Britain and the United States
agreed to regard a threat to EDC as a threat to their own security. The U.S.
Senate ratified the NATO protocol on July 1, 1952. See August 30, 1954.

June 23, 1952   *TUNISIAN NATIONALISTS REJECT A FRENCH OFFER FOR GREATER*
                         AUTONOMY.

In Tunisia, the local national leaders wanted greater home-rule as a step to
full independence. Since February 8, 1951, when Paris first agreed to pro-
vide some autonomy for Tunisia within the French Union, the two parties had
disagreed about continued French interference in local matters. Late in 1951,
Tunisia took the issue to the United Nations, but on January 14, 1952, the
Security Council denied the appeal to force the French to give home-rule.
     Subsequently, riots, violence, and near warfare took place between the
Tunisians and French forces. On June 23, the French presented new terms of
autonomy for Tunisia but the nationalist leaders claimed Paris retained too
much authority. Trouble continued in Tunisia, therefore, for the next 18
months.

June 26, 1952   THE McCARRAN-WALTER IMMIGRATION AND NATIONALITY ACT
                         IS PASSED BY CONGRESS OVER PRESIDENT TRUMAN'S VETO.

This act permitted naturalization of Asians and set a quota for their further admission. Truman objected, however, to the clauses which provided for the exclusion and deportation of aliens and the control of U.S. citizens abroad.

July 1, 1952   *THE SCHUMAN PLAN FOR INTEGRATING WESTERN EUROPE'S COAL AND STEEL INDUSTRIES GOES INTO EFFECT.*

This plan was proposed on May 9, 1950, by French Foreign Minister ROBERT SCHUMAN. On April 18, 1951, six nations agreed to establish a single market for coal and steel, an agreement which now became effective. The six nations were: France, West Germany, Italy, Belgium, the Netherlands, and Luxembourg.

July 23, 1952   *KING FAROUK OF EGYPT IS OVERTHROWN IN A COUP D'ÉTAT LED BY MAJOR GENERAL MOHAMMED NAGUIB BEY.*

The coup culminated nearly a decade of dispute between the nationalist WAFD PARTY and the monarch, whose main asset was his protection by the British government. As noted earlier, the WAFD Party gained control of Egypt's legislature and in 1951 acted to abrogate the Anglo-Egyptian Treaty of 1936.
Early in 1952, disputes between the British and the Wafd intensified, leading on January 18 to a clash between guerrilla forces and the British at Port Said. Subsequently, the Wafd leaders decided to eliminate King Farouk so that they could better control the administrative apparatus of the government. On July 23, Farouk offered little opposition, preferring to flee to France to exile. The Wafd Party under Naguib gained full control in Cairo.

October 20, 1952   *THE BRITISH GOVERNMENT SENDS TROOPS TO KENYA TO SUPPRESS THE FANATIC MAU-MAU SECT.*

November 1, 1952   THE UNITED STATES ANNOUNCES THE SUCCESS OF THE FIRST THERMONUCLEAR (HYDROGEN) BOMB.

The bomb yielded a force of 14 megatons (14 million tons of TNT). It was exploded on ENEWETAK (old spelling ENIWETOK), an atoll in the Marshall Islands.

November 5, 1952   DWIGHT D. EISENHOWER IS ELECTED PRESIDENT, DEFEATING THE DEMOCRATIC PARTY NOMINEE, ADLAI STEVENSON, FORMER GOVERNOR OF ILLINOIS.

The Republican Party also gained a slight majority in both houses of congress.
General Eisenhower's nomination by the Republicans was a victory for the liberal and progressive faction of the party which included such leaders as Governor Thomas Dewey, Earl Warren, and Nelson Rockefeller. This group hoped that Eisenhower would firmly establish control of the party for the "modern" progressive faction. They would eventually be disappointed in this matter, even though Eisenhower served two terms of office.
The conservative Old Guard Republicans continued to have great strength in the Senate and House. Eisenhower's nomination caused bitterness among proponents of Senator Robert Taft, such as Senators Everett Dirksen of

Illinois and William Knowland of California.

To placate the conservatives, Eisenhower chose Richard Nixon as his running mate. Yet the philosophical differences between the liberal and conservative Republicans were not healed by the 1952 presidential victory. Especially in foreign affairs, the Old Guard preferred an Asia-First policy
and a neo-isolationist, go-it-alone international policy. In contrast,
Eisenhower believed Europe deserved first priority in U.S. national security
and realized the value of NATO and other U.S. allies in world affairs.

Among the Democrats, the nomination of Stevenson revived hopes for the
continuation of a liberal foreign and domestic program such as the New Deal
of Roosevelt and the Fair Deal of Truman. Truman did not seek the nomination
because he believed in the idea of two terms for a president and felt he would
follow the 22nd Amendment even though he was exempt from it. Stevenson carried the liberal banner in satisfactory fashion, but General Eisenhower's
popularity was too great to overcome in 1952 or, later, in 1956.

XIV. STRUGGLES IN THE COLD WAR: EUROPEAN SECURITY;
SUEZ CRISIS; CASTRO IN CUBA; THE VIETNAM ESCALATION (1953-1968)

1953

January 20, 1953   PRESIDENT DWIGHT D. EISENHOWER IS INAUGURATED AS THE
                        34th PRESIDENT OF THE UNITED STATES.

He appointed John Foster Dulles as Secretary of State and Charles Wilson,
former president of General Motors Corporation, as Secretary of Defense.
     Dulles was eminently qualified to serve as Secretary of State. He had
been an advisor to President Wilson during the Paris Peace Conference and a
member of the Reparations Commission in 1919. During World War II, he became
an internationalist who was interested in urging Republicans to act in a bipartisan fashion in foreign policy. He had been a delegate to the San Francisco Conference on the United Nations in 1945 and served as a special representative of President Truman to negotiate the Japanese Peace Treaty of
1951. He served as secretary from January 21, 1953, until illness forced
him to resign on April 22, 1959. He died on May 24, 1959.

March 5, 1953   JOSEPH STALIN DIES AND IS INTERRED IN THE LENIN MAUSO-
                     LEUM ON RED SQUARE.

Outside Russia two related questions arose after his death. Did Stalin die
a natural death? Would his successors adopt new policies?
     In the six months prior to his death, Stalin had taken steps to ASSURE
A CONTINUED HARD-LINE POLICY in Russia. At the 19th COMMUNIST PARTY CONGRESS
IN OCTOBER, 1953, he declared that the Soviet economic programs must stress
heavy industry and agricultural collectivization. He also asserted that tight
party controls should be adopted against capitalist aggression which could
be expected at any time.
     Stalin's continued hard-line contrasted with recent statements of some
politburo members. Georgi MALENKOV had urged stress on consumer products
and cooperation with Western powers. Stalin seemed to disagree. More seriously, perhaps, Stalin seemed to be ready for another party purge. In October, he added 14 members to the politburo and renamed the Central Committee
the "PRESIDIUM." More threateningly, on January 13, 1953, Stalin disclosed
the "Doctor's Plot," arresting a group of Kremlin doctors, charged as British
and American agents who killed Andrei Zhadanov in 1948. By February, rumors
in Moscow threatened party members such as Malenkov, M. Vyacheslav MOLOTOV,
and Anastas MIKOYAN.
     Thus, when Stalin died, Western observers suspected a plot against his

life and the rise of new leadership which would change Soviet policy.

Initially, new policies did seem apparent. On MARCH 6, GEORGI M. MALEN-
KOV became premier and First Secretary of the Communist Party, although he
gave party leadership to NIKITA KHRUSHCHEV on March 20. Both Malenkov and
Khrushchev, who gained full control by May 27, 1958, spoke of "collective
leadership." They also relaxed Stalin's tight controls both at home and
abroad. In economics, they placed more investment in consumer goods such as
textiles and housing, and allowed farmers to sell vegetables in the markets
for individual incentives. Internationally, they mixed claims of military
build ups with speeches on "peaceful coexistence." A period known as the
"thaw" in cold war relations lasted from 1954 to 1960.

March 27, 1953   THE U.S. SENATE CONFIRMS THE NOMINATION OF CHARLES
                           BOHLEN AS AMBASSADOR TO THE SOVIET UNION IN SPITE OF
                           SENATOR McCARTHY'S ATTEMPTS TO PREVENT IT.

This incident was the first effort of the Eisenhower administration to stand
firm against McCarthy's intemperate charges against a government official.

Bohlen's appointment as ambassador had been supported because of his
excellent qualifications and Eisenhower's personal acquaintance with him in
Paris. McCarthy and his followers charged that Bohlen was a security risk.
They claimed that as an Assistant Secretary of State and interpreter at the
1945 Yalta Conference, he had a role in those decisions. McCarthyites claimed
that Roosevelt sold out Chiang Kai-shek at Yalta.

The Senate hearings gave Bohlen an opportunity to clarify the record on
the Yalta agreements. He pointed out that Chiang in 1945 greatly appreciated
being able to have a pact signed with Stalin to accept his regime. Only the
later violations of the Yalta agreements by Stalin caused difficulty, not
the Yalta agreements.

During the Senate debate on Bohlen, McCarthy went too far in his charges.
After reviewing Bohlen's personnel and FBI files, both Senator Robert Taft
and Senator William Knowland, two Republican conservatives who had previously
backed McCarthy, reported that they accepted Bohlen's nomination. McCarthy
sought to challenge the report of Taft and Knowland and was seriously rebuffed. Secretary of State Dulles and President Eisenhower expressed support
for Bohlen and the Senate voted approval, 74 to 13.

Senator McCarthy's fanatic efforts continued for another 18 months before the U.S. Senate voted to condemn his method; see December 2, 1954.

April 16, 1953   PRESIDENT EISENHOWER IS CAUTIOUS IN REACTING TO THE
                           NEW RUSSIAN LEADERSHIP'S DESIRE FOR RELAXATION OF THE
                           COLD WAR.

Eisenhower declared that better relations with the United States would be
possible if Russia FIRST DEMONSTRATED its policy by actions such as "free
elections in Korea"; approving U.N. control and inspection of "disarmament
agreements"; restoring "free choice" in eastern European nations; and giving
similar evidence of policy changes.

In contrast, WINSTON CHURCHILL on May 11 desired more appreciation of
the new Soviet rulers. He suggested a summit conference "on the highest level" to prepare an agenda of problems to resolve. He indicated that President
Eisenhower should not, perhaps, expect too much at one time.

Generally, the continued strong anti-Communist feelings in America prevented Washington from responding more positively to Soviet overtures for an
easing of tension.

June 16, 1953   *AN UPRISING OF WORKERS IN EAST GERMANY RESULTS IN RUS-*
                        SIAN TANKS AND TROOPS BEING SENT TO RESTORE ORDER.

*In May, the Soviet Union had abolished its control commission in East Germany
and relaxed controls on protests. It demanded, however, an increase in production for the same wages. Marching in Stalinallee on June 16, the workers
protested the low wages. Strikes soon spread throughout East Germany until
Russian tanks rolled into Berlin, Dresden, Leipzig, and other cities to smash
the demonstrations.*
*In order to placate the workers, the Communist government instituted a
10-point reform plan on June 22. This plan increased wages, improved living
conditions, ended travel restrictions between East and West Berlin, and announced that martial law would end on July 11.*

July 10-14, 1953   THE UNITED STATES, FRENCH, AND BRITISH FOREIGN MINIS-
                        TERS CONFER IN WASHINGTON.

Their final communique invited Russia to meet and discuss German unity and
an Austrian treaty. They also warned the Communists that the Korean war would
reopen if there were truce violations or other Communist aggression in Asia.

July 26-27, 1953   AN ARMISTICE AGREEMENT IS SIGNED AND BECOMES EFFECTIVE
                        IN KOREA.

The armistice agreement came slowly despite Eisenhower's visit to Korea on
December 14 to seek an end to the war. Not until March 30, when the Chinese
suggested letting the prisoner-of-war issue be decided by an international
authority, was progress made.
On June 18, Syngman Rhee, president of South Korea, opposed the agreement
and tried to sabotage the negotiations by releasing 27,000 Chinese and North
Korean prisoners. Rhee's attempt to stop the talks failed and an armistice
was reached in July.
The armistice did not, however, result in a peace treaty or Korean unity.
Further negotiations continued on a sporadic basis but without success. The
United States assisted South Korea by giving Seoul over $6 billion in the
next decade and stationing American troops south of the 38th parallel. But
the negotiations for permanent peace would become stalemated.

August 8, 1953   *THE UNION OF SOVIET SOCIALIST REPUBLICS SUCCESSFULLY*
                        EXPLODES A HYDROGEN THERMONUCLEAR DEVICE.

*Premier Malenkov announced the successful test in a speech to the Supreme
Soviet in which he emphasized that Russia was ready to ease tension and seek
peace if western Europe would agree, but that she also retained power to prevent aggressive war by the capitalists.*

August 19, 1953   PREMIER MOSSADEGH'S GOVERNMENT IS OVERTHROWN BY A COUP
                         IN IRAN. THE REZA SHAH PAHLAVI REGAINS CONTROL.

The coup concluded Mossadegh's attempt to bring social and economic modernization to Iran by nationalizing the Anglo-Iranian Oil Company.
        Soon after the Iranian MAJLIS voted full dictatorial control to Mossadegh
on August 11, 1952, disagreement led to a break in diplomatic relations between Teheran and London on October 22, 1952.
        On January 8, 1953, Mossadegh's power was extended for 12 months and
his relations with the SHAH AND THE UNITED STATES BECAME DIFFICULT. On June
29, 1953, America stopped all aid to Iran, and soon after the SHAH FLED TO
EXILE IN IRAQ.
        By early August, the CIA and the U.S. Embassy gave support to ROYALIST
FORCES WHO DEPOSED MOSSADEGH AND BROUGHT THE SHAH BACK. The Shah appointed
Major General FAZOLLAH ZAHEDI as the new premier.
        On September 5, Washington gave the Shah a grant of $45 million and by
December 5, IRAN restored diplomatic relations with Great Britain. The Shah
and the British negotiated a new oil pact, which the Iranian majlis approved
on October 21, 1954.

September 15, 1953   *COMMUNIST CHINA ANNOUNCES THAT THE SOVIET UNION HAS*
                        MADE AN AGREEMENT TO PROVIDE MASSIVE ECONOMIC AID TO
                        HELP CHINA BUILD ITS HEAVY INDUSTRY.

The agreement permitted China to carry on the Five-Year Plan begun in January,
1953, but did not specify funds in addition to the $300 million, five-year
loan agreed to by Moscow in 1950. In 1954, however, Khrushchev visited Peking
and approved a second loan of $130 million.

September 21, 1953   ANDREI VISHINSKY, THE U.S.S.R. DELEGATE TO THE UNITED
                         NATIONS, OFFERS THE GENERAL ASSEMBLY A PROPOSAL TO
                         REDUCE ALL ARMED FORCES OF THE GREAT POWERS BY ONE-
                         THIRD, AND TO BAN THE USE OF ATOMIC WEAPONS.

The proposal became the basis for the U.N. disarmament commission to ask a
five-power subcommittee (United States, Union of Soviet Socialist Republics,
Great Britain, France, Canada) to consider the question of an inspection system,
a means to prevent surprise attacks, and a nuclear test ban. The subcommittee
met from May 13 to June 22, 1954, but achieved no results.

September 26, 1953   THE UNITED STATES AND SPAIN AGREE THAT THE UNITED
                         STATES MAY ESTABLISH AIR AND NAVAL BASES IN SPAIN IN
                         RETURN FOR $250 MILLION OF ECONOMIC AND MILITARY AID.

This action culminated more than four years of effort by conservative Senators Pat McCarran, Robert Taft, and Owen Brewster working with Franco to
end the U.S. "communist-front philosophy." On August 25, 1953, Spain awarded
McCarran the Special Medal of the Grand Cross for his devotion to Spain.
Truman despised Franco but he allowed negotiations because U.S. military men
advised him that forward bomber bases were essential to strike the Soviet
Union. The agreement was not made, however, until Eisenhower and Dulles accepted the idea of "working with a Fascist."

October 30, 1953   PRESIDENT EISENHOWER'S "NEW LOOK" POLICY IS DESCRIBED
                          IN NSC-162.

The Eisenhower administration wanted to continue Truman's CONTAINMENT POLICY
but undertook a new national security plan to replace NSC-68 and its revised
defense plan of 1952 (NSC-141). Eisenhower believed the Truman methods failed
to give a balanced federal budget and were not adapted to the "long-haul"
defense program designed to outlast communism and demonstrate capitalism's
superiority.
    Showing his concern for budgetary matters, Eisenhower appointed Secretary
of the Treasury George Humphrey to the NSC, where he could comment on the
fiscal significance of defense plans.
    To relate fiscal, foreign, and defense policies, Eisenhower's plan em-
phasized the primary U.S. effort in maintaining a SUFFICIENT NUCLEAR STRIKE
FORCE TO HIT THE SOVIET UNION IF A CRISIS NECESSITATED A NUCLEAR ATTACK. To
save U.S. expense in conventional army and navy forces, a greater reliance
on having allies who could provide for their own defense was desired. Finally, as an overall goal, Eisenhower's plan aimed to avoid the large new
$74 billion defense costs envisioned in Truman's 1952 budget plan, and to
stabilize defense expenditures at between $38 and $40 billion per year.
    The particular cuts in the army and navy budget became clear in February,
1954, when Secretary of Defense Wilson told a congressional committee that
the army would be decreased from 20 to 17 divisions; the navy would modestly
reduce its ships; and the air force would seek 137 wings, not 143. The major
defense increase would be $1 billion over 1954, "for continental air defense."
    The following tables indicate the shift in defense emphasis involved in
the "new look" policy. They also explain why the army and navy eventually
sought aid from congress and the public to oppose Eisenhower's "new look"
which met its fiscal and military priority goals by cuts in army and navy
budgets and personnel.

Manpower Proposals

	December 1953	October 1954	June 1955
Army	1,500,000	1,500,000	1,000,000
Navy/Marines	1,000,000	920,000	870,000
Air Force	950,000	960,000	970,000

Defense Budget - Billions of Dollars

	Fiscal Year 1954	Fiscal Year 1955
Army	$12.9	$8.8
Navy/Marines	11.2	9.7
Air Force	15.6	16.4

October 30, 1953   THE UNITED STATES AND JAPAN AGREE THAT JAPAN MAY EN-
                          LARGE HER "SELF-DEFENSE" FORCES TO PROTECT HER FROM
                          AGGRESSION.

The Eisenhower administration followed its "New Look" policy of both reducing
U.S. costs of Japan's defense and enabling local forces to protect themselves
from aggression.

November 21, 1953   *CONFLICT BETWEEN ITALY AND YUGOSLAVIA IS AVERTED WHEN*
                          BOTH NATIONS AGREE TO A CONFERENCE PROPOSED BY THE
                          FOREIGN MINISTERS OF THE UNITED STATES, FRANCE, AND
                          GREAT BRITAIN.

The Italian-Yugoslav dispute arose over the disposition of Trieste which had
been pending since 1945. On October 8, the British and American governments
announced they would end the occupation of Trieste by giving Italy Zone A
and Yugoslavia Zone B.
*   Tito opposed this plan and threatened to march troops into the Italian*
Zone. The conflict caused the Big Three Western Powers to ask the two con-
tending nations to a meeting on the problem. On October 5, 1954, the dispute
was resolved according to terms which divided Trieste between Italy and Yugo-
slavia.

December 8, 1953   PRESIDENT EISENHOWER PROPOSES AN ATOMS-FOR-PEACE PLAN
                          TO THE UNITED NATIONS.

Speaking before the U.N. General Assembly, Eisenhower suggested that all nations should pool their fissionable nuclear material to use for peaceful industrial purposes.
    The U.S. delegation presented the American atoms-for-peace plan to the
United Nations on September 23, 1954. Specifically, the United States suggested that an agency be established for promoting the BENEFICIAL USES OF
ATOMIC ENERGY. The U.N. General Assembly unanimously ENDORSED THIS PLAN ON
December 4, 1954.

1954

January 12, 1954 SECRETARY OF STATE JOHN FOSTER DULLES DELIVERS A SPEECH OUTLINING THE "MASSIVE RETALIATION" DEFENSE POLICY OF EISENHOWER'S "NEW LOOK" PROGRAM.

Dulles emphasized that the United States would respond to Communist aggression by building "a great capacity to retaliate" instantly "by means and at places of our choosing."
 Although Dulles' speech cited the "New Look's" desire to have local defense forces and to prefer to stress the deterrent aspects of the policy, news accounts and critics oversimplified the complex purposes of Eisenhower's concepts and emphasized "massive retaliation" as the whole focus of the "New Look."

January 25-February 18, 1954 IN BERLIN A BIG-FOUR FOREIGN MINISTERS CONFERENCE DISCUSSES BUT FAILS TO AGREE ON TREATIES FOR GERMANY AND AUSTRIA.

An important by-product of the conference was an agreement to hold a GENEVA CONFERENCE ON FAR EASTERN PROBLEMS OF KOREA AND INDOCHINA and to INVITE COMMUNIST CHINA TO ATTEND.
 Secretary of State Dulles reluctantly agreed to a Chinese presence at Geneva. He did so after Anthony Eden offered a compromise by which all countries representing the U.N. command in Korea would be present on one side, with the delegates of the Union of Soviet Socialist Republics, Communist China, and North Korea on the other side. Dulles made it clear, however, that this did not mean American diplomatic recognition of the Peking government. See April 26, 1954.

January 26, 1954 THE U.S. SENATE RATIFIES A MUTUAL SECURITY TREATY WITH SOUTH KOREA.

The United States would assist South Korea if it were attacked, but would not assist any attempt by Seoul's government to unite Korea by force.

February 25-26, 1954 THE SENATE REJECTS VARIOUS VERSIONS OF THE "BRICKER AMENDMENT" AS WELL AS OTHER PROPOSALS TO LIMIT THE TREATY-MAKING POWERS OF THE PRESIDENT.

Senator John Bricker of Ohio, one of a group of conservative Republicans who claimed that the presidential decisions of Franklin Roosevelt and Harry Truman caused problems for the nation, proposed that EXECUTIVE AGREEMENTS BY THE PRESIDENT AS WELL AS ALL TREATIES MUST BE RATIFIED BY BOTH HOUSES OF CONGRESS AND EVERY STATE. If ratified as a constitutional amendment, Bricker's proposal would have drastically curtailed the presidential and State Department conduct of foreign affairs, and both Eisenhower and Dulles opposed it. Yet in the Senate, the amendment lost by only one vote.

March 1, 1954   THE UNITED STATES SUCCESSFULLY TESTS A HYDROGEN BOMB DROPPED FROM AN AIRPLANE AT BIKINI ATOLL IN THE PACIFIC.

The 15 megaton (15 million tons of TNT) bomb unleashed a heavy amount of radioactive debris. Radioactive particles carried over 100 miles where some landed on and caused illness for the crew of a Japanese fishing boat, the "Lucky Dragon" ("FUKURYU MARU"). This incident revived anti-American emotions in Japan, especially after the boat's radio operator, AIKICHI NAGAKUBO, died of radiation sickness on September 23, 1954.

March 14, 1954   VIETMINH FORCES ATTACK 10,000 FRENCH SOLDIERS AT DIENBIENPHU.

The Vietminh attack was exactly what French General Henri Navarre had hoped for in November, 1953, when he concentrated his forces at the small, northern, rural outpost of Dienbienphu. The "Navarre plan" wanted to entice the Vietminh's General VO NGUYEN GIAP from his *protracted war* guerrilla tactics so that he would engage the French in conventional war where Navarre's crack Legionnaires could decisively beat the Communists.

Navarre's plan backfired because like many French and, later, American military officers, he underestimated the Vietnamese. The Vietminh fought aggressively and Giap used his artillery in superior fashion to besiege Dienbienphu. Monsoon rains also handicapped the French, because they could not adequately resupply their forces.

By March 22, a decisive Communist victory appeared possible, causing Paris to appeal for help to Washington. General Paul Ely came to Washington to seek U.S. air support. The French wanted aircraft from the U.S.S. *Boxer* and U.S.S. *Essex* to help the besieged French forces.

In Washington, Ely's request precipitated a lengthy consideration of whether the United States should intervene in this French colonial war.

April 4-5, 1954   PRESIDENT EISENHOWER DECIDES NOT TO SEND IMMEDIATE ASSISTANCE TO THE FRENCH BESIEGED AT DIENBIENPHU.

When General Ely first arrived in Washington, rumors in the newspapers suggested that America would intervene. Thorough consideration and a desire for Allied and congressional backing caused the president to refuse France such aid.

On March 24, the president stated that the defeat of communism in Southeast Asia was critical to American interests. He and Dulles agreed, however, with a military study (the Erskine Report) prepared in March, 1954, that recommended that the United States should act only in coordination with Great Britain and France. Eisenhower also asked Dulles to consult with congressional leaders to gain their support.

Neither Britain nor France wanted a joint action with the United States. The British were unwilling to aid French colonialism; the French did not want

to internationalize the war because Paris wished to retain control over the
solution to Indochina's rebellion.

When Secretary of State Dulles and Admiral Arthur D. Radford, chairman
of the JCS, met with congressional leaders, they were also refused cooperation. The congressmen asked how many of the JCS supported action, learning
that only Radford did. General Matthew Ridgeway and others opposed this action. In addition, the congressmen agreed that a multinational force to assist France would be best.

Although Vice-President Richard Nixon urged action despite the lack of
support, Eisenhower preferred a united action and the backing of congress.
Therefore, on April 5, he avoided U.S. action on the terms sought by General
Ely.

From early April to June 17, Dulles and Eisenhower searched for some
other formula to gain "united action" with allies to help the French. The
president wrote to Churchill, who rejected his request for British action.
Later, Dulles flew to London to try to convince Churchill and Anthony Eden
that the Communists should not be permitted to win Indochina. But Dulles
could not convince them that Vietnam was a critical world region. Yet, until
June 17, when a new French premier, who was committed to secure "peace" in
Indochina, took office, Dulles believed that there should be some means to
secure French control in Indochina. See June 4, 1954.

April 26, 1954   THE GENEVA CONFERENCE ON KOREA AND INDOCHINA BEGINS.

As agreed at the Berlin Conference (January-February, 1954), the delegations
included the Soviet Union, North Korea, Communist China, France, Great Britain, the United States, and 13 other non-Communist nations which contributed
to the U.N. forces in the Korean War.

During the first month, the delegates argued the question of Korea. By
June 15, no solution was in sight and the 16 non-Communist delegates issued
a statement that further talks "would serve no useful purpose." They blamed
the three Communist states for rejecting the principle of Korean independence
and unity through free elections.

Several compromises were achieved on the Indochina issue. See under
July 20, 1954.

May 19, 1954   THE UNITED STATES AND PAKISTAN SIGN A MUTUAL DEFENSE
                        PACT BY WHICH WASHINGTON HELPS TO ARM PAKISTAN AGAINST
                        COMMUNISM.

Secretary of State John Foster Dulles was willing to provide a similar pact
for INDIA, but Prime Minister NEHRU preferred to remain neutral in the cold
war. India bitterly opposed U.S. aid to Pakistan because of the frequent
threats of war between these neighboring nations. Nehru believed Pakistan's
arms would be used against India not the Soviet Union.

June 1, 1954   THE PERSONAL SECURITY BOARD OF THE ATOMIC ENERGY COM-
                    MISSION UNANIMOUSLY FINDS DR. J. ROBERT OPPENHEIMER
                    IS "LOYAL" IN HANDLING ATOMIC SECRETS. NEVERTHELESS,
                    IT VOTES 2 TO 1 NOT TO REINSTATE HIM AS A GOVERNMENT
                    CONSULTANT ON ATOMIC ENERGY.

Although Oppenheimer was one of America's most renowned physicists and had
directed the Los Alamos laboratory in producing the atomic bomb in 1945, he
had been criticized for opposing the H-BOMB development in 1949, joining many
scientists who desired international controls on nuclear weapons.

The Oppenheimer case of 1954 indicated Senator McCarthy's influence on
American life. Later, Thomas E. Murray, an AEC member who voted not to rein-
state Oppenheimer, admitted his vote was cast in the "exigencies of the moment," the "moment" being McCarthyism.

June 4, 1954   *FRENCH PREMIER JOSEPH LANIEL AND VIETNAMESE PREMIER*
                    BAO DAI SIGN TREATIES GRANTING VIETNAM "COMPLETE INDE-
                    PENDENCE" IN "FREE ASSOCIATION" WITH FRANCE.

Since February, 1953, Paris had negotiated an arrangement to transfer defense
and security affairs to the government in Saigon. The agreement on June 4
stopped just short of recognizing complete Vietnamese independence, which
France was still reluctant to grant. The Emperor Bao Dai remained as head
of state.

June 9, 1954   A LEFT-WING GOVERNMENT IN GUATEMALA IS OVERTHROWN WITH
                    ASSISTANCE FROM THE AMERICAN CENTRAL INTELLIGENCE
                    AGENCY (CIA).

Since 1944, GUATEMALA'S POLITICAL LEADERS HAD TALKED ABOUT LAND REFORM AS A
MEANS OF RESOLVING SOCIAL UNREST IN RURAL AREAS. Until the 1951 election of
COLONEL JACOBO ARBENZ GUZMAN, the reformers had accomplished little. ARBENZ
decided that real reform required the takeover of the UNITED FRUIT COMPANY,
an American company that profited from Guatemala's banana plantations. In
1953, ARBENZ's government CONFISCATED 225,000 acres of UNITED FRUIT's 300,000
acres of land.

The U.S. State Department protested on behalf of United Fruit, demanding
compensation for the property. Arbenz claimed Guatemala could not afford
the payment expected by United Fruit and argued that Guatemala's land belonged
to its people.

Secretary of State Dulles believed Arbenz was a Communist and must be
acted against. In March, 1954, Dulles took the issue to the Tenth Inter-
American Conference session at Caracas, Venezuela. Without specifying Guatemala, Dulles persuaded the conferees to adopt a declaration that communism
was "incompatible with the concept of American freedom" and nations should
act to "eradicate and prevent subversive activities." The vote was 17 to 1:
Guatemala voted no; Mexico and Argentina abstained; Costa Rica was absent.

On May 15, U.S. opposition to Arbenz heightened when Guatemala acknowledged receipt of 900 tons of arms from communist Czechoslovakia. In retaliation, Washington airlifted arms to Nicaragua and Honduras, where an Arbenz
opponent, Colonel Carlos Costillo Armas, was forming an army.

Armas' insurrectionary force invaded Guatemala on June 18, 1954, and with CIA help easily overthrew the Arbenz regime by June 28. Although Arbenz and his government appealed to the United Nations, where the Soviet Union supported their cause, the United States refused to allow Security Council intervention.

On July 8, Colonel Armas was chosen as president of the ruling junta of military officers.

June 12, 1954　　　　　*THE FRENCH NATIONAL ASSEMBLY VOTES NO CONFIDENCE IN GEORGE BIDAULT'S MINISTRY; ON JUNE 17, THE ASSEMBLY APPROVES PIERRE MENDES-FRANCE AS HEAD OF A NEW MINISTERIAL COALITION.*

Bidault's government fell as a result of criticism of his Indochinese policies. Mendes-France promised to solve the problem and vowed to resign if an "honorable peace" had not been concluded in Indochina by July 20, 1954.

June 15, 1954　　　　　NGO DINH DIEM REPLACES BUU LOC AS PREMIER OF THE FRENCH-RECOGNIZED VIETNAMESE GOVERNMENT.

Diem, whose rule greatly influenced both Vietnam and the United States from 1954 until his assassination in November, 1963, was born in Vietnam of a Mandarin family. During the 1930's, he favored moderate reform to obtain some local government from the French, but by 1933 he abandoned the possibility of cooperating with the French and retired from active politics. In 1948, Diem refused to accept the French terms which Bao Dai agreed to when he became head of state. Diem spent the early years of the 1950's in the United States at Maryknoll seminaries. In America, he gained many influential friends including Supreme Court Justice William O. Douglas, Francis Cardinal Spellman, and Senators Mike Mansfield and John F. Kennedy. Thus, when Bao Dai selected Diem as premier in 1954, he chose a person who was acceptable to the United States.

Although Bao Dai appointed Diem on June 15, he did not announce the new ministry until July 5, 1954.

July 20, 1954　　　　　THE GENEVA CONFERENCE APPROVES A SETTLEMENT OF THE INDOCHINESE WAR.

In May, the conferees had become deadlocked on the status of the governments of Laos and Cambodia. On May 31, the delegates approved a British proposal to invite both sides in each Indochinese state to hold cease-fire talks at Geneva. The United States opposed this concept of negotiating with the Communists and, while never completely abandoning the conference, became generally less active in cooperating in or leading the decision-making process. Dulles never returned to the conference, sending Walter Bedell Smith as the U.S. representative.

The final Geneva agreements provided for the cessation of hostilities in each of the three Indochinese states (July 20) and for a Final Declaration of the Geneva delegations (July 21). Together, the agreements recognized Laos and Cambodia as independent nations, and temporarily divided Vietnam into two parts separated by a demilitarized zone (DMZ) at the 17th parallel. An election in 1956 would unify and decide on a future government of Vietnam.

In Vietnam, each side's forces would regroup on its side of the DMZ. The Vietminh government of Ho Chi Minh controlled the north with its capital at Hanoi; the Vietnamese Nationalist Government of Bao Dai controlled the south from Saigon. French forces could remain in the south but no new forces were to be introduced or rotated by either side. No new military equipment could be added, but replacement of destroyed, damaged, or worn equipment was allowed. Refugees from either side would be able to move freely to the north or south, according to their wishes. Finally, an International Control Commission with representatives from India, Poland, and Canada would supervise the cease-fire accords and the election procedures.

The United States announced it COULD NOT ACCEPT THE CONFERENCE DECLARATION, but agreed not to use force or threat to disturb the accords. Furthermore, the United States would view a violation of the accords as a threat to international peace.

Speaking for the National Vietnamese government at Saigon, Tran Van Do informed the final conference session that his government had reservations about the Geneva accords but would not use force or threat to resist the cease-fire. He said his government would support "every effort to reestablish a real and lasting peace in Vietnam."

July 23, 1954   *CHINESE COMMUNIST FIGHTER PILOTS SHOOT DOWN A CATHAY-*
                         PACIFIC AIRWAYS COMMERCIAL AIRLINER. LATER, THE CHI-
                         NESE GOVERNMENT APOLOGIZES TO GREAT BRITAIN, OWNER OF
                         THE AIRLINE, AND AGREES TO PAY COMPENSATION. TEN PAS-
                         SENGERS DIE IN THE CRASH; EIGHT SURVIVE.

The Cathay-Pacific plane was shot down in the South China Sea near Hainan Island. Following a strong protest by Prime Minister Churchill, the Chinese government admitted its pilots had mistaken the plane for a Chinese Nationalist airplane. Mao's government apologized and offered to compensate the victims' families and the British airline.

August 30, 1954   *THE FRENCH NATIONAL ASSEMBLY REJECTS THE EUROPEAN DE-*
                         FENSE COMMUNITY (EDC) TREATY.

The EDC plan had been agreed to on May 27, 1952, but conflicts over French foreign policy in Indochina and Europe prevented the French assembly from voting on the EDC until 1954.

The French veto required the NATO allies to seek another method for attaining a united European defense plan. Secretary of State JOHN FOSTER DULLES WAS DETERMINED TO HAVE GERMAN TROOPS IN THE NATO DEFENSE STRUCTURE. French intransigence was the only factor preventing this.

September 8, 1954   THE SOUTHEAST ASIA TREATY ORGANIZATION (SEATO) IS
                         FORMED AT MANILA TO PROTECT THE REGION FROM AN ATTACK
                         AGAINST THEMSELVES OR "ANY STATE OR TERRITORY HEREAFTER
                         DESIGNATED."

The designated states were Cambodia, Laos, and Vietnam. If any state were threatened by subversion or aggression, the signatory states would consult on appropriate action. The members of SEATO were the United States, France,

Three Parts of Indochina: Cambodia, Laos, Vietnam. From Wayne S. Cole, An Interpretive History of Foreign Relations, *Homewood, Illinois: Dorsey Press, 1968. Used with permission.*

Great Britain, Australia, New Zealand, Thailand, Pakistan, and the Philippines.

In hearings on the SEATO treaty, Senator Alexander Wiley asked Secretary Dulles if agreeing "to counter subversive activity" is not different from agreeing to resist armed attack. Dulles acknowledged that it was different because it involved a Communist threat within a foreign country. Significantly, Dulles added that "We are confronted by an unfortunate fact--most of the countries of the world do not share our view that Communist control of any government anywhere is in itself a danger and a threat." In fact, France, Britain, and most U.S. allies would not accept the unusual U.S. concept expressed by Dulles, that America must fear *any nation* with a Communist government. This reflected the MONOLITHIC MYTH PREVALENT IN AMERICA THAT ALL COMMUNISTS RECEIVED ORDERS FROM MOSCOW as part of the universal Communist threat to capitalism. See October 23, 1954.

October 21, 1954   AMERICAN OIL COMPANIES SECURE A SHARE IN IRAN'S OIL
                          CONCESSIONS AS A RESULT OF A STATE DEPARTMENT DEAL
                          WITH BRITAIN AND THE IRANIAN GOVERNMENT.

On August 19, 1953, the Iranian nationalist leader Mossadegh had been ousted with U.S. aid on behalf of the Reza Shah Pahlavi. Because the Shah did not wish to retain exclusive British ownership of Iranian oil, President Eisenhower's advisor on petroleum, Herbert Hoover, Jr., undertook negotiations to form an international consortium to take over the Anglo-Iranian oil concessions. Basically, Hoover and the Eisenhower administration conceived of this as a cold war necessity to keep Soviet interests out of Iran.

Hoover had to convince not only the British but also the U.S. oil companies that the Iranian consortium was in everyone's best interests. Although long-range studies of U.S. oil requirements anticipated an excess of demand relative to production during the next 20 years, there was an oil glut on the world market in 1953 and the U.S. companies did not want Iranian oil competing in the U.S. market. Hoover, however, gained assurances from the U.S. Justice Department that joint ownership by five American companies would not violate the anti-trust laws, and Jersey Standard, Mobil, Gulf, California Standard, and the Texas Company agreed to participate in the consortium.

By October 21, the oil consortium arranged by Hoover concluded a pact with the Shah's government which the Iranian Majlis (parliament) ratified. The National Iranian Oil Company was set up. For this company, Iranian oil would be extracted, refined, and marketed by the international oil consortium. Iran received 50% of the profits, and the other 50% were divided by the consortium members as follows: Anglo-Iranian Company, 40%; Royal Dutch Shell, 14%; French Petroleum Company, 6%; and each of the five American companies, 5% for a total 40% U.S. shares. The consortium was named the Iranian Oil Exploration and Producing Company.

October 23, 1954   A LETTER FROM PRESIDENT EISENHOWER OFFERS AID TO NGO
                          DINH DIEM.

This letter and the SEATO alliance formed the basic "commitment" for U.S. aid to South Vietnam, the region of Vietnam below the 17th parallel established by the Geneva cease-fire agreement.

In his letter, Eisenhower limited aid in accordance with the "New Look"

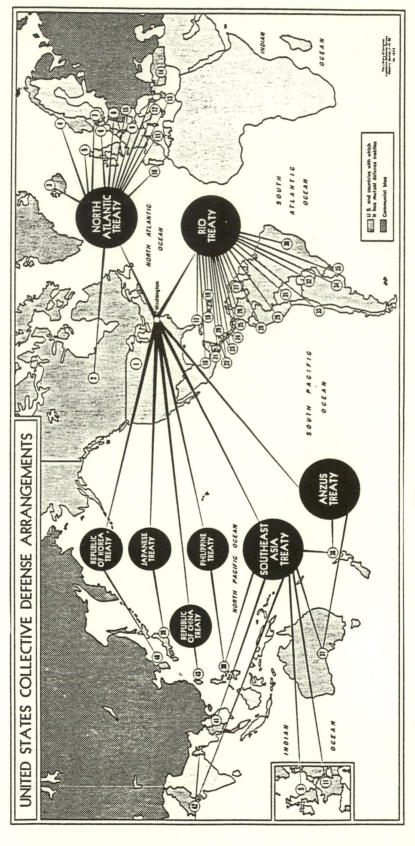

U.S. Collective Defense Arrangements, 1955.

which expected Diem to establish satisfactory local defense capabilities. In sum, Eisenhower agreed:

1. to provide a "humanitarian effort" for assisting refugees from the north;

2. to give aid for the "welfare and stability of Diem's government" provided Diem gave "assurances as to the standards of performance" his government would maintain;

3. to provide aid to help Vietnam develop and maintain "a strong, viable state, capable of resisting attempted subversion or aggression through military means";

4. to expect Diem's government to begin "needed reforms" which would establish an independent Vietnam "with a strong government" that would be respected "at home and abroad...."

Eisenhower's letter had one other significant consequence: U.S. ECONOMIC AID BEGAN TO GO DIRECTLY TO DIEM'S GOVERNMENT IN SAIGON, NOT THROUGH FRENCH OFFICIALS IN PARIS as it had since 1950. French Premier Mendes-France thought Washington had agreed to continue sending aid through Paris, a belief that resulted in increased friction between the French and American governments in 1954 and 1955 (see also the French veto of EDC, August 30, 1954).

November 2, 1954　　CONGRESSIONAL ELECTIONS RETURN CONTROL OF BOTH HOUSES TO THE DEMOCRATIC PARTY BY A MAJORITY OF ONE IN THE SENATE, AND 29 IN THE HOUSE.

This change did not affect Eisenhower's foreign policy at first because the Democratic congressmen held positions closer to the president than many Republican congressmen such as Senator William Knowland of California. After 1957, however, Senate Democratic leader Lyndon Johnson attacked Eisenhower's "new look" reduction in conventional forces and his "peaceful coexistence" discussions with Premier Khrushchev.

November 23, 1954　　A COMMUNIST CHINESE MILITARY COURT CONVICTS 13 AMERICAN AIRMEN OF SPYING AND SENTENCES THEM TO LONG PRISON TERMS.

The airmen had disappeared while flying missions during the Korean War. In response to the court's action, the United States protested both to Peking through the British embassy and to the United Nations.

On December 10, the U.N. General Assembly voted 47-5 to condemn China's treatment of the airmen and instructed U.N. Secretary General Dag HAMMERSKJOLD to confer with the Chinese. On December 17, after meeting with Hammerskjold, China's Premier CHOU EN-LAI agreed to release the American airmen.

December 2, 1954　　THE UNITED STATES AND NATIONALIST CHINA (TAIWAN) SIGN A MUTUAL DEFENSE PACT.

The United States agreed to protect only TAIWAN and the Pescadores, NOT THE

OFFSHORE ISLANDS which TAIWAN OCCUPIED near the Chinese mainland.

This pact was negotiated by Secretary of State Dulles during a period when Communist Chinese batteries shelled Quemoy and Matsu. (For this crisis see January 25, 1955.) Although Dulles wanted the treaty to include a U.S. commitment to defend the offshore islands as well as Formosa, President Eisenhower declined to specify this. The president changed this clause to read that the U.S. commitment was to "such other territories as may be determined by mutual agreement."

In approving the Formosan treaty, Eisenhower also placed restraints on Chiang's incursions along the mainland Chinese coast. Not wishing to permit Chiang to involve the United States in a mainland attack, the president had Dulles exchange letters with Chiang on December 10, 1954, limiting the Nationalists' activity. The letters stipulated that the "use of force" from areas controlled by Chiang would be "a matter of joint agreement" with the United States.

December 2, 1954   A U.S. SENATE RESOLUTION CONDEMNS THE CONDUCT OF SEN-
                          ATOR JOSEPH McCARTHY BY A VOTE OF 67-22.

This action, together with the Democrats' regaining a majority in congress and removing McCarthy from his chairmanship of the Senate Internal Security Committee, ended the worst aspect of McCarthyism. Nevertheless, the fears, suspicions, and myths concerning Soviet spies continued to influence attitudes of intense anti-communism among Americans, even those who disliked McCarthy's extreme methods.

1955

January 25, 1955   CONGRESS AUTHORIZES PRESIDENT EISENHOWER TO USE AMERI-
CAN ARMED FORCES TO DEFEND FORMOSA AND THE PESCADORES
FROM AN ARMED ATTACK.

The congressional resolution to defend Taiwan resulted from a crisis over
the islands of Quemoy and Matsu which developed between 1953 and 1955 and
led to U.S. preparations for war with the People's Republic of China.

During his State-of-the-Union message on February 2, 1953, Eisenhower
"unleashed" Chiang Kai-shek by announcing that the U.S. Seventh Fleet would
no longer "shield Communist China" from Chiang's attacks. Democrats and Europeans told Eisenhower that the U.S. fleet under President Truman had not
protected Red China but had protected Chiang from being conquered by mainland
China.

Nevertheless, Chiang's supporters in the United States and Taiwan viewed
Eisenhower's statement as backing Chinese Nationalist operations against the
Communists. In 1953, Chiang began bombing attacks on the Chinese mainland.
He also fortified the islands of Quemoy, Matsu, and the Tachen Islands, which
were located a few miles off the coast of China.

In 1954, Peking retaliated against Chiang by shelling the off-shore islands. Soon after, the Chinese Communists announced they were prepared to
liberate Taiwan from the Chinese Nationalist dictator. While both Clement
Attlee and Churchill urged Eisenhower to get rid of Chiang, the president
and Dulles said the loss of Quemoy and Matsu would be a catastrophe. Dulles
visited Chiang in December, 1954, signing a defense pact by which America
would protect Formosa and the Pescadores.

Early in January, 1955, action by the Chinese Communists persuaded
Eisenhower to seek a specific resolution from congress to permit the president
to protect Chiang's regime. First, the Communists began constructing jet
airfields opposite Formosa. Later, on January 10, about 100 Chinese Communist
planes raided the Tachen Islands, 200 miles north of Formosa. On January 18,
nearly 4,000 Chinese Communist troops landed and captured the island of
Ichiang, seven miles north of the Tachens.

Eisenhower decided to draw a clear line beyond which Red Chinese attacks
would result in U.S. action. He modified U.S. policy by asserting that America would not protect the Tachens because they were not vital to the defense
of Formosa. He would, however, ask congress to approve the use of American
forces to protect Taiwan and the Pescadores Islands, especially Quemoy and
Matsu. In addition, he asked for authority, if necessary, to protect "closely
related localities" which might be vital to the defense of Formosa. Acting
on this decision, on January 24, Eisenhower requested a congressional resolution permitting the president to protect Formosa, the Pescadores, and "certain
territories" under the jurisdiction of the Republic of China. In his speech
to Congress, Eisenhower said these "related localities" might be essential
to the defense of Formosa under some circumstances.

The House of Representatives passed the Formosa resolution almost immediately by a vote of 410 to 3. The Senate debated the issue until January 28, passing the resolution by a vote of 83 to 3.

Although the Red Chinese responded to the congressional resolution by beginning a heavier bombardment of the islands, Peking stopped its shelling by the end of April, 1955. During these two months, however, Eisenhower undertook preparations for a preventive war to protect Quemoy and Matsu. He also considered massive retaliation against China with nuclear weapons. On March 10, 1955, Dulles told the president that "we'll have to use atomic weapons" if we want to protect Quemoy and Matsu. Later in March, while Dulles and Chief of Naval Operations Robert B. Carney talked of preventive nuclear war to prevent a Chinese attack, Eisenhower remained circumspect about any decision regarding a Chinese attack on Quemoy or Matsu, saying that Formosa was the island deserving to be protected. As usual, in a crisis, Eisenhower, not Dulles, controlled American policy. See March 23, 1955.

On April 28, Eisenhower told a press conference that he believed the Formosa crisis would soon end. Eisenhower had been in contact with his old friend Marshal Zhukov of the Soviet Politburo. On April 23, at the Bandung Conference, Chinese Premier Chou En-lai said he was ready to negotiate over Formosa. Three days later, Secretary Dulles responded to a news conference question by saying he was willing to talk about a cease-fire with Red China although he did not want to imply recognition for that regime.

On May 22, news reports said there was an informal cease-fire in the Formosa Straits. Communist vessels did not attack Nationalist ships or fire on Chiang's patrol planes. The shelling of Quemoy and Matsu diminished and finally stopped. The crisis ended. See August 23, 1958.

February 5, 1955   *THE FRENCH NATIONAL ASSEMBLY VOTES "NO CONFIDENCE" IN*
                          THE MINISTRY OF MENDES-FRANCE.

This ministry had arranged the Geneva declarations of July, 1954, but ran into difficulty by seeking a compromise with the REBELLION IN ALGERIA. ALGERIAN MUSLIMS HAD STARTED A NATIONALIST UPRISING IN MID-1954 AND MENDES-FRANCE SOUGHT TO RESOLVE THE PROBLEMS BY COMPROMISE. Conservatives in the French assembly opposed the proposed reforms in Algeria. They wanted to use the army to regain French glory and defeat the rebels.

THE OVERTHROW OF MENDES-FRANCE'S CABINET LED TO TWO YEARS OF POLITICAL INSTABILITY which eventually led to General de Gaulle's return to power in 1958.

February 12, 1955   THE U.S. ARMY AGREES WITH FRANCE TO TAKE CHARGE OF
                          TRAINING THE ARMY OF THE VIETNAMESE NATIONAL GOVERN-
                          MENT.

Under this arrangement, General Paul Ely announced that French forces would cease training operations but would continue defensive activity in the northern provinces near the DMZ prior to their final withdrawal in 1956. American General John O'Daniel commanded the training mission in Vietnam after February 12.

This agreement was a vital step toward the United States' replacing France as the Western power in Vietnam. U.S. military experts believed that the French had not allowed sufficient independence for Vietnam's officers and that they could more ably prepare Diem's army to fight communism.

February 18, 1955   *BAGHDAD PACT CREATES A DEFENSIVE ALLIANCE BETWEEN TUR-*
                         KEY AND IRAQ.

Soon after, Great Britain, Iran, and Pakistan joined the alliance. The United
States gave wholehearted support to the pact, but never joined it. On April
19, 1956, the United States established economic ties with this pact. On
June 3, 1957, the United States joined the Military Committee of the Baghdad
Pact.

March 23, 1955   PRESIDENT EISENHOWER SEEKS TO CLARIFY DULLES' "MASSIVE
                       RETALIATION" ASSERTIONS BY DECLARING THAT THE UNITED
                       STATES WOULD NOT USE NUCLEAR WEAPONS IN A "POLICE AC-
                       TION."

Actually, Eisenhower's comments to a news conference on March 23 were not
intended to "clarify" but to confuse the newsmen. The question which had
been asked was whether or not the president would use atomic weapons to defend
Chinese off-shore islands under Chiang Kai-shek's control. (For the Quemoy-
Matsu crisis see January 25, 1955.) On March 12 and 15, Secretary of State
Dulles had spoken of the United States' using tactical nuclear weapons against
Chinese airfields and troops near Quemoy and Matsu. On March 16, Eisenhower
told a reporter that the tactical weapons Dulles referred to could be used
for "strictly military targets and for strictly military purposes." The pres-
ident hoped this statement would warn Peking of the dangers of the Quemoy-
Matsu crisis.
      In the context of these previous statements, a war scare developed in
America. Hawks in the United States wanted war on Red China; doves feared
an all-out nuclear war with the Soviet Union would result. Thus, on March
23, the president withdrew slightly from his March 16 remarks. He told the
newsmen that he could not predict how war would occur or what would result.
Eisenhower said it would depend on the circumstances at the time the decision
was made. There would be no automatic nuclear attack by the United States
in the manner that some Americans interpreted as "massive retaliation."

April 18-24, 1955   *BANDUNG CONFERENCE OF ASIAN-AFRICAN NATIONS AGREES TO*
                       PROMOTE THE SELF-DETERMINATION OF ALL NATIONS.

Twenty-nine governments from Asian and African nations attended. This con-
ference was a milestone along the way to the liberation of many former colo-
nial nations from western European control between 1955 and 1960. Because
anti-colonialists often used Marxian terminology to explain the imperialist-
capitalist use of colonies to exploit nations of Asia and Africa, many Ameri-
cans associated these statements with Moscow's rhetoric, assuming that such
conferences as that at Bandung were Communist plots for "national liberation."
Such analysis disclosed how far some Americans had come from the anti-colonial
heritage of 1776, as renewed by Woodrow Wilson and Franklin D. Roosevelt in
the 20th century. Prior to the cold war, America had been a champion of self-
determination and the end of European colonial empires.

May 2, 1955   DIEM CENTRALIZES HIS POLITICAL POWER IN SAIGON BY DE-
FEATING LOCAL SECTS WITH WHOM FRENCH OFFICIALS HAD
COMPROMISED BY BRIBERY.

Three large non-Communist sects in the Saigon area had gained much local influence from 1946 to 1954, because France paid them to fight the Vietminh
and gave them much local control. These three were CAO DAI, HOA HAO, and
BINH XUYEN. CAO DAI was a religious sect with 2 million members, located
northwest of Saigon. HOA HAO was also a religious sect with an army that
controlled the Mekong River Delta region. The strongest sect was the BINH
XUYEN, a criminal-style organization which controlled Saigon's gambling, pros-
titution, drugs, and a police force of 8,000 men.

Using tactics of divide-and-conquer, Diem gained control over these sects
and other smaller ones by the summer of 1955. Between March 21 and May 2,
virtual civil war took place in Saigon, as Diem fought the Binh Xuyen and
drove them from the city.

Diem's success against the sects permitted him to increase his political
prestige. On May 1, he gained control of Vietnam's army from Bao Dai, and
on May 5, a political congress in Saigon urged that all Bao Dai's powers
should be given to Premier Diem, pending the formation of a new government.

May 7, 1955   THE WESTERN EUROPEAN UNION (WEU) IS ORGANIZED TO PRO-
VIDE A DEFENSIVE ALLIANCE WHICH WOULD INCLUDE WEST
GERMAN FORCES.

After the French assembly rejected the EDC in August, 1954, British Foreign
Secretary Anthony Eden proposed that a Western European Union, including German forces, four divisions of British troops, and American forces in Europe
could be coordinated into a west European defense program. German Chancellor
Konrad Adenauer cooperated by agreeing that West Germany would not "have recourse to force" as a means of uniting Germany.

Eden's plan was officially drawn up and signed on October 23, 1954. In
addition to creating the WEU with both West Germany and Italy as members,
the plan provided for ending the occupation of West Germany and admitting
West Germany to NATO.

Under Mendes-France's guidance, the WEU pact was approved by the French
National Assembly on December 24, 1954. Thus, on May 7, concluding formali-
ties organized the WEU, whose members were France, Great Britain, West Germany, Italy, Belgium, Luxembourg, and the Netherlands.

May 9, 1955   *THE WEST GERMAN FEDERAL REPUBLIC JOINS NATO, JUST TWO*
DAYS AFTER GAINING SOVEREIGN STATUS WITH THE IMPLEMEN-
TATION OF THE PARIS TREATIES (WEV) OF OCTOBER 23, 1954.

May 14, 1955   *THE WARSAW PACT DEFENSE ALLIANCE IS FORMED BY EUROPEAN*
COMMUNIST NATIONS.

The Warsaw Pact was the Soviet Union's answer to American integration of West
German troops into NATO. Eight eastern European nations signed the alliance
pact. Early in January, 1956, the EAST GERMAN ARMY became part of the Warsaw
Pact forces under Soviet MARSHAL IVAN S. KONIEV.

May 15, 1955   THE BIG FOUR POWERS AGREE TO AN AUSTRIAN PEACE TREATY.

The foreign ministers of Britain, France, the Union of Soviet Socialist Republics, and the United States accepted peace terms, agreeing to withdraw all foreign forces from Austria by December 31, 1955. Austria became a neutral nation.

    Ostensibly, Khrushchev accepted an Austrian treaty as evidence to Washington that the new Soviet leaders desired to be cooperative. Following the Austrian agreement, Eisenhower announced he would participate in the July, 1955, summit conference at Geneva.

June 25, 1955   SOVIET FOREIGN MINISTER MOLOTOV APOLOGIZES TO THE
                            UNITED STATES FOR THE SOVIETS' SHOOTING DOWN OF A U.S.
                            NAVY PLANE ON JUNE 24, OFFERING TO PAY PART OF THE
                            DAMAGES.

The Soviet apology for this incident was unusual because it was contrary to past Russian practice. Both in 1953 and 1954, the Soviets rejected U.S. protests and claims for damage. On July 29, 1953, the Soviets shot down a B-50 flying near the Siberian coast. On September 6, 1954, a U.S. Navy P2V-5 was downed near Siberia. In neither instance did the Soviets respond to U.S. protests, except to claim that the planes violated Soviet air space.

    On June 24, another P2V-5 on patrol in the Bering Sea was shot down by Soviet jet fighter pilots. The plane crashlanded on St. Lawrence Island, injuring seven members of the plane's crew.

    The next day, Molotov wrote to the United States, expressing the U.S.S.R.'s regrets for the incident and offering to pay 50% of the damages. Molotov insisted that the American plane was over Soviet air space. He stated, however, that the cloudy sky made errors possible on both sides.

    Later, on July 18, the U.S.S.R. proposed that some method should be found to prevent such incidents in the future.

    In Washington, President Eisenhower was willing to accept the Soviets' response. Secretary Dulles believed that the Russians should be made to pay a greater compensation, but this was a matter not pursued by the State Department.

July 18-23, 1955   PRESIDENT DWIGHT EISENHOWER, BRITISH PRIME MINISTER
                            ANTHONY EDEN, FRENCH PREMIER EDGAR FAURE, AND SOVIET
                            PREMIER NIKOLAI BULGANIN ATTEND THE BIG FOUR SUMMIT
                            CONFERENCE AT GENEVA.

The conference discussed the reunification of Germany, European security, and disarmament. The talks stalled, however, on the German issue. The United States desired that Germans should be free to join NATO if they wished; Russia wanted all foreign forces out of Germany and a neutral Germany.

    During the conference, EISENHOWER GAINED FAVORABLE WORLD REACTION WITH AN "OPEN SKIES" PROPOSAL. This plan would permit reconnaissance aircraft to photograph each nation's territory to ensure against a surprise enemy attack. In addition, each nation would exchange plans on military facilities.

    Although the U.N. General Assembly eventually supported this plan, the Soviet Union refused to permit such verification tactics as the "open skies" plan proposed. See December 6, 1955.

July 22, 1955   A REARMAMENT BILL IS ENACTED BY THE WEST GERMAN PARLIA-
                       MENT.

The bill authorized the enlistment of 6,000 officers as the nucleus of a
500,000-man army. Compulsory military service was enacted, to become effective on July 25, 1956.

July 27, 1955   BULGARIAN FIGHTER PLANES SHOOT DOWN AN EL AL (ISRAELI)
                       AIRLINER; 58 PASSENGERS ARE KILLED.

The El Al Constellation airliner was en route from London to Israel and
strayed off course, flying over Bulgarian territory. The Bulgarian government
admitted on August 3, following its investigation of the incident, that its
fighter pilots were "too hasty" in shooting down the aircraft. They pledged
to punish the pilots and to take steps to prevent a recurrence of the incident. They also agreed to pay compensation to families of the victims and
to share in the cost of the destroyed plane.
    During the fall session of the U.N. General Assembly, the member nations
approved a resolution on December 6 that asked all governments to avoid attacks on civilian aircraft which violated their international borders. For
a similar incident of the destruction of a commercial airliner, see July 23,
1954.

September 13, 1955   THE SOVIET UNION ESTABLISHES DIPLOMATIC RELATIONS WITH
                       WEST GERMANY.

The Soviets' recognition of West Germany came one week before the U.S.S.R.
conferred sovereignty on a separate East German government on September 20.
The Soviets also gave East Germany the control of civilian traffic between
West Germany and West Berlin.

September 16, 1955   AN ARGENTINE MILITARY JUNTA OUSTS PRESIDENT JUAN PERON.

On September 23, General EDUARDO LONARDI became provisional president, but
was replaced on November 13 by General Pedro ARAMBURU.
    Peron had experienced increased public dissatisfaction after his 1955
effort to deprive the Roman Catholic Church of its tax-exempt status and to
abolish teaching of Catholic religion in all schools. On June 16, the POPE
EXCOMMUNICATED PERON, while the Argentine navy and air force seized several
towns and bombed Buenos Aires. Peron's efforts at compromise with his opponents failed. Consequently, antagonism against Peron built up in the armed
forces and led to the coup d'état of September 16, 1955.

October 11, 1955   CANADA SIGNS AN AGREEMENT WITH THE SOVIET UNION GRANT-
                       ING MOST-FAVORED-NATION TRADE PRIVILEGES AND COOPERA-
                       TION IN ARCTIC RESEARCH.

Lester Pearson negotiated the treaty for Canada.

October 26, 1955   NGO DINH DIEM GAINS COMPLETE CONTROL OF THE SOUTH VIET-
                          NAMESE GOVERNMENT, PROCLAIMING A REPUBLIC WITH HIMSELF
                          AS THE FIRST PRESIDENT.

Since May 2, Diem had persistently prevented attempts by the French and Bao
Dai to unseat him. With American support, Diem rejected French plans to re-
organize the government under Bao and on October 18, he refused to resign as
Premier when ordered to by Bao Dai.

To gain power, Diem organized a referendum on October 23 which overwhelmingly voted for Diem against Bao Dai. This "election" permitted Diem to proclaim a republic, to end Bao Dai's emperorship, and to announce that elections
for a national legislature would follow in the near future.

November 8, 1955   PRESIDENT EISENHOWER AND SECRETARY OF DEFENSE WILSON
                          DECIDE TO GIVE INTERMEDIATE RANGE MISSILES (IRBM) EQUAL
                          PRIORITY WITH INTERCONTINENTAL (ICBM) MISSILES.

Within the U.S. Air Force during the early 1950's, internal disputes had
slowed the development of both ICBM's and IRBM's. On September 8, 1954, a
new ICBM organizational arrangement gave this missile the highest priority
for development, ending the Air Force's inclination to emphasize bomber delivery systems.

In the fall of 1954, the president appointed James Killian to head a
committee to review the entire missile program. In February, 1955, Killian's
group recommended that the IRBM's were "of utmost importance to national security" and should be made operational as early as possible.

To effect the IRBM development, Secretary Wilson established a Ballistic
Missiles Committee to oversee missile advances. A separate directive by
Wilson told the committee to assign the IRBM's equal priority with the pro-
curement of ICBM's. The IRBM would have a range of 1,500 to 2,000 miles.
Although the Air Force first interpreted the November directive as making
the IRBM "second" to the ICBM, this decision was corrected in January, 1956.
IRBM development required bases in Europe from which they could hit Soviet
targets. See December 19, 1957.

November 18, 1955   *PREMIER BULGANIN AND CHAIRMAN KHRUSHCHEV OF THE*
                          UNION OF SOVIET SOCIALIST REPUBLICS VISIT INDIA, BURMA,
                          AND AFGHANISTAN WHERE THEY PROMOTE FRIENDSHIP FOR THE
                          SOVIET UNION AMONG THIRD WORLD NATIONS.

December 14, 1955   *SIXTEEN NATIONS ARE ADMITTED TO THE UNITED NATIONS.*

They were: Albania, Austria, Bulgaria, Cambodia, Ceylon, Finland, Hungary,
Ireland, Italy, Jordan, Laos, Libya, Nepal, Portugal, Rumania, and Spain.

December 16, 1955   EISENHOWER'S "OPEN SKIES" PLAN IS APPROVED BY THE
                          U.N. GENERAL ASSEMBLY.

The U.N. action scored public opinion points for America, but the Soviet Union
opposed this or any other means for verification of its armament installations.

1956

January 1, 1956   THE SUDAN GAINS COMPLETE INDEPENDENCE FROM BOTH GREAT
BRITAIN AND EGYPT.

Since 1948, the question of the Sudan's future had been disputed. The Sudan
had been a part of the British protectorate of Egypt since 1898, but the Sudanese desired independence from Egypt as well as England. In 1952, the Egyptians rejected Britain's proposal for limited self-government for the Sudan
under Egypt's control. After the overthrow of King Farouk, the Egyptians
agreed to a referendum in the Sudan on whether it wished to be part of Egypt.
The Sudanese voted for complete independence, which was arranged to become
effective on January 1, 1956.

January 19, 1956   THE U.N. SECURITY COUNCIL UNANIMOUSLY VOTES TO CENSURE
ISRAEL FOR A DECEMBER 11, 1955, ATTACK ON SYRIA.

This attack was the most serious of several border engagements between Israeli
and Egyptian-Syrian forces during 1955. The 1955 raids occurred in the Gaza
strip near the Sinai desert and in the Lake Galilee region of the Israel-
Syrian border.
    Following the U.N. vote, the United States asserted on February 17 that
it would SUSPEND ALL ARMS SHIPMENTS TO BOTH ISRAEL AND THE ARAB NATIONS. On
April 9, the State Department said it fully supported the U.N. efforts to
secure peace in the Middle East. An Israeli-Egyptian cease-fire, arranged
by U.N. Secretary General Hammarskjold, became effective in April.

January 28, 1956   PRESIDENT EISENHOWER REJECTS A PROPOSAL FOR FRIENDSHIP
MADE BY SOVIET PREMIER BULGANIN.

As part of a so-called peace offensive, Premier Bulganin wrote to Eisenhower
early in January to propose a 20-year treaty of friendship and economic, cultural, and scientific cooperation. He called the president an outstanding
leader and recalled that only during the Russian Civil War of 1918-1920 had
the two nations clashed. The two nations had no territorial or interest conflicts. Therefore, U.S.S.R.-U.S. cooperation would be based on "vital and
long-term interests of both parties."
    Because Washington was astounded and uncertain how to receive Bulganin's
note and the accompanying treaty draft, Eisenhower replied in polite but evasive terms. He thought Russia should first cooperate on German unity or aerial inspection.
    Consequently, correspondence between Bulganin and the president continued
until the Suez and Hungarian crisis of October, 1956. Exactly why the Soviets
made this suggestion is not known. Adam Ulam, a U.S. Sovietologist, believes
the Russians either wished to frighten China into compliance with Soviet terms

or Moscow was trying to interest Washington in a treaty against Red China. These were the early days of the Sino-Soviet split during which Peking demanded nuclear capabilities and additional heavy industry from the Russians.

February 14, 1956   *SPEAKING BEFORE THE 20th COMMUNIST PARTY CONGRESS, KHRUSHCHEV CRITICIZED STALIN'S CRIMES AGAINST THE PARTY AND THE NATION.*

This "de-Stalinization" speech blamed Stalin for unnecessary party purges and terrorist tactics. Clearly, however, he blamed Stalin, NOT the Communist system, for the faults in Soviet policy since 1928. He justified the central party controls and overall objectives of the Soviet government.

In domestic affairs, Khrushchev's speech enhanced his power and assisted his shift of emphasis to consumer goods and worker incentives as a means to bolster the Soviet economy. The speech's greatest effects, however, were in the eastern European satellite nations where Khrushchev's message implied that Communist leaders could use a variety of methods of communism, not just Stalin's. Khrushchev also recognized this change by seeking to heal the breach with Yugoslavia's Tito whom, he said, Stalin mistreated in 1949.

April 7, 1956   *SPAIN TERMINATES ITS PROTECTORSHIP OVER ALL BUT SOUTHERN MOROCCO.*

COMBINED WITH THE FRENCH PROTOCOL ON INDEPENDENCE FOR FRENCH MOROCCO (March 2, 1956) an independent Morocco was established. Later, on October 20, the international administration for TANGIER, set up on October 11, 1945, was terminated and TANGIER was integrated with the MOROCCAN economy (April 19, 1960). On April 1, 1958, Spain gave independence to southern Morocco, creating a united Kingdom of Morocco.

April 17, 1956   *THE SOVIET UNION ANNOUNCES THAT THE COMINFORM HAS BEEN DISSOLVED.*

Since its inception in 1947 as a replacement for the Comintern, the single achievement of the Cominform was the expulsion of Tito and Yugoslavia from the world Communist movement. For this reason, Khrushchev hoped to reconcile Tito to renew his world socialist affiliation by abolishing the Cominform. Tito was not seduced by Khrushchev's ploy. Although the Yugoslavian ruler conducted negotiations with Moscow, Tito retained and strengthened his role as a neutralist between the two superpowers.

April 23, 1956   *KHRUSHCHEV, WHILE ON A VISIT TO ENGLAND, ANNOUNCES THAT RUSSIA WILL PRODUCE H-BOMBS CARRIED BY GUIDED MISSILE, GIVING THE SOVIETS LEADERSHIP IN NUCLEAR WEAPONS.*

May 9, 1956   SECRETARY DULLES REFUSES TO SUPPLY ARMS TO ISRAEL,
                                CLAIMING THAT THIS COULD LEAD TO A MID-EAST ARMS COM-
                                PETITION WITH THE U.S.S.R. BECAUSE THE ARAB STATES
                                SOUGHT MILITARY AID FROM THE SOVIETS.

As a crisis seemed imminent in the Middle East because of the demands of
Nasser of Egypt and incidents along the Arab-Israeli borders, Dulles hoped
to avoid providing U.S. arms for the Arabs or Israelis. He denied export
licenses for arms to Israel and all Arab states except Iraq and Saudi Arabia.
At the same time, however, Dulles encouraged Canada and France to sell F-86
aircraft and French Mystères to Israel. Although the Israeli leaders accepted
this tactic, they had already begun preparations with France to stake preemptive action in the Sinai-Suez area. See January 19, 1956 and October 29, 1956.

May 21, 1956   THE FIRST U.S. H-BOMB DROPPED FROM AN AIRPLANE IS DET-
                                ONATED AT BIKINI ATOLL.

In a series of nuclear tests code-named "Redwing," a B-52 dropped the bomb
which exploded at a height of from 10,000 to 15,000 feet. Although Japan
complained about the nuclear fall-out, U.S. experts said the radioactive debris was slight compared to the 1954 tests.

June 20, 1956   *YUGOSLAVIA'S PRESIDENT TITO CONCLUDES A THREE-WEEK
                                VISIT TO MOSCOW.*

This symbolized Khrushchev's promise to improve relations with TITO.
     *Later in the year (September 19) Khrushchev visited Belgrade. The talks
did not go well, however, and on February 19, 1957, Khrushchev said that because Tito rejected the Soviet proposals, Yugoslavia would not get further
economic aid from Russia. For several years, Khrushchev and Tito had both
favorable and unfavorable relations, each leader being suspicious of the other's intentions.*

June 28, 1956   *RIOTS BREAK OUT IN POZNAN, POLAND, AS WORKERS DEMON-
                                STRATE FOR BETTER ECONOMIC AND SOCIAL CONDITIONS.*

*This was the initial Polish reaction to Khrushchev's de-Stalinization speech.
Tensions continued in Russia throughout 1956, but WLADYSLAW GOMULKA, who be-
came Secretary of the Polish Communist Party on October 21, carefully steered
Warsaw's policy to gain concessions from Khrushchev without antagonizing the
Russian leader; see November 18, 1956.*

July 1, 1956   *THE FIRST THREE WEST GERMAN DIVISIONS JOIN THE NATO
                                COMMAND.*

Germany was committed eventually to provide 12 divisions to NATO.

July 17, 1956   *SOVIET PREMIER BULGANIN AND EAST GERMAN PREMIER OTTO*
                                GROTEWOHL DECLARE THAT THE UNIFICATION OF GERMANY
                                SHOULD BE WORKED OUT BY EAST-WEST GERMAN AGREEMENTS,
                                NOT BY THE FOUR POWERS THAT OCCUPIED GERMANY IN 1945.

July 19, 1956   SECRETARY DULLES CANCELS THE U.S. OFFER OF AID TO EGYPT
                                TO CONSTRUCT THE ASWAN DAM.

Although in December, 1955, the United States, Great Britain, and the World
Bank jointly offered funds to Egypt for their dam project, Colonel Nasser
persistently refused to discuss details of the loan with Washington. Instead,
Nasser undertook policies to upset the calm in Ethiopia, Uganda, and the Sudan. He also arranged arms purchases with Communist countries and held talks
with the Russians and Communist Chinese.

On July 19, Egyptian Ambassador to the United States Ahmed HUSSEIN ar-
rived back from Cairo and immediately told Dulles he wanted to finalize the
Aswan Dam loan. Negotiations were unnecessary, he said, for if the United
States did not guarantee the loan "the Soviet Union would do so."

Dulles rejected Hussein's abrupt "blackmail" demand. The United States,
the secretary said, had assumed Egypt did not want the loan because it had
rejected offers to negotiate the arrangement. Conditions in the Middle East
needed to improve, Dulles observed, before a loan could be concluded.

Commentators in July, 1956, showed surprise that Dulles had abruptly
withdrawn the loan. Actually, Dulles had discussed the loan with the British
and tentatively agreed to withdraw or not renew the offer to Egypt. In addition, Dulles indicated to Hussein that if Egypt desired, further talks on
the loan could be undertaken. Nasser chose to accept the Soviet loan.

July 26, 1956   EGYPT NATIONALIZES THE SUEZ CANAL COMPANY.

Acting in response to Secretary of State Dulles' refusal to fund the Aswan
Dam and because Egypt received only about $2 million as its share of the ca-
nal's annual $31 million profits, Egypt's President GAMAL ABDEL NASSER an-
nounced that, while Egypt would repay investors for their loss, his government
would henceforth operate and control the Suez Canal. The British had withdrawn the last of their troops from Suez on June 13, 1956, making it difficult
for them to protest as effectively as previously.

Nasser was especially chagrined at the American withdrawal of financial
support to construct the Aswan Dam, a project Egypt believed would benefit
its economy and help the nation become modernized. Dulles and British Prime
Minister Anthony Eden had promised to back the Aswan project in December,
1955. In February, 1956, Eugene Black, President of the World Bank, agreed
to provide $200 million for the Aswan Dam.

Between February and July, Dulles and Eisenhower changed their policy.
Due largely to criticism from congressional members, Dulles decided Nasser
was too close to his Communist friends to deserve a loan. Dulles underestimated Moscow, because he believed Russia would not aid Egypt's costly project
(see October 23, 1958). More important, during this presidential election
year, Dulles feared opposition from pro-Israeli groups; China lobbyists who
disliked Nasser's recognition of Red China in May, 1956; and ardent anti-
Communists who objected to Egypt's purchase of arms from eastern European
countries.

Therefore, in spite of prior promises, Dulles announced the withdrawal of U.S. aid for the Aswan Dam at the very time when Egypt's Ambassador returned to Washington to notify Dulles that Nasser was prepared to accept the terms of the loan.

Dulles announced the withdrawal of the loan on July 19, 1956. Within a week, Nasser declared Egypt would take over the Universal Suez Canal Company. Profits from the canal, he claimed, would help build the Aswan Dam. Nasser's action caused extreme concern in London and Paris, giving rise to the Suez Crisis (see October 29-November 6, 1956).

October 19, 1956   *THE UNION OF SOVIET SOCIALIST REPUBLICS AND JAPAN ISSUE A DECLARATION ENDING THEIR 11-YEAR STATE OF WAR.*

Because the two nations could not settle the issue of the KURILE ISLANDS, IT WENT UNRESOLVED.

October 21-November 14, 1956   *HUNGARIAN UPRISING OCCURS AGAINST COMMUNIST POWER.*

As in several east European countries, Hungarian dissenters believed Khrushchev's de-Stalinization speech permitted them to criticize party policy and to get rid of Stalinist-style dictators in their government.

In Hungary, these protests first led to the end of MATYAS RAKOSI's government by a new Communist leader, ERNO GERO, on July 18.

By October 21, however, students requested greater freedoms and threatened to strike. Their demonstrations, especially in Budapest, led to a new government on October 24 after Russian troops tried to stop the uprising.

The new Hungarian leader was IMRE NAGY who became Premier. On October 25, Nagy yielded to student demands to replace ERNO GERO with JANOS KADAR as head of the Hungarian Communist Party.

IMRE NAGY persuaded the Soviet Union to withdraw Russian troops from Budapest and permit some members of the Old Smallholders Party to join his cabinet. Nagy's effort succeeded until November 2, when his call for free elections and his denunciation of the Warsaw Pact caused Khrushchev to realize that the Hungarian leader was going too far in his compromises.

On November 4, Soviet tanks moved back into Budapest and violently smashed the rebellion, ousting and later arresting Nagy and making JANOS KADAR the head of the government. Although the United Nations condemned the Soviet assault on Budapest, the Russians ignored the General Assembly resolution.

The last rebel stronghold at Csepel Island was overthrown by Soviet forces on November 14, 1956. During the next six months, the Kadar Ministry restored prior policies of internal controls and its subservience to Soviet demands.

October 26, 1956   DIEM PROMULGATES A NEW CONSTITUTION FOR SOUTH VIETNAM.

Early in 1956, Diem's cabinet approved the appointment of an assembly to draw up a constitution. The assembly's recommendation was completed and ratified by Diem on October 26.

Establishment of the new government occurred during the period when, according to the Geneva agreements, an election was to take place to unite

Vietnam and choose a government that would end the division of the nation.
Diem refused to work with the International Control Commission regarding elections and, despite Hanoi's protests, elections never took place. The United
States approved Diem's decision because it was obvious from American intelligence reports that in a "free election," Ho Chi Minh and the Vietminh would
win.

     In this manner, Diem and the United States by-passed the Geneva Confer-
ence attempt to provide self-determination for all Vietnamese to decide on
their future government and national unity.

October 29-November 6, 1956   THE SUEZ CRISIS IS CAUSED WHEN ISRAELI,
                                            BRITISH, AND FRENCH FORCES ATTACK EGYPT.

The attack on Suez was one of several Israeli-Egyptian engagements during
the years since Israel became a nation in 1948. The British and French joined
the attack in an attempt to regain some control of the Suez Canal following
Egypt's nationalization decree of July 26, 1956. Israel had an interest in
the canal's status because Egypt had denied Israeli ships the use of the canal, a situation Israel wished to abolish. London and Paris wanted to be
certain Cairo never denied them use of the canal because west European nations
depended on oil supplies going through Suez.

     After Nasser's nationalization decree, England and France rushed naval
units and paratroopers into the region between Cyprus and Suez, threatening
to use force if Nasser did not accept joint control plans for the canal.

     Compromise efforts had failed between July and October. Secretary of
State Dulles proposed the formation of a SUEZ CANAL USER'S ASSOCIATION (SCUA)
to operate the canal, but Nasser refused. Next, the U.N. Security Council
worked out a compromise for an international canal agency. On October 13,
the Soviet Union vetoed the plan even though it appeared Egypt would accept
it.

     As compromise talks went on, French, British, and Israeli representatives
held secret military talks. On October 24, at Sevres, near Paris, the three
nations AGREED TO A SECRET JOINT ATTACK ON SUEZ.

     As planned at Sevres, ISRAELI TROOPS FIRST LAUNCHED A RAID IN THE SINAI
DESERT on October 29. London and Paris sent cease-fire requests to Cairo
and Tel Aviv which, as expected, Nasser rejected. On October 31, Anglo-French
planes bombed Cairo, Egyptian air bases, and the canal. On November 2, British naval forces and paratroopers occupied Port Said forcing Egyptian forces
to retreat west of the Canal Zone.

     U.N. action to halt the crisis was, initially, ineffective. The British
and French vetoed an October 31 Security Council resolution to "refrain from
the use of force." On November 2, a U.N. General Assembly resolution called
for a cease-fire and mutual troop withdrawal, but included no method of implementation. Therefore, on November 4, Lester Pearson of Canada proposed
that a U.N. EMERGENCY FORCE should supervise the cease-fire.

     Pearson's proposal passed the U.N. Assembly by a vote of 57-0 with 19
abstentions. At 12:15 a.m. on November 5, the assembly authorized General
E.L.M. BURNS of Canada to recruit and lead an international force to Suez,
with the force to exclude troops from any permanent members of the Security
Council.

     On November 6, the Soviet Union supported Egypt, when Khrushchev threat-
ened to send Soviet forces to stop the aggressors if a cease-fire did not
occur immediately.

Eisenhower and Dulles (who had emergency cancer surgery on November 3) opposed the British-French-Israeli attacks from the outset. They sought to use the United Nations and backed Pearson's attempt to intervene through the assembly. On November 6, EISENHOWER DECIDED TO APPLY GREATER PRESSURE ON BRITAIN AND FRANCE. Financial pressure was applied by the United States' selling British pounds on the exchange to damage British currency rates and cutting off oil supplies from Latin America to Europe. Before the end of the day, November 6, the fighting in Suez had stopped because the British, French, and Israelis accepted the cease-fire and the intervention of the U.N. supervisory force.

The U.N. supervisory force still had to overcome obstacles before the Suez situation reached peaceful terms; see June 13, 1957.

November 6, 1956   THE REPUBLICAN TICKET OF EISENHOWER AND NIXON WINS
                          THE PRESIDENTIAL ELECTION, EISENHOWER RECEIVING 57%
                          OF THE VOTE. THE DEMOCRATS RETAIN CONTROL OF BOTH
                          HOUSES OF CONGRESS.

Regarding foreign policy, commentators thought Eisenhower best expressed two major points about which *most* liberals and conservatives agreed in 1956: (1) the underdeveloped nations, not Europe, were becoming the central area of conflict in the cold war; and (2) the United States must find a means to keep the "neutrals" and new developing nations tied to American interests or they would become "virtual allies" of the Soviet Union.

November 18, 1956   *POLISH PREMIER GOMULKA SIGNS AN AGREEMENT WITH KHRU-*
                          SHCHEV AND BULGANIN AT MOSCOW TO GIVE POLAND EQUALITY
                          IN ITS RELATIONS WITH RUSSIA.

This agreement settled disturbances in Poland against the Soviet Union. Gomulka had to walk the narrow line between gaining some reforms without an- tagonizing Russia as Hungary had done.

On October 20, the Polish crisis had heightened when Soviet and Polish border troops exchanged fire and students demanded that Soviet officers leave the Polish army. Gomulka secured some independence for Poland, including the release (October 29) of Cardinal WYSZINSKI from army custody. Gomulka agreed to a limited role for Soviet troops in Poland. As a result, while gaining some local control and religious freedom but retaining other Russian controls, the Polish rising never became as serious a threat to Khrushchev as had Imre Nagy's efforts in Hungary.

1957

January 5, 1957   THE EISENHOWER DOCTRINE IS PRESENTED IN AN ADDRESS TO
                      CONGRESS.

The President asked CONGRESS TO AUTHORIZE THE USE OF U.S. ARMED FORCES IF
THERE WERE COMMUNIST AGGRESSION IN THE MIDDLE EAST. Congress approved the
resolution on March 5, 1957. The congressional resolution stated that
a nation must *request assistance* from the United States.
     The doctrine was seldom used, however, because American forces could
not check the growth of Soviet diplomatic influences in the Middle East and
Arab nations hesitated to request aid because the United States supported Israel.

February 8, 1957   SAUDI ARABIA RENEWS THE U.S. LEASE ON THE DHAHRAN AIR
                      BASE IN EXCHANGE FOR AMERICAN ARMS.

The agreement was announced after King Saud visited Washington for 10 days.

March 6, 1957   *THE BRITISH GOLD COAST COLONY BECOMES THE INDEPENDENT*
                      STATE OF GHANA.

In accordance with a 1956 plebiscite, TOGOLAND united with Ghana. GHANA re-
tained membership in the British Commonwealth.

March 13, 1957   *JORDAN GAINS INDEPENDENCE WHEN GREAT BRITAIN TERMINATES*
                      THE 1948 ALLIANCE AND AGREES TO WITHDRAW ITS ARMED
                      FORCES WITHIN SIX MONTHS.

KING HUSSEIN I, who became monarch of Jordan on May 2, 1953, also acted vig-
orously to purge his national army of Egyptian and Syrian sympathizers.
     Although the United States sympathized with Hussein's actions and later
sent arms to aid him, Hussein refused to make any commitments to America and
claimed to seek a neutral policy in the cold war.

March 24, 1957   BRITISH AND U.S. LEADERS MEET AT BERMUDA TO REPAIR
                      STRAINED RELATIONS RESULTING FROM THE SUEZ CRISIS.

Great Britain was represented by Prime Minister HAROLD MACMILLAN who replaced
Eden following his Suez policy failure in 1956. President Eisenhower and
Macmillan discussed the improvement of British defenses. The British explained their need to cut their number of troops in NATO from 75,000 to 50,000
(accepted by the WEU on March 19) and Eisenhower agreed to supply Britain
with intermediate range guided missiles.

March 25, 1957   *THE EUROPEAN COMMON MARKET (EUROPEAN ECONOMIC COMMU-*
                       NITY) IS AGREED TO IN THE TREATY OF ROME.

France, West Germany, Italy, Belgium, Luxembourg, and the Netherlands were
the charter members.

April 25, 1957   THE EISENHOWER DOCTRINE IS APPLIED TO HELP KING HUSSEIN
                       OF JORDAN AGAINST THE THREAT OF "INTERNATIONAL COM-
                       MUNISM."

Although historians disagree on whether or not the Eisenhower Doctrine applied
to the Jordanian crisis, the president ordered the U.S. Sixth Fleet to the
Eastern Mediterranean and Secretary Dulles advised that this action was designed to protect Jordan from Syrian and Egyptian pressure. Both Syria and
Egypt received Soviet aid, causing Dulles to link them with Moscow's clandestine activity to promote communism.
    On March 13, 1957, Great Britain had agreed with King Hussein to end its
treaty of alliance of 1948 and to withdraw British troops in six months.
Hussein also lost Britain's financial subsidies, and although Saudi Arabia
helped to replace these funds, Hussein had financial problems which Egypt's
Colonel Nasser hoped to exploit by forcing Jordan to join Syria and Egypt in
forming a United Arab Republic. Hussein opposed the efforts of Syria and
Egypt and President Chamoun of Lebanon asked the United States to act on behalf of Jordan. Partly due to Eisenhower's show of force in the Mediterranean, Hussein maintained power in Jordan and the United States offered him a
grant of $10 million. See September 5, 1957.

May 1, 1957   THE UNITED STATES AGREES TO PROVIDE AID TO POLAND IN
                       THE FORM OF $95 MILLION WORTH OF COMMODITIES AND MINING
                       MACHINERY.

Loans to Poland of $48.9 million were arranged on June 7, 1957.

May 15, 1957   *GREAT BRITAIN SUCCESSFULLY EXPLODES A HYDROGEN BOMB*
                       AT CHRISTMAS ISLAND.

May 30, 1957   *PRESIDENT BATISTA OF CUBA ORDERS THE ARMY TO INTENSIFY*
                       ITS FIGHT AGAINST FIDEL CASTRO'S REBELS IN ORIENTE
                       PROVINCE.

Since his election in 1954 under charges of "rigged elections," Batista had
been increasingly provoked by rural raids by guerrilla armies. On May 20,
FIDEL CASTRO APPEALED TO THE UNITED STATES TO STOP ARMING BATISTA.
    The Cuban rebellion continued to grow for the next two years, in spite
of Batista's attempts to crush Castro's underground activity. See December
28, 1958.

June 12, 1957   *THE CHINESE COMMUNISTS INDICATE THEY ARE RELAXING THEIR*
                       SEVERE RESTRICTIONS ON THE POPULACE.

The Chinese Communist press printed part of the text of two of Mao Tse-tung's
recent speeches. Mao reported that the government had had to liquidate
800,000 persons in China from 1949 to 1954 because of "contradictions" between
the ruler and the ruled. He hoped, however, that there would be freer expres-
sion in the future, declaring, "Let a hundred flowers bloom, let a hundred
schools of thought contend."

June 13, 1957   THE AFTER-EFFECTS OF THE SUEZ CRISIS OF OCTOBER, 1956,
                       ARE FINALLY RESOLVED WHEN EGYPT APPROVES TERMS FOR ALL
                       NATIONS TO USE THE CANAL.

After the November 6 cease-fire, Britain and France delayed removing their
forces until December 22, 1956, in order to assume negotiations for use of
the canal. Israel refused to withdraw from the GAZA STRIP AND AQUABA until
Washington agreed to support Israel's free passage through the Gulf of Aquaba
(February 11, 1957), and U.N. forces agreed to build a mined-fence and to
patrol the Gaza border (March 29, 1957). Finally, Israel demanded that terms
for the use of the Suez Canal include permission for their ships to navigate
the canal. Terms satisfying France and England were approved by Egypt on
June 13.

June 18, 1957   THE U.S. SENATE APPROVES THE ATOMS-FOR-PEACE TREATY.

This treaty evolved from President Eisenhower's December, 1953, proposal
through the United Nations where 80 nations had joined in forming the International Atomic Energy Agency, a group including the Soviet Union. The treaty
provided for the sharing of fissionable materials for peaceful uses.

June 30, 1957   THE INTERNATIONAL GEOPHYSICAL YEAR (IGY) BEGINS.

Scientists from 64 countries cooperated in an intensive study of physical
geographic phenomena during an 18-month period.

July 26, 1957   *A MILITARY JUNTA IN COLOMBIA ASSUMES CONTROL OF THE*
                       GOVERNMENT, ANNOUNCING THERE WILL BE ELECTIONS ON MAY
                       4, 1958.

The coup against GENERAL ROJAS PINILLA arose because Rojas violated the con-
stitution in seeking reelection as president on May 8, 1957. Student riots
followed and the Roman Catholic Church accused Rojas of murder in suppressing
the students. Rojas resigned on May 10, but demonstrations continued in Co-
lombia until the junta agreed to fix new election dates for 1958. On May 4,
1958, ALBERTO ILLERAS CAMARGO was elected president.

August 26, 1957   *THE SOVIET UNION ANNOUNCES IT SUCCESSFULLY TEST-FIRED*
                         THE FIRST INTERCONTINENTAL BALLISTIC MISSILE, A WEAPON
                         CAPABLE OF CARRYING A NUCLEAR WARHEAD TO TARGETS IN
                         THE UNITED STATES.

September 5, 1957   PRESIDENT EISENHOWER ANNOUNCES PLANS TO AIRLIFT ARMS
                         TO JORDAN AND TO ASSIST LEBANON, TURKEY, AND IRAQ
                         AGAINST COMMUNIST PLOTS FROM SYRIA: THE SYRIAN CRISIS
                         OF 1957.

Tensions increased between Washington and Damascus during the summer of 1957
and the United States concluded that a "takeover by the Communists would soon
be completed" in Damascus. A Syrian agreement with the Soviets provided Damascus with $500 million of assistance and military aid. On August 13, Syria
charged three American embassy officials with plotting to overthrow President
Shukuri al-Kuwatly and forced them to leave the country.
     Joined by diplomats from Turkey, Lebanon, Iraq, Israel, Jordan, and Saudi
Arabia, the Eisenhower administration became convinced that Moscow wanted
Communists to take power in Syria. Eisenhower reaffirmed his Middle East
doctrine and took action to prevent Russian subversion. With assurances of
help from the United States, forces of Turkey, Iraq, Jordan, and Lebanon
massed around Syria's borders. U.S. air forces were sent to a base in Adana,
Turkey, and the Strategic Air Command was placed on alert. The U.S. Sixth
Fleet proceeded to the Eastern Mediterranean.
     Whether or not Eisenhower overreacted to the Syrian situation is not
certain. Following the preparations in territory surrounding Syria, the
United Nations undertook to calm the affair. Of the nations which sent forces
to Syria's borders, only Turkey desired to intervene. Arguments in the United
Nations thoroughly aired charges and countercharges but mediation efforts
were rejected. Finally, King Saud informed Washington that the crisis was
not necessary. By October 31, the dispute faded. Russia had gained influence
in Syria but no Communist takeover was attempted in Damascus.

October 5, 1957   *"SPUTNIK" BECOMES THE FIRST ARTIFICIAL EARTH SATELLITE.*

*The Soviet Union fired Sputnik into an earth orbit by which it circled the
world at 18,000 miles per hour. A second satellite, "Sputnik II," was
launched on November 3, carrying a live dog aboard for experimental purposes.*

October 23-25, 1957   BRITISH PRIME MINISTER MACMILLAN VISITS WASHINGTON TO
                         DISCUSS THE CONSEQUENCES OF RUSSIA'S "SPUTNIK" LAUNCH-
                         ING.

Following the October 17-20 visit of Queen Elizabeth II to Washington, this
session helped to reestablish the "special relationship" between England and
America which had become part of U.S. policy since 1941.

October 26, 1957   *POLITICAL TROUBLES IN GUATEMALA FOLLOW THE ASSASSINA-*
                          TION OF PRESIDENT CASTILLO ARMAS (JULY 26) AND THE
                          ELECTION (OCTOBER 20) OF MIGUEL ORTIZ PASSARELLI.

On October 26, a military junta annulled the election and installed GUILLERMO
FLORES AVENDANO as interim president. On March 2, 1958, General MIGUEL
YDIGURAS FUENTES was elected and installed as president for six years.

November 7, 1957   THE GAITHER REPORT IS PRESENTED TO THE NATIONAL SECUR-
                          ITY COUNCIL.

Based on a series of studies in the summer of 1957 by a group of private citizens chaired by H. Rowen Gaither, the report went beyond its purpose of
studying shelter programs in civil defense to comment on the entire U.S. defense posture. The Gaither Committee claimed the U.S. strategic air force
was highly vulnerable to Soviet Intercontinental Ballistic Missiles (ICBM's),
making the American population critically vulnerable. It advocated a build
up of U.S. strategic offensive weapons by diversifying missile bases and increasing the U.S. forces for conventional war. The committee did not believe
bomb shelter programs should be given much priority.

November 7, 1957   EISENHOWER BEGINS A SERIES OF "CONFIDENCE" SPEECHES
                          TO REASSURE THE NATION THAT U.S. DEFENSES ARE EXCELLENT
                          AND CAPABLE OF COUNTERING ANY SOVIET THREAT.

The launching of SPUTNIK by the Russians in October and the rise of critics
of the "new look" policies in congress, the army, and the navy caused Eisenhower to better inform the public about U.S. force capabilities and the value
of his "long-haul" defense policy related to sustaining a prosperous U.S. economy. See October 30, 1953, and December 17, 1957.
     Between October, 1957, and the end of his second term of office, Eisen-
hower's massive-retaliation policy with a cost-effective defense program was
disputed by former Army Chief of Staff Maxwell Taylor; Senators Lyndon
Johnson, John F. Kennedy, and Stuart Symington; and academic commentators
Henry Kissinger and Herman Kahn. These and others argued that the United
States needed "flexible response" forces, which required a large army and
navy as well as strategic and tactical nuclear forces and would necessitate
a huge defense budget, far beyond the budget needs Eisenhower believed necessary.
     By 1960, the "new look" critics also raised the issue of a "missile-gap"
which asserted that the Soviet Union would soon gain superiority over America
in missiles. Eisenhower denied the missile-gap theory but the concept continued to be advocated by John F. Kennedy and his supporters through the election of 1960. Later, early in 1961, Kennedy's Secretary of Defense would
admit that Eisenhower had been correct; *there was no missile-gap.*
     Nevertheless, in congress and among many persons concerned about U.S.
defense, both the "flexible response" policy and the "missile-gap" were concepts which opposed Eisenhower's "long-haul," economy-concerned, "new look"
program.

November 7, 1957   *SPEAKING ON THE 40TH ANNIVERSARY OF THE 1917 REVOLUTION*
                            IN MOSCOW, MAO TSE-TUNG PROVIDES AN OVERT INDICATION
                            OF THE DIVISIONS BETWEEN PEKING AND MOSCOW WHICH EVEN-
                            TUALLY LEAD TO THE SINO-SOVIET SPLIT.

*Mao stated that the international situation was at a turning point because
"There are two winds in the world today: the East wind and the West wind."
In addition, he said that "I think the characteristic of the situation
today is the East wind prevailing over the West wind." Mao was urging strong
Communist backing for revolution in the former Asian-African colonial attempts
to become free from Western control. He believed the Chinese victory in 1949
demonstrated the proper tactics to use in the emerging nations and criticized
Khrushchev for his program of "peaceful coexistence" with capitalism.
     During 1958, the differences became more emphatic. Mao began the "Great
Leap Forward" program in China, a program forcing collectivization of land
into communes and indoctrinating peasants with Communist ideas. The Russians
insisted on heavy industry first, and preferred to seek mass support from the
people as only a secondary part of their Communist-Bolshevik ideology.
     Mao, of course, was also striving to devise unique Chinese Communist
programs that would be aided but not controlled by the Soviet Union.*

November 14, 1957   *EAST AND WEST GERMANY SIGN A $260 MILLION TRADE AGREE-*
                            MENT FOR 1958.

November 15, 1957   PORTUGAL EXTENDS THE U.S.-AZORES ISLAND DEFENSE PACT
                            TO 1962.

The original pact was made in 1951.

December 5, 1957   *PRESIDENT SUKARNO OF INDONESIA EXPELS ALL DUTCH NA-*
                            TIONALS FROM THE COUNTRY.

*Throughout the previous three years, Sukarno's government had had political
problems with the Netherlands; with rebels in parts of his country such as
the Celebes and Borneo; and with competing political groups in Jakarta.
     To help resolve the economic costs of these constant problems, Sukarno
had repudiated $1 billion of debts to the Netherlands (August 4, 1956) and
received a loan from the Soviet Union of $100 million (September 15, 1956).
     The immediate 1957 dispute with the Netherlands focused on the continued
occupation of West New Guinea by the Dutch. On October 28, 1957, Sukarno
threatened to seize West New Guinea if the United Nations failed to solve
the issue. Finally, in December, Sukarno protested against the Dutch by a
24-hour strike (December 1) and a decree to expel Dutch Nationals. Indo-
nesians' problems had not been resolved by 1958, but the United States was
concerned about Soviet influence in the islands through its loans to Sukarno
and the privileges given to the Indonesian Communist Party. Sukarno had been
trying to secure support of all parties in the islands but had trouble bringing Communists and moderate national groups to agree on policy.*

December 17, 1957   THE FIRST SUCCESSFUL TEST OF AMERICA'S INTERCONTINENTAL BALLISTIC MISSILE, *ATLAS*, IS MADE.

The Air Force program for the ICBM began on July 27, 1955. On November 28, 1958, the Series B-ATLAS missile performed a full-range test of 5,506 nautical miles.

The American intermediate range missile, THOR, had its first successful flight on September 20, 1957.

December 19, 1957   NATO MEMBERS CONCLUDE THEIR PARIS MEETING.

The session indicated the European concern about recent Russian technical developments. A major issue among the delegates centered on the American desire for missile bases in Europe and the Europeans' desire for the United States to pursue disarmament talks. The issue resulted in compromise; the EUROPEANS AGREED TO ACCEPT U.S. INTERMEDIATE RANGE MISSILE BASES, and the United States said it would discuss any "reasonable proposal" for "comprehensive and controlled disarmament." This dual-related issue constantly reappeared at NATO meetings during future sessions.

In 1957, NATO described the deployment of IRBM's as a temporary measure to deter Russia until American ICBM's became operational from U.S. bases. NATO also indicated that missile deployment was subject to American agreement with the countries where missiles were based. Only Great Britain, Italy, and Turkey accepted the U.S. offer to permit missile bases in their countries.

A large part of the difficulty in persuading NATO allies to permit U.S. missile bases was the American desire to keep monopoly control of atomic weapons. As an anonymous French general told a reporter in November, 1957, the risk of the absolute weapon was too grave to allow "a single one of the allies the monopoly of a retaliation which in the hour of danger, could be neutralized by the enemy or by the opposition of its own press or public opinion." Although Eisenhower wanted to cooperate further with the allies in nuclear plans and control, congress and the Joint Committee on Atomic Energy would not permit him to share U.S. "secrets." The U.S. distrust of Europeans as indicated by this unwillingness to share responsibility for nuclear decisions became a persistent point of dispute in NATO.

1958

January 23, 1958   *IN VENEZUELA, PRESIDENT PEREZ JIMENEZ IS OVERTHROWN*
                        BY A MILITARY JUNTA LED BY ADMIRAL WOLFGANG LARRAZABAL.

Jimenez had been named provisional president by the national assembly on Jan-
uary 9, 1954, after several years of political conflict. He was empowered
to rule until "constitutional government is reestablished." The new consti-
tution required three years to prepare, but after its approval Jimenez can-
celled the elections scheduled for December 15, 1957. Subsequently, a revolt
broke out against Jimenez on December 31, leading to the military takeover
on January 23.
*   At the time of Vice-President Richard Nixon's visit in May, 1958, Vene-*
zuela's political difficulties were still in transition with future political
control under dispute. A new constitution was adopted later in 1958 and on
December 7, ROMULO BETANCOURT was elected president, taking office on February
13, 1959. Also see April 28-May 14, 1958.

January 27, 1958   THE UNITED STATES AND THE SOVIET UNION SIGN A CULTURAL
                        EXCHANGE AGREEMENT.

This pact provided for visits by educators, technicians, sports teams, and
musicians on a mutual interchange basis.

January 31, 1958   THE FIRST U.S. EARTH SATELLITE, EXPLORER I, IS PLACED
                        IN ORBIT BY A MODIFIED JUPITER-C ROCKET.

This began a series of experiments in the next two years with U.S. earth satellites known as Explorer, Vanguard, Discoverer, Tiros, Nimbus, and Essa.

February 1, 1958   *THE UNITED ARAB REPUBLIC (UAR) IS FORMED IN A PROCLA-*
                        MATION OF EGYPT'S PRESIDENT NASSER AND SYRIAN PRESIDENT
                        SHUKRI AL-KUWATLY.

Nasser apparently hoped other Arab nations would join the UAR, meeting the
Arab world's most important need: Arab unity. Nasser's dream was not real-
ized, however. Only YEMEN agreed to associate itself with the UAR (March 8,
1958). By September 29, 1961, the UAR broke up when Syria withdrew from the
pact.

February 22, 1958   THE UNITED STATES AGREES TO SUPPLY ENGLAND WITH 60
                       "THOR" INTERMEDIATE RANGE MISSILES CAPABLE OF CARRYING
                       ATOMIC WARHEADS.

This was an essential follow up to the October, 1957, meeting between
Macmillan and Eisenhower which reviewed the effect of SPUTNIK on Western defense capabilities.

February 22, 1958   *ARTURO FRONDIZI IS ELECTED PRESIDENT OF ARGENTINA,*
                       TAKING OFFICE ON MAY 1, 1958.

After the overthrow of Peron in 1955, a provisional government ruled, first
under Lonardi, but then, following a November 13, 1955, coup, under General
PEDRO ARAMBURU.
   In 1957, a constituent assembly voted to restore the Constitution of
1853. Frondizi was selected under this constitution.

March 27, 1958   THE UNITED STATES ANNOUNCES A SPACE FLIGHT PROGRAM IS
                       HEADED FOR THE MOON.

Secretary of Defense Neil McElroy reported the president's approval for a
program to explore space in order to "obtain useful data concerning the moon,
and to provide a close look at the moon." Officially, the exploratory "PIO-
NEER-RANGER" programs would be part of the U.S. contribution to the International Geophysical Year.
   Although John F. Kennedy later publicized the "race to the moon" featur-
ing a human landing, the PIONEER-RANGER PROGRAM, which started in 1958, provided essential data on moon-landing sites. It also proposed to counter the
Soviet SPUTNIK feat of October, 1957, by promoting U.S. space technology.
   Unfortunately, the Pioneer program's initial rocket launchings failed
on August 17, October 11, November 8, and December 6, 1958. Pioneer 4 made
a successful fly-by the moon on March 3, 1959. On January 2, 1959, the Soviets beat the United States by successfully flying LUNA I by the moon; and
on September 12, 1959, the Soviet's LUNA 2 impacted on the moon.
   Not until July 28, 1964, did a U.S. moon shot begin to surpass the Soviets' achievements. Ranger 7, using television, returned the first high-
resolution pictures of lunar mare, which was the basic objective of the Ranger
program as a prelude to the manned Apollo flights. The first clear Russian
pictures were transmitted from the moon on July 18, 1965, with the flight of
Zond 7.

March 27, 1958   *NIKITA S. KHRUSHCHEV BECOMES PREMIER AS WELL AS HEAD*
                       OF THE PARTY IN THE SOVIET UNION.

In replacing Bulganin as premier, Khrushchev demonstrated he had gained firm
control of the central party organization. According to Western Soviet-
watchers, Khrushchev had nearly lost his position in June, 1957. The Com-
munist Party Presidium sought to dismiss him in favor of Bulganin and old
Stalinists such as Molotov, Malenkov, and Kaganovich. By appealing to the
whole Central committee, Khrushchev saved his power because the Central Com-
mittee reversed the Presidium decision. This enabled Khrushchev to remove

*Molotov and his other opponents and in March, 1958, to get rid of Bulganin
as well.*

April 28-May 14, 1958   VICE-PRESIDENT NIXON EXPERIENCES INTENSE ANTI-
AMERICAN FEELINGS WHILE TOURING LATIN AMERICA.

In some cities, mobs hurled eggs and stones at Nixon. On May 13, in Caracas,
mobs attacked his limousine, nearly overturning the car before the vice-
president escaped.

These events awakened some Americans to the fact that U.S. assistance
went to other parts of the world but neglected its neighbors' economic problems. Between 1945 and 1960, for example, the United States gave three times
more aid to the Benelux countries than to all 20 Latin American countries.
U.S. private capital investment continued, but these funds increased the im-
balance of the Latin American economies because they profited citizens of
the United States.

Nixon's experience led the Eisenhower administration to reconsider its
Latin American policy. In December, 1959, an Inter-American Development Bank
was established with $1 billion to channel low-interest development loans to
Latin American nations. In September, 1960, a meeting at Bogota made long-
range economic aid plans designed to benefit Latin America's economic growth.

May 31, 1958   *GENERAL CHARLES DE GAULLE HEADS AN EMERGENCY GOVERNMENT
AND BEGINS TO ORGANIZE A NEW FRENCH CONSTITUTION.*

*Since the National Assembly's "no confidence" vote in MENDES-FRANCE'S Cabinet
in February, 1955, France had experienced a succession of coalition governments that failed to resolve the nation's economic problems or the rebellion
in Algeria. The assembly's reform bill on January 31 was rejected by Algeria's nationalists and a full-scale civil war threatened to begin.*

*On May 31, 1958, President René Coty named de Gaulle as premier, and on
June 1, the assembly voted him emergency powers by 329-244.*

*On September 28, 1958, the CONSTITUTION OF THE FIFTH REPUBLIC was ap-
proved, and following elections (November 23 and 30), de Gaulle became president of the Fifth Republic.*

June 13, 1958   SIX NATIONS AGREE TO DISCUSS TECHNICAL PROBLEMS OF
NUCLEAR TEST DETECTION AT GENEVA.

The participants were the United States, Great Britain, the Soviet Union,
France, Poland, and Czechoslovakia.

Two months later a panel of scientific experts concurred in a report
that it was technically feasible to build a system to detect violations of a
nuclear test ban.

July 10, 1958   *CAMBODIAN PREMIER PRINCE NORODUM SIHANOUK GRANTS REC-
OGNITION TO THE CHINESE COMMUNIST REGIME.*

*Sihanouk's action indicated his desire to be neutral in the cold war between
communism and capitalism by following other neutralists who de facto*

recognized Mao Tse-tung's government.

The recognition of China was one of Prince Sihanouk's earliest acts after gaining control of the Cambodian government. On March 23, 1958, his Communist-Socialist Party won all 61 seats in the national assembly. While the prince now ruled as prime minister, his father, NORODOM SURAMARIT, was king. On June 5, 1960, on the death of his father, Prince Sihanouk became chief of state after a nationwide referendum voted approval.

Prince Sihanouk was not a Communist, although his party's name confused most Americans. His main goal was to keep Cambodia independent by following a neutralist foreign policy.

July 14, 1958   *IN IRAQ, AN ARMY COUP LED BY GENERAL ABDUL KARIM AL-KASSEM ASSASSINATES KING FAISAL II AND PROCLAIMS A REPUBLIC.*

Soon after, the new government met with representatives of the UNITED ARAB REPUBLIC to announce that the UAR and IRAQ "stood together as one nation."

July 15, 1958   AMERICAN FORCES INTERVENE IN LEBANON AS 1,400 U.S. MARINES LAND ON THE BEACHES NEAR BEIRUT.

Lebanon's President, CAMILLE CHAMOUN, requested U.S. help because he feared possible intervention by President Nasser's United Arab Republic (Egypt and Syria).

Lebanon's political system had for some time hinged on cooperation of the three competing religious factions--Christians, Moslems, and Druze. This precarious triad of power was disrupted in 1958 as street fights and riots advocated a new political alignment. Christian Lebanese such as President Chamoun believed that the UAR had incited the Moslem population to oppose the existing regime. On June 6, Lebanon's Foreign Minister, Charles Malik, asked the U.N. Security Council to halt the aggression of the UAR. On June 11, U.S. observers were sent to Beirut. As more Arab pressure grew, President Chamoun feared a civil war. He asked Eisenhower for assistance.

Washington responded quickly. On July 15, the U.S. forces landed but met no resistance. They remained until October 25, after a political compromise was again renewed in Beirut. The Lebanese parliament chose General Faud Chehab as president and approved a cabinet of four Christians, four Moslems, and one Druze. Meanwhile, Lebanon's neighboring Arab nations promised not to interfere in Lebanon's internal affairs.

Eisenhower demonstrated that the United States could intervene in the Middle East with its Sixth Naval Fleet if necessary. Critics charged that the president acted in haste and that Dulles incorrectly blamed the Communists for difficulties in Lebanon and the Middle East in general.

July 26, 1958   *THE RUMANIAN GOVERNMENT ANNOUNCES THE WITHDRAWAL OF ALL SOVIET OCCUPATION FORCES.*

This did not end Russian influence in Bucharest but gave the Rumanians more political latitude without the disrupting riots that occurred in Hungary and Poland.

August 3, 1958   THE U.S.S. *NAUTILUS*, AMERICA'S FIRST NUCLEAR-POWERED
                  SUBMARINE, COMPLETES AN UNDERSEA CROSSING OF THE NORTH
                  POLE.

August 13, 1958   PRESIDENT EISENHOWER OUTLINES A NEW U.S. POLICY TOWARD
                  THE MIDDLE EAST WHICH RECOGNIZES ARAB NATIONALISM AND
                  ENDS THE TENDENCY TO VIEW THE AREA IN COLD WAR TERMS.

On August 13, Eisenhower's speech at the United Nations suggested a new attitude toward the Middle East. Rather than think simply in terms of extending
aid committing the Arab states to anti-communism as the Eisenhower Doctrine
implied, the president recognized "positive neutralism" as a factor in the
Middle East.

As a consequence of his new approach, Eisenhower agreed to send wheat
to Egypt in 1959 and to deal even-handedly with Arabs and Israelis. Some
historians discount the concept that Eisenhower began this new approach, at-
tributing it to President Kennedy.

August 23, 1958   CHINESE COMMUNISTS' ARTILLERY ON THE MAINLAND BEGINS
                  A HEAVY BOMBARDMENT OF THE OFF-SHORE ISLANDS OF QUEMOY
                  AND LITTLE QUEMOY, WHICH CHIANG KAI-SHEK'S GOVERNMENT
                  OCCUPIED.

Initial fighting for these off-shore islands began in 1955. On February 5,
1955, the U.S. Seventh Fleet had evacuated Nationalist Chinese from TACHEN
Islands, but Chiang's government announced on February 25 that it would retreat no further.

The bombardment of Quemoy in 1958 did not seem to be preceding Communist
invasion. Commentators believed it was intended to show Mao's hard-line policy and, perhaps, his desire to entice Washington to threaten or bomb China,
thereby forcing Moscow to aid Peking. Whatever China's reasons, Eisenhower
and Dulles decided to permit the Seventh Fleet to escort Nationalist troops
and supplies to Quemoy. The new supplies included eight-inch howitzers capable of firing tactical nuclear shells. Washington also reinforced the
Seventh Fleet with an aircraft carrier and four destroyers.

Before sending supplies to Quemoy, Secretary Dulles declared American
forces would aid the defense of Quemoy and nearby Matsu Islands (September 4).
As a result, the Chinese Communists did not fire on the Seventh Fleet escort
of supply ships (September 7). In order to settle the off-shore island dispute, the United States and Communist China began ambassadorial discussion
of the Taiwan issue in Warsaw, Poland (September 15, 1957).

The issue was not fully resolved, however. On October 20, the Chinese
Communists again resumed shelling of Quemoy. Subsequently, Chinese shelling
was sporadic over the next decade, with Peking and Taiwan continuing to dispute the status of the off-shore islands. The 1958 Quemoy crisis abated by
November, however. See October 23, 1958.

August 26, 1958   PRESIDENT EISENHOWER BEGINS A 12-DAY VISIT TO GERMANY,
                  FRANCE, AND BRITAIN.

The good-will visit was designed to reassure American allies of the U.S.

desire and ability to protect western Europe. Since the Geneva Conference
of 1955, Britain and France complained that Washington did not understand
their economic and defense problems. Dulles often used little tact with the
Europeans; Eisenhower, it was hoped, would be more capable of gaining continued support and good will in the NATO organization and its member nations.

September 2, 1958   EISENHOWER SIGNS THE NATIONAL DEFENSE EDUCATION ACT.

Enacted largely in reaction to the fear of Soviet leadership in science and
technology, this bill provided loans to college students, grants for science
and foreign-language instruction, and graduate school fellowships for students
preparing to teach.

September 28, 1958   *FRANCE ESTABLISHES THE FRENCH COMMUNITY FOR ITS OVER-
                            SEAS TERRITORY.*

*Each former colonial state could join the community, vote for complete inde-
pendence from France, or remain as an overseas territory of France. Only
FRENCH SOMALILAND chose to remain a territory. Other former French colonies
opted for independence or very loose ties to the French community. These
included: Guinea, Senegal, Mauritania, Dahomey, Voltaic, Niger, Mali, Chad,
Togo, Ivory Coast, Cameroun, Congo (Brazzaville), Gabor, Malagasy, and the
Central African Republic.*

October 7, 1958   *A COUP IN PAKISTAN ANNULS THE REPUBLICAN CONSTITUTION
                           OF 1956, LEADING TO MILITARY CONTROL BY GENERAL
                           MOHAMMED AYUB KHAN ON OCTOBER 30, 1958.*

October 23, 1958   *THE SOVIET UNION AGREES TO LOAN EGYPT $100 MILLION
                           TOWARD BUILDING THE ASWAN DAM.*

Construction was scheduled to start on January 1, 1959.

October 23, 1958   AFTER CONCLUDING TALKS IN FORMOSA WITH SECRETARY OF
                           STATE DULLES, CHIANG KAI-SHEK ANNOUNCES HIS GOVERNMENT
                           WILL NOT USE FORCE TO RETURN TO MAINLAND CHINA; THE
                           SECOND QUEMOY-MATSU CRISIS ENDS.

In August, the Chinese Communists renewed their shelling of the off-shore
islands which they had begun in 1955 (see August 23, 1958). Because of U.S.-
Red Chinese talks in Warsaw and the British desire that the United States
should settle the Taiwan Straits issue, Secretary of State Dulles visited
Chiang from October 20 to 23 to have a candid discussion on U.S.-Nationalist
Chinese relations. Both Dulles and President Eisenhower believed changed
circumstances since 1955 required new policies by Chiang. The United States
was Chiang's only vigorous ally but could not overlook other American allies'
concern about Chiang forcing the United States to war over a less-vital interest. World opinion, Dulles said, required Chiang to end his civil war
attitude toward Red China. Therefore, Dulles told Chiang to call for an

armistice on existing lines--a two-China policy. The Nationalists should
stop commando raids on China and neutralize Quemoy and Matsu.

Whether Chiang fully understood the new circumstances Dulles described
is a moot question. At the end of the talks on October 23, Dulles stated
the United States would continue to recognize Chiang's regime; the Nationalists stated they would not attempt to return to the Asian mainland by force
and they would reduce their forces on Quemoy and Matsu.

This communique ended the 1958 crisis because the Peking government
stopped bombing the off-shore islands. It did not finally settle all problems, however. On October 31, the State Department revealed that Chiang had
reserved the right to use force if there were a large-scale anti-Communist
uprising on the mainland. On October 7, 1959, Undersecretary of State Douglas
Dillon stated that Mao would risk "total war" if he attacked Taiwan or the
off-shore islands.

October 31, 1958   CONFERENCE ON A NUCLEAR TEST BAN OPENS AT GENEVA BE-
                            TWEEN DELEGATES OF THE UNITED STATES, BRITAIN, AND THE
                            SOVIET UNION.

During the 1950's, the testing of nuclear weapons caused radioactive particles
to travel around the world's atmosphere, and some scientists deplored the
present and future hazards of such radioactive rain.

In March, the U.S.S.R., Britain, and the United States each announced
unilaterally that they would suspend nuclear tests, reserving the right to
renew tests if other nations did so.

The October, 1958, sessions opened with optimism but no agreements were
accepted during the next two years. The discussion did provide a foundation
for more successful talks in the 1960's. See August 5, 1963.

November 4, 1958   THE DEMOCRATS ENLARGE THEIR CONTROL OF CONGRESS IN
                            NATIONAL ELECTIONS; THEIR SENATE MAJORITY BECOMES 64
                            TO 34; THE HOUSE MAJORITY, 283 TO 153.

November 10, 1958   KHRUSHCHEV DEMANDS THAT WESTERN FORCES LEAVE WEST BER-
                            LIN, MAKING IT A "FREE CITY."

The Soviet premier wanted to give East Germany control over access to Berlin,
requiring that the United States recognize the East German regime. The NATO
allies held fast, however, asserting that they would use military force if
necessary to retain their rights in Berlin. The unity of NATO in support of
the American stand caused Khrushchev to back down. He did not carry out his
threat to give East Germany such controls, but continued to seek some means
to end the Berlin occupation by the Western powers.

On November 27, Khrushchev sent a note to the Western powers declaring
the Soviet intention of signing a peace treaty with East Germany if a negotiated agreement on Berlin could not be achieved. He gave the Western nations
six months, indicating that by May 27 the allies should settle the German
problems with Russia. See December 14, 1958, and May 11, 1959.

December 14, 1958   THE U.S., BRITISH, AND FRENCH FOREIGN MINISTERS RE-
                          ASSERT THEIR RIGHTS AND DUTIES IN BERLIN.

On November 27, Soviet Premier Khrushchev asserted that the four-power occupation of Berlin should end and the city should be demilitarized. The foreign
ministers of the three Western powers rejected the Soviet demand, but requested talks with the U.S.S.R. on Berlin in the context of German unity and
European security (December 31).

December 28, 1958   A STATE DEPARTMENT MEMO ON CUBA OUTLINES THE NEED TO
                          REMOVE BATISTA FOR A CENTRIST PARTY PROPONENT.

In 1958, the struggle between Batista and Fidel Castro's rebels in Cuba began
to cause difficulties. Batista's repression and corruption led the State
Department to prefer that he resign in favor of another moderate leader but
no method to achieve this could be found. Although some U.S. writers such
as Jules Dubois of the *Chicago Tribune* liked Castro's reform proposals, U.S.
diplomats disliked his anti-Americanism and left-wing associates. The report
of December 28 indicated that there were Communists in Castro's camp but that
the rebels did not appear to be dominated by Communists.
    Thus, the report principally outlined the U.S. dilemma: how to get a
moderate reform leader in Cuba. Some Latin American nations assisted in the
search for a moderate to replace Batista, but no solution was found. By early
January, Castro gained power. See January 1, 1959.

1959

January 1, 1959   *CUBAN PRESIDENT BATISTA RESIGNS AFTER FIDEL CASTRO'S FORCES CAPTURE SANTA CLARA (DECEMBER 31, 1958).*

Castro's forces marched on Santiago and Havana, giving Castro control of all of Cuba by January 3.

January 3, 1959   ALASKA BECOMES THE 49th STATE AFTER EISENHOWER SIGNS FINAL DOCUMENTS OF APPROVAL.

January 19, 1959   THE UNITED STATES REJECTS A RUSSIAN REQUEST TO LOWER U.S.-U.S.S.R. TRADE BARRIERS.

This request came during a two-week Washington visit by the Soviet First Deputy Premier ANASTAS I. MIKOYAN.

January 27-February 5, 1959   *AT THE 21ST COMMUNIST PARTY CONGRESS, KHRUSHCHEV CLARIFIES SEVERAL OF HIS IDEAS ON "PEACEFUL COEXISTENCE."*

Two basic parts of Khrushchev's strategy for "Peaceful Coexistence" with capitalism were: (1) a declaration that war between Socialist and capitalist states was not inevitable. In Khrushchev's view, the Soviets were young and would grow in strength; the Western capitalists were old, becoming weaker, and would collapse as wars of national liberation damaged their imperial-based economy; (2) a proposal to construct an atom-free zone in the Far East and the entire Pacific Ocean. This would preserve the continuance of two real superpowers, preventing China and Japan from developing nuclear weapons. The premier warned that without such an agreement, the Soviets would continue to mass produce their ICBM's which gave them a lead in nuclear weapons.

The 21st Congress also disclosed new rifts in Moscow's relations with Tito's Yugoslavia. The Communists declared their united opposition to Tito's revisionist methods.

February 19-20, 1959   PRESIDENT EISENHOWER AND MEXICAN PRESIDENT ADOLFO LOPEZ MATEOS CONFER AT ACAPULCO.

They agreed on construction of the Diablo Dam to enhance U.S.-Mexican economic collaboration.

March 2, 1959   SERIOUS ANTI-AMERICAN RIOTS BEGIN IN BOLIVIA.

Although there were reports of at least 14 anti-American demonstrations in Latin American nations during 1959, the most serious was in La Paz, Bolivia. It resulted when *Time* magazine's Latin American edition published the story that a U.S. embassy officer in Bolivia had said that the way to solve Bolivia's economic problem was for "her neighbors to divide up the country and the problems."

For three days, rioters in La Paz and other cities shouted anti-Yankee slogans, attacked U.S.-owned buildings, and burned American flags. American citizens had to be gathered together for protection by police, and the State Department considered evacuating all Americans.

The riots finally ended. To calm things, Secretary Herter informed the Bolivian ambassador that he could not believe the reported statement was correct. *Time* would not retract its report but printed a story which said the "jest" was a quip which both Bolivians and foreigners had repeated for many years.

Together with Vice-President Nixon's experiences during his Latin American tour of April 27 to May 15, 1958, the Bolivian riots indicated poor U.S. relations in Latin America.

March 5, 1959   THE UNITED STATES SIGNS BILATERAL DEFENSE PACTS WITH
                           IRAN, PAKISTAN, AND TURKEY.

The death of King Faisal of Iraq during the military coup which brought General Abdul Karin al-Kassem to power in Iraq led to Iraq's proposed withdrawal from the Baghdad pact, which was formalized on March 24, 1959. To replace this alliance the United States undertook separate treaties with the states along the southern border of the Soviet Union. Soon after forming the alliance with Turkey, the United States obtained permission to establish Intermediate Range Ballistic Missile bases in Turkey.

After the Baghdad pact ended, the alliance, without Iraq, was recreated as the Central Treaty Organization (CENTO). The United States did not join the pact but supported its objectives.

March 31, 1959   *COMMUNIST CHINA COMPLETES ITS POLITICAL TAKE-OVER OF*
                           TIBET.

Fighting between Communists and the populace of Tibet began on March 13, 1959, following Chinese infiltration of this small Himalayan country. The Chinese had always claimed sovereignty over Tibet and began actively to seek control in 1956 when they concluded a treaty with Nepal (September 24, 1956) which surrendered Nepalese rights to the area in recognition of Chinese sovereignty.

The Tibetans stood little chance against Chinese forces and on March 28, 1959, China's Premier CHOU EN-LAI declared the Tibetan government of the Dalai Lama dissolved, so that a new government for the Tibetan autonomous region could be organized. The Communists gained full control when the Dalai Lama fled to India on March 31.

April 15, 1959   CUBA'S PRESIDENT, FIDEL CASTRO, VISITS WASHINGTON,
                         WHERE HE DECLARES HIS REGIME IS "HUMANISTIC" BUT NOT
                         COMMUNIST.

Nevertheless, talks with the Americans about his desired reforms soon caused
U.S. opposition. Castro wanted national control over the Cuban economy which
heretofore was manipulated by Americans who owned 80% of Cuba's utilities,
40% of its sugar, and 90% of the mining wealth. Washington also controlled
how much Cuban sugar could enter the U.S. market.
     Although Castro's arbitrary arrests and executions of his opponents in
January and February alarmed some of his U.S. followers, his April visit generally left many believing he was a moderate.
     During a three-week period, Castro had executed 250 Cubans and many oth-
ers had been threatened with imprisonment. The United States had, however,
sent a new ambassador to Havana, Philip Bonsal, on January 19 and recognized
Castro's government. In addition, Castro's demands for U.S. economic and
sugar quotas, as well as his promise to pay for any expropriated property in
Cuba, caused his moderate image to be again projected during April, 1959.
See June 4, 1959.

April 22, 1959   CHRISTIAN A. HERTER REPLACES JOHN FOSTER DULLES AS
                         SECRETARY OF STATE.

Mr. Dulles had been suffering from cancer for several years, having had emergency surgery in November, 1956, during the height of the Suez Crisis. Dulles
died on May 24, 1959.
     Herter had extensive experience to qualify him as Secretary of State.
He had served on the U.S. Peace Commission at Paris in 1918-1919 and as
Herbert Hoover's personal assistant in the Commerce Department to 1924. He
was elected a representative from Massachusetts in congress from 1943 to 1953
and was on the House Select Committee for the Marshall Plan. Prior to becoming secretary, he served as the Undersecretary of State from 1957 to 1959.
He served as secretary until January 20, 1961.

May 11, 1959   A FOREIGN MINISTERS MEETING CONVENES IN GENEVA TO SET-
                        TLE THE GERMAN AND BERLIN PROBLEMS.

This conference evolved from the Soviet Union's November 27, 1958, ultimatum
by which Khrushchev threatened to sign a separate peace treaty with East Germany if the four powers did not resolve their disputes over the German treaty
by May 27, 1959.
     The three Western powers took a firm stand in backing up their continued
rights in Germany and Berlin under the Potsdam Accords of 1945 (see December
14, 1958). President Eisenhower explained to the British and French that
while doing everything possible to avoid confrontation with Russia, the Western nations could not yield to their demands. While U.S. conventional forces
in Europe were not adequate to protect West Berlin, Eisenhower remained ambiguous about what he would order if the Russians did not agree to negotiate.
As in the case of Quemoy and Matsu in 1955, the president said he would make
a decision on Berlin when he saw exactly what the Russians did.
     Britain's Foreign Minister, Harold MACMILLAN, desired to avoid a war in
which Russia's IRBM's would obliterate England. Therefore, in March,

Macmillan visited Moscow and learned that Khrushchev would cancel his ultimatum if there were a summit conference on Germany. Eisenhower responded
that the United States could attend a summit meeting only if preliminary talks
showed there would be positive results. The president suggested a foreign
ministers conference at Geneva, and the Russians agreed. This conference
opened on May 11, 1959, but no results were attained during the next three
months. When a deadlock occurred at the Geneva talks, Eisenhower invited
Khrushchev to tour America and have a talk with the president. Khrushchev
accepted the invitation and began a visit to the United States on September
15, 1959.

May 24, 1959   A FIVE-YEAR ANGLO-RUSSIAN TRADE AGREEMENT IS SIGNED
                            IN MOSCOW.

*Unlike the United States, Great Britain and most Western European governments
welcomed Khrushchev's détente and peaceful coexistence overtures, especially
hoping to get new markets for their products. Thus, while Washington rejected
trade agreements (see January 19, 1959), the European nations pursued negotiations with Moscow.*

June 4, 1959   CASTRO'S AGRARIAN REFORM DECREE BECOMES A SIGN OF HIS
                            MORE RADICAL INTENTIONS.

The Cubans had approved land reform legislation on May 17 which Castro put
into operation on June 4. The law abolished all large sugar plantations and
decreed that sugar mill operators could not own sugar-growing operations.
Both foreign and Cuban landowners were affected. They would be paid by Cuban
bonds over a 20-year period at $4\frac{1}{2}\%$ interest. Proceeds from the bonds had to
be reinvested in Cuba and could not be converted into dollars. Finally,
Castro asserted that the property value would be based on the most recent
tax assessment values of the property.
    Obviously, property owners protested. On July 12, the U.S. State Depart-
ment objected to the method of valuation and bond payment and said the action
amounted to confiscation not expropriation of property. Castro denounced all
protests and told television audiences in Cuba that anyone opposing land reform was a traitor. By August, 1959, many of Castro's moderate backers began
to flee to the United States for safety.

June 26, 1959   THE ST. LAWRENCE SEAWAY OPENS OFFICIALLY TO LINK THE
                            GREAT LAKES AND THE ATLANTIC OCEAN.

President Eisenhower and Queen Elizabeth II were present at the official ceremonies.

July 8, 1959   THE UNITED STATES ANNOUNCES THAT 200 AMERICAN PLANES
                            WILL BE MOVED FROM FRANCE TO WEST GERMANY AND GREAT
                            BRITAIN.

French President Charles de Gaulle disagreed with Washington's European defense plans and advocated France's "separate" role in NATO defenses, in preference to an integrated role.

On March 14, U.S.-French defense talks ended in dispute because de Gaulle refused to place one-third of his Mediterranean fleet under NATO as previously arranged. De Gaulle believed French "grandeur" required a separate French nuclear force. He also argued that the United States would not use its nuclear forces to defend Europe and, therefore, France needed its own means to deter and defeat the Soviet Union.

July 24, 1959   "KITCHEN DEBATE" BETWEEN VICE-PRESIDENT RICHARD NIXON AND PREMIER KHRUSHCHEV TAKES PLACE.

Nixon made a good-will visit to the Soviet Union at the time that an American national exhibit opened in Moscow. He and the Soviet premier attended the opening together and visited a model of an American home on display. As they surveyed the technology of a U.S. kitchen, they began an impromptu argument on the virtues of communism and capitalism which the news media highlighted.

August 19, 1959   THE CENTRAL TREATY ORGANIZATION (CENTO) REPLACES THE BAGHDAD PACT.

Because Iraq withdrew from the Baghdad Pact on March 24, CENTO formed to continue the defensive alliance of Turkey, Iran, Pakistan, and Great Britain. As in the case of the Baghdad Pact, the United States supported but did not join the alliance. America's bilateral defense pacts (see March 5, 1959) served the same purpose in the Middle East.

August 21, 1959   HAWAII BECOMES THE 50TH STATE.

September 15, 1959   PREMIER KHRUSHCHEV TOURS THE UNITED STATES.

The Soviet leader visited Washington, the United Nations, Iowa, Los Angeles, and Hollywood's 20th Century-Fox movie studio for the filming of "Can-Can." His request to visit Disneyland was turned down because his security could not be guaranteed.

During his Iowa visit, Khrushchev went to the farm of Roswell Garst who had visited Russia earlier to inform the Soviets of U.S. seed corn growing and pig-raising. On Garst's farm in Coon Rapids, Iowa, as elsewhere during his visit, Khrushchev made a hit with many Americans because of his humor and display of common sense.

On the final three days of his visit, Khrushchev met with President Eisenhower at his Camp David retreat. Their meeting appeared to end cordially and the two leaders agreed to discuss further such pending issues as Germany, Berlin's status, and a nuclear test ban. Over the winter, reporters talked about "the SPIRIT OF CAMP DAVID" as defining better relations between Moscow and Washington.

The Camp David meetings did not accomplish anything specific, but served to diffuse the 1959 tensions over Germany. Khrushchev dropped his previous time limit on negotiations regarding Germany, and Eisenhower agreed to a summit meeting in 1960 without the necessity for successful lower-level agreements preceding the summit.

December 1, 1959   THE UNITED STATES, THE U.S.S.R., AND 10 OTHER NATIONS
                         APPROVE A TREATY TO RESERVE THE ANTARCTIC FOR SCIEN-
                         TIFIC AND PEACEFUL PURPOSES.

December 19-21, 1959   EISENHOWER, DE GAULLE, MACMILLAN, AND ADENAUR CONFER
                         IN PARIS.

They decided to invite Khrushchev to a summit meeting in Paris early in 1960.
The Soviet Premier agreed and a meeting was arranged for May 16, 1960.

December 22, 1959   PRESIDENT EISENHOWER MAKES A GOOD-WILL TOUR OF THREE
                         CONTINENTS, VISITING ITALY, TURKEY, PAKISTAN, AFGHAN-
                         ISTAN, INDIA, IRAN, GREECE, TUNISIA, FRANCE, SPAIN,
                         AND MOROCCO ON A JOURNEY OF 22,370 MILES.

1960

January 19, 1960   THE U.S.-JAPANESE TREATY OF MUTUAL SECURITY (1951) IS
                          RENEWED.

The treaty renewal caused intensive leftist riots in Japan in an effort to
prevent the treaty ratification by the Japanese house of representatives.
Japan's Premier NOBUSUKE KISHI and his Liberal Democratic cabinet held firm,
however, and the treaty was ratified on June 19, 1960 (also see June 12-21,
1960). The treaty continued to permit American military bases on Japanese
soil, which was the principal clause detested by the critics of Kishi's government. See June 12, 1960.

January 28, 1960   *BURMA AND COMMUNIST CHINA SIGN A 10-YEAR NON-AGGRESSION
                          TREATY.*

February 13, 1960   *CUBA AND THE U.S.S.R. SIGN AN ECONOMIC PACT.*

*The Soviets agreed to buy 5 million tons of Cuban sugar and to give Castro
$100 million of Soviet trade credits.*
    *The Russian-Cuban agreement was offered by Anastas MIKOYAN, Deputy Pre-
mier of the Soviet Union, who visited Cuba in February. In addition to the
credits and sugar purchase, the Soviets would provide technical assistance
to build factories in Cuba.*

February 13, 1960   *FRANCE EXPLODES ITS FIRST ATOMIC BOMB IN THE SAHARA
                          REGION OF ALGERIA.*

*This successful test fulfilled President de Gaulle's desire to create an in-
dependent French nuclear capability.*

March 7, 1960   THE UNITED STATES RENEWS DIPLOMATIC RELATIONS WITH
                          BULGARIA AFTER A NINE-YEAR DISRUPTION.

U.S. Minister Edward Page, Jr., arrived in Sofia on March 7.

April 25, 1960   KHRUSHCHEV AGAIN RAISES THE BERLIN ISSUE, ASSERTING
                          THAT A SEPARATE PEACE TREATY WITH EAST GERMANY WOULD
                          END ALLIED RIGHTS IN BERLIN. EISENHOWER REPLIES THAT
                          WESTERN TROOPS WOULD NOT EVACUATE WEST BERLIN.

Throughout 1959, several attempts to resolve the Berlin issue failed. Most

notable was the foreign ministers conference at Geneva between May 11 and
August 5, 1959, which discussed the issues of Berlin, German unification,
and the guarantee of free elections.

In October at Camp David, there was hope that the Khrushchev-Eisenhower
sessions had established a time-table to resolve the Berlin issue. Now, on
the eve of the Geneva conference of May, 1960, Khrushchev again talked in
threatening terms about settling the question unilaterally.

April 27, 1960   IN SOUTH KOREA, SYNGMAN RHEE RESIGNS AS PRESIDENT FOL-
                             LOWING FOUR WEEKS OF DEMONSTRATIONS AGAINST HIS GOV-
                             ERNMENT.

On March 15, RHEE RAN UNOPPOSED AND WAS REELECTED FOR HIS FOURTH FOUR-YEAR
TERM. There had been protests against Rhee's repressive and conservative
administration before the 1960 election, and in March, demonstrators claimed
the election was rigged to favor Rhee's Liberal Party in the assembly ballot-
ting. Before Rhee resigned, his police fired on the rioters, killing 127
people. This caused greater protests against Rhee.

On July 29, an election voted a majority of assembly delegates from John
M. CHANG'S Democratic Party. Within a year, however, the military overthrew
Chang and established a dictatorship (July 3, 1961) under Major General CHUNG
HEE PARK.

May 3, 1960   *THE "OUTER SEVEN" ECONOMIC GROUP FORMS THE EUROPEAN*
                            FREE TRADE ASSOCIATION (EFTA).

Nations surrounding the COMMON MARKET NATIONS had signed the STOCKHOLM TREATY
in 1959, to cooperate in economic trade as a means of counteracting Common
Market policy. The Free Trade group included Great Britain, Sweden, Norway,
Denmark, Switzerland, Austria, and Portugal.

May 5, 1960   THE U-2 INCIDENT BEGINS AFTER KHRUSHCHEV ANNOUNCES
                            THAT A HIGH RECONNAISSANCE AMERICAN AIRPLANE HAS BEEN
                            SHOT DOWN WHILE SPYING OVER SOVIET TERRITORY ON MAY 1,
                            1960.

The incident assumed controversial proportions because after MOSCOW's initial
announcement, the U.S. State Department denied it was a spy plane, saying
that a weather plane may have flown off course in Turkey or Iran. Khrushchev
then produced films taken from the plane and stated that the pilot, FRANCIS
GARY POWERS, had been captured after he parachuted to safety. Powers had
not pulled the destruct mechanism, designed to demolish the aircraft.

Eisenhower stepped in and told newsmen he accepted responsibility for
the incident, but hoped that the Soviets would not use the affair to disrupt
the positive results which could be achieved at the forthcoming PARIS summit
between Khrushchev and the American, British, and French leaders.

Later, the United States disclosed such U-2 flights had been made several
times since 1956 when the air and photo technology became feasible. These
flights gave Eisenhower the secret data on Russian technology to establish
firmly that there was no missile-gap as Kennedy, Johnson, and other U.S. experts alleged from 1957 to 1960. Eisenhower kept the information secret so

that the Soviets could not learn what the photos disclosed. The photos were
not declassified and publicly released until 1975.

The U-2 data, as secret information which the president could not offer
to the public, provides a note of pathos for historians studying the intense
criticism of Eisenhower's defense program and the missile-gap myth which
played such a large role in U.S. politics at that time.

From 1957 to 1960, Lyndon Johnson and John F. Kennedy created an atmosphere of distrust about Eisenhower's alleged complacency in national defense
matters. Even when Eisenhower declared that there was no missile-gap and
the Russians did not have a lead in missile strength, his critics and many
reputable journalists accepted the 1957 Gaither report's findings and the
expert claims of Maxwell Taylor, Henry Kissinger, and others. The release
of the U-2 photos not only could have proved Eisenhower's case but also might
have influenced the critical changes in U.S. defense policy to which Kennedy
became committed before his election and tried, therefore, to carry out after
1961. See November 7, 1957 and February 6, 1961.

May 16, 1960   THE PARIS SUMMIT CONFERENCE IS ABORTED BECAUSE KHRU-
                         SHCHEV DEMANDS THAT EISENHOWER APOLOGIZE FOR THE U-2
                         FLIGHTS.

Eisenhower was willing to cancel future flights but refused to apologize.
Khrushchev walked out of the conference, blaming the United States for preventing peaceful solutions to world problems. Although British Prime Minister
Harold Macmillan tried to heal the differences between Eisenhower and Khrushchev, he could not persuade the Soviet leader to compromise and stay at
the conference.

After the Geneva Conference of 1955, summit sessions became highly publicized and open to television cameras and newsmen. As a result, the Big
Power leaders could not negotiate on the give-and-take basis that is possible
behind closed doors. At the 1960 Paris session, Khrushchev used the TV-news
media to berate the president and to claim great powers for the Soviet Union.
Diplomatic yielding was difficult or impossible in the glare of the public
news media. Summits of the world leaders had, of necessity, become sessions
to ratify previously accepted treaties, not to engage in negotiations, a matter not often understood by journalists and their public.

May 27, 1960   *A MILITARY COUP IN TURKEY OUSTS PREMIER ADNAN MENDERES.*

*The overthrow was led by Lieutenant General JEMAL GURSEL who established a
junta known as the TURKISH NATIONAL UNION, and promised eventually to organize
free elections. The new regime announced its continued support for NATO and
Turkey's U.S. treaties.*

June 5, 1960   PRINCE NORODOM SIHANOUK WINS CONTROL OF CAMBODIA IN
                         A NATIONAL REFERENDUM.

Prince Sihanouk had been elected premier of Cambodia on April 7, 1957, as a
member of the People's Socialist Communist Party. Following the death of
King Norodom Sumarit on April 3, the Prince resigned his office and appealed
to the nation for acceptance of his control of the country without a new

monarch. The referendum of June 5 provided Sihanouk with this authority.
Sihanouk wanted his country to be neutral in the U.S.-Communist dispute in
Southeast Asia, which disturbed many Americans who disliked Sihanouk's Com-
munist Party affiliation.

June 12-21, 1960   PRESIDENT EISENHOWER MAKES A GOOD-WILL TOUR OF THE
                           FAR EAST, VISITING THE PHILIPPINES, TAIWAN, OKINAWA,
                           AND KOREA.

The Far East tour caused difficulty regarding relations with JAPAN. Eisenhower
had scheduled a visit to Tokyo, but anti-American riots escalated to such a
degree that he CANCELLED HIS JAPANESE VISIT. The rioting focused on the January, 1960, renewal of the U.S.-Japanese alliance on terms that left-wing
critics in Japan claimed were not favorable to their nation. Eisenhower's
visit was planned for the week the treaty ratification was being debated in
Japan's house of representatives, a time when the left-wing parties staged
their most violent demonstrations. As a result, Premier Kishi recommended
that the president should not visit Tokyo at that time.

June 27, 1960   COMMUNIST BLOC COUNTRIES WITHDRAW FROM TALKS BY THE
                           10-POWER COMMITTEE ON DISARMAMENT MEETINGS IN GENEVA.

The meeting had begun optimistically on March 15, 1960, but Khrushchev stopped
Communist participation after the U-2 incident damaged his "peaceful coex-
istence" concepts and indicated the United States knew of his weakness in
ICBM missiles despite the premier's public claims of superiority.

June 30, 1960   *BELGIUM GRANTS THE CONGO REPUBLIC FULL INDEPENDENCE*
                           UNDER PRESIDENT JOSEPH KASAVUBU AND PREMIER PATRICE
                           LUMUMBA.

The Belgians decided in 1959, after nationalist demonstrators in the Belgian
Congo demanded independence, to give their colony freedom as soon as possible.
Elections took place in the Congo on December 20, 1959, and the elected Congo
assembly demanded immediate, unconditional independence.
     Within two weeks after gaining separation, the new Congo government faced
dissident groups which wanted tribal or provincial separation from the central
government. The most serious uprising occurred in KATANGA PROVINCE where
dissidents led by MOISE TSHOMBE proclaimed independence for the province.
Tshombe was backed by European and American copper and cobalt mining inter-
ests, desiring to keep control of these vital resources and their investments.
     Because of the problems, Lumumba asked for U.N. aid, and on July 14,
the Security Council voted to send a U.N. force to replace Belgian troops
and attempt to secure peace among the contending factions. U.N. forces and
negotiators led by Secretary General Dag Hammarskjold began a four-year effort
to mediate amid the contending Congolese factions and to secure an orderly
government. While working at this effort, Hammarskjold was killed in an air-
plane crash in the Congo on September 18, 1961.

July 1, 1960   THE SOVIETS SHOOT DOWN AN AMERICAN PLANE OVER THE
                       BERENTS SEA, CLAIMING IT VIOLATED RUSSIAN BORDERS.

The plane was a reconnaissance bomber (RB-47) which the United States contended was on an IGY mission to collect data on electromagnetic activity in
arctic waters. NATO ships and planes had searched the area for two days,
giving it up for lost on June 3.

        Finally, on July 11, Moscow announced that a Soviet fighter plane shot
down the RB-47 as it flew over the territorial waters of Russia, heading for
Archangel. The Soviets captured the two American airmen who survived out of
a crew of six. Moscow said the two rescued men confessed to being on a spy
mission.

        The United States reported that when it last radioed to a Norwegian Air
Force base, the RB-47 was 300 miles outside Soviet territory. Washington
asked for an impartial U.N. investigation of the incident and for return of
the rescued pilots. A U.N. Security Council resolution to conduct an inquiry
was vetoed on July 26 by the Soviet Union. The U.S.S.R. also vetoed a proposal to let Red Cross workers see the two rescued airmen.

July 6, 1960   CONGRESS APPROVES AND EISENHOWER LEVIES CUTS IN CUBA'S
                       SUGAR QUOTA; CASTRO RETALIATES BY NATIONALIZING ALL
                       U.S. PROPERTY IN CUBA.

On March 15, 1960, President Eisenhower asked congress to renew the Cuban
sugar quota, which had given special prices to Cuba since 1934. He also asked
congress to include authority for the president to change the quota if it
was in the national interest. Congress passed this quota law, which Eisenhower signed on July 6, 1960. The only change congress made in Eisenhower's
March request was to permit the president to fix but not increase the sugar
quota until April 1, 1961.

        After signing the law, the president immediately cut Cuba's 1960 quota
by 95% from 700,000 tons to 39,752 tons. While this action constituted economic intervention in Cuba, congress approved the law because Castro's connections with Russia had become apparent since February 13, 1960.

        As soon as Eisenhower announced the sugar cut, Castro retaliated by de-
creeing the Nationalization Law, which applied exclusively to Americans. This
law ordered the seizure of all U.S. property without compensation. The United
States protested this law on July 16, but there was no response from Havana.

        As tensions increased between the United States and Cuba, Khrushchev
added to the difficulties. On July 9, the Soviet leader pledged Russia's
fullest support of Cuba. Soviet rockets, Khrushchev said, could "figuratively
speaking support the Cubans in case of Pentagon aggression."

July 20, 1960   A POLARIS MISSILE IS LAUNCHED FROM A SUBMERGED SUB-
                       MARINE.

This success gave the U.S. Navy a new role in nuclear weapons; the United
States gained a new form of deterrent power because the submarines were mobile
and difficult to detect by the Soviet Union.

August 1, 1960   *THE BREAKUP OF THE FRENCH COMMUNITY BEGINS WHEN THE*
                         REPUBLIC OF DAHOMEY DECLARES INDEPENDENCE.

President de Gaulle had established the French Community on September 28,
1958, as a means of compromising the nationalism of the former French colonies
with some degree of French control and trade. Nationalists in most of these
areas eventually preferred independence. On April 27, Togo, which had been
a U.N. trust territory under French rule, became independent. Dahomey's dec-
laration to be free of the French Community began an exodus of other states.
Former French colonies to gain independence were: Niger (August 3), Voltaic
Republic (August 5), Ivory Coast (August 7), Chad (August 11), Central Africa
(August 13), Gabon (August 17), Senegal (August 20), Sudan, renamed Mali (Sep-
tember 23), and Mauritania (November 28).

August 9, 1960   IN LAOS, A COUP LED BY KONG LE RETURNS SOUVANNA PHOUMA
                         TO POWER AND RESULTS IN TENSIONS BETWEEN RUSSIA AND
                         AMERICA.

After the Geneva Accords of 1954 gave Laos independence, international conflict increased over the failure of this state to achieve political order.
The Geneva agreements called for the regrouping of all Communist Pathet Lao
in the two northern provinces of Laos. In 1957, the neutralist Premier
Souvanna Phouma compromised with the Communists and brought his half-brother,
who was a Communist, into the cabinet.
     The compromise failed because Communist election gains in 1958 threatened
a left-wing takeover. As a result, civil war began as the extreme right-
and left-wing groups fought. Disliking the turn of events, Premier Souvanna
resigned on July 23, 1958. Pro-Western ruler Phoui Sanaikone took charge of
the government. In October, 1958, Phoui promised to bring economic and political reforms to Laos and the United States provided about $25 million of
aid to Laos for 1959.
     During 1959, Phoui complained that Communist guerrilla war had begun in
Laos and appealed to the United Nations to stop the invasion of North Vietnamese in Laos. On September 7, the U.N. Security Council sent a subcommittee
to make an "inquiry" in Laos, and in October the subcommittee reported that
the North Vietnamese sent arms and supplies to Laos but that it could not
clearly establish whether North Vietnamese troops crossed the border.
     The U.N. report led to the resignation of Phoui in December, 1959; Kou
Abhay then became provisional head of the government. Elections were conducted in April, 1960, but they were rigged to favor the government, and the
Pathet Lao protested. As a result, guerrilla war increased and on August 9,
a coup overthrew Abhay, making Tiao Somsanith the head of the new regime.
The power behind Tiao was a young army captain, KONG LE. Soon after the government ended its fight against the Communists and brought the neutralist
Souvanna Phouma back to office, the coup resulted in a dilemma for America
because there were three factors in Laos: the neutral Souvanna Phouma controlled the government but he lost his army control because the pro-Western
Phoumi Nosavan headed a conservative group that refused to cooperate with
Souvanna. The third faction was the Soviet-supported Pathet Lao. By the
end of his term of office in January, 1961, Eisenhower had reached no solution
to the Laotion imbroglio. See January 17, 1961.

August 12, 1960   *U.N. FORCES REPLACE BELGIAN TROOPS IN KATANGA PROVINCE*
                           OF THE CONGO.

*Following its acceptance of independence from Belgium on June 30, 1960, the
Congo became politically chaotic because the provinces of Katanga and Kasai
tried to secede and several troop mutinies occurred. On July 12, the Congolese Premier Patrice LUMUMBA appealed to the United Nations for aid and
the Security Council set up a multi-national U.N. force to replace the Belgian
troops at Leopoldville. After Moise TSHOMBE declared Katanga was an independent nation, the U.N. forces moved to take over that area and prevent its
secession. The problems of the Congo had just begun. See September 18, 1961.*

August 16, 1960   *CYPRUS BECOMES AN INDEPENDENT REPUBLIC.*

*This government was arranged as a compromise between Greek and Turkish fac-
tions after many years of negotiation to end British control of the island.
On February 19, 1959, the compromise was designed to give each ethnic group
a proportionate share of the assembly seats: 70% for Greeks; 30% for the Turkish. Some British forces remained at two military enclaves in order to safeguard the agreement.*
     *On December 15, 1960, GREEK ARCHBISHOP MARKARIOS was elected president;
FAZIL FUTCHUK, a Turk, became vice-president.*

August 28, 1960   *THE SAN JOSÉ DECLARATION OF THE OAS CONDEMNS INTER-
                           VENTION "BY ANY EXTRACONTINENTAL POWER," AN INDIRECT
                           WARNING AGAINST RUSSIAN INTERFERENCE IN CUBA.*

*The United States asked for a special OAS meeting in July, 1960, following
Soviet Premier Khrushchev's threat to support Cuba with rockets. Khrushchev
also told the State Department that the Monroe Doctrine had "outlived its
time." During the conference sessions, Secretary of State Herter wanted the
group to condemn Castro for violating principles of the inter-American system.
The other delegates refused to specify Cuba as a guilty party, preferring to
issue a declaration which reaffirmed American "solidarity and security" and
opposed intervention by an outside power.*

September 8, 1960   *EAST GERMANY INSTITUTES A PERMANENT RESTRICTION ON
                           TRAVEL BY WEST GERMANS TO EAST BERLIN.*

*West Germans would be required to obtain a police pass to enter East Berlin.
THE ALLIES PROTESTED THIS VIOLATION OF THE FOUR-POWER PACT ON BERLIN.*

September 10, 1960   THE ORGANIZATION OF PETROLEUM EXPORTING COUNTRIES
                           (OPEC) IS FORMED IN BAGHDAD.

This group was formed by Sheik Abdullah Tariki, the Minister of Petroleum of
Saudi Arabia. The original members were Iraq, Iran, Kuwait, Saudi Arabia,
and Venezuela. These nations agreed to demand stable oil prices from oil
companies.
     The impetus to form OPEC occurred when Standard Oil of New Jersey

unilaterally cut posted oil prices in 1960, drastically hurting Saudi Arabia's revenues. To enable OPEC to function, they set up a secretariat at Geneva with a budget of £150,000.

September 12, 1960   THE INTER-AMERICAN CONFERENCE AT BOGOTA, DURING WHICH THE UNITED STATES AGREES TO ESTABLISH A SPECIAL SOCIAL DEVELOPMENT FUND FOR LATIN AMERICA, CONCLUDES.

The U.S. delegation, headed by Undersecretary of State Douglas Dillon, proposed an act to promote a "broad dimension of social development" which would aid "social justice in our hemisphere." Although the President of Colombia, Dr. Alberto Lleras, hailed the spirit of the act, he warned that Latin America was on the edge of an unprecedented economic and social crisis. The U.S. proposal hoped to promote a plan to provide the people of the region with land, jobs, homes, schools, hospitals, and a fairer share of the products of their labor.

   The Act of Bogota underwrote the new awareness in the United States of Latin American needs. In 1961, President Kennedy's Alliance for Progress resulted. See March 13, 1961.

September 20, 1960   THE 1960 SESSION OF THE U.N. GENERAL ASSEMBLY INCLUDES KHRUSHCHEV, TITO, AND FIDEL CASTRO AS HEADS OF THEIR NATIONS' DELEGATIONS.

Before the session concluded, the Soviet premier displayed amazing methods of debate. Khrushchev used the United Nations as a forum to woo the support of Third World nations for Russian policy. Sixteen nations, mostly from Asia and Africa, joined the United Nations during this 15th session of the General Assembly. U.N. membership by October, 1960, totaled 98 nations, of which the Asian-African bloc numbered 44.

   Khrushchev's September 24 speech at the United Nations attacked Secretary General Dag Hammarskjold's policy in the Congo as pro-colonial. He demanded ousting Hammarskjold and replacing the Secretary General with a three-man (TROIKA) executive. Both of these proposals were defeated by the assembly.

   On October 12, the chairman of the General Assembly, Frederick H. Boland of Ireland, had to suspend the assembly's session due to Khrushchev's outburst. Khrushchev had argued strongly for a resolution to end all colonialism in the world. The Philippine delegate, Lorenzo Sumulong, responded by speaking against *all* colonialism by contending that the debate should include Russian imperial controls over countries in eastern Europe. Khrushchev interrupted Sumulong, calling him a U.S. "lackey." As Boland tried to bring order, breaking his gavel in the process, Khrushchev remarked, laughingly, on the weakness of the United Nations in breaking a gavel. The Soviet premier then took off his shoe and banged on his desk to protest Sumulong's speech. The assembly became chaotic before Boland finally adjourned the meeting.

September 23, 1960   AT AMERICAN URGING, NATO MEMBERS ACCEPT A WEST EUROPEAN AIR DEFENSE COMMAND AND OTHER POLICIES TO STRENGTHEN THE ALLIANCE.

October 1, 1960   FOR THE FIRST TIME SINCE 1903, THE U.S. AND PANAMANIAN
                         FLAGS ARE FLOWN TOGETHER OVER THE CANAL ZONE.

Although the Panama flag issue was not the only question about which the Panamanians complained, it symbolized Panama's desire for national respect.
Thus, President Eisenhower's decision on September 17 to permit both flags
to fly together also symbolized Eisenhower's attempt to relieve some of the
difficulties between the United States and Panama.

In February, 1955, Eisenhower had agreed to a treaty with Panama regarding U.S. commissary practices and increasing the Canal Zone annuities from
$430,000 to $1,930,000. By 1957, however, congress had not appropriated funds
for the 1955 treaty and, when Panama objected, Eisenhower persuaded congress
to act by providing funds and averting a crisis.

Nevertheless, demonstrations for Panamanian sovereignty and nationalism
continued on a sporadic basis. On November 3, 1957, anti-American demonstrators in Panama destroyed much U.S. property and burned the American flag.
Although Secretary of State Herter wished to compromise the flag issue with
Panama, the U.S. congress showed its nationalism on February 2, 1960, when
the House of Representatives passed a resolution by a vote of 380 to 12 which
said that Panama's flag could *not* fly in the Canal Zone unless a treaty specifically approved this action.

The Senate did not act on this resolution, and in the fall of 1960,
Eisenhower, Herter, and U.S. Ambassador to Panama Joseph S. Farland all agreed
that the president should permit the Panamanian flag to be flown. Soon after
congress adjourned in September, Eisenhower issued a statement that approved
the flying of both flags over the zone beginning on October 1, 1960.

On April 19, 1960, Eisenhower issued a nine-point program to improve
wages and living conditions of the unskilled and semi-skilled Panamanian workers in the Canal Zone. He also sought to improve schools and set up appren-
tice programs for training the Panamanians. Americans living in the zone--
the "Zonians"--loudly opposed Eisenhower's program because it threatened their
special way of life. Yet Eisenhower's reforms only began to help improve
the life of the natives in Panama.

October 19, 1960   THE U.S. EMBARGOES ALL EXPORTS TO CUBA EXCEPT MEDICINES
                         AND CERTAIN FOOD PRODUCTS.

The embargo was intended to put further pressure on Fidel Castro to moderate
his anti-American policies.

The next day, Eisenhower recalled the U.S. Ambassador to Cuba, Philip
Bonsal. Castro had refused to talk with the ambassador since a brief conversation on September 3, 1959. Since January 1, 1959, the United States
had requested negotiations with the Cubans on 9 formal and 16 informal occasions. Only once, on February 22, 1960, did the Cuban government respond,
and then it offered absurd conditions for undertaking negotiations.

November 8, 1960   JOHN F. KENNEDY DEFEATS RICHARD M. NIXON IN THE PRES-
                         IDENTIAL RACE.

Although the election was close, the Democratic Party enlarged its majority
in both the House (260 to 172) and Senate (65 to 35). Kennedy's victory margin was 114,000 votes out of 68.3 million ballots.

During the campaign, neither candidate offered unique foreign policy programs. Both emphasized the importance of the newly developing nations. On defense policy, Kennedy continued to be critical of Eisenhower's complacency toward Russia and the "loss" of Cuba, and advocated Maxwell Taylor's "flexible response program for a vigorous defense budget increase. Nixon never provided a firm challenge to the criticisms of Eisenhower's program.

November 11-12, 1960   IN SAIGON, PRESIDENT DIEM REGAINS POWER AFTER A PARA-
                           TROOP BRIGADE OF HIS ARMY TEMPORARILY OUSTS HIM FROM
                           OFFICE.

The paratroop uprising reflected opposition to Diem's policies in the military and among other non-Communist politicians in South Vietnam. In addition to the unsuccessful plot of the paratroopers, 18 old-time non-Communist politicians showed their displeasure with Diem in August, 1960, by issuing the so-called Caravelle Manifesto.

The Caravelle group urged Diem to evaluate his policies by recognizing that all his critics were not Communists. They asked that he hold free elections, end censorship, and end political repression by releasing political prisoners who filled the jails "to the rafters." They asked Diem to secure dedicated civil servants to end army factionalism, and to stop exploiting the farmers and workers. They concluded by saying they were not seeking to overthrow Diem but to appeal to his reason by telling him "hard truths" which those close to him were afraid to report.

Diem reacted like a tyrant. He saw no difference between the Caravelle group and Communists. Therefore, he arrested and imprisoned the 18 signatories of the petition.

Diem eliminated political reformers easily. During the next three years, he discovered that eliminating dissent in the army and among Buddhist religious leaders was not so easy.

By 1960, Diem's publicity in the United States made him as popular in America as he was disliked in South Vietnam. The American Friends of Vietnam had been formed in 1955, and its letterhead cited Senator John F. Kennedy as a founding member. By 1960, the American media called Diem the "tough little miracle man" and *Newsweek*'s Ernest Lindley exclaimed that he was "one of the ablest free Asian leaders." In 1960, both Diem and Chiang Kai-shek won Freedom Foundation awards from a Valley Forge-based organization. See also December 5, 1960.

November 19, 1960   THE UNITED STATES AND CANADA JOIN 18 MEMBERS OF THE
                           OEEC TO FORM THE ORGANIZATION FOR ECONOMIC CO-OPERATION
                           AND DEVELOPMENT (OECD).

The purpose of the OECD was to expand trade and economic cooperation and to aid underdeveloped states to promote their economy.

December 5, 1960   THE U.S. AMBASSADOR TO SOUTH VIETNAM, ELBRIDGE DURBROW,
                           ISSUES A FINAL CRITICAL REPORT ON DIEM'S POLICIES.

After serving four years in Saigon, Ambassador Durbrow grew increasingly disillusioned with Diem. He said there was a weak internal backing of Diem, blaming the problems on corruption in the officer classes and the influence of Diem's family members who held high office, especially Ngo Dinh Nhu, Diem's brother, and Madame Nhu. Durbrow wanted Diem replaced if he did not bring economic reform, broaden the non-Communist base of his cabinet, and eliminate the corrupt leaders in the army and government.

While Durbrow's reports indicate the internal causes of South Vietnamese opposition to Diem, they were not implemented because Kennedy replaced Durbrow with a European expert, Frederick E. Nolting, Jr.

December 5, 1960   CLEARER SIGNS OF THE SINO-SOVIET SPLIT ARE EVIDENT
                        AT A MOSCOW MEETING OF WORLD COMMUNIST PARTIES.

At the end of the meeting (November 7-December 5, 1960) 81 parties signed a
COMMUNIST MANIFESTO which pledged Communist victory by peaceful means and
affirmed the Soviet leadership of all Communist parties.

The Chinese Communists objected to these views, reflecting the prevailing
arguments on policy between Peking and Moscow, which had increased during
1960. On May 14, 1960, Mao Tse-tung published an interview in which he
taunted Russia about permitting U-2's to spy on them and for believing they
could work cooperatively with Western imperialists.

In June, Khrushchev sent letters to a Communist meeting in Rumania. The
letters attacked Chinese views on Communist policy and blamed Mao for being
a revisionist. Khrushchev said the Chinese were madmen and "left adventur-
ists" desiring to unleash a nuclear war.

The November-December sessions in Moscow failed to heal the division
between China and Russia. However, the only country joining China in criti-
cizing Khrushchev was Albania.

December 20, 1960   THE NATIONAL LIBERATION FRONT (NLF) IS CREATED IN SOUTH
                        VIETNAM.

The NLF said it represented all Vietnamese peoples south of the 17th parallel in their fight against Diem's tyranny.

The formation of the NLF indicated efforts of the South Vietnamese to overthrow Diem's government. After securing control of Saigon in 1955, Diem did not display equal skill in bringing economic reform and political prestige to his government. He failed to carry out land reform for the peasants and increasingly repressed all who dissented from his policies.

In 1958, the first anti-Diem organizations appeared in the south. In resisting Diem's army, police, and local rulers, the rural groups used sabotage and attacks on village chiefs or informers who were loyal to Diem. As resistance grew in the country, Diem used greater repression, until by 1960 those opposing Diem decided to organize as the NLF in order to coordinate their attacks on Saigon and Diem's officials.

1961

January 3, 1961   THE UNITED STATES SEVERS DIPLOMATIC RELATIONS WITH
                     CUBA.

While the United States had recalled Ambassador Bonsal from Havana only on
October 20, Castro had assigned no ambassador to Washington since he took
office in 1959.

On January 2, 1961, Castro charged that the U.S. Embassy was a center
for counter-revolutionaries. He ordered that the embassy staff must be reduced to 11 persons in 48 hours. This convinced President Eisenhower to break
diplomatic relations with Cuba.

January 4, 1961   CASTRO'S CLAIM THAT THE UNITED STATES IS PREPARING AN
                     INVASION IS IGNORED BY THE U.N. SECURITY COUNCIL.

First on October 18, 1960, Cuba asked the U.N. General Assembly to investigate
U.S. plans to invade Cuba. The assembly refused to act. Later, on January
4, 1961, Castro petitioned the U.N. Security Council, asking it to prevent
U.S. intervention in Cuba. Again, Castro's charges were rebuffed.

Historians know that on March 17, 1960, President Eisenhower secretly
ordered the Central Intelligence Agency (CIA) to train Cuban exiles for possible guerrilla operations against Castro. By the end of 1960, nearly 1,200
men were being trained by the CIA, most of them in Guatemala.

January 6, 1961   *SOVIET PREMIER KHRUSHCHEV ASSERTS THAT HIS GOVERNMENT
                     WILL SUPPORT WARS OF NATIONAL LIBERATION.*

*Addressing a Communist Party meeting in Moscow, the Soviet leader reiterated
his desire for peaceful coexistence with the Western world. The only excep-
tion, he stated, was for Soviet backing for "just" wars of liberation from
capitalist imperialism. Khrushchev's speech reflected the emphasis on the
end of the Western nations' colonial empires, which had accelerated after
Ghana gained independence in 1957. National uprisings against foreign control
had become one of the major areas of conflict throughout the world. This
damaged British, French, and U.S. policies the most because they were the
powers whose trade and financial policies had become global since the 18th
century. When Khrushchev spoke of national liberation, he did not include
the many national minorities in the Soviet Union.*

January 17, 1961   EISENHOWER'S "FAREWELL ADDRESS" WARNS AMERICANS OF THE
                         DANGEROUS POWER OF THE AMERICAN MILITARY-INDUSTRIAL
                         COMPLEX.

During debate on Eisenhower's "new look" policy, the president had become
acutely frustrated with the "conjunction of an immense military establishment
and a large arms industry" whose "total influence" was felt throughout the
nation. Americans, Eisenhower warned, "must guard against the acquisition
of unwarranted influence, whether sought or unsought, by the military-
industrial complex." Because of this connection, "the potential for the disastrous use of misplaced power exists and will persist."

January 17, 1961   THE LAOTIAN PROBLEM IS REVIEWED FOR SECRETARY OF STATE-
                         DESIGNATE DEAN RUSK BUT NO SOLUTION IS OFFERED.

Following the return to office of neutralist Premier Souvanna on August 9,
1960, the Laotian issue became more difficult for Washington to assess. The
Russians worked with Souvanna's attempt to form a coalition government, but
right-wing leader Phoumi refused to do so and the United States did not approve the concept of joining a coalition that included the Communist Pathet
Lao.
      Unable to form a left-neutralist-right government, Souvanna left for
Cambodia on December 9. The Laotian king gave power to the right-wing government of Phoumi and his cohort, Prince Boun Oum. Because Souvanna never
resigned, the legitimacy of the Phoumi-Oum government was challenged by the
Communists. The United States recognized the new right-wing ruler but the
French and British preferred a neutralist regime in Laos.
      In order to get other nations to back the rightist Boun Oum, the United
States called a meeting of the SEATO Council on January 2, 1961. SEATO Secretary General Pote Sarasin reported that, while weapons were coming to the
Pathet Lao from North Vietnamese Communists, there was no definite evidence
of North Vietnamese troops in Laos. The SEATO council therefore voted to
seek a "peaceful" settlement of the Laotian question, backing no specific
government in Laos. Eisenhower decided, however, to back Phoumi and sent
him six fighter bombers in January, 1961.
      When Herter reviewed the situation with Rusk on January 17, he said that
a neutral government without Communists was needed but could not be found.
The CIA wanted to back Phoumi and Oum fully; State Department analysts wanted
to form a right-center coalition. Laos, he told Rusk, was "a good example
of no solution." Moreover, few other nations were willing to cooperate with
America in assisting the Phoumi-Oum regime in Laos. See May 3, 1961.

January 20, 1961   PRESIDENT JOHN F. KENNEDY'S INAUGURAL ADDRESS CALLS
                         ON THE NATION TO RENEW ITS COMMITMENT TO EXTEND FREEDOM
                         THROUGHOUT THE WORLD.

An energetic cold-warrior in the mold of Truman and Dulles, President Kennedy
believed that the relative calm of the Eisenhower years could be equated with
weakness or lack of will. In contrast, Kennedy projected the go-do-it style
and a can-do quality.
      In his inaugural address, the president eloquently called on the American
people to defend freedom in this hour of need. He asserted:

Let every nation know, whether it wishes us well or ill, that we
shall pay any price, bear any burden, meet any hardship, support
any friend, oppose any foes, in order to assure the survival and
success of liberty. This much we pledge, and more.

January 21, 1961   DEAN RUSK IS COMMISSIONED AS SECRETARY OF STATE UNDER
                        PRESIDENT JOHN F. KENNEDY.

Although Rusk was well qualified to be secretary, President Kennedy desired
to be the dominant force in foreign affairs, selecting Rusk as a person who
would be loyal and hard working but not try to capture the headlines or become
controversial. During World War II, Rusk served as a deputy chief of staff
in the China-Burma-India theater. Between 1945 and 1952, he held several
positions in the State Department, achieving the post of Assistant Secretary
for Far Eastern Affairs in 1950-1951. From 1952 to 1961 he was president of
the Rockefeller Foundation. Rusk was secretary throughout the administrations
of Kennedy and Johnson, leaving office on January 20, 1969.

February 6, 1961   THE MISSILE-GAP THEORY IS A MYTH: SECRETARY OF DEFENSE
                        McNAMARA TELLS NEWSMEN THAT THE "MISSILE-GAP" CRITICISM
                        LEVIED AGAINST THE EISENHOWER ADMINISTRATION HAS NO
                        FOUNDATION IN FACT.

Between 1957 and 1961, the widespread criticism of Eisenhower's "new look"
policy had been based partly on the incorrect claim that Eisenhower's nuclear
sufficiency program to build 200 ICBM's to protect America would create Russian superiority in nuclear weapons during the early 1960's.
     Eisenhower insisted that there was no "missile-gap," but acceptance of
this theory became so popular that both Republican and Democratic candidates
for their parties' nomination assumed its validity. It was used effectively
by Kennedy to assert that Eisenhower's foreign programs had been weak and
ineffective. It also was part of Maxwell Taylor's plan to build up counterinsurgency forces of the army to win brush-fire wars under the protection of
a superior nuclear force umbrella. See November 7, 1957.
     Soon after McNamara took over the Defense Department, he saw evidence
that Eisenhower's denials of a missile-gap were based in fact. In a background briefing, McNamara admitted that there was no missile-gap. Nevertheless, neither the Kennedy administration nor the news media played up the
fact that the claims of a missile-gap were false.
     McNamara and Kennedy wanted to build a superior nuclear force whether
or not there was a missile-gap. As Richard Aliano has noted, Kennedy wanted
a missile-gap in reverse, with the gap being on the Soviet side. Therefore
the rapid build up of U.S. ICBM's became one part of the large defense expenditures Kennedy promoted for all branches of the armed forces after 1961. In
nuclear weapons, by 1967 the United States had increased ICBM's from 200 to
1,000. In addition, the United States had 41 Polaris submarines with 656
missile launchers and 600 long-range bombers for nuclear attack. By 1967,
however, the Soviets had responded to the U.S. nuclear race by matching the
U.S. nuclear arsenal.

February 28, 1961   SECRETARY RUSK INFORMS THE SENATE FOREIGN RELATIONS
                        COMMITTEE THAT KENNEDY'S ADMINISTRATION, LIKE EISEN-
                        HOWER'S, SUPPORTS U.N. ACTION IN THE CONGO.

Since the Congo dispute first went to the U.N. Security Council during the
summer of 1960 (see August 12, 1960), the United States had voted with most
nations in backing the U.N. peacekeeping mission in the Congo and U.N. Secretary General Dag Hammarskjold's policy which recognized the Leopoldville government against both the pro-Belgium faction in Katanga and the Russian-backed
forces led by Antonio Gizenga, who had replaced Patrice Lumumba.

      The only problem in the United States was the support given to Tshombe
and the rebels in Katanga whose independence was urged by such conservatives
as Senator Barry Goldwater and news editor William F. Buckley. The opponents
of the U.N. position increased during the summer of 1961 when the United Nations attempted to use force to defeat Katanga. See September 18, 1961.

March 1, 1961   PRESIDENT KENNEDY ISSUES AN EXECUTIVE ORDER CREATING
                       THE PEACE CORPS.

The Peace Corps was set up to train Americans to go to underdeveloped nations
which requested U.S. services and to provide teaching and technical services.
Ideally, the corps would allow Americans and people of other nations to work
side by side to promote both economic development and the democratic way of
life. Kennedy believed the cold war in the Third World nations could be won
by demonstrating U.S. virtues on a person-to-person basis.

      Kennedy conceived of the Peace Corps as an important cold war weapon.
He argued that many technicians from Russia and China "spend their lives
abroad in the service of world communism." Young Americans dedicated to freedom, he said, "are fully capable of overcoming the efforts of Mr. Khrushchev's
missionaries who are dedicated to undermining that freedom."

March 13, 1961   PRESIDENT KENNEDY ANNOUNCES THE ALLIANCE FOR PROGRESS
                       PROGRAM TO AID LATIN AMERICA.

This program, Kennedy said, would extend previous aid of the Eisenhower administration by committing America to a 10-year program of $20 billion. De-
tails of the program would be finalized at an Inter-American Conference in
Punta del Este, Uruguay, in August. See August 17, 1961.

April 17, 1961   THE BAY OF PIGS FIASCO: BACKED BY THE UNITED STATES,
                       A CUBAN REBEL FORCE FAILS TO INVADE CUBA.

Preparations for possible guerrilla operations in Cuba began on March 17,
1960. After the 1960 election, the CIA appraised Kennedy of its plans. Although Secretary Rusk opposed the operation, Kennedy decided to go ahead with
it. Thus, on April 17, 1,600 Cuban exiles who had been trained in Guatemala
landed at the Bay of Pigs in southern Cuba and for two days held a beachhead.
The CIA's expectation that the Cuban people would rise up against Castro never
materialized. The CIA's plan had been based on a false premise because only
a major U.S. invasion force could have averted the disaster, but Kennedy did
not want a larger war.

On April 15, Cuban exiles used B-26 bombers in an attempt to destroy Castro's air forces. The effort failed but led Castro to appeal to the United Nations to stop U.S. invasion plans. Consequently, Kennedy cancelled a second air strike scheduled to cover the April 17 landing at the Bay of Pigs. This cancellation and the lack of a mass uprising against Cuba doomed the expedition. The invaders were killed, captured or driven back to their ships.

In the United Nations, Ambassador Adlai Stevenson had on April 15 unknowingly denied U.S. involvement. Thus the Bay of Pigs episode embarrassed the usually forthright Stevenson and damaged America's explanations to the United Nations and the Organization of American States. America's unilateral intervention in Latin America reaped another harvest of ill will. To paraphrase Kennedy's inaugural address, he had paid a price but also lost in both results and reputation.

May 3, 1961   A CEASE-FIRE IS ACHIEVED IN LAOS SOON AFTER THE UNITED STATES THREATENS MILITARY INTERVENTION.

Less noticed than the Cuban Bay of Pigs incident of April, 1961, was the fact that the United States seriously considered war in Laos if the Communist advances continued in that state. American support for the rightist regime of Phoumi and Oum in Laos resulted in that government's growing unpopularity and the strengthening of Communist and neutralist unity. By March, 1961, the Communist drive in Laos left Phoumi's forces in disarray, causing Kennedy and Rusk to seek some means to obtain a neutral, non-Communist state in Laos.

On March 23, Kennedy ordered U.S. forces to move to areas near Laos. The aircraft carrier *Midway* was sent to the Gulf of Siam, a marine unit to Thailand, and forces on Okinawa were placed on alert. At the same time, Secretary Rusk went to a SEATO meeting in Bangkok to obtain support for U.S. military action if necessary.

At Bangkok, Rusk added a clear global dimension to the Truman Doctrine, telling the SEATO delegates that U.S. assistance to "freedom-loving nations" had "no geographical barriers." The French and British, however, did not desire military action in Laos, which they considered to be an area of non-vital interest. Nevertheless, Rusk persuaded SEATO to endorse "appropriate" victory in South Vietnam, assuming Laos might fall.

While Rusk and Kennedy prepared for possible unilateral military intervention in Laos, British Prime Minister Harold Macmillan arranged for a cease-fire in Laos and a conference at Geneva. Premier Khrushchev also favored a conference and on May 3, a cease-fire was announced in Laos. The Geneva meetings began on May 16 but did not reach agreement until 1962. See July 23, 1962.

May 5, 1961   A NATO COUNCIL MEETING AT OSLO DISCLOSES EUROPEAN CONCERN FOR A GREATER ROLE IN NATO DEFENSE OPERATIONS.

Europeans did not look favorably on Kennedy's shift from the Eisenhower-Dulles "massive retaliation" to a "flexible response" strategy. The Kennedy program to use conventional forces wherever necessary, and to build a superior nuclear force which might or might not be used, seemed to President de Gaulle and other European leaders to be a design to keep America aloof from the interests of European powers. In addition, the Europeans had grown less dependent on the United States and asked for some degree of control over nuclear weapons and the NATO forces in Europe.

At the Oslo meeting, Secretary Rusk indicated that America would steadfastly support Europe. He could not, however, offer an end to U.S. monopolistic control of the alliance's strategic nuclear weapons. In addition, by asserting that all areas of the world were important and would be defended, Rusk by definition lowered Europe's former rating as the first priority of U.S. concerns.

Rusk offered the Europeans five Polaris submarines as part of the NATO command. He insisted, however, that Americans must command the subs and control nuclear missiles. The Europeans wanted more. They wanted a respectful position in the NATO command and spoke of a multilateral defense force (MDF) which would include nuclear weapons under European control. The United States was not willing to relinquish its control of the NATO forces, especially the nuclear forces.

May 16, 1961   *A MILITARY JUNTA IN SOUTH KOREA OVERTHROWS PRESIDENT*
                      POSON YUN AND DECREES A MILITARY DICTATORSHIP. ON
                      JULY 3, GENERAL PARK BECOMES SOUTH KOREA'S MILITARY
                      HEAD.

The United States initially opposed the military take-over in Seoul and pressured Major General Chung Hee Park to restore civilian government. Subsequently, Park arranged elections in Korea. On October 15, 1963, he designated himself a civilian, restricted the opposition from campaigning, and won a plurality of votes to become president of South Korea.

May 25, 1961   PRESIDENT KENNEDY LAUNCHES A "MOON RACE" TO BEAT THE
                      SOVIET UNION IN LANDING THE FIRST MAN ON THE MOON.

Kennedy had asked Vice-President Johnson on April 20 to study U.S. space capabilities and determine if the United States had a chance of beating the Soviet Union in the moon race or some other dramatic space program. This feat, Kennedy believed, would reassert U.S. technical superiority over the Soviets.

Johnson, as Chairman of the Space Council, conducted a study and reported that the Soviets had larger boosters for a possible moon flight. With a strong U.S. effort, however, the Space Council believed the United States could accomplish a moon mission by 1966 or 1967.

On May 25, Kennedy told congress that it was time for the United States to organize a "great new American enterprise" and "take a clearly leading role in space achievement." He committed the nation to achieve the goal, "before the decade is out, of landing a man on the moon and returning him safely to earth." This launched the Apollo program, which was successful on July 20, 1969.

May 30, 1961   *GENERAL RAFAEL TRUJILLO, THE REAL POWER IN THE DOMINI-*
                      CAN REPUBLIC, IS ASSASSINATED.

Trujillo had directly or indirectly ruled the Dominicans since the 1930's. President Joaquin Balaguer, who had fronted for Trujillo since 1960, had difficulty in keeping political order in his nation as opposition groups initiated strikes and demonstrations against his government. To resolve the problems, Balaguer formed a National Civil Union on December 19, 1961, and

promised to conduct elections for a constituent assembly in August and to
hold general elections by December, 1962. See December 20, 1962.

June 3-4, 1961   KENNEDY AND KHRUSHCHEV HOLD A SUMMIT CONFERENCE IN
                         VIENNA.

This meeting was designed to resolve the Berlin issue. On February 17, Premier Khrushchev informed the Bonn government that West Berlin should become
a "free city." In addition, he wished to conclude a final German peace
treaty. If not, Khrushchev said, he would sign a separate pact with East
Germany.
     The Vienna meetings did not settle either the German or the pending Lao-
tian problem. Khrushchev stated he would act unilaterally with East Germany
on a German peace treaty if none were achieved by December, 1961. If the
West interfered, there would be war. Kennedy countered by warning the Russians that the United States would fight to keep access routes to Berlin.
Russia must not take unilateral action.
     Regarding Laos, both leaders expressed their desire for a neutral Laotian
state. Khrushchev said, however, that the Pathet Lao would eventually win.
Kennedy expressed the American determination to protect Laos. Thus, on both
Laos and Germany the two leaders defended a strong position to maintain their
status in those areas. As Kennedy told the U.S. public on his return, the
Vienna visit was "a very sober two days."

July 25, 1961   PRESIDENT KENNEDY DELIVERS A SPEECH STRONGLY BACKING
                         THE IMPORTANCE OF BERLIN AS VITAL TO AMERICA.

Because Khrushchev had indicated at Vienna that the Russians would unilaterally act in Berlin and East Germany by December, 1961, Kennedy decided to
assert explicit American rights and duties in Berlin. He refused to negotiate
access to Berlin or the U.S. military presence in that city. The president
also placed National Reserve troops on duty and announced a 25% increase in
U.S. military power.
     Kennedy declared the American position on Berlin without prior consulta-
tion with American allies, which Rusk had recommended. The president's attitude toward U.S. allies was to avoid reliance on these people. Unlike Eisenhower, who strongly emphasized close cooperation with the NATO allies, Kennedy
and Johnson believed the United States must act as it believed necessary.
In July, 1961, Prime Minister Macmillan approved Kennedy's action; President
de Gaulle and Chancellor Adenauer were troubled by its bellicose overtones.

August 13, 1961   THE SOVIETS BEGIN CONSTRUCTION OF THE BERLIN WALL BE-
                         TWEEN EAST AND WEST BERLIN.

One of the Soviets' principal concerns in Berlin was the drain of East Germany's educated and technical elite resulting from the flow of exiles to West
Germany. After the Vienna Conference of June, 1961, this flow increased to
30,000 in July and 4,000 on August 12.
     On August 13, East German police erected barriers to cut off East and
West Berlin. Because Kennedy had never argued for direct access to East Berlin, he and Secretary Rusk protested the barriers but did not take any

military action to stop the wall's construction, although some critics argued that Kennedy should have challenged the Soviets with U.S. soldiers. Kennedy, however, emphasized the wall as a symbol of the Communists' failure to provide adequately for their own people. During the next year, East Germany replaced the original barbed wire barricade with a more elaborate concrete wall and machine-gun nests to prevent East Germans from fleeing to the West.

August 17, 1961   THE ALLIANCE FOR PROGRESS CHARTER IS SIGNED AT THE INTER-AMERICAN CONFERENCE IN PUNTA DEL ESTE.

This meeting finalized a U.S. agreement which all Latin American nations except Cuba had signed. Over 10 years the United States would provide $20 billion for a public and private investment program in Latin America. There would also be another $300 million annual investment from private capital in America. The Latin American governments pledged $80 billion of investments over 10 years. In addition, they pledged to enact land, tax, and other socio-economic reforms in their nations.

Unfortunately, the Alliance for Progress did not function as well as expected. Brazil, Argentina, and Mexico did not want close scrutiny of their programs. Thus, many Latin American governments did not enact the necessary reforms. Although some benefits resulted from the program, orderly, stable, and improved political and economic developments did not occur in Latin America in the next decade.

September 18, 1961   U.N. SECRETARY GENERAL HAMMARSKJOLD IS KILLED IN A PLANE CRASH WHILE SEEKING A TRUCE IN THE CONGO.

At the time of Hammarskjold's death, he and Secretary of State Rusk disagreed about the use of U.N. forces against Tshombe's regime in Katanga. The dispute on the Congo had narrowed to a struggle between Cyrille ADOULA, who was elected premier of the Leopoldville government backed by the United Nations, and Tshombe's state, backed by some European nations, South Africa, and Southern Rhodesia as well as many U.S. conservatives.

Rusk backed U.N. support for Adoula as the moderate candidate in the Congo but objected to Hammarskjold's use of U.N. forces against Tshombe. Rusk desired negotiations between Tshombe and Adoula to solve their dispute.

On September 20, two days after Hammarskjold died in a plane crash in the Congo, the opposing Congolese leaders agreed to a cease-fire. The truce did not end successfully, however. By November 11, Kennedy agreed to Rusk's recommendation to allow the United Nations to use force if necessary against Katanga. See January 20, 1962.

September 21, 1961   SOVIET FOREIGN MINISTER ANDREI GROMYKO AGREES TO DELAY RUSSIA'S DECEMBER DEADLINE FOR SETTLEMENT OF THE GERMAN ISSUE.

The United States was greatly disturbed by Khrushchev's threat on June 3, 1961, to act unilaterally on Germany's peace treaty. Therefore, in September, Secretary Rusk and Gromyko discussed the dangerous implications of the situation. During a series of three discussions, Gromyko indicated that the Soviet deadline could be delayed if negotiations began. Rusk agreed to talk, suggesting that a four-power agreement could guarantee Western access to Berlin. In addition, Rusk said that if the German problem were settled, arms limitations in central Europe might be discussed.

The September talks did not finalize but did relieve East-West tension over Germany. Although General de Gaulle and some U.S. critics such as Harvard Professor Henry Kissinger believed Rusk's "weakness" bordered on "appeasement," it had not. Rusk had not committed any nation to arms limits but had obtained a delay in the Soviet deadline on Germany. Rusk's talks, combined with Kennedy's frequent assertions of U.S. support for West Berlin, resulted in the end of the Berlin crisis of 1961. Further talks on Berlin and Germany continued, but Khrushchev's ultimatum no longer added to the tense atmosphere.

October 28, 1961   AN EAST BERLIN CRISIS ENDS AFTER BOTH THE RUSSIAN AND
                            AMERICAN GOVERNMENTS REMOVE THEIR TANKS.

A crisis began on October 26, when East German border guards demanded that U.S. civilians must submit identification before they could enter East Berlin. At the Friedrichstrasse crossing point both Soviet and American forces moved tanks to protect the crossing. The crisis faded quickly, however, when each government ordered its military officers to pull their tanks back from the border.

November 22, 1961   PRESIDENT KENNEDY APPROVES THE "FIRST PHASE OF VIETNAM
                            PROGRAM" WHICH BROADENS THE U.S. COMMITMENT TO VIETNAM
                            BY ADDING AMERICAN "COMBAT SUPPORT" TROOPS.

Although in April, 1961, President Kennedy had added 100 advisors to the U.S. contingent and thereby exceeded the number permitted by the Geneva Accords of 1954, his frist critical decision on Vietnam was made on November 22. This decision was largely based on a report by General Maxwell Taylor and Walter W. Rostow who visited Saigon in October, 1961. Taylor, who had been the leading critic of Eisenhower's "New Look" policy in the late 1950's, became Kennedy's principal military advisor. Rostow was a White House advisor to the president. These two men discounted the 1960 report of Ambassador to Saigon Elbridge Durbrow which severely criticized Premier Diem of South Vietnam. Taylor and Rostow thought Diem had "extraordinary stability, stubbornness and guts." They recommended a "limited partnership" with Diem.

The November 22 "First Phase ..." was based on the Taylor-Rostow recommendations, which were changed to provide fewer combat troops and to delete the objective to "save South Vietnam."

Kennedy ordered a gradually increased number of "combat support" troops to Vietnam. General Taylor, who expected a few highly qualified "Green Berets" to deal easily with "brush-fire wars," did not believe many troops would be needed, but he was uncertain just how many because estimates varied from 8,000 to 25,000 men. In December, 1961, 400 men in two helicopter companies and 33 H-21 aircraft reached Saigon. By November, 1963, Kennedy had ordered 16,263 "combat support" troops to Vietnam; combat support, according to the White House, meant they would not fire until fired on but would accompany South Vietnamese army patrols.

In addition to these forces, the November 22 plan called for a Strategic Hamlet Program. Based on British counterinsurgency plans used in Malaya, the

"Hamlets" were fortified villages for the rural populace to occupy while the Communists were driven out of their home region. Then the peasants could return home in peace. In South Vietnam, unfortunately, the program was headed by Diem's unpopular and corrupt brother and sister-in-law, Ngo Dinh Nhu and Madame Nhu.

December 2, 1961   FIDEL CASTRO ANNOUNCES THAT HE IS A MARXIST-LENINIST.

Although conservative Americans had suspected throughout the 1950's that Castro was a Communist, the Cuban leader had previously shaded his reform efforts in Cuba with promises of election and compensation for nationalized property. Now, Castro had become dependent on the Soviet Union for economic aid. On December 2, he called for the formation of a united Cuban party to bring communism to Cuba.

1962

January 18, 1962   RUSK INFORMS THE SENATE FOREIGN RELATIONS COMMITTEE
THAT THE UNITED STATES MUST SUPPORT ADOULA AND THE
UNITED NATIONS IN THE CONGO AS THE BEST ANTI-COMMUNIST
MEASURE.

Following Hammarskjold's death on September 18, 1961, a truce was arranged
between Tshombe of Katanga and Adoula of the central Congolese government.
The truce was not sustained, however, and by November 11, Rusk and Kennedy
agreed to allow the United Nations to use whatever force was necessary to
persuade Tshombe to negotiate. Tshombe and Adoula agreed on December 21 to
end Katanga's secession. Tshombe was slated to have a role in the Leopoldville government.

On January 18, Rusk explained that the United States would continue to
back the U.N. program as the best solution to keep the integrity of the Congo
and to defeat Communist efforts. Those who backed Tshombe, Rusk said, followed a policy which would weaken Adoula's government and allow the Soviets
to defeat both the moderate Adoula and the conservative Tshombe.

Within six months, Tshombe violated the December 21 Kitonia agreement.
Therefore, the United Nations was required to apply force to restore Katanga
to the control of Leopoldville's government. See December 17, 1962.

January 31, 1962   CUBA IS EXCLUDED FROM THE INTER-AMERICAN SPHERE.

At the end of a 10-day meeting at Punta del Este, Uruguay, the American foreign ministers approved by a two-thirds vote a resolution which excluded Cuba
from the Inter-American system. Brazil, Argentina, Chile, Ecuador, and Mexico
abstained on the vote.

February 10, 1962   RUSSIA AND THE UNITED STATES EXCHANGE "SPIES."

Francis Gary Powers, who piloted the U-2 which crashed in Russia in 1960,
was released in exchange for the American release of Colonel Rudolf Abel, a
Soviet spy who had been convicted of espionage in 1957.

February 20, 1962   LIEUTENANT COLONEL JOHN H. GLENN, JR., IS THE FIRST
U.S. ASTRONAUT TO ORBIT THE EARTH.

On his flight Glenn circled the earth three times before landing in the Pacific Ocean, where U.S. naval vessels picked him up.

A Russian had been the first to orbit the earth. On April 12, 1961,
Major Yuri A. Gagarin in spaceship Vostok I circled the earth for 108 minutes
at a maximum altitude of 203 miles.

March 28, 1962   MILITARY LEADERS IN ARGENTINA OVERTHROW PRESIDENT
                        ARTURO FRONDIZI.

*Frondizi had, in 1958, become Argentina's first elected president in 12 years.
The military junta named José Maria Guido as president. On July 24, Guido
banned both the rightist Peronist Party and the Communist Party and provided
government control over the internal affairs of all parties.*

April 8, 1962   FRENCH VOTERS APPROVE DE GAULLE'S PLAN TO GRANT INDE-
                        PENDENCE TO ALGERIA.

*Since 1955, the Algerian nationalist rebellion had cost the French many lives
and much money. De Gaulle finally agreed to make peace with the rebels and
grant them independence. Although right-wing Algerian insurgents rejected
the proposal, a campaign to eliminate their army succeeded during the next
year.*

April 25, 1962   EXPLODING A NUCLEAR DEVICE AT CHRISTMAS ISLAND, THE U.S.
                        RESPONDS TO THE SOVIETS' RESUMPTION OF NUCLEAR TESTS IN
                        1961.

On August 31, 1961, Moscow announced the Russians were renewing nuclear tests,
ending the informal 1958 agreements of Khrushchev and Eisenhower which had ended
such tests. Soon after, the U.S.S.R. conducted a series of nuclear tests.
        Following a thorough review of the situation, President Kennedy announced
on March 2, 1962, that the United States would resume its tests in April unless
an effective test ban agreement was reached with the Soviet Union during the
interim. In announcing his decision, Kennedy stated that the United States
needed to check the effectiveness of high-altitude explosions in order to counter
gains made by the Soviet Union during its 1961 test series. He said no "super-
bombs" would be detonated and that radiation fallout would be minimized.
        The president's decision divided public opinion in America and in other
free world nations. At home, the White House admitted that the telegrams it received were divided evenly among those in favor and those opposed to the tests.
There were large peace and anti-nuclear demonstrations in New York and other
American cities as well as in London and, especially, Japan. The Japanese
government warned Washington that it would seek compensation for possible damages to its citizens.
        Nevertheless, after Khrushchev spurned a special message from Kennedy and
British Prime Minister Macmillan which urged him to accept an effective test
ban, Kennedy authorized the tests to begin on April 24. The tests in the region
of Christmas Island and, later, Johnson Island and Nevada were conducted between
April 25, and November 4, 1963. The test's time schedule was extended from July
to November because the explosions of high-altitude bombs failed on several
occasions. Eventually, a total of 36 bombs were exploded by the U.S. during 196
        On September 2, the Atomic Energy Commission and the Defense Department ad-
mitted that the high-altitude test of July 9 had increased space radiation more
than anticipated. In particular, the radiation in the earth's Van Allen belt
was extended lower in the atmosphere where it would remain for at least five
years. U.S. scientists disagreed on the effect which radiation in food would
have on Americans. Increased levels of iodine were found in milk taken from
cows in parts of the Middle West. Some scientists thought the dosage was

approaching dangerous levels.   There was no agreement on exactly what level was "dangerous."

On February 2, 1963, Kennedy threatened another series of U.S. nuclear tests if the U.S.S.R. did not agree to an effective test ban treaty. Discussions had been held between diplomats in London, Moscow, and Washington during the fall and winter of 1962-1963. These talks eventually succeeded. See July 25, 1963.

May 26, 1962   THE NETHERLANDS ACCEPTS A U.S. PLAN TO SETTLE THE WEST
                             NEW GUINEA DISPUTE WITH INDONESIA.

A dispute over the possession of West New Guinea had resulted in war between the Netherlands and the Indonesian forces of President Sukarno. The United States proposed to end the struggle by mediation on ownership while the United Nations administered the territory and arranged a plebiscite to permit the Papuan inhabitants to decide their future.

After the Dutch accepted the American plan, U.N. Secretary General U Thant obtained a cease-fire, and on May 29, the two nations began discussions. Subsequently, on July 31, Indonesia and the Netherlands agreed to transfer West New Guinea (renamed West Irian) to the United Nations on October 1, with the United Nations to transfer it to Indonesia on May 1, 1963. Within six years, Indonesia was to hold a plebiscite of self-determination for the Papuan natives of the area. Kennedy and Rusk hoped this process would keep Sukarno and Indonesia from appealing to the Soviet Union for aid.

June 25, 1962   IN ACCRA, GHANA, A "WORLD WITHOUT THE BOMB" CONFERENCE
                             BEGINS.

More than 100 delegates, including those from the United States and the Soviet Union, attended this meeting. During the seven-day conference, the delegates recommended that the United Nations train disarmament inspection teams and called on African states to disarm throughout their continent. The group also recommended the admission of Communist China to the United Nations.

July 4, 1962   KENNEDY INFORMS THE EUROPEANS THAT THEY CAN HAVE NU-
                             CLEAR WEAPONS AS SOON AS THEY ACHIEVE POLITICAL UNITY.

Kennedy's message of July 4 responded to the European desire for a multilateral nuclear defense force for NATO. It did not, however, provide the answer de Gaulle and other Europeans desired.

Kennedy's speech was a plan by George Ball, the Undersecretary of State to whom Rusk delegated European problems. Ball's dream was an integrated Europe, allied with America and generally under U.S. control. Because European unity was, at best, in the distant future, Kennedy's agreement to give Europeans a greater role in a European defense force meant nothing. It did not satisfy President de Gaulle or other Europeans.

July 19, 1962   TO DETER FUTURE AMBITIOUS GENERALS IN LATIN AMERICA,
                         KENNEDY SUSPENDS DIPLOMATIC RELATIONS WITH AND ECONOMIC
                         AID TO PERU FOLLOWING A MILITARY COUP ON JULY 18.

The military junta displeased the United States by suspending all constitutional rights. In order to act quickly against the regime, Kennedy immediately cut off benefits to Peru from the United States. Only after the junta
agreed to return to constitutional practices did Kennedy renew assistance to
Peru on August 17, 1962.
     In 1963, the Kennedy administration made similar agreements with right-
wing military groups which had usurped the governments of Argentina, Guatemala, and the Dominican Republic. The military leaders in these states all
agreed to be anti-Communist. The Alliance for Progress of 1961 had not
brought democratic regimes to power in Latin America.

July 23, 1962   THE CONFERENCE ON LAOS AT GENEVA AGREES TO GUARANTEE
                         THE INDEPENDENCE AND NEUTRALITY OF LAOS.

The Geneva Conference had convened on May 16, 1961, as a means of avoiding a
large-scale U.S. intervention in Laos. (See May 3, 1961.) Over the next 14
months, the delegates met to gain an effective cease-fire and to form a neutral government acceptable to the three competing factions in Laos. Throughout the year, full-scale war threatened to disrupt the conference, but eventually the three rival princes of Laos reached a settlement. The three rivals
were the neutralist Souvanna Phouma, the U.S.-backed rightist Boun Oum, and
the leftist Communist-supported Souphanouvong.
     By May, 1962, Pathet Lao military actions in Laos had advanced over 100
miles. President Kennedy protested these movements and, on May 12, again
ordered U.S. naval ships and marines to the Gulf of Siam, and 2,000 U.S. soldiers to Thailand. As a result, the Communist advances stopped and the three
Laotian princes again met to negotiate.
     In June, the Laotian leaders announced that a 19-member coalition gov-
ernment had been formed under the neutralist Souvanna Phouma. King Savang
Vathana installed this ministry on June 22, and political calm returned to
Laos. On July 23, delegates at the 14-nation conference in Geneva recognized
the Souvanna coalition government. They also signed an agreement to withdraw
all foreign troops and guarantee the neutrality of Laos.

August 18, 1962   *VENEZUELA ASKS THE UNITED NATIONS GENERAL ASSEMBLY TO
                           INVESTIGATE ITS BOUNDARY WITH BRITISH GUIANA.*

*Although Venezuela had accepted the arbitration of its boundary with the Brit-
ish in 1899 (see February 20, 1895, and October 1, 1899), Caracas claimed
that later evidence in the reports of one of its legal advisors of 1899,
Severo Mallet-Prevost, showed the arbitration tribunal had not been just but*

had made a political deal in favor of the British. Therefore, Venezuela continued to hold its claims of 1896 against the British.

     Although the U.N. General Assembly referred the issue to a Special Po-
litical Committee, the issue was not resolved. Venezuela wanted the border
settled before the British granted independence to the state of Guyana. Because Guyana's independence was scheduled for 1966, the British insisted that
Venezuela should form a mixed commission to arbitrate the boundary with Guyana. The mixed commission was established on February 17, 1966, but Venezuela
and the independent state of Guyana could not agree on a new boundary settlement. The agreement of 1899 remained operative although Venezuela continued
to adhere to its previous land claims east of the Orinoco River into the territory of Guyana.

October 11, 1962   THE TRADE EXPANSION ACT OF 1962 BECOMES LAW--THE
                            KENNEDY ROUND IN AMERICAN TRADE POLICY.

By 1961, many U.S. international financial experts realized that the United
States needed new legislation to give the president greater authority in dealing with foreign tariff and trade policy. The success of the European Common
Market after 1957 required special attention. In addition, the U.S. balance
of international payments had turned adverse since 1958. During the three-
year period 1958 to 1960, the United States lost $4.7 billion in gold to for-
eign payments. In contrast, the EEC had collectively increased its gold reserves by over $6.5 billion. Because of these conditions, the United States
hoped to regain an increase in its exports by obtaining lower trade barriers
with Europe and other parts of the world.

     The 1962 Trade Expansion Act was designed to gain multilateral reductions
for U.S. exports to Europe and Japan. After four years of negotiation among
the major GATT members, a protocol signed on June 30, 1967 provided for significant tariff reductions. The United States gained a 35% reduction in nonagri-
cultural exports. While the agricultural agreement varied, the new tariffs
favored U.S. exports in all cases excepting Denmark. The United States gained
especially favorable reduction from Japan and the United Kingdom.

October 20, 1962   *CHINA AND INDIA BEGIN LARGE-SCALE FIGHTING IN A DIS-*
                            PUTED BORDER AREA.

Although Indian border police and Chinese forces had clashed on October 26,
1960, the Chinese-India issue had confined itself to small attacks before
October, 1962. India claimed that China unlawfully occupied 12,000 square
miles of its territory and demanded its return.

     During the three weeks after October 20, Chinese forces made successful
incursions into Indian territory. On October 31, India's Premier Nehru asked
the United States for aid, and in November, Kennedy sent transport planes
and crews to transport Indian troops. The U.S. aid was not necessary. On
November 21, Peking announced that the Chinese would withdraw to their 1957
borders and the fighting ended.

     In the United States, the India-China war affected American evaluations
of the Sino-Soviet split and China's relations with the West. Although Dean
Rusk, Chester Bowles, and other U.S. leaders wanted to negotiate with China
to take advantage of their poor relations with Moscow, President Kennedy

disagreed; he had, in fact, made an agreement with Chiang Kai-shek in 1961
to continue American support in the United Nations for the Formosan govern-
ment. Kennedy's cold war perceptions of Asia prevented him from comprehending
the potential significance of the Sino-Soviet split.

October 22, 1962   KENNEDY INFORMS THE NATION THAT THERE ARE RUSSIAN-BUILT
                          MISSILE SITES IN CUBA. HE ANNOUNCES A NAVAL QUARANTINE
                          ON ALL MISSILE EQUIPMENT BEING SHIPPED TO CUBA AND
                          CALLS ON KHRUSHCHEV TO REMOVE THESE WEAPONS.

The Executive Committee of the National Security Council (NSC), which President Kennedy ordered to examine alternative responses to the presence of Soviet missile sites in Cuba, had met regularly from October 16 to October 21.
The committee included McGeorge Bundy and Secretary Rusk from the State Department; Secretary of Defense McNamara; CIA Director John McCone; Attorney
General Robert Kennedy; and others. In addition, Vice-President Johnson,
U.N. Ambassador Adlai Stevenson, and the president met with the committee on
occasions.
     After considering a variety of alternative responses to the Russians,
the Executive Committee, the full NSC, and the president agreed to begin action against the Soviets with a naval blockade of Cuba, escalating subsequent
actions only if necessary. Other alternatives considered included such suggestions as an invasion or air strike of Cuba, secret negotiations with Cuba,
appeals to the United Nations, and doing nothing. By October 19, the consensus favored a blockade because it could be effective but would leave up to
Khrushchev the decision of acting as an aggressor to break the blockade. It
also left later alternatives for U.S. action if it failed.
     On Sunday, October 21, the full NSC decided to act as follows:

1. The president was to inform the public of the Russian missiles on
    October 22 over national television.

2. The naval quarantine was to be announced on television.

3. An appeal for support from the OAS and the United Nations was to be
    made on Tuesday.

4. Khrushchev was to be asked to remove all missiles from Cuba.

5. Dean Acheson and David Bruce would be sent to tell de Gaulle and
    Macmillan, respectively, of Kennedy's speech in advance.

On Monday, these plans went into operation beginning with Acheson's early
morning flight to London to inform Ambassador Bruce and to Paris to visit
de Gaulle. At 5 p.m., Kennedy met with congressional leaders to explain his
decision. At 7 p.m., the president outlined his quarantine plans to the U.S.
public, explaining to them that the United States found definite evidence of
missile sites in Cuba although there were no nuclear warheads as yet. Finally, he told the audience that his plan was a difficult and dangerous effort, "But the greatest danger of all would be to do nothing." Kennedy explained that the course chosen was most in keeping with the American character, to seek to avoid war but not to submit or surrender. He concluded: "Our
goal is not the victory of might, but the vindication of right--not peace at
the expense of freedom, but both peace and freedom, here in this hemisphere,
and, we hope, around the world."

The next day, Secretary Rusk obtained approval from the OAS to quarantine Cuba and take measures, including force if necessary, to end the crisis. All OAS members but Uruguay approved the quarantine decision. Brazil, Mexico, and Bolivia abstained from the section authorizing the use of force. At the same time, Adlai Stevenson indicted the Soviet Union for its aggressive action in Cuba. Because of the Soviet veto power, no action was sought in the Security Council.

The U.S. quarantine went into effect on October 24. A naval task force of 19 ships set up a picket line in the Atlantic, 500 miles from Cuba. See October 28, 1962.

October 23, 1962   PRESIDENT KENNEDY SIGNS A $3.9 BILLION FOREIGN AID BILL.

This bill included clauses which forbade aid to 18 Communist nations and to any nation which shipped arms to Cuba.

October 28, 1962   AN EXCHANGE OF PERSONAL LETTERS BETWEEN PRESIDENT KENNEDY AND PREMIER KHRUSHCHEV ENDS THE CUBAN MISSILE CRISIS. PREVIOUSLY, ON OCTOBER 24, RUSSIAN SHIPS DID NOT TRY TO BREAK THROUGH THE NAVAL BLOCKADE.

The days from October 24 to 27 were especially critical as Kennedy and his advisors waited to learn what the Russian ships en route to Cuba would do when they reached the U.S. naval blockade. On October 23, U.S. reconnaissance planes spotted 25 Russian ships in the Atlantic, most of which seemed to be headed for Cuba. Early on the morning of October 24, the first Russian vessels approached the quarantine line but until the last moment the Americans did not know what to expect.

On October 23, Khrushchev sent two divergent messages about his intentions. In a formal letter to President Kennedy the Soviet leader denounced the blockade as an act of piracy, bringing the world to the brink of nuclear war. He declared that Russian ships on their way to Cuba would defy the American blockade. At about the same time, he wrote a note to Bertrand Russell, a British pacifist who had appealed to Khrushchev to avoid war. The Soviet Chairman told Russell that he was not reckless, the Americans had acted aggressively. Khrushchev understood the disaster which nuclear war would bring. Therefore, he said, he was ready to do anything to avoid war. If the United States agreed, he would consider a top-level meeting to settle the Cuban crisis.

Consequently, as Russia's ships neared the U.S. blockade on October 24, the Americans did not know which orders Khrushchev had given to the Russian ships, the peaceful one or the bellicose one. About 10 a.m. two Russian ships neared the blockade point. Then the U.S. naval observers radioed that a Soviet submarine was between the Russian ships and the American ships. The captain of the U.S. carrier *Essex* was ordered to signal the sub to surface. More tension built at the White House. Then, at 10:25 a preliminary message arrived: the Russian ships appeared to be stopping. By 10:32, navy reports confirmed that 20 Russian ships in the area of the blockade line had stopped or were turning to head back to Europe. The quarantine had not been broken.

Kennedy now needed to arrange to move the Russian missile sites out of Cuba. To achieve this goal two steps were taken on October 25 and 27.

First, the navy was told to let the Russian ship *Bucharest* pass the blockade because visual sighting indicated it carried no cargo connected with missiles. The ship *Marcula*, however, was stopped and searched. After a two-hour search had found no missile equipment, the *Marcula* was allowed to proceed to Cuba. This process was followed with all Soviet ships that had not turned away from their sea route to Cuba.

Second, Kennedy had to consider two recent notes from Chairman Khrushchev, each of which suggested a settlement. The first, received on October 26 was a personal letter to Kennedy in which Khrushchev offered to remove the missiles from Cuba if Kennedy gave assurances that the United States would not invade Cuba. The second, received on October 27, was a more formal message in which Khrushchev offered to dismantle Cuban missiles if the United States dismantled missile bases in Turkey. Although the Turkish bases were obsolete, Kennedy did not want to swap them under pressure from Moscow. In light of the second note, the Joint Chiefs of Staff recommended that an air strike or an invasion of Cuba would be necessary. Kennedy opposed this at that moment.

Robert Kennedy suggested the method that worked. He told his brother to ignore the second letter and answer the first, in which Khrushchev asked only for a no-invasion pledge. The president followed this advice, writing a personal letter to transmit by teletype to Moscow. Kennedy's message accepted Khrushchev's proposal that Russia would remove its weapons system from Cuba if the United States would end the quarantine and give assurances against an invasion of Cuba. That same evening Robert Kennedy visited Soviet Ambassador Anatoly Dobrynin to explain the president's agreement as well as his determination not to back down, and his assurance that the Turkish missiles could be removed in the near future.

The next morning at nine o'clock, Moscow Radio broadcast Khrushchev's reply, which accepted Kennedy's proposal of October 27. On noon that day, Kennedy used the Voice of America to broadcast his acceptance of Chairman Khrushchev's "statesmanlike decision."

Only Fidel Castro's opposition blocked a final settlement of the dispute during the next several weeks. Castro refused to admit U.N. officials so Russian technicians had to dismantle the missile sites. When Castro refused to allow on-site inspection, the United States relied on visual inspection at sea. Russian crews pulled back tarpaulins so the U.S. Navy men could see the missiles on the decks of their ships. The final problem was the Cubans' desire to keep the IL-28 bomber planes stationed on their island. Not until November 20 could the Russians announce that these bombers would be sent back to the Soviet Union.

During the crisis, Khrushchev had backed away from violence by not running the blockade. Kennedy, however, had pledged that the United States would not invade Cuba.

December 17, 1962   KENNEDY AND THE NATIONAL SECURITY COUNCIL AGREE TO
                          GIVE MILITARY AID TO THE UNITED NATIONS TO FIGHT KA-
                          TANGA.

During the summer of 1962, Moishe Tshombe violated the Kitonia agreement with Adoula's Leopoldville government by refusing to forward tax funds from Katanga and continued to act independently backed by the Belgian mining company which paid for Tshombe's mercenary soldiers.

In October, 1962, U.N. Secretary General U Thant wanted to place an economic boycott on Katanga. He agreed, however, to try to negotiate again so

that the U.S. November elections would end before forceful action began
against Tshombe. By December, fighting began between Tshombe and Adoula's
forces and U Thant decided the United Nations had to take action. Although
American opponents of Adoula opposed U.S. military assistance against Tshombe,
the National Security Council and President Kennedy agreed on December 17 to
provide airlift operations and military equipment to aid the U.N. forces' invasion of Katanga. The U.N. troops attacked in January, and on January 15,
Tshombe again ended his secession. On June 14, Tshombe fled to exile and
the crisis in the Congo finally ended. This was a victory for the Leopoldville government backed by the United Nations and America.

December 20, 1962   *GENERAL ELECTIONS IN THE DOMINICAN REPUBLIC CONCLUDE*
                            WITH THE ELECTION OF JUAN D. BOSCH AS PRESIDENT.

*During 1962, a council of state under Rafael Bonnelly had weathered at least
two coup attempts before finally holding elections. On December 20, Juan
Bosch won the election, taking office on February 27, 1963. His rule lasted
only seven months. On September 25, 1963, a group of military leaders overthrew Bosch.*

December 21, 1962   PRESIDENT KENNEDY AGREES TO REPLACE THE BRITISH SKYBOLT
                            PROJECT WITH U.S. POLARIS MISSILES.

The U.S. military supported by Secretary of Defense Robert McNamara objected
to giving the Europeans independent nuclear capabilities and did not want to
let them share control of U.S. nuclear weapons in Europe. Consequently, in
the fall of 1962, McNamara unilaterally cancelled the Skybolt missile program
which would have given Great Britain an independent intermediate-range missile. Secretary Rusk warned McNamara that the cancellation would provide
problems for the British government, but McNamara agreed to settle it with
Britain's defense minister, Peter Thorneycroft. This issue arose, however,
at the Nassau meeting between Kennedy and Macmillan, because McNamara had
not clearly told the British of his Skybolt cancellation decision. As a result, Macmillan had not been prepared to accept the cancellation and strongly
objected because this decision would ruin his parliamentary backing. Therefore, Kennedy offered to give Britain Polaris missiles *without* nuclear warheads, agreeing to do the same for France. If Britain and France built submarines and warheads for the missiles, they would have to assign the vessels
to the NATO forces and not be independent. Macmillan did not like these restrictions but accepted them because he at least had something to soften the
blow to British pride. U.S.-British relations did not improve, however, because the British felt Americans did not trust them as an ally.

December 24, 1962   CUBA RETURNS 1,113 CUBAN REBELS CAPTURED IN APRIL,
                            1961.

Castro agreed to exchange his captives for $53 million worth of food and med-
icine.

1963

January 29, 1963   *FRANCE VETOES GREAT BRITAIN'S APPLICATION TO JOIN THE*
                        EUROPEAN ECONOMIC COMMUNITY (THE COMMON MARKET).

Urged by the United States, England reluctantly began discussions in 1962
with France and other EEC members for admission to the Common Market. The
British application was approved by all members except France. President
de Gaulle opposed Britain's entry into the European economic partnership.

March 30, 1963   THE UNITED STATES ANNOUNCES IT WILL "TAKE EVERY STEP
                      NECESSARY" TO PREVENT CUBAN REFUGEE RAIDS ON CUBA OR
                      ON SOVIET SHIPPING TO CUBA.

This announcement was made jointly by the U.S. Departments of State and the
Treasury. It was a follow up to President Kennedy's October 28, 1962, agreement not to permit an invasion of Cuba from the United States.

May 8, 1963   *BUDDHIST LEADERS IN SOUTH VIETNAM ORGANIZE DEMONSTRA-*
                   TIONS PROTESTING DIEM'S REPRESSIVE POLICIES.

Between 1961 and 1963, Diem had not enacted any significant reforms but en-
larged his repression because he envisioned every opponent as a "Communist"
enemy. Until 1963, the Buddhists had patiently avoided public demonstrations
of their dislike for Diem's thought-control methods which terrorized peasants
and discriminated against Buddhists.
*   Diem's methods against the Buddhists reached the breaking point in May,*
1963, when he forbade them to fly their religious banners in celebrating Bud-
dha's birthday on May 8. The Buddhist leaders at the religious center in
Hue defied Diem by carrying their banners and rallying the people to demon-
strate against Diem.
*   Diem moved to stop the Buddhists. South Vietnamese army units used ar-*
mored vehicles to break up the crowds. The soldiers opened fire and 9 people
were killed, 14 wounded.
*   The Buddhist leaders endeavored to negotiate a solution with Diem but*
he refused. As a result, American news reports of Buddhist opposition showed
clearly for the first time that Diem's problem was not simply the threat of
communism but his failure to gain the support of his own people. Buddhist
protests continued throughout 1963 and were reported in the United States.
One photograph which became famous for its dramatic effect showed a young
Buddhist monk aflame on a busy Saigon street. The monk had poured gasoline
over himself and put a lit match to his yellow saffron robes to show his dis-
dain for Diem. When Diem's sister-in-law, Madame Nhu, ridiculed these events
as "barbecues," her following in America dropped drastically.

May 12, 1963   *PAKISTAN AND COMMUNIST CHINA SIGN A TERRITORIAL AGREE-*
                         MENT.

*By this treaty, China ceded 750 square miles of land to Pakistan. This treaty
fostered good relations between China and Pakistan, both of whom had disputes
with India. On August 29, Pakistan signed an agreement with China to provide
scheduled air service to Peking. This was the first Western agreement for
air service with the People's Republic of China.*

May 22, 1963   NATO'S FOREIGN MINISTERS COUNCIL FORMS A 10-NATION
                         MULTILATERAL NUCLEAR STRIKING FORCE.

The United States had urged the creation of this multinational force as a
symbol of its willingness to cooperate with European defense plans. President
de Gaulle of France did not approve the plan and on June 21 began withdrawing
many French naval ships from the NATO Fleet Command.

May 25, 1963   *THE ORGANIZATION OF AFRICAN UNITY IS CHARTERED.*

*At Addis Ababa, 30 leaders of African states formed a regional bloc to work
together for their economic well being. On August 5, delegates of 32 African
countries formed an African development bank with a capitalization of $250
million.*

June 14, 1963   THE CHINESE COMMUNIST PARTY INDICTS MOSCOW FOR "RE-
                         VISIONIST" DOMESTIC POLICIES AND SAYS IT PLANS TO SPLIT
                         ANY COMMUNIST PARTY SUPPORTING THE SOVIET UNION.

Since the Communist Party meetings in Moscow on December 5, 1960, signs of
Sino-Soviet division had appeared more frequently. Each side urged other
national Communist groups to back their views on foreign and domestic policy.
The Peking declaration of June 14 was a most bellicose statement demonstrating
the split between Mao and the Soviet Presidium. In foreign policy, the Chinese rejected the idea of "peaceful coexistence" and seemed more willing to
risk a nuclear war. By early 1964, Peking began recognizing pro-Chinese factions in various nations as the legitimate Communist party in opposition to
Russia's party controls.

June 20, 1963   THE UNITED STATES AND THE SOVIET UNION AGREE TO CREATE
                         A COMMUNICATIONS "HOT LINE" TO REDUCE THE RISK OF AC-
                         CIDENTAL WAR.

Following the Cuban missile crisis of 1962, the idea of direct emergency communication between the Kremlin and the White House was proposed as a method
of averting any misunderstanding which might lead to war. The Soviet Union
accepted this idea on April 5 and on June 20, 1963, formal arrangements were
agreed to which established this instant communication means.

June 26, 1963   PRESIDENT KENNEDY VISITS WEST BERLIN, PROMISING TO
                       DEFEND FREE BERLIN FROM COMMUNIST ENCROACHMENT.

Kennedy's speech in Berlin enthralled the West Germans, as he concluded his
speech on defending freedom with the words, "Ich bin ein Berliner!"

July 11, 1963   *A MILITARY COUP IN ECUADOR OVERTHROWS PRESIDENT CARLOS
                       AROSEMENA.*

*The government came under the control of a four-man junta headed by Captain
Ramon Castro Jijon. The junta outlawed the Communist Party and promised to
wipe out Fidel Castro's terrorist guerrillas who had infiltrated Ecuador.
The United States recognized the new regime on July 31, 1963.*

July 31, 1963   ALTHOUGH THE CIA ESTIMATES THAT CHINA'S POLICIES ARE
                       NOT AGGRESSIVE, PRESIDENT KENNEDY AND SECRETARY RUSK
                       BELIEVE OTHERWISE: RESULTS OF A NATIONAL SECURITY COUN-
                       CIL MEETING.

Following the Cuban missile crisis of 1962, the president and Rusk spoke about
Russia's compliant policies and China's "blatant aggression" in India and
elsewhere. Their concern led to a special NSC session on July 31, 1963.
     At the meeting, the CIA presented a special estimate of the Chinese sit-
uation which discounted Chinese military ambition against India, indicating
as others had done that India, not China, had been the aggressor in October,
1962. The CIA also dismissed the view that China was acting aggressively in
Southeast Asia or elsewhere. The Peking government spoke often of support
for anti-imperial wars but showed respect for U.S. power and most feared the
Soviet Union.
     Nevertheless, Kennedy had always disliked Red China, continued to back
Chiang Kai-shek, and deplored Mao's aggressive talk against America. Although
Rusk was less opposed to Peking than Kennedy, he too accepted the president's
views. Later attempts by Kennedy's apologists to assert that he planned to
change his China policy are assertions which have not been well documented.

July 31, 1963   THE UNITED STATES ABSTAINS IN A U.N. SECURITY COUNCIL
                       VOTE ON A RESOLUTION TO STOP ALL ARMS SHIPMENTS TO
                       PORTUGAL'S COLONIAL GOVERNMENT OF ANGOLA.

Native uprisings against Portuguese rule began in Angola in 1961. As a result, on January 30, 1962, the U.N. General Assembly voted 99-2 to urge Portugal to stop its repressive measures against the "people of Angola." Because
the Angola rebel leader Holden ROBERTS had become "friendly" in accepting
aid from the Soviet Union and later (January 3, 1964) from Communist China,
the United States, Britain, and France faced a dilemma. They wanted Portugal
to give independence to Angola but did not like Roberts' policies. As a result, the three Western powers abstained on a Russian-sponsored resolution
to stop all arms going to Portugal's colonial government.

August 5, 1963   A LIMITED NUCLEAR TEST BAN TREATY IS SIGNED BY BRITAIN,
                          THE SOVIET UNION, AND THE UNITED STATES.

Three-power talks on a test ban began in Moscow on July 15. The representatives were Foreign Minister Gromyko, U.S. Undersecretary of State W. Averell
Harriman, and British Minister for Science Viscount Hailsham.
    The three powers signed the treaty on August 5. When it became effective
on October 10, over 100 nations had agreed to it. The treaty prohibited tests
in space, the atmosphere, and underwater. It did not eliminate underground
tests. See October 31, 1958.

September 25, 1963   *DOMINICAN PRESIDENT JUAN BOSCH IS OVERTHROWN BY A*
                         RIGHT-WING GROUP HEADED BY GENERAL ELIAS WESSIN Y
                         WESSIN AND DONALD REID CABRAL.

*Bosch's election as president of the liberal reform government had been per-
sonally approved by Kennedy in 1962. Therefore, Kennedy cut off aid to the
new military junta and tried to pressure it to conduct new elections. In
December, 1963, President Johnson agreed to recognize Reid's government and
renewed its economic assistance. See April 28, 1965.*

October 19, 1963   *SIR ALEC DOUGLAS-HOME BECOMES PRIME MINISTER OF ENGLAND*
                         FOLLOWING THE RETIREMENT OF HAROLD MACMILLAN.

November 1-2, 1963   A MILITARY COUP IN SAIGON OVERTHROWS AND KILLS NGO
                         DINH DIEM.

The increased domestic pressure against Diem which corresponded to the Buddhist protests (see May 8, 1963) resulted in several plots by South Vietnamese military generals against Diem. As early as August, U.S. Ambassador
to Saigon Henry Cabot Lodge heard of these plots and asked Secretary of State
Rusk how to react. Lodge recommended that he should give assurances to any
anti-Communist groups who opposed Diem.
    The White House was not certain how to respond because Kennedy heard
two opposing views. Taylor and Rostow clung to their 1961 plan, urging that
the U.S. strategic hamlet and combat-support missions should be continued,
claiming they would succeed by 1964 or 1965. They blamed the Nhus, not Diem,
for Saigon's problems. Two senior U.S. diplomats who had spent much time in
Vietnam disagreed. Joseph Mendenhall and Rufus Phillips, who headed the
hamlet-assistance program, reported that Diem seldom followed U.S. advice
and that the Nhus had corrupted the purposes of the hamlet program. In addition, Phillips said, the Nhus gave Taylor and Rostow falsified reports of
the pacification program, which made the military evaluations incorrect. Marine General Victor Krulak was enraged by Phillips' charges but neither he
nor Taylor would investigate Phillips' data. Phillips' reports showed that
the Viet Cong (South Vietnamese Communists) had captured 50 hamlets in recent
weeks in the southern delta region near Saigon. The Viet Cong controlled
80% of Long An province in the south.
    Krulak and Taylor preferred to base their reports on the northern prov-
inces because they argued that Diem's problem was the invasion of North Vietnam along the 17th parallel. Phillips told them they should look at the

heavily populated southern delta area where local Communists as well as non-Communists opposed Diem. The dispute, which became a classic between the military and the civilian American advisors, had appeared. The U.S. military saw the war as a Communist invasion from the north; most U.S. civilian advisors saw the domestic South Vietnam economic problems as the basis for the threat to the Saigon regime.

Kennedy preferred the military viewpoint. As he told Chet Huntley during an NBC interview on September 9, China instigated the problems in Vietnam and if South Vietnam fell, the Chinese could capture all of Indochina and Malaya. He told Huntley, "the war in the future in Southeast Asia was China and the communists." Neither Kennedy nor Johnson wanted to be accused of another "China cop-out," as Truman had been in 1949. As David Halberstam observes in his ironically titled *The Best and the Brightest*, seldom has so much Washington talent been so misguided by its incorrect assessment of circumstances, which led in turn to poor policy planning in Vietnam.

Nevertheless, in the fall of 1963 the White House estimates shifted enough to enable Ambassador Lodge to inform the plotters in Saigon that the United States would accept a new government. McNamara and Taylor visited Saigon in September and on their return indicated that while there was "great progress" in U.S. military action, Diem was not popular. The United States, they told Kennedy, should "work with the Diem regime but not support it."

This curious recommendation enabled Secretary Rusk to inform Lodge on October 6 that America would accept a new government led by General Duong Van Minh (Big Minh). Subsequently, on the night of November 1-2, 1963, General Minh and his allies staged an attack on the presidential palace where they captured Diem and the Nhus. Diem tried to rally his loyal troops in Saigon but outside of his personal guards, he had no loyal troops. The assassination of Diem and his brother and sister-in-law does not appear to have been planned by Big Minh. The United States expected they would be exiled. Allegedly, a long-time enemy of Diem led the armored unit which captured the three family leaders. He had them shot before they reached Big Minh's headquarters.

November 22, 1963   PRESIDENT KENNEDY IS ASSASSINATED IN DALLAS, TEXAS. KENNEDY DIES ALMOST IMMEDIATELY AND VICE-PRESIDENT LYNDON B. JOHNSON IS SWORN IN AS PRESIDENT.

December 12, 1963   *KENYA, A FORMER BRITISH COLONY, BECOMES INDEPENDENT.*

Just two days earlier, Zanzibar became independent.

Problems in Kenya did not end, however. On January 24, there was a troop mutiny in Kenya. President Jomo Kenyata asked British forces to restore order.

Zanzibar and Tanganyika also experienced problems because of an uprising on January 20 at Dar es Salaam. On January 25, the British restored order. Eventually Zanzibar became part of Tanzania under Jules Nyerere's presidency on October 29, 1964.

December 26, 1963   SECRETARY McNAMARA INFORMS THE PRESIDENT THAT POLITICAL
                           CONDITIONS IN SAIGON ARE UNSTABLE.

The coup against Diem on November 1, 1963, did not solve South Vietnam's political problems. Big Minh's new regime lacked support and came under attack
from opposing military groups. Following a visit to Vietnam in December,
the Secretary of Defense made a gloomy report to Johnson. Present trends,
he wrote, "will lead to neutralization at best and more likely to a communist
controlled state." The new government was "indecisive and drifting." The
internal reform program lacked leadership. Viet Cong progress had been great.
     McNamara's recommendation was ominous. The United States must watch the
situation but prepare "for more forceful moves if the situation does not show
early signs of improving." For more on Saigon's continuing political problems
see January 25, 1965.

1964

January 1, 1964   *THE FEDERATION OF RHODESIA AND NYASALAND IS DISSOLVED.*
THREE SEPARATE STATES ARE FORMED: NYASALAND, NORTHERN
RHODESIA, AND SOUTHERN RHODESIA.

On October 23, 1953, Great Britain had overseen the establishment of the fed-
eration of these three states within the British Commonwealth. Black African
majorities within the federation opposed the federation because they were not
effectively represented, and on February 21, 1961, the British revised the
federation constitution to rectify this complaint. The new system did not
satisfy the black Africans. Although blacks outnumbered whites in the fed-
eration by 26 to 1, the electoral rolls gave whites a 10 to 1 superiority of
votes.

Between October, 1962, and January 1, 1964, Great Britain had to nego-
tiate a settlement which evolved separate status for each of the three states.
Both Nyasaland and Northern Rhodesia set up legislatures with black African
majorities. In Southern Rhodesia, however, a white majority gained control
and Great Britain opposed its request for independence.

Consequently, after the federation was dissolved on January 1, 1964,
Northern Rhodesia was renamed Zambia and became independent, with Kenneth
Kaunda as prime minister. Nyasaland (later renamed Malawi) was an independent
nation with Hastings Banda as prime minister.

Southern Rhodesia's all-white government presented greater problems to
the British. On April 13, a radical right government gained control under
Ian D. SMITH. On April 16, Smith banished, without trial, four black African
leaders including Joshua Nkomo. The first of a series of riots and demonstra-
tions by black Africans had to be suppressed by Smith's government.

January 27, 1964   *FRANCE GRANTS RECOGNITION TO THE PEOPLE'S REPUBLIC OF*
CHINA.

February 11, 1964   *FIGHTING BEGINS ON CYPRUS BETWEEN GREEKS AND TURKS.*

This struggle to dominate the island of Cyprus continued throughout 1964 and
tensions continued between Greece and Turkey for over a decade.

February 21, 1964   A CRISIS WITH CUBA ENDS WHEN CASTRO AGAIN TURNS ON
THE WATER SUPPLY TO GUANTANAMO NAVAL BASE.

This crisis began on February 2 when the U.S. Coast Guard arrested four Cuban
fishing boats in U.S. waters off the Florida Keys. Thirty-six fishermen were
turned over to Florida authorities for legal disposition; two fishermen requested political asylum in the United States. Two of the Cuban captains

admitted that they had been selected for this "historic venture" as a means
of testing "U.S. reactions."

Cuba protested to the United States through Swiss Ambassador Emil
Stadelhofer, and also complained to the U.N. Security Council. On February
6, Cuba's Foreign Minister, Raul Roa, sent word that Cuba was cutting off
the water to the U.S. naval base at Guantanamo. It would be turned on only
when the fishermen were released.

The U.S. Navy had contingency plans to supply water at the base on a
limited basis, and these were put into effect. In addition, Johnson and the
U.S. Navy agreed immediately to take steps to make Guantanamo self-sufficient
by obtaining a permanent water supply and ending the employment of Cubans on
the base.

On February 21, the Florida court dropped charges against the Cuban crews
but fined the four captains $500 each. All the men were released and Cuba
immediately turned on the water to Guantanamo.

Johnson proceeded to carry out the plan to make the base self-sufficient.
The 2,000 Cuban employees at the base were released from work and on April 1,
construction of a desalination plant began at Guantanamo. This water proces-
sor was completed in December, 1964, and the U.S. base was then self-reliant.

March 31, 1964   *IN BRAZIL, MILITARY LEADERS OVERTHROW PRESIDENT JOAO*
                          GOULART.

Goulart had undertaken reforms in line with Kennedy's Alliance for Progress.
These changes included distributing federal land to landless peasants, dou-
bling the minimum wage, and expropriating land adjacent to federal highways.
Conservatives opposed these reforms, leading to the revolt which sent Goulart
into exile. On April 11, Army Chief of Staff General Humberto Castelo Bianco
was selected to replace Goulart as president.

April 3, 1964   A CRISIS WITH PANAMA ENDS WHEN PRESIDENT JOHNSON
                          AGREES TO "REVIEW EVERY ISSUE" WITH PANAMA, AND DIP-
                          LOMATIC RELATIONS RESUME.

President Eisenhower's September 17, 1960, agreement to permit Panama's flag
to fly with the American flag in the Canal Zone had satisfied a symbolic but
not a substantive complaint of Panamanians regarding their rights in the
Canal Zone. On October 1, 1961, President Robert Chiari formally asked the
United States to revise the Panama Canal Treaty to provide just rights for
Panamanians. The Kennedy administration ignored this request, and the growing
discontent led to large-scale riots in Panama beginning on January 7, 1964.
Panama broke relations with the United States and demanded a new canal treaty.

The OAS council set up a 17-member committee to find a solution to the
U.S.-Panamanian dispute. While its efforts failed, the committee succeeded
in obtaining President Johnson's agreement to review all issues in the treaty
relations. With this understanding, President Chiari agreed to renew diplomatic relations with America.

Although U.S. and Panamanian election-year politics prevented a decision
during 1964, a new treaty was formalized in 1965. See September 24, 1965.

April 20, 1964   PRESIDENT JOHNSON ANNOUNCES THAT HE AND SOVIET CHAIRMAN
                          KHRUSHCHEV HAVE AGREED TO REDUCE THE PRODUCTION OF
                          U-235 FOR NUCLEAR WEAPONS.

President Johnson had sought some means to curb the arms race, and in his
January 8 state-of-the-union message announced that the United States was
cutting its production of enriched uranium 235 by 25% and was closing several
nonessential nuclear military installations.

Between February 22 and April 20, Johnson corresponded with Chairman
Khrushchev to determine if he would take parallel action in further reducing
the Soviet output of U-235, which was used to produce hydrogen bombs. Just
as Johnson reached New York to deliver his address of April 20 to the annual
Associated Press luncheon, he received a message from Moscow that Chairman
Khrushchev agreed on parallel action to reduce U-235 production and to allocate more fissionable material for peaceful uses. He gave this information
to the public in his speech of April 20. Johnson believed that small steps
such as this would lead to limits on nuclear weapons and to the decline of
the threat of a nuclear holocaust.

April 22, 1964   *RUMANIA'S COMMUNIST PARTY INSISTS ON THE INDEPENDENCE
                          OF ALL COMMUNIST NATIONS AND PARTIES.*

*The Rumanians desired greater freedom from Moscow's interference and began
economic negotiations with the United States, France, and other nations. The
Rumanian Communists agreed, however, to support Moscow in its ideological
dispute with Communist China.*

April 28, 1964   *PRESIDENT DE GAULLE ANNOUNCES THAT FRENCH NAVAL STAFF
                          OFFICERS WILL NO LONGER SERVE UNDER NATO COMMANDS.*

*Since 1962, de Gaulle had begun to disassociate his nation from NATO organi-
zations. President Kennedy had rejected his suggestion of a pact by which
Paris, London, and Washington would jointly oversee Western affairs. Thereafter, de Gaulle began an independent foreign policy program. On January 14,
1963, he rejected a NATO proposal for a multilateral defense force. On January 28, 1964, he signed a five-year trade agreement with the Soviet Union.*

July 10, 1964   THE FORMER KATANGA SECESSIONIST, MOISE TSHOMBE, BECOMES
                          PREMIER OF THE CONGO; THE UNITED STATES ASSISTS THE
                          CONGO IN ENDING THE REBELLION.

In March, 1964, Averell Harriman recommended that Johnson should provide
planes and pilots to assist the Congolese in putting down rebels, some of
whom were aided by the Chinese Communists. Harriman wanted to support the
Government of National Reconciliation groups headed by Cyrille Adoula. Therefore, Johnson sent planes to "train" the Congolese. Soon after, exiled Cubans
recruited by the CIA were flying U.S. aircraft against the Congolese rebels.

As the rebel raids increased, Adoula resigned on June 30, leaving the
National Reconciliation party leaderless. Then on July 10, Tshombe returned
from exile where he had fled on June 14, 1963, and took over as prime minister
in the coalition government. Because Tshombe's former secessionist plots

made him unacceptable to other black African leaders, only the United States
and Belgium helped him against the rebels.

August 7, 1964   CONGRESS PASSES THE TONKIN GULF RESOLUTION AUTHORIZING
                                THE PRESIDENT TO TAKE "ALL NECESSARY MEASURES TO REPEAL
                                ANY ARMED ATTACK" IN SOUTHEAST ASIA.

Although the congressional Tonkin Gulf Resolution resulted from North Vietnamese gunboat attacks on U.S. destroyers off the coast of Vietnam, congress
did not investigate nor did President Johnson accurately report the developments in the United States of secret plans during 1964 which led to the North
Vietnamese attack. (Later, in 1966, the Senate did investigate the Tonkin
Gulf incident.)

On February 1, 1964, Johnson authorized the use of military plan 34a
for covert action against North Vietnam designed to pressure Hanoi to withdraw
from South Vietnamese territory. Plan 34a provided a variety of sabotage
and psychological and intelligence-gathering operations against North Vietnam.
These included U-2 flights to gather intelligence on targets; assisting South
Vietnamese commando raids on North Vietnam to destroy railways, bridges, and
coastal defense installations; air raids by U.S. fighter-bombers disguised
as Laotian Air Force planes; and destroyer patrols in the Gulf of Tonkin to
collect data on Communist radar and coast defenses. Although the Pentagon
later claimed the destroyer patrols and commando raids just happened to occur
on the nights when the North Vietnamese attacked the American destroyers,
Hanoi could not be expected to disassociate the two types of U.S. interference
on its coastline and assumed the commandoes and the destroyers worked together.

These covert operations are the only explanation for the small North
Vietnamese PT boat attacks on the larger destroyers. On August 2, the commander of the U.S.S. *Maddox* fired on a group of torpedo boats which he said
launched their missiles at his ship. Whatever torpedoes were fired were off
target, but the U.S. ships and planes from the carrier *Ticonderoga* damaged
two PT boats and destroyed a third. Two nights later, on August 4, there
was another PT boat-destroyer encounter. While the Communist boats were alleged to have launched one or two torpedoes, they never reached their target.
This time the Americans sank two PT boats.

President Johnson saw the naval incidents on August 2 and 4 as the opportunity to stand tall. At 11:30 p.m. on August 4, Johnson went before a
nationwide TV audience, interrupting all programs to announce the "unprovoked"
attack by Communist boats on the U.S. destroyers in the Tonkin Gulf. Communist subversion in South Vietnam "has now been joined by open aggression on
the high seas against the United States of America." The president announced
he would act with restraint with a simple reprisal raid on North Vietnam but
he urged congress to give him greater authority to repel future attacks.

On May 23, McGeorge Bundy had prepared a resolution for Johnson to obtain
authority from congress. The president gave this draft to the House and Senate for quick action. Congress acted quickly. Although Senator Wayne Morse
wanted an extended investigation before voting, Senator J. William Fulbright,
Chairman of the Senate Foreign Relations Committee, refused. The committee
supported Fulbright, and with little debate, congress passed the resolution.
The House vote was 416 to 0; the Senate vote, 88 to 2.

The Tonkin Gulf Resolution was the closest congress ever came to a declaration of war in Vietnam. It was not, however, a declaration of war. The

resolution declared Southeast Asia was "vital to the national interest and world peace"; therefore, it gave the president the right to "take all necessary steps, including the use of armed forces" to aid any member or protocol state (South Vietnam) of SEATO to defend the region from communism. Only the presidential campaign of 1964 prevented Johnson from immediately taking steps to further escalate the war in 1964.

Johnson did, however, make reprisal raids against North Vietnam. On August 4, within six hours of the reported Tonkin Gulf incident, the Joint Chiefs selected targets and the National Security Council supported the reprisal raids on North Vietnam. Two and a half hours later, planes from the carriers *Ticonderoga* and *Constellation* attacked North Vietnam. Their targets were four torpedo boat bases and an oil storage depot which held 10% of Hanoi's petroleum supply. Following this attack, Johnson ordered U.S. bombers to be deployed in the southwest Pacific pending orders for future raids on Vietnam. See January 28, 1966 and June 12, 1970.

October 14, 1964   KHRUSHCHEV IS OVERTHROWN BY KOSYGIN AND BREZHNEV.

An intraparty struggle had arisen in Moscow between 1962 and 1964. To counter his opposition, Khrushchev tried a new method of open deliberations of the Central Committee before hundreds of "plain folk." The attempt to silence the opposition did not succeed because it threatened to undermine the power of the highest party groups of the Soviet organization. Khrushchev was ousted apparently because Brezhnev and Kosygin persuaded all members of the Presidium to vote against the Chairman. Members of the Central Party Committee could not resist. Khrushchev went into exile at a dacha near Moscow and wrote his memoirs, which were published in the West as Khrushchev Remembers.

October 15, 1964   JAMES HAROLD WILSON BECOMES BRITISH PRIME MINISTER
                      FOLLOWING A LABOUR PARTY VICTORY WITH A MAJORITY OF
                      FOUR SEATS OVER THE CONSERVATIVES, LED BY DOUGLAS-
                      HOME.

November 3, 1964   LYNDON JOHNSON WINS A LANDSLIDE VICTORY OVER BARRY
                      GOLDWATER.

The election of 1964 was the first in which the Republican candidate directly challenged the cold war consensus policies of containment and the socio-economic programs begun under the New Deal. In domestic affairs, Goldwater opposed such basics as agricultural subsidies and social security. Abroad, he wanted "total victory" over communism, not containment, and made many Americans fear he might launch a nuclear war. Whether or not he actually said, as alleged, that the United States should "lob a nuclear bomb into the men's room at the Kremlin," both his avid followers and his opponents believed he did.

Against Goldwater, Johnson became a symbol of restraint and progress. Even during the Tonkin Gulf crisis, Johnson's single reprisal raid did not accurately indicate the more bellicose secret plans which Johnson prepared for use in 1965 if necessary. Therefore, Johnson said as little as possible about Vietnam or other foreign issues.

The 1964 election was the apogee of Johnson's political career. He won

the greatest vote (43 million to 27 million), and the greatest percentage
(61.1%) in recent American history. If the southern whites had not deserted
Johnson on the Civil Rights issue, the victory would have been larger. The
electoral college vote was Johnson 486, Goldwater 52.

1965

January 27, 1965   THE U.S. DEFENSE DEPARTMENT REPORTS ON SOUTH VIETNAM'S
CONTINUED POLITICAL DETERIORATION.

When interfering in Third World conflicts, American political leaders had a
consistent lack of comprehension of how to deal with the government they supported against the apparently more vigorous and focused leadership of the
Communists. In Vietnam as in Nationalist China before 1949, the problem was
that the right-wing non-Communists were concerned about themselves and their
families, gathering about them equally self-centered generals and political
underlings. By the end of 1964, Maxwell Taylor, who became the U.S. Ambassador to Saigon in June, 1964, discovered that the Vietnamese did not want Americans to interfere in their domestic affairs, they only wanted the United
States to fight the war for them.
      Reports by Taylor, and on January 27, 1965, a summary analysis of the
Vietnamese situation by John T. McNaughton (an assistant to McNamara), described the difficulties of the internal political conflicts of 1964 during
which Taylor's advice was seldom heeded by the Vietnamese. In January, 1964,
Big Minh was overthrown by General Nguyen Khanh. In August, a coup against
Khanh by General Lan Van Phat aborted and gave power to a triumvirate of
Nguyen Cao KY, Nguyen Chanh THI, and Nguyen Van THIEU. These three younger
officers tried to please Taylor by forming a High National Council. On December 20, however, General Khanh eliminated the National Council and joined
Thi and Ky in a new military junta. With the military, religious, and social
factions running amok in Saigon, the South Vietnamese army could not function
effectively. Because a new government seemed incapable of improvement,
Taylor and McNaughton said the war would be won only if America controlled
the war. A vital step to Americanize the war was taken in 1965.

February 6-7, 1965   PRESIDENT JOHNSON ORDERS REPRISAL AIR RAIDS ON NORTH
VIETNAM AFTER A COMMUNIST ATTACK ON U.S. BARRACKS AT
PLEIKU.

The plan to escalate the war in Vietnam in stages had been decided upon on
November 6, 1961. These "slow squeeze" techniques were designed to force
North Vietnam and the Viet Cong to stop their war against Saigon. The plan
required reprisal raids as the first escalation stage. The second stage would
be the increase of U.S. ground troops for combat in South Vietnam.
      Johnson's decision of November 6 was critical and is often misunderstood
because it was based on the limited-war theory of war for political objectives. The Joint Chiefs of Staff urged Johnson to turn the entire conflict
over to the military so that they could take all necessary actions, short of
nuclear attack. Johnson and his advisors fought the war for political purposes, which were to contain communism at the 17th parallel and to protect
South Vietnam and other non-Communist areas of southeast Asia. Thus, military

tactics were given political objectives, a strategy which the U.S. armed
forces had not traditionally followed until the Korean War in 1950-1953, when
Truman and MacArthur dramatically disagreed on the primacy of political,
limited-war objectives.

The Communist attack on Pleiku created a circumstance that enabled the
reprisal raids to begin. In the raid on Pleiku, the Viet Cong killed nine
U.S. soldiers and wounded 76 severely. They damaged or destroyed six airplanes and 16 helicopters. Following a brief NSC meeting, Johnson ordered
reprisals code-named Flaming Dart I. Two attacks by navy carrier jet planes
hit a North Vietnamese barracks at Dong Hui and a communications center at
Vinh Linh.

In announcing the reprisals, the White House cited the Viet Cong attacks
on two southern villages as well as at Pleiku. This announcement linked
"their" war with "our" war--the Pleiku attack on U.S. facilities with an attack on South Vietnam villages.

Subsequently, Johnson told General Westmoreland that while reprisal attacks should not be given the same character as the Stage Two sustained bomber
raids, he could make necessary reprisals in retaliation for particular Communist attacks on villages or U.S. facilities. The reprisal Stage One policy
lasted less than six weeks. See March 19, 1965.

March 19, 1965   "ROLLING THUNDER," SUSTAINED BOMBER ATTACKS, BEGIN
                          AGAINST NORTH VIETNAM.

Johnson ordered Stage Two of his "slow squeeze" tactics to begin against North
Vietnam on March 19. Except for specific periods when President Johnson
halted these raids in order to consider possible cease-fire agreements, the
Rolling Thunder air attacks continued from March 19, 1965, to March 31, 1968.

The first bombing pause came between May 10 and 18, soon after the initial attacks inspired many international leaders to seek negotiation methods
that would alleviate the problems in Vietnam. Great Britain and the Soviet
Union proposed to reconvene the 1965 Geneva Conference. Neither this effort
nor others were successful during the next three years.

In operation, the Rolling Thunder attacks took place at least two or
three times each week. Johnson and McNamara controlled the dates and target
selection for the raids. Although this control dismayed the U.S. military,
Johnson wanted to retain political authority in deciding whether to increase
or decrease targets as well as when attacks took place. Nevertheless, the
quantity of Rolling Thunder attacks against North Vietnam was astonishing.
During a three-year period, 309,996 U.S. bombers dropped 408,599 tons of bombs
on North Vietnam, most of these in the area between Hanoi and the 17th parallel. Generally, the area around Hanoi, the port of Haiphong, and the Chinese
border were avoided. By 1967, Johnson gradually eased this restriction, enu-
merating new targets such as rail yards or oil installations near Hanoi and
Haiphong.

By July, 1965, Johnson also embarked on Stage Three of the slow squeeze,
sending combat troops to Vietnam after April 6, 1965. Johnson did not admit
this publicly until July. See July 28, 1965.

March 24, 1965   AMERICAN OBJECTIVES IN VIETNAM ARE GIVEN A QUANTITATIVE FORMULATION BY JOHN T. McNAUGHTON.

The Assistant Secretary of International Affairs in the Defense Department, McNaughton prepared a memo which justified the U.S. bombing campaign against North Vietnam. This memo stated that U.S. aims in Vietnam were:

70% - to avoid a humiliating defeat (to our reputation as guarantor).

20% - to keep Vietnamese (and adjacent) territory from Chinese hands.

10% - to permit the people of South Vietnam a better, freer way of life.

Also - to emerge from crisis without unacceptable taint from methods used.

NOT - to "help a friend," although it would be hard to stay if asked out.

Except for the statement of percentages, President Johnson's, Rusk's, and McNamara's speeches from 1965 to 1968 appeared to verify McNaughton's listing. McNaughton's memo was secret and confidential, not reaching the U.S. public until the publication of the *Pentagon Papers* in 1971.

March 24, 1965   PROTESTS AGAINST THE VIETNAM WAR ARE MADE DURING A "TEACH-IN" AT THE UNIVERSITY OF MICHIGAN, BEGINNING A NEW METHOD OF DISSENT.

Although there were a few war dissenters before March, 1965, the criticism against the White Paper's explanation of the war in January, 1965, the Pleiku reprisal raids of February, and the first Rolling Thunder bombings of March inspired the start of a slow but growing opposition to the Vietnam war.

Significant dissent arose on college campuses where professors trained in international studies, foreign policy, and Asian or Vietnamese culture opposed the administration's methods. The teach-ins became a means to disseminate information about an area of the world which few Americans knew and about which there were misconceptions based on myth or misinformation. The teach-ins lasted from two hours to all day and night. Some were conducted as debates for and against Johnson's policies; others were informative or were held to explain why U.S. policies erred. Some were argued by moderate dissenters who wanted better U.S. global strategy; others, by radical opponents who described the emotional and inhumane results of napalm bombs and B-52's on helpless South Vietnamese families.

The dissenters were aided by the fact that although Johnson talked about funding both guns and butter programs, the president's military program received much funding, his war on poverty received little. In 1965, the key program in Johnson's "Great Society" was the Office of Economic Opportunity (OEO). It received *less than* $1 billion for 52 weeks; the Vietnam war cost *more than* $1 billion for *each* of 52 weeks in 1965. All social programs in 1965 cost $2 billion, the equivalent cost of two weeks of war. Persons in the United States living below the poverty level were eligible for an average of $532 from the federal budget; the Pentagon estimated it cost $322,000 for each Communist killed in Southeast Asia. In 1968, the military budget was $76 billion; the budget for health, education, welfare, and social programs was $15 billion.

The failure of guns and butter both to be funded affected foreign policy because it increased dissent. During the summers of 1966 and 1967, there were major riots in Los Angeles, Chicago, Newark, and Detroit and smaller riots elsewhere as demonstrators opposed Johnson's failure to fulfill his rhetoric on either the Vietnam war or the war on poverty.

The growth of dissent was indicated in public opinion polls. When Rolling Thunder began in 1965, 50% of the public supported Johnson's Vietnam policy; by December, 1965, this rose to 65%. During 1965, the president's acceptance rate by the public stabilized at 54%. In 1967, his popularity steadily declined. Only 44% agreed with the war program and a smaller percentage, 23%, thought he did a good job as president. By early 1968, Johnson, who was a devotee of opinion polls, watched the support of the war effort collapse even more. (See March 31, 1968.) For other factors in dissent against the war see October 14, 1965, and January 28, 1966.

April 7, 1965   PRESIDENT JOHNSON EMPHASIZES THAT AMERICA MUST PROTECT
                               THE FREEDOM OF THE VIETNAMESE PEOPLE.

In a speech at Johns Hopkins University, President Johnson sought to counteract the first signs of dissent on his Vietnam policy by describing America's idealistic role in fighting in Vietnam. The United States had a "promise" to keep in Vietnam and must show our allies they can depend on us. In addition, China and North Vietnam were allegedly stepping up their attacks on the "brave people of South Vietnam," and only America could slow this Communist aggression.

Johnson ended his speech with dramatic but ironic words--ironic because he had just introduced the Rolling Thunder bombing campaign in Vietnam. Johnson said at Johns Hopkins that the American people have a very old dream "of a world where disputes are settled by law and reason." They also have a dream "of an end to war." We must make these so, he said, concluding:

> Every night before I turn out my lights to sleep, I ask myself this question: Have I done everything that I can do to unite this country? Have I done everything I can do to help unite the world, to try to bring hope to all the peoples of the world?
> This generation of the world must choose: destroy or build, kill or aid, hate or understand.
> We can do all these on a scale never dreamed of before.
> We will choose life. And so doing will prevail over the enemies within man, and over the natural enemies of all mankind.

April 28, 1965   IN VIOLATION OF THE OAS CHARTER, PRESIDENT JOHNSON
                               SENDS U.S. MARINES TO INTERVENE IN THE DOMINICAN RE-
                               PUBLIC, CLAIMING THERE IS A THREAT OF COMMUNISM.

Dominican politics had been in flux since May 30, 1961, when Trujillo was assassinated. Juan Bosch had been elected president in 1962, but was overthrown in a coup on September 25, 1963. During 1964, there was frequent unrest in the Dominican Republic when the possibility of another military coup appeared possible. President Reid was not popular. U.S. Ambassador W. Tapley Bennett backed Reid, but a CIA poll showed only 5% of the people favored Reid.

A revolt began on April 24, led by officers who favored the return of Juan Bosch. Secretary of State Rusk disliked Bosch and wanted to prevent

his accession to power. Rusk thought Bosch had been ineffective in 1962 and
that he was under Communist influence. Neither Rusk nor Johnson wanted another Cuba in the Caribbean. When a CIA report said the Communists supported
Bosch, Rusk became convinced that he should not gain control.

As a result, when General Wessin counterattacked against Bosch supporters
on April 26, Johnson encouraged the general, asking him only to act moderately
against the rebels. Wessin failed, however, and when the U.S. embassy called
for marines to save the country from communism, Johnson responded quickly to
Wessin's request for aid because the government could not protect U.S. lives.

On April 28, 500 marines landed; soon after, 20,000 more soldiers arrived. Johnson gave the U.S. public lurid details of the Communist threat,
saying the United States acted on behalf of humanity. His action saved
Wessin's counterrevolution from the victory of Bosch's rebels.

The United States never proved that there was a real Communist threat
in the Dominican Republic. There was danger to Americans in the country because of conflict, but until the U.S. forces arrived, Bosch had hoped to get
U.S. support because Kennedy had helped him in 1962. In early May, Johnson
sent John Barlow Martin to Dominica to check on Communist influence. Martin
reported that one rebel, Colonel Francisco Caamano Deno, was a potential
Castro because he had an advisor who was a Communist. This inspired Rusk
and Johnson to further action to back the loyalists in the island republic.

Somewhat ironically, by May 21, Rusk told the Senate Foreign Relations
Committee that the danger of communism had vanished. The administration, he
said, could accept either Bosch or his leading opponent, Balaguer. Also by
mid-May, Rusk had referred the intervention to the OAS Council. The OAS
agreed to send a multinational force to oversee the return of stability to
the Dominican Republic. Later, in June, 1966, the OAS held elections and
Balaguer won. The fear of Castro had led Johnson to overreact in April, 1965.

June 12, 1965   GENERAL THIEU AND MARSHAL KY GAIN CONTROL OF THE SOUTH
                         VIETNAMESE GOVERNMENT, APPEARING TO GIVE UNITY TO SOUTH
                         VIETNAM.

Following further political difficulties in Saigon from December, 1964, to
June 12 (see January 25, 1965), the government achieved a semblance of order
after Thieu and Ky replaced Prime Minister Phan Huy Quat. Thieu became chief
of state; Ky became prime minister.

In reality, the Ky-Thieu government created a decentralized order by
dividing up the political spoils of South Vietnam with four other generals.
The so-called National Leadership Committee which made up the six-man junta
set up four corps areas. General Thi held the First Corps area, Vinh Loc
the Second, Bao Tri the Third, and Dang Van Quang the Fourth. Each general
was in complete charge of his corps area, awarding military and civilian posts
to the highest bidder, friends, or relatives. These posts were profitable
for the generals--reports were that a province chief's job cost three million
piatres plus a 10% kickback each month. Ky was the head of the baronies because his charismatic personality suited the U.S. newsmen, TV cameras, and
visiting politicians. Thieu was in the shadows but was the brains behind
the junta and he eventually gained complete power. As David Halberstam and
other reporters documented, in their corps areas the generals' basic motives
were personal power and profit. They conserved their troops for personal
use, letting the Americans do the fighting as much as possible.

Outwardly, however, Ky and Thieu created a political scheme which looked good compared to the difficulty of frequent political changes between November, 1963, and June, 1965.

July 28, 1965   PRESIDENT JOHNSON ANNOUNCES THE ADDITION OF MORE AMER-
                         ICAN FORCES IN VIETNAM BUT TRIES TO EXPLAIN THAT IT
                         IS A "RESTRAINED" RESPONSE.

Because of recent "leaks" to the press in Washington about American troops in South Vietnam, President Johnson held a press conference to explain his decisions. On June 8, Robert McClosky of the State Department told reporters that U.S. forces would "fight alongside Viet forces when and if necessary." Although the State Department clarified McClosky's statement on June 9 by saying there had been "no recent change in mission" of U.S. forces, Secretary McNamara on June 16 acknowledged that U.S. combat troops would "act as was necessary" to cope with the enemy.

President Johnson was enraged by the news headlines of June 9 and 17 generated by McClosky's and McNamara's statements. As the *Pentagon Papers* of 1971 indicated, Johnson had specifically instructed everyone on April 1 that the role of U.S. troops should not be reported as a "sudden change in policy." On April 1, the Third Stage of the slow squeeze had been secretly approved. By this decision, 20,000 American troops were ordered to Vietnam, and there was a policy change in the role of U.S. forces. Kennedy's "combat support" role ended. American officers and their troops would assume direct control over actions against the Viet Cong and North Vietnamese forces south of the 17th parallel.

Johnson wanted this decision to appear not as a change but as action consistent with Kennedy's commitments. Thus, NSAM-328 of April 6 (whose contents had been approved on April 1) stated that:

> The President desires that ... premature publicity be avoided by
> all possible precautions.... The President's desire is that these
> movements and changes should be understood as being gradual and
> wholly consistent with existing policy.

American troop increases had begun in a limited fashion before July 28. Two Marine Battalion Landing Teams of 3,500 men arrived at Danang on March 8 and by mid-June, 75,000 U.S. troops were in South Vietnam. Moreover, the April 1 policy called for forces to come from Australia, South Korea, New Zealand, and the Philippines. At Ambassador Taylor's request, the government of South Vietnam asked other nations for assistance. One Australian battalion arrived in June, 1965. Because Britain and France opposed the U.S. operations, SEATO never sanctioned Johnson's "war" in Vietnam.

U.S. air operations south of the 17th parallel were also ordered on April 1. These included both tactical and strategic aircraft operations. General Westmoreland had charge of the fighter and bomber planes assigned to South Vietnam. These planes substituted for ground artillery by bombing and strafing enemy-held areas. They also dropped napalm fire-bombs and chemical defoliants to burn out or kill vegetation in jungle areas under Communist control. These attacks caused civilian protests both in South Vietnam and the United States because they indiscriminately damaged combatant and non-combatant areas, but the U.S. Air Force claimed they served a useful purpose. By the end of 1965, the U.S. Air Force stationed 500 aircraft and 21,000 men at eight major air bases in South Vietnam.

The air force's strategic bombing by B-52's in the south was code-named Arc Light. Beginning in June, 1965, B-52's flew area bombing missions from Guam. These area destructive capabilities coming from high altitude flights gave an extra dimension of fear to both VC and non-VC in the south because the people usually never saw the high-flying planes.

Although the April 1-6 decisions involved the Americanization of the war in South Vietnam, Johnson and his advisors were not certain what term to use in news releases to the U.S. public. When the marines landed in March, their mission was described as "security force" for the U.S. bases at Danang. General Westmoreland's reports called these operations "active counterinsurgency" to give ambiguity to the missions. McClosky on June 8 used the term "fight alongside."

On July 28, the president announced that another 50,000 U.S. forces would go to South Vietnam (the *Pentagon Papers* showed the figures approved by July, 1965, to be 125,000). This increase, the president said, was minimal and non-provocative because of the large number of North Vietnamese units fighting in the south. The spring offensive of the Communists had made large advances during June, 1965, and South Vietnam needed greater assistance. When a reporter asked the president if the troop increase implied less reliance on South Vietnam's troops, Johnson assured him: "It does not imply any change in policy whatsoever."

Johnson's attempt to deceive the newsmen failed. Too many reports of the U.S. "search and destroy" mission in South Vietnam contradicted the president's words. For many reporters, the July 28 press conference began their realization that the president purposely misled them. A "credibility gap" grew larger and larger between the president and the Washington press corps after 1965, further serving the groundswell of U.S. dissent between 1965 and 1968.

At various times after July, 1965, U.S. ground troops increased in size in South Vietnam as the war was Americanized. By December, 1965, there were 267,500 U.S. ground combat troops in South Vietnam; in December, 1966, 385,300; in December, 1967, 449,800. The peak number of U.S. ground troops in Vietnam occurred in April, 1969, when there were 543,400 U.S. military forces in Vietnam.

September 24, 1965   THE UNITED STATES AND PANAMA SIGN A NEW CANAL AGREEMENT.

Negotiations to change the U.S. treaty with Panama began in 1964 following a series of riots in Panama (see April 3, 1964). During the next year, the United States and Panama agreed to a treaty which granted Panama sovereignty over the Canal Zone, provided economic aid to Panama, and allowed U.S. bases to protect the canal.

October 3, 1965   A NEW IMMIGRATION ACT REPLACES THE QUOTA SYSTEM OF 1921.

As passed by congress and signed by Johnson, this law set overall immigration limits, including 120,000 from the Western Hemisphere and 170,000 from the rest of the world. Generally, however, it allowed 20,000 immigrants from most nations on a first-come, first-served basis.

October 14, 1965   THE DEPARTMENT OF DEFENSE ANNOUNCES THE LARGEST DRAFT
                        CALL SINCE THE KOREAN WAR.

One consequence of the escalation of U.S. ground forces in Vietnam was the
call for more draftees aged 18 to 35. Although the Defense Department preferred to call up trained military reserves or the National Guard, Johnson
opposed this method of enlarging the armed forces. The president believed
calling reserves and the National Guard was tantamount to a national crisis
that would require a declaration of war. He did not want to engage congress
in that debate, preferring to act under the Gulf of Tonkin resolution permitting him to do "all things necessary" to defend Vietnam.

The call up of more young men from colleges or their first job opportunities was not popular. During the two days after the Defense Department's
October 14 draft call, there were anti-draft demonstrations on college campuses and in all major U.S. cities. Some young men burned their draft cards
to symbolize their determination not to go to Vietnam. The "burn your draft
card" campaign became so extensive that congress passed legislation in 1966
which punished such acts with a $5,000 fine and up to five years in prison.

Anti-draft tactics varied during the next decade. Counseling centers
were set up to advise young men on how to fake physical and mental tests in
order to fail the army's physical examination. Two Catholic priests, Daniel
and Phillip Berrigan, led a group of draft resisters in a raid of the Baltimore Selective Service offices to destroy draft files by pouring ox-blood on
the records. Some young men avoided the draft by going into exile in Canada
or Europe. Nearly 40,000 men deserted from the U.S. Army in 1968.

Returning war veterans also questioned the war and the draft. On May 8,
1966, Lloyd Shearer published an article in *Parade* magazine based on interviews with 88 wounded soldiers at U.S. hospitals. Eighty of the soldiers
"declared flatly" that the "South Vietnamese could not be trusted." One said,
"maybe the Vietnamese like us, but after spending 10 months there, I can tell
you--they sure do a great job hiding it." These men, said Shearer, fought
because the president said they should but they were confused about U.S. war
objectives and could not understand why most Vietnamese disliked Americans.

Parade was a widely read Sunday supplement magazine and these reports
could not help raising questions about Johnson's policy in Vietnam.

November 20, 1965   *IN THE LAST OF THREE RESOLUTIONS AGAINST SOUTHERN RHO-*
                        DESIA, THE U.N. SECURITY COUNCIL ORDERS AN OIL EMBARGO
                        ON RHODESIA.

Because a series of negotiations between Great Britain and Rhodesia in 1963-
1964 had failed to reach a compromise to provide an integrated government
for Rhodesia, IAN SMITH, the white supremacist President of Rhodesia, had
unilaterally declared independence from Britain on November 11, 1965.

On November 13, the first Security Council resolution condemned Rhodesia
for its action. The second resolution, on November 17, ordered Britain to
put down the Rhodesian revolution. Finally, on November 20, an oil embargo
was voted against Rhodesia. Ian Smith defied each of these actions. Because
the Rhodesians refused to negotiate, the Security Council voted economic sanc-
tions against Rhodesia on December 16, 1965.

November 25, 1965   *TWO YEARS OF POLITICAL DIFFICULTIES END IN THE CONGO*
                       AS GENERAL MOBUTU BECOMES PRESIDENT.

Maneuvering in the Congo between Moise Tshombe on the right and a left-wing
rebel group which took over Stanleyville on August 5, 1964, placed the Congo
in political disorder. The Stanleyville group was put down, and on October
13, 1965, General Kasabuva removed Tshombe as prime minister of the Leopold-
ville government. Finally, on November 25, Mobutu overthrew Kasabuva and
order came to the Congo for the first time since June, 1960.
    On June 30, 1966, Leopoldville was renamed Kinshasha.

December 7, 1965   THE UNITED STATES AND INDIA SIGN AN AGRICULTURAL AID
                       TREATY IN WHICH INDIA ALSO AGREES TO GIVE AGRICULTURAL
                       MODERNIZATION MORE ATTENTION.

India had been experiencing severe food shortages in 1964-1965. President
Johnson was willing to help, but urged Secretary of Agriculture Orville
Freeman to link future U.S. food shipments to India's readiness to emphasize
food progress as well as industrial advance.
    Meeting in Rome with India's Minister of Food and Agriculture, Chidambaro
Subramaniam, Freeman worked out an agreement based on Johnson's position.
In its next Five-Year Plan, India agreed to give greater attention to supplying more food for itself. In turn, the United States agreed to make necessary
wheat shipments to meet India's requirements. The India Treaty became the
basis for Johnson's "Food for Peace" program. See November 12, 1966.
    In spite of India's new efforts, the United States had once again to
assist India with food in April and December, 1966. Johnson limited this
aid because he claimed other nations should also respond to India's needs.
See January 15, 1967.

December 27, 1965   PRESIDENT JOHNSON AGREES TO MAKE THE CHRISTMAS BOMBING
                       PAUSE IN THE ROLLING THUNDER ATTACKS A LONGER PAUSE
                       WITH A WIDESPREAD DIPLOMATIC ATTEMPT TO ACHIEVE PEACE.

Since early November, Secretary of Defense McNamara had favored a bombing
pause in order to permit North Vietnam a chance to react positively to the
fact that the United States had escalated air and ground action in Vietnam
during the past nine months. Both the Joint Chiefs of Staff and Secretary
Rusk opposed McNamara's request. In early December, however, the Soviet Ambassador Anatoly Dobrynin indicated that the Russians would help obtain an
agreement if there was a bombing pause. This convinced Rusk that a bombing
pause would succeed or, at least, demonstrate to the American public that
Johnson tried everything possible to seek peace.
    With the backing of both the Secretary of State and the Secretary of
Defense, Johnson concurred. On December 24, the United States and South Vietnam had agreed to call a Christmas halt to aggressive action. Therefore, on
December 27, Johnson simply extended this pause in order to permit the State
Department to examine a peaceful solution.
    In spite of a large-scale and much publicized U.S. diplomatic effort to
use the pause as a method of gaining negotiations on Vietnam, the bombing
pause failed. Between December 27 and January 31, 1966, U.S. diplomats visited Rome, Belgrade, Warsaw, Paris, and London to seek aid in gaining a

settlement.   Rusk believed the most hopeful effort was a mission from Hungary, Poland, and Russia which visited Hanoi to try and convince Ho Chi Minh to seek a settlement.   This mission failed.

On January 28, Radio Hanoi broadcast Ho Chi Minh's message that America's "so-called search for peace" was "deceitful" and "hypocritical." He insisted that the United States must first pull out of Vietnam and recognize the Communist National Liberation Front as the legitimate representative of the people of South Vietnam. On January 31, Johnson ordered the resumption of Rolling Thunder's bombing raids on North Vietnam.

1966

January 17, 1966 THE UNITED STATES LOSES A HYDROGEN BOMB IN AN AIR COL-
LISION OVER SPAIN.

A U.S. plane carrying four unarmed H-bombs crashed near Palomares, Spain.
The consequences were less harmful than expected, although several bombs rup-
tured sufficiently to poison farmland nearby.

January 19, 1966 *MRS. INDIRA GANDHI BECOMES PRIME MINISTER OF INDIA
FOLLOWING THE SUDDEN DEATH OF LAL BAHADUR SHASTRI ON
JANUARY 11.*

January 28, 1966 THE SENATE FULBRIGHT COMMITTEE HEARINGS ON VIETNAM
OPEN IN WASHINGTON.

Senator J. William Fulbright had been a close friend of President Johnson
and led Senate action in quickly passing the Tonkin Gulf Resolution in August,
1964, persuading senators such as Sherman Cooper and Gaylord Nelson that
Johnson needed the resolution as soon as possible even if the wording appeared
to be open ended in granting presidential authority. Fulbright believed
Johnson meant it when he told the senator that the resolution was limited
and was designed only to steal ground from Senator Goldwater's criticism.
During 1965, Fulbright realized that the president had lied to him and
misled him in August, 1964. Gradually, the senator turned bitterly against
Johnson and the escalation of the war. Joining with other Democratic Party
members on the Senate Foreign Relations Committee, Fulbright opened hearings
on the Vietnam war on January 28, 1966, which heard both sides of the question
but were designed to provide the television audience and news media with the
opportunity to hear and propagate the views of dissenters against the war
such as George Kennan and Lieutenant General James Gavin. In so doing, the
Senate hearings caused the liberal "egghead" wing of the Democratic Party to
turn against the war.
During the Senate hearings between January 28 and February 18, 1966,
Dean Rusk explained how the war resulted from North Vietnam's "invasion" of
South Vietnam and contended that the United States had to keep its pledge to
help Saigon. Maxwell Taylor and others also defended Johnson's policy, but
their version of the war had already been heard frequently on national television.
More significant was the opportunity for the ideas of Kennan and Gavin
to reach a large audience. Kennan believed the war was foolish and not vital
to the United States. Gavin urged that different tactics were required to
minimize the U.S. role and maximize the role of South Vietnam. Finally,
Robert Kennedy testified in favor of new policies in Vietnam. Kennedy thought
a coalition with the Communists might be better than with the corrupt regime

in Saigon. In brief, Fulbright's hearings added to the growth of dissent
against Johnson's policies in Vietnam.

February 6, 1966   FRANCE WITHDRAWS ITS TROOPS FROM NATO AND REQUESTS
                           NATO TO MOVE ITS HEADQUARTERS FROM FRANCE.

President de Gaulle of France had been hostile toward the United States since
1962 because Washington refused to grant the French a more equitable position
in their partnership. In particular de Gaulle disliked the multilateral (MLF)
NATO force proposed by George Ball and urged by the United States from 1963
to 1966. Having previously withdrawn French naval forces from NATO, de Gaulle
now extended French independence by withdrawing all French forces from NATO.
In addition, at France's request, NATO headquarters were moved from Paris to
Brussels. Soon after, the idea of the MLF was dropped by the United States.

February 8, 1966   PRESIDENT JOHNSON IS OPTIMISTIC AT THE CONCLUSION OF
                           MEETINGS IN HAWAII WITH THE LEADERS OF SOUTH VIETNAM,
                           KY AND THIEU.

Between June 12 and early 1966, the system Ky and Thieu established on June
12, 1965, seemed to keep political order. Johnson was pleased and on January
31, 1966, invited the two leaders to meet with him in Honolulu.
    Ky knew all the right words to satisfy Johnson. Their regime was defeat-
ing the enemy, pacifying the countryside, stabilizing the economy, and building democracy. Ky told Johnson that any government may launch a program for
a better society "but such a program cannot be carried forward for long if
it is not administered by a really democratic government, one which is put
into office by the people themselves and which has the confidence of the people."
    At the conclusion of the Honolulu meeting on February 8, the Declaration
of Honolulu was issued. In the first part of the decree, the Vietnamese government stated its goals, which included:

1. defeating the Viet Cong and those "illegally fighting with them";

2. eradicating social injustice among our people;

3. maintaining a viable economy to build a "better material life for
    our people ...";

4. building "true democracy for our land and for our people," including
    a constitution in a "few months."

The United States promised to support the goals and programs stated by
the Vietnamese. See September 11, 1966.

February 24, 1966   *KWAME NKRUMAH, THE GHANIAN DICTATOR WHO HAD ALIGNED*
                           WITH RUSSIA, IS OVERTHROWN IN AN ARMY COUP LED BY GEN-
                           ERAL J.A. ANKRAH.

May 14, 1966   THE KY GOVERNMENT ATTACKS DANANG AND HUE FOLLOWING
                        RECENT OUTBREAKS OF BUDDHIST-LED UPRISINGS.

The Buddhist riots of 1966 which in many respects reenacted those of 1963
had been precipitated by Prime Minister Ky's attempt to remove General Thi
as commander of the First Corps area. With strong support from the Buddhists
and the Dai Viet organization of Southern Vietnamese Nationalists, Thi had
become very independent of Saigon's control. When Ky sought to remove Thi,
Buddhists led by Thich Tri Quang began protests on March 10, 1966. Students,
trade unionists, and the Dai Viet aided the Buddhists. A nun and eight young
Buddhist bonzes set themselves aflame to protest against Ky's government.
The U.S. consulate at Hue was burned.

     On May 14, Ky ordered South Vietnamese troops to quell the uprising.
Paratroopers landed at Danang airport but were repelled. Next, loyal Vietnamese marines and infantry besieged Hue, causing Buddhist hunger strikes
throughout South Vietnam in sympathy with Hue. By June 8, however, Ky's armies conquered Hue and Danang. Ky alienated the Buddhist leaders by banning
their religious processions and all political acts. Many of the leaders in
Hue and Danang were imprisoned or exiled. In his memoirs, President Johnson
said he "always believed" Thi Quang and his followers were either pro-
Communist or their movement was "deeply penetrated" by Hanoi's agents.

June 29, 1966   ROLLING THUNDER'S FIRST ATTACK ON "POL" TARGETS BEGINS
                        ALTHOUGH SECRETARY McNAMARA AND OTHERS HAD OPPOSED
                        THEM.

Since September 2, 1965, the air force and Joint Chiefs had urged Johnson to
permit the bombing of POL (petroleum, oil, lubricants) targets near Hanoi as
well as the aerial mining of North Vietnam's seaports. Secretary McNamara
opposed these targets because of the increased risk of war with China or the
Soviet Union. Moreover, he claimed, the POL storage areas contained only
10% of North Vietnam's needs and their loss would not seriously damage the
economy. The JCS favored all efforts to remove the president's restraints
on their targets and strongly believed the POL and seaport mines would help
the war effort.

     Johnson decided in May, 1966, not to mine the seaports but to permit
the attacks on POL targets. His final orders were delayed, however, first,
because British Prime Minister Harold Wilson asked Johnson to reconsider;
later, in June, because Canada sent an ambassador to Hanoi to discuss possible
peace terms with Ho Chi Minh. After Ambassador Chester Ronning's mission
failed, Johnson ordered the POL attacks which began on June 29. See November
11, 1966.

August 18, 1966   *THE "CULTURAL REVOLUTION" BEGINS IN CHINA.*

*The complete Chinese title of Mao's policy from 1966 to the early 1970's was
the "great revolution to establish a propertyless class culture." Edgar Snow
described Mao's version of this in his book* The Long Revolution *(1972), which
was based on interviews with the Chairman of the Chinese Communist Party.*

     *According to Snow, Mao realized by the mid-1960's that the Peking Party
Committee led by Liu Shao-ch'i was making Mao a cult figure in order to decrease his power. This group had been strongly influenced by the Russian*

*apparatus of party controls and bureaucratic prerogatives. As a result, Mao
secured supporters in Shanghai as well as the backing of the army under Lin
Piao. They organized the masses and the Red Guards to overthrow Liu Shao-
ch'i.*

*In practice, the cultural revolution emphasized agriculture and the vil-
lage tradition. It sought to train village youths at the University so they
could return to their homes and boost village production and culture. In
this sense, it was a conflict between the modernization tendencies of the
city, technology, and expertise versus the Chinese village and communal life
around which Mao had rallied the Communist Party from 1930 to 1949.*

September 6, 1966   *PRIME MINISTER VERWOERD OF SOUTH AFRICA IS ASSASSI-
                           NATED.*

*Despite this killing, the white supremacist leadership of South Africa was
undisturbed. B.J. Vorster became prime minister on September 13, 1966.*

September 11, 1966   ELECTIONS IN SOUTH VIETNAM SELECT DELEGATES FOR A CON-
                           STITUENT ASSEMBLY.

These elections were set up by the Ky-Thieu government in order to fulfill a
long-sought desire of U.S. advisors to have a "free" election to prepare a
constitution for South Vietnam. The election went well; more than two-thirds
of the south's adults registered to vote and 81% of those registered voted,
electing 117 delegates who represented all political factions except the Buddhists, who boycotted the election. Neither U.S. reporters nor European observers found any significant fraud at the ballot box.
    Between October, 1966, and March, 1967, the assembly delegates met to
prepare a constitution. There was much dissension over the type of government
to create. A document was finally drawn up on March 19, 1967, the day before
Ky and Thieu met with President Johnson at Guam.

October 25, 1966   THE MANILA CONFERENCE IS ATTENDED BY PRESIDENT JOHNSON
                          AND REPRESENTATIVES OF NATIONS CONTRIBUTING TROOPS TO
                          THE VIETNAM WAR.

At the invitation of President Marcos of the Philippines, President Johnson
met in Manila with General Thieu and Prime Minister Ky of South Vietnam; President Chung Hee Park of South Korea; and Prime Ministers Harold Holt of Australia, Keith Holyoake of New Zealand, and Thanom Kittikachorn of Thailand.
    Following a two-day review of the military and non-military situation
in Vietnam, the delegates issued three statements:

1. *Goal of freedom* - The seven nations at Manila declared their unity
    in seeking freedom for Vietnam and other Asian Pacific areas.

2. *Allies seek no permanent bases in Vietnam.* In this statement, South
    Vietnam asserted she would ask the seven nations to leave Vietnam
    when peace was restored. The seven allies declared they were in
    Vietnam only to aid the victim of aggression. They would withdraw
    within six months after peace was restored.

Soviet Foreign Minister Andrei Gromyko told Johnson on October 10 that a specific statement on withdrawal would aid peace arrangements. Therefore, Johnson said, the second statement of the Manila Conference clarified Gromyko's suggestion.

3. *Declaration of peace and progress in Asia and the Pacific.* The seven allies said their objectives were to oppose aggression, poverty, illiteracy, and disease. They would search for peace, reconciliation, and economic, social, and cultural cooperation in Asia.

November 1, 1966 ALBANIA'S COMMUNIST PARTY BREAKS WITH MOSCOW AND ALLIES WITH CHINA AS THE "TRUE" COMMUNIST PARTY.

November 11, 1966 PRESIDENT JOHNSON COMPROMISES BETWEEN PROPOSALS OF SECRETARY McNAMARA AND OF THE JCS ON ACTIVITY IN VIETNAM.

Following the inauguration of POL bombing raids on June 29, Secretary McNamara's aides watched the results closely while a special group of leading scientists prepared the code-named JASON report for devising new methods against North Vietnam. Between August 29 and October 15, 1966, a flow of reports from JASON, the CIA, and the Defense Intelligence Agency all concluded that the POL bombings had no critical effect on North Vietnam. On September 4, 1966, the Commander in Chief for the Pacific had redirected the air force from a POL emphasis to targets causing "attrition on men, supplies and equipment" in North Vietnam.

The conflict over war priorities between Secretary McNamara and the Joint Chiefs focused on new recommendations in October, 1966. McNamara's JASON group recommended the construction of an electronic anti-infiltration barrier across the 17th parallel of Vietnam. In addition, McNamara recommended stabilization of the air war or a bombing pause, and the addition of 40,000 combat troops. The JCS disagreed with the secretary, urging an escalation of attacks against the north and requesting an added 150,000 men with the call-up of military reserve units.

Johnson's orders of November 11 sought a middle ground between McNamara and the JCS. He agreed to add 70,000 troops but rejected the call-up of military reserves. At the same time, he rejected the electronic barrier, agreeing with the JCS that it could not work. Finally, Johnson agreed to stabilize the Rolling Thunder attacks. The bombing stabilization was coordinated with an effort by Prime Minister Harold Wilson to push Moscow and Hanoi to agree to reconvene the 1954 Geneva talks on Vietnam. See February 14, 1967.

November 12, 1966 JOHNSON SIGNS THE FOOD FOR PEACE ACT OF 1966.

On December 7, 1965, the United States and India signed an agreement to encourage India to modernize its agriculture. President Johnson liked this concept and on February 10, 1966, recommended that congress approve a program for the United States to assist other nations in agricultural progress by offering U.S. know-how on irrigation, pesticides, and farm equipment to less developed nations. Congress adopted this program and the president signed the bill into law on November 12.

November 13, 1966   *ISRAEL LAUNCHES A LARGE-SCALE REPRISAL ATTACK ON JOR-*
                          DAN: THE UNITED STATES LATER VOTES TO CENSURE ISRAEL
                          IN THE UNITED NATIONS.

During 1965-1966, tensions increased on the Syrian-Israel border as Syria's
new radical government under Premier Salah el-Bitar sent Arab guerrillas
across the border causing the Israelis to retaliate. In addition, a Palestin-
ian group, al-Fatah, operated from bases in Lebanon and Jordan to raid Israel.
On August 15, Syria and Israel had a serious conflict at Lake Tiberias using
planes, tanks, and patrol boats.

On November 13, Israel launched a large reprisal attack on the Jordanian
towns of al-Samu, Jimba, and Khirbet Karkoy. Jordan appealed to the United
Nations where the Security Council voted to censure Israel. President Johnson
also sent military aid to bolster the army of Jordan's King Hussein. Jordan
had generally been pro-Western in its policies but the increase of Palestinian
refugees and the al-Fatah Party made it difficult for Hussein to restrain
these guerrilla raids on Israel.

1967

January 15, 1967   PRESIDENT JOHNSON SENDS EUGENE ROSTOW ON A WORLD MIS-
                        SION TO PERSUADE OTHER NATIONS TO HELP ALLEVIATE IN-
                        DIA'S FOOD PROBLEMS.

Although the United States had supplied wheat shipments to India on various
occasions after 1947, including the U.S.-India agreement of December 7, 1965,
Johnson believed nations other than the United States should develop responsibility to assist India.

When India appealed to the president for wheat in March, 1966, he sent
a small amount but decided to restrict the shipments to the "must" requirements, while encouraging India to ask other nations for aid. To emphasize
his point, Johnson held up some shipments of wheat between August and December, 1966. Some observers criticized him for this policy but Johnson persisted.

By mid-December Australia and Canada each provided 150,000 tons of wheat
for India; other nations did not. The French, in particular, irritated
Johnson because they offered only to sell 200,000 tons at the "usual commercial terms."

To get his message more directly to other nations, Johnson asked George
Woods, President of the World Bank, to talk with other nations about aid to
India. On January 15, he sent Eugene Rostow, the Undersecretary of State,
on a round-the-world mission to solicit greater assistance. Eventually in
1967, other governments helped India including Canada, Australia, the Soviet
Union, Britain, France, West Germany, Japan, Belgium, Austria, and the Scan-
dinavian countries. With this additional aid India obtained nearly 10 million
tons of wheat in 1967. During 1965 and 1966, the United States alone had
sent 8 million tons and 6 million tons, respectively.

This aid from 1965 to 1967 and India's new agricultural program brought
the "green revolution." India's agricultural output increased considerably
after 1967. Unfortunately, India's large population increase outran its food
increase in Malthusian fashion.

January 26, 1967   SECRETARY OF DEFENSE McNAMARA INFORMS A SENATE COMMIT-
                        TEE OF U.S. NUCLEAR STRATEGY: THE CONCEPT OF MUTUAL
                        ASSURED DESTRUCTION (M.A.D.) IS EVOLVED.

On January 26, McNamara's testimony before the Senate Armed Services Committee
was made public. His information indicated the Soviets' "faster-than-expected
build up of ICBM's and their deployment of an antiballistic-missile defense
(ABM) around Moscow." Although the secretary stated that the United States
would presently have superiority by three times in the number of ICBM's until
the early 1970's, the Soviets were catching up and their ABM program represented a new menace the United States should meet.

McNamara said the American nuclear strategy needed two basic capabilities:

1. *"Assured destruction"* as a deterrent. To absorb a surprise first strike and be able to inflict an "unacceptable degree of damage" on any combination of aggressors;

2. *"Damage limitation"* ability to restrict destruction of the U.S. population and industry. This required a build up of America's ABM missiles--the Nike-X program.

Together these strategic goals would achieve a mutual nuclear deterrent power (MAD). "U.S. fatalities from a Soviet first strike could total about 120 million; even after absorbing that attack, we could inflict on the Soviet Union more than 120 million fatalities." With an American ABM system the increase in the Soviet ICBM system would give it a second-strike ability to kill 120 million Americans.

Because both sides would spend money--the United States on ABM's; Russia on ICBM's--it seemed in both nations' interests that negotiation would permit each to save money. Thus, McNamara wanted to talk with Moscow about an ABM limitation. Meanwhile, the Nike-X program had to continue until an agreement was reached.

January 27, 1967   THE UNITED STATES, THE SOVIET UNION, AND 58 OTHER COUNTRIES SIGN THE OUTER SPACE TREATY.

This treaty embodied a variety of potential outer space contingencies which the signatories agreed to follow including: no nation can claim sovereignty over a celestial body such as the moon or planets; outer space will not be used for military purposes; astronauts or equipment forced to land on foreign territory will be returned; the launching country is liable for damage by its rockets, satellites, or space vehicles. The most notable of the clauses in this treaty was the agreement to prohibit weapons of war in outer space.

This treaty formalized a resolution of October, 1963, in which the General Assembly of the United Nations called on all nations to avoid placing nuclear weapons in orbit around the earth. At that time, both the United States and the U.S.S.R. independently declared that they would abide by the U.N. resolution. On April 25, 1967, the U.S. Senate ratified the treaty unanimously.

February 14, 1967   *IN MEXICO CITY, 14 LATIN AMERICAN NATIONS SIGN A TREATY BANNING NUCLEAR WEAPONS.*

February 14, 1967   PRIME MINISTER WILSON'S ATTEMPT TO RECONVENE THE GENEVA CONFERENCE ON VIETNAM IS NOT SUCCESSFUL.

During the fall and winter of 1966-1967, Wilson and Johnson agreed that Washington would stabilize its bombing activity while the prime minister persuaded Premier Alexsei Kosygin of the Soviet Union to invite participants in the 1954 Geneva talks to reconvene and resolve the Vietnamese dispute. In addition, other tactics were used to seek negotiations with Hanoi.

Initially, in October and November, Ambassador Lodge and Janusz Lewandowski, the Polish delegate on the International Control Commission, conducted "Marigold" talks to arrange meetings in Warsaw between U.S. and North Vietnamese delegates. On December 6, 1966, U.S. delegates waited in

Warsaw but the North Vietnamese never showed up, saying they refused because the United States had bombed targets near Hanoi on December 4.

On February 8, 1967, Johnson wrote a personal letter to Ho Chi Minh and also ordered a halt to the bombing as part of a Tet holidays general truce arrangement. The North Vietnamese never responded positively to Johnson's request for direct talks with Ho Chi Minh.

Throughout this period, Harold Wilson contacted Kosygin, inviting him to London for discussion of various matters including Vietnam. The Soviet premier agreed and visited London early in February, 1967. Wilson's plans did not succeed. Johnson wanted Hanoi to stop sending supplies to the south before a bombing halt; Ho Chi Minh demanded that the bombing should stop while there was only a partial cessation of supplies reaching the south. Prime Minister Wilson blamed Johnson for requiring too much in order to achieve peace, growing dismayed by the president's intransigence. Subsequently, there was a diplomatic misunderstanding between London and Washington about Johnson's minimum requirements.

Johnson extended the Tet truce until February 13, but Wilson and Kosygin could find no grounds for an agreement between Hanoi and Washington. On February 14, Johnson ordered the renewal of the bombing of North Vietnam.

February 22, 1967   PRESIDENT JOHNSON ESCALATES THE VIETNAMESE AIR WAR.

After the Tet truce failed on February 14, 1967, Johnson decided to take more vigorous action against North Vietnam. Thus, on February 22, he approved the JCS plan for the aerial mining of North Vietnam's waterways (except Haiphong Harbor) and authorized Rolling Thunder attacks on the Thai Nguyen Iron and Steel Works near Hanoi. The aerial mining began on February 27, 1967; the attack on the iron-steel complex was made on March 10, 1967.

March 20, 1967   AT GUAM, PRESIDENT JOHNSON LEARNS ABOUT SOUTH VIETNAM'S
                         NEW CONSTITUTION AND DISCUSSES NON-MILITARY PROBLEMS
                         WITH KY AND THIEU.

At their first meeting on March 20, Johnson received a copy of the Vietnamese constitution which had been finalized by the constituent assembly the night before in Saigon. The document was patterned on the U.S. government, having a president, Senate, and House of Representatives. Ky told Johnson there would be a "popularly chosen government" selected later in the year. Most of the Guam sessions were spent discussing Vietnam's economy and such matters as inflation, blackmarkets, corruption, land reform, and food supplies. Johnson said he would send former TVA Chief David E. Lilienthal to aid the Vietnamese economists and planners.

The only military matter discussed was the need for regular South Vietnamese army units to undertake greater effort to provide security for the hamlets and villages which U.S.-directed pacification teams helped to rid of Communist influence. Whether President Johnson and his advisors realized the full implication of this shortcoming is not clear. This involved the relationship between South Vietnamese army leaders and the local populace, which was seldom a beneficent relation. It also related to the manner in which the generals of the four corps areas elected to use or not use the army forces at their command. This is where corruption thrived and the local populace suffered. Consequently, villagers resented the South Vietnamese soldiers and many joined the Viet Cong. As General Westmoreland told President Johnson in 1967, the Communists continued successfully to recruit southerners to their ranks, enabling the Viet Cong to replace their losses faster than the U.S. attrition tactics killed the Viet Cong. There is no evidence that Johnson asked: How could this be if democracy was progressing so well?

April 21, 1967   *A MILITARY COUP IN GREECE OVERTHROWS THE KING. CONSTANTINE KOLLIAS BECOMES PRIME MINISTER OF GREECE.*

The King of Greece, Constantine, went into exile in Rome on December 14, 1967.

May 19, 1967   McNAMARA RECOMMENDS THAT MILITARY ESCALATION OF THE VIETNAM WAR SHOULD STOP AND GREATER ATTENTION SHOULD BE GIVEN TO THE POLITICAL AND ECONOMIC PROBLEMS OF SOUTH VIETNAM.

McNamara's lengthy memo of May 19 reflected the growing division between the JCS and the Defense Department on the methods to be used in South Vietnam. The split between the civilian and military groups in the U.S. defense establishment was an argument not between "hawks and doves" but about the proper strategic goods and methods to be used in Vietnam. Both groups wanted to defeat the insurgents and protect Saigon. They divided on the war's limitations as correlated with America's specific objectives in Vietnam.

In 1967, McNamara believed the air attacks on the north had not been effective. He did believe, however, that the basic U.S. goal in the south was attained because America had prevented the fall of South Vietnam to communism. Now, McNamara contended, the United States should continue to protect the south militarily but attention must be given to the precise means for gaining a strong, viable government in Saigon which could win the "hearts and minds" of the South Vietnamese. Until this objective was finished that nation would always be threatened by revolution. Military death and destruction could not achieve this goal because political problems required different methods.

The JCS solidly opposed McNamara, never fully understanding the Clausewitzian principle of war for political ends. The U.S. armed forces wanted more planes, troops, and military authority to force North Vietnam to a virtual unconditional surrender, although that term was never used. The military wanted more bombing targets and another 100,000 men during the spring of 1967.
. Thus by May, 1967, the conflicting objectives and methods in South Vietnam intensified friction between McNamara and the JCS. Although McNamara was supported by McGeorge Bundy, William Bundy, the CIA's senior analysts, and the Pentagon's Systems Analysis Team, the president deferred to the military, making the secretary's position difficult.

The May 19 memo of McNamara intended to provide a detailed argument favoring the program of the civilians in the Defense Department. Using data prepared by Alain Enthoven's computer systems office, the memo showed that each troop escalation yielded fewer results. Assuming the "body-kill" counts were accurate, 100,000 added soldiers would kill 431 enemies each week, a rate which would require 10 years to gain complete surrender. Errors of assumption in the system would, the report said, make the time longer.

Computer data also showed that the Rolling Thunder attacks achieved few results. The air raids on POL targets, Hanoi, and communication links to

China had cost heavy losses of men and material but yielded no long-term results. In addition, the will to survive of the North Vietnamese increased
as bombing attacks increased. Thus, more bombs would be counterproductive
in forcing Hanoi to surrender.

On the positive side, McNamara wanted to step up the pacification program
in South Vietnam. Counterinsurgency, he said, meant building a viable economy
and government, not laying waste to the country. The army's attrition tactics
were exactly those which could not win in South Vietnam. If there were a
ceiling on U.S. troop additions, Westmoreland and the U.S. military would
have to use forces more efficiently as well as strive to pacify South Vietnam.
If American troops were used passively, the government and army of South Vietnam could have a greater role in maintaining their own security. Perhaps
the South Vietnamese Army could learn to be as effective as the South Korean
forces, which had been known for their fighting ability since 1953.

Finally, McNamara argued that stabilizing U.S. troop levels would bring
an economic benefit to South Vietnam. Inflation in South Vietnam was 20%
during the first quarter of 1967, and those figures seemed ready to increase.
The unstable economy handicapped Thieu's government, the secretary said.

Therefore, for economic, political, and military reasons, the May 19
program proposed new approaches to this war. First, it asked for 30,000 more
troops which would become the maximum for U.S. combat forces. Second, it
proposed concentrating all air attacks between the 17th and 20th parallel in
order to interdict troops and supplies entering the South. Finally, and most
crucially, McNamara wanted a broadly based representative government set up
in Saigon, committed to economic and social reforms to win the people's loyalty. This political phase of the war had to be won while the limited U.S.
troops prevented a Communist victory. These methods would secure South Vietnam's peace and contain communism south of the 17th parallel.

McNamara's memo of May 19 was considered a bureaucratic declaration of
war by the JCS and Westmoreland. To counterattack on the civilians, the JCS
turned to their main supporters: congress, the president, and especially the
Preparedness Subcommittee of the Senate Armed Forces Committee. See August
25, 1967.

May 23, 1967   PRESIDENT JOHNSON CHARGES THAT EGYPT'S BLOCKADE OF
                         THE GULF OF AQABA VIOLATES INTERNATIONAL LAW; HE RE-
                         AFFIRMS PRESIDENT EISENHOWER'S 1957 COMMITMENT TO IS-
                         RAEL TO KEEP THE STRAIT OF TIRAN OPEN TO AQABA.

A Middle East crisis had been brewing for nearly a year. On November 13,
1966, the Israelis made a large reprisal raid on Jordan. On April 7, 1967,
the Syrians and Israelis had a large border skirmish. Subsequently, Damascus
urged Egypt's Nasser to assist it against their common enemy.

To show his solidarity with Syria, Nasser asked the U.N. forces to leave
Sharm el Sheikh at the mouth of the Gulf of Aqaba. The Multinational U.N.
force had been in the Sinai area since 1956 as part of the agreement which
ended the Suez crisis. U.N. Secretary General U Thant decided to withdraw,
and Egyptian troops entered the area. At the same time Nasser warned Israel
that if it attacked Syria, Egypt would attack. To further pressure Israel,
Nasser announced on May 22 that Israeli ships could no longer pass through
the Strait of Tiran leading to the Israeli port of Aqaba.

In Washington on May 22, Johnson asked both Israel and Egypt to maintain
peace. To emphasize America's concern, Johnson conferred with Eisenhower on

his commitment to Israel. After this meeting, Johnson declared that the United States had been pledged to keep the port of Aqaba open. Egypt, he said, must stop its illegal blockade.

Johnson took two other steps to avert the conflict. On May 31, the United States asked the U.N. Security Council to appeal to all parties in the Middle East to use diplomacy to resolve the dispute. Both the Arabs and the Soviet Union opposed this resolution.

When the United Nations could not act, Johnson accepted the British suggestion that a multilateral naval force should assemble and move through the Strait of Tiran. When other nations doubted the value of this method, the United States and Britain tried to obtain a compromise with Egypt to permit all neutral flags to carry goods to Israel at Aqaba. Egypt refused, but so did Israel. Tel Aviv's government wanted its right to free passage with no strings. Israel agreed, however, to give the United States two weeks to work out a settlement. Yet war seemed imminent, sooner or later. See June 5, 1967.

May 30, 1967   *A CIVIL WAR BEGINS IN NIGERIA AS BIAFRA, THE EASTERN*
                        REGION OF THE NATION, PROCLAIMS INDEPENDENCE UNDER
                        LT. COLONEL ODOMEGWU OJUKWA.

The war ended on January 15, 1970, when Biafran rebels agreed to surrender.

June 5, 1967   *ISRAELI FORCES LAUNCH AIR ATTACKS ON AIRFIELDS IN*
                        EGYPT, IRAQ, SYRIA, AND JORDAN; THEN ISRAELI INFANTRY
                        ATTACK ON THREE FRONTS: THE SIX-DAY WAR.

Although President Johnson was still attempting to organize a multinational naval force to keep the port of Aqaba open and to persuade the United Nations to approve a resolution on the right of innocent passage in the Strait of Tiran, the Israeli Cabinet secretly voted for war on June 3 and began its attack on June 5.

The Israeli campaign was highly successful. In three days, the Israelis overran the Gaza strip and most of the Sinai peninsula, including Sharm el Sheik. In the east, they captured the west bank of the Jordan River and the city of Jerusalem. In the northeast, they occupied the strategic Golan Heights on the Syrian border. Israel agreed to a cease-fire on June 11. See June 6, 1967.

June 5, 1967   ALEKSEI KOSYGIN, CHAIRMAN OF THE SOVIET UNION'S COUNCIL
                        OF MINISTERS, CALLS PRESIDENT JOHNSON REGARDING THE
                        MIDDLE EAST WAR: THE FIRST USE OF THE "HOT LINE" IN A
                        CRISIS.

At 7:57 a.m., Secretary of Defense Robert McNamara called Johnson to inform him that the "hot line" was activated for a call from Moscow. This special line had been installed on August 30, 1963, but was previously used only for tests and to exchange New Year's greetings.

On June 5, some trouble arose because the communications line from the Pentagon to the Situation Room of the White House did not work. McNamara had to find a technician to repair this defect while Chairman Kosygin waited on the Kremlin end.

Fortunately, the line was fixed so that Kosygin and Johnson could agree to work for a cease-fire. Johnson was to exert influence on Israel; Kosygin, on Syria and Egypt. Thus, both nations' leaders understood their peaceful intentions to settle the dispute.

In addition, Johnson informed Kosygin that the Egyptian charge that U.S. carrier aircraft helped Israel was not true. Because the Soviet navy had intelligence-gathering ships in the eastern Mediterranean, Kosygin knew that Egypt's claims were false. Johnson asked the Soviet chairman to explain this to Cairo.

June 6, 1967　　　　　THE U.N. SECURITY COUNCIL PASSES RESOLUTION 234, DE-
　　　　　　　　　　　MANDING A CEASE-FIRE IN THE MIDDLE EASTERN WAR.

Although Egypt and Jordan agreed immediately to the cease-fire, Syria and Israel did not. Finally, on June 9, Syria accepted a cease-fire and the United States had to pressure Israel to do likewise. Tel Aviv agreed to do so on June 11, and the six-day war ended in victories for Israel. The postwar details now had to be dealt with in the United Nations because Resolution 234 did not state what the boundaries would be following the cease-fire.

During the final efforts to get Israel and Syria to accept a cease-fire on June 9-11, Johnson and Kosygin again used the hot line to keep one another aware of developments. Both Israel and Syria were prepared to accept the cease-fire, but their mutual mistrust prevented either from quickly obtaining an effective halt in the fighting. At 3 a.m. on June 10, the cease-fire seemed to have been accepted. It was not fully implemented until June 11.

June 8, 1967　　　　　AN ISRAELI GUNBOAT MISTAKENLY TORPEDOES AN AMERICAN
　　　　　　　　　　　NAVAL COMMUNICATIONS SHIP, THE *LIBERTY*. USING THE
　　　　　　　　　　　MOSCOW "HOT LINE," JOHNSON TELLS KOSYGIN THAT U.S.
　　　　　　　　　　　CARRIER PLANES WERE FLYING ONLY TO INVESTIGATE THE
　　　　　　　　　　　INCIDENT.

The *Liberty* was in international waters when torpedoed by an Israeli ship. This occurred early in the morning, but not until 11 A.M. did the Israelis report that their gunboat attacked in error and offer their apologies.

To avoid confusion when the incident was first announced, Johnson phoned Kosygin to tell him why U.S. carrier planes were present off the Sinai coast. Earlier, on June 5, Egypt had falsely charged that U.S. carrier planes had participated in the attacks on Arab airfields. Johnson wanted the Russians to know exactly what U.S. aircraft were doing on June 8.

June 9, 1967　　　　　*ARAB OIL MINISTERS DECLARE AN OIL EMBARGO AGAINST BRIT-*
　　　　　　　　　　　AIN AND FRANCE FOR ASSISTING ISRAEL IN THE EGYPTIAN
　　　　　　　　　　　WAR.

This was the first political oil boycott by the Arab oil states. The boycott was short-lived, ending immediately after the Six-Day War. It indicated, however, a possible future boycott of more serious consequences in case of political problems in the Middle East. Western Europe was dependent on the Middle East for 20% of its oil needs.

June 17, 1967   *CHINA EXPLODES ITS FIRST HYDROGEN BOMB.*

June 25, 1967   PRESIDENT JOHNSON AND CHAIRMAN KOSYGIN CONCLUDE MEET-
                        INGS AT GLASSBORO, NEW JERSEY, WITH NO SPECIFIC RE-
                        SULTS.

The Glassboro meetings took place because the Russian leader visited the
United Nations to support the Arab cause in discussions following the Six-Day
War of June 5 to 11, 1967. Desiring to arrange future talks on nuclear arms
limitations, Johnson asked Kosygin to visit the White House. The Russians
did not wish to come to Washington because such a visit might be misconstrued
by the Arabs. Therefore, Johnson arranged for the use of the home of the
president of Glassboro State College in New Jersey.

      The sessions lasted for two days with many warm feelings exchanged but
no specific agreements. Johnson wanted to set dates for disarmament talks;
Kosygin wanted the United States to qualify some of its strong support for
Israel and to compromise on the Middle Eastern problems. Thus, except for
the fact that the two leaders learned to appreciate each other's position
better, the Glassboro meetings did not accomplish anything.

August 25, 1967   THE SENATE ARMED FORCES COMMITTEE SUPPORTS THE JCS,
                        STRONGLY OPPOSING McNAMARA'S IDEAS AND BLAMING JOHNSON
                        FOR NOT USING THE "UNANIMOUS WEIGHT OF PROFESSIONAL
                        MILITARY JUDGMENT."

Following a June 1, 1967, rebuttal of Secretary McNamara's May 19 report, the
Joint Chiefs, led by Chief of Staff General Earle G. WHEELER and U.S. Commander, Pacific Vice Admiral U.S.G. Sharp, Jr., contacted their friend Senator
John Stennis who chaired the Senate Armed Services Committee. Stennis arranged secret committee hearings between August 9 to 25 to review the military
aspects of the war.

      Wheeler and Sharp presented the JCS views on the war. They admitted
the air war was not effective but blamed this on Johnson's bombing restrictions. They wanted the air targets enlarged and to be permitted to make the
U.S. air presence felt over Hanoi and Haiphong. They gave the subcommittee
a list of 57 targets which should be bombed in North Vietnam.

      Although McNamara testified on behalf of his proposals, the Stennis re-
port was a foregone conclusion. The senators could not comprehend Enthoven's
computer analysis nor differentiate between attrition and counterinsurgency
strategy. Generally, as usual, the Armed Services Committee gave the military
what they wanted. The Stennis Report, which came after the hearings ended
on August 25, reflected that attitude. It urged Johnson to end his restriction on troops and bombing targets. Most surprising, it attacked their fellow
Democrat, Lyndon Johnson, for not following the opinion and recommendations
of military experts. Because Johnson cherished the support of the generals
and the Senate, the president and Secretary McNamara had reached the parting
of the ways. See November 2, 1967, and November 28, 1967.

September 3, 1967   THE SOUTH VIETNAMESE PRESIDENTIAL ELECTION IS WON BY
                        THE THIEU-KY SLATE ALTHOUGH THE ELECTION IS NOT WELL
                        CONDUCTED.

Unlike the 1966 election for the constituent assembly, the election for control of the government had to be managed by Ky and Thieu to keep the "delicate
balance" which the military junta established during the summer of 1965. The
constituent assembly had designated 12 candidates for the presidency, one
for each political faction in the assembly. Only Ky and Thieu seemed capable
of winning, but a problem developed because both wished to be president.
South Vietnam's military commanders met to resolve the conflict, persuading
Ky to be vice-president while Thieu became their presidential nominee.

     The campaign and election were seen by observers in South Vietnam as a
farce. Two of the 12 assembly nominees could not run: one, because he advocated a neutrality agreement with North Vietnam; the other, Big Minh, was in
exile. An effort to get the 8 civilian candidates to unite against Ky and
Thieu did not succeed.

     Thus, Thieu's victory on September 3 was no surprise. The surprise was
his campaign manager's ineptness in stuffing the ballot boxes. In Saigon,
where U.S. observers congregated, Ky and Thieu ran poorly. As a result, their
advocates stuffed thousands of votes into the ballot boxes after the polls
closed. Following the election, the 8 losing candidates accused Thieu of
fraud and tried to invalidate the vote. Before 1967 ended, however, Thieu
retaliated by imprisoning 20 of his leading political, religious, and labor
opponents. Any opponents who refused to conform with Thieu's presidency suffered a similar fate after 1967.

     Despite the election fraud, Thieu gave a semblance of political order
to South Vietnam. Order is what Johnson preferred. Political calm and a
lack of coups d'état in Saigon became equated with a politically sound government. Thieu's system did not, however, encourage the South Vietnamese to
opt for anti-communism as a way of life. Rather, it spawned apathy, immoral-
ity, and corruption in South Vietnam. It answered the question often asked
by U.S. reporters: "Why don't our Vietnamese fight as well as the Communist
Vietnamese?"

September 29, 1967   PRESIDENT JOHNSON SAYS THE UNITED STATES WILL STOP
                        BOMBING NORTH VIETNAM WHEN THE COMMUNISTS ACCEPT "PRO-
                        DUCTIVE DISCUSSIONS" FOR PEACE: THE SAN ANTONIO FOR-
                        MULA.

During the summer of 1967, dissenting demonstrations to stop the U.S. bombing
intensified in the United States and Europe, eventually leading to the large
protest of 500,000 in Washington, D.C., on October 21, 1967.

     In a speech to the National Legislative Conference on September 29,
Johnson publicly announced a proposal to which he had privately agreed with
French intermediaries during August, 1967. In July, two Frenchmen, Herbert
Marcovich, a scientist, and Raymond Aubrac, who knew Ho Chi Minh, returned
from Hanoi with news that Hanoi would negotiate as soon as the U.S. bombing
ended. The Frenchmen contacted Henry Kissinger, who was Nelson Rockefeller's
advisor on foreign policy, asking him to find out if Washington would accept
Hanoi's position. Johnson agreed that the United States would halt the bombing if "productive discussions" followed and if North Vietnam agreed not to
build up its forces and supplies during the truce period. To allow Hanoi to

realize that the French delegates were authentic representatives, Johnson informed Kissinger that they could inform Hanoi that the United States was reducing its bombing in the Hanoi area as a signal of Washington's intent.

The effort of the two Frenchmen failed. On August 24, Johnson learned that Hanoi would not renew visas for Marcovich and Aubrac. Later, Hanoi's delegation at Paris informed the two Frenchmen that there could be no negotiations until America stopped bombing and removed its forces from Vietnam.

Subsequently, Johnson decided to announce publicly the formula which he had previously given to the two Frenchmen, although he did not mention the French effort during the San Antonio speech. While observers in September thought Johnson made a "new" proposal, it was one which Hanoi had already rejected.

October 9, 1967   *REPORTS FROM BOLIVIA ARE THAT CHE GUEVARA HAS BEEN KILLED BY BOLIVIAN TROOPS.*

Che, who symbolized the radical, Castro-type of Communist reform for Latin America, had been leading guerrilla groups in Bolivia against the government when he was reported to have been killed. While the initial stories of Che's death were dubious, they were later confirmed.

October 12, 1967   SECRETARY OF STATE RUSK TELLS NEWSMEN THAT THE VITAL U.S. INTEREST IN VIETNAM IS THAT IN A DECADE OR TWO "THERE WILL BE A BILLION CHINESE ON THE MAINLAND, ARMED WITH NUCLEAR WEAPONS WITH NO CERTAINTY ABOUT WHAT THEIR ATTITUDE TOWARD THE REST OF ASIA WILL BE."

Rusk had previously told the newsmen that the United States was in Vietnam to "defend our vital national interests." Because the Johnson administration often used this term but never defined it, Jon Finney of the *New York Times* asked Rusk what the United States had at stake in Vietnam.

Rusk referred to the future threat of China, saying Peking had nominated itself as the enemy by proclaiming a "militant doctrine of the world revolution." Peking had inspired the Vietnamese to engage in the war against Saigon.

Rusk's words surprised many commentators in the United States. Most leading Far Eastern scholars in universities and in the Far East Section of the State Department did not see China as a menace. Peking's leaders always spoke passionately against Western powers, but Mao Tse-tung usually acted with caution. Thus Rusk appeared intentionally to mislead Americans by raising the specter of the Chinese threat. Moreover, if China were the enemy, then wasting U.S. resources in Vietnam was nonsense; the United States should plan strategies against Peking, not Hanoi. Rusk seemed therefore simply to be repeating the anti-Chinese rhetoric which had been popular in the United States since 1949.

November 2, 1967   PRESIDENT JOHNSON CONFERS WITH "THE WISE MEN," HIS SPECIAL GROUP OF RESPECTED ADVISORS, REGARDING McNAMARA AND THE VIETNAM WAR STRATEGY.

Johnson assembled this group of advisors for a White House meeting because

he faced McNamara's opposition to his plan to escalate the war. Following
the Stennis Report of August 25, 1967, Johnson decided in October to increase
U.S. forces by 45,000, compared with McNamara's recommendation for 30,000 and
the JCS's desire for 100,000. More important, Johnson rejected the Secretary
of Defense's proposal to place a ceiling on future additions of forces. He
also ordered Rolling Thunder to target 52 of the 57 targets listed by the
JCS for the Stennis Committee (see August 25, 1967).

On October 31, McNamara discussed his opposition with Johnson and prepared a memo which essentially summarized the arguments and proposals made
on May 19, 1967. McNamara recommended a troop ceiling and suggested a cut
in bombing raids coupled with a truce appeal to Hanoi. Finally, he asked
for a study of military operations to reduce U.S. casualties and give South
Vietnam's army more responsibility for self-defense.

The "wise men" met with Johnson to discuss McNamara's recommendations
and future policy in Vietnam. The group included Dean Acheson, George Ball,
Maxwell Taylor, and McGeorge Bundy. These advisors believed the war was going
well and thought the gradual escalation should continue. They could not accept McNamara's proposal to cut Rolling Thunder because they believed North
Vietnam should be ready to surrender soon.

In addition to the "wise men," Johnson asked Clark Clifford and Abe
Fortas to comment on the secretary's proposal. They both agreed with Johnson.
Significantly, however, none of these men was briefed by McNamara, by
Enthoven's systems analysis studies, by any explanation of the difference between attrition war and counterinsurgency which McNamara made (see May 19,
1967). On the basis of these talks with other advisors, Johnson agreed to
have McNamara resign. See November 28, 1967.

November 17, 1967   THE U.N. SECURITY COUNCIL RECOMMENDS SANCTIONS AGAINST
                           PORTUGAL UNTIL SHE GRANTS INDEPENDENCE TO HER OVERSEAS
                           COLONIES.

November 22, 1967   U.N. SECURITY COUNCIL RESOLUTION 242 STATES TERMS FOR
                           A LONG-TERM SOLUTION TO THE SIX-DAY WAR CONFLICT OF
                           JUNE 5, 1967.

From June 11 to November, a variety of proposals to settle the Middle East
crisis had been debated in the United Nations. Because the cease-fire agreement did not propose boundaries, Russia and the Arab nations wanted Israel
to withdraw to its borders of June 4, 1967, evacuating the strategic military
areas Israeli forces won from June 5 to 8, 1967. Backed by America, Israel
insisted she could not withdraw unless there were guarantees of her security
in the future.

U.N. Resolution 242 was based on suggestions by President Johnson which
favored a peace favorable to all parties. It provided for free navigation
of international waterways, justice for refugees (i.e., the Palestinians),
recognition of the sovereignty of all states with secure borders, and the
withdrawal of Israel from all occupied territories. This resolution, interpreted as an entity by the United States and Israel, reestablished close "special relations" between Israel and the United States. The Arab world became
critical of the Americans for fully backing Israel against the Arab rights
in the Middle East.

November 26, 1967   THE PEOPLE'S REPUBLIC OF SOUTH YEMEN IS PROCLAIMED.

On November 5, President Sallal of Yemen was deposed and a three-man presiden-
tial committee formed. The radical left group had gained power and adopted
a Communist-Bolshevik style of government, aided by the Soviet Union.

November 28, 1967   SECRETARY OF DEFENSE McNAMARA RESIGNS BUT AGREES TO
                        CONTINUE SERVING UNTIL CLARK CLIFFORD CAN REPLACE HIM
                        ON MARCH 1, 1968.

Between May 19, when the secretary outlined his detailed recommendations for
action in Vietnam, and October 31 when he stated his opposition to the Joint
Chiefs, relations between the president and the secretary became tense. After
meeting with the "wise men" and others in November, Johnson decided he should
replace the secretary. As Johnson later confessed to his biographer, Doris
Kearns, he once thought McNamara had become a loyal friend. In November,
however, the president realized the secretary was too much of a Kennedy man
who imbibed Robert Kennedy's dissenting ideas.
    On November 28, McNamara tendered his resignation to Johnson who arranged
for him to become the head of the World Bank. Johnson's concern about dropping McNamara continued to haunt him, however. In his memoirs, Johnson says
he decided on December 18, 1967, to write himself a special memorandum giving
his personal views on McNamara's October 31 proposals. The memo is reproduced
in the Appendix to Johnson's *The Vantage Point* (1971). While it responds to
the secretary's proposals, the memo is notable as evidence that Johnson lacked
the imagination necessary to visualize the strategic implications of
McNamara's counterinsurgency ideas compared to the military's attrition strategy of direct force against the enemy. On McNamara's October 31 views see
November 2, 1967.

November 30, 1967   SENATOR EUGENE McCARTHY ANNOUNCES HE WILL BE A "PEACE
                        CANDIDATE," SEEKING THE DEMOCRATIC PRESIDENTIAL NOMI-
                        NATION IN 1968.

Although Senator McCarthy of Minnesota agreed with Senator Fulbright's opposition to Johnson's policy in Vietnam, he had been reluctant to campaign
against the president. In November, however, Allard Lowenstein, who headed
a student group of dissenters, persuaded McCarthy to run because he could
expect seven million college students to assist. Although McCarthy's "children's crusade" enlisted many young people, the senator's amateur politicians
were not well organized. McCarthy played one significant role in U.S. politics, however, in the New Hampshire primary. See March 12, 1968.

December 1, 1967   FRANCE VETOES THE ADMISSION OF GREAT BRITAIN INTO THE
                       EUROPEAN ECONOMIC COMMUNITY (COMMON MARKET).

Prior to the British application for Common Market membership on May 11, the
question of joining was a controversial political issue in England. France
objected to the membership because she wanted Great Britain to end its British
Commonwealth trade agreements before being admitted.

1968

January 16, 1968   THE UNITED KINGDOM ANNOUNCES IT MUST WITHDRAW ITS
                       FORCES FROM THE PERSIAN GULF AND THE FAR EAST.

The British government was further retreating from its previous imperial commitments east of Suez, a not unusual decision inasmuch as its east coast African colonies gained independence between 1958 and 1967.

January 23, 1968   NORTH KOREA SEIZES THE U.S.S. *PUEBLO*, A NAVY ELECTRONIC
                       SPY SHIP, IN INTERNATIONAL WATERS.

During the night of January 22-23, a North Korean submarine chaser and three patrol boats challenged the *Pueblo* and boarded the U.S. ship with an armed party. North Korea claimed the *Pueblo* was 7 miles off shore. According to the *Pueblo*'s commander, the ship was 15½ nautical miles from shore, outside North Korea's 12-mile limit. During the foray, one American was killed and four injured. As a surveillance ship, the *Pueblo* was virtually unarmed and unprotected.

North Korea also took 82 Americans captive, and in order to obtain their release, Johnson used diplomatic channels. Other U.S. methods were considered by the National Security Council but appeared too risky to the lives of the American captives. Although Johnson sent 350 airplanes to bases in South Korea in case of further aggression, he tried to work through the United Nations, the Kremlin, and other nations to obtain the captives' release. It took 11 months to gain the release of the *Pueblo*'s officers and crew.

January 26, 1968   GENERAL WESTMORELAND'S YEAR-END REPORT FOR 1967 IS
                       OPTIMISTIC ABOUT THE DESPERATION OF THE COMMUNIST ENEMY
                       IN VIETNAM.

Accurately or not, the U.S. Commander in Vietnam and the U.S. Ambassador to Saigon, Ellsworth Bunker, had been making favorable reports. In November, 1967, the two leading U.S. figures in South Vietnam had visited Washington to spread the good word about U.S. successes. Before congressional committees and such luncheon groups as the National Press Club, they characterized the Vietnam struggle as nearing a victory. According to Westmoreland, the United States would soon "weaken the enemy and strengthen our friends until we have become superfluous." On invitations to the 1967 New Year's Eve party at the Embassy in Saigon, the party message read, "Come and see the light at the end of the tunnel," the code-words for winning the war.

Just before Westmoreland composed his annual report, the North Vietnamese attacked exactly where the U.S. military preferred, at Khe Sanh on the strategic border between Laos, South Vietnam, and the 17th parallel. Attacking on January 21, the North Vietnamese fought the type of battle favorable to

U.S. fire power, in the north, away from urban areas where American military and air forces could fight without concern for the South Vietnamese populace.

Thus, Westmoreland's January 26 report reflected an added touch of optimism. He wrote that the enemy was "resorting to desperation tactics" in order to attain a "military/psychological victory" and had failed in these attempts since October, 1967.

From November to January 26, this optimistic news enabled President Johnson to look forward eagerly to the 1968 presidential campaign. However, the euphoria reaped contrary results. Four days after Westmoreland reported, the Communists launched the Tet offensive.

January 30-31, 1968   THE TET OFFENSIVE OF THE COMMUNISTS BEGINS IN SOUTH VIETNAM.

In retrospect, the North Vietnamese attack on Khe Sanh on January 20 had been only diversionary. (See January 26, 1968.) While U.S. forces rushed north to engage the enemy at Khe Sanh, the Communists initiated their Tet offensive farther south. Its initial assaults appeared successful and, thereby, damaged Johnson's credibility in having publicized optimistic reports of successes after November, 1967.

During the first days of Tet, in attacks on Saigon the VC hit the U.S. embassy, the Presidential Palace, the South Vietnamese military headquarters, and Saigon's air bases. Although they were supposed to be subdued, the VC soon appeared to be everywhere. Communist troops overran the old capital and its religious centers at Hue and raided 39 provincial capitals and 76 other cities and towns. Unfortunately for North Vietnam's General Giap, the South Vietnamese did not rise up to join the Communists as he had planned they would. The southern populace was apathetic to both the Communists and the American efforts. During Tet, this helped the United States because without their anticipated local support, the Communists had to withdraw or be chased from the cities after February 13.

Giap had miscalculated. Using Mao's doctrine of protracted war, Giap believed the time had come to move his rural armies to gain control of the urban areas. Tet 1968 was not the time. As a result, the Tet offensive eventually cost the Communists heavily. It made new enemies for Communists in the south, and it caused the loss of 45,000 Communist soldiers and much equipment. Khe Sanh and Hue held out for several weeks until mid-March, but captured documents of Giap's forces showed that Tet failed to meet Giap's basic objectives.

Nevertheless, if Tet proved to be a blow to the Communists, it was also a disaster for the American perspectives on the war. Although the full implications of Tet 1968 may always be controversial, Tet probably paved the way for both North Vietnam and President Johnson to be prepared to start negotiations. For the Tet results in the United States see March 25-26 and March 31, 1968.

March 12, 1968   SENATOR McCARTHY NEARLY DEFEATS PRESIDENT JOHNSON IN THE NEW HAMPSHIRE PRIMARY.

Senator McCarthy's near victory surprised Johnson and most observers because the "children's crusade" had not been well organized after November 30, 1967. Moreover, Johnson's campaign experts had predicted an easy victory with

landslide figures of 70 to 80%. Johnson obtained only 49.5% of the votes to
McCarthy's 42.2%. Political pundits interpreted McCarthy's near victory as
a blow to the president's Vietnamese policy.

March 16, 1968   ROBERT KENNEDY ANNOUNCES HE WILL CAMPAIGN FOR THE PRES-
                          IDENTIAL NOMINATION.

In November, 1967, some Democratic liberals had urged Kennedy to campaign
against Johnson but he refused. Traditionally, party loyalty ruled that in-
siders should not challenge an incumbent president and Kennedy's advisors
preferred to wait until 1972. McCarthy's near victory in New Hampshire on
March 12 and the disaster which appeared to befall America in the Tet offensive of January-February convinced Kennedy that he should challenge the president. Kennedy's candidacy surprised and dismayed Johnson and probably was
one influence in determining the president's decision to withdraw as a nominee
on March 31.

March 25-26, 1968   PRESIDENT JOHNSON MEETS WITH THE "WISE MEN" TO GAIN
                          ASSISTANCE IN DECIDING FUTURE POLICY IN VIETNAM FOLLOW-
                          ING THE TET DEBACLE.

North Vietnam's Tet offensive, Eugene McCarthy's near victory in New Hampshire, and Robert Kennedy's announced candidacy left President Johnson in a
quandary. The JCS wanted more troops and more extensive bombing in Vietnam
while a report by the new Secretary of Defense, Clark Clifford, sought a compromise. Finally, economic problems over taxes and an unfavorable trade balance added to Johnson's perplexities. To help him decide on a course of action, Clifford persuaded the president to convene the "wise men," his trusted
advisors from outside the bureaucracy.
      The Tet offensive had been quelled by mid-March, but its psychological
effects on the American public had been disastrous. The optimistic reports
of Westmoreland and Bunker at the end of 1967 had led Americans to believe
the Communists were nearly wiped out. Tet demonstrated that the Communist
fighting capabilities remained enormous. Johnson compounded this problem
because two days after the Tet offensive began, he asserted that the U.S.
military had prior knowledge of the attacks and would immediately counterattack. His analysis was wrong. For the next 10 days, Communist advances
continued and Hue was captured.
      Johnson lost the backing of middle-of-the-road moderates during the Tet
offensive. News cartoonists poked fun at the president, depicting him weeping
crocodile tears because of destruction in Vietnam. Humorist Art Buchwald
wrote a parody of Johnson as General George Custer just before the Little
Big Horn massacre; Custer (Johnson) asserted: "We have the Sioux on the run,"
because the battle "had just turned the corner" and he could see "the light
at the end of the tunnel." The Indian massacre of Custer's men followed.
      Other small things added to the American disillusionment in Vietnam. A
U.S. army major at Ben Tri remarked that "It became necessary to destroy the
town to save it." *Life* magazine published the gruesome picture of Saigon's
police chief shooting a Viet Cong prisoner in cold blood on the street. The
president's press secretary claimed that Walter Cronkite, America's most prominent TV news anchorman, had turned against Johnson when he stated "we weren't
winning the war" despite Johnson's statements to the contrary. Reportedly

Johnson remarked, "Well, if I've lost Cronkite, I've lost Middle America."

Unlike Cronkite, the military officers' reaction to Tet was to seek fewer restraints on their battle tactics. As early as February 3, the JCS asked Johnson to give air force commanders complete authority to select targets. Generals Wheeler and Westmoreland wanted 206,000 additional troops as well as the mobilization of all military reserves.

Wheeler's mobilization request alarmed Johnson. The president knew the difference between a limited containment action and an all-out World War II-type war. He was never prepared to support the latter in South Vietnam because that nation was not that vital to the United States. Thus, as previously, Johnson rejected proposals to call up the National Guard and reserve units. Wheeler's request so disturbed Johnson that he asked Secretary of Defense Designate Clifford to organize a committee to study the problem "from A to Z."

The Clifford Committee's report of March 4 startled the president further. Unlike McNamara, who had been taunted with Kennedy's influence, Clark Clifford was a long-time Washington friend of Johnson. In November, Clifford had counseled Johnson to follow his own policy, not McNamara's. Yet between November and March, Clifford changed his perspectives on Vietnam.

Looking back later, Clifford remembered that his first doubts about U.S. policy in Vietnam had been planted during the summer of 1967. During a trip to Asian nations, Clifford discovered that none of America's allies shared Washington's great fear of communism in Vietnam. His requests for more troops in Vietnam had largely been shunned by the leaders of Australia, New Zealand, Thailand, the Philippines, and South Korea. Each of them sent token forces to South Vietnam in order to please the United States, not because they feared Hanoi's victory. By March, 1968, Clifford altered his Vietnam analysis completely, largely because of the Tet offensive, General Wheeler's request for greater military control, and the policy review board he headed from February 26 to March 4.

During the review, Clifford became familiar with the civilian-military division inside the Pentagon. He talked with and studied the computer data used by McNamara's advisors, Paul Nitze, Paul C. Warnke, and Enthoven. He began to grasp the political dimensions of South Vietnam's problem, realizing that U.S. military strength could not solve the internal problems of South Vietnam. At the same time, he heard fully the all-out war opinions of Generals Wheeler and Taylor, and National Security Advisor Walter Rostow as they sought full mobilization of U.S. forces.

The Clifford Committee's report of March 4 represented a compromise, not the new attitudes of its chairman. Because it was a composite of the civilian and military proposals, the March 4 report simply made Johnson less certain of how to proceed. While Johnson pondered the report and observed the final defeat of the Communist Tet offensive, he experienced a new crisis during mid-March--an economic crisis.

Johnson's attempted guns-and-butter economy began to come unhinged by early 1968. In 1967, Johnson sought an income tax surcharge to finance his programs, but the Democratic leaders in congress rejected the tax. In January, 1968, Johnson again asked congress for a 10% tax surcharge. This time southern Democrats, led by Wilbur Mills of the House Committee on Ways and Means, preferred to spend more on the war but less on Johnson's social program as the best method to cut the budget deficits.

In March, the tax conflict became complicated by the rapid decline in the value of the dollar on the gold market. The American international trade balance had been experiencing trouble during the 1960's. The Kennedy Round of trade and tariff reforms tried to band-aid the problem (see October 11, 1962), but by 1967 the difficulty became more acute. During the last quarter of 1967, U.S. trade imbalances were $7 billion and this trend continued into 1968. The Tet offensive caused a flurry of international speculation, and during the first 10 weeks of 1968, the dollar value declined on the gold market by $327 million.

To stem the gold dollar decline in March, the United States and its European partners arranged temporary relief by buying dollars to raise their value artificially. Because other "free world" currencies were pegged to dollar value, U.S. economic shortfalls affected the currency and budget of many countries. The instability of the dollar was temporarily rectified in March, but the international financial community informed the United States that America must correct its budget and tax problem. Both the Great Escalation and the Great Society were jeopardized by financial problems in 1968.

Johnson's call to the "wise men" to meet on March 25 came at a difficult time, militarily, diplomatically, economically, and with regard to domestic dissent. Clifford had urged Johnson to consider a bombing halt and negotiations; the "wise men" could, he said, focus on this issue as the central problem requiring an answer.

Clifford handled the "wise men's" March meeting discreetly. For their first meeting on March 25, Clifford gave Johnson's advisors a briefing at the State Department. During this session, Clifford familiarized the "wise men" with detailed computer data prepared by Nitze, Enthoven, and Warnke as well as with the military proposals of Wheeler and Westmoreland. Their data was updated to reflect the Tet offensive information.

As a result of the March 25 briefing, Johnson's White House meeting with the advisors took a divergent turn on March 26. During a breakfast session, the advisors heard an up-to-date report on Tet by General Wheeler, who had just flown in from Saigon at 6 a.m. Wheeler was optimistic. Tet had damaged the Communist forces. The South Vietnamese army had fought "commendably," although Wheeler avoided mentioning his request for full mobilization, which he knew Johnson disliked. He asked only for 13,000 troops to aid the pacification effort. Johnson had already agreed to send an additional 30,000 combat troops.

Following Wheeler's report, General Taylor spoke strongly in favor of escalation of the bombing targets and of more combat troops for Vietnam. But Taylor stood almost alone. Most of the "wise men" told Johnson that a new counterinsurgency strategy was necessary. The military, they believed, had prevented the fall of South Vietnam. Now the United States should stabilize its combat role by emphasizing internal reform in South Vietnam. In addition, they said, the political divisions and dissent at home were serious disturbances of national harmony. Although each advisor emphasized different concepts, the same men who backed the military attrition war in November now supported the Pentagon civilians who stressed counterinsurgency.

Johnson was distraught. Someone, he said, "had poisoned the well." The men whose opinions Johnson most respected had changed their views, but Johnson could not believe that Tet alone had done this. Clifford later remarked: "The meeting with the Wise Men served the purpose that I hoped it would. It really shook the president."

At first, Johnson was angry. He asked to hear the briefing which the "wise men" received at the State Department on March 25. He learned they had been fully informed of both the civilian and the military perspectives in the Pentagon. He also learned that his good friend Clark Clifford agreed not with Wheeler but with McNamara.

Johnson was resilient, however. His long political experience permitted him to roll with the punches, to accept the good and the bad. He decided to change his policy. See March 31, 1968.

March 31, 1968   PRESIDENT JOHNSON ANNOUNCES DRAMATIC CHANGES: A BOMBING
                         HALT, A REQUEST FOR NORTH VIETNAM TO NEGOTIATE, HIS
                         WITHDRAWAL AS A 1968 PRESIDENTIAL CANDIDATE.

Sometime after the "wise men's" meeting of March 25-26, the president decided to salvage what fame he might as a statesman. Although he never admitted any past errors nor directly proposed the counterinsurgency strategy desired by McNamara and Clifford, he changed the terms of U.S. involvement in Vietnam between March 31, 1968, and January, 1969. The change began with a television address on March 31.

The most dramatic part of Johnson's address came last, his decision not to run for reelection. Exactly when Johnson decided not to be a nominee is not certain. In his memoirs, Johnson said he had decided early after 1964 but waited for the right moment to announce it. Various sources indicate he mentioned retirement between 1965 and 1968. On March 31, Johnson believed his decision to retire would be a special signal of his sincerity in seeking negotiations with Hanoi. The proposal to talk would not be seen as a political tactic.

The other two announcements on March 31 were vital to developments in Vietnam, demonstrating that Johnson had not wavered since 1965 in his determination to fight a limited war in Vietnam. First, he announced that U.S. aircraft and naval ships would no longer attack North Vietnam except in the "area of the demilitarized zone," that is, between the 17th and 20th parallels. called on Ho Chi Minh to "respond positively and favorably" by agreeing to negotiate.

Second, the president announced the moderate increase of U.S. troop strength in South Vietnam. This moderate increase (30,000) would protect South Vietnam. Our first priority, Johnson said, would be to improve South Vietnam's ability to defend itself militarily and politically. Although he did not specify this, his statement reflected the counterinsurgency policy which the civilians in the Defense Department advocated.

Without saying so, Johnson ended the escalation policy of 1965-1968. He privately rejected the JCS's full mobilization plan and retained presidential control of the war to attain political objectives. His subsequent activity in striving to open negotiations with Hanoi indicated both his presidential control and his desire to make certain that North Vietnam did not perceive his March 31 speech as a sign of weakness. See May 13, 1968.

April 4, 1968   MARTIN LUTHER KING, JR., IS ASSASSINATED IN MEMPHIS,
                         TENNESSEE.

Dr. King had become the symbol and leading spokesman for the broad moderate group of liberal Americans who sought social justice. Because the Vietnam war siphoned funding from Johnson's social programs and the army drafted a disproportionate number of black youth into the army, King had dissented from Johnson's war policy. His assassination left more radical leaders of black Americans to vie to replace King's nonviolent methods.

On June 8, 1968, Scotland Yard arrested James Earl Ray in response to a

U.S. request for Ray's extradition for the murder of Dr. King. An escaped convict, Ray waived extradition hearings and returned to the United States for questioning. Ray confessed to the crime and was sentenced to life in prison. Later, he recanted his confession but the courts found no sufficient reason for changing the verdict. He remained in prison.

May 13, 1968   U.S. AND NORTH VIETNAM DELEGATES OPEN DISCUSSIONS IN
                         PARIS TO TALK ABOUT NEGOTIATIONS.

Although on April 4 Hanoi officials denounced Johnson's speech of March 31 as an imperialist plot, they secretly contacted the United States to indicate their willingness to talk. They wanted the United States to stop all bombing and other acts of war, but Johnson refused. Finally, the two sides agreed to talk about conditions for beginning talks. They held their first session at Paris on May 13. W. Averell Harriman represented the United States at Paris; Xuan Thuy represented North Vietnam. Neither the VC nor Saigon regimes had direct representation. See October 31, 1968.

June 5, 1968   ROBERT F. KENNEDY IS ASSASSINATED IN LOS ANGELES ON
                         THE DAY OF HIS PRESIDENTIAL PRIMARY VICTORY IN CALI-
                         FORNIA.

Kennedy was shot by an Arab named Sirhan B. Sirhan who opposed Kennedy's pro-Israel views. Kennedy had become the leading contender for the Democratic presidential nomination. His death left Vice-President Hubert Humphrey as the likely nominee.

June 24, 1968   FEDERAL TROOPS AND POLICE DISPERSE DEMONSTRATORS IN
                         THE POOR PEOPLE'S CAMPAIGN.

In order to dissent against Johnson's guns-and-butter policy which sacrificed the butter, demonstrators moved into Washington to protest to congress. Coming just after a series of riots in April which resulted from Dr. King's assassination, the poor people's campaign dismayed the president. The "poor people" built a shanty-town called "Resurrection City" on the mall near the Capitol, from which they moved out each day to protest before congress and at the White House gates. Finally, Johnson and the Washington, D.C., city fathers decided to abolish "Resurrection City." They drove the people from the mall and destroyed the shanty homes on June 24. At one time, 50,000 people participated in the "poor people's" protest.

July 1, 1968   AMERICA, THE SOVIET UNION, AND 51 OTHER NATIONS SIGN
                         A NUCLEAR NON-PROLIFERATION TREATY.

Under this agreement, nations with nuclear weapons pledged to work for arms control and disarmament; nations without nuclear weapons promised not to make them or receive them from others. The United States, the Soviet Union, and Great Britain, the three signatories with nuclear weapons, assured the non-nuclear countries that they would assist them in obtaining the necessary nuclear power for peaceful uses. The U.S. Senate ratified the treaty on March 13, 1969.

Following the signing of the treaty on July 1, Johnson and the Soviet Union announced that in the near future there would be talks to limit offensive strategic nuclear weapons as well as defensive ballistic missiles. These meetings were never held in 1968. See August 20, 1968.

July 1, 1968   PRESIDENT THIEU ACCEPTS RESPONSIBILITY FOR THE CONDUCT OF THE AMERICAN CIA'S OPERATION PHOENIX TO ELIMINATE THE VIET CONG'S LEADERSHIP INFRASTRUCTURE (VCI).

This project had been designed by the CIA as a method to reduce VC operational ability after the United States had withdrawn its troops. Thieu's officials would arrest and punish captured VCI who directed the insurgency efforts in South Vietnam. About 50 U.S. civilian CIA advisors and 600 U.S. military men assisted Thieu's government.

Phoenix operations were clandestine and used strong-arm methods to eliminate the VCI. Paid informants were recruited, normal search and arrest procedures were avoided, and torture was used to interrogate suspects. There was a large number of killings in the process (see the table at the end of this item). Other VCI suspects were imprisoned or rallied to support the Saigon government.

In 1970, information on Phoenix leaked to American newsmen, and the morality of its methods became controversial. Although the White House–CIA view was that the VC were terrorists who deserved their fate, the critics charged that Phoenix methods of totalitarianism were not only wrong but also punished or "neutralized" many innocent people. Newsmen discovered gruesome stories of assassination and misinformation causing persons to be killed because of a grudge, of doors broken down, and homes invaded at night. Robert Komer's 1971 study of Phoenix concluded that although 20,000 VC leaders were allegedly killed or otherwise neutralized, the project was a "largely ineffective effort."

Phoenix Operations Against VC, 1968–1971

Year	Captured	Rallied to Thieu	Killed	Total	% Killed
1968	11,288	2,229	2,559	15,776	16
1969	8,575	4,832	6,187	19,534	32
	Sentenced*				
1970	6,405	7,745	8,191	22,341	37
1971 (May)	2,770	2,911	3,650	9,331	39

Source: U.S. House, Committee on Government Operations, *U.S. Assistance Program in Vietnam*, Hearing, 92nd Congress, 1st Session, July 15–August 2, 1971, p. 83.

*After January, 1970, all VC sentenced to jail were considered neutralized.

August 20, 1968   THE SOVIET UNION MOVES TROOPS INTO PRAGUE TO OVERTHROW
THE CZECH GOVERNMENT OF ALEXANDER DUBCEK: IN WASHING-
TON, PRESIDENT JOHNSON CANCELS PROPOSED NUCLEAR ARMS
TALKS WITH RUSSIA.

During the ceremonies attendant on the signing of the Nuclear Non-Proliferation Treaty on July 1, 1968, President Johnson and the Soviet Union had announced their mutual agreement to begin strategic arms talks in the near future. Between July 1 and August 20, Johnson pressed the Soviet Union to set
a time for formal talks and on August 19, Soviet Ambassador Dobrynin informed
Secretary Rusk that they were willing to open negotiations on October 15.

Following meetings with Rusk and National Security Advisor Rostow, President Johnson agreed to visit Russia during the first week of October to exchange opinions of mutual concern and begin discussions to limit the uses of
strategic arms.

The only difficulty remaining was the White House awareness that the
problems in Czechoslovakia might erupt into a conflict, preventing the talks
from beginning. In Prague, the Dubcek government had replaced the older
Stalinist government of Antonin Novotny, and had undertaken reforms to make
its Communist government more liberal. Although Dubcek tried to convince
Moscow he would not take the Czech reforms too far from the Soviet model, he
defied some Russian requests sufficiently to upset the Soviet Presidium. As
a result, on August 20, Soviet tanks led a Warsaw Pact force into Czechoslovakia to replace the Dubcek government with a "loyal" and "peaceful" regime.

On the evening of August 20, Ambassador Dobrynin visited President
Johnson. He read a statement from Moscow explaining that it was necessary
for the Soviet Union to put down the external and internal aggression in
Czechoslovakia. The message concluded that the Soviets assumed that these
"current events" would not harm Soviet-American relations, to which "the Soviet Government as before attaches great importance." Ambassador Dobrynin
privately realized that the Soviet action against the Czechs did make a
difference to President Johnson.

Nevertheless, President Johnson tactfully said he would inform Dobrynin
of his reaction later. The president, Rusk, and Rostow required little time
to decide. Secretary Rusk had issued a statement on July 28 that the United
States could not intervene in the Prague crisis. Thus, the only considerations were the arms talks and Johnson's proposed visit to the Soviet Union
in October.

The president and his advisors believed they could not begin negotiations
under the circumstances. Later that evening, Secretary Rusk spoke with
Dobrynin and said the announcement of Johnson's visit could not be made. The
pending arms discussions were delayed until after President Nixon took office
in 1969.

August 28, 1968   THE DEMOCRATIC PARTY CONVENTION NOMINATES HUBERT
HUMPHREY FOR PRESIDENT WHILE POLICE FIGHT DISSENTERS
IN DOWNTOWN CHICAGO.

While the Democratic party divided seriously on foreign policy during the
convention, 11,900 Chicago police, 7,500 members of the Illinois National
Guard, and about 1,000 FBI and Secret Service agents tried to protect the
delegates and the city from radical dissent groups. For several days before
and during the convention, police had tried to subdue and disperse the Students for a Democratic Society (SDS), the Youth International Party (YIPPES)

and other dissent groups which made Chicago a focal point of protest against the war in Vietnam.

The protests climaxed on August 28, the same day Humphrey was nominated for president. In Grant Park and at the Michigan Avenue Hilton Hotel, demonstrators and police clashed with tear gas, clubs, rocks, and waterbags dropped from hotel windows. Television scenes of the riots interspersed with Humphrey's nomination scenes at Convention Hall. The rioters were kept away from the convention by a mile-square chain link fence topped by barbed wire. Convention delegates were screened by an electronic pass system.

Inside the convention from August 26 to 28, the groups opposing Johnson's Vietnam policy lost but issued a minority statement. The official platform backed Johnson policy, opposing a complete bombing halt and promising a Vietnam government chosen by "free election." The minority groups advocated the unconditional end of the war, halting all bombing and forming a coalition government in Saigon which would include the VC. Although the minority was led by Senator George McGovern and Edward Kennedy, they did not name another person to run for president.

Right-wing Democrats did run another candidate in the Dixiecrat style of 1948. Governor George Wallace of Alabama formed the American Independent Party. See November 5, 1968.

October 5-6, 1968 *VIOLENCE BEGINS IN NORTHERN IRELAND WITH RIOTS IN LON-DONDERRY BY CATHOLICS CLAIMING CIVIL RIGHTS FROM THE PROTESTANT GOVERNMENT.*

Although the government of Northern Ireland instituted some reforms on November 22, tensions increased. The radical provisional Revolutionary Army of the Irish Catholics began fighting the radical Protestants under Rev. Ian Paisley on November 30. These riots and virtual civil war continued into 1969.

October 9, 1968 PERU NATIONALIZES THE INTERNATIONAL PETROLEUM CORPORATION, A SUBSIDIARY OF EXXON.

Peru's government expropriated the property of Exxon and filed a claim against the U.S. oil company for $690 million in past excess profits.

American relations with Peru had been deteriorating throughout 1968. On May 16, the State Department suspended economic aid to Peru after that government spent $20 million to purchase military jet planes from France. Washington claimed its military aid legislation required a cut-off of aid if a developing nation used funds to purchase military equipment.

Anti-American rioting began in Peru during the period from June to September, ending in the overthrow of President Belaunde's government by a military junta headed by General Juan Alvardo Velasco. The new regime decreed the nationalization of the International Petroleum Corporation.

October 31, 1968 THE UNITED STATES AND NORTH VIETNAM AGREE TO CONDUCT FORMAL NEGOTIATIONS FOR PEACE; PRESIDENT JOHNSON HALTS ALL BOMBING IN NORTH VIETNAM; HANOI AGREES TO STOP ROCKET ATTACKS AND RAIDS ON CITIES IN SOUTH VIETNAM.

From May 13 to October 30, Harriman and Xuan Thuy pursued a joint process of formal and secret talks in order to try to arrange a cease-fire and the beginning of formal truce agreements. Unofficially, the success of these talks was opposed by the Joint Chiefs of Staff and Thieu's government in Saigon, both of whom thought that discussions and any bombing restrictions benefitted Hanoi. President Johnson tended to support the JCS view that Thieu had to be satisfied and grow stronger. Harriman and the Democratic presidential nominee, Hubert Humphrey, wanted a more complete turn-around in U.S. policy, hoping for a return to the divided Vietnam of 1954. They believed the first steps in this process were to stop the bombing, get negotiations started, and move to a complete cease-fire in Vietnam.

Until October 15 Johnson would not accept any concession in addition to those he made on March 31. The talks became stymied by October, meaning that Johnson could not end his administration on a positive note unless he agreed to halt the bombing. To accomplish this, Harriman got Hanoi to agree that Thieu's government could have a direct role in the peace negotiations while the National Liberation Front represented the VC.

Having arranged this compromise, Johnson reported on October 31 that all bombing would cease in North Vietnam; that is, the bombing from the 17th to the 20th parallel which had continued after March 31. The president announced that peace talks would begin, involving four parties but with two sides in negotiations: the United States/South Vietnam as one side; the NFL/Hanoi as the second. On the negative side, there was no cease-fire or truce. Negotiations would proceed while fighting continued, except for the restrictions against Rolling Thunder's bombing of the north and Hanoi's attacks on South Vietnam's cities. Thus began the lengthy negotiations, which continued until January, 1973, under President Nixon.

November 5, 1968   RICHARD NIXON IS ELECTED PRESIDENT.

Nixon had won an easy Republican nomination for president, winning many primaries by cultivating a new image of maturity after his political loss to Kennedy in 1960 and for the California governorship in 1962. The split in the Democratic party over foreign policy caused many liberal Democrats to boycott the election (see August 28, 1968). In addition, George Wallace's party cost Humphrey votes in the south. Although Humphrey broke with Johnson on Vietnam in October, his late surge in public opinion polls came too late for a victory.

In the November 5 ballot, Nixon's popular vote was 31,785,148; Humphrey's was 31,274,503; Wallace received 9,901,151. The electoral college vote was Nixon, 301; Humphrey, 191; Wallace, 46. The Democratic Party retained control of congress.

XV. DÉTENTE OR COLD WAR? NIXON DOCTRINE; VIETNAM TRUCE; PROBLEMS IN ASIA, AFRICA, AND LATIN AMERICA; CRISES IN IRAN AND AFGHANISTAN (1969 TO JANUARY 20, 1981)

1969

January 20, 1969   NIXON'S INAUGURAL ADDRESS INDICATES HIS DESIRE TO CHANGE U.S. POLICY TO REALISTIC POWER-BALANCE DIPLOMACY ALTHOUGH THE IMPLICATION OF HIS WORDS AND PRIOR WRITING ON FOREIGN POLICY DO NOT CLEARLY DEFINE THIS FOR HIS AUDIENCE.

Although Nixon had explained some of his foreign policy views in an October, 1967 article for the quarterly *Foreign Affairs*, his inaugural address and his selection of Henry Kissinger as National Security Advisor enabled a wider group of persons with international concerns to realize that a major new approach to U.S. foreign relations was to be attempted.

Throughout the 1950's and 1960's, scholars of U.S. foreign policy often deplored America's emphasis on ideological, crusading-style approaches to the cold war. George Kennan disliked this emphasis in the Truman Doctrine speech of March, 1947. Balance-of-power realists traced this ideological flaw of U.S. policy back to Woodrow Wilson's "new diplomacy" of 1917 or before. Hans Morgenthau and other "realists" believed the idea of national interest had been dealt with in proper power relations by U.S. leaders between 1789 and 1823 when John Quincy Adams epitomized such power politics relations. Gradually, however, the United States dispensed with these realities in the 20th century.

During the 1960's realists such as Henry Kissinger advocated a return to power politics as the best style of diplomacy. Thus, Kissinger's ascension to a position of power indicated that Nixon would launch a new era of U.S. realistic power diplomacy. Nixon and Kissinger did so during their term of office until August, 1974. They failed, however, to persuade the majority of Americans or the subsequent administrations of Presidents Carter and Reagan to comprehend and follow the methods of balance-of-power relations. As President Ford's Secretary of State, Henry Kissinger used "realism" as much as possible but he never sufficiently schooled Ford in the nuances of this non-traditional U.S. policy.

Although a complete understanding of U.S. power politics diplomacy requires a study of books such as Hans Morgenthau's *The Politics of Nations*, it is possible, at the risk of oversimplification, to contrast the idealistic tradition in the United States and the realistic concepts of Nixon and Kissinger. These may be explained as follows:

1.   *Ideological conflicts vs. power relations* - Truman and other U.S.
     leaders emphasized the cold war as a confrontation between freedom
     and tyranny, good and evil, democracy and communism. These ideolog-
     ical terms were dangerous according to the realists who saw all in-
     ternational disputes as the struggle of one nation's interests with
     another nation's interests. The danger was that ideological rhetoric
     could not be negotiated or compromised, whereas the interests of
     nations could be given priorities and negotiated. To realists, the
     form of government or society did not decide a nation's policy, its
     interests did. Monarchies, republics, democracies, Communist states,
     or any other type of government had political, economic, social,
     territorial, or other interests to defend for their nation. Power
     determined the outcome of a conflict whenever interests clashed.
     Diplomats, however, could avoid war by skillfully balancing one na-
     tion's interests with the opposing nation's interests. Wars resulted
     only when negotiations failed, but were fought on a limited basis
     in order to settle a particular dispute. This last statement is
     critical because while ideological quarrels became win-lose situa-
     tions between good and evil, realistic interests quarrels were lim-
     ited to particular interests at particular times in a never-ending
     diplomatic game. Thus, for realistic power-balance advocates, Amer-
     icans failed to understand limited wars to contain communism as op-
     posed to "total victory" slogans which proposed to eliminate all
     Communists and their evil ideas.

2.   *Collective security or power balance* - Generally, realists believed
     an alliance worked only if all parties shared common interests. Be-
     cause collective security concepts assumed an interest greater than
     the nation's interest, this method could work only when the entire
     group shared common interests. No nation acted in a manner contrary
     to its interest. Thus, any collective agreement failed if a proposed
     course of action did not satisfy a participant's interests. Collec-
     tive security, like world law, was a nice idea but in a world of
     nations and nationalism, it could not operate.

3.   *Open diplomacy vs. secret diplomacy* - Power politics disdained open
     discussion because no nation could openly admit to a compromise un-
     less it had full authority over its citizens. Thus, ironically,
     the openness which made a nation's democracy work in the interests
     of its citizens on a domestic level precluded satisfactory inter-
     national decision making. As Kissinger claimed, the "most success-
     ful" democracies were those based on "essentially aristocratic
     forms." Europe's power balance had worked best under strong monar-
     chies. Within a monarchy, secret diplomacy was possible because
     the state's authority could not be subject to question. In an open,
     democratic society, secrecy in foreign affairs had to be accepted
     or power politics would be difficult.
         The attempts of Nixon and Kissinger to conduct secret activity
     abroad and at home resulted in severe criticism of the Nixon admin-
     istration, leading also to Nixon's fall from power in 1974. The
     association between secret decisions and power politics in a democ-
     racy represents, therefore, one of the most serious issues for real-
     istic politics.

4.   *Cold war vs. détente* - To a great extent the divergence between the
     confrontation tactics of cold warriors such as Acheson, Dulles,

Kennedy, and Johnson and the *consultation* efforts of Eisenhower's "peaceful coexistence" and Nixon's "détenté" serves to explain the tendency in much American diplomacy from 1945 to 1980. Although confrontation does not imply a total absence of diplomacy with the Soviet Union, it does imply an attitude in which compromise is called "appeasement" in the adverse sense of that term because talks with Communists meant that someone wins and someone loses. Thus, summit meetings were not valued by some Americans because their cold war attitudes led them to believe that the satanic forces will win in any compromise of "good" interests. For realists, détente simply means to consult. Power diplomacy requires consultation especially among the big powers who are the most active in playing the national interest game in a chess-like fashion. To a realist, whenever talking stops, movements to war (confrontation) begin. Moreover, because nations each pursue their own interests (including the United States), negotiations are possible. These talks can induce good relations which are in the mutual interests of all antagonists. Therefore, trade, tourist and scientific exchanges, financial deals, and other avenues of international intercourse permit both sides to benefit to some degree.

The four factors of power politics described above are seldom all operative or non-operative at any given instance. All are present, but some are emphasized, others played down. There were some détente developments under Kennedy and Johnson; there would be some cold war attitudes expressed by Nixon and Kissinger. Nevertheless, the comprehension of the polarity of the ideological and realistic perspectives enables one to determine the attitude and tendencies of particular policies. Because both Nixon and Kissinger accepted the basics of power politics, many of their decisions from 1969 to 1974 can be understood as the first clear effort to break with the ideological emphasis of U.S. policy after 1947.

Nixon's inaugural speech outlined some of the attitudes of the power politics which the Nixon Doctrine later asserted more definitely. Thus, the president stated: "After a period of confrontation, we are entering an era of negotiation.... We seek an open world--open to ideas, open to the exchange of goods and people--a world in which no people, great or small, will live in angry isolation.... We cannot expect to make everyone our friend, but we can try to make no one our enemy.... [But] let us leave no doubt that we will be as strong as we need to be for as long as we need to be...."

January 21, 1969   WILLIAM PIERCE ROGERS IS COMMISSIONED AS SECRETARY OF STATE IN PRESIDENT RICHARD NIXON'S CABINET.

Rogers had much experience in Washington, having served as President Eisenhower's Attorney General from 1957 to 1961. Nixon selected Rogers not for his foreign policy expertise but for his talents at handling congress and the press. President Nixon wished to control foreign policy himself, selecting Henry Kissinger as his National Security Advisor in order to centralize international policy-making in the White House.

Kissinger was a former Harvard professor of international relations and had served as Nelson Rockefeller's foreign advisor. He agreed with Nixon's basic policy views on balance-of-power diplomacy, being a scholar of the two leading 19th-century power balance diplomats, Prince Metternich of Austria and Otto von Bismarck of Germany (see January 20, 1969).

Kissinger and Nixon had moved immediately on January 20 to give the White House direct access to American ambassadors abroad. He and Nixon drafted messages to the ambassadors and personal letters to 15 heads of foreign governments, including the Soviet Union's Brezhnev. Kissinger obtained Rogers' consent to address the ambassadors. The messages to the heads of state were delivered to their Washington Embassies by NSC aides. Subsequently, Nixon and Kissinger consulted Rogers only when he could be useful. In decision making, the State Department was generally by-passed.

February 23, 1969   NIXON SEEKS TO EMPHASIZE HIS DESIRE TO CONSULT MORE
                           WITH AMERICA'S EUROPEAN ALLIES AS HE LEAVES ON A ONE-
                           WEEK VISIT TO EUROPEAN NATIONS.

When the president embarked on his European trip on February 23 he told dignitaries at Andrews Air Force Base that he believed progress in settling world affairs made it "necessary to consult with our friends." The grave problems he wished to discuss with others included Vietnam, the Mideast, monetary affairs, and others.

Nixon's itinerary included Brussels where he visited King Baudouin and the NATO Council; London to renew assurance of the Anglo-American "special relation"; Bonn and West Berlin; four days with de Gaulle in Paris; and Rome and Vatican City to meet Italian leaders and Pope Paul VI. Nixon returned to America on March 2, having launched his term of office with a gesture he hoped would gain better relations with Europe.

March 2, 1969   *RUSSIAN AND CHINESE TROOPS CLASH ON THE BORDERS AT*
                          THE USSURI RIVER.

This was one of several border skirmishes in 1969-1970, indicating that the nadir of the Sino-Soviet split had been reached.

March 11, 1969   *MRS. GOLDA MEIR BECOMES PRIME MINISTER OF ISRAEL.*

On February 26, Levi Eshkol died, requiring a change in the Israeli cabinet.

March 14, 1969   NIXON REQUESTS CONGRESS' APPROVAL FOR THE "SAFEGUARD"
                          ANTI-BALLISTIC MISSILE (ABM) SYSTEM.

Early in March, Kissinger's NSC staff completed NSSM-3, a study of the U.S. military posture regarding the strategic arms limitation talks (SALT) which President Johnson had almost begun with the Soviet Union prior to the Czechoslovakian incident (see August 20, 1968). Based on NSSM-3, Nixon decided to seek ABM funding in order to buy time prior to the SALT negotiations and to gain a bargaining chip against Russia's ABM defenses under construction around Moscow.

As a result, on March 14, Nixon announced the United States would ask congress for a Safeguard ABM system to replace President Johnson's plans for a "thin line" ABM Sentinel system allegedly for defense from a Chinese nuclear attack. Because Rusk and Johnson had attempted to solicit better relations with Moscow in 1967-1968, they had announced that the Chinese "menace" required the Sentinel ABM defense.

Nixon's Safeguard ABM's would begin their deployment around two Minuteman ICBM sites in North Dakota, increasing further deployments as warranted by Soviet responses. By defending America's second-strike capability at the Minuteman bases, Nixon said the United States demonstrated it did not intend a first-strike nuclear objective. The second-strike strategy required that U.S. ICBM's must be able to survive a Soviet first strike in order to retaliate in kind. Thus, Nixon argued, Russia's "Galosh" ABM defense of Moscow was creating a first-strike capacity because the Russian defenses of their cities protected them from the American second strike aimed at the centers of Soviet population. In reality, of course, the rhetoric of first- and second-strike tactics partly obscured the fact that, as Secretary of Defense McNamara had indicated in 1967, M.A.D. had given each side sufficient nuclear weapons to blow the entire world apart once nuclear war began.

Nevertheless, in the nuclear limitations games that the United States and Russia played from 1969 to 1979, ABM and other tactical claims and preparations became part of the complex methodology by which the United States and the U.S.S.R. negotiated to forestall a nuclear war. For the start of SALT I negotiations see November 17, 1969.

March 18, 1969   THE FIRST SECRET BOMBING ATTACKS ON CAMBODIA ARE
                          LAUNCHED BY ORDER OF PRESIDENT NIXON.

President Nixon's orders secretly to extend the Vietnam war into neutral Cambodia led to the first in a series of bombings between March 18, 1968, and April, 1970. The secrecy of the operations was maintained until 1973 when congressional investigations followed a report on the operation by Major Hal Knight, a radar officer near Saigon, who objected because he thought the falsification of records violated Article 107 of the Military Code of Justice.

Major Knight's disclosure was necessary because Nixon, Kissinger, and other high U.S. officials conspired in an intricate pattern to keep information on this extension of the war from congress and the U.S. public. Prince Sihanouk of Cambodia, Moscow, Hanoi, and Peking officials knew about it, but not Americans. Nixon did not want to risk the criticism of dissenters in the United States. Or, as some analysts claim, the secrecy was to demonstrate to Moscow President Nixon's willingness to use realistic power politics to act secretly to accomplish his goals.

The Cambodian bombings had been recommended for some time by U.S. military officers who contended that Communist "sanctuaries" in eastern Cambodia were the principal base of supplies for North Vietnam's and the VC's forces in the southern delta area. President Johnson had tried to obtain Prince Sihanouk's permission to eliminate the sanctuaries but would not permit the Pentagon to attack without that approval.

In January, 1969, Nixon asked the Joint Chiefs for recommendations on Cambodia, indicating his willingness to violate Cambodian neutrality if necessary. On February 9, General Abrams recommended "a short-duration, concentrated B-52 attack of up to 60 sorties" to destroy the central headquarters of the Communists (COSVN) in eastern Cambodia. Pentagon intelligence located the headquarters at Base Area 353 in the "fish-hook" area of Cambodia which geographically jutted into South Vietnam northwest of Saigon. Abrams believed that the B-52 attacks would minimize the violation of Cambodian territory to one minute per sortie and that few Cambodian civilians would be killed. The destruction of COSVN, Abrams said, would "have a very significant effect on enemy operations throughout South Vietnam."

President Nixon approved Abrams' proposal but insisted on strict secrecy, objecting to Secretary of Defense Laird's desire to inform congressional leaders. To maintain secrecy, a devious "dual reporting" system was devised by the Pentagon. The B-52's would leave Guam for Vietnamese targets. Once over South Vietnam, ground radar controllers would redirect the planes to Cambodia without the pilot or navigator realizing the location of the new target. The radar controllers knew, however, and would send two reports to General Abrams, one for the original targets and one for the revised target. Officially, the bombs fell on Vietnam. Major Knight was a radar controller who had first appealed to his superiors to amend the false documents. When they refused to follow through, Knight later appealed to congress.

General Abrams' February 9 recommendation for a few low-level attacks never did the job, assuming his assumptions about the sanctuaries were correct. Following the March 18 bombing of Base 353, a U.S. Special Forces team code-named "Daniel Boone" entered the area to survey the damage. The team of 12 men commanded by Captain Bill Orthman flew helicopters to the area, but after they landed and moved toward the jungle, the enemy attacked, slaughtering Daniel Boone. Nine men were killed; three Vietnamese and Orthman were wounded but got back to the helicopter and survived.

Overlooking Abrams' miscalculation, Nixon ordered additional bombings, but the objectives of these attacks were never fulfilled. During the next year there were 3,875 sorties in which the B-52's dropped 108,823 tons of bombs. The Communist bases survived, being relocated farther inland. Only Cambodia suffered from the bombings. The American incursion into Cambodia in April, 1970, led to the complete end of Cambodian neutrality. See April 30, 1970.

May 10, 1969   IN VIETNAM, OPERATION *APACHE SNOW* INDICATES THE ARMY
                        HAS NOT ADJUSTED TO THE USE OF GENERAL ABRAMS' "AREA
                        SECURITY" STRATEGY.

Although General Abrams, who succeeded Westmoreland as U.S. Commander in Vietnam on April 10, 1968, had introduced new strategic methods for the war, Abrams' "area security" plan broke so severely with the U.S. Army's traditional attrition warfare that American officers either could not or would not forsake the attrition methods. As designed by Abrams and approved by President Nixon early in 1969, U.S. and ARVN army action would cooperate with the People's Self-Defense Forces (PSDF) to clear and secure an area of Communist influence. Because the PSDF had knowledge of local conditions, the United States and ARVN would work closely with them. There would be small unit actions which would emphasize every effort to avoid destruction and killing so that the local population and PSDF could avoid the disaster and dislocation of battle affecting the population such as occurred from attrition fire power. Together ARVN and PSDF would protect the future security of a region step by step. Thus, Abrams' methods deemphasized "body count," and stressed "local loyalty" at all costs. The area security plan would counteract the Communist-protracted warfare. It was approved by Nixon because it fit his Vietnamization plans effectively.

There was one major problem with Abrams' plan. It radically changed the way U.S. officers were trained to fight. West Point taught big-unit action, fire power, attrition ways of death and destruction. From the Indian frontier to Korea these methods had won. Thus, U.S. army doctrine eschewed political goals; military goals were ends in themselves. Area security might win the Vietnamese "hearts and minds" but as Major General Julian Ewell wrote in 1969, "I guess I basically feel that the 'hearts and minds' approach can be overdone. In the Delta, the only way to overcome VC control and terror is by brute force applied against the VC." Another senior officer criticized Abrams' methods more succinctly: "I'll be damned if I permit the United States Army, its institutions, its doctrine, and its tradition to be destroyed just to win this lousy war." As Guenter Lewy concluded: "Abrams' campaign plan, for the most part, remained a paper exercise."

About one year after Abrams took command, Operation Apache Snow, including the famous battle of Hamburger Hill, represented U.S. "old-style" heroism and the inability of the United States or its trained ARVN units to accept Abrams' plans. Apache Snow was a big-unit action by the U.S. 101st Airborne Division and the First ARVN Division in the 30-mile-long A Shau Valley near the borders of South Vietnam, Laos, and the 17th parallel.

The first day, B-52's, artillery, and naval guns bombarded the valley. The second day, U.S. Airborne troops and ARVN helicopters entered the valley. Eventually, the decisive location focused on Hill 937 where a strong enemy force held out. Lodged on a rugged, densely forested, heavily fortified hill, the Communists held out for 10 days. The U.S. Field Commander, Major General Melvin Zais, threw more and more men into battle, where they were "chewed up like meat" on "Hamburger Hill." The U.S. Air Force flew 272 sorties and dropped one million pounds of bombs including napalm. The artillery fired 21,732 rounds at the hill. Finally, fighting bunker to bunker, the U.S. soldiers secured Hill 937. U.S. losses were 56 killed, 420 wounded; the enemy lost 505 troops.

Once Hill 937 was secured, however, it was abandoned. The search-and-destroy operation had killed the enemy. Hill 937 had no political or military value such as Abrams had prescribed. In fact, the U.S. pacification agency reported that Communist terrorism increased in formerly "pacified" areas while the battle of Hamburger Hill raged.

Abrams' area security plans tumbled before the search-and-destroy attrition methods. Old army methods still needed to be attuned to new world conditions. American soldiers fought heroically, but their gallant efforts provided no results.

May 14, 1969   NIXON OFFERS PEACE TERMS TO NORTH VIETNAM WHICH ARE
                                  TOTALLY UNACCEPTABLE TO HANOI.

Speaking on nationwide television, President Nixon announced a peace plan for Vietnam. His proposal called for a cease-fire, the withdrawal of all American and North Vietnamese troops, an exchange of prisoners of war, and the creation of an international commission to conduct free elections in South Vietnam.

News commentators noted that this proposal had no chance to be accepted by North Vietnam. Its terms would have accomplished what the United States had not achieved during the last five years: the withdrawal of North Vietnamese forces and an election to divide Vietnam, with Thieu in charge in the south. At best, Nixon's so-called eight-point plan expressed the extreme bargaining position for U.S. truce negotiations at the Paris peace talks.

June 8, 1969   PRESIDENT NIXON AND PRESIDENT THIEU ANNOUNCE THE INI-
TIAL WITHDRAWAL OF U.S. FORCES FROM SOUTH VIETNAM: THE
VIETNAMIZATION PROCESS BEGINS.

Nixon had approved the initial "Vietnamization" plans on May 14 but waited
to announce the decision until after a meeting at Midway Island during which
Thieu had little choice but to accept the plan. Significantly, the initial
study--NSSM-1--by Kissinger's national security team in January, 1969, recommended plans for the gradual U.S. withdrawal from Vietnam. These plans were
reviewed and redesigned slightly in NSSM-36 and 37 during April before Nixon
accepted them.

Thus, following talks with Thieu and General Creighton ABRAMS, Nixon
announced the Vietnamization program on June 8. On Thieu's recommendation,
Nixon told reporters that 25,000 U.S. combat troops would be withdrawn as
the first step in allowing South Vietnamese forces to take over their nation's
self-defense. Thieu and Abrams agreed that with proper training by U.S. officers and with U.S. equipment, the Army of the Republic of Vietnam (ARVN)
could protect their country from communism. Training of the Vietnamese had
begun under Abrams' orders in 1968 and it showed every sign of success.

Nixon did not give a precise timetable for withdrawal of U.S. troops.
He said the situation in Vietnam would be reviewed regularly and future withdrawals would be in accord with ARVN's capacity to take charge. Later, in
Washington, the president asserted that "no action will be taken" in the Vietnamization process which would "threaten the safety of our troops and the
troops of our allies" or "the right of self-determination for the people of
South Vietnam." The initial secret plans of the NSC indicated that the summer
of 1972 would be the earliest date when South Vietnam might be able to defend
itself.

As Nixon explained to reporters at Guam on July 25, Vietnamization fitted
the Nixon policy by which local defense forces would be aided, trained, and
equipped to defend themselves. Not stated, but a part of the Nixon-Kissinger
balance-of-power strategy (see January 20, 1969), Vietnam was not considered
a vital interest of the United States in global power relations. The United
States could not withdraw rapidly because of historic commitments. From a
power politics perspective, the United States should never have been in Vietnam because U.S. commitments from 1950 to 1968 had been based on ideological
not realistic political grounds. From 1969 to 1973, however, Moscow's Communist considerations regarding its support of Hanoi would be linked to other
power objectives desired by Nixon and Kissinger.

The table on page 1046 shows the declining role of U.S. combat forces
between 1968 and July, 1972.

June 15, 1969   *GEORGES POMPIDOU IS ELECTED PRESIDENT OF FRANCE FOL-
LOWING DE GAULLE'S RESIGNATION.*

*French economic problems increased in 1968, causing serious student riots in
Paris and Nanterre. The Gaullists in parliament held only a one-vote majority, making it difficult to rule efficiently.*

*In 1968, a change in Ministers to Couve de Murville as premier did not
solve the problem. There was a currency crisis against the franc on November
13.*

*To strengthen the presidential power, de Gaulle suggested reforms of
the French Senate, but in a referendum the majority rejected this by 52.87%*

Decline of U.S. Combat Role

1968-1972

	U.S. Troop Strengths	U.S. Ground Operation Batallion Size	U.S. Deaths from Hostile Acts	U.S. Deaths per 1,000 Strengths
January, 1968	498,000	NA	1,202	2.4
July, 1968	537,000	71	813	1.5
January, 1969	542,000	56	795	1.5
July, 1969	537,000	89	638	1.9
January, 1970	473,000	58	343	0.7
July, 1970	404,000	64	332	0.8
January, 1971	336,000	64	140	0.4
July, 1971	225,000	40	65	0.3
January, 1972	133,200	9	16	0.1
July, 1972	45,600	0	36	0.8

Source: OASD (Comptroller), SEA Statistical Summary, Table 6, August 18, 1973; Table 9, November 7, 1973.

on April 28, 1969. De Gaulle resigned and Alain Poher became interim president.

Pompidou was elected president on June 15 with 58% of the votes. The new prime minister was Jacques Chaban-Delmas.

On August 10, Pompidou devalued the franc in order to solve some of the economic difficulties.

July 15, 1969   NIXON SENDS A SECRET LETTER TO HO CHI MINH.

Although U.S. negotiations with North Vietnam had been conducted in Paris since January 25, these were public meetings conducted with both South Vietnamese and NLF delegates present, as agreed to in October, 1968. Nixon had designated Henry Cabot Lodge to head the U.S. delegation, replacing Harriman and the team Johnson had appointed in May, 1968.

Kissinger suggested to Nixon in February that the open Paris sessions could never reach an agreement. He believed, however, that there could be success by high-level secret discussions in Paris with a North Vietnamese delegate. To achieve this without Ambassador Lodge's knowledge, Kissinger arranged for Jean Sainteny, a retired French diplomat and friend of Kissinger, to deliver to Xuan Thuy, Hanoi's delegate in Paris, an oral message regarding secret talks as well as a written letter from Nixon to Ho Chi Minh.

Following Nixon's world tour and the beginning of Vietnamization in July, the president decided to enact Kissinger's proposal with Sainteny acting as the go-between. Although Ho did not respond to Nixon's letter for over four weeks, he responded immediately to the suggestion for secret talks. The first session began in Paris on August 4, 1969.

July 20, 1969   U.S. ASTRONAUTS MAKE THE FIRST MOON LANDING.

Neil A. Armstrong and Edwin E. Aldrin, Jr., landed the lunar module *Eagle* on the moon. Armstrong became the first man to walk on the moon's surface. After 21½ hours on the moon, the *Eagle* rejoined *Apollo 11* which had been orbiting the moon after ejecting *Eagle* for the landing. Astronaut Michael Collins commanded the *Apollo 11*. Live TV broadcasts sent pictures of the landing back to earth for viewers around the world to watch.

A second U.S. moon landing was made on November 19-20, 1969. Four more moon visits were made by Americans between 1970 and 1972. Only one moon mission experienced difficulty: *Apollo 13*. This mission was aborted but the three astronauts landed safely in the Pacific Ocean on April 17, 1970.

The moon landing program was the consequence of John F. Kennedy's call for a U.S. program to land the first man on the moon. See May 25, 1961.

July 25, 1969   AT GUAM, NIXON INFORMALLY TELLS REPORTERS THE POLICIES
                           WHICH WILL BECOME BASIC TO THE NIXON DOCTRINE REGARDING
                           ASIA AND, BY IMPLICATION, OTHER REGIONS OF THE WORLD.

Unlike the Truman Doctrine which derived essentially from one presidential speech on March 12, 1947, the Nixon Doctrine was first disclosed casually by the president in July and November, 1969, before it was formally described in a report to congress during January, 1970.

Nixon arrived in Guam as part of a world tour during which he first greeted the U.S. astronauts on their return from the first moon flight. During the evening of July 25, he met with news reporters for an off-the-record conversation which the White House later made public. In somewhat rambling fashion, Nixon told the reporters that nationalism had changed matters in the world, especially in Asia. The United States needed to recognize this fact and, while keeping commitments, let other countries develop on their own. The United States had to avoid policies which made others "so dependent on us that we are dragged into conflicts such as the one that we have in Vietnam."

During later questioning by reporters, Nixon summarized his ideas more precisely. He said the United States in its Asian relations must be

> quite emphatic on two points: one, that we will keep our treaty
> commitments ... for example, with Thailand under SEATO; but, two,
> that as far as the problems of internal security are concerned, as
> far as the problems of military defense, except for the threat of
> a major power involving nuclear weapons, that the United States is
> going to encourage and has a right to expect that this problem will
> be increasingly handled by, and the responsibility for it taken by,
> the Asian nations themselves....

The president also said that the policy of letting Asians protect themselves would be effective only after the Vietnam War ended. Until then, the United States had of necessity to remain in command.

During his subsequent visits to Manila, Djakarta, Bangkok, and Saigon, Nixon made much the same point regarding Asians' eventually assuming control of their own internal and defense needs. On July 31, Nixon flew to India where relations with the United States were not satisfactory, and continued on to Pakistan and Rumania before flying back to Washington. See August 3, 1969.

August 3, 1969   NIXON RETURNS FROM A WORLD TOUR WHICH HAD ENDED WITH
                              A VISIT TO RUMANIA.

Following a trip to greet the moon astronauts in the Pacific and visit Guam and four capitals of Southeast Asia (see July 25, 1969), Nixon's final stops were in India, Pakistan, and Rumania. Relations in neutralist India were tense because that government seemed to lean toward Moscow and wanted the United States to leave Vietnam. In pro-American Pakistan, the Yahya Kahn was more congenial, giving Nixon the nation's highest medal, the Nishan-e-Pakistan.

The visit to Bucharest, Rumania, impressed Nixon the most. On August 2, thousands of citizens in this Communist state greeted the president. Subtly, of course, the Rumanian enthusiasm was more anti-Soviet than pro-American because the government of Nicholae Ceausescu wanted to show the nation's limited independence of Russia. Both Nixon and Ceausescu expressed the desire for open contacts with all nations.

Having traveled around the world, Nixon arrived back at Andrews Air Force Base near Washington on the evening of August 3.

August 4, 1969   KISSINGER AND XUAN THUY CONDUCT THEIR FIRST SECRET
                          NEGOTIATIONS IN PARIS.

On July 26, Ho Chi Minh sent word to President Nixon that North Vietnam would
empower Xuan Thuy to hold high-level secret talks in Paris. Nixon selected
Kissinger to represent him, and by-passing Lodge and the State Department,
Nixon entrusted the secret arrangements to his old friend Lieutenant General
Vernon A. Walters, the U.S. defense attaché at the Paris Embassy.

On August 3, Nixon's plane en route from Rumania stopped briefly in London for a presidential visit with Prime Minister Wilson. Kissinger and two
of his aides, Anthony Lake and Helmut Sonnenfeldt, left Air Force One and
boarded a U.S. military aircraft for Paris. The Americans spent the night
at General Walters' Neuilly apartment and Kissinger met publicly with President de Gaulle to brief him on Nixon's recent trips. De Gaulle also agreed
to help Kissinger preserve the secrecy of his future talks with Xuan Thuy in
Paris.

On the afternoon of August 4, Kissinger and his assistants went to Jean
Sainteny's apartment where they were introduced to Xuan Thuy and his aide.
The first talks led to an agreement to hold future secret talks although no
date was set for the next meeting.

August 13, 1969   *FIGHTING BREAKS OUT ON THE SINO-SOVIET BORDER.*

*This border clash was the last in a series of Chinese-Soviet border incidents
during 1969, highlighting 1969 as reaching a low point in relations between
Moscow and Peking. Following a clash on March 2 along the Ussuri River border, the two governments exchanged heated accusations intermixed with border
engagements. The most serious fighting took place on March 15, June 11, and
August 13. Soviet Premier Kosygin stopped in Peking on September 11 following
the funeral of Ho Chi Minh in Hanoi. Talks to resolve the border problems
began on October 19 but were not resolved during the next month.*

September 1, 1969   *IN LIBYA, COLONEL MUAMMAR AL-QADDAFI LEADS A SUCCESSFUL
                            MILITARY COUP OVERTHROWING KING IDRIS I.*

*A strong pro-Arab, who some claimed wanted to replace Nasser as the Arab's
leading spokesman, Qaddafi took a hard line against the Western powers and
Israel.*

September 3, 1969   HO CHI MINH DIES, SOON AFTER ANSWERING NIXON'S PERSONAL
                            LETTER ON AUGUST 25.

Although Nixon and Kissinger believed Ho's death was good news because it
would leave Hanoi leaderless, they, as often true of other Americans, underestimated the North Vietnamese political structure. In Hanoi, power appeared
to be taken by the Politburo, but Washington saw only deep divisions in this
between the LeDuan faction and the Truong Chinh faction. Actually, the North
Vietnamese leaders were united in their devotion to expelling the Americans
and reuniting Vietnam.

On August 25, Ho had sent his reply to Nixon's letter of July 15, 1969.
Ho's response showed the gulf between the perceptions of the two leaders

regarding Vietnam. Whereas Nixon believed the United States was rightfully fighting in Vietnam for its Saigon ally, Ho saw the U.S. role as that of direct aggression to preserve imperialism and in violation of the "fundamental rights" of the Vietnamese people. He told Nixon that only if the U.S. left Vietnam could Vietnamese rights and world peace be secured.

The letters exchanged between Nixon and Ho were released by the State Department for publication on November 4, 1969.

October 21, 1969   *IN WEST GERMANY, WILLY BRANDT BECOMES CHANCELLOR, LEADING THE SOCIAL DEMOCRATIC PARTY.*

Brandt was an exponent of building better relations with Eastern European countries and the Soviet Union.

October 21, 1969   THE SHAH OF IRAN VISITS WITH PRESIDENT NIXON, THE PRESIDENT TELLING THE SHAH THAT IRAN SHOULD BECOME THE DOMINANT POWER IN THE PERSIAN GULF.

Although the visit to Washington of the Shah Reza Pahlevi was largely ceremonial, Nixon indicated to Reza the important role Iran had in the Middle East. The National Security Council Study NSSM-66 indicated that as Great Britain abdicated more and more power east of Suez, the United States needed allies such as Iran to control the Straits of Hormuz in the Persian Gulf oil area.

In public, Nixon referred to Iran "as one of the strongest, the proudest among all nations of the world." The shah, Nixon said, had made land reforms which were a "revolution in terms of social, economic, and political progress.

November 17, 1969   AMERICA AND THE SOVIET UNION BEGIN SALT I NEGOTIATIONS IN HELSINKI.

Discussions between Moscow and Washington about limiting offensive and defensive nuclear weapons had been considered, but had been delayed since August 20, 1969. Not until October 20 did Ambassador Dobrynin inform Nixon and Kissinger that Russia was ready to begin arms discussions. Because the U.S. Senate had finalized the law approving ABM construction on August 6, the United States was also ready to undertake talks. On October 25, the two governments jointly announced that discussions would begin at Helsinki on November 17. The secret talks would cover offensive and defensive weapons. All substantive announcements would be made jointly.

The principal issues confronting the SALT I negotiations from the U.S. viewpoint were: the ABM, offensive MIRV weapons, and verifications. Nixon and Kissinger had agreed that the United States wanted to eliminate the ABM systems if possible. They had sought ABM funding only as a chip to throw away during the talks. The greatest concern to the United States was to retain its leadership in MIRV technology. MIRV warheads--multiple independent reentry vehicles--have clusters of separately targeted nuclear warheads. These MIRV could be deployed on the Minuteman and U.S. submarine launchers. Considered by technicians to be the biggest breakthrough since the hydrogen bomb, MIRV gave the United States a qualitative advantage over the Soviet

Union. Nixon believed Russia delayed the SALT discussions in order to perfect its own MIRV. In fact, there was a dispute in the Nixon administration between Melvin Laird, the Secretary of Defense, and Richard Helms of the CIA. Laird insisted that the Soviets already had minimum MIRV's available with three separate warheads. Helms's intelligence data indicated it would be 1972 before the Russians had this minor capability. Although the Soviets did not gain MIRV technology until 1973, Kissinger assumed Laird was correct because he used this to obtain limits on Soviet offensive missiles.

Finally, the verification issue was always one of the most problematic for U.S. negotiators. Here again, Laird and Kissinger differed with CIA head Helms. The CIA believed that electronic surveillance and telemetry permitted the United States to keep aware of Soviet weapons including such capabilities as MIRV. Kissinger, who apparently disliked Helms personally, argued that Helms and the CIA had a "vested interest" in verification and could not therefore be relied on to judge the requirements of verification. Moreover, doubts about verification made Kissinger appear "hard" in negotiations with Russia.

Thus, when the SALT talks convened, the principal U.S. concerns were to stop ABM systems, to protect U.S. advantages in MIRV, and to seek the most satisfactory verification methods possible. To conduct the U.S. discussions, Nixon named Special Ambassador Gerard C. Smith, who was director of the U.S. Arms Control and Disarmament Agency. The first round of talks lasted until December 22, 1969.

November 21, 1969   THE UNITED STATES AGREES TO RETURN OKINAWA TO JAPAN AS A RESULT OF WASHINGTON DISCUSSIONS BETWEEN PRESIDENT NIXON AND JAPAN'S PRIME MINISTER EISAKU SATO.

During 1969, two issues disturbed relations between Japan and America: Japan's desire to regain Okinawa and the importation of Japanese textiles. As a lawyer for U.S.-owned corporations during the 1960's, Nixon had often visited Tokyo and liked the conservative political-business circles of that country. He was eager therefore to satisfy Japan's major request in 1969, the return of Okinawa. Nixon had convinced the Joint Chiefs of Staff that U.S. planes and nuclear weapons requirements would not be damaged if they later had to be removed from Okinawa. Consultation with Tokyo on these affairs was necessary.

Thus, when Sato reached Washington on November 19, Nixon was prepared to agree on details of the U.S. withdrawal from Okinawa. Sato stated that the U.S. Treaty of Mutual Cooperation would be extended to Okinawa. Thus, U.S.-Japanese consultations on air bases in Okinawa would have the same terms as those in the Japanese home islands. In addition, the prime minister approved the continued use of B-52 bases on Okinawa for action in Indochina where the United States fought for "self-determination for the people of South Vietnam." The treaty on Okinawa was finalized in April, 1970.

The textile issue was not easily resolved. In April, Maurice Stans, the U.S. Secretary of Commerce, visited Tokyo but bungled efforts to reach a textile agreement because he made harsh statements against Japan. In November, 1969, Sato told Nixon he would place self-export limits by Japanese on their textiles. Sato's promise was vague, however, and this trade issue was not resolved for two more years.

November 25, 1969   NIXON PROCLAIMS AMERICA'S RATIFICATION OF THE NON-
                             PROLIFERATION TREATY AND ANNOUNCES THAT AMERICA WILL
                             RENOUNCE CHEMICAL-BIOLOGICAL WEAPONS BY HAVING THE
                             U.S. SENATE RATIFY THE GENEVA PROTOCOL OF 1925.

The non-proliferation treaty had been signed by the United States on July 1,
1968, but was not ratified by the U.S. Senate until March, 1969. In the interim, 108 nations (but not China or France) signed the treaty which Nixon
proclaimed for the United States.

On the same day, Nixon committed the United States not to make first
use of chemical, incapacitating, or biological weapons. He would submit the
1925 protocol to the Senate because the United States had not previously accepted this pact. Henceforth, said Nixon, America would confine its chemical-
biological research to "immunization and safety methods."

In 1975, U.S. Senate investigators found that the CIA ignored Nixon's
1969 suggestion to destroy its stocks of toxins used in biological warfare.
It retained stocks of cobra venom and Saxitonit, a toxin causing instant
death. The 1925 protocol was not ratified until 1975. See January 22, 1975.

December 8, 1969   IN A PRESS CONFERENCE, PRESIDENT NIXON REFERS TO THE
                            MY LAI "MASSACRE" AS AN ISOLATED INCIDENT NOT REPRE-
                            SENTING U.S. POLICY.

The My Lai massacre had taken place on March 16, 1969, but had not been reported by U.S. newspapers until November 16. During this action, U.S. troops
led by Lieutenant William L. Calley shot 450 unarmed South Vietnam villagers.
Although there were other reports of individual atrocities in North Vietnam,
My Lai and the Phoenix operations of 1968-1972 became the most notorious il-
lustrations of the type of degrading incident associated with guerrilla warfare.

During his press conference, Nixon was asked to react to the My Lai report. He said, "We cannot ever condone or use atrocities against civilians"
in order to bring security to Vietnam. He hoped this event would not "smear
the decent men that have gone to Vietnam" on a vital mission.

December 19, 1969   SECRETARY OF STATE ROGERS EXPLAINS THAT HIS OCTOBER
                             PLAN FOR THE MIDDLE EAST HAS BEEN REJECTED BY RUSSIA
                             AND EGYPT.

Nixon and Kissinger had decided in March, 1969, to have Secretary Rogers conduct discussions with the Soviet Union regarding a solution to the Arab-
Israeli quarrels which continued from the Six-Day War of 1967 and U.N. Reso-
lution 242's interpretation. Nixon believed the two big powers should de-
termine a plan for their client states--Israel and Egypt--which would have
to be accepted by them. With Joseph Sisco of the State Department's Near
Eastern Division conducting most of the day-to-day negotiations with Soviet
Ambassador Dobrynin during the spring and summer of 1969, the so-called
Rogers Plan emerged by September and was "signed off on" (approved) by the
National Security Council on October 19.

Although the White House never fully supported the Rogers Plan, its principal features were (1) that the Sinai would be demilitarized with Israel's
security guaranteed in the Strait of Tiran; (2) that after Israel withdrew

from the occupied territory, the Arabs and Israelis would negotiate details of peace "in some manner"; and (3) that special discussions would settle the issue of the Gaza Strip. The precise definition of where Israel would withdraw was not provided.

When Israel's Prime Minister Golda Meir visited Washington on September 25-26, Nixon did not confide in her about the Rogers Plan or U.S.-Soviet discussions. He told her the White House fully supported Israel, but that he had trouble dealing with others in the State Department and the NSC.

After the NSC approved the Rogers Plan on October 19, the secretary held extensive talks with Soviet Foreign Minister Andrei Gromyko in New York. The two worked out an agreement for the approval of Egypt and Israel. By their terms, the territories which Israel would withdraw from were those taken from Egypt in 1967 except for "insubstantial alterations," which was one of Rogers's phrases. In return, Egypt would assure the security of the Israeli borders.

The Rogers plan, as he explained in December, did not survive long. Late in October, after the United States had orally explained the plan to Israel, Tel Aviv announced that the Soviet-American plan called for "direct negotiations" between Israel and Egypt. Egypt's foreign minister, Mahmoud Riad, protested against this phrase. At best, he had told Moscow only that he would participate in "indirect talks," which itself was a concession because of strong Arab opposition to talks which would recognize Israel's right to exist as a state.

Although the Rogers plan might have survived if Nixon had fully pushed it, he did not. By December, Dobrynin informed Rogers and Sisco that they no longer backed the plan because of Egyptian opposition. Before the speech of December 19, in which Rogers explained the aborting of his proposal, Rogers had neglected to inform Israel of the Russian notification. Abba Eban, Israel's Foreign Minister, objected strongly to any effort of outside parties to impose a peace on Israel. As a result, U.S.-Israeli relations were strained by the end of 1969.

1970

January 8, 1970   PRESIDENT THIEU OF SOUTH VIETNAM INFORMS NEWSMEN THAT
IT WOULD BE "IMPOSSIBLE AND IMPRACTICAL" TO WITHDRAW
ALL U.S. TROOPS FROM VIETNAM IN 1970.

Since the announced Vietnamization program of June 8, 1969, there had been
extensive speculation in Vietnam and the United States regarding the time of
America's complete withdrawal.

A vital part of Vietnamization was the question of South Vietnam's preparations to take charge of local defense. During the summer of 1968, President Thieu had called a general mobilization in South Vietnam. All army reserves were called up and a draft began of men 18 and 19 years old. In addition, men aged 16-17 and over 38 years could be drafted into Socialized People's Self-Defense Forces (PSDF). By 1972, the ARVN and other regular South
Vietnamese forces totaled 516,000, fewer than the American total of 542,000
at its peak in January, 1969 (see table on page 1046).

U.S. military advisors expected that the trained and equipped PSDF of
nearly 500,000 would add to Saigon's total defense establishment. The critical problem was for the Saigon government to obtain the respect and loyalty
of local leaders of the PSDF. This local loyalty had been a persistent problem of Saigon's dictatorial regime since 1954. Enlarging the PSDF was simple;
gaining their affection and motivation was a different question. The table
on page 1055 summarizes the number of the South Vietnamese forces from 1964
to 1972.

January 20, 1970   U.S. AMBASSADOR TO POLAND WALTER STOESSEL, JR., AND
CHINA'S CHARGÉ D'AFFAIRES LEI YANG CONDUCT TALKS IN
WARSAW.

The U.S. and Chinese representatives had had 133 sessions in Warsaw since
1955 but since 1965 these had dwindled to only one or two a year with only
one in 1968 on January 8. On November 26, 1968, the Chinese chargé had sent
Stoessel a note suggesting a formal meeting with a U.S. representative on
February 20, 1969. Later, Chinese diplomats said they had read president-
elect Nixon's article in the October, 1967, issue of *Foreign Affairs* and were
impressed by his advocacy of normalizing American relations with China. Although Nixon, through Secretary of State Rusk, agreed to a meeting with the
Chinese in Warsaw in February, the session was cancelled because a Chinese
diplomat in the Netherlands defected to the West and Peking blamed America.

Both Nixon and Kissinger were willing to hold talks with the Chinese
and sought in various ways to encourage this during 1969. On May 24, Secretary of State Rogers visited Pakistan and, along with other matters, told
Yahya Khan, who had good relations with China, that the United States desired
to make diplomatic contact with Peking. On July 21, the State Department
announced that certain professional persons could obtain valid passports for

Armed Forces
Strength of the Republic of Vietnam*
1964-1972

	Army	Air Force	Navy Marines	Total Regular	PSDF		Grand Total
					Regional Forces	Popular Forces	
1964	220,000	11,000	19,000	250,000	96,000	168,000	514,000
1967	303,000	16,000	24,000	343,000	151,000	149,000	643,000
1968	380,000	19,000	28,000	427,000	220,000	173,000	820,000
1969	416,000	36,000	41,000	493,000	190,000	214,000	897,000
1970	416,000	46,000	53,000	515,000	207,000	246,000	968,000
1971-72**	410,000	50,000	56,000	516,000	284,000	248,000	1,048,000

Source: James L. Collins, Jr., *The Development and Training of the South Vietnamese Army, 1960-1972* (Washington, 1975).

* Appropriations

** Decline due to desertions and recruiting shortfall

China and that U.S. residents abroad or tourists could buy a limited amount of Communist Chinese goods to bring back with them to America.

Finally, on December 12, Ambassador Stoessel, acting on instructions from Nixon, informally contacted Lei Yang at a Yugoslavian reception, telling Lei's interpreter that the United States would like to arrange a meeting. Two days later, Lei sent Stoessel an invitation to visit him at the Chinese embassy on January 20, 1970.

At the January meeting and again at a meeting in the U.S. embassy on February 20, Stoessel and Lei exchanged formal and polite views. Stoessel also suggested that perhaps a "high-level emissary" from America could visit Peking. No firm agreement resulted from this overture but Stoessel and Lei decided to hold monthly sessions thereafter.

February 18, 1970   THE NIXON DOCTRINE IS DESCRIBED IN A REPORT TO CONGRESS TITLED "FOREIGN POLICY FOR THE 1970's."

Although Nixon had informally COMMENTED ON THE PRINCIPLES OF HIS POLICY DURING A NEWS CONFERENCE in Guam on July 25, and in a national TV speech on November 3, 1969, the Nixon Doctrine was not precisely spelled out until his report to congress of February 18, 1970.

This report identified three basic points of the Nixon Doctrine:

1. The United States would keep all of its commitments to allies.

2. The allies should provide their own troops for self-defense against communism.

3. The United States would provide a nuclear shield and economic aid for its allies.

Nixon principally wanted America to "participate" but no longer undertake all the defense" for its allies. To provide American aid, funds for the Military Assistance Programs increased in 1971 by $2 billion over Johnson's last budget. The United States also sold more arms to the allies. By 1973, Iran alone obtained $205 billion worth of U.S. weapons. Nevertheless, American allies would, said Nixon, "define the nature of their own security and determine the path of their own progress."

March 18, 1970   *PRINCE SIHANOUK OF CAMBODIA IS OVERTHROWN BY HIS PRIME MINISTER, LON NOL.*

Since becoming leader in Cambodia on June 5, 1960, Sihanouk often irritated U.S. officials because of his desire to remain neutral in both the cold war and the Vietnam conflict. American claims of Communist sanctuaries in eastern Cambodia were shrugged off by the prince as "illegal" or "under control." Essentially, Prince Sihanouk believed his people would fare best if he kept his nation as aloof as possible from direct involvement in the north-south conflict in Vietnam.

Although the leaders of the March 17-18 coup, Lon Nol and Prince Sirik Matek, had advocated strong anti-Communist methods and greater support for America, there is no evidence that the CIA engineered the March 18 coup. William Shawcross, whose study Sideshow *is generally critical of Nixon and Kissinger, believes the CIA knew about Lon Nol's plans but did not promote them.*

Nixon's secret Cambodian bombings which began on March 18, 1969, did

*influence Sihanouk's ouster. By driving the Communists deeper into Cambodia,
the North Vietnamese Communists and the Cambodian Communists, the Khmer Rouge,
joined forces and increased their conflicts with the Cambodian Royal Army.
These incidents gave credence to Prime Minister Lon Nol's desire for stronger
anti-Communist efforts.*

*On March 12, while Prince Sihanouk vacationed in France, Lon Nol decided
to attack the Communists. He closed Sihanoukville port to Communist supply
ships and ordered Hanoi to withdraw its troops from Cambodia in 72 hours.
He also organized anti-Communist street demonstrations in the capitol, Phnom
Penh. Finally, on March 17-18, Lon Nol and Prince Matek became emboldened
enough to arrest Sihanouk's political supporters and to take over the government.*

*Although Sihanouk quickly flew to Peking via Moscow and organized resist-
ance to Lon Nol, he was too late to regain power. The new government was on
shaky ground, however. Although the Nixon administration recognized the Lon
Nol regime, enemies of Lon Nol united. Sihanouk allied with the Khmer
Rouge and the North Vietnamese against Lon Nol, asserting that he would overthrow the U.S.-supported "lackey," Lon Nol. Cambodia's tragic destruction
was just beginning.*

March 19, 1970   *GOVERNMENT HEADS OF EAST AND WEST GERMANY MEET AT
                          ERFURT.*

*This meeting of the two German leaders reflected Chancellor Brandt's desire
to improve relations with east Europe.*

April 30, 1970   PRESIDENT NIXON ANNOUNCES TO THE U.S. PUBLIC THAT
                          AMERICAN AND SOUTH VIETNAMESE FORCES HAVE MADE AN
                          "INCURSION" AGAINST CAMBODIAN SANCTUARIES OF THE COM-
                          MUNISTS.

The U.S.-ARVN attack on Cambodia began on April 29. To his television audience on April 30, Nixon explained that Cambodia had been neutral since 1954,
and U.S. policy "had been to scrupulously respect the neutrality of the Cambodian people." Failing to acknowledge the U.S. bombings which began in Cambodia on March 18, 1969, Nixon asserted that only North Vietnam "has not respected that neutrality." The Communists, Nixon stated, had large bases in
Cambodia for training, weapons, ammunition, air strips, prisoner-of-war compounds, and planning headquarters. Previously the United States had not moved
against these bases, Nixon lied, "because we did not wish to violate the territory of a neutral nation."

Nixon noted that the Communists had recently stepped up their attacks
on Cambodia and were encircling the capital city of Phnom Penh. Therefore,
the U.S. and South Vietnamese forces had to clean out the Communist bases in
order to secure the freedom of South Vietnam and permit the process of Vietnamization to be successful.

Nixon asked the American people to understand and support his decision.
"Free institutions," he said, "are under attack from without and within."
America cannot be a "pitiful, helpless giant" in a totalitarian world. "I
would rather be a one-term president and do what I believe is right than to
be a two-term president at the cost of seeing America become a second-rate
power and to see this nation accept its first defeat in its proud 190 year

history." America, he concluded, was being tested. If we fail, "all other nations will be on notice that despite its overwhelming power the United States, when a real crisis comes, will be found wanting."

Nixon's decision to send 74,000 troops into Cambodia originated in October, 1969, when General Abrams and the Joint Chiefs of Staff recommended that ground forces should invade both Cambodia and Laos to destroy the Communist bases. By October, Abrams realized that his February 9 bombing proposal had been incorrect. The military-bureaucratic game, however, is not to admit mistakes, but to propose additional effort to compound mistakes.

Nixon delayed action on the October request until April, 1970. By then, many things had changed. The bombing had clearly failed, Sihanouk had been ousted, and in the secret Paris peace negotiations during early 1970, the North Vietnamese had not offered any significant compromises. Nixon did not ally with Lon Nol because the Cambodian leader was as much anti-Vietnamese as he was anti-Communist. In April, Lon Nol had appealed to the United Nations to help Cambodia get rid of both the Communists and the South Vietnamese who operated on the western borders of his state.

Although Kissinger claims in his memoirs that he obtained approval for the Cambodian "incursion" from Senator John Stennis, Chairman of the Senate Armed Forces Committee, the security advisor unwittingly gives his case away. He wrote that Stennis like other southern senators "sometimes lagged behind the moral currents of their time, but on national security and foreign policy they were towers of strength." No other congressmen were told in advance about the April 29-30 decision. Both Secretary of State Rogers and Secretary of Defense Laird cautioned Nixon about the constitutional question involved in ordering a ground attack on neutral Cambodia, but the president ignored their advice.

The Cambodian incursion became a 90-day raid with, at best, limited success. As another "search and destroy" mission, there were some benefits. U.S. forces encountered little resistance in their 21-mile invasion. The tanks, planes, and armored vehicles destroyed small towns such as Snuol and Mimot. At Snuol, the 11th Armored Cavalry Regiment of tanks bombed and shelled the village for 24 hours. On occupying the village they found seven dead bodies, one a small Cambodian girl. Elsewhere, U.S. forces captured large caches of rice, arms, and ammunition. They killed an estimated 11,000 "Communists."

Generally, however, the U.S. objective of destroying significant sanctuaries failed. An August, 1970, Defense Department study stated that Communist attacks had been disrupted "to some extent." The incursion had not "substantially reduced NVA capabilities in Cambodia." The Communists lost 25% of their supplies, but these would be replenished in 75 days or less.

Neither Kissinger nor Nixon agreed with the Pentagon's August report. Kissinger claimed the attacks bought two years' time to carry out Vietnamization. The Communists did not launch another offensive action in Vietnam until 1972. Of course, the Communists may have simply been awaiting a better time to make their next major attack.

As in the case of the secret bombing, Cambodians suffered. The Khmer Rouge stepped up its attacks on Lon Nol's forces. Although the Nixon administration gave Phnom Penh $273 million of economic aid and military equipment for an army of 220,000, the new government had the impossible task of defending itself. During the next decade Cambodia experienced destruction, starvation, and genocide. First the Khmer Rouge under Pol Pot and later the Vietnamese conquered the ancient kingdom.

May 4, 1970   AT KENT STATE UNIVERSITY, FOUR STUDENTS ARE KILLED BY
OHIO NATIONAL GUARDSMEN. TEN DAYS LATER, POLICE AT
JACKSON STATE COLLEGE KILL TWO ANTI-WAR DEMONSTRATORS.

A major consequence of Nixon's "incursion" into Cambodia was the greatest
outburst of anti-war dissent since Nixon took office. Demonstrations at colleges and universities began on May 1. In both Ohio and Mississippi, inspired
perhaps by Nixon's claim that dissenters were disloyal, national guardsmen
and police responded by shooting, and killed six dissenters. At Kent, Ohio,
Governor John Rhodes denounced the demonstrators as "worse than brown shirts
and the communist element," ordering 750 guardsmen to the campus after someone set fire to an Army ROTC building. On May 4, Kent State students staged
a peaceful assembly to protest the war. For still unclear reasons, a group
of guardsmen moved to disperse the crowd, advancing in full battle gear and
carrying loaded M-1 rifles. The guardsmen fired at the unarmed students,
later asserting there was sniper fire, an unsubstantiated charge. Two young
women and two young men died; nine students lay wounded, one permanently par-
alyzed. An investigation disclosed that the students had no weapons other
than a few rocks.
        On May 14, a similar protest at Jackson State College had similar re-
sults. Drawn to the campus by reports of rock and bottle throwing, city and
state police found a large crowd protesting the Cambodian invasion. For reasons which a later investigation called "completely unwarranted and unjusti-
fied," the police fired 150 rounds of ammunition into the assembly and a nearby women's dormitory. Two students were killed, 12 wounded. The President's
Commission on Campus Unrest found that a combination of racial animosity and
pro-war feelings probably caused the police to open fire.
        During the spring of 1970, over 448 colleges experienced some form of
protest. At the end of May, 100,000 dissidents marched in Washington. Police
used tear gas and made mass arrests to stop the protestors.

June 9, 1970   A CRISIS ERUPTS IN JORDAN WHEN THE PALESTINIAN LIBERA-
TION FRONT REBELS AND HOLDS A GROUP OF AMERICANS HOS-
TAGE AT AMMAN'S INTERCONTINENTAL HOTEL.

The crisis in Jordan began as a conflict between the Popular Front for the
Liberation of Palestine (PFLP) and King Hussein of Jordan. Hussein was a
moderate and usually pro-Western Arab ruler. Because Jordan had become a
major haven for Palestinian refugees after the Arab-Israeli war of 1948-1949,
Hussein had increasing difficulty preventing the Palestinians in Jordan from
conducting raids into Israel. This resulted in Israeli retaliatory attacks
on Jordan and disrupted Hussein's society. In 1970, Hussein used his army
to prohibit future Palestinian raids. This caused anger among the PFLP as
well as the more moderate Palestine Liberation Organization headed by Yasser
ARAFAT.
        When the Palestinian uprising began on June 9, members of the PFLP took
some Americans hostage in the Intercontinental Hotel to express their opposition to U.S. support for Israel. Moreover, some American homes in Jordan
were looted and Major Robert P. Perry, an embassy military attaché, was killed
by shots fired into his home.
        The U.S. Ambassador to Amman, Harry L. Odell, reported that it was too
dangerous to evacuate U.S. personnel from the airport because of heavy fighting in the city. As a result, the White House undertook contingency

discussions to prepare either a paratroop drop at Amman or to ferry Americans by helicopter to aircraft carriers in the Mediterranean Sea.

Fortunately, on June 12, King Hussein had battled the guerrillas until they accepted a truce. The hostages were released and the fighting ended. The uprising indicated a factor in Middle Eastern affairs not previously given much attention: the status of Palestinian refugees who had become organized and were ready to demand the rights to their homeland in territory controlled by Israel.

June 18, 1970   *EDWARD HEATH BECOMES PRIME MINISTER OF BRITAIN AFTER A CONSERVATIVE ELECTORAL VICTORY.*

June 22, 1970   THE U.S. SENATE TERMINATES THE TONKIN GULF RESOLUTION OF 1964. THIS IS ONE OF SEVERAL CONGRESSIONAL ATTEMPTS TO CHALLENGE THE CONTINUED U.S. INVOLVEMENT IN SOUTH-EAST ASIA.

Although the Senate repealed the Tonkin Gulf resolution overwhelmingly, most congressional measures to restrict Nixon's activity were limited or unsuccessful. Included among these actions were:

1. May - Senate approved section of Cooper-Church amendment to prohibit funds for Cambodia after July 1, 1970, unless authorized by congress. President Nixon had promised to have all troops out of Cambodia by July 1.

2. June 10 - Senate rejected a proposal authorizing the president to send troops back into Cambodia if necessary to protect Americans in Vietnam.

3. June 23 - Senate rejected the "end-the-war" McGovern-Hatfield amendment to ban all funds expended in Vietnam after December 31, 1970, unless congress declared war.

4. June 29 - Senate rejected a proposal to allow Nixon to aid "other nations such as Thailand" in helping Cambodia.

5. June 30 - Senate approved Cooper-Church amendment to ban all funds for training Cambodians. This bill was rejected by the House of Representatives on July 7.

Although none of these measures specifically tied the president's hands, they all represented extensive dissent in congress regarding Nixon's policy in Vietnam and Cambodia.

August 7, 1970   THE UNITED STATES ARRANGES A CEASE-FIRE IN THE MIDDLE EAST: ROGERS PLAN II.

Throughout the first seven months of 1970, border conflicts between Israel and its three neighbors--Syria, Jordan, Egypt--had steadily escalated to status as an undeclared war. In addition, the Soviet Union extended its influence in the region by increasing its arms and missiles in Egypt as well as using Russian "experts" to fly missions protecting Egypt. The United

States wanted some means to lessen Soviet influence or, as Kissinger told reporters in a "backgrounder" in early July, to expel the Russians. A "backgrounder" was a remark which could not be publicly attributed to Kissinger
but which, by mid-July, 1970, most diplomats knew meant "Kissinger."

Beginning as border skirmishes in 1969, the conflicts in the Middle East
multiplied. On the Golan Heights border of Syria and Israel there often were
heavy tank and artillery duels in addition to border raids. Along the Jordanian border, Palestinian raids became frequent until the Hussein-Palestinian
dispute of June 9-12 finally calmed down some of the PFLP-PLO raids.

The Egypt-Israeli border became the most serious area, however, for a
war of attrition had begun. After the breakdown of the 1969 Rogers Plan (see
December 19, 1969) the Soviets rapidly increased the delivery of modern weapons to Egypt. Advanced jet fighter bomber MIG-23's and SAM's (surface to air
missiles) gave Egypt a new integrated air-defense system. Soviet personnel
also manned the SAM-3 batteries while Soviet pilots flew jets against Israeli
invasion planes. At the same time, Israel urged the United States to send
Phantom and Skyhawk jets to bolster their defenses. Nixon and Kissinger restricted these deliveries, however, in order to persuade Moscow to limit arms
to the area as a method of moving toward permanent peace arrangements.

Egypt and the Soviets had become closer allies after the Israelis
launched "deep penetration" air raids against Egypt beginning in January,
1970. By February, the Israeli air force had controlled Egyptian skies from
Alexandria to Aswan, even attacking Cairo-West air base. Reportedly, the Israelis shot down five MIG's flown by Russians and killed a Soviet general during one air raid.

The Soviets' response between February and July was to rapidly deploy
more planes and SAM bases in Egypt. Eventually, Israeli plane losses became
so risky that during April and May, they curtailed penetration attacks, limiting their raids to the Suez area. The situation became so tense that Israel
had to consider large-scale invasion plans to destroy SAM bases along the Suez
before they were completed by Egypt and Russia.

Following the end of the Jordanian crisis on June 12, Nixon, Kissinger,
and Rogers agreed to launch a new peace effort in the Middle East. On June
25, after prior consultations without agreement by the various parties involved, Rogers announced his cease-fire plan. His hope was to obtain an
Egyptian-Jordanian-Israeli cease-fire while the U.N. mediator, Gunnar Jarring,
undertook negotiations to implement U.N. Resolution 242 or some other acceptable proposal. Syria was left out of Rogers' proposal because Damascus never
accepted in principle 1967's U.N. Resolution 242. The same day he offered
his proposal Rogers announced that the United States would withhold plane
shipments to Israel. Privately, Rogers explained to Israeli Ambassador
Yitzhak Rabin that if the cease-fire did not work shortly, U.S. aircraft deliveries would resume.

In order to pressure Moscow and Cairo to accept the cease-fire, Kissinger
and Nixon made tough statements about expelling the Soviets or giving Israel
huge new arms supplies. At the same time, Rogers, who was not fully aware
of Kissinger's "power" tactics, had qualified these tough statements by, for
example, distinguishing between "expelling" the Russians and "lessening" their
influence.

The Soviet Union played its own "power game." While considering Rogers
Plan II and encouraging Cairo and Amman to accept the plan, Kosygin delayed
any commitment while rushing additional SAM-3's to be deployed along the Egyptian side of the Suez Canal. Moscow would protect its client by providing
more secure air defense if a cease-fire broke down.

By late July, Egypt and Jordan had accepted Rogers' June 25 plan in principle. Israel had to comply before the details could be worked out for a cease-fire arrangement. Before the August 7 cease-fire went into effect, the United States had to obtain a secret agreement that none of the parties would increase their arms or defense units during the cease-fire. Israel also wanted assurances that the Soviet Union would respect the agreements. Rogers talked with Soviet Ambassador Dobrynin, receiving a Russian commitment, but not an absolute one, to respect the cease-fire as well as the arms "standstill" agreements.

Finally, on August 7, the cease-fire went into effect. The situation remained precarious, however, and hardly had the arrangements begun before violations of the agreement took place.

September 6, 1970   THE SECOND JORDANIAN CRISIS OF 1970: THE PFLP HIJACKS
                          THREE COMMERCIAL AIRLINERS, HOLDING 475 HOSTAGES NEAR
                          AMMAN.

Although the cease-fire of August 7, 1970, did not settle the difficulties in the Middle East, the Palestinian radicals wanted to prevent any settlement by disturbing the equilibrium of the region. To demonstrate their ability to disrupt, the PFLP organized four skyjackings of airliners on September 6-7, 1970. Three of these succeeded, and the planes and passengers on Trans-World Airways, Swiss Air, and British Overseas Airways were commandeered and flown to an abandoned British airfield 35 miles from Amman which the PFLP called Revolution Field.

The fourth skyjack attempt, on an El Al (Israeli) plane, failed. Shortly after taking off from London, two Arabs ordered the airplane's crew to fly to Amman. An Israeli security guard aboard the El Al acted quickly. He shot one Arab, a man, and subdued his companion, a woman named Leila Khaled, who was arrested when the plane returned to London.

In Jordan, the PFLP demanded the release of all Palestinian and pro-Palestinian prisoners jailed in Israel, West Germany, Switzerland, and Britain. While the Swiss complied, the United States joined Britain and Israel in rejecting the demands but offering to negotiate. They asked the International Red Cross to contact the PFLP for possible discussions.

Nixon decided to prepare to intervene in Jordan if necessary. On September 9, he announced that the United States was delivering 18 Phantom jets to Israel. He also sent six C-130 U.S. Air Force transports to a Turkish base at Incirlik, 350 miles from Amman, where they would be ready to bring out the PFLP hostages. The U.S. Sixth Fleet was ordered to the Israeli-Lebanese coast and 25 U.S. Air Force Phantom jets were sent to Incirlik.

At Revolution Field near Amman, the Red Cross negotiators achieved a compromise with the PFLP by September 12. Although the Palestinians blew up the three airliners, they took the hostages to a camp near the village of Zerqua preparatory to working out a deal with the Red Cross. Israel agreed to release 450 Arab prisoners it had taken since September 6 and the British agreed to release Miss Khaled. In exchange, the PFLP released all but 55 Jewish passengers. The Jewish passengers were held until September 29 when the PFLP secured the full release of the 450 Israeli-held Palestinians.

September 15, 1970   *KING HUSSEIN OF JORDAN ATTACKS THE PALESTINIAN REFUGEE*
                        CAMPS TO ABOLISH THE PFLP AND PLO POWER IN JORDAN.

*While the last non-Jewish hostages of the PFLP were being released from the
camp at Zerqua (see September 6, 1970), King Hussein decided the moment was
opportune to eliminate the Palestinian "state-within-a-state" which the PFLP
and PLO had created in their refugee camps in Jordan. The Royal Army and
tank corps moved to take over the camps, forcing the Palestinians to relocate
or go into exile in Syria or Iraq.*

*Hussein's action was a civil war with international dangers. Both Syria
and Iraqi forces with Moscow's quiet support moved to their borders in a
threatening menace to aid the Palestinians. The Israeli government of Golda
Meir preferred a viable Jordanian government under the Hasemite King Hussein
and considered the possibility of backing him against the Arabs and Palestinians. In this context, the U.S. government had to decide on a satisfactory
response. See September 22, 1970.*

September 22, 1970   AT THE PEAK OF THE CRISIS OVER HUSSEIN'S FIGHT WITH
                        THE PALESTINIANS, NIXON AGREES TO PROTECT ISRAEL IF
                        SHE ASSISTS JORDAN. WITHIN 48 HOURS, THE TENSIONS
                        ABATE.

Because the Soviet Union's "client states" of Syria and Iraq backed the Palestinian organizations in Jordan as a way to keep the refugees out of their
own lands, King Hussein's campaign to eliminate the *fedayeen* caused widespread
international concerns. Nixon was ready to back Hussein as far as necessary
but hoped he would not have to commit American troops to intervene.

Initially, on September 16 and 17, the president publicly warned Moscow
that the United States and Israel might intervene if Syria and Iraq attacked
Jordan. He talked with Israeli Prime Minister Golda Meir who was on a scheduled visit to the United States, telling her that the United States favored
Hussein but Israel should use restraint as long as possible. He also contacted the Russian Chargé in Washington (Ambassador Dobrynin was on leave)
and asked Russia to restrain its two Arab associates.

Although the Russians said they would restrain Syria, they did not or
could not. On September 19, 300 Syrian tanks attacked Jordan, bringing a
severe world crisis. If Hussein fell, Israel and perhaps the United States
would have to move to help Jordan.

Hussein survived, however. On September 20, Hussein asked for Israeli
air support in order to make an all-out offensive against Syria and the Palestinians. The Israelis were reluctant to do so without American guarantees
of protection on their southern (Egyptian) border. Nixon and his staff reviewed their options. On September 19, the president had alerted American
troops in the United States and Europe, while ordering emergency preparations
by airborne battalions at Fort Bragg, Georgia, and in West Germany. Now at
Meir's request the president agreed on September 22 to protect Israel from
Russia and Egypt if she helped Hussein maintain his authority in Jordan.

Nixon's commitment brought the United States and Russia to the brink of
war. Fortunately, the crisis stopped. All Hussein needed was enough encour-
agement to commit his tanks and air force to an all-out war on Syria and the
Palestinians. The promises of Israel and America supplied this, and by September 23, Hussein's army turned the Syrians back to a forced retreat home.
Perhaps Moscow, too, had pressured Damascus to stop the attacks.

Consequently, tensions relaxed temporarily in Jordan. Hussein had established his position against the Palestinians. Soon after, however, the PFLP, the PLO, and other Palestinian groups moved to reestablish a position of strength in Lebanon.

September 25, 1970   AN ALLEGED "CUBAN CRISIS" ARISES ABOUT THE POSSIBLE CONSTRUCTION OF A SOVIET NUCLEAR-SUBMARINE BASE AT CIENFUEGOS, CUBA.

While there is some evidence that the Russians had begun some new type of activity at Cienfuegos during the summer of 1970, exactly what was done is not clear. During July, Admiral E.P. Holmes of the Atlantic Fleet told a congressional committee that the Soviets *might* build a submarine base in Cuba. According to Kissinger, U-2 flights on September 10 showed construction activity which he interpreted to be a nuclear sub base. He indicated this in a press background briefing on September 16. The article appeared in the *New York Times* on September 25, causing other congressmen to accuse Russia of deception.

Subsequently, Kissinger claimed a diplomatic triumph for putting pressure on Russia to stop its construction. After the *Times* story appeared, Ambassador Dobrynin denied it. Kissinger later claimed he confronted the ambassador with photoevidence and Dobrynin turned "ashen," asking to consult Moscow. On October 5, Dobrynin, followed on October 13 by the Tass news agency in Moscow, denied that Russia was building a sub base in Cuba. The "crisis" disappeared as fast as Kissinger had inaugurated it during his September 16 briefing. Neither Nixon nor the NSC chairman forced Russia to explain what was taking place.

September 28, 1970   *PRESIDENT NASSER OF EGYPT DIES OF A HEART ATTACK.*

On September 29, Vice-President Anwar Sadat was sworn in as acting president. On October 15, Sadat was elected president.

October 6, 1970   PRESIDENT NIXON ANNOUNCES A NEW PEACE INITIATIVE TO NORTH VIETNAM WHICH CONTRIBUTES NOTHING NEW. IT IS SEEN AS A POLITICAL PLOY TO HELP REPUBLICAN CONGRESSMEN IN NOVEMBER.

Nixon's much publicized "new initiative" called for a cease-fire-in-place in all of Indochina, the convocation of an Indochina Peace Conference, and the "immediate and unconditional release of all prisoners of war held by both sides." Hanoi saw no advantages to these proposals and, on October 9, dismissed them as "a maneuver to deceive world opinion." Nixon used the plan as evidence of his desire for peace, asking voters to provide Republican congressmen to support him in his effort.

October 17, 1970   *GREAT BRITAIN MAKES A MAJOR OIL FIND IN THE NORTH SEA.*

October 24, 1970   CIA EFFORTS FAIL TO INFLUENCE THE DEFEAT OF ALLENDE
AS PRESIDENT OF CHILE.

As disclosed by the Senate Select Committee on Intelligence Activities in
1975, the CIA had been attempting to prevent the rise to power of left-wing
liberal groups in Chile since at least the days of President Kennedy. Alarmed
apparently by the rise of Castro in Cuba, Kennedy ordered the CIA in 1962 to
use $180,000 to help the conservative Christian Democratic candidate Eduardo
Frei Montalvo defeat the Socialist Salvador Allende Gossens. Frei won in 1964
and, perhaps boastfully, a CIA report said that U.S. funds of $3 million made
the difference in the election.

Additional funds were continually used in Chile to aid pro-American candidates but, by 1970, Allende's chances of victory appeared to increase. Both
the U.S. business community and Ambassador Edward Korry, who backed U.S. business interests, feared that if elected, Allende would nationalize copper
mines and other U.S. investments. Thus, in March, 1970, the Forty Committee
of the NSC, which regulated covert intelligence operations, agreed to spend
$135,000 to subsidize "spoiling" operations critical of Allende. In June,
an additional $300,000 was authorized by the Forty Committee because Korry
flooded the State Department with alarming messages that Allende's victory
would be worse than Castro's. In addition to CIA funds, International Telephone and Telegraph and other U.S. business firms spent monies to assist the
National Party candidate, Jorge Alessandri.

On September 4, 1970, no candidate won a majority in the Chilean elections. Allende received 36.3%; Allesandri, 35.3%; and a third, left-wing
candidate, Radomiro Tomic, received 28.4%. Putting Tomic's left-of-center
vote with Allende's, the rightist candidate Allesandri clearly seemed likely
to lose. In accord with the Chilean constitution, the failure of a majority
victory sent the names of the two leading candidates to the congress to select the president. The ballot would be between Allende and Allesandri.

Although a CIA report in September, 1970, found that the United States
had "no vital interests within Chile" and the world balance would "not be
significantly altered by an Allende regime," it asserted that Allende's victory would be a "psychological setback to the U.S. as well as a definite advance for the Marxist idea." In reality, Allende was not pro-Russian or a
Communist, although many conservative U.S. cold warriors such as Ambassador
Korry believed anyone left of center was a Bolshevik working for Moscow.
Allende was an advocate of Marxian ideals. In Chile, he was the candidate
of *Unidad Popular*, a coalition of several leftist parties advocating economic
nationalism for Chile and broad social reforms. Like many Mexican nationalists between 1911 and 1941, Allende antagonized American business by espous-
ing a program to use Chilean resources to benefit the Chilean people. This
constantly translated into a candidate's being an advocate of Soviet Bolshevism when viewed through the prism of U.S. investors in underdeveloped nations.

Therefore on September 8 and 14, the Forty Committee authorized the CIA
and Ambassador Korry to use $350,000 of covert funds to bribe moderate con-
gressmen of those Christian Democrats who had backed Tomic. Their votes for
Allesandri in the congressional election for president on October 24 would
defeat Allende.

On September 15, however, Nixon and Kissinger went one step further,
ordering Richard Helms of the CIA to support military factions in Chile who
opposed Allende. The CIA had considered backing a military leader in Chile
since 1969. The political interference programs of the NSC were called "Track

I" and the military coup plans, "Track II." By September 15, Helms had evidently convinced Nixon and Kissinger that an Allende victory was akin to a Communist victory. Because Kissinger was notably lacking in knowledge of Latin America, he could easily be persuaded. Kissinger demonstrated his attitude during a news briefing on September 16. He told reporters that if Chile fell, then Argentina, Peru, and Bolivia would follow. What would happen to the "Organization of American States ... is extremely problematical." Such statements were unworthy of a high school freshman. But, of course, domino theories abounded in America after 1947.

Nixon's September 15 approval of Track II's aid to the Chilean military involved the CIA in a scenario which assured Allende's election. Although the exact connection of the CIA to the plot to kidnap General Rene Schneider is not known, this military plan went awry. The Chilean military wanted Schneider out of the way because he was a strong constitutionalist. Therefore, the abduction would be blamed on the left wing, giving the right wing an excuse to seize power. Unfortunately, Schneider was killed during the kidnap attempt and the right wing was implicated, not the left.

After anti-army protests arose, the Chilean generals showed their loyalty by joining to support the constitutional decision of congress on October 24. Allende was elected president. The plans of the CIA and the NSC were not laid aside, however.

November 10, 1970   GENERAL DE GAULLE DIES IN FRANCE.

To many Frenchmen de Gaulle had been the symbol of France's pre-1940's glories as a great empire and civilization. He had created the Fifth French Republic and been its first president after 1957.

November 21-22, 1970   A GROUP OF AMERICAN VOLUNTEERS STAGES AN UNSUCCESSFUL ATTACK ON A POW CAMP IN NORTH VIETNAM.

This raid against a POW camp at Sontay, 23 miles west of Hanoi, was made by volunteer troops from the U.S. Army's Special Forces and the Air Force's Special Operations Force. Reportedly, 70 to 100 Americans were prisoners at Sontay but when the U.S. helicopters landed, they found the place deserted. The POW's had been moved. Following a brief fire-fight with North Vietnamese in the area, the U.S. troops boarded their helicopters to return south. The raid was not reported in the United States until November 24.

The POW issue became one of the principal concerns of many Americans as Nixon's Vietnamization program proceeded. The Communists knew this and used the POW exchange as a trump card in all negotiations.

November 21-22, 1970   U.S. FIGHTER-BOMBERS FROM THAILAND STAGE HEAVY AIR ATTACKS ALL OVER NORTH VIETNAM.

Secretary Rogers told congress that these raids were retaliatory because the North Vietnamese and Viet Cong had shelled Saigon and Hue in violation of the October 31, 1968, agreement. Some observers believed these attacks were designed to warn Hanoi because she had recently infiltrated about 200,000 troops into South Vietnam. Others related them to the U.S. attack on the Sontay POW camp on the night of November 21-22.

December 7, 1970   POLAND AND WEST GERMANY SIGN A TREATY THAT RECOGNIZES
                         THE ODER-NEISSE RIVER LINE AS THE GERMAN-POLISH BOR-
                         DER.

*This treaty was signed by Polish Premier Jozef Cyrankiewicz and West German
Chancellor Willy Brandt. The border had been established by Stalin in 1944-
1945 to award Poland with former German territory in the west as compensation
for the extension of Russia's border into former eastern Polish land. Final
ratification of this treaty was delayed because it was coupled with the Quad-
ritite Agreement on Berlin by the West German government. See June 3, 1972.*

December 14, 1970   RIOTS OCCUR IN GDANSK, POLAND, AS WORKERS PROTEST THE
                         GOVERNMENT'S ECONOMIC POLICY.

*Polish workers' complaints against Communist rule had steadily increased in
1970, leading to a large-scale uprising of shipyard workers in Gdansk. In
response to these difficulties, the government promised to rectify some complaints. On December 24, the party followed Soviet advice by naming Edward
Giereck to replace Wladyslaw Gomulka as First Secretary of the Communist
Party.*

December 16, 1970   A REBELLION BEGINS IN ERITREA.

*About 10,000 insurgents threatened to overthrow the government of this East
African State. The conflict made the so-called horn of Africa on the Northeast Coast a new area of global strategic concern.*

December 28, 1970   THE UNITED STATES PERSUADES ISRAEL TO RESUME TALKS
                         WITH U.N. MEDIATOR GUNNAR JARRING.

The Middle East peace talks which resulted from the cease-fire of August 7,
1970, provided for mediation by the United Nations. Israel broke off these
discussions on August 27 because it claimed Egypt had violated the cease-fire
by basing more Soviet SAM-3's along the Suez Canal. CIA photos verified the
Israeli charge and in September and October, the United States passed new
legislation to add weapons to Israel's military power such as the Shrike missile which could neutralize the SAM-3.
        Following the Jordanian events of September and October, 1970, American
allies urged Washington to try again to keep peace by mediation in the Middle
East. Finally, on December 28, under pressure from Washington, the Israeli
government agreed to formal discussions with Jarring. The U.N. mediator hoped
to shuttle between Israeli and Egyptian delegations to seek a method to solve
the Sinai dispute.

1971

January 15, 1971   *EGYPT'S ASWAN HIGH DAM IS DEDICATED.*

*The construction of the Aswan Dam was a cooperative project between Egypt
and the Soviet Union following the Suez Crisis of 1956. The dam began operations on July 21, 1970, when its final generators were turned on.*

*On January 15, President Sadat of Egypt and the U.S.S.R.'s President
Nikolai Podgorny led dedication ceremonies for the project. Soon thereafter,
Moscow and Cairo signed a 15-year friendship pact. See May 27, 1971.*

January 25, 1971   *IN UGANDA, A MILITARY COUP LED BY GENERAL IDI AMIN,
                         IS SUCCESSFUL.*

February 8, 1971   SOUTH VIETNAM'S ARMED FORCES INVADE LAOS TO WIPE OUT
                        COMMUNIST SANCTUARIES AND THE HO CHI MINH TRAIL, BUT
                        THE ARVN EXPERIENCE A DISASTER.

Since the beginning of Rolling Thunder in 1965, the United States had tried
to eliminate the Ho Chi Minh supply route and other North Vietnamese sanctuaries on the border of Laos and the two Vietnams. To permit ground forces
to accomplish this task, General Abrams urged the ARVN leaders to plan an
operation into Laos. Code-named Lam Son 619 (Total Victory) the ARVN operation, aided by American air strike and U.S. helicopters, attacked the Laotian
border in a planned five-to-eight week invasion.

About the time that this maze was discovered, the North Vietnamese began
to attack not as guerrillas but in conventional warfare. Tanks aligned in
mass formation advanced on the ARVN food soldiers. Saigon's forces broke
ranks, beginning a retreat which turned into a rout. As TV cameras recorded
the scenes, ARVN troops crowded aboard or hung onto the tails and landing
gear of U.S. helicopters sent to rescue them. ARVN suffered heavy casualties
and lost large quantities of American equipment in the retreat. This Laotian
fiasco not only hurt Nixon's pride but also demoralized the ARVN troops which
the U.S. trainers had been seeking to build into a quality defense force in
South Vietnam.

During the first two weeks of battle, the ARVN succeeded. General Abrams
reported the ARVN "are fighting ... in a superior way." Nixon bragged to
newsmen about the qualities of South Vietnam's new army.

Late in February, however, ARVN ran into trouble, first with the Laotian
terrain, next with North Vietnamese forces. The Ho Chi Minh trail proved to
be a labyrinth of foot paths with criss-crossing single-lane dirt roads mean-
dering through thick jungles. The unguided person could not tell where
trails began or ended. The entire complex covered an area 5 miles wide and
100 miles long. It was not possible permanently to damage the so-called
trail.

February 11, 1971   EIGHTY NATIONS SIGN THE SEABED ARMS CONTROL TREATY
                         WHICH PROHIBITS NUCLEAR WEAPONS ON THE OCEAN FLOOR.

The U.N. Disarmament Committee in Geneva proposed this pact by which signatories agreed not to place nuclear missile launchers on the bottom of seas
or oceans. The United States, the Soviet Union, and Great Britain were the
important signators among the 80 nations. France and China refused to sign
it.

February 14, 1971   *WESTERN OIL COMPANIES AND SIX PERSIAN GULF OIL NATIONS*
                         AGREE TO RAISE PRICES: THE TEHERAN AGREEMENT.

*The Arab oil states accepted the leadership of the Shah Reza Pahlavi of Iran
in negotiating with oil companies to increase their demands for control of
their national oil resources. To do so, the shah threatened an oil embargo,
although he tried to separate his politics from the radical anti-Western policies of Libya's Quaddafi who had unilaterally forced a 30¢ oil increase on
Libyan oil companies in 1970.*
     *By the Teheran Agreement, the Western oil companies accepted an immedi-
ate posted oil price increase from $1.80 to $2.15 for 1971 and an annual 2.5%
increase annually between June 1, 1971, and January 1, 1975. The companies
also accepted a 55% income tax. The Western oil companies said the pact increased the stability of the oil supply. They simply added the extra oil
costs to their customers' bills in Western Europe and America.*
     *As inflationary prices resulted in the Western nations after 1971, the
Arab nations and Iran required the oil companies to amend their agreements
in 1972 to increase the posted oil prices to offset the decreased value of
the dollar. In January, 1972, prices increased another 8.94% and in April,
1972, they went up another 7.5%. The Shah of Iran was a leader in these moves
to gain oil revenue and continued to be until his overthrow in 1979. See
January 16, 1979.*

March 16, 1971   SECRETARY ROGERS PROPOSES A MID-EAST PEACE PLAN BECAUSE
                         THE U.N. DISCUSSIONS HAVE BROKEN DOWN; ISRAEL REJECTS
                         IT AND ANOTHER DEADLOCK RESULTS.

Following Israel's agreement to renew mediation on December 28, 1970, Jarring
undertook discussions in Egypt, Jordan, and Israel. Jarring did not handle
the affair well. On February 8, he made the impossible proposal that Israel
withdraw to its 1948 borders, following this by making the Israeli rejection
public. Consequently Israel withdrew from further talks even though Egypt
had agreed to extend the truce of August, 1970.
     In March, Secretary of State Rogers undertook to resolve the dispute.
After working quietly to review the situation Rogers offered a plan on March
16. If Israel withdrew to the pre-June, 1967, borders, Egypt would guarantee
peace in the Sinai and an international force including U.S. troops would
back up peace in the area.
     Egypt rejected this plan. By March, 1971, Prime Minister Golda Meir
said Israel "cannot trust Rogers' offer, even if it is proposed in good
faith." As a result, another deadlock occurred in the Middle East. Although
Rogers visited both Sadat and Meir in May, 1970, both sides were inflexible.
Mrs. Meir was especially upset that the United States was again restricting

arms sales to Israel while the Soviet Union bolstered its military aid to
Egypt. See May 27, 1971.

March 24, 1971   CONGRESS REJECTS PUBLIC FUNDING FOR A SUPER-SONIC
                        TRANSPORT PLANE (SST).

Extensive debates in the United States at large, as well as in congress,
showed a general uneasiness about the necessity for a superfast airplane.
Environmental concerns as well as the technical and economic viability of
the project caused its rejection. Not even the nationalistic claim that the
Soviets and Europeans had developed an SST aroused significant support for
the project.

April 6, 1971   PING-PONG DIPLOMACY: WHILE IN JAPAN, CHINESE PING-
                        PONG TEAM MEMBERS INVITE THE U.S. TEAM TO VISIT THEM
                        IN CHINA AS SOON AS THE NAGOYA TOURNAMENT ENDS.

Although the United States and China had been quietly but frequently sounding
each other out to renew normal relations, the Peking government followed an
unusual method to indicate its willingness to negotiate with Washington.
Prior talks had begun in Warsaw (January 20, 1970) and through contacts by
way of Lahore, Pakistan, and Rumania. On March 15, 1971, the State Department strongly signaled Peking because it completely lifted the travel ban
by Americans to China which had been partly raised on July 21, 1970.
    The April 6 invitation came from the Chinese ping-pong team, which had
participated in an international tournament in Nagoya. On the last day, Chinese team members invited the Americans to come and play against them in
China. Graham B. Steenhoven, president of the U.S. Table Tennis Association,
contacted the American ambassador in Tokyo. By telegram, the State Department responded positively.
    The American group arrived in Peking on April 10. It included nine
team members, four officials, two wives, and three American journalists. Chou
En-lai put out the red carpet. Although the Chinese easily won at ping-pong,
the U.S. team had an unusual reception at the Great Hall of the People. Chou
En-lai told them: "You have opened a new page in the relations of the Chinese
and American people. I am confident that this beginning again of our friendship will certainly meet with majority support of our two peoples." The U.S.
team invited China's ping-pong team to visit America, and Chou accepted.

April 14, 1971   NIXON QUICKLY PICKS UP CHINA'S "PING-PONG" OVERTURE,
                        ANNOUNCING HE PLANS SOON TO END RESTRICTIONS ON OB-
                        STACLES TO "CREATE BROADER OPPORTUNITIES FOR CONTACTS
                        BETWEEN THE CHINESE AND AMERICAN PEOPLES."

Nixon had eagerly awaited Chou En-lai's indication that better relations were
needed. After learning of Chou's favorable speech to the U.S. table tennis
team on April 14, he indicated that the NSC recommended and he approved the
following actions which did not require legislation or negotiation:

    1. to expedite visas for visitors from the People's Republic of China
        to America;

2. to relax U.S. currency controls on China;

3. to end oil sales restrictions on Chinese-owned or chartered ships or aircraft;

4. to allow U.S. vessels to carry Chinese cargo again;

5. to create a list of non-strategic materials that could soon be exported to China.

April 16, 1971   PRESIDENT NIXON EXPLAINS TWO VITAL PARTS OF HIS VIETNAM STRATEGY: (1) TO USE AIR POWER AND SMALL U.S. GROUND FORCES UNTIL PEACE IS MADE; (2) TO HAVE ALL U.S. POW'S RELEASED AS A TRUCE CONDITION OF WITHDRAWAL OF ALL U.S. FORCES.

On April 16, the president specified this particular part of his plan for Vietnam. Earlier, on April 7, Nixon announced on national television that 100,000 American forces would be brought home between May 1 and December 1. This would leave about 175,000 men in Vietnam in 1975 with only 60,000 to 75,000 in combat units. Thus, Nixon explained to the American Society of Newspaper Editors on April 16 that he hoped after the peace treaty was made to bring all U.S. troops home so that Saigon's government could defend itself. Again, as he had more and more in 1970, Nixon stressed the POW issue as one the United States would insist on before it withdrew completely. In his speech of April 16, he made the POW release a *sine qua non* condition of final U.S. withdrawal.

May 3, 1971   A MASSIVE ANTI-WAR DEMONSTRATION IN WASHINGTON, D.C., LEADS TO THE ARREST OF NEARLY 12,000 PEOPLE.

May 27, 1971   *CAIRO AND MOSCOW ANNOUNCE AN EGYPTIAN-SOVIET TREATY OF FRIENDSHIP AND COOPERATION.*

Article 8 of this treaty pledged Russia to help Egypt in the military field. Since September, 1970, Egypt received 100 MIG-21 fighters and 16 MI-8 troop-carrying helicopters.

June 13, 1971   THE *NEW YORK TIMES* BEGINS PUBLISHING THE TEXTS OF SECRET VIETNAM DOCUMENTS: *THE PENTAGON PAPERS.*

The multivolume series of documents known as the *Pentagon Papers* had been compiled by aides of Secretary of Defense McNamara in 1967-1968 as a systematic study of exactly how the United States became involved in Vietnam between 1945 and 1968. In addition to an analytical text, it included copies of secret documents available in Pentagon files which included any circulated from the White House and State Department.

     Later, Nixon learned that these documents had been "leaked" to the *Times* by Daniel ELLSBERG, a former member of Kissinger's NSC staff who went to work in 1969 at the Rand Corporation. At Rand, Ellsberg read and made photocopies of the *Pentagon Papers*, a document available to Rand because it was a "think

tank" for the Defense Department. In addition to the *Times* edition, which
was a selected version of the papers, the *Pentagon Papers* were later published
in a five-volume Senator Michael Gravel edition (1971) and a 12-volume Government Printing Office edition.

Ellsberg's act had future repercussions for Nixon. Concerned about
"leaks," the president established a "Plumbers Unit" in the White House which
became involved in a variety of clandestine activity during the next two
years. Its first project was a covert operation to obtain Ellsberg's file
from the office of his psychiatrist, Dr. Lewis J. Fielding, on August 25.
This operation was the White House's first authorization of illegal action,
which ultimately led to Nixon's resignation in 1974.

July 9, 1971   NSC CHAIRMAN KISSINGER SECRETLY DISRUPTS AN AROUND-
                         THE-WORLD TRIP TO FLY TO PEKING FROM RAWALPINDI, PAKI-
                         STAN. IN CHINA, KISSINGER CONSULTS WITH CHOU EN-LAI,
                         CHINA'S FOREIGN MINISTER.

Arrangements for Kissinger's secret trip to Peking originated late in April,
1971. Chou's invitation--by way of Pakistan--for a high-level delegate to
visit Peking had been made and accepted. A specific date for the visit was
set in mid-June, and on July 1, Kissinger left on a world tour which took
him to Pakistan by July 8. After visiting Saigon, Bangkok, and New Delhi,
Kissinger arrived at Rawalpindi where Pakistan's Foreign Minister Khan Sultan
took great pains to assure the secrecy of Kissinger's departure and return
from China.

On the evening of July 8, Kissinger cancelled a dinner because of illness, slipping from his room to an automobile which took him back to the airport. The next morning a Secret Service agent disguised as the NSC Chairman
set out to recover from his illness by resting at Nathia Gali.

Meanwhile, Kissinger flew by Pakistani Airlines to Peking where he met
on July 9-10 with Chou En-lai. These sessions went splendidly as their per-
sonalities were compatible. Their discussions included the following points:

1. The United States would recognize that Taiwan was part of China;
    the issue would be settled by the Chinese themselves. Kissinger
    accepted this because on April 26, a special U.S. presidential com-
    mission recommended that the United States should approve the seating
    of the People's Republic in the United Nations but without expelling
    Nationalist China. This commission included fairly conservative
    Republicans such as Henry Cabot Lodge and Senators Robert A. Taft,
    Jr., and Bourke B. Hickenlooper.

2. Chou indicated that he expected the United States would some day
    sever relations with the Nationalist government, but he set no date
    or precondition on this.

3. Kissinger said Nixon could not break with Chiang Kai-shek immediately
    but hoped for good relations with Peking anyway.

4. The People's Republic would be accepted in the United Nations but
    the precise question of Nationalist China was left unsettled.

5. Kissinger said the United States believed mainland China was one of
    the five great power centers of the world, as Nixon had stated in a
    speech on July 6, 1971.

6.   Chou invited President Nixon to visit China in 1972; Kissinger accepted.

7.   Future contact would be through the U.S. and Chinese embassies in Paris.

July 15, 1971   PRESIDENT NIXON ANNOUNCES ON TELEVISION THAT HE WILL VISIT THE PEOPLE'S REPUBLIC OF CHINA SOMETIME BEFORE MAY, 1972.

Kissinger returned to Washington from his Peking visit on July 13. Following extensive discussions, the president decided to announce the visit on July 15, as Chou and Kissinger had agreed. Nixon relaxed most of the day, then flew to California in order to make the broadcast from San Clemente. This sequence of events is important because until he reached Los Angeles about 5:30 California time, he did not notify Secretary of State Rogers so that U.S. allies could be contacted in advance.

When Rogers phoned the State Department, its Asian specialist, Marshall Green, was concerned that Japan must know in advance. He telegraphed Ambassador Armin Meyer in Tokyo but the message arrived too late. Nixon was on television and the Armed Forces radio station while Meyer was having his hair cut. Rogers did call the ambassadors of Japan, Nationalist China, and Russia in advance. Nationalist Chinese Ambassador James C.H. Shen was shocked, calling Nixon's move a "shabby deal."

Although American allies concurred generally with Nixon, they all felt dismayed by not being consulted, especially the Japanese. Nixon and Kissinger's style, however, was often to work outside the normal diplomatic apparatus and protocol channels of the State Department.

Nevertheless, Nixon surprised many Americans by announcing he had changed an American policy which went back to October, 1949. He told his audience that the United States sought "friendly relations with all nations." The visit would reduce tensions with China and promote peace "not just for our generation but for future generations on this earth we share together."

August 9, 1971   *INDIA AND THE SOVIET UNION SIGN A 10-YEAR TREATY OF FRIENDSHIP AND COOPERATION.*

Similar to the Soviets' May 27 treaty with Egypt, this pact provided for Soviet military aid to India. Although both nations claimed the pact was to maintain peace in South Asia, the United States and Pakistan believed it aimed at the latter country as a threat of war. They were correct. See December 3, 1971.

August 12, 1971   *THE SOVIET UNION AND WEST GERMANY SIGN A TREATY MAKING THE EUROPEAN FRONTIERS ESTABLISHED IN 1945 "INVIOLABLE."*

German Chancellor Willy Brandt negotiated this treaty with Moscow as part of his Ostpolitik. In particular, West Germany recognized the Oder-Neisse border between Poland and Germany and the border states dividing East and West Germany. See December 7, 1970, and June 3, 1972.

August 15, 1971   NIXON ANNOUNCES A "NEW ECONOMIC POLICY." THIS INCLUDES
                        A 10% IMPORT TAX SURCHARGE WHICH HAS INTERNATIONAL
                        CONSEQUENCES.

The American economic difficulties in foreign trade and domestic expenses
had been growing since the crisis of March, 1968, affected President Johnson's
decisions on Vietnam (see March 25-26, 1968). American balance of payments
deficits continued to multiply during the next three years and European nations wanted the United States to devalue the gold value of the dollar to a
more realistic ratio. Gold had held at $35 per ounce since 1933. By 1971,
the speculative gold exchange no longer valued dollars sufficiently, causing
the currency and trade of all nations based on the dollar to suffer.
     Following a lengthy meeting of the NSC, the Treasury Department, and
others, Nixon decided to take three important actions on August 15. These
were:

1. A wage-price freeze was set up for America.

2. The convertability of the dollar to gold was temporarily suspended.

3. There would be a 10% import surcharge. Nixon claimed the surcharge
   would stabilize the dollar better than devaluation. He announced
   it would be temporary, but did not specify for how long.

The trade surcharge shocked America's allies who had not been consulted
before the announcement by Nixon. In reality, these policies were temporary
expedients, not a new program. They were band-aids which did not cure but
only covered over the economic crisis for another day. Especially in international economies, additional changes were needed. See December 17, 1971.

September 3, 1971   THE QUADRIPARTITE AGREEMENT ON BERLIN IS SIGNED TO
                        SOLVE SOME OF THE PAST TENSIONS IN THAT DIVIDED CITY.

Ambassadorial-level talks regarding Berlin began among the four powers during
February, 1970. The talks dragged on until May 14, 1971, when Soviet Chairman Brezhnev agreed to discuss possible mutual reductions of Warsaw Pact and
NATO forces if the West would discuss the confirmation of the postwar borders
in Europe.
     Following detailed discussions between June and August, the four-power
pact in Berlin was signed on September 3. The agreement's main clauses were:

1. Traffic to and from West Berlin would be unimpeded.

2. West Berliners could visit East Berlin and East Germany for up to
   30 days per year.

3. East Berliners could enter the West, but their departures were to
   be controlled by East Germany.

4. The three Western powers agreed that Berlin's western sectors were
   not a "constituent" part of West Germany and would not be governed
   by it.

5. Four-power rule was kept in Berlin.

The Berlin accords were ratified by East Berlin and the West Germans on

December 17, by West Berlin and East Germany on December 20. The Berlin Wall remained operative as East Berlin's symbol of keeping its people locked in. The force-reduction talks did not begin as scheduled in October, 1971, because the Russians would not receive the NATO delegation in Moscow.

The final protocols on the Quadripartite Agreement of 1971 were not ratified until 1972. See June 3, 1972. Also see West Germany's treaties with the Soviet Union and Poland of August 12, 1971, and December 7, 1970.

September 5, 1971   A *NEW YORK TIMES* REPORT INDICATES THE SOVIET UNION
                         HAS DEVELOPED AN INTERCONTINENTAL SUPERSONIC BOMBER--
                         THE BACKFIRE.

This was the world's first supersonic bomber. The White House learned of its successful testing in March, 1971. The *Times* article was based on a CIA study, including drawings of the plane. The Pentagon refused officially to discuss the "sensitive" intelligence on the Backfire bomber.

September 30, 1971   THE UNITED STATES AND THE U.S.S.R. SIGN TWO MINOR
                         AGREEMENTS TO TRY TO AVOID AN ACCIDENTAL NUCLEAR WAR.

These two agreements stated that: (1) the nation under nuclear attack would try to ascertain if it were an accidental launch or not. This pact tried to strengthen "fail-safe" procedures although no specific actions in case of an attack could be precisely predetermined; (2) the Washington-Moscow "hotline" was switched to space satellite communications to make it swifter and less vulnerable to disruption in case of an accidental launch.

October 3, 1971   *PRESIDENT THIEU WINS REELECTION IN SOUTH VIETNAM WITH*
                         82% OF THE VOTE.

Although Thieu staged an election in 1971 because it pleased his American advisors, the campaign threatened for a while to become a real contest with former South Vietnamese politicians Marshal Ky or General Big Minh. In particular, Big Minh ran as an advocate of neutrality and negotiations with Hanoi, a program which, in Paris, Le Duc Tho told Kissinger was a favorable possibility for North Vietnam to consider.

Neither Ky nor Minh remained as a candidate for president until October 3. On August 5, the Supreme Court of the Republic of Vietnam ruled that as a former vice-president, Ky could not run for election. Big Minh first tried to get the United States to guarantee a fair election. On April 12, Minh gave the U.S. embassy a document in which Thieu instructed all government and military officers in South Vietnam to ensure his victory. The Americans claimed, however, to be "neutral" in the election and, therefore, unable to interfere with Thieu. On August 20, Minh withdrew from the race charging that the election process was corrupt.

With no opposition, Thieu won 82% of the votes on October 3. He had learned that the Americans did not like election results of 94 to 98% favoring Thieu; yet even 82% was large for a "democratic" candidate.

By 1971, most observers of Thieu's government either criticized or excused his political methods. Critics said his government had less support than that of Diem in 1963; at least Diem had the Catholic backing which Thieu

had lost by 1971. After 1968, Thieu talked about political, economic, and
military reform but never took any significant action to change these areas.

October 12, 1971   WASHINGTON AND MOSCOW ANNOUNCE THAT NIXON WILL VISIT
                          THE SOVIET UNION IN MAY, 1972.

While reporters believed the signing of SALT I was near, the president cautioned that this pact might or might not have been achieved by that time.
In other respects, the announcement of Nixon's visit was no surprise. Since
his July 15 decision to visit China, most observers believed the Russian
visit would come sooner or later.

October 15, 1971   THE UNITED STATES AND JAPAN SIGN A THREE-YEAR AGREE-
                          MENT ON TEXTILES.

Since Nixon's meeting with Prime Minister Sato in November, 1969, a better
atmosphere for trade negotiations had gradually been created. In March,
1971, the Japanese Textile Federation in Washington struck a bargain with
Wilbur Mills, Chairman of the House Ways and Means Committee, by which they
unilaterally agreed to limit their exports. This irritated Nixon, who disliked Mills' action, but it began to solve the U.S. trade deficit with Japan
which reached $3 billion in 1971.
     On September 26, 1971, Japan's Emperor Hirohito and his empress visited
Alaska and were warmly greeted by the president. This symbolized better relations and helped the two countries reach a trade agreement in October.

October 25, 1971   THE PEOPLE'S REPUBLIC OF CHINA IS ADMITTED, THE NA-
                          TIONALIST GOVERNMENT OF TAIWAN EXPELLED, FROM THE
                          UNITED NATIONS.

Although the U.S. State Department acted as if it wished to have both Chinese
governments in the United Nations, Chou En-lai told Kissinger in July that
the Peking regime could not be represented unless Taiwan left the United Nations.
     Beginning on August 2, however, Secretary Rogers stated that the United
States would support the seating of the Peking regime but opposed Taiwan's
expulsion. The United States submitted such a resolution to the U.N. General Assembly on August 20 and solicited votes to support Taiwan. Until September 16, the United States left undisclosed its view of the Chinese seat
as one of the Big Five permanent members of the Security Council if Taiwan
remained. Then Nixon announced that the United States would vote for Peking's
position on the council because it reflected "realities." After that statement, the United States lost all but a small hard core of followers on the
U.N. vote.
     The U.N. action on October 25 was essentially a foregone conclusion.
In the General Assembly, the U.S. vote to keep the Nationalists as members
lost by a vote of 59 to 54. Ninety minutes later, an Albanian resolution to
admit the People's Republic and expel Nationalist China carried by a vote of
76 to 35. The United States voted for this resolution. Taiwan's delegation,
led by Liu Chieh, quietly gathered its papers and left the hall. The Peking
delegation arrived in New York on November 12.

October 26, 1971   HENRY KISSINGER LEAVES PEKING TO RETURN TO AMERICA
                        WITH NEWS THAT NIXON'S 1972 VISIT IS ARRANGED.

Kissinger made his second visit to see Chou En-lai beginning on October 20,
realizing that the details of the president's visit could be finalized following the U.N. vote on October 24 or 25. Thus, on the day after the U.N.
vote which expelled the Taiwanese government, Peking was assured that the
United States had complied with its July request. Officially, the White House
announced on November 29 that Nixon's visit to China would begin on February
21, 1972.

December 3, 1971   *WAR BEGINS BETWEEN INDIA AND PAKISTAN.*

There had been a build up of tension between these two old antagonists since
1970 following the outbreak of a rebellion in Bengali, East Pakistan. Be-
cause of Pakistani persecution, 5 million refugees fled from Bengali to India
where Indira Gandhi championed their cause. The rebels had proclaimed the
independent republic of Bangladesh on March 26, 1971, causing the Pakistanis
to take further measures to suppress the rebellion.

On December 3, Indian troops invaded Bengali and with help from the reb-
els trapped 90,000 Pakistani troops. In West Pakistan, Indian armies took
over land in the disputed areas of Kashmir. See December 17, 1971.

December 17, 1971   THE "GROUP OF TEN" AGREE ON NEW INTERNATIONAL MONETARY
                        ARRANGEMENTS BY WHICH THE U.S. DOLLAR IS DEVALUED AND
                        EXCHANGE RATES "FLOAT."

Because America's major economic partners could no longer accept the 10% surcharge and continued declining value of the dollar which Nixon permitted by
his August 15 "new economic policy," the United States as one of the leading
financial nations worked out a new exchange program with the European community, Canada, and Japan.

Negotiations for the December 17 agreement had been conducted at the
Portuguese Azores between U.S. delegates and a French group headed by French
President Georges Pompidou. Meeting on the Azores island of Tercerira beginning December 13, Nixon and Pompidou reached the basic agreement that was
formalized on December 17 in Washington with delegates of the other nations.
Nixon in particular had to overrule Secretary of the Treasury John Connally's
belief that the United States should "strongarm" other nations such as Germany
and Japan to devalue their currencies. To the contrary, Secretary of Labor
George Shultz argued that there should be floating currency rates. Nixon
rejected Shultz's theory in August, but it was accepted during the Azores
meeting with Pompidou. Unlike Connally, Shultz had extensive business experience in international trade.

Bypassing Connally, Nixon and Kissinger accepted the floating currency
concept and dollar devaluation during the Azores sessions, an idea on which
Pompidou agreed. This basic pact was announced as the Azores Pact on December
14 and ratified by the other European nations, Canada, and Japan on December
17. The agreement permitted all national currencies to float on the exchange
market within "broader permissible margins" around a devalued dollar rate.
The immediate devaluation of the dollar was from $35 to $38 an ounce of gold.
This was a 9% dollar devaluation, compared to Japan's devaluation of the yen

by 17%, the West German mark's change by 13½%, and the British pound and French franc change of 8½%. The United States ended the 10% import surcharge and the non-convertibility of the dollar decreed on August 15. Extensive trade negotiations between the United States and the other nine nations would also begin.

December 17, 1971   PAKISTAN AND INDIA AGREE TO A CEASE-FIRE, PARTLY DUE
                             TO AMERICAN ACTION TO PREVENT A WIDER WAR.

After war broke out on December 3, President Nixon sought a truce through the United Nations and took action which "tilted" toward Pakistan in order to limit the war. The U.N. resolutions did not gain a truce because the Soviet Union vetoed three attempts to pass them.

Although publicly claiming U.S. neutrality on December 6, Nixon acted in a fashion that prevented a disastrous defeat for Pakistan. He persuaded Jordan and Iran to send obsolete F-5, F-86, and F-104 jets to Pakistan. He also ordered a naval task force led by an aircraft carrier to move from the Pacific to the Bay of Bengal. This let India and its ally, Russia, know that the United States would probably act to help Pakistan if necessary.

Whether or not Nixon would have acted further is unclear. In America, public opinion favored the Bengalis as victims of Pakistani persecution. Thus, presidential action would have been difficult to justify. Fortunately, India agreed to a cease-fire in East Pakistan on December 14 and in West Pakistan on December 17. The major result of the war was that the independence of Bangladesh was secured.

1972

January 22, 1972   *THE UNITED KINGDOM IS ACCEPTED AS A MEMBER OF THE*
                       COMMON MARKET.

*Because de Gaulle had vetoed the British membership application on December
18, 1967, Prime Minister Heath held discussions with President Pompidou of
France on May 21 to agree on terms of Britain's admission. As a result the
EEC voted in favor of English membership on June 23, 1971. On October 28,
the British Parliament approved the terms of membership and on January 22,
1972, the EEC formally voted to admit the British. On the same day, Ireland
and Denmark also were accepted as members of the Common Market. The membership of these three nations became effective on January 1, 1973.*

January 25, 1972   TO A NATIONAL TELEVISION AUDIENCE, NIXON OUTLINES A
                       PLAN TO END THE VIETNAM WAR AND DISCLOSES KISSINGER'S
                       SECRET TALKS IN PARIS.

President Nixon told the public he was presenting a plan for peace to North
Vietnam which would "end the war now" because it was "both generous and far-
reaching." In reality, the proposal Nixon described was a slightly revised
version of a plan offered to Le Duc Tho in Paris on October 11, 1971. The
proposal included withdrawal of all U.S. forces within six months of an agreement, new elections in South Vietnam after Thieu's prior resignation, an independent body to conduct elections in which the Communists could run candidates, and a U.S. aid program to help rebuild Vietnam.
     In order to impress the nation with his willingness to "try to break
the deadlock in the negotiations," Nixon informed the public about Dr.
Kissinger's secret talks in Paris since August 4, 1969. The National Security
advisor had met 12 times with either Le Duc Tho, Xuan Thuy, or both. Nixon
reported that until recently, the secret talks had appeared to progress, but
the Communists late in 1971 again became reluctant to yield on any compromise.
     Nixon's speech indicated that, contrary to public reports, he had been
making extra efforts to seek peace. North Vietnam appeared for the first
time to have been the party blocking a successful truce arrangement. Nixon's
1972 peace suggestions had been rejected by Hanoi in October, 1971. Nevertheless, he had made a fresh proposal and the Communists had not responded
seriously to it between October and January.

January 30, 1972   *PAKISTAN WITHDRAWS FROM THE BRITISH COMMONWEALTH AFTER
                       GREAT BRITAIN RECOGNIZES THE INDEPENDENCE OF BANGLA-
                       DESH.*

*Although the truce with India of December, 1971, virtually assured the inde-
pendence of Bangladesh, Pakistan refused to recognize the loss of its eastern*

territory. As a result, London's recognition of the government of Prime Min-
ister Shaikh Mujibur Rahman was opposed by Pakistan. On April 18, 1972,
Bangladesh became a member of the British Commonwealth.

February 17, 1972   PRESIDENT NIXON LEAVES FOR CHINA, MAKING HIS ENTIRE
                           JOURNEY A TELEVISION SPECTACULAR.

From his departure before an honor guard, the Vice-President, members of
congress, and 8,000 well-wishers until his return on February 28, Nixon used
the China tour to promote his 1972 presidential campaign. After stopping in
Hawaii and Guam, Air Force One reached Peking at 11:40 a.m. on February 21.
Nixon and Kissinger went immediately to visit with Chairman Mao Tse-tung.
Subsequently, live television reports carried to American homes his visits
to the Great Hall of the People, the Great Wall, Hangchow, and Shanghai. On
the final day in Shanghai, Nixon and Chou En-lai issued what became known as
the Shanghai Communique, which described the working relations between Washington and Peking. The important parts of this message were:

1. On Vietnam, the United States declared that after a truce the Amer-
    ican forces would withdraw and permit the peoples of Indochina to
    "determine their destiny without outside intervention." America,
    the message incorrectly stated, had always sought "a negotiated so-
    lution" to the Vietnam war.

2. The United States said it would retain strong ties with South Korea
    and Japan.

3. In South Asia, Nixon promised U.S. support for the rights of peoples
    in India, Pakistan, and elsewhere to "shape their own future in
    peace, free of military threats, and without having the areas become
    the subject of great power rivalry."

4. Chou declared China wanted all nations to be treated as free and
    equal; "it opposes hegemony and power politics of any kind."

5. China supported the "peoples of Vietnam, Laos and Cambodia in their
    efforts ...," but said nothing about the U.S. presence in the area.

6. China opposed any Japanese "revival and outward expansion" of "mili-
    tarism," favoring a "peaceful and neutral Japan."

7. China said it backed Pakistan in its "struggle to preserve ... its
    independence and sovereignty." This referred indirectly to China's
    alliance against India.

8. The United States and China agreed to conduct relations on the "prin-
    ciples of respect for the sovereignty and integrity of all states,
    non-interference in the internal affairs of other states, equality
    and mutual benefits, and peaceful coexistence."

9. Regarding Taiwan, China stated that it could have no full diplomatic
    relations with the United States as long as Washington recognized
    the Taiwan regime. Without a definite date, Nixon promised the
    gradual U.S. withdrawal of its forces from Taiwan, agreeing that
    there is but one China and Taiwan is part of it.

10. China and the United States promised to broaden "people to people"
    exchanges, bilateral trade, exchanges in science, technology, sports,

and journalism. The two nations would remain in direct contact and establish "liaison missions" in lieu of normal diplomatic representation.

February 25, 1972   SECRET BOMBINGS OF NORTH VIETNAM ARE DISCLOSED IN A
                           LETTER TO SENATOR HUGHES OF THE SENATE ARMED SERVICES
                           COMMITTEE.

Similar to the secret Cambodian bombings of 1969-1970, the aggressive U.S. Air Force attacks on North Vietnam between November, 1971, and March, 1972, were made public after February 25. Air Force Sergeant Lonni Douglas Franks wrote to Senator Harold E. Hughes to describe these actions and request a public investigation. Subsequent hearings of the Senate committee between June and September, 1972, indicated that the Nixon administration had condoned, if not approved, these violations of the 1968 agreement with Hanoi.

The secret bombings of 1971-1972 had been conducted by the Seventh Air Force, commanded by General John D. Lavelle. To justify the attacks, U.S. Air Force personnel filed reports that reconnaissance planes had been attacked and the fighter escorts had retaliated. A second set of reports for General Lavelle only would list the planes and the targets struck by the B-52's. The targets were not the surface-to-air missile (SAM) bases but truck parks, petroleum depots, troop concentrations, and other suitable targets such as "Rolling Thunder" used before 1968.

General Lavelle explained that he designed the attacks and the report system in order to impede the pre-invasion build up of Communist forces. He said "higher authorities" encouraged him to use "protective air strikes" to attack other targets. He considered his method similar to the navy's practice of sending an aircraft as bait over North Vietnam's coast and retaliating after the Communists' fire had been provoked. General John D. Ryan told the committee that the Defense Department had issued "liberal interpretations" of Communist targets during 1971 and that by January, 1972, the revised regulations justified the targets Lavelle had hit. Thus, the committee tried to locate exactly by whom the changes in guidelines had been ordered. They could not obtain evidence from the Defense Department to either corroborate or refute that a "higher authority" was responsible. These documents were refused to the committee.

General Lavelle suffered the consequences. He was relieved of command, reduced in rank, and retired from the service. According to the Senate committee report, Lavelle had ordered 28 unauthorized missions with 147 sorties by B-52's in a three-month period of 1971-1972.

March 13, 1972   *THE UNITED KINGDOM GRANTS FULL DIPLOMATIC RELATIONS
                        TO THE PEOPLE'S REPUBLIC OF CHINA.*

*In their agreement with China, the British raised their recognition to the
ambassadorial level for the first time since 1950. They also withdrew their
consulate from Taiwan's Nationalist Chinese government. The British were
one of many nations granting the Peking government recognition during 1972.*

March 30, 1972   NORTH VIETNAM BEGINS OFFENSIVE ACTION IN SOUTH VIETNAM
                          WHICH LASTS UNTIL EARLY JUNE.

Although General Giap began to build up his forces in the fall of 1971 for
an attack, President Nixon ignored these reports in favor of more optimistic
omens in order that planned U.S. withdrawals could continue. Thus, although
Ambassador Bunker warned the White House that it underestimated the Communist
preparations, the Vietnamization process continued. When the Communists began their "Easter Offensive" on March 30, only 6,000 U.S. combat troops remained in South Vietnam. As a result, ARVN bore the brunt of the March-June
offensive.

     Giap's forces attacked on three fronts: across the demilitarized zone
and the Laotian border into the northern and central highlands, then, later,
after ARVN forces moved north from Saigon, into the southern delta region
near Saigon. Using 200 Russian T-54 tanks and large numbers of 130-mm. guns,
the Communists overran the outposts north and west of Highways 9 and 13 leading to Hue and An Loc. By April, An Loc and Kontum were besieged and the
Communists had nearly cut the country into two parts.

     After Thieu sent ARVN troops north, other Communists attacked the delta
regions. Lacking ground forces, General Abrams ordered B-52's from Guam to
hit the delta. Previously, the United States had avoided B-52 raids in the
populous delta. Now these planes struck in this area, destroying many peasant
villages and homes as much as they hurt the Communists. The B-52 attacks
and the VC attacks severely damaged America's pacification program in the
south. An estimated 365,000 villagers went under Communist control in the
delta area during this period.

     In June, ARVN counterattacks began to succeed. Parachute drops relieved
An Loc although the siege dragged on until September. At Kontun, ARVN's 23rd
Division troops moved in and held the city. The tide of battle favored ARVN
after June 1. Some ARVN forces did commendably well; others did not hold up,
however. The People's Self-Defense Force functioned well in the north but
seemed to be demoralized in the delta region.

     The military consensus was that U.S. air support was the decisive factor
in the successful defenses. Air strikes at An Loc and Kontum allowed the
besieged cities to hold fast. In Quang Tri province air attacks knocked out
enemy tanks and 130-mm. guns. How ARVN would do without U.S. air cover remained a question.

April 4, 1972   NIXON ORDERS RENEWED B-52 RAIDS ON NORTH VIETNAM, THE
                          FIRST SUCH SINCE 1969. THE PRESIDENT BELIEVES THE
                          LARGE COMMUNIST EASTER OFFENSIVE JUSTIFIES HIS ACTION.

Since Johnson's October 31, 1968, announcement to halt Rolling Thunder, the
only U.S. air attacks on North Vietnam had been low-level retaliatory fighter-
bomber attacks. After General Giap's large-scale offensive of March 30 began
while the United States had only 6,000 troops remaining in the south, Nixon
wanted to reaffirm America's resolve by a strong attack against the enemy.

     The initial B-52 bombing raids were limited to the area from the 17th to
20th parallel. Nixon decided also to test Moscow's link to Hanoi by an additional bombing escalation plus the mining of Haiphong harbor. In order to
enact this maneuver, Nixon sent Henry Kissinger on a special mission to Moscow
before this new escalation began. See April 20 and May 8, 1972. For
data on Nixon's secret bombing of North Vietnam, see February 25, 1972.

April 20, 1972   NATIONAL SECURITY ADVISOR KISSINGER BEGINS A SECRET
FOUR-DAY MEETING WITH SOVIET LEADER BREZHNEV TO OBTAIN
THE KREMLIN'S REACTION TO AN ESCALATION OF U.S. AC-
TIVITY AGAINST NORTH VIETNAM AND TO PROMOTE NEW CON-
DITIONS FOR THE PEACE NEGOTIATIONS IN PARIS.

Kissinger's secret mission to Moscow from April 20 to 24 was summit power
politics at its most dramatic. He and President Nixon kept the mission so
secret that Secretary of State Rogers did not know of it, nor did U.S. Ambassador to Russia Jacob D. Beam until, on the last day, Kissinger called
him.

Nixon and Kissinger achieved two objectives during these secret talks.
First, they learned that Moscow's détente relations with the United States
took precedence over the events in Vietnam. This resulted because Kissinger
told Brezhnev that Nixon believed he had to do two things to punish North
Vietnam for the Easter offensive: (1) begin a general bombing of North Vietnam, and (2) mine Haiphong harbor as the strongest U.S. action yet taken
against Hanoi. Brezhnev understood this necessity. Although Moscow had protested the B-52 attacks of April 4, Brezhnev and Kissinger realized this was
a matter of form. In addition, Brezhnev would not interfere with the U.S.
escalation in the north but would continue supplies to Hanoi as best he could.

The crucial question Brezhnev answered was: yes, he would receive Nixon
on his long-planned visit to Moscow on May 22, 1972. The U.S.-planned escalation would not damage the Soviet Union's reception of Nixon on this historic visit. Thus, Brezhnev's response demonstrated that détente with America
took precedence over the Moscow-Hanoi relationship.

The second objective of Kissinger's visit was to gain Brezhnev's backing
for a U.S. proposal to break the deadlock in Kissinger's secret peace talks
with Le Duc Tho. Because Brezhnev had yielded regarding the bombing escalation as a sign of Russia's interest in détente, Kissinger showed the U.S.
desire for big-power détente by yielding on a significant point in the truce
talks with Hanoi: the United States would agree to a cease-fire-in-place on
the basis of North Vietnam's troops in the south before the March 30 Easter
offensive. This meant that Hanoi could keep 100,000 North Vietnamese in
the south after the truce and until a final settlement between North and
South Vietnam. Kissinger asked only that Hanoi must permit Thieu to remain
in power in Saigon from the time of the cease-fire until the final settlement.

Brezhnev realized that Kissinger made a major concession to allow Hanoi's
troops to remain in the south. The Thieu matter appeared inconsequential to
the Kremlin leaders. Therefore, Brezhnev accepted Kissinger's offer. He
immediately dispatched Konstantin KATUSHEV, the Politburo member in charge
of allied relations, to Hanoi to deliver Kissinger's new proposal and to arrange a renewal of the secret Paris talks between Kissinger and Le Duc Tho.

Kissinger was elated. On April 24, before leaving Moscow, he called
Ambassador Beam. He told Beam that not even the State Department must know
about the secret visit. Beam knew because he would be Kissinger's contact
point with Brezhnev in working out arrangements for the new truce talks with
Katushev. He said the president demanded secrecy to avoid any leaks. Regarding Nixon's escalated attacks on Hanoi see May 8, 1972.

May 8, 1972   PRESIDENT NIXON ORDERS THE MINING OF HAIPHONG HARBOR
                       AND RENEWS LARGE-SCALE B-52 ATTACKS ON NORTH VIETNAM
                       AS LINEBACKER I.

Whereas the April 4 B-52 attacks were limited to the 20th parallel, Linebacker
I duplicated much of Rolling Thunder's most extensive North Vietnamese targets. Only the 30-mile limit of China's border was restricted. New targets
included the Paul Doumer bridge in Hanoi; bridge and rail lines leading to
China; fuel dumps; power plants; pipelines to China; and all missile or anti-
aircraft sites. The B-52 now had TV- and laser-guided bombs for more accuracy
and fewer plane losses. Linebacker I continued until October 23, 1972.

The order to mine Haiphong harbor was the most critical escalation ordered by Nixon. The Joint Chiefs had urged the mining of Hanoi's port since
1965, but heretofore, the risk of possible war with China or the Soviet Union
seemed too great in case one of the ships of those nations was hit. Nixon's
détente policy negated the previous risks. His February, 1972, visit to Peking and Kissinger's secret talks in Moscow of April 20-24 guaranteed that
those two major powers would not interfere but would subtly cooperate with
the closing of the harbor.

Because the secret arrangements made by Nixon with Brezhnev were unknown
to the president's critics, Nixon could chuckle at their boisterous denunciation of his announcement that Haiphong harbor would be mined. The dissenters said nuclear war was risked with Russia. Not until Nixon arrived in
Moscow to begin talks on May 22 could the dissenting pundits really concede
that President Nixon had pulled off the mining without Soviet opposition.

Soon after May 8, the mining of the sea areas around North Vietnam began. Flying criss-cross patterns, U.S. planes laid the mines in the water,
setting them to explode at various water depths. The aircraft placed over
8,000 mines in the coastal port areas and 3,000 in the inland waterways.
Prior to the aerial mining, foreign ships had been given three days' notice
to leave the area. The warning was effective. All ships, including the Com-
munist-bloc vessels, left the region without any serious incidents.

Only General Giap and Hanoi's Communists were surprised that neither
Peking nor Moscow did more than issue mild protests to Washington. While
U.S. planes completed the mining process late in May, Brezhnev and Nixon wined
and dined in Moscow; China's diplomats arranged new trade deals with the
United States. Hanoi's party newspaper, *Nhan Dan*, bitterly complained that
Brezhnev's reception of Nixon was like "throwing a life preserver to a drown-
ing pirate."

Nevertheless, the Joint Chiefs' expectation that mining the harbor would
seriously hurt Hanoi was another miscalculation. Much of North Vietnam's
foreign trade simply went overland. Highways from China to Hanoi became
clogged with trucks carrying supplies. New oil pipelines kept fuel plentiful,
and the French news correspondent in Hanoi found no evidence of a critical
lack of supplies during the summer of 1972. As some observers had previously
told the JCS, 90% of North Vietnam's supplies always came overland, making
the earlier risk of mining the sea areas unimportant. For "hawks" in America,
however, the mining of the North Vietnamese port areas had become a symbol
of the "hard line" against the Communists.

June 3, 1972   THE QUADRIPARTITE AGREEMENT ON BERLIN IS FULLY RATIFIED.

The final exchange of ratifications of the agreement signed on September 3,

1971, awaited the ratification of West Germany's 1970-71 treaties with the Soviet Union and Poland. (See August 12, 1971 and December 7, 1970.) These treaties had been delayed by the German Bundestag because the opponents of the treaties wanted to be certain that Germany retained its right to self-determination, to membership in the European Common Market, and to some-day reuniting with East Germany. Their doubts satisfied, the Bundestag ratified the two treaties on May 19. The Soviet Union and Poland ratified the treaties by May 31, 1972. This action cleared the way for the ex-change of ratifications on the Berlin pact on June 3. A new relationship had been formalized between the two Germanies and Poland.

June 17, 1972   THE WATERGATE BREAK-IN AT THE DEMOCRATIC NATIONAL HEAD-QUARTERS IS LINKED TO THE COMMITTEE TO RE-ELECT THE PRESIDENT (CREEP).

Watergate was an apartment-hotel complex in Washington, D.C. Initially a relatively small incident, Nixon's denials of involvement prevented it from affecting his 1972 campaign. However, further investigation resulted in disclosures which led to his resignation as president in August, 1974.

July 18, 1972   *EGYPT'S PRESIDENT SADAT EXPELS 20,000 SOVIET "ADVISORS."*

Ostensibly, Sadat was upset with Moscow because Brezhnev refused to supply him with modern military technology to prepare for conflict with Israel. The only Russians permitted to remain were 200 advisors on SAM missile sites.

July 19, 1972   HENRY KISSINGER AND LE DUC THO RENEW TRUCE NEGOTIATIONS IN PARIS THAT FINALLY LEAD TO A SETTLEMENT.

The renewed discussions in Paris came 10 months after Kissinger and Le Duc Tho reached an impasse during a session on September 13, 1971. Kissinger's April 20-24, 1972, talks with Brezhnev opened the door for both to renew ne-gotiations and to find a settlement in the formal and secret discussions which had been held intermittently in Paris since May, 1968.
    The formal talks in Paris had become a sideshow because of the many secret and separate discussions which Kissinger held with either Le Duc Tho or Xuan Thuy. They were important as a symbol of four parties negotiating and as the group which would finalize any treaty resulting from the secret talks. The U.S. head of the formal delegation in July, 1972, was William Porter. The first head of the delegation, Henry Cabot Lodge, resigned on November 20, 1969. From July 1, 1970, to July, 1971, David Bruce led the U.S. delegation. Finally, Porter took over for Bruce in July, 1972.
    Kissinger's secret talks had resulted in 12 meetings between August, 1969, and September 13, 1971, when the talks became deadlocked. His first discussions with Le Duc Tho were in February, 1970. The lengthiest series of secret discussions occurred between May 31 and September 13, 1971. On at least six different trips to Paris in 1971, Kissinger and Le Duc Tho exchanged various proposals, but all talks broke down by September 13. Although Kissinger made another proposal on October 11, 1971, the North Vietnamese refused to meet again until more substantive changes were made by the United States.

The principal deadlock in 1971 resulted from U.S. insistence on two points: (1) mutual withdrawal of all "foreign" troops from South Vietnam because to Kissinger "foreign" included North Vietnam; and (2) leaving President Thieu in charge in South Vietnam to negotiate a final settlement with the Communists. The second proposal had particularly concerned Hanoi during 1971 because Hanoi did not want the United States to allow Thieu to be re-elected again as president of South Vietnam during the October 11 elections.

By July, 1972, both Kissinger and North Vietnam had become aware of the need for each side to compromise. Kissinger had outlined a new U.S. position on the cease-fire-in-place when he talked with Brezhnev on April 20, 1972. During a press conference in Paris on May 12, Le Duc Tho indicated his willingness to make a major concession: to permit Saigon to be represented on a three-party "government of broad national concord reflecting the real political situation in South Vietnam." Tho's only qualification was that Thieu could not be chosen by the South Vietnamese as a representative.

Before July, a variety of developments enabled the new discussions to begin. The Communists' spring offensive, Nixon's retaliatory B-52 strikes, and the successful defense of their territory by the ARVN with U.S. air support were factors causing the North Vietnamese to become more conciliatory when the July 19 meetings began. The most vital reality to North Vietnam, however, was that both Peking and Moscow urged Hanoi to negotiate a U.S. withdrawal from Vietnam. Hanoi had hoped China and Russia would reject Nixon's détente overtures unless the United States stopped all military action in Vietnam. By cancelling the Moscow summit and halting Chinese-U.S. trade discussions, Hanoi's Communist brothers could have pressured Nixon to withdraw more rapidly from Vietnam. This policy had been rejected by the Soviet Union and the People's Republic of China, each of whom had their *own national* reasons for encouraging détente with America.

North Vietnam, therefore, had both military and diplomatic reasons for moving toward a truce. Until U.S. air support was taken away from Saigon, the Communists could not win in Vietnam. Without Russian or Chinese diplomatic backing, a coalition government in the south would have to precede a definite Communist victory.

For Nixon and Kissinger, the desire to pull out of Vietnam was part of their realistic global politics and part of the president's 1972 campaign strategy at home. Détente and satisfactory power relations with Moscow and Peking required that the United States relinquish its exaggerated concern for the minor issue of Vietnam in its big power relations, that is, to release the U.S. foothold in Southeast Asia which the Chinese disliked. Vietnam, not Taiwan, was the primary obstacle to Nixon and Kissinger's rapprochement with Peking. At home, the increased dissent against the prolonged war in Vietnam which Nixon had promised to end during the 1968 campaign and the belief that George McGovern was a serious contender for a presidential victory required Nixon to demonstrate that the Vietnamization process was nearly fulfilled. As Nixon's exaggerated concern in planning the Watergate burglary of June 17 demonstrates, the president wanted to avoid all possible risks of defeat in 1972.

On July 19, therefore, Le Duc Tho and Kissinger began what became their final round of discussions for truce arrangements. For the outcome see October 26, 1972.

September 5, 1972   PALESTINIAN GUERRILLAS TAKE HOSTAGES AT THE OLYMPIC
VILLAGE IN MUNICH.

On September 5, Black September guerrillas killed two members of Israel's
Olympic team and held nine others hostage. The terrorists wanted Israel to
release 200 Arab prisoners. When the Israeli government refused, the West
German government flew the guerrillas by helicopter to a military airport at
Furstenfeldbruck, telling them that a Lufthansa plane would fly them to Egypt.
At the airport, West German police attacked the terrorists. In the battle
the nine hostages were killed, along with five Arabs and one German police
officer.

October 26, 1972   NATIONAL SECURITY ADVISOR KISSINGER INFORMS NEWSMEN
THAT "PEACE IS AT HAND" IN VIETNAM; THE ONLY REMAINING
ISSUES ARE THE AMERICAN DESIRE TO REQUIRE THE PRECISE
LANGUAGE NEEDED FOR AN "HONORABLE WITHDRAWAL" AND TO
PROTECT THE CONTINUANCE OF PRESIDENT THIEU'S GOVERNMENT
OF SOUTH VIETNAM.

In light of the draft treaty which Kissinger negotiated with Le Duc Tho between July 19 and October 26, Kissinger's remarks to this press conference
misled reporters because the real affair delaying the peace process was
Nixon's desire to convince Thieu to accept the proposals drawn up by Kissinger
in Paris.

    Although Kissinger tried both on August 15 and from October 16 to 22 to
gain Thieu's approval, the National Security Advisor did not persuade Thieu
to concede. Kissinger had tried to persuade Nixon not to give Thieu veto
power over the treaty, but Nixon refused. For political reasons, the president could not risk loud protests from Saigon because the "peace with honor"
concept required Thieu's acceptance of any truce.

    Nevertheless, the basic framework of the January, 1973, truce terms had
been worked out by October 16. Briefly summarized, the agreements and the
controversial points accepted by Le Duc Tho and Kissinger between July 19 and
October 16 were:

1. *Cease-fire-in-place.* The important terms influencing this agreement
    were that all U.S. troops would withdraw within 60 days of the cease-
    fire and all U.S. prisoners of war would be released within 60 days
    of the cease-fire. While the agreement did not so specify, omission
    of withdrawal terms for the North Vietnamese meant that those forces
    would remain in place in South Vietnam.

2. *"Two-party" National Council of Reconciliation and Concord to imple-
    ment truce terms and reunify Vietnam.* The original Kissinger plan
    for a Tripartite Commission formed by Thieu's regime, the Provisional
    Revolutionary Government (formerly the National Liberation Front),
    and South Vietnamese neutralists had been rejected by Thieu. To
    attempt to satisfy Thieu, Kissinger on October 11 changed the name
    to "National Council" and referred only to the "two parties" in South
    Vietnam. Between October 11 and 26, however, Thieu also rejected
    this proposal. Thieu wanted to be the only government recognized
    in the south, a position which would have prevented any truce treaty.
    On October 26, therefore, Thieu had not accepted this idea.

3. *United States to stop bombing first.* The October 16 agreement called for the United States to stop bombing by October 23 so that the treaty could be signed on October 30-31. Linebacker I bombings ceased on October 23 but the treaty was not signed because of Thieu's objections.

4. *Replacement of war material.* When the first treaty draft was accepted on October 11, there was no agreement on this. Kissinger wanted loose terminology which would permit the United States to keep Thieu well supplied after the cease-fire; Tho wanted a narrow definition to prevent replacements as much as possible. The Communists accepted Kissinger's terms on replacement on October 22, 1972.

Because Thieu refused to sign the treaty on October 23 as provided for in the Kissinger-Tho plan of October 11, Hanoi broadcast a report which announced the terms it had agreed to and condemned Washington and Saigon for breaking their promise to sign and disturbing world peace. Peking and Moscow joined Hanoi's opposition to U.S. policy.

The Communist protests unintentionally served the Nixon-Kissinger problems with Thieu. Thus, at the press conference on October 26, Kissinger could appear to make the Nixon administration the champion of peace but also the champion of Thieu's governmental rights. Kissinger's "peace is at hand" statement indicated that only technical details needed to be resolved. One more round of talks with Le Duc Tho should resolve the matter, Kissinger said. At the same time, by requiring Thieu's agreement before signing, Nixon and Kissinger appeared to be defenders of "peace with honor," making certain that the technicalities of the truce would preserve the independence of South Vietnam. In this manner, Nixon's election campaign was not damaged but assisted on the eve of U.S. balloting.

November 7, 1972   PRESIDENT NIXON IS REELECTED BY A LARGE MARGIN.

Following his nomination on July 13 by the Democratic National Convention, George McGovern waged a poor campaign which included the withdrawal of Thomas Eagleton as the vice-presidential candidate when his history of psychiatric treatment was revealed. R. Sargent Shriver replaced Eagleton.

The Republicans nominated Richard Nixon and Spiro T. Agnew on August 23. Their platform supported Nixon's foreign policy, advocated welfare reform, and opposed the busing of school children to achieve racial integration. McGovern's platform emphasized the immediate end to the Vietnam war and a guaranteed income for the poor.

The war issue became insignificant after Henry Kissinger's "peace-is-at-hand" statement of October 26.

Nixon won 520 electoral votes to 17 for McGovern, who carried only Massachusetts and Washington, D.C.

November 9, 1972   THE UNITED STATES, FRANCE, GREAT BRITAIN, AND THE SOVIET UNION AGREE THAT BOTH THE EAST GERMAN AND WEST GERMAN GOVERNMENTS MAY JOIN THE UNITED NATIONS.

As a follow up to the Berlin agreement ratified on June 3, 1972, delegates of the four powers met in Berlin to decide on a method for accepting both governments as U.N. members.

This was part of an overall arrangement by which the East and West Germans cooperated to improve their relations as part of détente in central Europe. As early as March 19, 1970, Chancellor Willy Brandt of the Bonn government had visited Erfurt to conduct talks with Willie Stoph of East Germany.

December 16, 1972   KISSINGER INFORMS A PRESS CONFERENCE THAT THE PARIS PEACE TALKS ARE AT AN IMPASSE BECAUSE OF HANOI'S INTRANSIGENCE. THE UNITED STATES, HE SAID, MAY NEED TO MAKE RENEWED ATTACKS ON NORTH VIETNAM.

Between Kissinger's October 26 "peace is at hand" statement and his December 16 press conference, close observers realized that the differences between the negotiators in Paris were greater than "technical details." After the peace talks renewed in Paris on November 20, Saigon's demands for 69 changes in the draft treaty and Kissinger's initial attempt to support Saigon had nearly brought the negotiations to an end.

Nixon's attempts to placate Thieu in order to get his agreement had been unsuccessful during November. Nixon demonstrated U.S. support by speeding a rapid increase of military supplies to South Vietnam through Projects Enhance and Enhance Plus which began on October 14. But the rapid delivery of 70 tanks and 600 helicopters and fighter planes by early December did not persuade Thieu to yield.

Nixon also sent a personal letter to Thieu on November 14. He told Thieu the United States would take "swift and severe retaliatory action" against the Communists if they violated the truce terms. Moreover, he warned Thieu that his best security would be the sympathy of American and world opinion, a benefit which Thieu sacrificed by being an obstacle to the peace process. The South Vietnamese leader held firm; the destiny of all the people of South Vietnam was his to protect, Thieu claimed.

Because Saigon's demands precluded a truce solution, Kissinger asked Tho to renew secret and separate discussions on December 4. Kissinger was willing to return to the October draft treaty but he demanded a timetable by which the treaty would be signed on December 22, 1972. Kissinger wanted several changes in the October treaty in order to please Thieu, but Tho charged that the new concepts were complicated and could not be answered in the 48-hour limit which Kissinger desired. Kissinger became distraught and frustrated. First Thieu, now Tho gave him a hard time.

By December 11, the Kissinger-Tho talks reached an impasse. The security advisor returned to Washington on December 13. Kissinger and Nixon agreed that they must vigorously bomb North Vietnam as Kissinger frequently had threatened during the November, 1972, negotiations. Hanoi was sent a 72-hour ultimatum. It must agree to the issues pending during the December 4-11, 1972, peace talks or it would be bombed again.

At his December 16 press conference Kissinger never mentioned the ultimatum to Hanoi or the problem of Saigon's 69 demands. He emphasized that North Vietnam was responsible for the negotiating problems. Le Duc Tho, he stated, had raised "one frivolous issue after another...." Because Hanoi rejected these peace terms, the security advisor feared that America might have to renew its bombing raids on the Communists. On December 18 these attacks began on a larger scale than ever before.

December 18, 1972   THE UNITED STATES BEGINS PUNISHING BOMBING RAIDS ON
                          NORTH VIETNAM: THE "CHRISTMAS BOMBING" BY LINEBACKER
                          II.

Nixon and Kissinger decided to make the "Christmas" bombing raids with no
outside advice. Although Secretary of Defense Laird wrote the president a
letter which opposed a military response to the Paris deadlock, neither Laird
nor Secretary of State Rogers was trusted by Nixon and Kissinger. In addition, since the Cambodian incursion of April, 1970, Kissinger had lost most
of the highly competent NSC staff he recruited in 1969. Those who had resigned included Morton Halperin, Roger Morris, Anthony Lake, and William
Watts.

When, as expected, Hanoi rejected Nixon's 72-hour ultimatum, Nixon ordered the Linebacker II attacks to begin on December 18. For these attacks,
Nixon released the air force from almost all previous restrictions. The purpose of the bombing was alleged to be to cripple daily life in Hanoi and Haiphong, the two major cities of North Vietnam. Between December 18 and 29,
except Christmas Day, incessant air raids were flown from Guam by 200 B-52's
aided by F-4's and F-111's from Thailand and South Vietnam. Using carpet-
bombing tactics, every three-plane B-52 mission attacked a target area one
and one-half miles long and one-half mile wide. The planes dropped 15,000
tons of bombs on their section of target, and little but rubble remained.
For example, on the night of December 27-28, whether by design or accident,
the Khan Thieu residential district of Hanoi was hit. Fortunately, most of
the 28,198 workers had evacuated that area. After the raid only a few houses
still had roofs or windows.

The bombing attacks of December 18-29 were controversial. Critics such
as Telford Taylor argue they hit civilian areas and were largely indiscriminate "terror" attacks. Military authorities emphasize that they targeted
only military areas, but that "spillage" caused residences and hospitals to
be hit off-target. In addition, Guenter Lewy's analysis shows that the 11-
day attack was not severe compared to attacks in Dresden and Tokyo during
World War II. In North Vietnam, reported deaths from the raids were 2,200
to 5,000 compared to the 35,000 who died at Dresden and 87,793 killed in Tokyo raids.

Undoubtedly, the bombings were denounced in America because the public
had been told "peace is at hand" and that "only technical details" had to be
worked out. The U.S. Vietnamization process seemed to be nearly completed
and U.S. military advisors in Saigon were optimistic about the capabilities
of the troops they had been training since 1968. Given these expectations,
the "Christmas" bombings appeared to be purposeless and vengeful attempts to
coerce Hanoi to accept some technicalities in Paris.

The results of the bombings are also controversial. Nixon and Kissinger
claim the bombings brought the Communists back to agree at the bargaining
table. Their critics argue that public opposition to the bombing caused Nixon
to agree to negotiate again. Somewhat paradoxically, Lewy claims the bombings
were *not terroristic* but did force Le Duc Tho to return to Paris. Bombing
critics such as Gareth Porter and Alan Goodman say the bombings were terroristic but were *not* the reason that negotiations began again.

Whatever the truth of the bombings, by December 30, President Nixon announced that the bombings above the 20th parallel had stopped and negotiations
would begin again in Paris in January. The official announcement of December
30 did not state why the bombing stopped or why talks would begin. Later,
the White House said it acted in response to Hanoi's pleas to stop bombing;

the Communists said they had never broken off the talks, and Kissinger returned to Paris because of world opinion and the "fact" that 34 B-52's had
been destroyed.   The U.S. Air Force acknowledged 15 losses.

Perhaps the greatest effect of the December Linebacker II raids was that
Nixon and Thieu lost the sympathy of a majority of U.S. congressmen.   A poll
of senators on December 20 indicated they opposed the bombing 45 to 19 and
favored legislation to end the war 45 to 25.   When congress returned to the
Capitol in January, most members were ready to cut off funds for the war, a
measure they had previously rejected.   World opinion blamed both Thieu and
Nixon for the "terror" attacks.   None of the NATO nations approved and Pope
Paul deplored the "resumption of harsh and massive war action" in Vietnam.
Thieu's Saigon regime could no longer be seen by most as an unwilling victim
or an embattled republic; this new attitude lasted until the fall of Saigon
in April, 1975.   As one commentator remarked, Kissinger violated one of the
principal rules of Bismarck's 19th-century power politics: never punish a
weaker enemy when his surrender is near.

1973

IN PARIS, THE FOUR DELEGATIONS IN THE VIETNAM NEGO-
TIATIONS SIGN THE TRUCE AGREEMENTS.

The Paris talks between Kissinger and Le Duc Tho resumed on January 8, 1973.
President Nixon wanted a truce before his second inauguration but did not
quite achieve that goal. Although the Paris delegates did not initial the
draft treaty until January 23, Nixon had ordered an end to all war action by
the United States on January 15 because Kissinger informed him the treaty
was practically agreed to. The cease-fire in Vietnam officially began at
2400 Greenwich Mean Time on January 27, 1973.

Actually, two separate treaties were signed in Paris because Thieu's
delegation refused to sign a document which specifically mentioned the Provisional Revolutionary Government (PRG). One treaty was signed by two parties, the Democratic Republic of (North) Vietnam (DRV) and the United States.
This treaty had the concurrent agreement of the other two parties. The second treaty was a four-party treaty signed by the DRV, the United States, the
PRG, and the Republic of South Vietnam.

During the last week of negotiations, Kissinger had yielded most disputed points to North Vietnam although, of course, he never admitted this.
The two scholars of the truce process, Allan Goldman and Gareth Porter, agree
that the January truce differed in no substantial ways from the October draft.

Despite Thieu's objections, the most critical clauses of the October
draft were intact (see October 26, 1972):

1. North Vietnamese troops would remain in place in South Vietnam, but
    the United States was to withdraw in 60 days.

2. Both sides were to exchange prisoners of war in 60 days, but Saigon's
    political "detainees" would be handled after the truce.

3. Military equipment could be replaced on a one-to-one basis.

4. An International Control Commission of 1,160 persons would implement
    the truce terms.

5. The National Council on Reconciliation and Concord would carry out
    elections and negotiate to reunite Vietnam. In the two-party treaty,
    both the Provisional Government and Thieu's Republic of Vietnam were
    included. In the four-party treaty the Council consisted of the
    "two parties in South Vietnam."

6. Contrary to Thieu's wishes, the 17th parallel was not a boundary be-
    tween states but remained, as in the 1954 Geneva Treaty, a "pro-
    visional and not a political or territorial boundary" until Vietnam
    was united as one nation.

Nixon had forced Thieu to agree to the Treaty. The same day the December

bombing began (December 18) Nixon sent Alexander Haig to Saigon to inform
Thieu that he must accept the settlement agreed to by Nixon or each party
would go his "separate way." Haig had been instructed not to negotiate.
Thieu had to decide whether "to continue our alliance" or whether Nixon should
"seek a settlement with the enemy which serves United States interests alone."

On January 5, Nixon again put pressure on Thieu. Nixon wrote him that
his "best guarantee" for survival was unity with Washington. This, he said,
"would be gravely jeopardized if you persist in your present course." Nixon
also promised to make certain that the Communists would not violate the truce
terms. This promise and other personal promises by Nixon held little substance in future years as the president moved toward his resignation as president in August, 1974.

February 9, 1973   THE UNITED STATES RESUMES THE BOMBING OF CAMBODIA,
                          CLAIMING THE COMMUNISTS HAVE NOT RESPECTED A CEASE-
                          FIRE AGREEMENT.

Between February and August, 1973, Nixon and his opponents in congress argued
continually regarding the renewed bombing of Cambodia after the Vietnamese
truce went into effect on January 27th. The administration contended that North
Vietnamese troops and the Khmer Rouge continued fighting in Cambodia and that
Lon Nol, the prime minister of Cambodia, requested U.S. aid. Congressional
critics such as Senator Stuart SYMINGTON pointed out that in every military
appropriations bill since October, 1970, a proviso forbade the bombing of
Cambodia except to protect Americans in Vietnam. Therefore, the continued
bombing after the 1973 Vietnam truce was illegal.

Henry Kissinger endeavored during the final Paris peace talks of 1972-
1973 to arrange cease-fires in Laos and Cambodia as well as Vietnam. Le Duc
Tho assured him this could be done in Laos because Hanoi had control over
the Laotian Communists. The same, Tho said, could not be done for Cambodia
because the Khmer Rouge were too independent. In fact, the traditional enmity
between the Khmer and Vietnamese ethnic groups caused all Cambodians to distrust and disdain the Vietnamese, who reciprocated these feelings. Kissinger,
however, was ill-informed about Cambodia, and apparently did not understand
or believe Tho's assertion.

On January 23, 1973, during the final discussions in Paris, Kissinger
read a unilateral statement saying that Lon Nol would suspend offensive attacks and the United States would stop bombing Cambodia. If the Khmer Rouge
and North Vietnamese reciprocated, there would be a *de facto* cease-fire. If
not, the U.S. Air Force would resume bombing until there was a cease-fire.

Kissinger did not advocate or engage in any talks between the Khmer Rouge
and Lon Nol. For Kissinger and the U.S. officials, Cambodia was a "sideshow" to the sustaining of South Vietnam. Although he urged Lon Nol and the
Communists to negotiate, Kissinger never actively fostered this process. Lon
Nol would have profited from a cease-fire because the Khmer Rouge were on
the verge of victory. Le Duc Tho and Hanoi encouraged the Khmer to stop
fighting. The Khmer leaders and, in Peking exile, Prince Sihanouk, believed
Hanoi simply wanted to damage the cause of Cambodia in order that the Vietnamese could conquer them at a later date. Therefore, the Khmer ignored Hanoi's requests.

By February 9, the *de facto* cease-fire had not materialized. Thus, Nixon
and Kissinger agreed to renew the bombing of Cambodia. This action would
not only support Lon Nol but demonstrate to Hanoi that Nixon was determined

to require North Vietnam to fulfill the 1973 truce. Indirectly, therefore, the White House viewed the Cambodian bombing as continuing evidence of its backing of Thieu. Nixon did not, however, ask congress to repeal its prior legislation against the Cambodian bombing as Symington suggested he should do.

The renewed bombing of Cambodia after February 9 was not a token bombing to indicate dissatisfaction to Hanoi, it was a large-scale, massive series of bombing attacks by B-52's from Guam and fighter bombers from Thailand. During 12 months of 1972, B-52's dropped 37,000 tons of bombs on Cambodia. In March, 1973, they dropped 24,000; in April, 35,000, and in May, 36,000 tons. The fighter bombers had used 16,513 tons in 1972. In April, 1973, these aircraft dropped 15,000 tons; the figure rose to 19,000 tons in July.

The 1973 U.S. bombings of Cambodia prevented the fall of Lon Nol's government but, as in the case of Thieu in Vietnam, U.S. military action weakened rather than strengthened Lon Nol's support among his people. Internally, the Khmer Rouge successes between 1971 and 1973 caused the government of Lon Nol and Prince Sirik Matak to use repressive methods. Consequently, those Cambodians who opposed the Communist Khmer Rouge sought the return of Sihanouk. This tactic never succeeded because Sihanouk increasingly preferred an alliance with the Khmer Rouge against Lon Nol as the best way to regain control of Cambodia. In July, 1973, when Kissinger offered to talk with Sihanouk, it was too late. The exiled prince could not risk association with the United States.

For congressional action on the Cambodian bombing see July 1, 1973.

February 15, 1973   CUBA AND THE UNITED STATES SIGN AN ANTI-HIJACKING
                             AGREEMENT.

The number of incidents in which U.S. aircraft were hijacked and forced to fly to Havana caused difficulty for both nations. By this agreement, each country would try or extradite hijackers who forced aircraft to land in either the United States or Cuba.

February 21, 1973   *AN ISRAELI FIGHTER PLANE SHOOTS DOWN A LIBYAN COM-*
                             MERCIAL AIRLINER WHICH HAD STRAYED OVER THE ISRAELI-
                             OCCUPIED SINAI PENINSULA; 109 PERSONS ARE KILLED.

According to Israel, the Libyan airliner flew over highly sensitive military concentrations in the Sinai. The Libyan pilot acknowledged but ignored Israeli warnings. Later, tape recordings of the conversations between the Libyan pilot and the Cairo, Egypt, control tower indicated that the pilot believed he was over Egyptian territory and that the fighter planes were Egypt's. An Airline Pilots Association investigation, which condemned Israel for its act, stated that the principal problem was that the airline pilot and the fighter pilots had no method for communicating.

There were 113 passengers and crew on the Libyan plane; 109 died in the crash. Most passengers were Libyan and Egyptian because the plane's flight had been from Bengazi to Cairo. Four crew members who died were French. One passenger was an American.

On Febraury 24, Israel's Defense Minister Dayan stated that Israel made an error of judgment but that "serious responsibility" for the incident was that of the airline pilot. Israeli Premier Meir expressed regret for the loss of life in the incident. On March 6, Israel announced it would pay

$30,000 in compensation to families of the victims of the crash.

Libya's Foreign Minister Min Kikhia denounced the Israeli action as "criminal," claiming the plane lost its way because of communication difficulties and poor weather. A New York Times editorial on February 23 criticized the Israeli acts, stating that it was "at best a horrifying blunder ... an act of callousness that not even the savagery of previous Arab actions can excuse."

Both the Israeli and American governments expressed the hope that this incident would not interfere with discussions looking toward a peace settlement in the Middle East. For similar incidents see July 23, 1954, and July 27, 1955.

March 1, 1973   EIGHT GUERRILLAS OF THE PALESTINIAN BLACK SEPTEMBER GROUP SHOOT THEIR WAY INTO THE SAUDI ARABIAN EMBASSY IN THE SUDAN.

The guerrillas seized five hostages including the U.S. ambassador, his deputy, and a Belgian chargé d'affaires.

March 19, 1973   *TALKS BETWEEN THE REPUBLIC OF VIETNAM (RVN) AND THE PROVISIONAL REVOLUTIONARY GOVERNMENT OF VIETNAM (PRG) BEGIN AT ST. CLOUD, FRANCE.*

The first conference agenda item concerned setting a date for elections to the National Council on Reconciliation and Concord (NCRC). Immediately, disagreement occurred. The RVN wanted North Vietnamese troops to withdraw from the South before the election; the PRG wanted all fighting, including frequent skirmishes along the cease-fire line, to stop before elections. The NCRC was never elected. Formal but infrequent meetings continued at St. Cloud until January 25, 1974, when the delegates adjourned because their meetings were superfluous.

March 21, 1973   THE UNITED STATES VETOES A U.N. SECURITY COUNCIL RESOLUTION FAVORING THE RESTORATION OF PANAMANIAN SOVEREIGNTY IN THE CANAL ZONE.

In order to change the issue of the Panama Canal from a bilateral question with America to an international issue, Panama's head of state, General Omar TORRIJOS, invited the U.N. Security Council to conduct a meeting in Panama between March 15 and March 21. As a result, the council, with strong backing from all Latin American and Third World nations, offered a resolution stating that the United States should restore Panamanian national sovereignty over its entire territory. In the vote, 13 council members approved, Great Britain abstained, and the United States vetoed the resolution.

March 29, 1973   AMERICA'S LAST SOLDIER LEAVES VIETNAM; ALL AMERICAN PRISONERS OF WAR (POW) ARE RETURNED BUT THE FATE OF MANY MISSING IN ACTION (MIA) IS NOT KNOWN.

By March 29, about 1,000 POW's returned to America as did the last of the

6,000 combat troops which remained at the end of 1972. More than 2.5 million Americans served in Vietnam between 1961 and 1973. Over 50,000 were killed, 300,000 wounded. When the last U.S. soldier left on March 29, the war effectively ended for the United States.

May 17, 1973   THE SENATE WATERGATE HEARINGS BEGIN, PRESIDED OVER BY
                        SENATOR SAM J. ERVIN.

During the hearings, which lasted until August 7, John Dean testified that President Nixon was full party to the attempted cover-up of his reelection committee's role in the Watergate burglary. Presidential assistant Alexander Butterfield revealed the White House system for tape recording conversations, making the tapes and their content a critical factor in the further investigation of the president's methods of secrecy.

June 16, 1973   THE SOVIET LEADER, LEONID BREZHNEV, ARRIVES IN THE
                        UNITED STATES FOR A SUMMIT MEETING WITH PRESIDENT
                        NIXON.

The main achievement of this visit was a pact to prevent nuclear war which Brezhnev and Nixon signed on June 22. The two nations would conduct "urgent conversations" if needed to avert nuclear war between the two nations or with a third power. Nixon and Brezhnev also signed agreements on agricultural cooperation, oceanographical research, and cultural exchanges.

June 30, 1973   THE U.S. SELECTIVE SERVICE ACT EXPIRES.

On President Nixon's recommendation, congress did not renew the law providing for drafting of men into the armed forces. For the first time in 25 years, the armed forces became entirely voluntary.

July 1, 1973   CONGRESSIONAL LEGISLATION PROHIBITS THE USE OF FUNDS
                        TO BOMB CAMBODIA OR TO ENGAGE IN FURTHER MILITARY AC-
                        TION IN INDOCHINA WITHOUT PRIOR APPROVAL OF CONGRESS
                        AFTER AUGUST 15, 1973.

The arguments between Nixon and his critics about the renewed bombing of Cambodia on February 9, 1973, added to Nixon's difficulties with the hearings of Senator Sam Ervin's Watergate committee during the spring of 1973.

    The first evidence that congress no longer accepted Nixon's explanation of the Cambodian bombings came on May 10 when the U.S. House of Representatives voted 219-188 to stop funds for bombing Cambodia in the Supplemental Appropriations Bill. This bill also passed the Senate, but Nixon vetoed it on June 26. The House did not have sufficient votes to override the veto.

    Because Nixon needed the Supplemental Appropriations Bill, he agreed to compromise, accepting a statement on the Cambodian bombing which permitted it to continue until August 15 in order that truce arrangements could be worked out. Although some congressmen objected to the compromise, the majority accepted it as the "realistic" way. The bill was approved in congress on June 30; Nixon signed it on July 1.

Later, both Nixon and Kissinger claimed the peace talks on Cambodia in 1973 failed because congress had abdicated the bombing powers of the president on June 30. Kissinger said that "delicate negotiations" for a truce were underway but he never revealed any details of these transactions. In his book *Sideshow*, which was based on extensive research in documents secured under the Freedom of Information Act as well as interviews with various participants, William Shawcross could find no evidence of such talks. Nevertheless, the U.S. bombing of Cambodia stopped on August 15. At a farewell press conference in Phnom Penh on September 4, U.S. Ambassador Emory C. Swank said the war in Cambodia after 1970 was Indochina's most "useless war."

July 12, 1973   HEARINGS ON NIXON'S SECRET BOMBING OF CAMBODIA BEGIN AFTER THE SENATE ARMED SERVICES COMMITTEE LEARNS THAT THEY DID OCCUR.

Major Hal Knight, a radar operator who had handled the "dual bombing" reports on the Cambodian bombings (see March 18, 1969), wrote to Senator William Proxmire of Wisconsin in October, 1972, telling the senator of the secret bombing tactics and asserting that the American people should know about this. Knight protested the false record system to his commanding officer. His objections first resulted in low efficiency ratings for him and finally in the news that he would be discharged from the army. Thus, he asked Senator Proxmire to investigate the bombings.

Proxmire gave Knight's letter to Senator Harold Hughes, who was on the Senate Armed Forces Committee, and between March 28 and July, 1973, Hughes secured versions of the 1969-1970 bombing reports which were the sanitized official reports to which Knight had objected.

On July 12, Hughes searched further into the matter. During committee hearings at which General George Brown testified on his appointment to become Air Force Chief of Staff, Hughes asked Brown if the United States had conducted air strikes in Cambodia before May, 1970. Asking the committee to go into secret session, Brown told them that B-52's had bombed Cambodia in 1969-1970. Brown knew because he had been in Saigon as General Abrams' Deputy for Air Operations from August, 1968, to August, 1970.

Following the hearings on July 12, Brown returned to the Pentagon, reflected on his secret testimony, and decided to send the committee an explanation of the Cambodian raids. The "dual reports," he said, were not technically falsified reports because "they were not intended to deceive those with a security need to know...." This admission was hardly sufficient. During July and August, the Senate Armed Services Committee held hearings which fully disclosed Nixon's secret orders as well as the bombings between March, 1969, and April, 1970.

August 19, 1973   *GREECE PROCLAIMS A REPUBLICAN GOVERNMENT.*

Since the rebellion against King Constantine on April 21, 1967, the provisional leaders had elected a constituent assembly which ended the monarchy and approved a republican form of government. George Papadopoulos was elected President of Greece.

September 1, 1973   THE LIBYAN GOVERNMENT ANNOUNCES THE TAKE-OVER OF 51%
                          OF U.S. OIL CONCESSIONS.

During 1960 the discovery of oil reserves in Libya made that nation a major
producer of crude oil. Following the overthrow of the king in 1969, the military leaders under Qaddafi began to demand an increase in oil prices and new
treaty concessions with the West. In 1973, the government unilaterally declared that it must have a 51% share of all oil concessions held by U.S. investors.

September 11, 1973   A MILITARY COUP IN CHILE OVERTHROWS PRESIDENT ALLENDE,
                          WHO DIES. LATER, A U.S. SENATE INVESTIGATING COMMITTEE
                          INDICATES THAT NIXON AND KISSINGER HAD USED CIA OPERA-
                          TIONS TO DESTABILIZE CHILE'S ECONOMY AND ASSIST ANTI-
                          ALLENDE GROUPS.

The military coup against Allende was Chile's first overthrow of a democratic
government since 1932, a record unparalleled in recent Latin American history.
U.S. authorities had feared that Allende's electoral victory in 1970 was a
victory for Communist-inspired takeovers in Latin America. As a result, the
CIA used funds to buy anti-Allende votes and to aid opposition candidates.
The Nixon administration also suspended negotiations with Chile to rollover
its external debt. The United States wanted the debt to include funds covering Chile's expropriation of U.S. property in copper mines and the ITT Company. See October 24, 1970.
     By mid-1973, the Chilean economy was in disarray, leading to strikes
and demonstrations against Allende's rule. In June, miners, teachers, physi-
cians, and students went on strike. On June 21, Allende supporters and opponents fought a pitched, bloody battle in Santiago. Prior to the September
11 coup, Allende had averted several rebellions by diverse military factions.
     In August, shopkeepers, taxi drivers, truck owners, and professional
groups staged strikes. Allende had lost the support of the middle classes
and his overthrow appeared to be imminent. After General Carlos Gonzales
resigned as defense and army chief on August 23, Allende chose General Augusto
Pinochet Ugarte to replace him. Although Pinochet said he was loyal to
Allende, his loyalty proved shallow in September.
     The occasion for the military coup was Allende's announcement of his
intention to seek a national referendum creating a unicameral congress to
replace the two-house legislature.
     Pinochet now turned against Allende, taking charge of an organization
to overthrow the president. On September 11, army forces took over Moneda
Palace. Whether Allende was killed or committed suicide is uncertain; his
widow claimed the military murdered him.
     Following the coup, the CIA (according to the Senate Select Committee
on Intelligence Activities) spent $34,000 to finance a public relations cam-
paign which would give Pinochet a "positive" image and gain support for the
new regime. This was difficult because during the next months Pinochet executed many opposition leaders and enforced repressive measures against all
dissenters.

September 21, 1973   HENRY A. KISSINGER IS CONFIRMED BY THE SENATE AS SEC-
                        RETARY OF STATE.

On September 3, Secretary Rogers resigned in order to return to his law practice. The appointment of Kissinger was no surprise because as Assistant to
the President for National Security Affairs, Kissinger had worked closely
with Nixon to control U.S. foreign policy. Secretary Rogers had carried out
assignments in special areas such as the Middle East, but generally
Kissinger's NSC staff superseded most significant diplomatic activity of the
State Department. Kissinger's appointment as secretary returned the policy
apparatus to the State Department. Nevertheless, the power he had wielded
as head of the NSC allowed later appointees to this post to challenge the
role of the Secretary of State.

October 6, 1973   AN ARAB-ISRAELI WAR BREAKS OUT: THE YOM KIPPUR WAR.

Although throughout September there had been intelligence reports of war preparations by Egypt, Jordan, and Syria, Secretary of State Kissinger misread
the signals until the last moment. At 9 p.m. on October 5, Ray Cline of the
State Department's Bureau of Intelligence and Research concluded that war
would break out soon, but Kissinger continued to rely on his former NSC staff-
ers rather than the State Department. The NSC discounted Cline's report.
As a result, the secretary did not become alert to the imminence of war until
he received a telegram from Ambassador to Israel Kenneth Keating on October
6, reporting that Prime Minister Golda Meir expected a Syrian-Egyptian attack
that day.
      The timing of the secretary's information was vital because not until
the last moment did he realize that the Soviet Union was, apparently, not
following the expected détente prescription of influencing the Arabs to avoid
a war. Kissinger contacted Prime Minister Meir and successfully obtained
her agreement not to make a preemptive strike. In previous such situations
with the Arabs, Israeli strategy was to strike first. This time Golda Meir
altered tactics and Israel took only defensive action in the Sinai and the
Golan Heights when the Egyptian-Syrian attacks began.
      At 8 a.m. on October 6, Egyptian forces crossed the Suez into the Sinai,
and the Syrians attacked the Golan Heights. King Hussein of Jordan accepted
the role of simply mobilizing his army on the Israeli borders in order to
provide a threat which required Israel to man some defensive units along the
Jordan River.
      Although Kissinger believed the Israeli army and air forces would quickly
turn back the Arab armies, this situation did not materialize during the first
week of the war. Using Soviet-supplied surface-to-air missiles, tanks, and
MIG jet fighters, the Egyptian forces broke through the Bar-Lev defense lines
in the Sinai and made significant advances between October 6 and 15. In addition, the Soviet Union air-lifted huge quantities of arms to Damascus and
Cairo. Israel urged Washington to reciprocate by rushing Phantom jets and
other military equipment to Tel Aviv, but Nixon and Kissinger were slow to
respond. See October 13, 1973.

October 10, 1973   VICE-PRESIDENT SPIRO AGNEW RESIGNS.

Long the rhetorical champion of law, order, and "good faith," Agnew had been implicated in bribery and accused of income tax evasion. His resignation was part of an arrangement for dropping charges of bribery, conspiracy, and extortion. In return, Agnew pleaded no contest on the income tax charges and resigned as vice-president.

Nixon nominated Gerald Ford for vice-president and congress confirmed him. Constitutional provisions for this unusual process had just been provided for in the 25th Amendment to the Constitution, ratified in 1967. Ford was sworn in as vice-president on December 6.

October 13, 1973   NIXON AUTHORIZES A FULL-SCALE AIRLIFT OF EQUIPMENT
                        TO ISRAEL FOLLOWING A WEEK OF DELAY.

During the first week of the Arab-Israeli war, the United States failed to provide Tel Aviv with military supplies equaling those Russia sent to Syria and Egypt. Exactly why there was a delay is controversial. President Nixon was deeply involved in a crisis over the Watergate tapes and Vice-President Agnew's resignation. Therefore, most observers believe Secretary of State Kissinger played the leading role--with Nixon's backing--in the U.S. decisions. Kissinger, however, blamed Secretary of Defense James Schlesinger and his Deputy, William Clements, for the delay in aiding Israel.

More probable, however, is the interpretation that Kissinger hoped to manipulate Israel into realizing its dependence on the United States so that it would follow the secretary's plans to obtain a broad settlement between Arabs and Jews in the Middle East. In addition, Kissinger miscalculated Chairman Brezhnev's willingness to use the détente relationship to restrain Russia's Arab friends. Moscow knew in advance of the impending attack on Israel and, rather than warn Kissinger, Brezhnev sent large quantities of military supplies to the Arabs during the two weeks before October 6.

Between October 6 and 13, Kissinger's tactics were to seek a cease-fire resolution in the United Nations and to avoid sending Israel the equipment she desired. When talking with Israel's Ambassador to the United States, Simcha Dinitz, Kissinger implied that he was willing to send aid to Israel but that the Defense Department's bureaucracy handicapped his fast action. On one occasion, Kissinger asked Dinitz if Israel would pick up U.S. equipment in El Al aircraft whose tail emblem of the Star of David would be painted over. On another occasion, he told Dinitz he was seeking charter planes to fly equipment to the Portuguese Azores from where Israel could transport the equipment to Tel Aviv. These "games" of Kissinger's were designed to make him appear the champion of the Israeli cause even though his power politics objective was to demonstrate that he controlled Israel's fate.

Not until October 13 did Kissinger and Nixon agree to use U.S. military aircraft to rush supplies to Israel. During the first week of the war, Israeli forces had not been able to turn back the Egyptians, and the Soviet Union was rushing around-the-clock airlifts of equipment to Cairo and Damascus. In addition, proposals for a cease-fire had been rejected by Egyptian President Sadat. Finally, Ambassador Dinitz had threatened to go public regarding Washington's delay by appealing to friendly senators and the American Jewish community.

Once the White House approved aid to Israel the State Department quickly received Portugal's permission to refuel U.S. military planes in the Azores, and the Pentagon worked 24 hours a day to send Phantom jets, tanks, 155 mm. shells, and other equipment. Moreover, as soon as Israel knew the United States would replenish its military equipment, the Israeli army proceeded

with plans for a bold attack across the Suez into the African parts of Egypt.
This attack began on October 16 and quickly turned the war to Israel's favor.
See October 16, 1973.

October 16, 1973   THE ARAB STATES BEGIN A POLITICAL OIL EMBARGO THE SAME
                          DAY THAT ISRAEL LAUNCHES AN OFFENSIVE INTO AFRICAN
                          EGYPT.

Although the United States was not informed of the Arab oil embargo until
October 17, U.S. oil companies on October 16 began receiving telegrams informing them that oil shipments to the United States, Western Europe, and
Japan would soon cease. The Arab states had warned Secretary Kissinger that
if necessary, they were prepared to use oil as a weapon on behalf of Syria
and Egypt. After the U.S. airlift of supplies began for Israel, the Arab
leaders began to apply the embargo. On October 17, the Arabs announced a
10% cut in oil production. On October 18, Abu Dhabi instituted its oil embargo. Libya did likewise on October 19. On October 20 and 21, Saudi Arabia,
Kuwait, and Algeria inaugurated oil embargoes.
     As plans for the Arab oil embargo proceeded, Israel launched an offensive
into Egypt on the night of October 15-16. Using rafts to cross the canal,
Israeli commandoes reached Egyptian territory in force on the morning of the
16th and began their attack on Egypt. Led by General Ariel Sharon, the Israelis advanced rapidly. After 72 hours they were within 50 miles of Cairo.
At the same time, Israel began a counter-offensive against Syria, soon reaching artillery range of Damascus. The tide of battle had turned. By October
18, Syria, Egypt, and the Soviet Union desired a cease-fire as quickly as
possible. See October 25, 1973.

October 20, 1973   PRESIDENT NIXON FIRES ARCHIBALD COX, THE SPECIAL WATER-
                          GATE PROSECUTOR: THE SATURDAY NIGHT "MASSACRE."

Nixon's personal difficulties escalated during the summer of 1973 when knowledge of White House tape recordings of Oval Office conversations was disclosed. Nixon sought to withhold the tapes by suggesting that Senator John
Stennis should review the tapes and give summaries to the Senate Select Committee and to Circuit Court Judge John Sirica. Nixon's counsel also wanted
Archibald Cox, the Watergate Special Prosecutor, to agree to relinquish the
right to further subpoenas.
     When Cox rejected Nixon's proposals, President Nixon fired him and abol-
ished the special prosecutor's office. Attorney General Elliot Richardson
and his deputy, William Ruckleshaus, refused to fire Cox, who was Richardson's
appointee, and instead both resigned their positions.
     The American public responded with massive protests to Nixon's Saturday
night action. Over 250,000 telegrams of opposition reached the White House.
Subsequently, the president released the tapes to Judge Sirica and appointed
a new special prosecutor, Leon Jaworski.

October 25, 1973   A CEASE-FIRE IS FINALLY ACHIEVED IN THE ARAB-ISRAELI
                          WAR.

Within 48 hours after General Sharon's forces attacked Egypt on October 16,

President Sadat and the Soviet leaders realized that an early cease-fire was needed. On October 18, Ambassador Dobrynin gave Kissinger a copy of a Soviet proposal for a cease-fire and a total withdrawal of Israel from all occupied Arab lands including the Old City of Jerusalem. This proposal was quickly rejected by the Secretary of State.

Kissinger agreed, however, to fly to Moscow where he could work in consultation with Brezhnev in solving the Middle East crisis. Arriving in Moscow on October 20, the day that Nixon fired Archibald Cox as the Watergate prosecutor, Kissinger and Brezhnev worked out a cease-fire proposal which the United Nations passed on October 22 (Resolution 338). The cease-fire was soon violated because Egypt's Third Army Corps tried to break free of the Israeli army's encirclement. The Egyptian action and the arrival of more Soviet equipment in Cairo permitted Israel to tighten its grip on the Egyptians preparatory to a possible complete decimation of Egypt's forces.

Thus, another crisis occurred between October 22 and 25. A second cease-fire was approved on October 23 but it also failed on October 23. Blaming Israel for the violations, Brezhnev sent a personal message to Nixon which Ambassador Dobrynin read to Kissinger at 10 p.m. on October 24. The message seemed ominous. After urging that a joint Soviet-American force go to Egypt to restore peace, Brezhnev concluded:

> I will say it straight, that if you find it impossible to act together with us in this matter, we should be faced with the necessity urgently to consider the question of taking appropriate steps unilaterally. Israel cannot be allowed to get away with the violations.

About this same time, U.S. intelligence reported that seven Soviet airborne divisions had been alerted in Russia and Hungary and that additional Soviet ships had entered the Mediterranean Sea where Russia now had 85 ships. Although the accuracy of these reports was uncertain, Kissinger and Nixon assumed the worst, i.e., that Russia was ready for unilateral action in the Middle East.

Considering there was a "high probability" of Soviet action, Nixon took military and diplomatic action between 11:30 p.m. and 1:30 a.m. on October 24-25. He ordered a global alert of most U.S. forces. There are five degrees of U.S. alerts ranging from Defense Condition (Def Con) 5, which is the lowest form, to Def Con 1, which means war. At 1:30 a.m. Def Con 3 went into effect for all U.S. army, air force, and naval stations while Def Con 2 applied to the U.S. Mediterranean fleet.

At the same time, Nixon dispatched an answer to Brezhnev. He said Israel had not "brazenly" violated the cease-fire, asserting there was no need for a U.S.-Soviet force in the region. The United States could not permit unilateral Russian "action. Instead," he said, "non-veto and non-nuclear powers should comprise the peace force sent to the Middle East by the United Nations."

One flap of the Kissinger process on October 24-25 was his failure to consult with any NATO allies until the U.S. alert was underway. The British ambassador was piqued and reportedly told the secretary: "Why tell us, Henry? Tell your friends--the Russians." Other NATO allies were equally distraught, particularly because Nixon and Kissinger had frequently treated them in such cavalier fashion. If there was a genuine Russian threat as on October 25 as Kissinger later argued, the NATO allies might have to bear the brunt of Russian action.

Indeed, many observers thought Nixon conjured the Soviet threat and the alert in order to divert attention from Watergate and to show his decisive ability to deal with Russia. In such a context, there was no "probable" threat and no need for an alert. Nixon's letter to Brezhnev would have sufficed.

Whatever the circumstances which resulted in the effective cease-fire, it was achieved on October 25. U.N. Security Council Resolution 340 was passed 14-0 and accepted by the belligerents. The resolution provided for a cease-fire, a small-powers U.N. force to patrol the problem areas, and an international conference to finalize an armistice. The cease-fire became effective on October 26. The U.S. Defense Department ended its alert as quickly as it had been called.

Whether or not the alert was connected to Watergate, on October 26 Nixon implied in a news conference that it should be. In his usual rambling and unclear style, the president claimed the Soviets miscalculated because of Watergate. Nevertheless, he said, the Soviet leaders knew how Nixon had acted in Cambodia and in the mining of Haiphong Harbor in 1972. Thus, he argued on October 25, Brezhnev knew he had to yield when Nixon ordered the alert on October 24. See December 21, 1973.

November 7, 1973   NIXON INFORMS THE NATION THAT AMERICA MUST CHANGE ITS USES OF OIL AND GAS TO ACHIEVE OIL INDEPENDENCE BY 1980.

The Arab oil embargo, which began on October 16, had reduced the U.S. oil supply by 13%, which would reach 17% during the winter of 1973-1974, Nixon told the nation in a television address. Americans, he said, must conserve oil by reducing airplane flights, reducing home heating to 65° or 68°, and reducing automobile speed (50 to 55 miles an hour maximum).

On November 8, Nixon asked congress for legislation to provide $10 billion for Project Independence, in order that the United States could become self-sufficient in oil and therefore better able to conduct its foreign policy.

In addition to oil shortages, the Arab oil embargo led to large increases in oil prices. Iran did not join the embargo, but the shah more than doubled the price of his oil. Other OPEC countries such as Venezuela and Nigeria followed the shah's lead. These increases continued after the oil embargo ended in 1974, causing a new burden on America's already unfavorable balance of trade. See December 23, 1973.

November 7, 1973   BOTH HOUSES OF CONGRESS OVERRIDE NIXON'S VETO OF THE WAR POWERS ACT.

For some time, opponents of the U.S. war in Vietnam had sought legislation to limit presidential authority to involve the United States in war without the approval of congress or a declaration of war. President Truman, they said, set the precedent in acting against North Korea in June, 1950; the Vietnam war clearly indicated what they deemed to be the excessive power of the executive to act without the concurrence of the legislative branch.

The bill approved on November 7 began its legislative enactment on July 18, when the House passed the bill. This act required the president to report to congress within 48 hours after he committed U.S. troops to hostilities anywhere in the world. The president would have 60 days to gain congressional approval for the commitment. If he did not do so, the hostile action by the United States would have to stop. Congress retained power to act on its own to support ordering the commitment before 60 days passed.

Because the Senate version of this bill differed in details, it did not get through a conference committee to be approved until October 12. On October 24, President Nixon vetoed the bill. His veto did not hold, however. On November 7, the House overrode the veto by a vote of 284-135 (barely two-thirds); the Senate overrode the veto by 75-18.

November 25, 1973   *IN A BLOODLESS MILITARY COUP, GREEK PRESIDENT GEORGE PAPADOPOULOS IS OVERTHROWN.*

A military government was set up under General Phaidon Gizikis. On August 19, 1973, Greece had become a republic under President Papadopoulos.

November 30, 1973   DEFENSE SECRETARY SCHLESINGER ANNOUNCES THAT THE PENTA-GON WILL SEEK NEW WEAPONS PROGRAMS TO PRESERVE THE "ESSENTIAL EQUIVALENCY" OF U.S. NUCLEAR POWER SYSTEMS RELATIVE TO THE SOVIET SYSTEM.

The Middle East crisis and the Soviet violation of its détente pledges during the fall of 1973 caused the Department of Defense to calculate that the second round of the Strategic Arms Limitation Talks (SALT II) would not succeed. Therefore, as reinsurance, the United States had to equal or exceed the Soviet missile systems.

From this perspective, Schlesinger announced that the Pentagon desired the following:

1. a larger ICBM weapon because Russian ICBM weapons now had MIRV capabilities;

2. a mobile land-based missile system;

3. MIRV missiles for all existing U.S. missiles;

4. an accelerated production of ballistic missile submarines.

By the term "essential equivalency," Schlesinger indicated he wanted U.S. weapons to be equal or superior to Russia's in every nuclear category--land-based, manned bombers, and submarines. Opponents of this concept, including the NSC staff, calculated nuclear parity in terms of the overall equivalency of missiles possessed by Russia and America. Schlesinger's concept became popular with U.S. politicians who opposed détente and talked of Soviet superiority in land-based ICBM's, the one category the Soviets possessed in greater numbers than the United States. For this group the mobile land-based M-X missile became the weapon essential for U.S. defenses between 1974 and the early 1980's.

December 13, 1973   THE VIENNA CONFERENCE TO REDUCE CONVENTIONAL FORCES IN CENTRAL EUROPE ADJOURNS WITH NO PROGRESS.

The Vienna Conference of 19 nations opened on October 30. Its purpose was to achieve a mutual balanced-force reduction of conventional forces between

NATO and Warsaw Pact nations. After a month and a half of sessions, no agreements could be reached. On December 17, an article in the Soviet newspaper *Pravda* claimed that the Vienna conferees had developed more distrust because the NATO representatives proposed an alteration in existing force levels which would benefit the western European nations.

December 20, 1973   SECRETARY KISSINGER MEETS IN PARIS WITH VIETNAM'S LE
                           DUC THO.

This session, which proved to be Kissinger's final meeting with Tho, achieved no results. Kissinger urged that Vietnam should pull out of Cambodia but Tho refused.

Following the session, the State Department sent to all U.S. diplomatic posts a circular letter summarizing North Vietnam's frequent violations of the January, 1973, truce. The message concluded that "while we cannot predict their decision, the Communists clearly have a viable option to launch another major offensive" in Vietnam.

December 21, 1973   THE CONFERENCE ON THE MIDDLE EAST CONVENES IN GENEVA;
                           FOR THE FIRST TIME ARAB AND ISRAELI OFFICIALS EXCHANGE
                           VIEWS IN THE SAME ROOM.

Following the October 25 cease-fire agreement, Secretary Kissinger became the key figure in bringing together representatives of Israel, Egypt, and Jordan. On November 7, Kissinger met Egypt's President Sadat in Cairo. The meetings led to full-scale U.S.-Egyptian diplomatic relations as well as Sadat's agreement that Egypt would negotiate with Israel. Kissinger also visited Damascus, where he persuaded Syria's President Hofez Assed to offer a list of Israeli prisoners held by Syria. This gesture enabled Israel to justify the Geneva talks even though Syria refused to attend the December 21 sessions.

The formal Geneva sessions lasted only two days. With Kissinger and Soviet Foreign Minister Gromyko as observers, Egypt and Israel agreed that their military officers would meet on December 26 to settle the military problem along the Egyptian-Israeli borders of the Suez Canal. This was the beginning of a series of talks which returned those borders to their place as of October 5, 1973.

December 23, 1973   *THE SHAH OF IRAN ANNOUNCES INCREASED OIL PRICES.*

Rumors had begun circulating in October, 1973, that Iran and other nations which had not joined the Arab oil boycott after October 16, 1973, would increase their crude oil prices. On December 23, the Iranian government announced that its oil prices would increase from $5.10 per barrel to $11.65 per barrel. Other non-Arab members of OPEC (Nigeria and Venezuela) also adopted the $11.65 price. Thus, American oil shortages since November were now matched by the doubling of the price of available oil.

The shah first increased his oil prices on October 16 when the Arab boycott began. At that time, he unilaterally announced an increase in Iranian oil from about $3 to $5.10 per barrel. Thus the December 23 decree was Iran's second increase in three months in 1973.

1974

January 18, 1974   THE ISRAELI AND EGYPTIAN CHIEFS OF STAFF DISENGAGE
THEIR ARMIES IN THE SINAI. FOLLOWING FIVE DAYS OF
SHUTTLE DIPLOMACY, SECRETARY KISSINGER OBTAINS AN
AGREEMENT BETWEEN EGYPT AND ISRAEL.

After the Geneva Conference of December 21-22, Israeli and Egyptian officials
began to negotiate on December 26. When in early January the peace process
became stymied, Secretary Kissinger undertook a series of air flights between
Jerusalem and Aswan, where Sadat spent the winter months, in order to achieve
a peace formula. The final agreement grew out of a proposal by Israeli Defense Minister Moshe Dayan. It was based on the following five zones in the
Suez area:

1. an Egyptian Zone ten miles east of Suez in the Sinai with limited
   forces to patrol the area (ca. 7,000 men);

2. a U.N. buffer zone patrolled by a small-power U.N. force;

3. an Israeli zone in the Sinai;

4. two zones on each side of the Sinai in which no SAM missiles would
   be allowed for either Egypt or Israel;

5. the west bank of the canal, from which Israel would withdraw all
   forces.

In secret agreements, Kissinger gave Israel a memorandum saying that
Egypt would clear the Suez Canal, rebuild cities, and resume peacetime activities along the canal. The United States also agreed to "make every effort
to be fully responsive on a continuing and long-term basis to Israel's military equipment requirements." Sadat also agreed that Israel's non-military
barges could use the Suez Canal. Finally, both nations permitted the United
States to conduct aerial surveillance over the disengaged area.
On January 18, Israeli and Egyptian troops began withdrawal according
to the zonal plan.

February 7, 1974   SECRETARY KISSINGER VISITS PANAMA WHERE HE SIGNS A
STATEMENT OF PRINCIPLES FOR NEGOTIATIONS ON THE CANAL
ISSUE.

Following the U.S. veto of the U.N. Security Council resolution on Panama on
March 21, 1973, Secretary Kissinger decided to provide for a more conciliatory
American policy in Latin America. Consequently, in September, 1973, he appointed Ambassador at Large Ellsworth Bunker to renew discussions on the canal
with Panama. Previous negotiations begun with Panama in 1964 had resulted
in draft treaties rejected by Panama. Talks broke off in 1971 and were not

seriously undertaken again until Bunker's appointment in 1974.

Bunker's discussions with Juan Antonio TACK, Panama's Minister of Foreign Affairs, resulted in a Statement of Principles signed by Tack and Kissinger on February 7, 1974. In summary these principles were:

1. A new treaty will replace the 1903 treaty.

2. The United States will abandon the 1903 concept of "perpetuity" so that a fixed termination date can be negotiated. This was the most critical U.S. concession.

3. The treaty will provide for terminating U.S. jurisdiction in the future.

4. The new treaty shall return all canal territory to Panama but will provide for American transit and defense of the canal.

5. Panama shall have an equal share of the canal's benefits.

6. The new treaty will permit Panama to join in the canal's administration.

7. Panama and the United States will jointly protect and defend the canal.

8. The United States and Panama will agree on joint studies to enlarge the canal's capacity for new, larger ships.

Detailed negotiations to prepare the process for implementing these eight points would be continued between U.S. and Panamanian officials until a treaty was attained. See September 7, 1977.

February 11, 1974   A WASHINGTON CONFERENCE TO UNIFY THE WESTERN POWERS
                             ON AN OIL CONSUMER ACTION PROGRAM IS UNSUCCESSFUL.

On January 9, President Nixon invited the foreign ministers of Canada, West Germany, France, Italy, Japan, the Netherlands, Norway, and Great Britain to meet on February 11. The meeting's purpose was to unite the industrialized nations on a policy regarding oil supplies and prices. The nine nations could not agree, however, and disputes among the members caused bitterness, especially between the United States and European nations such as France, which preferred to arrange an independent deal with the Arab nations. Thus, the conference did not succeed.

February 13, 1974   *THE SOVIET UNION DEPORTS AND CANCELS THE CITIZENSHIP*
                             OF ALEXANDER SOLZHENITSYN, A NOBEL PRIZE-WINNING AUTHOR
                             AND DISSENTER AGAINST THE COMMUNIST GOVERNMENT.

Solzhenitsyn was sent to West Germany. Later he went to the United States where he argued strongly against the Communist government of Russia.

February 27, 1974   *AN ARMY COUP IN ETHIOPIA FORCES THE GOVERNMENT TO*
                             RESIGN.

Led by radical Marxists, the new leaders of Ethiopia gained complete control of the country on June 29, deposing the Emperor Haile Selassie on September 12, 1974.

February 28, 1974   THE UNITED STATES AND EGYPT RESUME FULL DIPLOMATIC RELATIONS.

Diplomatic relations between the two nations had ended during the Arab-Israeli war of June, 1967. On November 7, 1973, Secretary Kissinger and Egypt's President Sadat agreed to reopen their respective embassies and consular offices. This process was officially begun on February 28, 1974.

February 28, 1974   *BRITAIN'S GENERAL ELECTIONS GIVE NO PARTY A MAJORITY; ON MARCH 4, LABOUR PARTY LEADER WILSON FORMS A MINORITY CABINET.*

Both the Conservative and Labour Parties failed to gain 51% of the seats in Parliament. Between February 28 and March 4, Conservative Prime Minister Heath tried to gain sufficient Liberal Party votes to gain a majority. The Liberals rejected Heath's proposal, leading to Harold Wilson's decision to create a minority Labour cabinet, which gained sufficient votes to be installed on March 4.

March 1, 1974   A FEDERAL GRAND JURY INDICTS SEVEN KEY WHITE HOUSE AND CREEP OFFICIALS FOR VARIOUS FELONIES.

The grand jury wanted to indict President Nixon but Special Prosecutor Leon Jaworski persuaded them not to because of constitutional questions about indicting a president still in office.

March 17, 1974   THE ARAB OIL PRODUCERS LIFT THEIR OIL EMBARGO.

The Arab oil embargo had been set up in October, 1973, as a form of political pressure against the Western nations who tended to support Israel in wars against Arab nations, in this instance the current war between Israel, Egypt, and Syria.

In a meeting at Tripoli, Libya, on March 5, the majority of Arab countries agreed to lift the embargo. Led by the Saudi Arabian delegation, proponents of lifting the ban argued that the Israeli-Egyptian settlement indicated the crisis had ended. Libya and Syria wanted to retain the embargo, but were outvoted. Officially, the end of the embargo was announced on March 17.

April 25, 1974   *A MILITARY REVOLUTION IN PORTUGAL OVERTHROWS THE DICTATORIAL REGIME OF PREMIER MARCELLO CAETANO.*

Caetano and his predecessor, the dictator Antonio do Oliveira Salazar, had fought for 14 years in an attempt to keep control of Portugal's colonies of Angola, Mozambique, and Guinea-Bissau. The costly wars exhausted Portugal's economy. In addition, its young army officers learned to sympathize with the leftist ideas of the colonial nationalists.

   One of the revolution's first acts was to suspend the colonial wars and to grant independence to Portugal's three imperial possessions, to be effective at the end of 1975. Black rulers would gain control of Portugal's three African states; most of these leaders claimed to be Marxists.

May 18, 1974   *INDIA EXPLODES A NUCLEAR DEVICE.*

Using waste from the nuclear power plant's fuel supplied by Canada, India developed capabilities for nuclear weapons. India had been one of several nations which refused to sign the nuclear non-proliferation treaty.

May 31, 1974   ISRAEL AND SYRIA AGREE TO DISENGAGE THEIR ARMIES IN THE GOLAN HEIGHTS FOLLOWING 32 DAYS OF TALKS WITH SECRETARY OF STATE KISSINGER WHO SHUTTLES BETWEEN DAMASCUS AND JERUSALEM.

Although the Egyptians made peace with Israel on January 18, President Assad of Syria was adamant about his desire to obtain some territory such as the town of Quneitra from Israel. The Israeli government was not willing to give up its hard-won territory. As a result, these two nations continued a war of attrition both on the ground and in the air in the region surrounding the Golan Heights until May 29. The agreement provided for a U.N.-protected buffer zone between the two states and for limited-forces zones along the immediate boundary of each nation. The Israeli army pulled out of Syrian territory occupied during the war of 1973.

June 14, 1974   THE UNITED STATES AND EGYPT SIGN A STATEMENT OF PRINCIPLES OF COOPERATION WHICH CONTAINS A CLAUSE PROVIDING NUCLEAR FUEL TO EGYPT. SEVERAL DAYS LATER, A SIMILAR PROMISE IS MADE TO ISRAEL.

On a visit to the Middle East, President Nixon stopped in Egypt to meet with President Sadat. Before leaving Cairo on June 14, the two leaders issued a statement on the Principles of Relations and Cooperation Between Egypt and the United States. The controversial clause in this agreement provided U.S. aid in helping Egypt to develop nuclear power reactors and supplying fuel for this capacity. There were protests against this in both Israel and the United States because India had recently (see May 18, 1974) used waste fuel to develop a nuclear weapon.
   Nixon and Kissinger claimed that Egypt would have obtained this technology from the Soviets unless the United States offered it under strict regulations to prevent the Egyptians from using nuclear waste to develop weapons. Nevertheless, the reaction to this clause became so intense that the United States could not fulfill this agreement for Egypt.
   In addition to the statement of principles, later reports alleged that Nixon told Sadat that U.S. policy was for Israel to return to its pre-1967 boundaries. Reportedly, Nixon and Kissinger made similar statements to President Assad of Syria in a meeting in Damascus on June 15. Whether or not such verbal or written commitments on the Israeli borders were made has not been verified. If so, they were not considered binding on later U.S.

presidents but were part of the Nixon-Kissinger plan to appear to operate even-handedly with both Israel and the Arabs.

Meeting on June 17 with Israel as part of his tour, Nixon agreed that Israel would have access to the same nuclear power fuel and technology as Egypt. In addition, Nixon urged Israel to negotiate with Jordan regarding the west bank territory of the Jordan River. This was, however, an emotional issue in Israel because many Israelis believed the west bank should, like Jerusalem, remain under their nation's control. Prime Minister Meir said she could not negotiate this issue with King Hussein without a specific mandate from her people to do so.

On June 17-18, Nixon met with King Hussein. He explained the U.S. desire for Jordanian negotiations with Israel. Hussein was willing to conduct such talks but Israel was not. Nixon agreed to continue American military and economic aid to Jordan.

July 3, 1974   PRESIDENT NIXON LEAVES MOSCOW, HAVING ACHIEVED LITTLE
                        OF SIGNIFICANCE.

Nixon's visits to Brussels for NATO talks and to Moscow from July 3, 1974, had been designed for no reason except to boost the president's political status. In talks with Brezhnev on SALT II agreements, neither leader had cleared proposals in advance with their military leaders and, therefore, nothing could be accomplished. The ABM agreement of 1972 was amended to permit only one rather than two ABM sites. Agreements were signed to cooperate in energy, housing, and artificial heart research. But these pacts did not require a summit meeting. The concept of détente and goodwill was refurbished during the visit, but Nixon's future at home did not benefit, given the Watergate problem.

One incident during Nixon's visit caused him to be criticized on his return to America. U.S. television networks covering the visit had prepared a report on Russian dissidents to transmit to the United States. Just as a report began on Andrei D. Sakharov, the noted physicist and dissenter, the TV screens went black. Soviet technicians had shut off the reports. However, Nixon did not comment on this or urge Brezhnev to do something about Russia's repression of human rights. As George Will, a U.S. columnist said, perhaps Brezhnev knew Nixon's opinion of the press was not favorable.

July 20, 1974   *TURKISH FORCES LAND ON CYPRUS IN ORDER TO OPPOSE A*
                         GREEK TAKE-OVER AND PROTECT THE TURKISH MINORITY.
                         KISSINGER'S DIPLOMACY FAILS TO AVERT THE TURKISH IN-
                         VASION.

The Turkish attack resulted from a military coup d'état by the Greek military junta in Athens which overthrew Archbishop Makarios, who was president of Cyprus.

Although Kissinger knew in advance of the plan of General Dimitrious Ionnides to overthrow Makarios, he did not act to prevent the coup. Once it happened, Kissinger sought unsuccessfully to persuade Turkey not to send armed forces to Cyprus. The United States did arrange for a cease-fire on July 21, after Turkish army units were in position. Nevertheless, the groundwork was laid for renewed conflict in Cyprus. See October 18, 1974.

July 30, 1974   THE HOUSE JUDICIARY COMMITTEE VOTES THREE ARTICLES OF
                        IMPEACHMENT AGAINST PRESIDENT NIXON.

Following an extensive investigation of the Watergate cover-up and other reports of the president's activity since 1969, the House Judiciary Committee
found Nixon guilty of three impeachable offenses: obstruction of justice,
violation of his oath of office, and defiance of the impeachment process.
In an ironic twist, the president and vice-president (Nixon and Agnew) who
had campaigned for office on a "law and order" platform had been trapped by
their own rhetoric (see October 10, 1973, and August 8, 1974). This contributed to a general American disillusionment with politicians during the 1970's
thereby influencing foreign policy as well.

August 8, 1974   PRESIDENT NIXON ANNOUNCES HIS RESIGNATION, EFFECTIVE
                        AT NOON ON AUGUST 9, 1974.

Although the House committee's impeachment votes must have led the president
thoroughly to review his situation, Nixon did not refer to them in his letter
of resignation. The letter he tendered to Secretary of State Kissinger simply
stated that he resigned the office of president. Gerald R. Ford became president on August 9. He pardoned Nixon unconditionally on September 8.
     Once again using the 25th Amendment, Ford nominated Nelson A. Rockefeller
for the vice-presidency. Congress approved and on December 19, Rockefeller
was sworn in as vice-president.

September 30, 1974   *SEVERAL MONTHS OF POLITICAL DISPUTE END IN PORTUGAL*
                        AS GENERAL FRANCISCO COSTA GOMES BECOMES PRESIDENT.

A military coup in Lisbon overturned President Caetaro on April 25. General
Antonio de Spinola became president with Senhor Adelino de Palma Carolas as
prime minister on July 9. Carolas resigned and a new cabinet was created by
Colores Vasco Goncalves. Further difficulties led to Spinola's resignation
on September 30.

October 18, 1974   PRESIDENT FORD SIGNS LEGISLATION THREATENING TO CUT
                        OFF U.S. AID TO TURKEY.

Although the Ford administration opposed the congressional threat to stop
military and economic aid to Turkey, the movement to do so began in August,
1974, following the second Turkish attack against Greek rulers in Cyprus.
     The first Turkish troop landing on Cyprus occurred on July 20 following
the Greek military overthrow of Cypriot President Makarios. Soon after a
cease-fire in Cyprus on July 21, liberal opponents of the Greek military junta
in Athens overturned the rule of General Ionnides, bringing back a civilian
Greek regime under Constantine Caramanlis. Because the liberals continued
Greek efforts to dominate the Cypriot government, hoping to make it part of
Greece, Turkey broke the cease-fire on August 14, landed reinforcements, and
sought to conquer additional territory on Cyprus.
     Greeks in Athens and Greek-Americans in the United States strongly pro-
tested the Turkish invasion and blamed Secretary Kissinger for not restraining
the Turkish government. Pro-Greek lobbyists in Washington persuaded the House

of Representatives to pass an amendment to a funding bill for federal departments, cutting off aid to Turkey. The House amendment was vetoed by President
Ford on October 14. Because the House could not override the veto, a compromise was reached between Ford and the congressional leaders. According
to the compromise law, American aid to Turkey would continue until December
10, 1974, provided Turkey did not send additional military equipment to Cyprus.

This October 18 law did not end the crisis in U.S.-Turkish relations.
The Cypriot dispute continued and on February 5, 1975, U.S. aid to Turkey
halted. Turkey retaliated by closing down all NATO and U.S. bases in Turkey.
The U.S. bases had the vital function of monitoring weapons and missile activity in the Soviet Union. See July 24, 1975.

November 24, 1974   PRESIDENT FORD AND SOVIET LEADER BREZHNEV PLACE A CEIL-
                             ING ON OFFENSIVE NUCLEAR WEAPONS IN A MEETING AT VLAD-
                             IVOSTOK.

Since 1972, U.S. and Soviet negotiators had sought some formula to limit strategic nuclear weapons. As late as July 3, when Nixon left Moscow, the United
States wanted to limit the number of Soviet MIRV warheads.

Between July and October, negotiators sought a method to attain some
limit on offensive weapons because both nations already held overkill proportions of such weapons but for prestige neither wanted to have a total lower
than the other. In October, Kissinger visited Moscow to propose a formula
granting each side parity in overall offensive warheads. During their sessions Kissinger and Brezhnev reached an agreement which became the basis of
the Vladivostok formula. The Soviets agreed not to count the 500 U.S. bombers
based in Europe as part of the American strategic arsenal. This was a significant Soviet concession because U.S. aircraft in Europe could reach Soviet
territory and, heretofore, Brezhnev had insisted that they must be counted
in the total of U.S. warhead launchers. On the part of the United States,
Kissinger conceded that Russia could continue to fit its warheads with MIRV's.
The United States had been ahead in MIRV weapons and as part of the overall
parity, Russia could now build as many MIRV weapons as the United States held.

The Vladivostok formula as signed by Ford and Brezhnev was based on overall nuclear parity for the United States and the U.S.S.R. Specifically, the
agreement was an aide-mémoire designed to be the basic framework for a SALT II
agreement. The agreement included:

1. Each nation would have a 2,400 aggregate limit on nuclear delivery
    vehicles (ICBM's, SLBM's, and heavy bombers).

2. Each nation would have a 1,320 aggregate limit on MIRV systems.

3. No new land-based ICBM launchers would be built.

4. There would be limits on new types of strategic offensive weapons.

5. The new agreement would extend through 1985.

Originally there was expectation that SALT II might be finalized in 1975.
As negotiators began drafting a treaty to suit the Vladivostok formula, difficulties arose. The two critical concerns that prevented the conclusion of
SALT II in 1975 were: (1) how U.S. cruise missiles would be counted and
(2) whether the new Soviet Backfire bomber should be counted as a heavy bomber

under SALT II.   These questions were not addressed again until 1977 after President Carter had succeeded Ford.   See March 30, 1977.

December 7, 1974   *ARCHBISHOP MAKARIOS RETURNS TO CYPRUS.*

Between August and November, the new liberal Greek government agreed to re-store President Makarios as president of Cyprus and the Turkish Cypriot Rauf Denktash as vice-president.   Makarios immediately began seeking negotiations with Turkey to withdraw its invasion forces from the island.

December 20, 1974   CONGRESS REFUSES TO GRANT THE SOVIET UNION THE MOST-FAVORED-NATION TRADE STATUS, PLACING RESTRICTIONS ON U.S. TRADE WITH RUSSIA PENDING THE SOVIETS' LIBERAL-IZATION OF THEIR JEWISH EMIGRATION POLICY.

Opponents of détente with the Soviet Union complained that U.S. trade helped Russia but brought no reciprocal advantages to the United States.   They contended that the 1972 grain treaty resulted only in higher costs for U.S. consumers although U.S. farmers also profited from higher grain prices.

Senator Henry Jackson, a firm opponent of détente, proposed that U.S. trade policies should be linked with Russia's emigration policy, in particular, its limitations on exit visas for Jewish people desiring to leave the Soviet Union.   Thus, on December 20, 1974, congress approved the Trade Reform Bill with amendments which permitted lower tariffs for Russia only after the Soviets eased their emigration restrictions.   Both Jackson and Secretary Kissinger thought the Soviets were in sufficient need of U.S. trade to be convinced to increase the number of Jewish emigration visas.   Thus, Russia was not given the most-favored-nation status, an international trade principle which would have given the Soviets the trade benefits awarded to other nations friendly to the United States.   In addition, the bill limited Russian credits through the Export-Import Bank to $300 million, a sum which Secretary Kissinger denounced as being "peanuts."

Senator Jackson and Kissinger miscalculated the Soviets' reaction to the U.S. trade amendments.   On January 14, 1975, the Soviets rejected the American trade agreement.   The Kremlin considered its emigration policy an internal issue.   Rather than easing the Jewish emigration restrictions, the Soviets tightened them, cutting such visas to 13,200 for 1975, down from 35,000 Jewish visas in 1973.   The Jackson amendments were a grave blow to the détente policy of Nixon and Kissinger.

1975

January 8, 1975   TWENTY NATIONS MEET IN WASHINGTON AND AGREE TO RECYCLE
                    "PETRODOLLARS" TO AVOID A GLOBAL DEPRESSION.

Unlike the Washington Conference of February 11, 1974, which failed to deal
with the oil problem, the 1975 session was attended by representatives of
the developing nations and oil producing nations as well as the industrial
powers. The 20 nations agreed to add a $6 billion oil facility to the Inter-
national Monetary Fund (IMF) to help consuming nations pay their oil bills
and to give interest rate subsidies to 30 very poor nations. The $6 billion
would be borrowed from oil producers in order to recycle the assets those
nations held as a consequence of the greatly increased oil prices since October, 1973.
     During a separate session, 10 industrial nations agreed to set up a $25
billion "safety net" fund for emergency use by the "poor" nations. In future
meetings, the quota payments for each industrial country would be established.
The United States would contribute the greatest single amount, probably about
$7 billion.

January 8, 1975   *NORTH VIETNAM'S GENERAL VAN TIEN DUNG LEARNS OF UN-*
                    EXPECTED SUCCESSES BY HIS FORCES IN SOUTH VIETNAM AND
                    DECIDES TO STEP UP HIS ATTACKS.

During 1974, the truce of 1973 had completely broken down in South Vietnam.
The disputes at St. Cloud between the conflicting parties ended on January 25,
1974, and the International Control Commission could persuade neither the PRG
nor President Thieu to cooperate in settling disputes and the constant skir-
mishes along the cease-fire line (see March 19, 1973).
     Initially, from February, 1973, to February, 1974, Thieu succeeded in
grabbing territory and extending his control over the south. U.S. analysts
estimated in February, 1974, that the RVN had siezed 15% of the land con-
trolled by the PRG in January, 1973, including 779 hamlets and one million
people. Thieu also tightened his controls in the south, a policy which did
not endear him to his people.
     During 1974, however, the Communist leaders moved from a passive to an
aggressive effort to counteract Thieu's control. Once American forces had
withdrawn and U.S. bombing stopped in Cambodia, Hanoi secured a major advan-
tage because U.S. air support had been Thieu's biggest asset. Although in
1974 Nixon asked congress to give more money to Saigon, he could offer little
evidence to support his views because all reports from Vietnam indicated both
sides violated the truce and that until the fall of 1974, Saigon was the major
violator.
     Preceding the fall of 1974, Hanoi had built subtle but long-term needs
for their efforts against Saigon. Where the Ho Chi Minh trail had existed,
they built a road eight meters wide through the Truong Mountains. They laid

a pipeline into the central highlands of South Vietnam and recruited North Vietnamese men to help "unify" the nation. Because these build-ups did not appear as confrontational in South Vietnam, they seemed less harmful than Thieu's land-grabbing and suppression of all dissenters or "neutralists" in South Vietnam.

Subsequently, while Americans experienced the unusual historic events of Nixon's resignation and Gerald Ford's ascension to power, the North Vietnamese undertook small-scale aggression in the south during the fall of 1974. These probing actions disclosed weak support for Thieu among the local populace and the People's Defense Forces in South Vietnam. On January 8, General Dung learned that all of Phuoc Long province had been placed under Communist control.

Surprised but pleased, Dung speeded his plans for a 1975 offensive. He hoped to be able to make sufficient inroads into the south in 1975 so that he could win a victory in 1976. These plans, which Dung published in a 1976 account of the war, miscalculated the weakness of the Army of the Republic of Vietnam. After Dung began his large-scale offensive on March 1, 1975, ARVN's defense efforts crumbled quickly. See March 14, 1975.

January 22, 1975   PRESIDENT FORD APPROVES THE GENEVA PROTOCOL OF 1925 AND THE 1972 BIOLOGICAL CONVENTION, WITH U.S. AFFIRMATIONS ON THE SCOPE OF CHEMICAL OR BIOLOGICAL USES UNDER THE PROTOCOL.

Unlike the United States, many nations had ratified the 1925 agreement on gas and biological war weapons. Consequently, several attempts had been made from 1945 to 1975 to obtain the approval of the United States. In 1969, the issue arose in the United Nations, leading President Nixon to resubmit the treaty to the Senate. See November 25, 1969.

Between 1969 and 1974, the protocol had not been ratified by the Senate because of interpretations about its application to non-lethal chemical herbicides and tear-gas. To resolve these questions, President Ford affirmed in 1974 that under the protocol, America would renounce first use of herbicides in war excepting use "applicable to their domestic use" or their riot-control use in "defensive military modes to save lives...." Under these guidelines, the Senate ratified the Geneva Protocol on December 16, 1974. President Ford signed the ratification on January 22, 1975.

At the same time that the Senate ratified the Geneva Protocol, it also approved the Convention on the Prohibition of the Development, Production, and Stockpiling of Bacteriological (Biological) and Toxin Weapons and on Their Destruction. This treaty had been signed by the U.S.S.R., Great Britain, and the United States on April 10, 1972. Its ratification was delayed by the Senate until the U.S. position on chemical weapons was clarified. Following the guidelines adopted by the Ford administration for the Geneva pact, the Senate ratified the 1972 convention on December 16, 1974; Ford signed it on January 22, 1975.

March 14, 1975   *PRESIDENT THIEU OF SOUTH VIETNAM DECIDES TO WITHDRAW*
                      HIS FORCES FROM THE HIGHLAND AREAS AND CONCENTRATE
                      THEM ALONG THE COAST LEADING TO SAIGON. THIS BECOMES
                      A CRITICAL DECISION BECAUSE ARVN COMMANDERS HAD NO
                      PRECISE PLANS FOR THE RETREAT WHICH BECAME A ROUT.

President Thieu's decision reflected the quick success of the Communist of-
fensive which began on March 1, 1975. After cutting Highway 19 and 21 be-
tween the coast and the central highlands, North Vietnamese forces captured
Ban Me Thuot and threatened Pleiku and Kontum. Pleiku was the former center
of a large U.S. support base and had prospered during the war years. The
local populace was not secure, however, because General Nguyen Van Toan, whom
Thieu appointed in 1972, controlled the heroin trade and ARVN troops had been
corrupted by this illegal traffic as well as the addiction of 30% of the sol-
diers.
     On March 14, after conferring with other ARVN officers, Thieu decided
to retreat from Pleiku and Kontum and concentrate the ARVN defenses along
the coastal areas. The retreat from the two cities was a disaster. The
upper-ranked officers left quickly; the lower-ranked officers had no plans
to retreat. Command of the troops vanished. Soldiers mutinied, looted
stores, raped women, and left Pleiku burning as the Communists arrived. Many
ARVN troops had their families with them and they fled in trucks, wagons, or
by backpacking down Highway 19 toward the coast. About 250,000 people fled
the highlands.
     General Dung followed his advantage as quickly as logistical control
allowed. In the north on March 18, Communists captured Quang Tri and moved
south. Between March 24 and 28, the Pleiku chaos was repeated at Hue and
Danang. At Danang's docks, refugees and troops vied for the last boats to
Saigon while Communist forces shelled the beaches. Between March 1 and March
28, Thieu's forces lost two-thirds of their territory, half of their 1.1
million-man army and local defense forces, and most of the air force. Former
U.S. military equipment at Pleiku and Danang fell into Communist hands because
the retreating ARVN troops did not take time to destroy it. See April 29,
1975.

March 25, 1975   *KING FAISAL OF SAUDI ARABIA IS MURDERED BY HIS NEPHEW,*
                      PRINCE FAISAL.

The prince was disgruntled with politics in the royal palace. After an ex-
amination found him to be mentally sane, the prince was publicly beheaded
for his crime in June, 1975. The new Saudi ruler was King Khaled, with Prince
Fahd exercising the role of prime minister. The new regime did not alter
the relatively moderate policy of Saudi Arabia in the Middle East.

April 5, 1975   *CHIANG KAI-SHEK DIES IN TAIWAN.*

On April 6, Yen Chin-kar became the president of the Republic of China.
Following Chiang's death, his son Chiang Ching-kuo gained primary power in
Nationalist China.

April 12, 1975   *MOSLEM AND CHRISTIAN FACTIONS FIGHT IN LEBANON.*

Open warfare shook the precarious political balance between Moslems and

Christians in Lebanon. Phalangist Christian military forces, a private army led by Pierre Gemayel, fought against the Palestinian guerrilla bases which moved into Lebanon after King Hussein ejected them from Jordan in 1971. Fighting between the Phalangists and Palestinians first took place in May, 1973, leading the Syrian army to enter Lebanon in November, 1973. Cease-fire arrangements had been attempted but broke down in early April, leading to the large-scale battle on April 12 in which an estimated 150 Lebanese died.

April 13, 1975   *FIGHTING ERUPTS BETWEEN PALESTINIANS AND CHRISTIAN MILITIA IN LEBANON.*

There had been increased tensions in Lebanon since 1971 because the Palestinian refugees in that state had become aggressive under the leadership of Yasir Arafat of the Palestine Liberation Organization (PLO). The precarious balance between Moslem and Christian political officers became unhinged because the Moslem leaders claimed Christian army officers allowed extremists of the Phalangist militia to use anti-Arab tactics to quiet the Palestinians. Early in 1975, the Moslem leaders demanded the formation of military councils on which they and the Christian officers would jointly make decisions. Lebanon's President Camille Chamoun and the Phalangists rejected these demands.

An incident on April 13 caused large-scale conflict after gunfire was exchanged between Phalangist troops and Palestinian militants. Each side claimed the other fired first when a busload of Palestinians engaged Christian troops in a small-scale battle. Fighting spread to Beirut and other parts of Lebanon and large-scale rocket and machine gun attacks occurred during the next three days. Attempts to resolve the dispute and reassert the government's authority were not successful. No one knew at the time, but the April 13 incident ignited a conflict which totally despoiled Lebanon during the next decade.

April 17, 1975   *CAMBODIA FALLS TO THE FORCES OF THE KHMER ROUGE AS PHNOM PENH SURRENDERS AFTER A LONG SIEGE.*

Former president Lon Nol had left Cambodia for exile on April 1, turning the government over to General Saukham Khoy.

April 25, 1975   *PORTUGAL CONDUCTS ITS FIRST FREE ELECTION IN 50 YEARS.*

In the election, moderate political candidates received 70% of the votes; the Communists won only 16%. The Ruling High Council of the Revolution was still in power, however. The election offered the non-communists on the council--a mixture of military men and Communists--the opportunity to press for less radical economic measures.

April 29, 1975   THE LAST AMERICAN "CHOPPER" EVACUATES THE U.S. EMBASSY IN SAIGON.

The collapse of the South Vietnamese forces and government of President Thieu came faster than anyone, even the Communists, anticipated. Thieu's trained and well-equipped armies of 1973 displayed all the basic corruption, decay,

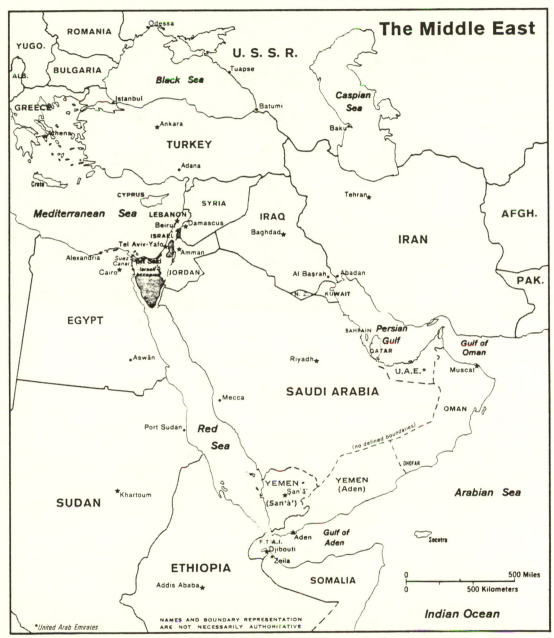

The Middle East

ROMANIA

YUGO.

ALB.

BULGARIA

GREECE

Odessa

Black Sea

U. S. S. R.

Tuapse

Batumi

Istanbul

Athens

Crete

Caspian Sea

Baku

★ Ankara

TURKEY

Adana

CYPRUS

Mediterranean Sea

LEBANON
Beirut
Damascus

SYRIA

IRAQ

Baghdad ★

Tehran ★

AFGH.

ISRAEL
Tel Aviv-Yafo

Amman

IRAN

PAK.

Alexandria

Suez Canal
Port Said
Israeli Occupied

JORDAN

Al Baṣrah

Abadan

Cairo ★

N. Z.

KUWAIT

EGYPT

Aswān

BAHRAIN

Persian Gulf

QATAR

Gulf of Oman

Riyadh ★

U.A.E. *

Muscat

Mecca

SAUDI ARABIA

OMAN

Port Sudan

Red Sea

(no defined boundaries)

DHOFAR

Arabian Sea

SUDAN

Khartoum ★

YEMEN
Ṣan'ā'
(Ṣan'ā')

YEMEN
(Aden)

Socotra

F.T.A.I.
Djibouti
Zeila

Aden

Gulf of Aden

ETHIOPIA

SOMALIA

0   500 Miles

0   500 Kilometers

Addis Ababa ★

Indian Ocean

*United Arab Emirates

NAMES AND BOUNDARY REPRESENTATION
ARE NOT NECESSARILY AUTHORITATIVE

The Middle East, January, 1975.

and self-centeredness of the high-level officer corps which Generals Ky and
Thieu created as a facade of power in 1967. While a few ARVN soldiers showed
skill and bravery during the final weeks, they could not make up for the
general decay of South Vietnam's military and political structure, which the
United States had been unable to influence between 1954 and 1973.

Throughout most of March, 1975, President Ford and Secretary of State
Kissinger worried more about Cambodia than about Saigon. Phnom Penh had been
surrounded for some time and the Khmer Rouge tightened its grip on the city
early in 1975. Eventually, Phnom Penh fell on April 17 after the United
States evacuated the embassy on April 12.

Regarding Vietnam, Washington officials were constantly beguiled by the
allegedly successful Vietnamization program of 1968 to 1973. Even after
Pleiku fell (see March 14, 1975), the Pentagon expected the "well-trained"
ARVN to counterattack as they had during the 1972 Easter Offensive. On March
24, *Time* magazine quoted U.S. military officials as predicting that Saigon
would soon establish "battle-field equilibrium." On March 31, *Time* praised
Thieu for his "gritty gamble to evacuate the highlands" and save the "body
of South Vietnam." U.S. experts gave Thieu "high ranks for his strategy of
retreat."

In retrospect, Saigon would have fallen earlier except for the gallant
defense of ARVN units at Xuan Loc on Highway 4 near Saigon. On April 28,
the RVN National Assembly announced that General Duong Van Minh had replaced
President Thieu. Because the North Vietnamese had previously offered to negotiate with a neutralist advocate such as Minh, the assembly hoped Saigon
would be spared. It was too late for negotiations. The Communists refused
to negotiate with Minh but accepted his surrender on April 30.

The U.S. embassy and its "friends" completed their evacuation late in
the evening of April 29. U.S. Ambassador Graham Martin delayed the evacuation
in order to provide exit for pro-American Vietnamese. On April 20, President
Ford ordered the immediate departure of U.S. personnel, and until April 29,
helicopters relaying refugees to U.S. ships tried to board all the people
they could. American TV cameras relayed the chaotic evacuation scenes back
to U.S. firesides. Less influential Vietnamese "friends" crowded to climb
the embassy walls and reach a departing helicopter. Finally, the last U.S.
helicopter left. Saigon had fallen to the Communists, following a "decent
interval" of 27 months since the truce of January, 1973.

May 15, 1975   THE *MAYAGUEZ* INCIDENT ENDS AFTER U.S. MARINES RESCUE
                            THE SHIP'S CREW FROM CAMBODIA.

This incident began on May 12 when President Ford learned that a private U.S.
cargo ship, the *Mayaguez*, had been fired on, boarded, and captured by Cambodian patrol boats 55 miles off their coastline in the Gulf of Thailand. Because the United States had no diplomatic relations with the Pol Pot regime
in Phnom Penh, Washington found it difficult to learn exactly what Cambodia
intended. Two other foreign boats had recently been harassed by Cambodian
patrol boats, but there had been no warnings sent to keep ships out of the
region.

On Tuesday, May 13, the president ordered 1,000 marines to fly from Okinawa to Utapao air base in Thailand although the Thai government, which had
not been consulted, protested this action. In addition, the aircraft carrier
Coral Sea and two destroyers were sent to the Gulf of Thailand.

On Wednesday, Ford appealed for aid to U.N. Secretary General Kurt

Waldheim. At the same time, however, the president and the NSC decided to take military action as soon as possible. Thus, without waiting for the United Nations to act, the United States began an assault against Cambodia on the evening of May 14 (Thursday morning in Cambodia). While U.S. helicopters carried marines to Koh Tang, the island where the *Mayaguez* had been taken, the destroyer U.S.S. *Holt* approached the cargo ship and marines boarded the vessel. They found it was empty. At 11:13 a.m. Cambodian time, a Thai fishing boat approached the destroyer. The fishing boat flew a white flag and carried the 39 *Mayaguez* crew members.

During the attack, one marine and one air force officer were killed; 14 Americans were missing. The casualties occurred during the landing operations when three helicopters were shot down. The assault may not have been necessary, however, because from 7:07 to 7:26 a.m. (Cambodian time) a Phnom Penh radio message received in Bangkok indicated Cambodia would surrender the *Mayaguez*. The marine assault began at 6:20 a.m.

June 5, 1975   *PRESIDENT SADAT REOPENS THE SUEZ CANAL TO INTERNATIONAL SHIPPING.*

The canal had been closed since the 1967 Six-Day War with Israel. During his discussion with Secretary Kissinger in November, 1973, Sadat had agreed to return the Suez operations to normal and to permit non-military ships of Israel to use the canal.

June 10, 1975   THE ROCKEFELLER COMMISSION'S REPORT ON THE CIA FINDS ITS OVERALL RECORD GOOD BUT NOTES SOME AREAS OF IL-LEGAL ACTION WHICH MUST BE REMEDIED.

Because there were extensive claims of illegal CIA activities, President Ford appointed Nelson Rockefeller on January 5 to head an investigative commission to study the organization's activity.

Following five months of study, the commission report, entitled "CIA Activities Within the United States," found that the agency overstepped the bounds of legality in some areas. The violations involved errors of judgment, not crime, in seeking to protect the national security. The areas where the CIA overstepped its bounds included: (1) opening the mail of private citizens since 1959; (2) preparing computer files on the names and actions of over 300,000 citizens; (3) experimenting with mind-expanding drugs on unknowing subjects; (4) giving President Nixon secret data on the Kennedys which was used for political purposes; (5) keeping a Soviet defector in solitary confinement for three years while checking on his credibility.

The commission also uncovered material regarding CIA plots of attempted or actual assassinations of foreign leaders during the Eisenhower and Kennedy administrations. President Ford directed that this data should not be made public, but it was turned over to a congressional committee on the intelligence services. The Rockefeller Commission recommended that a joint congressional committee should have oversight of intelligence agencies.

The Rockefeller Commission recommended that there should be an administrative reorganization of the CIA to prevent a recurrence of what did go wrong. It did not propose a fundamental alteration of the CIA's power as the predominant agency for U.S. intelligence gathering. Critics of the CIA claimed, however, that the Rockefeller Commission did not go far enough and that there were more serious actions and attitudes of the CIA which needed to be corrected. See November 21, 1975.

June 26, 1975   *INDIA'S PRIME MINISTER INDIRA GANDHI DECLARES A STATE*
                       OF EMERGENCY AND ARRESTS SEVERAL HUNDRED POLITICAL
                       OPPONENTS.

On June 12, the High Court of Allahabad disqualified Mrs. Gandhi for office for six years on the grounds of corrupt practice in the 1971 election in Uttar Pradesh. Mrs. Gandhi appealed the ruling and was allowed to stay in office.
    On June 26, Mrs. Gandhi said the emergency decree was necessary to safe-guard the country's unity and stability. Her opponents claimed she acted to secure her continuance in political power. On November 7, India's Supreme Court invalidated the Allahabad Court ruling against Mrs. Gandhi.

July 1, 1975   *VIETNAM IS UNITED AS ONE NATION.*

Following the fall of Saigon on April 29 and the unconditional surrender of the Republic of Vietnam, the effort to unite an independent Vietnam which began in September, 1945, became de facto. *See April 25, 1976.*

July 11, 1975   *BLACK NATIONALIST GROUPS IN ANGOLA BEGIN TO FIGHT FOR*
                       DOMINANCE AS PORTUGAL PROCEEDS WITH PLANS TO GRANT
                       INDEPENDENCE.

In January, 1975, Portugal's plans to give Angola independence by November 11 seemed to be going smoothly because the three nationalist factions said they would cooperate in forming an interim government. During the next four months fighting broke out, becoming more serious by July 11. In Luanda, the capital city of Angola, the Marxist Popular Front for the Liberation of Angola had gained control. It expelled from Luanda the Conservative National Front for the Total Independence of Angola. The third group, the National Union for the Total Independence of Angola, was much smaller and had not yet been involved in the fighting.
    Portugal tried to mediate the dispute but, thus far, had failed. There was a minority of 400,000 white settlers in Angola, but many of these had fled into exile in order to avoid involvement in the fighting.

July 15-17, 1975   APOLLO 18--SOYUZ 19: A JOINT U.S.-SOVIET SPACE VENTURE
                       TAKES PLACE.

As one of President Nixon-Premier Brezhnev's détente achievements, a joint space program was agreed upon. This was completed in July, 1975. The U.S. and Soviet spacecraft rendezvoused and docked while orbiting the earth, link-ing the two ships. Their crews exchanged visits and shared meals in space. Prior to the launching of the mission, the astronauts visited the space facil-ities of each other's nation. The American astronauts were Vance D. Brand, Thomas P. Stafford, and Donald K. Slayton. The Soviet astronauts were Alekseiv A. Leonov and Valeriy N. Kubasov.

July 24, 1975   THE HOUSE OF REPRESENTATIVES REJECTS PRESIDENT FORD'S
                        REQUEST TO LIFT THE ARMS EMBARGO ON TURKEY.

Ford requested $185 million in military aid for Turkey to make up for the
Turkish aid program which congress cut off on October 18, 1974, after Turkey
used U.S. weapons to invade Cyprus. Ford wanted the aid restored in order
that the activity of American military installations in Turkey could return
to normal. These bases monitored Soviet missile and troop movements.

      Arguing that Turkey violated the Foreign Military Assistance Act in using
the weapons in Cyprus, House members refused to renew aid to Turkey. In Washington, a large "Greek lobby" opposed aid to Turkey; the Turks had no similar
Turkish-American interest group.

      Immediately after the House vote rejected the aid bill, Turkey halted
all activity at 20 U.S. military bases within her borders. At President
Ford's urging, the House reconsidered the July 24 vote and on October 2 voted
to ease the Turkish embargo. The Senate rejected the change, however. Congress continued the embargo until 1978. See September 26, 1978.

August 1, 1975   REPRESENTATIVES OF 35 NATIONS SIGN THE HELSINKI AGREE-
                        MENTS WHICH LEGITIMIZE THE SOVIET UNION'S TERRITORIAL
                        GAINS IN EUROPE SINCE 1940 AND GUARANTEE HUMAN RIGHTS
                        AND THE FREE FLOW OF IDEAS IN BOTH EAST AND WEST EU-
                        ROPE.

After several months of negotiation at Vienna in 1974-1975, the Helsinki document was finalized in a three-day conference on European security. It was
called officially the "final act of the conference on security and cooperation
in Europe."

      A principal part of the agreement confirmed the eastern European bound-
aries established by the Soviet armies in 1945. These border "realities"
included the Soviets' absorption of three Baltic states (Estonia, Latvia,
Lithuania); Russia's takeover of Ruthenia (formerly part of Czechoslovakia)
and Bessarabia (formerly Rumanian territory); the shift of Poland's border
to the west, whereby Poland lost territory in the east to the Soviets but
gained German territory in the west; Rumania's acquisition of Transylvania
(formerly Hungarian); and the partition of Germany. This "ersatz peace
treaty" declared that the new frontiers were "inviolable." It also stated
that borders might be changed by peaceful agreement, a clause West Germany
desired in the hope that the two Germanys might one day reunite.

      The second part of the Helsinki document was designed to guarantee cer-
tain human rights in Europe. All nations ascribed to the concept that they
would permit more human freedom and free contacts between the peoples of their
nations. In order to evaluate better the "human rights" accords, the security
conference agreed to reconvene in June, 1977, to assess the situation. The
U.S. State Department emphasized the advantages of having the Soviets agree
to improve these rights; the Soviets emphasized the Helsinki agreement which
recognized the political boundaries which had existed since 1945.

      During the three-day meeting marking the Helsinki agreement, speeches
by Soviet Party Chairman Brezhnev and U.S. President Ford showed the divergence of interests of the two superpowers in signing the Helsinki accords.
Brezhnev's address emphasized that under the agreement, states could no longer
interfere in the internal affairs of another nation. Although some observers
thought Russia might no longer interfere in the affairs of its Warsaw Pact

allies, Brezhnev really meant the United States should not complain about human rights in or the emigration policies of the Soviet Union.

President Ford's message to the Helsinki delegates emphasized the accords as a method to improve the daily life of people living in both eastern and western Europe. Ford said, however, that the new agreement would be judged "not by promises made but by promises kept."

August 29, 1975   *VENEZUELA NATIONALIZES ITS OIL INDUSTRY, WHICH HAD BEEN LARGELY CONTROLLED BY THE SHELL, EXXON, AND GULF OIL COMPANIES.*

On August 29, President Carlos Andres Perez signed a bill passed by the Venezuelan congress which nationalized, with compensation, all foreign-owned oil companies. The companies, which were largely American-owned, would receive government bonds according to the net book value of their assets. On October 9, the Venezuelans fixed this compensation to the oil companies at $1 billion.

President Perez wanted foreigners to remain in the oil industry to provide expertise. Therefore, technical assistance contracts were to be made with the oil companies for the continued operation of the oil wells.

Unlike response to earlier nationalization projects (for example, that of Mexico during the 1930's), the U.S. response was calm. This was largely due to President Perez's efforts to retain the friendliness of the oil operators and to the State Department's prior experience with the need to recognize such oil take-overs.

September 1, 1975   EGYPT AND ISRAEL SIGN AN ADDITIONAL AGREEMENT ON BUFFER ZONES IN THE SINAI, SETTING UP AN EARLY WARNING SYSTEM ENTRUSTED TO THE UNITED STATES.

The agreement of September 1 was based on the January 18, 1974, Israeli-Egyptian pact. It provided a more sophisticated means of avoiding aggression by Egypt or Israel through the Giddi or Mitla Passes in the Sinai desert. At those locations the two nations would establish surveillance stations. The United States would set up three watch stations to be operated by 200 U.S. civilian personnel. Electronic sensor fields would be set up at each end of the pass. Any movement of armed forces other than the U.N. Emergency Forces would be reported by the American surveillance teams. See map of the Suez-Sinai area on page 1124.

September 5, 1975   PRESIDENT FORD ESCAPES AN ASSASSINATION ATTEMPT.

The assassination attempt was made by Lynette Fromm in Sacramento, California. Ford was saved when Secret Service bodyguards pushed the gun aside. Miss Fromm was a follower of Charles Manson, who was serving life imprisonment for the murder of actress Sharon Tate and others in 1969. Seventeen days later (September 23) Sara Jane Moore fired a shot at President Ford but missed. Both Fromm and Moore were tried and convicted of attempts to murder the president and given terms of life in prison, Fromm on December 18, 1975; Moore on January 16, 1976.

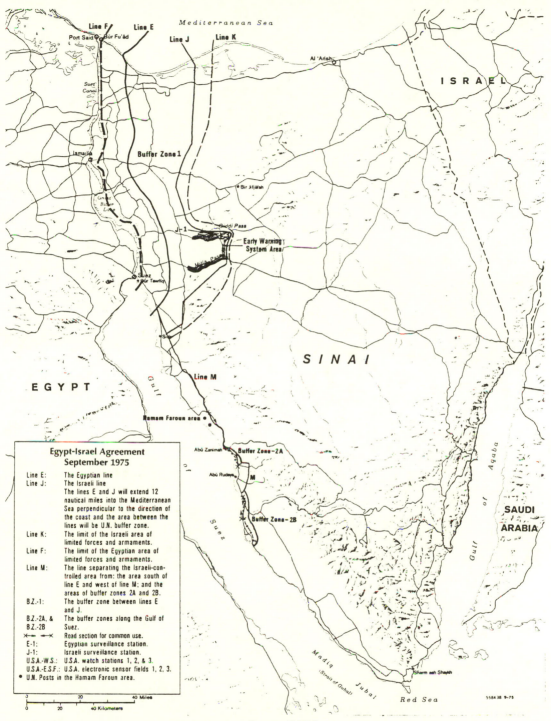

Line F   Line E   *Mediterranean Sea*
Port Said   Bûr Fu'âd   Line J   Line K

Al 'Arish

ISRAEL

Suez
Canal

Ismailia

Buffer Zone 1

Great
Bitter
Lake

Bir Jifjâfah

J-1   Giddi Pass
Mitla Pass   **Early Warning
System Area**

Suez
Bûr Tawfiq

Sir

SINAI

Line M

Hamam Faroun area

Abû Zanimah   **Buffer Zone-2A**

Abû Rudays   M

**SAUDI
ARABIA**

Buffer Zone-2B

Gulf of Aqaba

E G Y P T

Suez

Madiq
Jubal (Strait of Jubal)

Jubal

Sharm ash Shaykh

Red Sea

558438 9-75

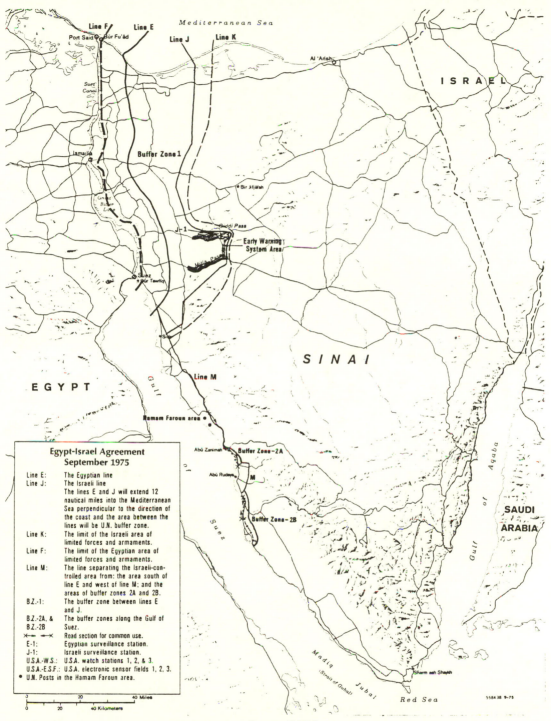

**Egypt-Israel Agreement
September 1975**

Line E: The Egyptian line
Line J: The Israeli line
           The lines E and J will extend 12
           nautical miles into the Mediterranean
           Sea perpendicular to the direction of
           the coast and the area between the
           lines will be U.N. buffer zone.
Line K: The limit of the Israeli area of
           limited forces and armaments.
Line F: The limit of the Egyptian area of
           limited forces and armaments.
Line M: The line separating the Israeli-con-
           trolled area from: the area south of
           line E and west of line M; and the
           areas of buffer zones 2A and 2B.
B.Z.-1:   The buffer zone between lines E
           and J.
B.Z.-2A, & The buffer zones along the Gulf of
B.Z.-2B   Suez.
✕—●— ✕   Road section for common use.
E-1:   Egyptian surveillance station.
J-1:   Israeli surveillance station.
U.S.A.-W.S.: U.S.A. watch stations 1, 2, & 3.
U.S.A.-E.S.F.: U.S.A. electronic sensor fields 1, 2, 3.
●   U.N. Posts in the Hamam Faroun area.

0   20   40 Miles
0   20   40 Kilometers

Egypt-Israel Agreement: September, 1975.

October 2, 1975   EMPEROR HIROHITO OF JAPAN BEGINS HIS FIRST STATE VISIT
                         TO THE UNITED STATES.

November 10, 1975   A U.N. GENERAL ASSEMBLY RESOLUTION CONDEMNS ZIONISM
                         AS A FORM OF RACISM.

This U.N. action was a strong rebuff to both Israel and the United States,
which had fought to prevent its passage. It indicated that the General Assembly make-up had changed since 1945. The United Nations had tripled its
membership in 30 years, most of the new nations coming from former imperial
and colonial regions previously dominated by the United States and western
Europe. These less developed nations were poor, non-democratic, non-white,
and hostile to the U.S. policy of promoting conservative and repressive governments which would accept imperialist controls over their people. The
United States had become identified, in the minds of oppressed nations, with
non-democratic and non-self-governing foreign policies outside its own borders. See November 5, 1977.

November 10, 1975   *ANGOLA OBTAINS INDEPENDENCE FROM PORTUGAL.*

*The Lisbon government decided to grant Angola independence even though the
three factions seeking power in Luanda had not given the nation a united government. Fighting for dominance continued. See July 11, 1975.*

November 20, 1975   *GENERAL FRANCO, SPAIN'S FASCIST LEADER, DIES. ON NO-
                         VEMBER 22, KING JUAN CARLOS IS SWORN IN AS SPAIN'S
                         RULER.*

November 21, 1975   THE CHURCH COMMITTEE OF THE SENATE REPORTS PREVIOUS
                         CIA INVOLVEMENT IN PLOTS TO ASSASSINATE FOREIGN LEAD-
                         ERS.

Between 1970 and 1974, there were many accusations of illegal covert activity
by the Federal Bureau of Investigation and the Central Intelligence Agency.
Because CIA action directly affected U.S. foreign relations, the investigation
of its activity particularly affected U.S. diplomacy.
     Two committees investigated the CIA during 1975. One, a "blue-ribbon"
panel chaired by Vice-President Rockefeller, began its investigation on January 5. On June 10, its report indicated the CIA exceeded its charter by conducting surveillance on U.S. citizens at home.
     The second, the Senate Investigative Committee, headed by Frank Church,
delved into CIA activity abroad. The most sensational finding of the committee was the CIA's involvement in assassination plots. Among nations where
the CIA's involvement was identified were Cuba, Zaire, the Dominican Republic,
South Vietnam, and Chile. The involvement varied in method, usually being
to encourage or pay parties already willing to conduct an assassination.
     Later in December, the Church Committee cleared the CIA of direct re-
sponsibility for the overthrow and murder of Salvador Allende. The CIA and
the Nixon administration had assisted anti-Allende groups in Chile, however.

December 5, 1975   PRESIDENT FORD CONCLUDES A FIVE-DAY VISIT TO CHINA.

There was no significant agenda for Ford to pursue in his talks with Chinese
officials. The tour was largely designed to project a favorable public relations image for the president and to confirm prior U.S.-Chinese friendship.
During this visit, Ford and China's leader, Deng Xiaoping, renewed the commitment of their two nations to the Shanghai communique of February, 1972.
Ford also restated orally the American commitment to remain a major power in
the Pacific Ocean.

1976

January 8, 1976   *CHINESE PRIME MINISTER CHOU EN-LAI DIES.*

Chou, who conducted the diplomatic discussions with Nixon and Kissinger in 1971-1972 was replaced as Prime Minister by HUA GUOFENG on February 8. Hua also became Chairman of the Chinese Communist Party on October 12, 1976.

January 11, 1976   *THE ORGANIZATION OF AFRICAN UNITY DEADLOCKS ON THE ISSUE OF ANGOLA'S GOVERNMENT.*

The OAU called an emergency meeting to resolve the Angolan issue but adjourned with no results on January 11. Twenty-two African states favored recognition for the Soviet-backed government of the Popular Movement for the Liberation of Angola; 22 other African states opposed this government. The 50-50 split prevented the OAU from acting. See November 10, 1975, and January 27, 1976.

January 26, 1976   THE UNITED STATES VETOES A U.N. SECURITY COUNCIL RES-OLUTION CONDEMNING ISRAEL'S SETTLEMENTS ON THE WEST BANK OF THE JORDAN AND CALLING FOR AN INDEPENDENT PAL-ESTINIAN STATE.

During the debate preceding the Security Council vote, U.S. Ambassador Daniel Moynihan strongly objected to a council decision to permit the Palestine Liberation Organization to sit at the council table and participate in the discussions, which began on January 12. The U.S. veto of this decision did not apply to the procedural vote of 11 to 1 which seated the PLO. As a result of this action, Israel refused to be present at the council debate.

The council debate of January 12 followed a series of violent demonstrations by Arabs in the West Bank territory occupied by Israel in June, 1967. The Israelis had begun settlements in this area and had conducted midnight searches of Arab homes in the West Bank. They had also detained many Arabs suspected of causing trouble. Between 1967 and 1975, Israel had set up 55 Jewish settlements in territory occupied in 1967.

On January 26, the Security Council voted on a resolution which stated that Israel should withdraw from all Arab territory and called for an independent Palestinian state. The vote, as on January 12, was 11-1, the U.S. veto preventing the resolution from passing. Great Britain, France, and Italy abstained.

Following a similar debate and resolution vote on March 22, the United States cast a veto against condemning Israeli settlement policy in the occupied area.

January 27, 1976   CONGRESS REJECTS PRESIDENT FORD'S REQUEST FOR AID TO
ANGOLA. THE HOUSE OF REPRESENTATIVES CONCURS WITH
PRIOR SENATE ACTION IN REFUSING TO PROVIDE $28 MILLION
FOR ANGOLA'S ANTI-COMMUNIST FACTIONS.

Between May and December, 1976, reports surfaced of the Ford administration's
covert aid of $32 million to support Angolan rebels opposing the Luanda gov-
ernment, which held the dominant position in that African state. According
to State Department officials, the Soviets had provided $200 million and
11,000 Cuban troops to support the Popular Movement in Angola. In December,
1976, U.S. news reports indicated the United States had given covert military
aid to two Angolan groups opposing the Luanda government: the Bakongo tribal
group, which led the National Liberation Front of Angola; and the Ovimbudu
tribal group, which formed the Union for the Total Independence of Angola.
The White House denied that Americans were recruited to fight in Angola but
would not comment on reports that Cuban refugees fought on behalf of the U.S.-
backed factions in Angola. South Africa also supported the U.S. factions in
Angola, but the apartheid policies of the Johannesburg government only served
to detract from the arguments which favored the U.S.-backed factions in Angola.
    In December, President Ford asked congress for additional military aid
to Angola even though he and Secretary of State Kissinger refused to apply
direct pressure on Moscow to stop assisting the Luanda government. The president rejected a proposal to restrict grain shipments to Russia and Secretary
of State Kissinger objected to suggestions that SALT II be halted unless Russia cooperated in Angola.
    Thus, in presenting the case for Angola to congress, Ford used only rhet-
oric to imply that the domino theory might lead to the spread of further Communist victories in Africa. Congress rejected these arguments, especially
because the United States appeared to be backing the weaker side in Angola.
The Bakongo and Ovimbudu tribal groups were not effective and refused to cooperate against the Luanda government. The breadth of congressional opposition to Ford's request is seen in the House vote of 323 to 99. Votes to end
aid to Angola were cast by 251 Democrats and 72 Republicans. See December 1,
1976.

February 6, 1976   LOCKHEED AIRCRAFT CORPORATION ADMITS BRIBERY PAYMENTS
TO OFFICIALS OF JAPAN, SWEDEN, THE NETHERLANDS, AND
ITALY.

In hearings of the Senate Subcommittee on multinational corporations, Lockheed
officials indicated that about $24.4 million had been spent in bribes to as-
sist its business operations in foreign countries. Later disclosures indicated bribes were also made to officials of Colombia, Spain, South Africa,
Nigeria, and Turkey.

March 1, 1976   PRESIDENT FORD TELLS NEWSMEN HE WANTS TO DROP THE WORD
DÉTENTE FROM HIS POLITICAL VOCABULARY.

Criticism from the right wing of the Republican Party, headed by Ronald
Reagan, caused Ford to move away from détente because it was a concept which
many Americans seemed unable to comprehend.

President Nixon and his advisor, Henry Kissinger, had never been careful to school the U.S. public in the nuances of power politics and the advantages of reaching mutual agreements with the Soviet Union. Following Nixon's resignation in August, 1974, Secretary of State Kissinger endeavored to deliver more speeches throughout the country to clarify his policies with Russia. From August 20, 1974, to early 1976, he made 16 such speeches in various parts of the country. He also sent four of his principal advisors around the nation to conduct town-meeting sessions on foreign policy.

Generally, however, these meetings convinced Kissinger and his aides that there was widespread disagreement with the administration's policies. Although experts on international affairs continued to laud détente and the power realities espoused by Kissinger, the U.S. public did not. Nixon's radical change from the moralistic, anti-Communist rhetoric begun under President Truman and carried on by Ronald Reagan and Senator Henry Jackson continued to rouse the anti-Communist pulse of Americans.

By January, 1976, many European observers stated they found Kissinger's rhetoric becoming more flamboyant in talking of "domino" Communist victories in Africa. One British editor stated that Kissinger's private comments were "reminiscent of John Foster Dulles" as he talked of dominoes in Europe if the Italian Communists should be elected, leading to Communist governments in Paris, Madrid, and Lisbon as well. Such signs indicated that Kissinger as well as Ford was ready to end détente as a U.S.-Soviet policy whose time had not yet arrived.

March 11, 1976   THE NEW YORK PORT AUTHORITY BANS THE LANDING OF THE
                        BRITISH-FRENCH SUPERSONIC AIRCRAFT *CONCORDE*.

The *Concorde*'s flights from Paris and London to Washington began in April but were delayed in gaining permission to land in New York.

The State of New York had passed legislation barring any planes with excessive noise levels from landing in the state. The New York Port Authority, which had jurisdiction over Kennedy International Airport, ruled that the *Concorde* could not land until its noise levels were evaluated elsewhere.

As a consequence, while the *Concorde* began scheduled flights to the Washington, D.C., airport on May 24, it did not receive this privilege from Kennedy Airport until 1977. During the intervening year and a half, courts in New York continued the ban against the *Concorde*. The French government protested to the State Department, causing ill will between France and the United States. Eventually, on October 19, 1977, the U.S. Supreme Court ruled that the New York ban was illegal because it conflicted with federal regulations approving the landing of the *Concorde* in New York. On November 22, the French and British SST airliners began regular service from Kennedy Airport.

March 14, 1976   *EGYPT ENDS ITS 1971 TREATY OF FRIENDSHIP WITH THE SO-*
                        VIET UNION.

Prime Minister Sadat distrusted the Soviet advisors in Egypt. Soon after, Sadat undertook talks for a treaty with Communist China.

March 18, 1976   THE UNITED STATES STOPS ALL AID TO INDIA.

The halting of U.S. aid to India resulted because negotiations about economic assistance broke down in February, 1976. Washington was upset because Prime Minister Indira Gandhi accused the CIA of trying to undermine her government. The amount of aid involved totaled about $65 million for 1976.

March 24, 1976   *A MILITARY COUP IN ARGENTINA OVERTHROWS PRESIDENT MARIA ESTELLA PERÓN.*

Señora Perón was found guilty of embezzlement by Argentinian courts on October 25. Following the coup, General Jorge Videla was named president by the military junta.

March 28, 1976   *SEVERAL NATIONS IN SOUTHEAST ASIA FORM A TREATY OF FRIENDSHIP AND COOPERATION.*

The nations signing this agreement were the Philippines, Singapore, Malaysia, Thailand, and Indonesia.

April 5, 1976   *JAMES CALLAGHAN REPLACES HAROLD WILSON AS PRIME MINISTER OF BRITAIN'S LABOUR CABINET.*

Wilson announced his retirement on March 16, 1976. On the third ballot of the Labour members, Callaghan received 176 votes to 137 for Michael Foot.

April 5, 1976   *CAMBODIA'S PRINCE NORODOM SIHANOUK RESIGNS AS HEAD OF STATE IN FAVOR OF KHIEU SAMPHAN.*

April 7, 1976   *RIOTS IN PEKING, CHINA, LEAD TO THE DISMISSAL OF DENG XIAOPING AND APPOINTMENT OF HUA GUOFENG AS PRIME MINISTER AND FIRST DEPUTY CHAIRMAN OF THE CHINESE COMMUNIST PARTY.*

April 25, 1976   *ELECTIONS IN VIETNAM REUNITE THE TWO HALVES OF THE NATION, WHICH HAD BEEN DIVIDED SINCE THE GENEVA CONFERENCE OF 1954.*

The official unification became effective on June 24, 1976.

May 28, 1976   THE UNITED STATES AND THE U.S.S.R. SIGN A TREATY ON NON-MILITARY NUCLEAR EXPLOSIONS.

The treaty limited any single underground nuclear test to the equivalent of 150,000 tons of TNT. If any explosion exceeded this limit, the other side had the right to an on-site inspection. In practice, no inspections were anticipated because neither nation planned larger explosion tests.

June 4, 1976   *THE PALESTINE LIBERATION ORGANIZATION (PLO) GAINS REC-*
                      OGNITION AS A MEMBER OF THE INTERNATIONAL LABOR ORGA-
                      NIZATION AT THE WORLD EMPLOYMENT CONFERENCE IN GENEVA.

Under Yasar Arafat's leadership, the PLO sought greater recognition from vari-
ous U.N. affiliates such as the ILO. On January 27, 1976, the PLO became a
member of the U.N. Conference on Trade and Development. On September 6, it
became a member of the Arab League.

June 16, 1976   IN LEBANON, THE U.S. AMBASSADOR, FRANCIS E. MELOY, JR.,
                      AND HIS ECONOMIC COUNSELOR, ROBERT O. WARING, ARE SHOT
                      AND KILLED.

The two Americans were shot while en route to a meeting; their bodies were
abandoned in a garbage dump. The United States and Great Britain immediately
planned to evacuate Americans and British in Lebanon. For further data on
Lebanon's problems see April 13, 1975, and November 8, 1976.

June 30, 1976   *A TWO-DAY MEETING OF EUROPE'S COMMUNIST PARTIES ENDS,*
                      DECLARING THAT EACH NATIONAL PARTY IS INDEPENDENT AND
                      EQUAL TO OTHER PARTIES.

Although this conference ended the myth of the Communist monolith as con-
trolled by Moscow, it also reflected realities because Moscow continued to
control wherever it had military forces, while Communist Parties outside the
Soviet orbit followed, as they often had previously, their own national at-
titudes toward Communist methods and local policies. Nevertheless, the con-
ference dramatized the new tactic of non-Soviet parties which emphasized their
separate programs for their nation's particular Communist Party needs.

July 4, 1976   *ISRAELI COMMANDOS ATTACK THE AIRPORT AT ENTEBBE,*
                      UGANDA, FREEING 98 JEWISH CAPTIVES AND THE CREW OF A
                      HIJACKED AIR FRANCE AIRCRAFT.

Palestinian terrorists took over the Air France plane in the air near Athens,
forcing the pilot to fly to Entebbe, Uganda, on June 30. The next day, all
non-Jewish passengers were released.
     The Israeli commandos flew to Entebbe where they attacked the hangar
where the hostages were held. Three hostages were killed; one was wounded
and taken to an Entebbe hospital where she (Dora Block) was allegedly mur-
dered. Generally, the Israeli raid was successful.

July 20, 1976   THE U.S. SPACECRAFT *VIKING* LANDS ON MARS AND TRANSMITS
                      PHOTOGRAPHS TO EARTH.

On September 3, *Viking 2* landed on Mars.

August 18, 1976   AT PANMUNJOM, KOREA, NORTH KOREAN FORCES ATTACK AND
                        KILL TWO U.S. ARMY OFFICERS. THE INCIDENT ENDS WITH
                        A NORTH KOREAN APOLOGY ON AUGUST 21.

The North Koreans attacked a U.N. Forces contingent in the Joint Security
Area at Panmunjom. The U.N. group was trimming trees in the area in order
to permit two U.N. command posts to see each other, when 30 North Korean soldiers appeared on the scene. They asked the U.N. officials to stop their
work, and when they refused, the North Koreans attacked the U.N. forces personally, beating them with axe handles and clubs. The U.N. commanders suffered the worst beatings and died. They were Captain Arthur G. Bonifas and
Lieutenant Mark T. Barrett.

American officials in Korea believed the incident was part of North Korea's attempt to publicize tensions between U.S. and Korean troops, hoping
the United States would withdraw.

The American reaction was to order U.S. F-4 and F-111 aircraft to move
up from Okinawa and Idaho. The Pentagon also sent the Midway naval task force
into the area and raised the region's alert status to Def Con 3. In addition,
on August 21, a U.N. work team under heavy guard went to the Security Defense
Area at Panmunjom and cut down the tree which previously was only being
trimmed.

On August 21, North Korea's President Kim Il-sung sent an unprecedented
message to the Korean U.N. headquarters. Kim expressed his regret at the
incident and hoped such incidents could be prevented in the future. The U.N.
command believed its response affirmed U.N. rights in the area and successfully
calmed the incident.

September 9, 1976   *MAO TSE-TUNG DIES.*

As leader of the Chinese Communist Party since 1927, Mao directed the People's
Republic of China from 1949 until his death. On November 12, HUA GUOFENG
became the new Chinese Communist Chairman. He and his colleagues soon
launched attacks against the radical leaders of the "Cultural Revolution."
Mao's widow, Chiang Ch'ing, and the radical "gang of four" were arrested
by Hua's regime, pending later trial by the courts. On November 2, Li Hsien-
nieu became the Prime Minister of China. Li and Hua redirected China's poli-
cies toward modernization in contrast to the rural-oriented program that the
"gang of four" gave to China from 1966 to 1976.

November 2, 1976   JAMES EARL "JIMMY" CARTER IS ELECTED PRESIDENT.

Running against Gerald Ford, whom the Republicans nominated on August 19,
Carter advocated reforms in Washington to cut government costs and emphasized
human rights in foreign affairs. Ford's platform upheld the Nixon-Kissinger
policies except for deemphasizing détente with the Soviet Union (see March 1,
1976). Ford's principal opponent before the August convention was Ronald
Reagan, whose strong conservative group claimed that Nixon's détente policy
had weakened the United States in relation to the Soviet Union. Carter
avoided making any definitive statements on détente, and his foreign policies
were never clarified prior to the election.

In the November 2 ballot, Carter received 297 electoral votes to Ford's
241. This was the closest election since the Nixon-Kennedy campaign of 1960.

November 8, 1976   *SYRIA OCCUPIES LEBANON IN A "PEACEKEEPING" ROLE DE-*
                       SIGNED TO END 19 MONTHS OF CIVIL WAR IN LEBANON.

Fighting between PLO, Lebanese Christian, and Lebanese Muslim forces had de-
fied solution for over a year. Between April and August, 1976, Syrian forces
moved into eastern Lebanon to restore peace, and in October an Arab League
plan provided for Syria's temporary occupation until Lebanon restored an or-
derly government. On November 8, Syrian forces entered the regions of western
Lebanon and on November 10 occupied Beirut. Lebanon's President Elias Sarkis
now had to reorganize a new compromise government, hoping to regain the peace
that had existed before 1975.

November 15, 1976   THE UNITED STATES VETOES VIETNAM'S APPLICATION TO JOIN
                        THE UNITED NATIONS.

The principal reason that Washington opposed Vietnam's membership was the
claim that Hanoi did not cooperate in giving data about 795 Americans listed
as missing in Vietnam. Although the two countries were conducting talks in
Paris about the missing Americans, Vietnam had not satisfied the U.S. delegates by the information provided.

December 1, 1976   WITH THE UNITED STATES ABSTAINING, ANGOLA BECOMES THE
                       146TH MEMBER OF THE UNITED NATIONS.

Following the end of U.S. aid to the opponents of the government of President
Agestinho Neto of Angola, the triumph of the Luanda regime became certain
(see January 27, 1976). By October 1, 1976, Portugal recognized Neto's government as the successor to the former Portuguese colony. On November 10,
Neto and Leonid Brezhnev signed a 20-year friendship treaty in Moscow. Nevertheless, when Angola's membership in the United Nations was voted on, the
United States decided to abstain rather than veto the membership. As early
as February 21, 1976, the State Department told the Gulf Oil Company and
Boeing Aircraft Corporation they could undertake business deals with Neto's
government.

December 1, 1976   *JOSÉ LOPEZ PORTILLO BECOMES PRESIDENT OF MEXICO.*

December 16, 1976   *OPEC INCREASES OIL PRICES IN A MEETING AT QATAR.*

Although Saudi Arabia and the United Arab Emirates agreed only to a 5% in-
crease, the other 11 OPEC members raised their oil prices by 10%. Saudi Ara-
bia not only announced a smaller price increase but indicated it would in-
crease its oil production. Some observers believed that the Saudi oil min-
ister, Sheik Ahmed Zaki Yamani, was indicating to President-elect Carter that
he should pressure Israel to be more flexible in solving Middle East problems.

1977

January 20, 1977   CYRUS VANCE IS COMMISSIONED AS SECRETARY OF STATE.

Vance was a New York lawyer who had held diplomatic posts in both the Kennedy and Johnson administrations. Thus, he provided a link of continuity with the eastern foreign policy establishment.

As his National Security Advisor, President Carter selected Zbigniew BRZEZINSKI, a professor of international relations whose views often differed from Henry Kissinger's. Vance and Brzezinski soon began competing to determine whose advice Carter would follow.

January 26, 1977   TWO YOUNG AMERICANS ARE INDICTED FOR SELLING THE SOVIET
                            UNION DATA ON U.S. SPACE SATELLITE SYSTEMS USED TO
                            GATHER INTELLIGENCE ABOUT SOVIET WEAPONS.

Christopher Boyce and Andrew Daulton Lee of Palos Verdes, California, were indicted by a federal grand jury in Los Angeles on 12 counts of espionage. Lee had been arrested near the Russian embassy in Mexico City on January 6, 1977. A heroin addict and fugitive from justice in California, Lee had relayed data obtained by Boyce to Russian agents in Mexico between 1975 and January, 1977. Boyce was a $140-a-week clerk at the TRW Defense and Space Systems Group in Redondo Beach, California.

TRW was the Thompson-Ramo-Woolridge Corporation, which since 1959 had worked on U.S. intercontinental missile systems such as Atlas, Titan, Thor, and Minuteman. Since 1960, TRW had experimented with and operated for the Defense Department more than a dozen earth satellite projects in order to collect data about Soviet weapons. It also processed and analyzed the data for the Pentagon.

Within five months after going to work for TRW in 1974, Boyce had a security clearance for the highest TRW special project at the Redondo Beach plant: Project Rhyolite. This was a covert electronic surveillance system, which monitored activity in the U.S.S.R. and China. Boyce worked as a clerk in the code room which linked ground stations placed secretly in Australia with the CIA in Washington. During the next two years, Boyce also had contact with Project Argus, an advanced Rhyolite system. He also handled plans for Project 20,030-Pyramid, a futuristic scheme for TRW space satellite systems.

Following his arrest, Boyce cooperated with U.S. intelligence authorities in attempting to recall all the data he had photographed and given to the Russians through Lee, but he had not kept a systematic account of the data he copied. At the least, the Russians gained data to decode the telemetry reports used by the United States. They also changed all their codes for future messages sent from their satellites.

On September 12, 1977, having been found guilty on eight counts of espionage and conspiracy to commit espionage, Boyce was sentenced to 40 years in prison. In a separate trial, Lee was also found guilty of espionage and sentenced to life imprisonment. Boyce's lesser sentence was due to his cooperation in trying to recall all possible data he had delivered to Lee. On January 21, 1980, Chris Boyce escaped from Lompoc Prison, California. He was recaptured on August 22, 1981.

The data given to the Russians by Boyce and Lee seriously handicapped U.S. intelligence-gathering systems for the next several years. Some opponents of SALT II after it was signed by the United States and Russia in 1979 claimed that America's verification system of Russian weapons was in such disarray since 1977 that the United States could not know if SALT I had been violated or if SALT II might be violated by the U.S.S.R. Even though Project 20,030-Pyramid was cancelled by TRW, knowledge of its future U.S. expectations would assist Soviet intelligence operations in learning to counter the American satellite spy system. Prior to the Lee-Boyce case, U.S. spy satellite operations had been secret. President Carter did not publicly admit their existence until October, 1978.

February 17, 1977   PRESIDENT CARTER SENDS A PERSONAL LETTER TO SOVIET
                             DISSIDENT ANDREI SAKHAROV WHICH SUPPORTS SAKHAROV'S
                             DISSENTING BELIEFS.

In accordance with his 1976 campaign position on U.S. concern for human rights, President Carter issued a number of statements in February, 1977, criticizing human rights restrictions in the Soviet bloc. Carter's most dramatic effort was a letter to Soviet physicist Sakharov. Carter told Sakharov he would ask the U.N. Human Rights Commission to investigate the arrest of dissidents in Russia.

The Soviet government denounced Carter for interfering in their internal affairs, insisting that the United States should first improve human rights in some of the dictatorships it supported in Latin America and Africa.

March 9, 1977   PRESIDENT CARTER ANNOUNCES THE UNITED STATES WILL WITH-
                             DRAW ABOUT 30,000 TROOPS FROM SOUTH KOREA DURING THE
                             NEXT THREE OR FOUR YEARS.

Carter stated that the United States considered that during the past 25 years, South Korea's ability to defend itself had reached the point where the American reduction of forces was feasible. The decision, he said, did not affect America's continued treaty to defend South Korea if necessary. See July 20, 1979.

March 16, 1977   *IN LEBANON, KAMAL JUMBLATT, THE CHIEFTAIN OF THE DRUSE*
                           MUSLIM SECT, IS ASSASSINATED.

Although the Syrian occupation of November, 1976, was designed to resolve Lebanon's internal problems, it had not done so. Frequent riots and terrorist attacks by Druse, Christian Phalangist militia, and Muslims continued in 1977, and included Jumblatt's assassination. On March 18, 1977, Kamal's only son, Walid Jumblatt, became head of the Druse sect and leader of the Progressive Socialist Party in Lebanon.

March 24, 1977   THE UNITED STATES AND CUBA INAUGURATE OFFICIAL TALKS
                     REGARDING FISHING ZONES AND NORMALIZING RELATIONS.

During the next two months these talks made some progress in instituting new
diplomatic ties. In early June, the two nations announced that Cuba would
establish an "interest section" in Washington; the United States would do
likewise in Havana. Nevertheless, the negotiations were tense and each side
seemed reluctant to go too far in the direction of friendship.

March 30, 1977   SECRETARY OF STATE VANCE INFORMS REPORTERS THAT THE
                     SOVIETS HAVE REJECTED AN ARMS LIMITATION PROPOSAL PRE-
                     PARED BY THE CARTER ADMINISTRATION.

According to Vance, who met with reporters in Moscow after sessions with the
Soviets' General Secretary Brezhnev and Foreign Minister Gromyko, the Russians
simply rejected the Carter proposals as inequitable.
    Hoping to go beyond the Vladivostok formula of November, 1974, to achieve
a reduction of nuclear armaments, Vance and Carter suggested two proposals to
Brezhnev:

1. to sign a SALT II treaty based on the Vladivostok formula but to
    defer for the future the controversy over cruise missiles and the
    Backfire bomber;

2. to proceed with SALT III discussions to obtain a comprehensive pro-
    posal for progress in arms control by reducing nuclear weapons. This
    second proposal would (a) substantially reduce the aggregate number
    of strategic delivery vehicles; (b) reduce the number of modern large
    ballistic missile launchers; (c) reduce the MIRV (multiple indepen-
    dently retargetable vehicles) missile launchers; and (d) limit the
    number of ICBM launchers.

    According to Vance, the Russians would not accept these proposals because
they did not believe the deal would be to their advantage. Vance stated that
he did not believe the Russian decision on arms was connected to Carter's
complaints about the Soviet Union's violations of human rights.

April 10, 1977   *FRANCE SENDS PLANES AND MOROCCAN TROOPS TO AID THE
                     ZAIRE GOVERNMENT OF MOBUTU AGAINST REBELS IN SHABA
                     PROVINCE.*

*For some time rebels in the former Congo increased in strength, threatening
the regime of President Mobutu. France sent 1,500 Moroccan troops to assist
the government. The Carter administration hesitated to provide too much aid
for Mobutu but authorized $15 million for "non-lethal" equipment in March
and April, 1977.*

May 17, 1977   *ISRAEL HAS A SIGNIFICANT POLITICAL CHANGE AS THE LABOUR
                     PARTY LOSES AN ELECTION AFTER 29 YEARS IN OFFICE. THE
                     NEW PRIME MINISTER IS MENACHEM BEGIN OF THE LIKUD
                     PARTY.*

May 18, 1977   THE UNITED STATES, THE U.S.S.R., AND 32 OTHER NATIONS
                           SIGN A U.N. AGREEMENT BANNING ENVIRONMENTAL WARFARE.

This pact prohibited experiments with or the use of war methods which would
alter weather patterns or other environmental phenomena. From 1972 to 1974,
the United States conducted a study of "environmental war" which led to a
Senate resolution urging the president to negotiate a treaty prohibiting such
action. At a Moscow summit on July 3, 1974, Nixon and Brezhnev approved a
draft treaty which each nation submitted to the U.N. Conference of the Committee on Disarmament (CCD) in Geneva on August 21, 1975. This U.S.-Soviet
draft became the basis for the treaty signed on May 18, 1977.

June 3, 1977   A SERIES OF CONFERENCES BETWEEN RICH AND POOR NATIONS
                           (NORTH-SOUTH) ENDS WITH NO SIGNIFICANT RESULTS.

For over 18 months, dialogue had been conducted in Paris between 8 industrialized nations including the United States and 19 developing nations. The
rich nations wanted to pressure OPEC to cut its oil prices; the poor nations
wanted drastic reforms of the world's trade structure to redistribute the
world's wealth. The developing nations also requested a moratorium on the
$200 billion of debts they had; the rich nations offered only $1 billion of
funding.
        More North-South talks were scheduled for November, 1977, in Geneva.

June 15, 1977   *THE BRITISH COMMONWEALTH CONFERENCE CONDEMNS THE REGIME
                           OF UGANDA'S IDI AMIN, HAVING BARRED HIM FROM THE CON-
                           FERENCE SESSIONS.*

*Since gaining power in Uganda on January 25, 1971, Amin had become notorious for
his inhumane treatment of his political and tribal opponents. Efforts to rally
world opinion against Amin resulted in the decision of the Commonwealth nations,
meeting in London from June 8 to June 15, to condemn Amin for his "massive violations of basic human rights."*
        *By the end of 1977, a movement to oust Amin developed. Exiles formed a
"Ugandan National Liberation Front," and, helped by neighboring Tanzania, the
front succeeded in overthrowing Amin on April 1, 1979.*

June 15, 1977   *SPAIN CONDUCTS ITS FIRST ELECTION IN 40 YEARS. SENOR
                           ADOLFO SUAREZ'S DEMOCRATIC CENTRE UNION RECEIVES A
                           MAJORITY OF SEATS IN PARLIAMENT.*

June 21, 1977   *AT A COMMUNIST CONFERENCE IN WARSAW, THE SOVIET DELE-
                           GATION CONDEMNS EUROCOMMUNISM AS IDEOLOGICAL HERESY.*

*The Kremlin denounced Eurocommunism, a term used to designate the ideas of
Western Communist parties which renounced revolution and preferred parliamentary methods to gain power. In addition, Eurocommunists such as Santiago
Carillo of Spain and Enrico Berlinguer of Italy rejected Moscow's claim to
subservience and the first loyalty of all Communists because Russia was the
world's first Socialist country.*

July 1, 1977   PRESIDENT CARTER CANCELS PRODUCTION OF THE CONTRO-
                              VERSIAL B-1 BOMBER PROGRAM.

The president astounded newsmen at a press conference on July 1 by opening
the session with the statement that the expensive B-1 program would be ended
except for minimal testing developments in the unlikely event "that the cruise
missile system had trouble." Carter told the press: "I think that in toto
the B-1, a very expensive weapons system conceived in the absence of the
cruise missile factor, is not necessary."
        Carter's decision was logical, not political, but aroused resentment
from congressmen who hoped the B-1 would provide economic benefits in their
district or who believed the United States had to be superior to Russia in
all categories of weapons. The B-1's would cost more than $100 million each.
However, they would create 69,000 jobs directly and 122,700 jobs by ripple
effect. In contrast to the B-1, the cruise missile was, according to its
advocates, cheap, accurate, and powerful, able to avoid Russian detection
systems after being launched from existing B-52 planes outside the Soviet
defense. As a result, the cruise missiles could penetrate into Russia more
effectively than manned bombers.

July 8, 1977   PRESIDENT CARTER'S REQUEST TO CONGRESS FOR THE SALE
                              TO IRAN OF SEVEN AIRBORNE WARNING AND CONTROL SYSTEM
                              (AWACS) PLANES CAUSES OPPOSITION IN CONGRESS BEFORE
                              ITS APPROVAL.

Carter's request for the sale of AWACS might have been only a formality except
for the American demonstrations against the Shah of Iran which grew in 1977.
Both in and out of congress, many U.S. spokespersons opposed the repressive
political methods of the shah's government.
        Between July and October, intensive opposition in congress sought to ban
the sale of the seven AWACS to Iran. Led by Senators Hubert Humphrey and
Clifford P. Case, the ban proponents cited not only the shah's repression
but also the danger of risking the loss of the "sensitive technology" of the
AWACS to Iranian radicals. Nevertheless, with the help of Senate Majority
Leader Robert Byrd, Carter convinced congress on October 8 not to block the
sale. On November 9, Iran confirmed that it had purchased seven AWACS from
the United States.
        Opposition to the shah continued. When the Shah of Iran visited the
White House on November 15, a large demonstration took place outside the White
House gates. The police used tear gas to disperse the demonstrators; some
of the gas fumes blew to the area where President Carter conducted ceremonies
for the shah. The Iranian government consistently contended that it suppressed pro-Communists in its country although it became evident in 1977 that
Islamic religious groups were persecuted although they were not Communistic.

July 16, 1977   *LIBYAN AND EGYPTIAN FORCES CLASH, EGYPTIAN JET PLANES*
                              BOMBING AND STRAFING A LIBYAN AIR BASE NEAR TOBRUK.

President Sadat of Egypt and Colonel Qaddafi of Libya had often exchanged
antagonistic words, but their enmity nearly caused war in mid-July. Following
a border raid by Libyan forces in early July, Egypt retaliated by the attack
on Tobruk. Later, on July 22, Sadat said his forces gave Qaddafi a "lesson

he could never forget." Qaddafi had been verbally attacking Sadat for seeking
peace negotiations with Israel.

July 20, 1977   VIETNAM IS RECOMMENDED FOR U.N. MEMBERSHIP BY THE SE-
                           CURITY COUNCIL.

Vietnam's membership became certain because the United States announced in
May that it would not use its Security Council veto again to prevent Hanoi
from joining the United Nations. In May, Hanoi's delegates told U.S. diplomats in Paris they would intensify their search for 800 Americans missing
in Indochina. By September 30, Hanoi delivered the remains of 22 U.S. servicemen to American representatives. About the same time, the U.N. General
Assembly finalized Vietnam's admission to its organization.

August 8, 1977   ETHIOPIA AND SOMALIA ARE ENGAGED IN FULL-SCALE WAR ON
                           THE HORN OF AFRICA.

Each side claimed the other began this conflict. Somalia appeared, however,
to be the aggressor. It captured most of the southern third of Ethiopia which
it claimed to be Somalian territory. Russia had the most to lose in this
conflict because Moscow supported Ethiopia's government and had naval facilities at the port of Berbera in Somalia. See November 13, 1977.

September 7, 1977   THE UNITED STATES AND PANAMA SIGN THE TREATIES ON THE
                           FUTURE OPERATION AND DEFENSE OF THE PANAMA CANAL.

President Carter and Panama's Chief of Government General Torrijos signed the
treaties in the presence of representatives of 25 other American republics
and Canada. The treaties resulted from negotiations begun in 1964 and conducted at various times under Presidents Johnson, Nixon, Ford, and Carter.
The key decision permitting successful negotiations had been a statement of
eight principles signed by Torrijos and Secretary of State Kissinger on February 7, 1974. The first treaty dealt with the transition of canal ownership over a period of 20 years, to end on December 31, 1999. The second
treaty provided for U.S.-Panamanian relations after the Panamanians assumed
full jurisdiction over the canal in the year 2000.
     The first treaty provided for a Joint Commission of five Americans and
four Panamanians gradually to phase out U.S. control of the canal and prepare
the way for Panama's operation of the canal. Until 1999, a Joint U.S.-Panama
Defense Commission would regulate the defense of the canal. The second treaty
provided for the neutrality of the canal, future canal toll charges, and the
joint U.S.-Panamanian defense of the canal. The agreement also provided for
a joint study on the feasibility of a new sea-level canal. If this canal
were built, terms for its construction would be negotiated.
     In addition to the two treaties, the United States pledged outside the
treaty to arrange loans of up to $200 million of Export-Import Bank Credits
to Panama; up to $75 million in AID housing guarantees; and a $20 million
Overseas Private Investment Loan Corporation guarantee for Panama. The United
States also agreed that all U.S. civilians employed in the Canal Zone could
keep their jobs until retirement. See June 16, 1978.

October 17, 1977   *A WEST GERMAN COMMANDO UNIT SUCCESSFULLY LIBERATES 87*
                           HOSTAGES HELD BY FOUR ARAB SKYJACKERS AT AN AIRFIELD
                           IN MOGADISHU, SOMALIA.

The Lufthansa aircraft was captured by 4 terrorists on October 13. They de-
manded the release of 11 terrorists held in Germany and 2 held in Turkey.
The German commando unit used stun grenades to attack the plane. All the
hostages were freed, although the terrorists had previously killed the plane's
pilot. Three of the terrorists were killed; the fourth was wounded.

November 5, 1977   THE UNITED STATES WITHDRAWS FROM THE INTERNATIONAL
                           LABOR ORGANIZATION (ILO).

This U.N. agency had become increasingly politicized by Arab and Communist
delegations. In 1974, the ILO voted a resolution to condemn Israel for "rac-
ism" in administering Arab territory and Secretary Kissinger warned the ILO
the United States would withdraw unless the group concerned itself only with
labor conditions. President Carter decided to withdraw U.S. membership until
the ILO changed its rules and policies. See also November 10, 1975.

November 13, 1977   *SOMALIA EXPELS 6,000 SOVIET ADVISORS AND BREAKS DIP-*
                           LOMATIC RELATIONS WITH CUBA.

Somalia had been a Soviet ally for eight years but was angered by Russian aid
to Ethiopia in the conflict which broke out on August 8, 1977. Somalia ob-
tained aid against Ethiopia from France and the conservative Arab states.

November 15, 1977   *PRIME MINISTER BEGIN INVITES EGYPT'S PRESIDENT SADAT*
                           TO VISIT ISRAEL; SADAT ACCEPTS, HERALDING A NEW RELA-
                           TIONSHIP BETWEEN EGYPT AND ISRAEL.

Early in November, Sadat had suggested he would be willing to visit Israel.
Nevertheless, Begin's invitation surprised most observers.
*   After 29 years of enmity Egypt and Israel finally began a search for*
peaceful relations. On November 19, Sadat flew to Israel where he talked
with Begin. He addressed Israel's Knesset on November 20. When Sadat re-
turned to Cairo on November 21, cheering crowds indicated many Egyptians
lauded these new peace overtures. See December 14, 1977.

December 2, 1977   *RADICAL ARAB LEADERS MEET IN TRIPOLI TO UNITE AGAINST*
                           EGYPT'S MOVES TOWARD PEACE WITH ISRAEL.

Leaders of Libya, Algeria, Iraq, South Yemen, Syria, and the PLO opposed Pres-
ident Sadat's new policy of negotiating with Israel.
*   On December 5, Egypt expelled the ambassadors of each of these radical*
Arab states except Iraq.

December 14, 1977   A CAIRO SUMMIT MEETING OF REPRESENTATIVES OF THE UNITED
                           STATES, EGYPT, AND ISRAEL CONVENES TO DISCUSS PEACE
                           PROPOSALS.

Following his visit to Israel, President Sadat of Egypt offered to negotiate
directly with Israel, and Prime Minister Begin agreed (November 27). As a
result sessions began in Cairo on December 14 and included U.S. representatives.

      Initially, Sadat hoped to persuade Russia and the other Arab states to
join the talks, but Syria led the Arab radicals in rejecting the Egyptian
proposal. Moscow also refused to join a multi-national meeting on the Middle
East. Therefore, Sadat called for direct Israeli-Egyptian talks with only
U.S. representatives involved in the discussions. Although American diplomats
preferred a multi-national agreement on Middle Eastern problems, President
Carter decided to encourage the new initiatives of Begin and Sadat. Nevertheless, both Sadat and Carter continued to seek support for the Cairo talks
from moderate Arab leaders in Jordan, Saudi Arabia, and the Persian Gulf
states. See September 17, 1978.

December 29, 1977   PRESIDENT CARTER ARRIVES IN WARSAW, HIS FIRST STOP
                           ON A TOUR TO POLAND, IRAN, INDIA, SAUDI ARABIA, FRANCE,
                           AND BELGIUM.

The reasons for Carter's trip included:

1.   a desire for East-West accords with such Communist nations as Poland,
     Hungary, and Rumania;

2.   a desire to improve the image of the Shah of Iran in America. The
     United States depended on the shah as a major ally in the Middle
     East although the shah had been severely criticized in the U.S. news
     media because of his repressive measures against dissenters;

3.   a desire to improve relations with India, whose President Morarji R.
     Desai had indicated his desire to end the tensions created with Amer-
     ica by Indira Gandhi's policies;

4.   a desire to show Saudi Arabia that the United States welcomed its
     friendship as well as its "friendly" oil policies;

5.   a desire to bolster continued good U.S. relations with French Presi-
     dent Valery Giscard d'Estaing;

6.   a desire to visit NATO offices in Brussels and symbolically reaffirm
     the American commitment to NATO as the keystone of U.S. alliances.

1978

January 13, 1978   THE UNITED STATES AND JAPAN SIGN A TRADE AGREEMENT IN
AN ATTEMPT TO FORESTALL DEMANDS FOR PROTECTIONISM BY
SOME AMERICAN BUSINESS INTERESTS.

Robert STRAUSS, President Carter's trade negotiator, spent six months negotiating this treaty with Japan. At the signing, Strauss described his effort
as having "redefined the economic relations with our two great nations." U.S.
business interests believed Strauss exaggerated, although Japan had promised
some concessions.
        To reduce its trade imbalances with America, which totaled $8 billion
in 1977, Tokyo agreed to decrease its tariffs on 300 imports, to liberalize
its quotas on agricultural products such as California's citrus fruits, and
to stimulate a 7% growth rate in Japan's economy (it had been 5.3% in 1977).
Strauss admitted that the 1978 agreement was just one step in the direction
of Japan's further reduction of tariffs and agricultural quotas. He hoped
further Japanese changes would be forthcoming in the future.

*February 26, 1978   CHINA AND JAPAN SIGN A $20 BILLION TRADE AGREEMENT IN
SHANGHAI.*

*By this pact, Japan would buy over 47 million tons of oil from China and 9
million tons of coal. China would purchase Japanese steel and a variety of
other manufactured products.*

February 28, 1978   THE STATE DEPARTMENT ISSUES A SENATE FOREIGN RELATIONS
COMMITTEE REPORT WHICH FINDS THE SOVIET UNION HAS GEN-
ERALLY COMPLIED WITH THE 1972 SALT I AGREEMENTS.

The report on SALT I compliance had been prepared in order to counteract critics' arguments that Moscow had not fulfilled its agreements with Nixon.

March 3, 1978   THE UNITED STATES AND HUNGARY SIGN A TRADE AGREEMENT
GRANTING EACH OTHER THE MOST-FAVORED-NATION STATUS.

Paving the way for this trade arrangement with Communist Hungary, the United
States had returned to Hungary the Crown of St. Stephen. On January 6, Secretary Vance in elaborate ceremonies delivered the crown to Budapest. The
crown was Hungary's traditional symbol of nationhood, having been given to
King Stephen I by Pope Sylvester II in the year 1000. At the end of World
War II, American troops were given the crown by a Hungarian colonel. It had
been stored at Fort Knox, Kentucky, since that time. President Carter stated
that he returned the crown to Hungary because it belonged to no regime but to
the people of Hungary.

March 8, 1978   *SOMALIA WITHDRAWS ITS FORCES FROM ETHIOPIA AND SEEKS*
                            A NEGOTIATED SETTLEMENT.

*The withdrawal from Ogaden province seemed to make Ethiopia the temporary
victor together with its Cuban and Russian allies. Somalia had invaded Ogaden
province claiming this was its territory. On March 20, the United States
announced it would send $7 million of food aid to Somalia. See May 16, 1978.*

March 10, 1978   *PALESTINIAN TERRORISTS STAGE AN AMPHIBIOUS ATTACK ON
                            ISRAEL'S COAST NEAR TEL AVIV, KILLING 33 ISRAELIS.*

*The terrorists landed in rubber boats. They hijacked a tourist bus and at-
tacked other vehicles on the highway along the coast. Then they waged a suicide battle against Israeli forces. In the conflict four of the five terrorists were killed in addition to the 33 Israelis; 70 Israelis were wounded.*
     *At the time of the attack, Israel's Prime Minister Begin was in the
United States conducting peace talks with President Carter. The two leaders
hoped to end the stalled talks between Egypt and Israel. Because of the terrorist attack, Begin rushed home; the peace talks halted.*

March 14, 1978   *ISRAELI FORCES ATTACK PALESTINIAN BASES IN SOUTHERN
                            LEBANON, RETALIATING FOR THE MARCH 10 TERRORIST ATTACK.*

*About 20,000 Israeli troops crossed the border into southern Lebanon while
their jet aircraft bombed and strafed as far north as Beirut. The Israeli
purpose, said Prime Minister Begin, was to occupy a four- to six-mile-wide
"security strip" in Lebanon.*
     *On March 19, the U.N. Security Council called for an Israeli withdrawal
and established a 4,000-man U.N. interim force to patrol the border area between Lebanon and Israel. Israel announced a cease-fire on March 21 and U.N.
troops arrived on March 22. On June 13, Israel completed its withdrawal from
Lebanon but turned over the six-mile zone in southern Lebanon to Christian
Phalangist militia who were anti-Palestinian. This caused renewed fighting
in Lebanon with the Palestinians and Syrians opposing the Christians.*

March 21, 1978   THREE BLACK LEADERS IN RHODESIA BECOME MEMBERS OF AN
                            INTERIM GOVERNMENT UNDER THE WHITE LEADER, IAN SMITH.

This so called Salisbury Agreement, arranged on February 17 by Smith, had
been opposed by the United States and other Western powers because it omitted
more radical and stronger black Rhodesian leaders. Smith planned to have an
election on December 31 to provide for a transition to black majority rule
in Rhodesia.
     The December elections were, however, delayed until April 20, 1979. U.S.
and British efforts to obtain representation for all black factions continued
throughout 1978 but were not resolved. See July 30, 1979.

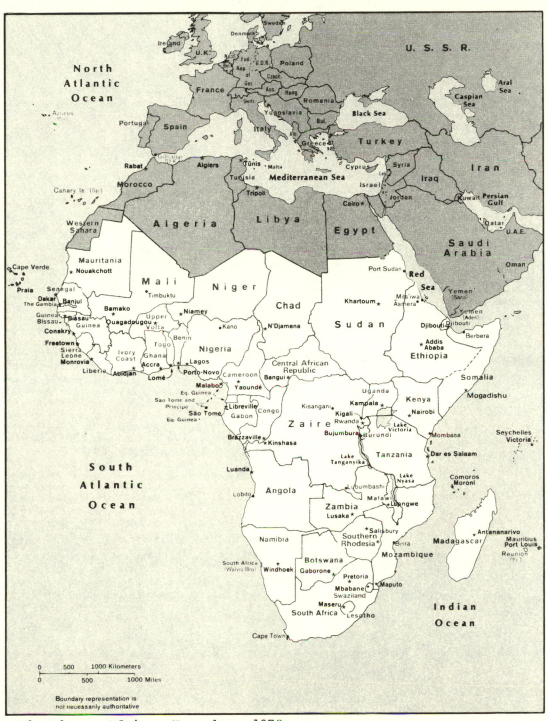

Sub-Saharan Africa, November, 1979.

April 7, 1978   PRESIDENT CARTER ANNOUNCES HE HAS DEFERRED PRODUCTION
                         OF THE NEUTRON BOMB.

During the summer of 1977, the neutron bomb had become public knowledge when
a budget item of the Energy Research and Development Administration included
an item for an "Enhanced Radiation Warhead." This was the neutron bomb, an
antipersonnel device which would damage humans more than buildings. It was
an intense radioactive bomb which would be deployed in Europe for use against
tanks attacking with the Warsaw Pact armies.

    In 1977, the neutron bomb became controversial. After congress approved
funds for its development, Carter had to decide whether or not to continue
to prepare the weapon for deployment. The bomb's critics claimed the use
of the neutron bomb would begin an escalation in the use of other nuclear
weapons if war should begin.

    During a NATO meeting in March, 1978, the European powers were divided
on use of the neutron bomb. The NATO Council finally voted that the United
States should produce the weapon. Its deployment in Europe, however, would
be delayed to determine if the Soviet Union would restrain its development
of SS-20 missiles which would be aimed against Western Europe.

    Evidently, President Carter decided not to produce the neutron bomb un-
less some European nations first agreed to deploy it. On March 20, he sent
the Deputy Secretary of State, Warren Christopher, to sound out England and
West Germany. Neither of these nations would agree to deploy it at that time.
Therefore, Carter decided to announce the delay in its production.

    On April 19, 1978, the NATO Nuclear Planning Group decided to keep the
neutron bomb option open for possible future use. Subsequently, after further
discussions with the NATO governments, President Carter decided on October 18
that components of the neutron bomb would be produced by the United States.

April 20, 1978   *SOVIET JET FIGHTER PLANES FORCE A KOREAN BOEING 707
                         JETLINER TO LAND NEAR MURMANSK; TWO PASSENGERS ARE
                         KILLED.*

*A Korean commercial airliner en route from Seoul to Paris flew 1,000 miles
off course, crossing into Soviet territory. Fired on by Soviet planes, the
airliner made an emergency landing on a frozen lake south of Murmansk, 390
miles northeast of Leningrad. Soviet authorities claimed the Korean plane
was forced to land but did not admit shooting at the plane as the Korean pilot
and his passengers averred. The passengers on the plane were immediately
released by the Soviets, but the pilot and navigator of the Korean plane were
held for questioning until April 29, 1978. For prior attacks on airliners
see July 23, 1954; July 27, 1955; February 21, 1973.*

May 16, 1978   *WAR BREAKS OUT AGAIN IN THE HORN OF AFRICA WHEN ETHIO-
                         PIA INVADES ERITREA.*

*Following Somalia's withdrawal from fighting in Ethiopia on March 8, the Ethi-
opians were aided by Russia in preparing to regain territory which Ethiopia
claimed in Eritrea. By November 29, Ethiopia claimed to have crushed the
Eritreans and to be victorious. Rebels in Eritrea began fighting guerrilla
warfare against Ethiopia.*

May 18, 1978   THE UNITED STATES, FRANCE, AND BELGIUM RUSH AID TO
                              ZAIRE WHEN A REBELLION RECURS IN SHABA PROVINCE.

President Mobutu of Zaire claimed that Cuba and the Soviet Union aided the
Shaba rebels. President Carter quickly sent $17 million of non-lethal aid
to Zaire. He also ordered U.S. transport planes to shuttle French and Belgian
forces to Kolwezi to rescue 3,000 stranded Europeans and Americans. The
president disclosed the U.S. action on May 19.
     The conflict in Zaire ended quickly. The Belgian and French forces left
the area by May 25. The United States charged that Cuba knew about the invasion, permitting the guerrillas to stage their operations in Angola before
launching their attack on Zaire.
     On June 5, the United States airlifted another 1,500 Moroccan troops to
Zaire. By July 29, the last Western forces evacuated Zaire after Zaire and
Angola agreed to prevent future guerrilla outbreaks along their borders.

May 24, 1978   *THE SOVIET UNION SUCCESSFULLY TESTS A HUNTER-KILLER*
                              SATELLITE.

This test followed Russia's agreement with Secretary of State Vance on April
10 to begin negotiations to suspend the testing of hunter-killer satellites.
These earth satellites were capable of finding and blowing up enemy satellites
in space. U.S.-Soviet negotiations for a ban on these space weapons began
on June 8 at Helsinki with Paul Warnke heading the U.S. delegation.

June 16, 1978   THE UNITED STATES AND PANAMA EXCHANGE RATIFICATION OF
                              THE TWO PANAMA CANAL TREATIES SIGNED ON SEPTEMBER 7,
                              1977.

In order to demonstrate U.S. good will toward Panama and its leader, Omar
Torrijos, President Carter visited Panama to participate in special ceremonies
for the final exchange of ratification of the canal treaties.
     Between September 7 and April, 1978, the Panama treaties had to overcome
intensive opposition from American congressmen prior to the Senate ratification of the treaties. U.S. treaty opponents, such as Senator Strom Thurmond
and former California Governor Ronald Reagan, made some valid and some pre-
posterous claims. Among their valid concerns were issues of how the joint
defense measures would function and whether the Panamanian people favored
the treaty as a friendly act. More Americans seemed impressed, however, by
critics' comments which had little or no substance. These comments included
such statements as "We bought the canal; we paid for it; it is ours"; or that
the treaty was a victory for communism and would promote victories for our
enemies in Latin America.
     After the Senate debate on the treaties began in January, 1978, President
Carter pulled out all stops to insure their ratification. He spoke on television; he enlisted support from Republicans such as Henry Kissinger, former
President Ford, and Senate Minority Leader Howard H. Baker, Jr.; and he gained
the support of all members of the Joint Chiefs of Staff.
     On March 16, before the Senate voted on the treaty guaranteeing the ca-
nal's neutrality, Carter telephoned 16 unfriendly senators to offer his aid
in passing their local-interest legislative bills provided they voted for
the Panama treaty. Led by Baker and Senate Majority Leader Robert C. Byrd,

a two-thirds majority of the senators approved the treaty by one vote (68) more than necessary. The second and more vital treaty, which replaced the 1903 treaty, did not come to a vote in the Senate until April 18. Again the Senate vote was 68 to 32, barely the two-thirds necessary to ratify the treaty.

Between March 16 and April 18, a serious problem arose because of an amendment introduced by Senator Dennis DeConcini, a Democrat from Arizona. The amendment stated that if necessary, the United States could intervene in Panama to secure the continued operations of the canal after the year 2000. This amendment was opposed by Panama's General Torrijos, and doubts arose as to whether Panama would accept the amendment. In addition, Torrijos circulated a letter among members of the United Nations complaining about the DeConcini reservation.

By April 18, however, pro-treaty senators had added a statement to DeConcini's amendment which asserted that the United States would not intervene in Panama's internal affairs. The DeConcini statement was thereby clarified as applying only to U.S. defense requirements during a war in which Panama was a participant. Torrijos indicated he would accept the revised DeConcini amendment.

Following the compromise on DeConcini's amendment, the Senate's approval was obtained. The final ratifications of the two treaties were exchanged in Panama on June 16, 1978.

June 29, 1978   *VIETNAM BECOMES A MEMBER OF COMECON, THE SOVIET BLOC ECONOMIC ALLIANCE.*

The admission of Vietnam to the Soviets' economic sphere indicated Russia's continued influence in seeking hegemony in South and Southeast Asia, a policy the Chinese disliked intensely. COMECON is the Soviet-backed Council for Mutual Economic Assistance. On November 3, 1978, Vietnam and the U.S.S.R. signed a Treaty of Friendship and Cooperation which further solidified their alliance.

July 10, 1978   DESPITE U.S. OPPOSITION THE SOVIET UNION BEGINS THE TRIAL OF ANOTOLY SHCHARANSKY ON CHARGES OF ESPIONAGE FOR THE CIA AND TREASON.

Following Shcharansky's arrest, President Carter denied the charges and warned the Soviets that a trial of Shcharansky would undermine the détente relationship.

Apart from Shcharansky's trial, détente seemed to many Americans to be inoperative because of Moscow's involvement in such African states as Angola, Ethiopia, and Zaire. On May 28, U.S. security advisor Brzezinski told a television audience that Russian acts in Africa violated détente.

Nevertheless, in accord with the Soviet Union's trial methods, within a week Shcharansky had been convicted and sentenced to 13 years in prison and a strict regime labor camp. See July 18, 1978, for the U.S. reaction.

July 18, 1978   PRESIDENT CARTER RETALIATES FOR THE SOVIETS' CONVICTION
                        OF SHCHARANSKY BY CANCELLING U.S. TECHNOLOGY SALES TO
                        MOSCOW.

The United States announced the prohibition of the sale of a $6.8 million
Sperry Univac computer to the Soviet news agency, Tass. In addition, all
sales of U.S. petroleum technology to the Soviets must now be approved on
a case-by-case basis by the Department of Commerce and by Zbigniew Brzezinski,
the National Security Advisor, and his staff. The Soviets were seeking over
$1 billion of U.S. oil equipment over the next three years, although some of
it could be obtained in Europe.

On December 4, in Moscow, U.S. Secretary of Commerce Juanita Kreps announced the issuance of licenses for $65 million of oil field equipment. This
effectively counteracted President Carter's July 18 announcement on oil equipment.

Within a year, the Carter administration also reversed its policy on
the Sperry Univac computer. On April 5, 1979, the Commerce Department permitted the sale of the computer to the Soviet Union's news agency.

July 18, 1978   *THE PEOPLE'S REPUBLIC OF CHINA CLOSES ITS BORDERS TO
                        ETHNIC CHINESE FLEEING FROM VIETNAM.*

*Trouble began on the Chinese-Vietnamese border after the Socialist Republic
of Vietnam expelled 70,000 Chinese on May 24, 1978. In retaliation on June 9,
China cancelled 70 aid projects in Vietnam and recalled 1,000 Chinese technicians. Between August 8 and 27, 1978, Peking and Hanoi attempted but failed
to reach a settlement on the status of the ethnic Chinese in Vietnam, most
of whom had lived in Indochina with their families for many years.*

July 27, 1978   THE U.N. SECURITY COUNCIL APPROVES A PEACE PLAN FOR
                        NAMIBIA (SOUTH WEST AFRICA) WHICH APPEARS LIKELY TO
                        END A 12-YEAR DISPUTE WITH SOUTH AFRICA.

Since 1965, the United Nations had sought a method to persuade South Africa
to yield the control over South West Africa which it had secured as a mandate
in 1920. The white apartheid government of South Africa refused to do so
unless the white minority of Namibia were secured and a moderate pro-South
African government was set up. These conditions were almost impossible to
meet because of the rise of black African nationalism.

During 1977-1978, the United States, Canada, West Germany, France, and
Great Britain conducted a series of talks with both sides and came up with a
plan whereby they put pressure on South Africa to accept by threatening economic sanctions. On March 23, the U.N. Council for Namibia adopted a declaration for sanctions, and on May 3, the U.N. General Assembly did the same.
On April 25, South Africa agreed to the five-nation plan. On July 12, the
South West African People's Organization (SWAPO) agreed to the plan. This
caused the optimistic belief that the problem would be settled.

When the U.N. Security Council met on July 27 the one outstanding question seemed to be South Africa's demand that Walvis Bay--the only seaport in
the state--should not be part of Namibia. The Security Council passed Resolution 431 which called for the independence of Namibia "at the earliest possible date." U.N.-supervised elections would decide the future government

of the state. The council also passed Resolution 432 making Walvis Bay part
of Namibia.

South Africa now decided to oppose the April 23 plan, rejecting Resolution 432. South Africa decided to hold its own internal election for South
West Africa on December 4, action the U.N. Security Council opposed on November 13 (Resolution 439). By the end of the year, the Namibia issue was
unsolved, and South Africa asked the United Nations to stop assistance to
SWAPO.

September 17, 1978   EGYPT AND ISRAEL SIGN TWO AGREEMENTS DESIGNED TO
                        BRING PEACE TO THE MIDDLE EAST: THE CAMP DAVID
                        ACCORDS.

President Sadat's visit to Jerusalem in November, 1977, heralded improved prospects for peace in the Middle East. During the first half
of 1978, however, these efforts became stalled as the two nations talked
with political leaders of the United States and other nations in an
attempt to resolve a priori such questions as Israel's settlements in the
land occupied on the West Bank and the Gaza Strip in 1967 and the status
of the PLO. In addition, the March attack of terrorists against Tel
Aviv and Israel's invasion of Lebanon caused further difficulty for the
peace process.

During the summer of 1978, several attempts to renew negotiations
were unsuccessful or short-lived. On July 5, Egypt offered a six-point
plan which Israel rejected. Sadat held meetings in Austria with both
Shimon Peres of Israel's Labour Party and Israeli Defense Minister Ezer
Weizman in July. Finally, on July 18-19, the Foreign Ministers of
Egypt, Israel, and the United States met at Leeds Castle in England.

Eventually, President Carter's August 8 invitation to Begin and
Sadat to meet on September 5 at Camp David was accepted and proved to
be fruitful. After 12 days of intense negotiations with Carter acting
as mediator and prodder, Begin and Sadat agreed to sign two documents:
"A Framework for Peace in the Middle East"; and "A Framework for the
Conclusion of a Peace Treaty Between Egypt and Israel." The first
treaty sought a solution to the problems involving Israel, Jordan, and
the Palestinians and proved to be the more difficult to carry out. The
second called for an Israeli-Egyptian peace treaty to be concluded in
three months and to provide for subsequent Israeli withdrawal from
Egyptian territory in the Sinai.

The treaties signed on September 17 in an atmosphere of hope and
euphoria were only guidelines for peace. Negotiations for the Israeli-
Egyptian peace treaty as well as with other Arab states were required
to carry out both treaties. See September 23, November 5, and December
14, 1978, and March 26, 1979.

September 23, 1978   *THE RADICAL ARAB STATES AGREE TO REJECT THE CAMP
                        DAVID ACCORDS AND TO BREAK DIPLOMATIC AND ECONOMIC
                        RELATIONS WITH EGYPT.*

*Meeting in Damascus, the Arab Front for Steadfastness and Confrontation
strongly denounced Sadat's agreements with Israel. These Arab governments
were Syria, Libya, South Yemen, Algeria, and the PLO, which claimed to
be the provisional government for Palestinians.*

September 26, 1978   THE THREE-YEAR-OLD TURKISH ARMS EMBARGO IS LIFTED WHEN
                        PRESIDENT CARTER SIGNS THE INTERNATIONAL SECURITY AS-
                        SISTANCE ACT OF 1978.

Although President Ford in 1974 and 1975 had opposed the arms embargo, congress required it after February 5, 1975, because of Turkey's intervention
to help the Turkish minority on Cyprus against the Greeks. Subsequent attempts by Presidents Ford and Carter to end the embargo had been resisted by
congress, due largely to the influence of pro-Greek lobbyists in Washington.
       Although the Cypriot issue had not been resolved in 1978, the Carter
administration persuaded congress to end the embargo by citing evidence of
U.S. military needs in Turkey as well as evidence that the Greeks prevented
a Cypriot solution as much as Turkey did. Although the Senate vote in July,
1978, required the certification that Turkey had contributed to settle the
Cyprus issue, both Carter and the House voted to approve this limit so that
the arms embargo could be ended for Turkey. Carter signed this legislation
on September 26, 1978.

September 30, 1978   *FOLLOWING EIGHT MONTHS OF INTERNAL TROUBLES IN NICA-*
                        RAGUA, PRESIDENT (DICTATOR) ANASTASIO SOMOZA ACCEDES
                        TO AMERICAN DEMANDS THAT HE ACCEPT THE INTERNATIONAL
                        MEDIATION GROUP TO SETTLE THE DISTURBANCES.

Nicaragua's internal problems began on January 24, 1978, when business and
labor groups joined the anti-Somoza Sandinista National Liberation Federation
(FSLN) in protesting the assassination on January 10 of La Prena's *anti-Somoza*
editor, Pedro Chamorro.
       For the first time since the beginning of the Sandinista's 45-year strug-
gle against Somoza, a broad spectrum of middle-class bankers and business
leaders acted against the Nicaraguan dictator. On August 28, a businessman's
strike took place, and fighting broke out between police and strikers. The
conflict grew and, on September 13, Somoza declared martial law.
       To end the trouble and investigate reports of Somoza's terrorist methods,
Carter sent Special Ambassador to Panama William Jorden to resolve the prob-
lems. On September 25, Jorden informed Somoza that the United States would
cut off its economic aid unless he accepted mediation by the United States,
the Dominican Republic, and Guatemala. Somoza agreed to mediate on Sep-
tember 30, but during the next several months he sought to delay any
reforms. On December 27, the Organization of American States planned a
plebiscite which the opposition groups accepted but Somoza rejected on
January 18, 1979. Somoza's intransigence led to his exile in 1979. See
July 17, 1979.

October 1, 1978   PRESIDENT CARTER CONCEDES THAT THE UNITED STATES HAS
                        USED SPY SATELLITES.

Public knowledge that the United States might have been using satellites in
space to gather intelligence first surfaced widely in America during 1977
when two young Americans were accused of selling spy satellite data to the
Russians. (See January 26, 1977.) In a speech on October 1, Carter indicated
that the United States had been covertly involved in using spy satellites for
more than a decade. This intelligence gathering, he said, was essential to
national security.

October 13, 1978   THE HOUSE OF REPRESENTATIVES COMMITTEE INVESTIGATING
                        BRIBERY BY SOUTH KOREAN OFFICIALS ISSUES A RELATIVELY
                        MILD REPORT.

The House had investigated the "Koreagate" scandal for 18 months. In its
final report, the committee found that four congressmen received between
$1,000 and $4,000 each for personal or state political use, although all four
denied the charge. Six congressmen were found not culpable. The House Majority Whip, John Brademas, was cleared of wrongdoing but was criticized for
accepting a foreign political contribution of $2,950 at the same time he urged
congress to outlaw such gifts. Speaker of the House Thomas "Tip" O'Neill
was cleared of all charges but was chastised for attending lavish parties
given by Tongsun Park, the central Korean figure in the investigation.

October 23, 1978   *THE U.S.S.R. TESTS A CRUISE-LIKE MISSILE.*

The cruise missile had been rapidly developed by the United States as a pos-
sible substitute for a manned bomber. Until announcement of this test, the
United States had been the only power with cruise technology. The October 23
test indicated that the Soviets had developed such technology and might soon
have these weapons operational.

November 5, 1978   *THE ARAB STATES, EXCLUDING EGYPT, MEET IN DAMASCUS TO*
                        TRY TO UNIFY THEIR RANKS AGAINST EGYPT AND ISRAEL.

During this Arab summit, the most significant result was that the disputes
between Iraq and the PLO and between Jordan and the PLO were reconciled. The
efforts of the radical Arab states to isolate Egypt completely were not suc-
cessful while Egypt and Israel still sought a final peace treaty. See March
31, 1979.

November 13, 1978   *MEXICO ANNOUNCES THAT BILLIONS OF BARRELS OF CRUDE*
                        OIL SHOULD BE AVAILABLE IN THE AREA AROUND TAMPICO.

This oil discovery inaugurated an optimistic development program in Mexico
based on the expected income from the Tampico oil wells.

November 26-27, 1978   *IN IRAN, THE SHAH'S DIFFICULTIES REACH CRISIS PROPOR-*
                        TIONS WHEN A SUCCESSFUL 24-HOUR STRIKE IS CALLED BY
                        IRAN'S RELIGIOUS LEADERS.

Opposition to the Shah Mohammed REZA PAHLAVI grew during 1978--first, in riots
at Tabriz on February 21; later, when Muslim extremists rioted in 24 cities
on May 9. By August 5, a coalition of left extremists, moderates, and con-
servative Muslims demonstrated against the shah, 16 people being shot by the
government's forces.
    Although the shah declared martial law on September 7, it was widely
ignored by students, workers, and religious leaders. On October 4, the shah's
main religious opponent, the Ayatollah Ruhollah KHOMEINI, was expelled to
France. Nevertheless, as the 24-hour strike of November 26-27 indicated,

Khomeini's influence continued to oppose the shah. See January 16, 1979.

December 3, 1978   VIETNAM BEGINS AN INVASION OF CAMBODIA.

There had been reports of fighting between Cambodia and Vietnam since Decem-
ber, 1977. On December 3, 1978, Hanoi radio said the Kampuchean (Cambodian)
United Front for National Salvation had been formed to overthrow the tyrant
Prime Minister Pol Pot. By December 30, Vietnam had joined Cambodian guerril-
las in capturing the Cambodian town of Kratie. Pol Pot had gained control
after the Khmer Rouge Communists overthrew Lon Nol's government in April,
1975. Pol Pot earned the anger of Hanoi because he refused to be subservient
to the Vietnamese and had purged Cambodia of all opponents in bloody execu-
tions in 1975-1976. By December, 1978, the "Communist" states of Vietnam
and Cambodia engaged in war, Vietnam being backed by the Soviet Union, China
giving some aid to Cambodia.

December 14, 1978   EGYPT AND ISRAEL ARE UNABLE TO MEET THEIR THREE-MONTH
                           DEADLINE FOR A PEACE TREATY DESPITE AMERICAN MEDIATION
                           ATTEMPTS.

The September 17 accords provided only a basis for peace; further diplomatic
negotiations began at Blair House in Washington on October 12 in an attempt
to reach a final agreement. In addition, Secretary of State Vance made frequent visits to Israel and Egypt to seek agreement on sticky points.
      In Vance's last attempt at reconciliation from December 10-14, he worked
out a peace formula with Sadat, but the Begin government continued to reject
Egyptian demands for clarity on the timing for Palestinian self-rule in the
West Bank and Gaza, and for recognition that Egypt had to consider its defense
pacts with other Arab states. Israel rejected the Egyptian ideas, saying
they could review the Sinai issue and the "target" date, not "fixed" date,
for Palestinian self-rule but not those parts regarding Egypt's relations
with other Arab nations. Generally the dispute focused on a major flaw in
the Camp David accords: there was no definite statement on the linkage between
the Egyptian peace treaty and Palestinian self-rule. Cairo claimed they were
linked; Begin said not necessarily. President Carter tended to agree with
Sadat, thus worsening relations between Israel and America. On November 5,
Carter and Vance insisted that linkage of the two agreements was essential.
The next day, Israel's cabinet rejected this concept. Thus on December 14
there was an impasse on this issue.

December 15, 1978   WASHINGTON AND PEKING ISSUE JOINT COMMUNIQUES AN-
                           NOUNCING THE ESTABLISHMENT OF DIPLOMATIC RELATIONS
                           AND THE TERMINATION IN 12 MONTHS OF THE U.S. DEFENSE
                           TREATY WITH THE REPUBLIC OF CHINA (TAIWAN).

On national television at 9 p.m., President Carter announced that the United
States and the People's Republic of China would establish normal diplomatic
relations beginning January 1, 1979. At the same time, in Peking, China's
Premier and Communist Party Chairman Hua Guofeng read a similar statement to
news reporters. It was Hua's first press conference.
      Although the normalization of U.S.-Chinese relations had been expected

since President Nixon visited China in February, 1972, the process was slowed because of Watergate, Mao's death, the Vietnam war, and the Chinese overthrow of the "gang of four." On May 20-22, National Security Advisor Brzezinski visited Peking where he proposed, with the agreement of Deputy Premier Deng Xiaoping, to negotiate the normalization. Subsequently, in secret sessions, the U.S. Liaison Officer in Peking, Leonard WOODCOCK, and the Chinese began discussions. In addition, Brzezinski met in Washington with the Chinese envoys, Han Tsu and Ch'ai Tse-min.

Early in December the negotiations moved quickly to a conclusion. On December 12, Woodcock visited with Deng who accepted an invitation to visit the United States in 1979. This signaled the Chinese willingness to normalize relations soon, and both sides worked on a communique to be issued on December 15. Prior to his television address, Carter briefed U.S. congressional leaders and met with Soviet Ambassador Anatoli Dobrynin to inform him that the U.S.-Chinese decision would not influence U.S. relations with Moscow.

In his message, Carter said normal relations would begin on January 1 with each nation opening embassies in the other's capitol city. Carter indicated that while the United States would give Taiwan the necessary 12 months' notice required to end the 1954 mutual defense treaty, the normalization would not "jeopardize the well-being of the people of Taiwan." The U.S.-Peking communique stated that "there is but one China, and Taiwan is part of China," a belief which Taiwan's government shared. Carter said that while the United States would recognize Peking as the "sole legal government of China," Peking had given assurances it would not seek to reunite Taiwan by force. The United States, Carter said, "will maintain cultural, commercial and other unofficial relations with the people of Taiwan." America could also continue to sell Taiwan "selective defensive weaponry" such as interceptor aircraft, antitank weapons, and artillery. Following his speech, Carter told a press conference that "The interests of Taiwan have been adequately protected."

Despite Carter's assurances on Taiwan, there remained a number of strong pro-Taiwan groups in the United States which protested strongly against Carter's action. Arizona Republican Barry Goldwater called the president's action "cowardly." On December 22, Goldwater and 14 other legislators filed suit in U.S. District Court to prevent the termination of the 1954 treaty with Taiwan. Goldwater argued that the Senate had ratified the 1954 treaty; therefore, the president needed Senate approval to end the treaty. Although a District Court ruled on October 17, 1979, that the president could not abrogate the 1954 treaty, a Federal Appeals Court reversed the decision on November 30, 1979, upholding the president's action. On December 13, the U.S. Supreme Court upheld the appeals court ruling.

December 17, 1978   *MEETING AT ABU DHABI, OPEC'S DELEGATIONS SET A 14.5% OIL PRICE INCREASE TO BE CARRIED OUT IN STAGES STARTING JANUARY 1, 1979.*

December 31, 1978   THE UNITED STATES AND THE PHILIPPINES SIGN A FIVE-YEAR AGREEMENT FOR CONTINUED AMERICAN USE OF FILIPINO MILITARY BASES.

The agreement provided $500 million of U.S. economic and military aid for the Philippines.

1979

January 1, 1979   AMERICA AND THE PEOPLE'S REPUBLIC OF CHINA RESUME DIP-
                         LOMATIC RECOGNITION WITH CEREMONIES IN PEKING AND WASH-
                         INGTON.

On February 26, the U.S. Senate confirmed Carter's appointment of Leonard
Woodcock as Ambassador to China. Woodcock had been serving as the U.S. Liaison Officer in Peking.

January 7, 1979   *VIETNAM AND THE KAMPUCHEAN NATIONAL UNITED FRONT CON-
                         QUER CAMBODIA AS PHNOM PENH FALLS.*

*The next day, Heng Samrin was named as head of the Kampuchean People's Revo-
lutionary Council. On January 15, the appeal of Prince Sihanouk of Cambodia
to the U.N. Security Council resulted in a resolution asking Vietnam to withdraw from Cambodia (Kampuchea). The resolution was vetoed by the Soviet Union.*

January 16, 1979   *THE SHAH OF IRAN LEAVES FOR ASWAN; HIS POWER IN IRAN
                         IS ENDED.*

*Between 1953 and 1973, the United States had come to rely on Mohammed Reza
Shah Pahlavi of Iran as a strong anti-Communist, pro-Western power in the
region of the Persian Gulf. To enhance his power, the shah undertook evolutionary methods giving Iran oil sovereignty following the overthrow of the
Mossadegh government in 1953. By agreements with British Petroleum and the
Consortium of International Oil Companies in 1954, the shah received 40% ownership of the oil corporations. He also was able to create the National Iranian Oil Company (NIOC) to exploit his nation's oil outside the concession
areas. The NIOC had about 10% of Iran's oil in 1961.*
    *After 1962, the shah combined an attempt to bring economic reforms and
modernization to Iran with efforts to obtain larger income from his oil concessions. Joining the newly formed OPEC (September 10, 1960) the shah worked
with other oil-producing nations to stabilize their prices and to unify their
policies toward the oil companies.*
    *Following the first oil boycott of the West (see June 9, 1967), the shah
moved to acquire leadership in the Middle East's oil politics. Appearing as
a moderate and non-boycotting nation on whom the United States could depend,
the shah persuaded the oil companies to give him 25% of their Iranian concession area in 1967 and began pressuring the oil companies to give the oil
nations greater influence. The shah avoided the radical confrontation style
of Libya's Qaddafi. Nevertheless, the February 4, 1971, Teheran Agreement,
which the shah and other Persian Gulf countries made with the oil companies,
established the dominant position for OPEC in future oil decisions. On March*

20, 1973, the shah obtained the St. Moritz agreement from Iran's oil companies. This pact brought all Iranian oil production under NIOC. Thus, before the October, 1973, Yom Kippur War, Iran was set to lead the OPEC nations in rapidly increasing oil prices to Western nations.

Although the shah led the Middle East powers in obtaining greater power for the OPEC nations, neither Nixon, Kissinger, nor subsequent U.S. presidents seriously criticized the shah for undermining the economic prosperity of the Western world. By 1973, the shah's political anti-communism required that the United States support him at almost any cost.

The U.S. backing for the shah continued even though the shah's economic modernization program in Iran did not envisage political and social reforms. As Iran's standard of living began to improve, social, economic, political, and religious critics began to demonstrate against the shah's repressive political methods. Claiming all opponents were "Communists," the shah organized the SAVAK secret police, which used torture, imprisonment, exile, and other methods to suppress all of his opponents. In addition, Iran's reform program was poorly planned and mismanaged, giving his reform efforts an unsatisfactory domestic structure. Such needs as education, the redistribution of wealth, and caring for Iran's minority Kurds and other groups were neglected. The bureaucracy which he created to bring reforms became both corrupt and incapable. By 1977, Iran experienced high inflation, political corruption, and economic and social inequities. The shah's absolute rule could not accommodate these problems.

In 1977, the shah appointed a new prime minister, Jamshid Amuzegar, who was expected to liberalize the government, end the corruption, and establish the human rights desired by President Carter. These measures were too little and too late. They opened the way for opposition groups which had been underground to rally public support against the shah. Among others, the Ayatollah Khomeini, the Shiite Moslem leader whom the shah exiled in 1964, returned to Iran. Khomeini was determined to overthrow the shah because he believed that SAVAK was responsible for the death of his son.

During the summer of 1978, Iranian protests developed into massive, nationwide anti-shah movements led by students, intellectuals, professionals, the middle class, workers, and religious zealots. The critics' rallying point became Khomeini who advocated an Islamic republic under traditional Islamic law. Many protesters who were leftist-Marxist or moderate republicans followed the crowds, being unable to oppose Khomeini lest they be denounced for their minority views. The shah's decision to exile Khomeini on October 4, 1978, inflamed the mass protestors even more. The shah's attempts to find ways to appease the opposition did not succeed.

By the end of 1978, Iran experienced much bloodshed, many strikes, and an ineffective political or military policy. Throughout 1978, President Carter supported the shah while urging him to establish a civilian government or become a constitutional monarch. In January, 1979, the shah looked for more moderate political supporters by turning to the National Front Party which Mossadeqh had established in the 1950's. The shah agreed to give most of his power to the National Front, appointing Dr. Shahpur BAKHTIAR as head of a new government. In addition, the shah agreed to leave the country temporarily and not return as an absolute monarch. This arrangement was completed on January 16, and the shah left for a "holiday" abroad. The plan did not succeed. For the outcome see February 1, 1979.

January 30, 1979   CHINA'S DEPUTY PREMIER DENG-XIAOPING BEGINS A VISIT
TO WASHINGTON.

While visiting the United States, Deng signed scientific and cultural accords.
He also made strong remarks against the Soviet Union, from which President
Carter had to disassociate the United States.

February 1, 1979   *KHOMEINI ARRIVES IN IRAN FROM EXILE AND FORMS HIS OWN
PROVISIONAL GOVERNMENT.*

*Khomeini rejected the government which the shah formed in Teheran before his
departure on January 16. Moreover, the populace in Teheran clearly favored
Khomeini over the shah's appointee Bakhtiar.*

*When the ayatollah returned from Paris to Iran on February 1, Bakhtiar
asked him to form a government of national unity, but Khomeini refused. On
February 5, Khomeini appointed Mehdi Bazargan as prime minister of a provisional government. Bakhtiar resigned on February 11 after the army leaders
withdrew support from his regime. Soon after, leftist and religious fanatics
in Iran began arresting, imprisoning, and executing persons associated with
the shah's regime.*

*The United States hoped to maintain normal relations with Iran's new
government. The American ambassador, William H. Sullivan, met with Bazargan
for the first time on February 21. Later, discussions began for American
businessmen to operate in Iran and for the United States to provide spare
parts for the military equipment it had supplied to the shah. Because of
the increased anti-Americanism in Iran, the establishment of normal relations
became a slow process, for the new government distrusted the United States.
This distrust built into dislike when America permitted the shah to come to
New York in October. See November 4, 1979.*

February 12, 1979   *FIGHTING BREAKS OUT IN CHAD, AFRICA, BETWEEN TWO IN-
TERNAL POLITICAL GROUPS.*

*With the support of France and Nigeria, a cease-fire was arranged and became
effective by March 20, 1979.*

February 14, 1979   THE AMERICAN AMBASSADOR TO AFGHANISTAN, ADOLPH DUBS,
IS ABDUCTED AND KILLED BY RIGHT-WING MUSLIM TERRORISTS.

The U.S. government protested to the Kabul regime, claiming that Soviet advisors had been involved in the assassination. On February 19, Kabul denied
this accusation.

In Afghanistan, disturbances by Muslim guerrillas had increased following
the military coup against President Mohammad Daud on April 27, 1978. On April
30, Nur Mohammed Taraki became both president and prime minister of the "Democratic Republic of Afghanistan." Under Taraki, Soviet influence increased
and on December 5, 1978, Taraki visited Moscow where he signed a 20-year cooperation treaty with the Soviet Union.

Since January 7, 1979, fighting between government troops and Muslim
guerrillas had begun in Afghanistan and continued throughout 1979. The number
of Soviet advisors steadily increased in Kabul. See December 28, 1979.

February 17, 1979   CHINESE FORCES INVADE VIETNAM ALONG A 480-MILE BORDER.

Although Peking stated the Chinese incursion was limited and intended to punish Vietnam for its exile of ethnic Chinese and the invasion of Cambodia, the Soviet Union threatened China, stating that it would support its Vietnamese ally. On March 5, the Chinese Premier, Hua Guofeng, announced the withdrawal of Chinese troops because the "punishment" of Vietnam had been completed. The Chinese reported on May 2 that they had lost 20,000 soldiers; Vietnam, Peking said, lost 50,000.

March 6, 1979   PRESIDENT CARTER ORDERS A U.S. NAVAL TASK FORCE TO THE ARABIAN SEA AFTER FIGHTING BEGINS BETWEEN THE YEMEN ARAB REPUBLIC (YAR) AND THE SOVIET-SUPPORTED PEOPLE'S DEMOCRATIC REPUBLIC OF YEMEN (PDRY).

The northern YAR had frequently exchanged harsh words with the southern PDRY. In 1979, however, intense fighting began along their borders, causing the YAR to ask the Arab League for help. While the league sought to arrange a cease-fire, President Carter sent a naval task force as a show of power. On March 9, the United States delivered $390 million of arms to the YAR.

Under Arab League auspices, north and south Yemen agreed to a cease-fire on March 30. The two states also agreed to negotiate methods to carry out cooperative relations in the future.

March 12, 1979   THE CENTRAL TREATY ORGANIZATION BREAKS UP WHEN PAKISTAN WITHDRAWS ON MARCH 12, TURKEY ON MARCH 15.

The United States had experienced increasingly poor relations with both Pakistan and Turkey. The latter nation disliked U.S. policy in the Cypriot crisis during which congress cut off aid to Turkey. Pakistan had been criticized by Carter for its arrest and later execution of former Prime Minister Ali Bhutto on April 4. On April 6, the United States cut off all economic and military aid to Pakistan because of reports that the government was acquiring a nuclear weapons capability. See November 21, 1979.

March 26, 1979   EGYPT AND ISRAEL SIGN A PEACE TREATY IN WASHINGTON.

President Carter's persistent pressure on Sadat and Begin to conclude a peace treaty finally achieved its purpose on March 13. Following the president's consultations in Cairo and Jerusalem, the Egyptian and Israeli leaders reached agreement on the issues of the West Bank and Gaza Strip. These questions continued to defy solution and had caused negotiations to break down on December 14, 1978. Israel made the issue more difficult by announcing its approval of new Jewish settlements on the West Bank on January 15, 1979. As a result, negotiations in Washington under Secretary Vance's mediation had failed on February 23.

Carter's successful diplomatic effort began on March 1-5 when, after meetings in Washington, Prime Minister Begin agreed to a set of U.S. compromises. On March 8, the president flew to Cairo where President Sadat accepted part of the agreement but desired several changes. On March 10, Carter flew to Jerusalem where, after three days of discussion, he convinced Begin to accept terms of compromise with Sadat. That same day, March 13, Carter stopped for 2½ hours in Cairo and gained Sadat's approval before returning to Washington in the evening. Before boarding his plane in Cairo, the president indicated to newsmen that if the Israeli cabinet approved, the treaty agreement could be concluded. Formal drafts of the treaty were prepared and ready for Sadat and Begin to sign on March 26 after Israel's cabinet had approved Begin's recommendations.

The important points of the Israeli-Egyptian peace treaty were:

1. Israel would submit to Egypt a detailed timetable to withdraw from the Sinai Peninsula. The first stage would be in nine months, and over a three-year period, Israel would withdraw all its troops and settlers from the Sinai. The area would generally be demilitarized, permitting Egypt to have only one division of troops there. Egypt could use the two existing airports only for civilian purposes. U.N. troops would remain along the Gulf of Aqaba and the eastern border of the Sinai.

2. One month after Israel made the first withdrawal behind the El Arish-Ras Muhammad line, the two nations would exchange ambassadors and create normal diplomatic relations.

3. Egypt would end its economic boycott of Israel and grant Israel the right of passage through the Suez Canal. Israel could buy oil from the Sinai fields at non-discriminatory prices. The United States would guarantee Israel a satisfactory oil supply for 15 years.

4. The two nations would conclude trade and cultural exchange arrangements and open their borders to each other's citizens.

5. Negotiations on Palestinian self-rule on the West Bank and Gaza Strip would be targeted for completion in 12 months. There would then be a five-year transition period to decide the final status of the West Bank and Gaza. These clauses did not set any deadline for settlement and later proved to be unworkable. The status of east Jerusalem was not mentioned in the peace treaty.

To help Egypt and Israel conclude their pact, President Carter promised that, with the consent of congress, the United States would provide about $4.8 billion of aid to the two nations over three years. Egypt and Israel would each get about $2 billion plus $500 million for economic support. Some observers expected these costs to be higher in the future.

Israel's cabinet formally ratified the treaty on April 1, Egypt on April 10. The two nations exchanged ratifications on April 25. In America, the U.S. Senate approved the military-economic aid package on May 14; the House did so on May 30.

March 30, 1979   *A WESTERN BANK CONSORTIUM ANNOUNCES LOANS OF $300 MILLION TO HUNGARY AND $550 MILLION TO POLAND.*

One consequence of détente was the increased loans from western European and American bankers to Warsaw Pact countries. This, of course, permitted east European purchases in the west.

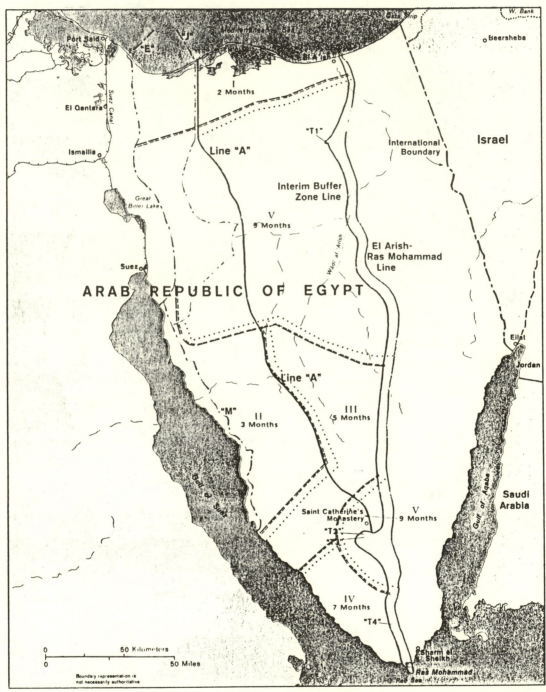

Sinai Peninsula: March 26, 1979.

March 31, 1979   *MEETING IN BAGHDAD, THE ARAB LEAGUE AND PLO APPROVE A*
                       COMPLETE BREAK IN ECONOMIC AND DIPLOMATIC RELATIONS
                       WITH EGYPT; THEY MOVE THE LEAGUE'S HEADQUARTERS FROM
                       CAIRO TO TUNIS.

On March 27, anticipating the league's decision, Egypt announced it would
freeze its relations with Arab League members. On April 8, the PLO Council
announced it would intensify its violent attacks on Israel, Egypt, and the
United States. On April 23, Saudi Arabia broke its diplomatic but not its
economic ties with Egypt.

April 10, 1979   PRESIDENT CARTER SIGNS LEGISLATION ESTABLISHING SPECIAL
                       U.S. TIES WITH TAIWAN: THE TAIWAN RELATIONS ACT.

This legislation established American relations with Taiwan to replace Washington's previous recognition of the Taiwanese government as the Republic of
China. Under the 1979 agreement, the two countries' embassies and consulates
were replaced by the Taiwan Coordinating Council for North American Affairs
in Washington and the American Institute in Taiwan. The agreement permitted
the United States to sell defensive arms to Taiwan and continued prior legal
and economic relations between America and Taiwan.

May 3, 1979   *IN BRITISH GENERAL ELECTIONS, MARGARET THATCHER, THE*
                       CONSERVATIVE PARTY LEADER, BECOMES BRITAIN'S FIRST
                       WOMAN PRIME MINISTER.

May 14, 1979   THE UNITED STATES AND CHINA SIGN A TRADE TREATY GRANT-
                       ING CHINA THE MOST-FAVORED-NATION STATUS.

This treaty was drawn up and signed in Peking by Commerce Secretary Juanita
Kreps and China's Trade Minister Li Qing.
     The Carter administration sent the Chinese Trade Treaty to congress for
approval on October 23, saying it hoped congress would also grant the Soviet
Union the most-favored-nation status. Congress approved the Chinese Trade
Treaty on January 24, 1980; it became effective on February 1, 1980. The
Soviet Union had not been granted most-favored-nation status, however.

May 22, 1979   *IN CANADIAN ELECTIONS, THE PROGRESSIVE CONSERVATIVE*
                       CHARLES J. CLARK DEFEATS THE LIBERAL PRIME MINISTER,
                       PIERRE TRUDEAU.

Clark's party obtained a majority of only six votes. On November 14 and 20,
1979, the conservatives lost five by-elections, reducing Clark's majority to
one.

May 25, 1979   *ISRAEL RETURNS EL ARISH TO EGYPT, THE FIRST STEP IN*
                       ITS WITHDRAWAL FROM THE SINAI.

On May 26, Secretary of State Vance, Begin, and Sadat met in Beersheba to
begin talks on an autonomy plan for the Palestinians.

June 8, 1979   PRESIDENT CARTER APPROVES FULL-SCALE DEVELOPMENT OF
                             THE MX MISSILE.

Carter announced the status of the MX before leaving for the Vienna summit
to sign SALT II. The MX was designed to modernize the American ICBM system
which, in terms of land-based missiles, lagged behind the new Soviet land-
based SS-18's and SS-19's. In order to make the MX less vulnerable to the
Soviet first strike, U.S. plans were to make the MX a mobile force, moving
it around on tracks in underground tunnels to varied launch sites in the
southwestern United States. The MX was permitted under SALT II.

On September 7, 1979, Carter announced that the United States would spend
$33 billion to deploy 200 MX missiles which would be fully operational in
1989.

June 10, 1979   *ELECTIONS FOR THE FIRST EUROPEAN PARLIAMENT ARE COM-*
                             PLETED.

*In direct elections where citizens cast 110 million votes, 410 members were
elected to form a European Parliament. On July 17, at the first session of
the group, Simone WEIL of France was elected president. Although the European Parliament had little political power, it was an additional, symbolic
step in the direction of a united Europe.*

June 18, 1979   AT A VIENNA SUMMIT MEETING, PRESIDENT CARTER AND CHAIR-
                             MAN BREZHNEV SIGN SALT II, A FIVE-YEAR TREATY LIMITING
                             MAXIMUM NUMBERS OF ICBM'S AND LONG-RANGE BOMBERS.

SALT II had been negotiated for nearly seven years, having been intended further to restrict strategic missiles which were limited by the United States
and U.S.S.R. in 1972. The final agreement on SALT II had been announced by
Secretary Vance on May 9, although at the Vienna meeting, Carter and Brezhnev
exchanged letters in which the Soviets agreed not to produce and deploy more
than 30 Soviet TU-26 (Backfire) bombers in any one year.

Because of prior criticism at home about SALT II, President Carter addressed congress two hours after he arrived back in Washington from the Vienna
meetings. In his speech and in later administration testimony to congress
on SALT II, Carter, Vance, and members of the JCS advocated ratification of
SALT by emphasizing the following points:

1. SALT II will help maintain a stable balance of missile forces between
America and the Soviet Union. According to SALT II each side would have an
aggregate of 2,250 missiles and heavy bombers; 1,320 cruise carriers and
MIRVed missiles; 1,200 MIRVed ICBM's. Because the Soviets were above these
numbers, they would destroy or dismantle 250 of their systems. While many
of those destroyed would be old, they had the power of America's Minuteman II
or Polaris missiles. Without SALT II, the Soviets could keep and add to
these 250 missiles or bombers.

2. Verification would continue to be based on U.S. systems, but for the
first time there was agreement not to encrypt telemetric information if it
impeded compliance with the treaty. In addition, regular data would be exchanged on strategic forces, rules for counting weapons were simplified, and

the U.S.S.R. would ban their SS-16 mobile missile, which was difficult to verify.

    3. Agreement on SALT II would open the way to negotiating further limits under SALT III.

    4. Ratification was important to America's allies and its leadership in the world. The NATO allies did not want Soviet superiority or the political tensions and pressure stemming from lack of agreement.

    For the results of the SALT II ratification process see January 2, 1980.

June 28, 1979   AS THE REFUGEE PROBLEM BECOMES ENORMOUS IN SOUTHEAST ASIA, CARTER DOUBLES THE U.S. REFUGEE QUOTA TO 14,000 PER MONTH FOR THE NEXT YEAR.

Other nations also had to be enlisted to assist the refugees fleeing from Cambodia and Vietnam. Thailand became the principal base of operations for refugee programs because people fled there from the neighboring states. By November 18, the Thais had a camp for 200,000 refugees, which proved insufficient. On August 3, a Red Cross Committee visited Cambodia, reporting that over 2.25 million people faced starvation due to policies of the Pol Pot regime and the Vietnamese invasion. Emergency food relief operations began on August 28.

July 14, 1979   *ETHIOPIAN FORCES LAUNCH AN OFFENSIVE AGAINST ERITREAN REBELS AS WAR AGAIN BEGINS IN THE HORN OF AFRICA.*

On August 3, U.S. officials estimated there were 11,000 to 14,000 Cuban troops and 1,000 to 1,200 Soviet military advisors and troops in Ethiopia.

July 17, 1979   *FOLLOWING U.S.-SPONSORED PROPOSALS, THE NICARAGUAN CONGRESS ACCEPTS PRESIDENT SOMOZA'S RESIGNATION. CONGRESS NAMES PRESIDENT FRANCISCO URCUYO MALAÑOS TO SUCCEED SOMOZA.*

Between October, 1978, and January, 1979, attempts to mediate Nicaragua's internal problems failed (see September 30, 1978). Consequently, Somoza became increasingly isolated from supporters at home and abroad because businessmen, the middle class, church leaders, and union members joined with the Sandanistas' FSLN group against the president. On June 4, a nationwide strike began and the rebels named a five-man junta to rule, headed by Sergio Ramirez MERCADO.
    Between June 21 and 23, the Foreign Ministers of the OAS met in Washington, adopting a six-point plan proposed by U.S. Secretary of State Vance. The plan set up a peace force and asked for the "immediate replacement" of Somoza's government.
    On June 27, U.S. Ambassador William G. Bowdler went to Panama where he met with FSLN leaders and demanded that two more moderates must be added to the junta. With Bowdler satisfied that the junta represented many groups, the unified junta named an 18-man cabinet on July 14, asking congress to recognize this cabinet and to replace Somoza.

On July 17, congress followed the peace plan. It accepted Somoza's resignation and exile to the Bahamas. On July 19 the rebel forces occupied Managua. The next day the junta's cabinet was sworn into office. The Somoza
regime ended in Nicaragua. See April 27, 1980.

July 20, 1979   PRESIDENT CARTER HALTS THE PULLOUT OF AMERICAN TROOPS
                         FROM SOUTH KOREA.

On February 17, 1979, delegates from North and South Korea began meetings to
seek cooperation and a process which would reunite their nation. After these
talks failed, Carter and President Park of South Korea proposed on July 10
that North Korea join them in a three-way discussion on national unity. Premier Kim Il-Sung of North Korea rejected this proposal. In addition, the
U.N. command at the 38th parallel truce zone reported that North Korea
built new fortifications within 100 yards of the truce border.

    As a result of the failure of unity talks and evidence of North Korea's
defense build-up, President Carter announced that the United States would
delay the withdrawal of American forces from South Korea until at least 1981.
Carter had announced withdrawal plans on March 9, 1977.

July 20, 1979   THE U.N. SECURITY COUNCIL PASSES A RESOLUTION URGING
                         ISRAEL TO HALT CONSTRUCTION OF WEST BANK SETTLEMENTS;
                         THE UNITED STATES ABSTAINS.

Since January 15, Israel had renewed its policy of approving Jewish settlements in territory occupied during the 1967 war. This issue had not been
specifically settled in the March 26, 1979, peace treaty between Egypt and
Israel although the two nations began negotiations on autonomy for the Palestinians on May 26. Begin claimed he had not agreed to stop these settlements
even though President Carter opposed these settlements. On September 18,
Carter said that Israel's decision of September 16 to permit Israelis to purchase land on the West Bank and Gaza Strip was "contrary to the spirit and
intent" of the negotiations between Egypt and Israel. Prime Minister Begin
did not agree with the president's assertion.

July 26, 1979   *NIGERIA NATIONALIZES THE BRITISH PETROLEUM AND SHELL
                         OIL COMPANIES.*

July 30, 1979   CONGRESS COMPROMISES WITH THE PRESIDENT ON A RESOLUTION
                         REGARDING ECONOMIC SANCTIONS ON RHODESIA.

Since April 24, when a new Rhodesian government was set up under Bishop Abel
T. MUZOREWA, head of the United African National Congress, some groups in the
United States had urged the president to lift U.S. economic sanctions on Rho-
desia, which was officially renamed ZIMBABWE on May 31, 1979.

    Carter was not willing to lift the sanctions because the new regime did
not involve the Patriotic Front black factions in the elections of April 17-
21. Great Britain, the United States, and other powers contended that the
groups headed by Joshua Nkomo and Robert Mugabe must be included in Muzorewa's
government. The Organization of African Unity agreed, asserting in a

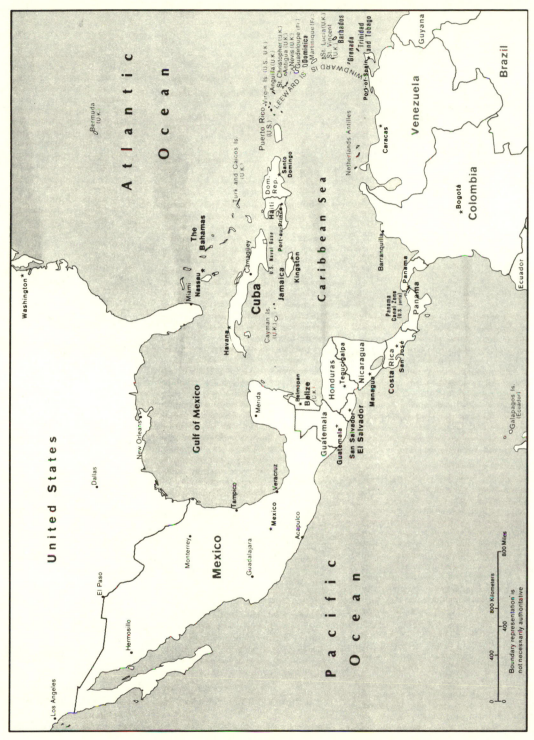

Middle America, 1979.

declaration of July 21 that the Patriotic Front was the legal representative
of Zimbabwe.

Both the U.S. Senate (June 13) and the House (June 28) passed resolutions
which called for the president to lift the economic sanctions on Zimbabwe.
On July 30, however, a Senate-House conference committee agreed to a compromise resolution which required Carter to lift sanctions by November 15, unless
he decided it was not in the national interest to do so.

Between August and October 22, British diplomats appointed by Prime Minister Thatcher worked out a compromise agreement to accept the British plan
for a cease-fire and the establishment of a new government. Because this
process had not been completed by December 3, Secretary of State Vance said
that Carter would lift the sanctions on Zimbabwe one month after the British
governor arrived in Salisbury to carry out the transition to a black majority
government of all black factions in Zimbabwe.

August 1, 1979   THE U.S. DEPARTMENT OF AGRICULTURE ENDS A SECRET SES-
                         SION WITH SOVIET DELEGATES IN LONDON BY ANNOUNCING
                         THAT AMERICA WILL SELL THE U.S.S.R. AN ADDITIONAL 10
                         MILLION TONS OF BOTH WHEAT AND CORN IN THE NEXT 14
                         MONTHS.

This agreement was followed on October 3 by an Agriculture Department announcement that over the next year the U.S.S.R. would buy a record 25 million
metric tons of corn and wheat. It was also disclosed that Secretary of Defense Brown had banned the sale of advanced computer technology to the Soviets.

August 6, 1979   THE UNITED STATES ANNOUNCES IT HAS OFFERED TO DEPLOY
                         FROM 200 TO 600 MEDIUM-RANGE PERSHING II AND CRUISE
                         MISSILES IN NATO COUNTRIES.

NATO had been considering the possible deployment of medium-range missiles
since January 19, 1979. These nuclear-warhead missiles were to counteract
the Soviets' deployment of SS-20 missiles aimed at western Europe. Medium-
range weapons were not part of the SALT I or SALT II pacts.

On October 4, the NATO High-Level Group approved deployment of these
weapons, and between December 11 and 14, both the NATO defense ministers and
the NATO Ministerial Council approved deployment of these missiles.

There were some limitations on these NATO decisions. On December 6,
the Dutch Parliament rejected the stationing of Pershing II missiles in their
territory. West Germany accepted deployment of the Pershing II and cruise
missiles on the basis that SALT II would be ratified and there would be new
talks with the U.S.S.R. on reducing nuclear forces in Europe.

On October 6, Brezhnev offered to withdraw 20,000 troops and 1,000 tanks
from East Germany but warned the Western nations not to deploy the Pershing II
missiles. Chancellor Helmut Schmidt of West Germany urged the NATO nations
to accept Brezhnev's offer as a means of reducing the conventional troops in
central Europe.

August 15, 1979   ANDREW YOUNG, THE U.S. AMBASSADOR TO THE UNITED NA-
                           TIONS, RESIGNS BECAUSE HE MADE UNAUTHORIZED CONTACTS
                           WITH THE PLO.

During his 2½ years as Carter's appointee to the United Nations, Young gener-
ated much good will for the United States in contacts with African leaders.
Often, however, Young had made incautious or impulsive statements. To replace
Young, Carter appointed Young's deputy at the United Nations, Donald F.
McHenry.

September 4, 1979   THE UNITED STATES AND THE DEMOCRATIC REPUBLIC OF GER-
                           MANY (EAST) CONCLUDE A CONSULAR AGREEMENT AFTER TWO
                           YEARS OF NEGOTIATIONS.

September 7, 1979   CARTER ASKS THE SOVIET UNION TO RESPECT AMERICA'S CON-
                           CERN FOR THE RUSSIAN MILITARY BRIGADE STATIONED IN
                           CUBA. THE PRESIDENT TELLS A NATIONAL TELEVISION AUDI-
                           ENCE THE BRIGADE POSES NO THREAT TO THE UNITED STATES.

Beginning on February 10, there were reports of added Soviet military activity
in Cuba. First the Defense Department confirmed that Cuba had received Soviet
submarines and two torpedo boats. On March 28, there were reports that the
U.S.S.R. was building submarine bases in Cuba, and on August 31, the president
stated that 2,000 to 3,000 Soviet combat troops had arrived in Cuba.
     On October 1, Carter announced the establishment of a new U.S. Caribbean
task force to offset Cuban-Russian activity in that region. The president
hoped this show of U.S. strength, plus Brezhnev's statement that the Soviet
forces were not in Cuba for combat purposes, would mollify senators who based
their opposition to SALT II on this Russian action. Carter's October 1 action
did not gain any new converts for SALT II, however.

September 19, 1979   AMERICA UNDERTAKES A LARGER ROLE IN THE SINAI BECAUSE
                           THE UNITED NATIONS ENDED ITS EMERGENCY FORCE IN JULY,
                           1979, AND ISRAEL REJECTED THE U.N. TRUCE SUPERVISORY
                           ORGANIZATION (UNTSO).

On July 24, the U.N. Security Council did not renew the emergency force and
voted to install the UNTSO to oversee the Sinai situation. The United States
and the Soviets had drawn up the UNTSO proposal on July 19, but could not
obtain the approval of Israel. Prime Minister Begin objected to the UNTSO
because he said unarmed observers could not enforce the duties required of a
U.N. neutral group. Moreover, the Israelis feared a possible repetition of
an early withdrawal by the United Nations as had happened in June, 1967, just
before the Arab-Israeli war.
     By September, 1979, the U.N. forces were nearly withdrawn, necessitating
a new plan to oversee the three stages of Israel's withdrawal and the Egyptian
occupation of the Sinai. In the trilateral agreement of September 19, the
United States agreed to enlarge the duties of its Sinai Security Mission (SSM)
which had been set up early in 1976 to operate an early warning system in
the Giddi and Mitla passes.
     As the U.N. emergency force began its withdrawal, the SSM assumed more

duties although they were not to begin officially until February 1, 1980. Diplomatic arrangements were not completed, however, until April 14, 1980, because the 1979 Trilateral Pact was not approved by the Israeli government until March 25 and by the Egyptians until April 2, 1980. Fortunately, no crisis occurred in the Sinai during the interim period from October to April.

September 21, 1979   MEXICO AND THE UNITED STATES AGREE ON NATURAL GAS PRICES TIED TO OPEC OIL PRICES.

This agreement had been negotiated after much dispute. During the fall of 1977, talks on natural gas prices broke off because the United States rejected Mexico's price requests as excessive. On April 3, 1979, another round of negotiations began, resulting in the agreement of September 21.

September 27, 1979   CARTER SIGNS LEGISLATION TO IMPLEMENT THE PANAMA CANAL TREATIES.

In order to operate the committees under the two canal treaties which would become effective on October 1, 1979, the president asked congress in January, 1979, to pass legislation including:

1. creating a Panama Canal Commission;

2. forming new bases for setting canal tolls;

3. arranging Joint U.S.-Panamanian Committees to carry out the treaties until 1999;

4. making special provisions for U.S. employees in the canal or for their emigration to the United States;

5. providing necessary funds to carry out the above provisions.

Although opponents of the Panama Treaties threatened to defeat the implementing laws, they were not successful. The House and Senate approved the laws and Carter signed them on September 27.

October 15, 1979   *EL SALVADOR'S PRESIDENT CARLOS HUBERTO ROMERO IS OVER-*
THROWN IN A BLOODLESS MILITARY COUP LED BY COLONELS
ADOLFO MAJANO AND JAIME GUTIERREZ.

There had been fighting between leftist rebels of the Popular Revolutionary
Bloc (PRB) and government forces since May 4 when the PRB occupied the French
and Costa Rican embassies as well as the San Salvador Cathedral, holding 11
hostages.
     Following the coup of October 15, a ruling junta was set up in El Salva-
dor on October 23, promising to reform the political and economic problems
of the state. Nevertheless, leftist guerrilla warfare continued in El
Salvador. On October 30, a rebel attempt to capture the U.S. Embassy in
San Salvador was repulsed; the State Department blamed Cuba for backing
the rebel attack. See October 24, 1970.

October 22, 1979   CARTER ANNOUNCES THAT THE UNITED STATES WILL SEND ARMS
                      TO MOROCCO TO AID KING HASAN II AGAINST THE POLISARIO
                      GUERRILLAS IN THE WESTERN SAHARA.

The Polisario group had secured aid from Syria, Ethiopia, and Algeria. On
December 6, 1979, the Organization of African Unity called on Morocco to withdraw from the Western Sahara, but King Hasan II refused. Through intermittent attacks on Morocco's southern and western borders, the Polisario continued
guerrila war against the king.

October 24, 1979   *IN EL SALVADOR, LEFTISTS OCCUPY TWO MINISTRIES AND
                      TAKE 130 HOSTAGES IN PROTEST AGAINST THE NEW JUNTA.*

*The Salvadoran leftists disliked the junta led by Majano and Gutierrez which
had gained power on October 15. Dramatizing their refusal to accept the regime, they occupied two ministries in San Salvador, asking for higher wages
and an investigation of Salvador's political prisoners.*

*On October 30, the leftists also raided the U.S. embassy, but were not
able to secure it or gain any hostages. Subsequently, on November 6, they
ended their occupation of the ministry quarters and released their hostages.
The junta promised to give the workers wage increases.*

October 26, 1979   *THERE IS A CRISIS IN SOUTH KOREA WHEN THE NATION'S
                      INTELLIGENCE SERVICE (KCIA) CHIEF ASSASSINATES PRESI-
                      DENT PARK, HIS BODYGUARD, AND FOUR OTHER KOREAN OFFI-
                      CIALS.*

*This incident resulted in a year of demonstrations, protests, and internal
fighting in Seoul. Not until September 1, 1980, did President Chun Doo Hwan
provide some degree of order in South Korean politics.*

November 4, 1979   THE U.S. EMBASSY IN TEHERAN IS STORMED BY IRANIAN STU-
                      DENTS WHO SEIZE 60 HOSTAGES AND DEMAND THE SHAH'S RE-
                      TURN BEFORE THEY WILL RELEASE THEM.

In some respects the crisis in Iran had begun in early October when the State
Department accepted pleas from Henry Kissinger and David Rockefeller to admit
the former shah of Iran to the United States in order that he could undergo
surgery and cancer treatments in New York. Iran's government had warned that
such a decision would provoke the Iranian people against America.

Following the November 4 embassy attack, the United States refused to
return the shah to Iran. The Carter administration did not, however, know
how to handle the unusual circumstances. Normally, a host country protects
foreign diplomats, but the Iranian government would not take action to free
the hostages. Rather, Khomeini and his followers supported the demand for
the shah's return, using the crisis as a means to rally the nation to oppose
the United States and to back Khomeini and the fundamentalist Islamic Republic
which had been established in a national referendum on April 1, 1979.

Although the United States sought to establish normal relations with
the government of Prime Minister Barzargun following the shah's exile in January, 1979, operating under the new government was difficult. The Islamic

Revolutionary Council and many of Iran's 60,000 religious mullahs seemed to share small degrees of the ayatollah's power. Barzargun held little real political power, and on November 5 he resigned as leader of the provisional government. The Revolutionary Council gained full control in Iran.

Subsequently, between November 4 and the end of 1979, various unsuccessful attempts were made to end the U.S. embassy crisis or to negotiate with Iran. The U.N. Security Council agreed unanimously to demand the release of the hostages; the PLO vainly sought to negotiate the hostages' release on November 8; U.N. Secretary General Kurt Waldheim could not persuade the Iranians to negotiate, and, although the International Court of Justice ordered the immediate release of the hostages on December 15, the court could not enforce its ruling. None of these methods worked because Khomeini rejected them as decadent Western policies.

The Iranians made only three concessions during the first 60 days of the crisis. On November 19 and 20 the students released five women and eight black male hostages; on November 22, they freed five non-American hostages. In addition, on December 24, Khomeini permitted three American clergymen, chosen by him, to come to the Teheran Embassy and conduct religious services for the American hostages. The crisis continued throughout 1980.

*November 15, 1979   ISRAEL RETURNS THE MOUNT SINAI REGION TO EGYPT TWO
                          MONTHS AHEAD OF SCHEDULE.*

Although Begin's government carried out its Sinai withdrawal agreement with Egypt, serious issues arose in the Middle East throughout 1979, because Israel continued to expand Jewish settlements on the West Bank and persistently raided southern Lebanon to attack PLO bases in that area.

The Arab autonomy talks between Egypt and Israel were stalemated. On October 21, Moshe Dayan resigned as Israel's Foreign Minister because he disagreed with Begin's policy on the West Bank Settlements and his arresting of moderate Palestinians in the West Bank. Begin claimed that both Jerusalem and the West Bank were part of Israel's traditional territory--Judea and Samaria. During the Camp David talks of 1978 and the Egyptian Peace Treaty negotiations of early 1979, President Carter avoided definite pledges from Begin on this issue because it would probably have ended the discussions. The Arab autonomy talks between Israel and Egypt had been unable to move Begin and his followers from their prior views on the West Bank territory or Jerusalem.

*November 20, 1979   AT THE GRAND MOSQUE IN MECCA, GUERRILLA FORCES LAUNCH
                          AN ATTACK FORCING SAUDI ARABIA TO CLOSE THE MOSQUE.*

The Saudis said the attackers were 500 organized guerrillas; other reports said the attack was led by fundamentalist Muslims who opposed the Saudi government. The army of Saudi Arabia dispersed or arrested the attacking force. The Grand Mosque was reopened on December 16, 1979.

*November 21, 1979   IN PAKISTAN, THE U.S. EMBASSY IS PARTLY BURNED AND A
                          U.S. MARINE GUARD IS KILLED.*

American relations with Pakistan had deteriorated rapidly in 1978-1979. (See

March 12, 1979.) In addition, Muslim extremists in Pakistan had been inspired
by the example of Khomeini in Iran to attack Western institutions which allegedly corrupted the traditions of Islam. In this atmosphere, the American
embassy in Islamabad was attacked by a mob and partly burned. Marine Chief
Warrant Officer Bryan Elis and two Pakistani employees were killed in the
attack. Pakistani troops had, however, fought the Muslim demonstrators and
rescued 100 Americans from the embassy grounds, ending the mob activity.

November 29, 1979   THE UNITED STATES CUTS CHILE'S MILITARY AND ECONOMIC
                           AID BECAUSE THE GOVERNMENT REFUSES TO EXTRADITE THREE
                           MEN ACCUSED OF INVOLVEMENT IN THE ASSASSINATION OF
                           ORLANDO LETELIER IN WASHINGTON.

Letelier had been foreign minister of Chile under Allende and was a critic
of President Pinochet's military government before he was killed in 1976.
On October 1, the Chilean Supreme Court upheld Pinochet's refusal to extradite
the Chileans as requested by the United States. Carter's November 29 action
halted a $6.6 million package of military spare parts for Chile. Loans to
Chile were also cancelled by the Export-Import Bank.

December 2, 1979   PRO-KHOMEINI GROUPS ATTACK THE U.S. EMBASSY IN LIBYA.

This incident in Tripoli was one of several radical Muslim attacks on U.S.
property and personnel in 1979. The United States protested to the government
of Qaddafi who had threatened to curtail oil exports to the United States.
On December 10, however, Qaddafi ended his threats, saying he had received
assurances that the United States would seek to become more neutral toward
the Arabs in the Middle East. Thus, U.S. oil producers in Libya could continue their operations.

December 28, 1979   REPORTS OF SOVIET TROOPS IN AFGHANISTAN CAUSE PRESIDENT
                           CARTER TO USE THE "HOT LINE" TO CALL BREZHNEV, WARNING
                           HIM OF THE POSSIBLE "SERIOUS CONSEQUENCES" UNLESS THE
                           SOVIET TROOPS ARE WITHDRAWN.

Since the assassination of U.S. Ambassador Dubs on February 14, 1979, the
guerrilla war in Afghanistan had gained in strength, leading to two changes
in Kabul's government.
     First, on September 16, President Taraki resigned on grounds of ill
health (his death was announced on October 9) and Hafizullah Amin of the Afghan Revolutionary Council replaced him. Guerrilla fighting continued, however, and on December 27, Amin was executed after a coup d'état was carried
out with the approval of the Soviet Union's advisors in Kabul. The Soviets
returned Babrak KARMAL from exile in east Europe, to take control of the Afghan government. Second, during the same period, the United States found
that the Soviets had steadily increased their forces in Afghanistan. This
build-up climaxed during a two-day airlift of 6,000 Soviet combat troops into
Kabul on December 26-27. These two 1979 developments resulted in Carter's
telephone call to Brezhnev on December 28. Carter also dispatched Deputy
Secretary of State Christopher to Europe to explain Carter's action to the
NATO governments. Unlike the United States, most European governments did

not find the Soviet action in Afghanistan to be a grave threat to their security. They believed Carter overreacted because of the Iranian hostage crisis.

On December 31, following Brezhnev's statement that the Afghan government
requested Moscow to send Soviet troops, Carter accused the Soviet leader of
"lying." A U.S.-Russian crisis over Afghanistan had begun.

1980

January 2, 1980   PRESIDENT CARTER ASKS THE SENATE TO DELAY ITS RATIFI-
CATION VOTE ON SALT II BECAUSE OF THE SOVIET INVASION
OF AFGHANISTAN.

Although the Senate Foreign Relations Committee voted 9-6 on November 9 to
send the SALT II treaty to the Senate with a recommendation favoring ratification, much opposition to the treaty had developed, especially among Republican Party members. On December 16, a group of 16 senators sent the president a letter requesting him to delay the Senate vote on SALT II until after
the presidential elections. Carter did not comply with this request but,
following the Soviet action in Kabul on December 27, he asked the Senate to
delay voting on SALT II. On June 6, 1980, the State Department announced
that SALT II and Afghanistan were "inseparable." Thus, the Senate never voted
on the ratification of SALT II.
    Upon announcing the decision on SALT II on January 2, the White House
indicated that the United States would continue to abide by the SALT I treaty,
which had been extended in 1977 after its original expiration date. On May 9,
President Carter told the Philadelphia World Affairs Council that he hoped
eventually to have SALT II ratified, saying the United States would observe
SALT II treaty terms as long as the Soviets did so.

January 3, 1980   THE UNITED STATES AGREES TO SELL THE REPUBLIC OF CHINA
(TAIWAN) $280 MILLION OF DEFENSIVE ARMS.

This deal did not include the advanced fighter jet planes requested by Taiwan.

January 4, 1980   PRESIDENT CARTER ANNOUNCES MEASURES AGAINST THE SOVIET
UNION BECAUSE OF ITS "INVASION" OF AFGHANISTAN.

The détente relationship between the United States and the Soviet Union had
grown shaky throughout 1979. Some observers attributed this to the fact that
Moscow feared Carter's rapid decision to normalize relations with China in
December, 1978; others viewed it as due to U.S. concern that Russia had violated the détente relationship in Angola, Ethiopia, and finally, on December
27-28, in Afghanistan. Whatever the reason, Carter's announcement of retaliatory measures against Russia for invading Afghanistan indicated that a cold
war relationship had developed between Washington and Moscow, a relationship
disturbing to many European statesmen who cherished the results of détente
between 1969 and 1979. Asked on New Year's Eve, 1979, whether the Afghanistan
affair had changed his perceptions of the Soviets, President Carter candidly
asserted: "This action of the Soviets has made a more dramatic change in my
own opinion of what the Soviets' ultimate goals are than anything they've
done in the previous time I've been in office."

On January 4, the president announced that the United States was placing an embargo on sales to Russia of high technology, grain, and other strategic items. He also said he would seek a Western boycott of the Summer Olympic Games scheduled to be held in Moscow during the summer of 1980 if the Soviet aggression continued.

On January 2, the president wrote a letter to Senate Majority Leader Robert Byrd, asking the Senate to delay its vote on ratification of SALT II until "congress and I can assess Soviet actions."

On January 8, Carter took additional measures to implement his hard line toward Moscow. He ordered the withdrawal of the American advanced consular group preparing to establish an office in Kiev and expelled 17 Soviet diplomats planning to open a consulate in New York. He also suspended current high technology licenses and shipments of such equipment to Russia.

Carter's reprisals continued in future weeks, including the following actions:

1. On January 18, he ordered curbs on Soviet phosphate ammonia exports. Although on February 3 the White House said there might be future phosphate export licenses, Carter made this embargo indefinite on February 25.

2. On January 21, Carter sent personal messages to 100 foreign government leaders asking them to boycott the Olympics if the Soviets did not leave Afghanistan by February 20.

3. Carter banned the export of all computer spare parts for the Kama River truck plant on January 21.

Carter's embargo actions were strongly criticized by some American politicians. As Senator Edward Kennedy said, "it's going to hurt the American farmer and taxpayer more than the Soviet aggressor." With regard to the embargo's effect on grain prices, the Carter administration pledged to buy up 14.5 million tons of corn, wheat, and soybeans (at a cost of $2.6 billion). On January 7-8, grain trading was suspended for two days to allow prices to stabilize but then, on January 9, prices dropped as far as regulations permitted. The administration did nothing to assist manufacturers of machinery and technology or their employees.

Carter endeavored to get U.S. allies around the world to impose a similar embargo, but failed to convince most of them. This enabled the Soviet Union to shop among other nations for replacements, especially of corn and wheat. It also caused tension with Japan and America's European allies who disagreed with the embargo.

January 6, 1980   *IN INDIA, INDIRA GANDHI'S PARTY RETURNS TO POWER BY WINNING 350 OF 542 SEATS IN PARLIAMENT.*

January 9, 1980   *THE SAUDI ARABIAN GOVERNMENT EXECUTES 63 MEMBERS OF THE EXTREMIST MAHDI SECT WHICH HAD ATTACKED THE GRAND MOSQUE AT MECCA ON NOVEMBER 20, 1979.*

In addition to beheading 63 radical Muslims, the Saudis sentenced 19 to prison terms, acquitted 38, and sent 23 women and minors to "re-education" centers.

January 14, 1980   THE U.N. GENERAL ASSEMBLY ADOPTS RESOLUTION ES-6/2
                           DEMANDING THE IMMEDIATE AND TOTAL WITHDRAWAL OF ALL
                           FOREIGN FORCES (SOVIET) FROM AFGHANISTAN.

The vote of the General Assembly was 104 to 18 with 18 abstaining and 12 absent. Although General Assembly votes are non-binding, this vote was the first in which many "non-aligned" nations voted against the Soviet Union. Only Moscow's 18 allies voted against the resolution. Libya and Rumania were notably absent when the vote was cast.

January 23, 1980   PRESIDENT CARTER PLEDGES THAT THE PERSIAN GULF AREA
                           IS A "VITAL AMERICAN INTEREST": THE CARTER DOCTRINE.

In his State-of-the-Union message to congress, the president extended U.S. global defense protection to the Arab oil states and the region along Russia's southern border. Specifically, Carter asserted that "any attempt by any outside force to gain control of the Persian Gulf region will be regarded as an assault on the vital interests of the United States.... Such an assault will be repelled by use of any means necessary, including military force."

In order to implement the new U.S. defense perimeter, Carter asked congress for a 5% increase in the defense budget for 1981, a sum he had resisted as "too much" during 1979. He also indicated that he would ask congress for authority to register young Americans for selective service, although he added, "I hope that it will not become necessary to impose the draft."

President Carter's message was warmly received by Americans who had become incensed at the Iranian crisis and appalled at the Soviet intervention in Afghanistan. Thus, during the next several months, Carter continued to display his hard line against the Communist menace. On February 11, the United States strengthened the American presence in the Persian Gulf and the Indian Ocean area by announcing agreements to obtain military facilities in Oman, Kenya, and Somalia. On April 8, Saudi Arabia refused to accept requests for U.S. military facilities but agreed (March 18) to provide financial aid for Yemen to replace aid formerly received from Moscow. The United States also agreed to provide 60 F-15 fighter planes for the Saudi Arabian defense forces.

Perhaps the most significant U.S. agreement in the Middle East was military cooperation with Egypt. On January 8, Cairo indicated that the United States had tested its Airborne Warning and Control (AWAC) planes by using Egyptian bases as a stopover for flights to Iran. On July 10, the United States and Egypt began a 90-day joint training exercise using American F-4E jet planes, paratroopers, and other forces of the two nations. On November 12, 1980, the United States sent advanced units of its Rapid Deployment Force (RDF) to Egypt for 12 days of joint exercises. The RDF was designed by the U.S. armed forces as a unit which could be quickly sent to any crisis area to counteract enemy (Communist) activity. Thus, the RDF could act as a method to carry out the Carter Doctrine with conventional forces in the Persian Gulf.

The one issue of the Carter Doctrine that was most questioned by some U.S. politicians was the status of U.S.-Pakistani relations. One unidentified senator was quoted as saying: "If Russian troops chase Afghan rebels into Pakistan, do we want American boys up in the Khyber Pass trying to stop them?" U.S. defenses under such contingencies would operate at an extreme logistic disadvantage compared with Soviet home bases. In addition, the questions of Pakistan's stability and reliability were raised. On January 13, Pakistan rejected a U.S. offer of $400 million of economic-military aid as "peanuts." Nevertheless, the United States continued to woo Pakistan, pledging on October 30 to assist Pakistan in case of Soviet attack. See March 12; November 21, 1979.

January 24, 1980   CONGRESS APPROVES THE U.S.-CHINESE TRADE ACT, GIVING THE MOST-FAVORED-NATION STATUS TO THE PEKING GOVERN-MENT.

Although the Carter administration had previously asked the most-favored-nation status for the U.S.S.R. as well as China, this condition no longer applied after the Soviet-Afghanistan affair of 1979. Therefore, congress granted Peking a trade position that the United States denied to Moscow.

January 29, 1980   *THE DAY AFTER CLOSING ITS IRAN EMBASSY, CANADA DIS-CLOSES THAT IT HELPED SIX U.S. EMBASSY EMPLOYEES ES-CAPE.*

After hiding the six Americans in its embassy for three months, Canada sup-plied them with forged Canadian diplomatic passports and smuggled them out on commercial air flights on January 26 and 27. Iran's government was angry, denouncing the Canadian government. Iran's Foreign Minister Sadegh Ghotbzadeh said, "sooner or later, somewhere in the world, Canada will pay."

February 13, 1980   PRESIDENT CARTER ANNOUNCES THE UNITED STATES WILL END ITS 27-MONTH BOYCOTT OF THE INTERNATIONAL LABOR ORGANI-ZATION, REJOINING THE GROUP ON FEBRUARY 18, 1980.

The State Department stated that the ILO had ceased its previous practice of making statements on political and other non-labor circumstances, a practice the United States had objected to in 1977. See November 5, 1977.

February 17, 1980   *PIERRE TRUDEAU IS REELECTED AS CANADA'S PRIME MINISTER.*

Trudeau's Liberal Party defeated Joe Clark's Progressive Conservatives who had won a narrow majority of parliamentary seats in 1979, holding office for less than one year.

February 19, 1980   THE EUROPEAN ECONOMIC COMMUNITY'S FOREIGN MINISTERS REJECT PRESIDENT CARTER'S REQUEST THAT THEY BOYCOTT THE 1980 MOSCOW OLYMPICS: CARTER ANNOUNCES THE U.S. BOYCOTT THE NEXT DAY.

Although the EEC members issued a resolution calling on the Soviet Union to pull its troops out of Afghanistan, the European ministers did not believe the Olympics should be mixed with political questions. Without EEC support, President Carter announced on February 20 that the United States would boycott the Olympics in 1980.

The EEC ministers also refused to support the U.S. embargo of high tech-nology equipment to the Soviet Union. They believed Carter overreacted to

Moscow's actions on December 27, not considering the Afghan buffer state as "vital to European interests" compared with better détente relations with the Soviets.

February 23, 1980   A U.N. COMMISSION OF INQUIRY ARRIVES IN TEHERAN, AS THERE IS SOME HOPE THAT THE HOSTAGE CRISIS MAY BE SETTLED.

The U.N. Commission was established by the Security Council on January 11, at Iran's request for an inquiry into its demands for the return to Iran of the shah and his wealth. Kurt Waldheim, the U.N. Secretary General, believed the U.N. group could settle the hostage crisis by discussions with Khomeini and Iran's Foreign Minister, Abolhassan Bani-Sadr.

On February 11, Bani-Sadr stated that the hostages could be released if the United States admitted its "crimes" in the last 25 years, pledged non-interference in Iran, and recognized Iran's right to extradite the shah. The shah had left New York in December, 1979, and remained in Panama until March 23, 1980, when he moved to Egypt.

Waldheim's optimism about the commission's work was not justified. Even as the U.N. group traveled to Iran, Bani-Sadr and Khomeini indicated they considered it the commission's duty to investigate the shah's crimes, not to settle the hostage issue. On the day the U.N. panel arrived, Khomeini stated that the fate of the hostages would be decided in April by the Islamic Consultative Assembly. In the light of such statements, the commission's members became demoralized. Following two weeks of interviews in Iran, the U.N. panel left on March 11, Secretary Waldheim admitting that its work had failed and that the commission was "suspended."

February 27, 1980   *A LEFTIST GUERRILLA GROUP OCCUPIES THE DOMINICAN REPUBLIC'S EMBASSY IN BOGOTA, COLOMBIA, TAKING 80 HOSTAGES INCLUDING U.S. AMBASSADOR DIEGO ASENCIO.*

Two dozen Colombians entered the Dominican embassy during a reception. They occupied the building and held the hostages. The rebels demanded $50 million, publication of a manifesto of their protests, and the release of 311 "political" prisoners in Colombia.

The hostages were held in Bogota until the negotiation of their release on April 27. The Colombian government released nine rebel prisoners and agreed to have observers from the Human Rights Commission of the Organization of American States at the trials of the other prisoners. In addition, the guerrillas at the Dominican Embassy were paid $2.5 million and allowed to take a plane to safety in Cuba.

March 3, 1980   PRESIDENT CARTER ANNOUNCES THAT THE AMERICAN VOTE ON A MARCH 1 U.N. SECURITY COUNCIL RESOLUTION THAT CENSURED ISRAEL SHOULD HAVE BEEN AN ABSTENTION.

Carter's statement of March 3 seems to have resulted from strong political complaints of pro-Jewish groups in the United States who said the U.S. vote in favor of the censure reversed all prior U.S. policy. Carter's political opponents in the presidential campaign also criticized the president.

Consequently, Carter explained on March 3 that there had been a failure of communication between Washington and New York which resulted in the "yes" vote rather than the usual U.S. abstention on such resolutions.

On March 1, the American Ambassador to the United Nations, Donald McHenry, had voted in favor of Security Council Resolution 454 which censured Israeli settlements on the West Bank of the Jordan. The West Bank issue arose again on February 10 when the Israeli cabinet agreed in principle that Jews could resettle in the Arab town of Hebron. Although world public opinion against this decision caused the Israelis to delay a final vote on the Hebron settlement on February 17, resolutions against such settlements were offered at the U.N. Security Council.

Apparently President Carter opposed the Jewish settlement problem and had instructed Ambassador McHenry to vote in favor of a resolution provided the statement simply said they were illegal. McHenry had negotiated with proponents of the resolution to obtain agreement on a statement the United States could accept. Keeping Secretary Vance informed of these talks, McHenry believed Secretary Vance accepted the wording of the resolution, which was voted upon on March 1.

Following the U.S. vote, critics protested. Therefore, on March 3, Carter explained that Vance accepted responsibility for the error. Vance and McHenry believed the agreed-on wording of the resolution would refer only to the illegality of the West Bank settlement. In fact, it also included a statement against Israel's control of Jerusalem, which Vance thought had been deleted.

Carter's March 3 explanation satisfied no one. The president's critics asked whether Carter was confused on the vote or really intended the vote to put pressure on Israel. Either way, they said, he had "botched up" the job. Generally, the failure of communications explanation appeared to be untenable for normal State Department operations.

March 4, 1980   ROBERT MUGABE'S PARTY WINS THE MAJORITY OF SEATS IN
                       ZIMBABWE'S ELECTION; HE BECOMES PREMIER ON MARCH 11.

The British conducted these elections in their former colony of Rhodesia, acting under the "Lancaster House" proposals accepted by the black Patriotic Front and Ian Smith's white government on November 15, 1979. Of the 80 seats allotted to blacks in the parliament, Mugabe's African National Front won 57, Joshua Nkomo's party won 20. Mugabe was a Marxist, but following his election he assured Rhodesian whites "there is a place for everybody in this country."

On April 14, President Carter named Robert V. Keeley as Ambassador to Zimbabwe and pledged $20 million in economic aid for both 1980 and 1981. On September 25, Zimbabwe joined the United Nations. Mugabe's conciliatory policies during the next year demonstrated that American predictions of a Communist radicalization of Zimbabwe were incorrect.

March 6, 1980   EL SALVADOR'S JUNTA, ACTING ON U.S. ADVICE, DECREES
                       LAND REFORMS, NATIONALIZES THE BANKS, AND DECLARES A
                       30-DAY STATE OF SIEGE.

The Salvador junta led by Colonels Majano and Gutierrez had gained power on October 15 with a promise to reform a nation in which previous military

leaders ran the state to benefit the small wealthy minority. As a U.S. offi-
cial said, El Salvador was a "classic setting for social and political unrest"
because 2% of the population owned 60% of the nation's arable land.

The United States sought to head off further unrest in El Salvador by
blocking a right-wing coup on February 23. In February, 1980, Washington
granted El Salvador $100 million in economic and military aid, asking the
junta to make social reforms. Thus, on March 6, the government confiscated
376 estates covering 700,000 acres of land, promising to redistribute it to
peasants. The government offered to pay the former land holders in govern-
ment bonds. The decree of siege, which banned demonstrations as a means of
maintaining order while the reforms were carried out, engendered much opposi-
tion from left-wing groups in Salvador.

March 24, 1980   *EL SALVADOR'S LIBERAL ARCHBISHOP OSCAR ROMERO IS AS-*
                          SASSINATED BY RIGHT-WING TERRORISTS.

Rather than ending violence by the left- and right-wing extremists in El Sal-
vador, the junta's March 6 announcement of economic reforms caused greater
disturbances. The right wing opposed the land reform as too radical; the
left-wing Marxists denounced the reforms as too little, while also protesting
the 30-day siege.

The slaying of Archbishop Romero led to more violence. During the fu-
neral on March 30, gunfire broke out near the cathedral causing the 30,000
mourners to panic. More than 30 people were killed. Who began the gunfire
was uncertain. Some people blamed Salvadoran army forces who occupied the
National Palace near the cathedral; others blamed the leftists, who, the
U.S. State Department claimed had now received aid from Cuba.

March 29, 1980   TURKEY AND AMERICA REACH A FIVE-YEAR AGREEMENT ON U.S.
                          BASES IN TURKEY AS WELL AS ON ECONOMIC AND MILITARY
                          COOPERATION.

Following the Cypriot crisis, Turkish and American relations had seriously
deteriorated. Throughout 1979, however, there was steady improvement in these
relations, due partly to American concern for the Middle East region following
the fall of the shah of Iran. Although Turkey rejected a U.S. request on
May 15 to permit U-2 flights from Turkish bases as a means for verifying the
Soviets' compliance with the SALT treaties, the renewal of talks between Greek
and Turkish Cypriot leaders on May 18 enabled the United States to undertake
negotiations to renew American aid to Turkey. Talks began on August 13 which
eventually resulted in the agreement signed on March 29, 1980. In the 1980
agreement, the United States did not gain Turkish agreement to provide bases
for U-2 flights over Russia. It received one air base, four intelligence-
gathering bases, and seven communications centers. Turkey received $450 mil-
lion per year.

In mid-June, 1980, the International Monetary Fund approved a three-year,
$1.6 billion loan to Turkey, the largest in the fund's history. During 1980,
Turkey received over $3 billion from sources in the Western alliance, becoming
the third largest recipient of American assistance after Israel and Egypt.
A portion of this made up for aid cut off by the United States during the
Cypriot crisis.

April 4-5, 1980   *OVER 10,000 CUBANS JAM PERU'S EMBASSY IN HAVANA AFTER*
                       CASTRO ANNOUNCES THAT ALL CUBANS WHO ENTER THE EMBASSY
                       PEACEFULLY ARE FREE TO LEAVE CUBA IF THEY OBTAIN FOR-
                       EIGN ENTRY VISAS.

*The Peruvian Embassy had been harboring 25 Cubans who had crashed a bus
through the embassy gate in order to get past a Cuban guard. Apparently to
retaliate against Peru, Castro issued his offer, which permitted any Cubans
who wished to emigrate to do so. On April 5, more than 10,000 citizens indicated they wanted to leave Cuba by arriving at the embassy. Castro's action
caused difficulty for the Peruvians because they could not permit 10,000 persons to immigrate. Lima's rulers called on her Andean Pact neighbors to help.
Peru also said most of the Cubans wanted to go to America. The initial U.S.
reaction was that the Latin American countries should take the lead in opening
their doors to the refugees. See May 5, 1980.*

April 7, 1980   PRESIDENT CARTER BREAKS DIPLOMATIC RELATIONS WITH IRAN
                       AND BANS U.S. EXPORTS.

From January to April 7, the United States conducted quiet diplomacy with
Iran's President Bani-Sadr, hoping to reach a compromise on the hostage question. Following the failure of Kurt Waldheim's U.N. inquiry group on March
11, Bani-Sadr asked the United States for time until the Iranian Revolutionary
Council met so that the government could persuade the militants to turn the
hostages over to the government. In this context, Carter believed a tough
U.S. stance would hinder Bani-Sadr's efforts.

On April 6, when the Revolutionary Council met, it placed the fate of
the hostages in the hands of Khomeini, not the government of Bani-Sadr.
Khomeini stated that the militants would continue to hold the hostages until
the Majlis (Parliament) met later in the summer.

These circumstances caused Carter to break relations with Iran on April
7. He imposed an economic boycott on Iran and asked American allies to join
in these sanctions. He also proposed legislation to allow Americans who held
debt claims against Iran to settle their bills by drawing on the $8 billion
of Iran's frozen assets in the United States.

While announcing these measures, the president said the United States
"will pursue every--and I repeat--every legal use of [U.S.] power to bring
our people home, free and safe." Later, Carter told a group of editors that
among his "legal" remedies he did not "foreclose the option of using military
force" or other punitive action.

April 25, 1980   A U.S. RESCUE MISSION TO LIBERATE THE AMERICAN HOSTAGES
                       IN IRAN ABORTS 250 MILES FROM TEHERAN DUE TO MECHANICAL
                       PROBLEMS.

President Carter ordered the clandestine rescue mission, which failed and
resulted in the accidental deaths of eight American servicemen.

The U.S. operation had been planned since November as one means of rescue
if negotiations failed. Volunteer anti-terrorist specialists from U.S. army,
navy, and marine units had rehearsed their plan under the leadership of Colonel Charles Beckwith. President Carter did not give the operation a "go-ahead"

until April 16. During the mission, six C-130 transport planes carried a 90-man commando team from an Egyptian base to Iran on Thursday evening, April 24. The transports also carried helicopter fuel, weapons, and communications jamming equipment. After refueling at a Persian Gulf base, the transports landed in Iran after dark.

To rendezvous with the C-130 transports, eight Sikorsky RH-53 helicopters left the aircraft carrier *Nimitz*, which had been stationed in the Gulf of Oman. Helicopter equipment failure began soon after take-off because one helicopter had to return to the carrier and a second was forced down during a sandstorm over southern Iran. The remaining six copters flew 600 miles to join the transport planes and commandos at 11:15 p.m. Iranian time. Their rendezvous point was near Tabas in the Dasht-i-Kavir salt desert, 200 miles southeast of Teheran.

The operational plans called for the helicopters to fly the 90-man team north to hide in a mountain area near Teheran. On the night of April 25, trucks driven by U.S. agents already in Iran would carry the team into the city. At a prearranged time the commandos would assault the U.S. compound and Foreign Ministry building to free the hostages. Helicopters would fly into the city and carry the team and hostages to an abandoned airstrip outside Teheran. Finally, two C-141's would fly to the airstrip, pick up the Americans, and carry them to safety in the desert area of Saudi Arabia.

The rescue operation never got beyond the initial salt desert rendezvous point. The landing team first had the unexpected problem of capturing a busload of Iranians who came on the scene. Next, as the helicopters refueled, one developed a hydraulic problem. The mission plan called for a minimum of six helicopters. With only five remaining, Colonel Beckwith recommended aborting the mission; the president agreed.

As the mission aborted and the C-130's prepared to carry out both the 90-man team and the helicopter crews, another disaster took place. While refueling in the desert darkness, a helicopter collided with a C-130. Ammunition aboard the transport plane exploded, killing eight servicemen. The commandos had to crowd aboard the remaining transport planes. At 4 a.m. the rescue team left behind the dead soldiers, six helicopters, and the wrecked C-130 and flew out to Masirah, a small island near Oman.

One consequence of the raid was that the Iranians scattered the U.S. hostages to various locations outside the U.S. embassy, making a second military rescue operation almost impossible. In America, the disaster caused further embarrassment for the president. Preparations for the mission seemed to have been incomplete, appearing to reflect the indecisiveness of the president about which critics complained.

April 27, 1980   *THE NICARAGUAN JUNTA LOSES TWO MODERATE MEMBERS WHO*
                          OPPOSED THE SANDINISTA POLICIES.

Since the overthrow of Somoza on July 17, 1979, there had been frequent disagreements in the mixed moderate-radical junta the United States had sanctioned. The formation of a Sandinist Popular Army on July 28 and the political-economic accords signed with Moscow on March 20, 1980, were the two most-criticized actions by the Sandinist members of the junta.

The announcement of the National Council of State that the number of Sandinist members would increase from one-third to a majority resulted in the resignation of the two moderates, Violeta Barios de Chamorro (April 19) and Alfonso Callejas (April 22). De Chamorro resigned for "reasons of health."

As the owner of La Prensa, *the nation's leading independent newspaper, she
had been troubled by a Sandinist-organized strike which shut down the paper.
Callejas, a businessman, resigned to protest the April 21 decree giving the
Sandinists a majority of council votes.*

   *On April 22, the council stated it would appoint other moderates to the
junta. On May 19, two moderates, Rafael Rivas and Arturo Cruz, joined the
National Council membership. Nevertheless, the new council moved rapidly to
undertake radical measures for full Sandinist control of Nicaragua. Having
gained a majority of council seats, the Sandinistas proceeded to obtain a
firm hold on the nation.*

April 29, 1980   EDMUND MUSKIE IS NAMED SECRETARY OF STATE FOLLOWING
                         SECRETARY VANCE'S RESIGNATION IN OPPOSITION TO THE
                         ABORTED HOSTAGE RESCUE ATTEMPT.

Vance had submitted his resignation to Carter on April 21, three days before
the aborted raid against Iran, which the secretary had opposed. He agreed,
however, not to announce his resignation until the raid ended.

   Edmund Muskie was a senator from Maine who had made his reputation in
domestic not foreign relations. He had been the Democratic vice-presidential
nominee in 1968 but lost the presidential nomination to McGovern in 1972.
Some observers said Muskie was named secretary because, unlike Vance, he would
not clash with the more aggressive proposals of National Security Advisor
Brzezinski, to whom Carter had turned increasingly after the Afghanistan crisis.

   In his first significant speech as secretary, Muskie told the Foreign
Policy Association on July 7 that the State Department would place less stress
on human rights issues and provide essential economic, social, and military
aid to non-Communist nations regardless of their civil rights agenda.

May 4, 1980   *MARSHAL TITO OF YUGOSLAVIA DIES.*

*Tito was replaced by Vice-President Lazar Kolsevski. In elections on May 15,
Cvijetin Mijatovic was elected president.*

May 5, 1980   PRESIDENT CARTER SAYS THE UNITED STATES WILL WELCOME
                       "WITH AN OPEN HEART AND OPEN ARMS" ALL REFUGEES FROM
                       CUBA.

On April 5, when Fidel Castro dropped all barriers to Cubans wishing to leave,
the U.S. government had hesitated about the proper response. Washington
agreed to take 3,500 of the 10,000 Cubans in Peru's embassy. Peru took 1,000;
Venezuela and Spain, 500 each; Costa Rica and Canada, 300; and Ecuador, 200.

   On April 21, Castro suspended the airlift of refugees to Costa Rica and
opened a ship-to-shore boat shuttle from Muriel, Cuba, to Key West. By May 5,
about 30,000 Cubans had reached the United States. Cuban-Americans attempted
to free their relatives and bring them to the United States but Castro decreed
that of the passengers on each boat only one-third could be relatives; one-
third would come from the group still at Peru's embassy; and one-third would
be Castro's "trash"--political dissidents, criminals, and those the government
wished to get rid of, including the mentally ill.

Carter's May 5 declaration meant that all Cuban-American relatives might eventually come to Florida. Therefore, the president declared a state of emergency in Florida and set aside $10 million to feed and clothe the refugees.

About this same time, refugees from Haiti began crowding onto boats in order to reach Florida and be accepted by the United States. Most Haitians, however, were declared economic not political refugees, even though it was also Cuba's poor economy that undoubtedly caused most Cubans to leave that island. As a result, lawyers for the Haitians went to court, claiming that their clients had been discriminated against because they were black and had fled a dictatorship that was on good terms with America. See May 14, 1980.

May 14, 1980   PRESIDENT CARTER QUALIFIES HIS "OPEN ARMS" FOR REFUGEES STATEMENT OF MAY 5 AND ORDERS LIMITS ON AIRLIFTS AND SEALIFTS TO SCREEN OUT UNDESIRABLES.

From April 21 to mid-May, 60,000 refugees poured into Key West from Cuba. Many boat owners had overloaded their vessels to obtain more profits from charging each refugee for the transportation. In one instance, an overcrowded boat capsized, drowning 12 persons. Therefore, Carter proposed to Castro that he assist in making the refugee flow orderly and assist in clearing people leaving Cuba for the United States. Castro chose to ignore Carter's suggestion and the exodus continued until September 26. Between April 21 and September 26, 125,262 refugees came to the United States from Cuba. Because Cuba did not screen the persons who left, the United States had to establish refugee centers in order to evaluate the status of each immigrant and assist each one in locating work or other support after leaving the refugee center.

May 16, 1980   SECRETARY MUSKIE MEETS IN VIENNA WITH SOVIET FOREIGN MINISTER GROMYKO IN THE FIRST HIGH-LEVEL U.S.-SOVIET MEETING IN EIGHT MONTHS.

Secretary Muskie described the sessions as "introductory." During other meetings at Vienna which included British and French delegates, Muskie spoke bluntly in asserting that "an act of aggression [i.e., Afghanistan] anywhere threatens security everywhere."

May 18, 1980   *IN RESPONSE TO AN AMERICAN REQUEST FOR EUROPEAN ACTION TO OPPOSE IRAN'S HOSTAGE POLICY, THE EUROPEAN ECONOMIC COMMUNITY LEADERS PLACE LIMITED SANCTIONS ON IRAN.*

The economic sanctions voted by the EEC became effective on May 22 and applied to all contracts made with Iran since November 4, 1979. The British government accepted slightly different sanctions on Iran, limiting them to new contracts only, that is, contracts made after May 22.

May 26, 1980   *THE TARGET DAY FOR EGYPT AND ISRAEL TO END WEST BANK AUTONOMY TALKS ENDS WITH NO RESULTS.*

The 1979 Egyptian-Israeli peace treaty had scheduled autonomy talks to resolve

the issue of Arab autonomy in lands occupied by Israel in 1967. Eight rounds
of talks had been held, but like the ninth-round discussions from February 27
to March 4, 1980, they ended in disagreement. Efforts by Carter to renew
talks were rejected by Sadat on May 15, because Israel's Knesset had approved
a bill declaring Jerusalem was the capital of Israel. On May 18, the Israeli
cabinet also opposed another round of autonomy talks.

    Israel's relations with Egypt and the United States reached a low point
during the spring of 1980. On May 2, six Jewish settlers were killed in Hebron. In retaliation, Israel deported three West Bank Arab officials to Lebanon for inflammatory criticism of Israel. On May 8, the U.N. Security Council voted for the fourth time in three months to censure Israel. The United
States abstained from voting on the resolution although the Carter administration disapproved Prime Minister Begin's West Bank settlement policy. On
June 2, 1980, Jewish terrorists placed bombs in automobiles; two bombs exploded, maiming two West Bank Arab mayors and an Israeli trying to defuse a
third bomb. Other Jewish terrorists threw hand grenades in Hebron, injuring
seven Arabs. Because of these tensions and the continuing Jewish settlement
of occupied West Bank territory, the autonomy discussions became impossible.

May 27, 1980   THE FIRST HEAD OF THE CHINESE STATE TO VISIT JAPAN IN
                          2,000 YEARS, HUA GUOFENG, ARRIVES IN TOKYO.

Hua and Japanese Prime Minister Ohira met to discuss trade relations and joint
cooperation against the U.S.S.R. in East Asia.

May 30, 1980   WEST GERMANY AND THE SOVIET UNION SIGN A TREATY ON
                          OIL AND GAS EXPLORATION AND USE.

West German and other European statesmen wished to separate détente in Europe
from the U.S.-Soviet tensions which appeared to have ended détente. Thus,
the Germans signed the oil-natural gas proposals which were being negotiated
with Moscow.

    Détente also continued to be pursued in relations between East and West
Germany. On April 30, the two German states signed a $282 million transporta-
tion agreement to permit road, railway, and water links between West Berlin
and West Germany.

June 16, 1980   CARTER SENDS WEST GERMANY'S LEADER, HELMUT SCHMIDT, A
                          LETTER WARNING HIM NOT TO AGREE WITH BREZHNEV ON FREEZ-
                          ING AMERICAN MISSILE DEPLOYMENTS IN EUROPE.

Apparently the president felt European leaders were acting with Moscow without
consulting with Washington. On May 19, French President Giscard d'Estaing
met with Brezhnev in Warsaw without consulting the United States. Carter
did not want Schmidt to do the same, even though Schmidt had announced his
meeting with Brezhnev as early as January 17, 1980. The publicity given to
Carter's letter caused many Europeans to object to the president's interference, especially because Washington frequently acted without first talking
with its European allies.

    On June 21, Carter held a meeting with Schmidt prior to the Venice eco-
nomic summit sessions. The United States was concerned that its alliance

with the European nations was drifting apart. Reportedly, Carter and Schmidt seldom got along personally and Carter's June 16 letter had upset the German Chancellor. Schmidt wanted to strengthen NATO but he disagreed with American proposals to stretch NATO forces into the area of the Persian Gulf. After their talk in Venice, the two leaders' outward sense of disunity temporarily dissipated. Carter stated that Schmidt supported the 1979 NATO decision to deploy missiles in Europe.

Nevertheless, both Schmidt and Giscard d'Estaing of France were disappointed with U.S. policy. From July 7 to 11, 1980, these two leaders met in Bonn to reaffirm the German-French alliance. Their joint communique on July 11 urged an independent role for Europe in world affairs. Such a role would not end the American alliance but would separate European national policies from Washington's authority in order to enact programs in the national interest of the West European states.

June 17, 1980   *VIETNAMESE FORCES ATTACK ACROSS THE THAI BORDER, STRIK-*
ING AT REFUGEE CAMPS HOLDING CAMBODIANS.

Following U.S. protest of these attacks, the Vietnamese withdrew. The raid resulted in 24 Thai and 1,000 refugees being killed. As these border incidents continued, the United States gave Thailand $32.5 million of military equipment on July 1. On October 22, the U.N. General Assembly passed a resolution calling for the Vietnamese to pull out of Cambodia. The United Nations continued to recognize the exiled government of Pol Pot as Cambodia's legitimate rulers.

June 18, 1980   FOLLOWING VISITS IN WASHINGTON WITH AMERICAN OFFICIALS,
JORDAN'S KING HUSSEIN INDICATES HE WILL JOIN MID-EAST
TALKS WITH EGYPT AND ISRAEL IF ISRAEL AGREES TO RETURN
THE OCCUPIED TERRITORY.

Seeking to revive and extend the West Bank autonomy talks, Carter hoped King Hussein would agree to participate, a maneuver which could end the Israeli-Egyptian deadlock (see May 26, 1980). Hussein refused to join the discussions on autonomy without specific commitments from Israel.

Nevertheless, the United States promised to sell Jordan 100 M-60 tanks with night-vision scopes and laser-range finders. Pro-Israel groups in congress opposed these sales, but the State Department said the arrangement was to prevent a Jordanian arms pact with the Soviet Union.

June 19, 1980   PRESIDENT CARTER ASKS CONGRESS TO APPROVE SHIPMENTS
OF ENRICHED URANIUM FUEL TO INDIA.

On May 7, the president indicated that the United States had agreed to send India nuclear fuel for the Tarapur plant. Although the U.S. Nuclear Regulatory Commission (NRC) voted against the proposal on May 16, Carter overruled the NRC. The NRC objected because India refused to comply with international regulations on the use of nuclear power and on the development of nuclear weapons. The president favored the agreement in order to prevent closer ties between India and the Soviet Union.

Congress held extensive debates before agreeing to allow the shipment of 38 tons of uranium fuel. The House had rejected the proposal on September 18 but the Senate removed the objection clauses, and a conference committee agreed to accept Carter's recommendation on September 24, 1980.

June 22, 1980   IN JAPANESE ELECTIONS, THE LIBERAL DEMOCRATIC PARTY
                       (LPD) WINS A 30-SEAT MAJORITY IN THE LOWER HOUSE AL-
                       THOUGH ITS LEADER, PRIME MINISTER MASAYOSHI OHIRA,
                       DIED ON JUNE 12.

On June 16, the LPD selected former Agricultural Minister Zenko SUZUKI as prime minister. On August 18, Suzuki reaffirmed Japan's commitment to the U.S.-Japanese security treaty.

June 25, 1980   CONGRESS APPROVES CARTER'S REQUEST FOR REVIVAL OF THE
                       SELECTIVE SERVICE SYSTEM.

There had been discussions about reviving selective service and universal military training for several years because voluntary enlistments often fell short of the armed forces requirements. Therefore, to indicate his continuing concern for the nation's defenses, Carter asked congress on February 8 to pass legislation for registering men and women under selective service for possible conscription "to resist further Soviet aggression." On February 26, the administration bill requested $45 million to make registration operative. The Senate approved this bill on the basis of $13.3 million on June 12; the House approved the bill on June 25.

June 26, 1980   FRANCE SUCCESSFULLY TESTS A NEUTRON BOMB.

This French weapon was experimental. The French government said it would decide in two or three years about whether or not to produce such weapons in quantity and deploy them.

June 26, 1980   A U.N. SECURITY COUNCIL RESOLUTION CONDEMNS SOUTH AF-
                       RICA'S INVASION OF ANGOLA, ASKING FOR ITS IMMEDIATE
                       WITHDRAWAL.

On June 13, South Africa said it had raided bases in Angola which were used by Namibian rebels for raids into South West Africa. On June 26, Angola claimed that 3,000 South African troops occupied its southern towns and had killed over 300 civilians. The Security Council backed Angola's demands that South Africa should withdraw. The vote was 12-0; the United States and two other members abstained.

July 1, 1980   CHANCELLOR SCHMIDT AND SOVIET CHAIRMAN BREZHNEV CONDUCT
                       DÉTENTE DISCUSSIONS IN MOSCOW.

Following two days of talks with Soviet officials, the West German leader reported that the Russians were prepared to negotiate with the United States on intermediate-range missiles to be stationed in Europe. He said he had

asked the Soviet leader to pull Soviet troops out of Afghanistan but had re-
ceived no commitment from Brezhnev. Finally, he said, the Germans and Soviets
continued plans for the $13.3 billion natural gas pipeline to be constructed
between Siberia and West Germany.

Following the Moscow talks, Schmidt sent West Germany's Foreign Minister,
Hans Genscher, to Washington on July 2, to provide details of his conversa-
tions to President Carter.

July 4, 1980   *THE ORGANIZATION OF AFRICAN UNITY (OAU) DEMANDS THAT*
                            THE UNITED STATES REMOVE ITS BASE ON DIEGO GARCIA AND
                            RETURN THE ISLAND TO MAURITIUS.

The U.S. Navy had occupied the Indian Ocean island of Diego Garcia during the
early 1970's, gradually replacing the British fleet which previously held the
island as a strategic naval base. The OAU protest was not acceptable to the
United States because Washington believed the base was more vital than ever
due to the Iranian and Afghanistan incidents of 1979 and the Carter Doctrine.

July 19, 1980   AS THE OLYMPICS OPEN IN MOSCOW, 59 NATIONS JOIN THE
                            UNITED STATES IN BOYCOTTING THE GAMES.

The most significant nations joining the U.S. boycott were West Germany,
China, Japan, Canada, and Kenya.

July 25, 1980   THE U.S. STATE DEPARTMENT TAKES ACTION TO OPPOSE
                            THE MILITARY COUP IN BOLIVIA.

Following a Bolivian election on June 29, Bolivia's armed forces staged its
fourth military takeover in 26 months on July 17. The junta headed by
General Luis Garcia Meza Tejada claimed that the Popular Democratic Party,
headed by Herman Siles ZUAZO, was communist. Zuazo gained the largest
percentage of votes (38.7%) of any of the fifteen presidential candidates.
General Meza began a program of arrest, torture, and execution which led
the Organization of American States, and the Andean Pact presidents to
condemn the military regime. On July 25, the State Department announced
the U.S. would withdraw its military advisors and economic aid from Bolivia
and "strongly" support the OAS condemnation of Bolivia.

July 27, 1980   *THE SHAH, MOHAMMED REZA PAHLAVI, DIES IN EGYPT.*

The shah died from cancer and circulatory shock after 18 months of exile and
a long illness.

July 30, 1980   *THE ISRAELI KNESSET APPROVES LEGISLATION MAKING JERU-*
                            SALEM THE "UNITED AND UNDIVIDED" CAPITAL OF ISRAEL.

Following this decision, Prime Minister Begin said he planned to move his
office to East Jerusalem. Israel's action made the autonomy talks with Egypt
more difficult because they implied that Israel would not compromise on its
occupation of East Jerusalem nor on its West Bank settlement policy.

August 5, 1980   WHITE HOUSE ADMINISTRATION AIDES DISCLOSE THAT CARTER
                           APPROVED PRESIDENTIAL DIRECTIVE 59, PROVIDING A NEW
                           AMERICAN NUCLEAR STRATEGY WHICH ACCEPTS THE CONCEPT
                           OF A "WINNABLE NUCLEAR WAR."

While Directive 59 was not made public and Secretary of Defense Harold Brown
said on August 10 it was not a "major break with past policies, but an evolutionary development," the implications of the directive were vitally significant to nuclear strategic and operational decisions.

   Since November, 1975, when Secretary of Defense James Schlesinger resigned after President Ford agreed with Secretary of State Kissinger on the
U.S. defense budget for fiscal 1977, scholars of nuclear strategy knew that
their dispute reflected the Pentagon's proposals greatly to increase the American military establishment by changing from the concept of mutually assured
destruction (M.A.D.) to a "counterforce" strategy which envisioned both a
limited and a winnable nuclear war.

   In explaining Directive 59, Secretary Brown and President Carter insisted
that the United States was not seeking a first-strike capacity. Brown said
the U.S. strategy was to give the president options to use "countervailing"
force; that is, the nuclear capacity to hit Soviet military targets or population centers and to do so at various levels of limited force which could be
retaliatory BUT MIGHT BE FIRST STRIKE. This selectivity of targets and force
levels would permit U.S. and Russian leaders to play a chess-like game during
which each sought to calculate what level of nuclear attack would be sufficient to obtain the surrender of the enemy. Whether called "countervailing"
or "counterforce," the strategy of Directive 59 reversed the strategy concepts which supported nuclear parity and détente. Nuclear "selectivity" war
replaced the previous concept of nuclear deterrent war in which neither power
would wish to begin a nuclear conflict.

   Since being described as M.A.D. by Secretary of Defense Robert McNamara
in 1967, U.S. nuclear strategy as well as the Nixon-Kissinger détente and
SALT I and SALT II programs had been based on limited strategic nuclear arms
and U.S. parity with the Russians. In this context, Directive 59 also indicated that the Carter administration had accepted the concept contained in
the Republican platform of Ronald Reagan adopted during the July, 1980, convention. This platform called for a "clear capability to destroy [Soviet]
military targets." Both this statement and the terminology and rhetoric used
by the Republican right wing and by Secretary of Defense Brown confused rather
than clarified the strategic substance of the two nuclear strategies: M.A.D.
and "counterforce."

   The "counterforce" strategy, which Pentagon officials claimed the Soviet
military had also adopted, was based on a scenario of nuclear war totally
different from M.A.D. Under M.A.D. doctrine, each side possessed sufficient
nuclear weapons to sustain a first strike and to retaliate against the other
nation's population centers in sufficient destructive force to prevent either
side from attempting a suicidal first strike--hence, assured destruction prevented war because no one would win. Nuclear war was considered to be a lose-
lose contest.

   During the 1970's, hawks in both the Russian and U.S. military hierarchy
began to write about the possibility of a LIMITED nuclear war, in which one
side could force the other side to surrender before striking back. By assumption, if one power could send nuclear warheads to knock out a sufficient number of the enemy's nuclear weapons in a first strike, the nation attacked
would decide not to commit its weapons to a second strike. Or, in another

scenario, if both powers attacked the nuclear weapons centers (*not the population centers*) of each other, the power receiving the greatest number of
knock-out blows would surrender to the other power. In either case, there
were two presupposed results: (1) the war would be limited and (2) one side
would surrender, the other side would win.

Although the counterforce strategy included weapons to conduct first
and, perhaps, second strikes against the weapons bases of the enemy, rather
than the population centers, critics of counterforce claimed these assumptions
were, like Dr. Strangelove's suicide-superbomb, based on a false premise.
In reality, they said, any first strike would soon escalate the war to a
global holocaust. Neither side would surrender as long as it held any nuclear
retaliatory weapons. The first strike could never knock out all the nuclear
warheads of the other side; so if one power dared to risk a nuclear attack,
the war would escalate to mutual destruction. What U.S. president, the critics said, would hesitate to strike back if his nation were attacked, especially if hesitation meant surrender to communism? Or what Communist leader
would surrender as long as he had a few weapons to unleash?

To the military planners in the Kremlin and the Pentagon, the counterforce strategy meant larger military budgets. For these hawks, M.A.D. and
parity resulted in an admittedly stable nuclear budget, including stability
in the highest priced and most sophisticated weapons under their control.
As a result, the Soviet and American military searched for bigger and better
weapons of greater accuracy and larger initial damage in order to be "certain"
to destroy the "military targets" of the enemy.

Even before approving Directive 59, Carter steadily moved in the direction of the new strategy by approving the MX-mobile missile system on September 7, 1979. The MX was one Pentagon answer to the Soviets' large SS-18's
and SS-19 intercontinental missiles. The MX bases would be mobile because
the U.S. analysts expected that under the limited-war plan, the American missiles would likely be used only on a second-strike basis. Mobility permitted
the MX to evade destruction and required the Soviets to target more warheads
to be certain to knock out all of the MX weapons.

In addition to the MX missiles, the Pentagon developed more powerful and
more accurate submarine missiles for its Trident submarines, including advanced Ballistic Re-entry Systems for accuracy. The American Air Force developed the Precision Guided Re-entry Vehicle to give the MX great accuracy.
This accuracy would provide a greater capability of destroying the weapons
of the opponent.

In strategic terms, opponents of SALT II used the counterforce strategy
to verify their claims that the Soviet Union developed its new weapons and
strategy to endeavor to "win" a nuclear war. On August 5, Carter adopted
the nuclear counterforce strategy. In part, of course, the president's decision reflected the hard line anti-Communist attitude he adopted after January 4, 1980. Hard-liners in America believed if the Soviets thought they
could "win," the United States must believe it could "win" a limited and sur-
vivable nuclear war.

As a follow up to the new strategy, Secretary Brown told an audience at
the Naval War College on August 20 that American I.C.B.M.'s may now be vulnerable to Soviet missiles. Brown significantly did not mention the American
bomber force and the navy submarine missiles, both of which had missile-
launching capacity that the Soviets could not knock out. As Brown's opponents emphasized, the Soviets relied almost completely on I.C.B.M.'s; the
United States had a triad of excellent nuclear launchers including submarine
missiles and a large manned bomber force as well as I.C.B.M.'s.

Also on August 20, the Pentagon announced it was developing the "stealth aircraft," a bomber invisible to Soviet radar because it would have aerodynamic features and technical features enabling it to fly low and evade detection by the Soviet warning system. In both "stealth" and cruise missile technology, the United States possessed future technology in advance of the Soviet technology.

August 13, 1980   *70,000 POLISH WORKERS STRIKE AT THE GDANSK SHIPYARDS,*
                           WITH OTHER STRIKES STAGED IN LODZ AND WROCLAW.

Economic difficulties had increased in Poland during the late 1970's, leading to the dismissal of Polish Prime Minister Piotr Jaroszewicz on February 15, 1980. Protests among Polish dissidents continued, however, and on March 20, the government arrested 20 dissident leaders. Between July 2 and 7 there were more scattered workers' strikes to oppose government increases in food prices and the government's announcement that workers' wage demands could not be met.

The first large-scale strike in Poland occurred on August 13 at the Gdansk shipyards. The workers demanded an independent union and the reinstatement of Lech Walesa, who had been dismissed in the 1970 riots.

On August 17, an Interfactory Strike Committee representing 21 factories presented a list of demands to the government. The next day, Poland's Communist leader, Edward Gierek, agreed to pay increases but asserted that the Socialist system could not be changed.

August 20, 1980   THE UNITED STATES ABSTAINS ON A U.N. SECURITY COUNCIL
                           RESOLUTION WHICH CENSURES ISRAEL FOR ANNEXING EAST
                           JERUSALEM AND REQUESTS ALL NATIONS TO REMOVE THEIR
                           EMBASSIES FROM JERUSALEM.

Significantly, the council vote demonstrated how Israel's West Bank policy isolated it from all other nations. The resolution vote was 14 in favor, none opposed, the United States abstaining. Soon after the resolution passed, 13 nations which had embassies in Jerusalem announced they would close them and relocate in Tel Aviv.

August 25, 1980   RONALD REAGAN, THE REPUBLICAN PARTY PRESIDENTIAL CAN-
                           DIDATE, ISSUES A "DEFINITIVE" STATEMENT THAT HE ACCEPTS
                           THE CURRENT UNOFFICIAL RELATIONSHIP BETWEEN THE UNITED
                           STATES AND TAIWAN.

Candidate Reagan issued the statement following news reports that Chinese officials in Peking, meeting with Republican Vice-Presidential nominee George Bush, told Bush that Reagan's previous views on Taiwan endangered Chinese-American relations and world peace.

Reagan had long been associated with right-wing Republican groups in America who supported Taiwan and opposed the recognition of Communist China. Until his statement of August 25, the presidential nominee's current views had not been clarified on the U.S. policy recognizing Peking's status as China's government, and on the U.S. special legislation on Taiwan.

August 27, 1980   *SOUTH KOREAN LEADER CHUN DOO HWAN ASSUMES THE PRESI-*
                              DENCY.

*Following student uprisings in Seoul, Kwangju, and other towns, Chun, who
had been made head of the Korean Central Intelligence Agency on April 14,
moved strongly to suppress the riots, close the universities, and extend martial law throughout South Korea. By August, Chun had solidified his power
and conducted an election which guaranteed his victory and selection as president on August 27.*

    *President Carter, who in the early years of his term of office champi-
oned human rights, told a Boston Globe reporter that Chun "favors complete
democracy" but "the Koreans are not ready for that, according to their own
judgment."*

August 30, 1980   *THE POLISH GOVERNMENT GRANTS WORKERS THE RIGHT TO
                              STRIKE AND FORM INDEPENDENT UNIONS.*

*Attempting to meet some of the workers' demands and end the extensive strikes,
the Polish government yielded to two principal demands of the workers. These
actions led Moscow to become concerned about Poland's situation. On September 3, the Soviets loaned Poland $100 million to help their economic problems.
They also decided that Gierek should be dismissed as the security chief of
the Polish Communist Party.*

    *By September 22, the unions had prepared a labor charter and registered
in the Warsaw Courts as a united organization known as SOLIDARITY with Lech
Walesa as their leader. The Warsaw court legalized the union on October 24
with the provision that it recognize the Communist Party's "leading role" in
Poland's unions.*

    *The Polish workers were not satisfied, however. Strike activity was
renewed in 200 plants in Czestochowa on November 15. As a result, on November 19, under a threat of a national Solidarity strike, Poland's Supreme Court
agreed to delete the lower court's wording on "the Communist Party's leading
role," inserting the phrase in a separate protocol to the union charter. The
protocol also guaranteed that the International Labor Organization would prevent government interference in the union.*

    *Solidarity's demands put more pressure on the Polish government from
Moscow where Soviet leaders watched to make certain that the party's compromises with the Polish workers did not become excessive. See December 3, 1980.*

September 4, 1980   *IRAQ AND IRAN GO TO WAR AS AN IRAQI ARMY SEIZES 90
                              SQUARE MILES OF TERRITORY NORTH OF THE SHATT AL ARAB
                              WATERWAY.*

*As the war began, there were immediate attempts by the PLO and the Arab League
to mediate the boundary dispute, but to no avail. The United States and the
Soviet Union both pledged neutrality in the conflict. The Iran-Iraqi conflict
became a lengthy war of attrition with neither side willing to compromise or
capable of launching a sustained major offensive to defeat the enemy.*

September 19, 1980   *THE BELGIAN GOVERNMENT AGREES TO DEPLOY 48 U.S. MIS-
                              SILES IF ARMS TALKS BETWEEN AMERICA AND THE SOVIETS
                              FAIL.*

October 2, 1980   *THE BRITISH LABOUR PARTY BACKS UNILATERAL DISARMAMENT*
                          TO PREVENT NUCLEAR WAR.

*This was the first time in 20 years that the leftist faction gained sufficient
votes in the Labour Party Convention to pass a resolution for unilateral disarmament. This vote was also a sign of the split developing between moderates
and radicals in that party. On November 10, 1980, Michael Foot, a radical
Laborite, was named as the British Labour Party Chief.*

October 5, 1980   *IN WEST GERMAN ELECTIONS, HELMUT SCHMIDT'S DEMOCRATIC*
                          COALITION WINS.

*As a result, Schmidt was reelected as the West German Chancellor on November
5, 1980.*

October 13, 1980   THE MARSHALL ISLANDS AND THE FEDERATED STATES OF MICRO-
                          NESIA ACCEPT A "FREE ASSOCIATION" ACCORD WITH THE
                          UNITED STATES.

These Pacific islands had been under U.S. trusteeship with the United Nations.
They now assumed a semi-independent status. The Federated States included
the islands of Truk, Yap, Ponape, and Kosrae. On November 15, 1980, a similar
accord was signed by the island Republic of Palau.

October 17, 1980   THE SOVIET UNION AND THE UNITED STATES BEGIN TALKS ON
                          LIMITING THEATER NUCLEAR FORCES.

Although Brezhnev told the State Department on January 3 that the TNF talks
on long-range, intermediate missiles in Europe could not be successful, discussions began on October 17, and the first round of discussions ended on
November 17. The Soviets wanted the United States and NATO to renounce the
December, 1979, decision to deploy Pershing II and cruise missiles prior to
negotiations. After the United States refused, the talks began but under
difficulties that handicapped their success. No results had been achieved
by November 17, 1980.

October 22, 1980   AMERICA SIGNS A GRAIN PURCHASE AGREEMENT WITH CHINA.

According to this grain accord, China would purchase up to nine million tons
of grain annually over the next four years. The grain purchase pact helped
Carter's presidential campaign because U.S. farmers had complained of price
decreases resulting from the Soviet grain embargo imposed by the president
in January, 1980.

October 24, 1980   *GREECE REJOINS THE NATO DEFENSE PACT AFTER ITS PARLIA-
                          MENT APPROVES A COMPROMISE AGREEMENT ON TURKEY.*

*The Cypriot crisis between Turkey and Greece led Athens to withdraw its mili-
tary cooperation with NATO forces to defend the Aegean Sea area in*

coordination with Turkey. Stressing the need to strengthen the Western alli-
ance in light of the Iranian and Afghanistan situations, the U.S. and Turkish
governments made concessions to Greece to obtain its reentry into NATO.
Greece and Turkey still had to negotiate the details of their NATO cooperation
in the Aegean.

November 4, 1980   RONALD W. REAGAN IS ELECTED PRESIDENT, WINNING A CLEAR-
                      CUT VICTORY OVER PRESIDENT CARTER.

Former Governor of California and spokesman for right-wing groups in the Republican Party, Reagan won the nomination at the national convention in Detroit on July 17. President Carter was nominated by the Democratic Convention
in New York on August 14. While Carter ran on his record, Reagan campaigned
on a platform emphasizing the renewal of America's preeminent military position against the Soviets and the return to concepts of supply-side economics
which would stimulate business investments, thereby revitalizing the American
economy.

     In the election, Reagan won 489 electoral votes to Carter's 49. The
Republicans gained control of the Senate by a six-vote majority; the Democrats
retained control of the House with a 57-vote majority.

November 11, 1980   SIGNS OF A POSSIBLE SETTLEMENT WITH IRAN APPEAR AS
                      THE UNITED STATES BEGINS TALKS IN ALGERIA, WHOSE GOV-
                      ERNMENT AGREES TO ACT AS AN INTERMEDIARY WITH IRAN.

The initial indication that Iran might discuss a solution to the hostage crisis came on September 12, 1980, when the Ayatollah Khomeini announced four
conditions for the release of the Americans. His terms were: to return the
shah's wealth, to cancel U.S. claims against Iran, to unfreeze Iranian assets,
and to promise future non-interference by the United States in Iran. The
Carter administration approached Khomeini's announcement cautiously, not wishing to raise unfounded hopes among Americans.

     On October 21, after President Bani-Sadr repeated Khomeini's terms,
Carter pledged he would unfreeze the assets and end U.S. sanctions. He had
agreed to noninterference in Iran on several occasions in the past. Carter
also asked Teheran to begin direct negotiations to settle the hostage crisis.
Bani-Sadr refused to negotiate directly.

     The final steps toward Algiers' offer to act as a go-between were taken
on November 2 and 3, when the Iranian Majlis approved Khomeini's four terms
and the student militants at the U.S. embassy agreed to give "responsibility"
for the hostages to the government.

     The next act was up to America. On November 11, Deputy Secretary of
State Warren Christopher went to Algiers for a 30-hour talk with Algerian
representatives. Christopher explained the American position; the Algerians
agreed to convey the details of the U.S. response to Teheran. The process
which finally gained the hostages' release had begun. See January 20, 1981.

November 13-14, 1980   NATO'S NUCLEAR PLANNING GROUP MEETS IN BRUSSELS AND AP-
                        PROVES THE AMERICAN "COUNTERVAILING" NUCLEAR STRATEGY.

(See August 5, 1980.)

November 28, 1980   SENATOR CHARLES PERCY MEETS WITH LEONID BREZHNEV IN
                        MOSCOW, REPORTING THAT THE SOVIETS WOULD LIKE TO START
                        SALT III TALKS AS SOON AS POSSIBLE.

Percy, who became the Chairman of the Senate Foreign Relations Committee in
January, 1981, was the first high U.S. official to speak with Brezhnev since
Carter signed SALT II in June, 1979. During his week in Moscow, Percy talked
for about 10 hours with Brezhnev and other officials. They discussed Poland,
Afghanistan, and oil, as well as arms limitations. Percy also appeared on
Soviet national television. Although the Illinois senator told the Soviets
that SALT II was dead regarding Senate ratification, Brezhnev indicated he
was ready to begin new talks on another strategic arms treaty.

December 3, 1980   PRESIDENT CARTER ANNOUNCES HE IS CONCERNED ABOUT THE
                        "UNPRECEDENTED" BUILD UP OF SOVIET FORCES ON THE POL-
                        ISH BORDER.

Since the formation of the independent Polish union, Solidarity, between August and October 22 (see August 30, 1980), there had been increased tensions
as the Polish government yielded to various workers' demands to end strikes.
The Russians had closed the border between East Germany and Poland (November
30) and the Polish Central Committee had ousted four Politburo members on
December 1, ostensibly in response to Soviet demands. As a result, rumors
increased in western Europe that the Soviet and Warsaw Pact neighbors of Poland were poised to invade if the Polish party experienced too great difficulties with the workers. See December 12, 1980.

December 4, 1980   AS TERRORIST RIGHT-WING VIOLENCE INCREASES IN EL SAL-
                        VADOR, THE BODIES OF FOUR U.S. WOMEN MISSIONARIES ARE
                        FOUND NEAR SAN SALVADOR.

The bodies found were those of three Roman Catholic nuns and one lay worker.
Their van had been ambushed and the women killed. The Carter administration
called for the suspension of $25 million in aid to the government and asked
for a thorough investigation because Salvadorean security forces were allegedly involved in the murder.
      Just six days before, rightist terrorists attacked a meeting of the Demo-
cratic Revolutionary Front at a San Salvadorean high school. They dragged
away 24 persons while 200 members of the National Guard and police stood by.
The bodies of the six leftist leaders were dumped outside the city including
those of the Front's president, Enrique Alvarez Cordova, and of the Popular
Revolutionary Bloc's leader, Juan Chacon.
      Carter had been providing only non-lethal aid to El Salvador because of
the government's human rights violations. There had been 8,000 political
killings in El Salvador during 11 months of 1980.
      In November, however, a group of right-wing Salvadoreans had met with
president-elect Reagan, reporting afterward that the new administration seemed
more receptive to their military aid requests. On January 18, 1981, Carter
authorized sending El Salvador $5 million of combat equipment. Reagan fol-
lowed with another $25 million and 20 military advisors on March 2, 1981.

December 6, 1980   REAGAN ISSUES A STATEMENT BACKING THE CAMP DAVID AC-
CORDS AS A CONTINUED BASIS FOR MIDDLE EAST PEACE.

The American Special Representative for the Middle East, Sol M. Lenowitz,
indicated that the president-elect assured him that he backed the autonomy
talks between Egypt and Israel although they had not borne fruit in 1980.
On December 18, Lenowitz ended a visit to Cairo and Tel Aviv by reading a
statement in which both President Sadat and Prime Minister Begin reaffirmed
the Camp David process. On December 27, however, Cairo asked to delay the
autonomy talks which were set to resume on January 13. The Egyptians gave
no reason for the delay.

December 11, 1980   *WAR BETWEEN SYRIA AND JORDAN IS AVERTED AFTER BOTH*
NATIONS PULL THEIR FORCES BACK FROM THE BORDER.

On November 29, Syria reportedly had 35,000 troops ready to invade Jordan
because King Hussein conducted an Arab League meeting in Amman which had been
boycotted by the radical Arab nations, including Syria. Jordan retaliated
by sending 24,000 troops to the border and, on December 1, asked the United
States to rush arms deliveries to Amman.
The crisis ended, however, because King Khalid of Saudi Arabia inter-
vened, telling both Arab states to calm down. On December 10, the Syrian
forces withdrew from the border; the next day, Jordan's forces drew back.
Allegedly, Syria feared that Hussein and the Saudis might agree to join Egypt
in negotiating with Israel. This fear did not materialize.

December 12, 1980   THE NATO COUNCIL WARNS THE U.S.S.R. THAT AN INVASION
OF POLAND WOULD END DÉTENTE.

Because of strikes and dissent in Poland, intelligence reports to the NATO
states indicated 55,000 Russian troops were billeted in tents on Poland's
eastern border as part of a Warsaw Pact force of 360,000 troops poised on
the three sides of Poland. Within Poland, Solidarity's leaders had stopped
speaking of strikes and Poland's political officials claimed the Western news
reports were a "hysterical campaign" with no basis in fact. The Roman Catholic church hierarchy asked the dissidents to avoid acts which "might expose
the homeland to the danger of losing independence."

December 16, 1980   *MEETING IN BALI, THE OPEC NATIONS ANNOUNCE ANOTHER*
INCREASE OF OIL PRICES TO A MAXIMUM OF $41 PER BARREL.

This was the third significant oil price increase in 1980. On January 27,
Saudi Arabia and other states had increased prices to $26; on May 14, the
price went to $28; and on June 10, it rose to $30 per barrel.

1981

January 3, 1981   IN EL SALVADOR, RIGHT-WING ASSASSINS KILL THE HEAD OF
THE GOVERNMENT'S LAND REFORM AND TWO U.S. AGRICULTURAL
EXPERTS.

The men assassinated were José Rodolfo Vivera and two Americans, Michael P.
Hammer and Mark David Pearlman. The three were killed while eating dinner
in the Sheraton Hotel of San Salvador.

The killing of the land reform head in El Salvador raised questions
about the success of the program during the nine months since it began.
Thus far only 15% of the land was affected, leaving 85% of the coffee,
75% of the cotton, and 60% of sugar cane in the hands of a few wealthy
families. Most peasants were still landless, others were members of
cooperative groups formed to organize production on the former plantations.
Apparently, some coops managed well, such as one at San Isidro. Others,
such as one at El Penon, had to pay much of its profit in protection money
to the local military commander and soldiers who "guarded" the ranch.

Since March, 1979, right-wing groups opposing land reform had killed
200 peasant cooperative leaders and five farm institute employees. The slaying of José Vivera enabled the rightists to get rid of the principal archi-
tect of the land program.

January 20, 1981   THE IRANIAN HOSTAGES ARE FREED, LEAVING TEHERAN FOR
ALGERIA JUST MINUTES AFTER PRESIDENT REAGAN IS SWORN
IN AS PRESIDENT.

The use of Algerian officials as intermediaries between Iran and Washington
began on November 11, 1980, and proved successful on January 19, 1981. Initially, it appeared that Khomeini was ready to release the American hostages
before Christmas Day, but his demand for $9 billion was rejected by Carter
as "ransom" which the United States would not pay.

On December 30, the U.S. negotiator, Warren Christopher, met with the
Algerians and worked out a plan to place $5 billion in an escrow account at
the time the hostages were released. Under Carter's instruction, Christopher
set a deadline for the offer of January 16, warning that when the new president replaced Carter on January 20, negotiations on the hostages would have
to begin anew. President-elect Reagan had given a qualified approval to fulfill any terms worked out by Carter, but he would not give Iran a "blank
check." Reagan's reputation as a hard-liner in foreign relations probably
led the Iranians to decide to end the discussions with Carter rather than
take a chance on the new president.

Subsequently, on January 3, the Algerians gave the U.S. proposal to Teheran. Khomeini accepted Algeria's offer to act as the guarantor of the hostage accord, and on January 14, Iran's Majlis approved a bill authorizing
the government to conduct binding negotiations with the United States. By

January 16, Iranian officers told Algiers there were no further obstacles to the hostages' release and the final details of the financial and legal terms of the accords had to be worked out in Algiers by British and American financial and legal experts. The accords were signed by Christopher on January 19. The next day, the 52 hostages flew from Iran to Algeria, ending 444 days of captivity. They were transferred to U.S. custody and flown to American military hospitals in Wiesbaden, Germany. On January 21, former President Carter flew to Germany and visited with the former captives.

The important terms of the Iranian-American agreements included what experts called the biggest single financial transaction in history. First, $8 billion was assembled in the Bank of England from $11 to $12 billion of the Iranian assets in the United States. Of that total, $5.5 billion was deposited in foreign branches of U.S. banks and $2.5 billion was in gold and securities in the New York Federal Reserve Bank of New York.

As soon as the hostages were released, Iran got nearly $2.9 billion; American and some foreign banks got $3.6 billion in loan repayments due from Iran. The balance of $1.5 billion went into an escrow account to settle disputes between the Western banks and Iran over loans and interest.

Other financial transactions would follow. Iran would get another $1 to $2 billion from different assets in America. Iranian bank deposits of about $2.2 billion would go to the Bank of England, which would put another $1 billion into the escrow account for other American claims against Iran.

After this complex arrangement resolved the issues of the shah's assets in the United States and American claims against Iran, the other condition set by Iran was simple to agree on: the American promise not to interfere in Iranian affairs.

SELECT BIBLIOGRAPHY

I. GENERAL WORKS

    Bailey, Thomas A. *America Faces Russia: Russian-American Relations
        from Early Times to Our Day*. Ithaca, N.Y.: Cornell University
        Press, 1950.

    Bemis, Samuel Flagg. *The Latin American Policy of the United States*.
        New York: Harcourt, Brace, 1943.

    Bemis, Samuel Flagg, ed. *The American Secretaries of State and Their
        Diplomacy*. 10 vols. New York: Knopf, 1928.

    Bemis, Samuel Flagg, and Ferrell, Robert, eds. *The American Secretaries
        of State and Their Diplomacy*. New series. 9 vols. to 1969, cover-
        ing secretaries from Frank B. Kellogg (1928) to Dean Rusk (1961-
        1969).

    Bevans, Charles I., comp. *Treaties and Other International Agreements
        of the United States of America, 1776-1949*. 12 vols. Washington,
        D.C.: G.P.O., 1968.

    Blumenthal, Henry. *France and the United States: Their Diplomatic Rela-
        tions, 1789-1914*. Chapel Hill: University of North Carolina Press,
        1970.

    Bryson, Thomas A. *American Diplomatic Relations with the Middle East,
        1784-1975: A Survey*. Metuchen, N.J.: The Scarecrow Press, Inc.,
        1977.

    Callahan, James M. *American Foreign Policy in Mexican Relations*. New
        York: Macmillan, 1932.

    Dangerfield, Royden J. *In Defense of the Senate: A Study in Treaty
        Making*. Norman: University of Oklahoma Press, 1933.

    Dulles, Foster R. *China and America: The Story of Their Relations Since
        1784*. Princeton: Princeton University Press, 1946.

    Fairbank, John K., Reischauer, Edwin O., and Craig, Albert M. *East
        Asia: Tradition and Transformation*. Boston: Houghton Mifflin Com-
        pany, 1973.

    Griswold, Alfred W. *The Far Eastern Policy of the United States*. New
        York: Harcourt, Brace and Co., 1938.

Hodson, H.V., and Hoffman, Verena, eds. *The Annual Register, a Record of World Events*. London: Longman Group Limited, annual publication since 1758.

Johnson, Robert. *Thence Round Cape Horn: The Story of United States Naval Forces on Pacific Stations, 1818-1923*. Annapolis, Md.: U.S. Naval Institute, 1963.

LaFeber, Walter. *The Panama Canal: The Crisis in Historical Perspective*. New York: Oxford University Press, 1978.

Langley, Lester D. *The Cuban Policy of the United States (1776-1962)*. New York: John Wiley, 1968.

Langer, William L., ed. *An Encyclopedia of World History*. Boston: Houghton Mifflin Co., 4th Edition, 1968.

Logan, John A., Jr. *No Transfer*. New Haven, Conn.: Yale University Press, 1961.

Logan, Rayford W. *The Diplomatic Relations of the United States with Haiti, 1776-1891*. Chapel Hill: University of North Carolina Press, 1941.

Miller, David Hunter. *Treaties and Other International Acts of the United States, 1776-1863*. 8 vols. Washington, D.C.: G.P.O., 1931-1948.

Morris, Richard B. *Encyclopedia of American History*. New York: Harper and Brothers, 1953; rev. 1965.

Paullin, Charles O. *American Voyages to the Orient, 1690-1865: An Account of Merchant and Naval Activities in China, Japan, and the Various Pacific Islands*. Annapolis, Md.: Naval Institute Press, 1971.

Paullin, Charles O. *Diplomatic Negotiations of American Naval Officers, 1778-1883*. Baltimore, Md.: Johns Hopkins Press, 1912.

Peterson, Harold F. *Argentina and the United States, 1810-1960*. Albany: State University of New York Press, 1962.

Tansill, Charles C. *The United States and Santo Domingo, 1798-1873*. Baltimore, Md.: The Johns Hopkins Press, 1938.

U.S. Department of State. *Department of State Bulletin*. Washington, D.C.: G.P.O., 1939- .

U.S. Department of State. *Foreign Relations of the United States*. Washington, D.C.: G.P.O., 1861- . Regular publications usually about 30 years after the events.

The United States in World Affairs, 1931-1967. New York: Simon and Schuster, 1932-1970.

United States Treaties and other International Agreements. Washington, D.C.: G.P.O., 1950–   . Vols. 1-30 cover to 1980 in 85 volumes.

Weigley, Russell R. *History of the United States Army*. New York: Macmillan, 1967.

Williams, William A. *American-Russian Relations, 1781-1947*. New York: Holt, Rinehart, and Winston, Inc., 1952.

Wriston, Henry M. *Executive Agents in American Foreign Relations*. Baltimore, Md.: Johns Hopkins Press, 1929.

II.   FROM 1607 TO 1828

Adams, Henry. *History of the United States During the Administrations of Jefferson and Madison*. 9 vols. New York: Scribner's, 1889–1891.

Allen, Gardner W. *Our Navy and the Barbary Corsairs*. Cambridge, Mass.: Harvard University Press, 1905.

Andrews, Charles M. *The Colonial Background of the American Revolution*. New Haven, Conn.: Yale University Press, 1931.

Bemis, Samuel F. *Diplomacy of the American Revolution*. Bloomington: Indiana University Press, 1955; reprint of 1935 edition.

Bemis, Samuel. *John Quincy Adams and the Foundations of American Foreign Policy*. New York: Knopf, 1949.

Bemis, Samuel F. *Pinckney's Treaty: A Study of America's Advantage from Europe's Distress*. Baltimore, Md.: Johns Hopkins Press, 1962.

Bolkhovitinov, Nikolai N. *The Beginnings of Russian-American Relations, 1775-1815*. Trans. Elena Levin. Cambridge, Mass.: Harvard University Press, 1976.

Burt, Alfred L. *The United States, Great Britain, and British North America from the Revolution to the Establishment of Peace after the War of 1812*. New Haven, Conn.: Yale University Press, 1940.

Combs, Jerald. *The Jay Treaty: Political Battleground of the Founding Fathers*. Berkeley: University of California Press, 1970.

De Conde, Alexander. *Entangling Alliance: Politics and Diplomacy Under George Washington*. Durham, N.C.: Duke University Press, 1958.

De Conde, Alexander. *The Quasi-War: The Politics and Diplomacy of the Undeclared War with France*. New York: Scribner's, 1966.

De Conde, Alexander. *This Affair of Louisiana*. New York: Scribner's, 1976.

Dickerson, Oliver M. *The Navigation Acts and the American Revolution.* Philadelphia: University of Pennsylvania Press, 1951.

Gilbert, Felix. *To the Farewell Address.* Princeton, N.J.: Princeton University Press, 1961.

Gipson, Lawrence H. *The British Empire before the American Revolution.* 15 vols. New York: Knopf, 1939-1958.

Gipson, Lawrence H. *The Coming of the Revolution, 1763-1775.* New York: Harper, 1954.

Horsman, Reginald. *The Causes of the War of 1812.* Philadelphia: University of Pennsylvania Press, 1962.

Irwin, R.W. *The Diplomatic Relations of the United States with the Barbary Powers, 1776-1816.* Chapel Hill: University of North Carolina Press, 1931.

Jensen, Merrill. *The New Nation: A History of the United States During the Confederation, 1781-1789.* New York: Knopf, 1950.

Kammen, Michael G. *Empire and Interest: The American Colonies and the Politics of Mercantilism.* Philadelphia: Lippincott, 1970.

Lint, Gregg. "The American Revolution and the Law of Nations, 1776-1789." *Diplomatic History*, I (1977), 20-34.

Madariaga, Isabel de. *Britain, Russia and Armed Neutrality of 1789.* New Haven, Conn.: Yale University Press, 1962.

Morris, Richard B. *The Peacemakers: The Great Powers and American Independence.* New York: Harper and Row, 1965.

Perkins, Bradford. *Castlereagh and Adams: England and the United States, 1812-1823.* Berkeley: University of California Press, 1964.

Perkins, Bradford. *The First Rapprochement: England and the United States, 1795-1805.* Philadelphia: University of Pennsylvania Press, 1955.

Perkins, Bradford. *Prologue to War: England and the United States, 1805-1812.* Berkeley: University of California Press, 1961.

Perkins, Dexter. *The Monroe Doctrine, 1823-1826.* Cambridge, Mass.: Harvard University Press, 1927.

Pratt, James W. *Expansionists of 1812.* New York: Macmillan Company, 1925.

Rippy, J. Fred. *Rivalry of the United States and Great Britain Over Latin America, 1808-1830.* Baltimore, Md.: Johns Hopkins Press, 1929.

Ritcheson, Charles R. *Aftermath of Revolution: British Policy Toward the United States, 1783-1795*. Dallas: Southern Methodist University Press, 1969.

Savelle, Max. *The Origins of American Diplomacy: The International History of Anglo-America, 1492-1763*. New York: Macmillan, 1967.

Savelle, Max. *Seeds of Liberty: The Genesis of the American Mind*. New York: Knopf, 1948.

Stinchcombe, William C. *The American Revolution and the French Alliance*. Syracuse, N.Y.: Syracuse University Press, 1969.

Van Alstyne, Richard W. *Our Rising American Empire*. New York: Oxford University Press, 1960.

Whitaker, Arthur P. *The Spanish American Frontier, 1783-1795*. Lincoln: University of Nebraska Press, 1927.

Whitaker, Arthur P. *The United States and the Independence of Latin America*. Baltimore, Md.: Johns Hopkins University Press, 1941.

III. FROM 1829 TO 1896

Adams, Ephraim D. *Great Britain and the American Civil War*. 2 vols. New York: Longmans, Green, 1925.

Binkley, William C. *The Texas Revolution*. Baton Rouge: University of Louisiana Press, 1952.

Blumenthal, Henry. *A Reappraisal of Franco-American Relations, 1830-1871*. Chapel Hill: University of North Carolina Press, 1959.

Brown, Charles H. *Agents of Manifest Destiny: The Lives and Times of the Filibusters*. Chapel Hill: University of North Carolina Press, 1980.

Cooling, Benjamin Franklin. *Benjamin Franklin Tracy: Father of the Modern American Fighting Navy*. Hamden, Conn.: Shoe String Press, 1973.

Corey, Albert B. *The Crisis of 1830-1842 in Canadian-American Relations*. New Haven, Conn.: Carnegie Endowment for International Peace, 1941.

Dennett, Tyler. *Americans in Eastern Asia*. New York: Macmillan, 1922.

Du Bois, W.E.B. *The Suppression of the African Slave Trade to the United States of America, 1638-1870*. New York: Longmans, Green, 1896.

Ferris, N.B. *Desperate Diplomacy: William H. Seward's Foreign Policy, 1861*. Knoxville: University of Tennessee Press, 1976.

Foner, Philip S. *A History of Cuba and Its Relations with the United States*. 2 vols. New York: International Publishers, 1962-1963.

Goebel, Julius. *The Struggle for the Falklands*. New Haven, Conn.: Yale University Press, 1927.

Graebner, Norman A. *Empire on the Pacific--A Study in American Continental Expansion*. New York: Ronald, 1955.

Jensen, Ronald J. *The Alaska Purchase and Russian-American Relations*. Seattle: University of Washington Press, 1975.

Johnson, Erwin. *For China Stations: The U.S. Navy in Asian Waters, 1800-1898*. Annapolis, Md.: Naval Institute Press, 1979.

Jones, Howard. *To the Webster-Ashburton Treaty: A Study in Anglo-American Relations, 1783-1843*. Chapel Hill: University of North Carolina Press, 1977.

Jones, Wilbur D. *The American Problem in British Diplomacy, 1841-1860*. Athens: University of Georgia Press, 1974.

LaFeber, Walter. *The New Empire: An Interpretation of American Expansion, 1860-1898*. Ithaca, N.Y.: Cornell University Press, 1963.

Latourette, Kenneth S. *The History of Early Relations Between the United States and China, 1784-1844*. New Haven, Conn.: Yale University Press, 1917.

McLemore, Robert A. *Franco-American Diplomatic Relations, 1816-1836*. Baton Rouge: University of Louisiana Press, 1941.

Merk, Frederick. *The Oregon Question: Essays in Anglo-American Diplomacy and Politics*. Cambridge, Mass.: Harvard University Press, 1967.

Miller, Stuart C. *The Unwelcome Immigrant: The American Image of the Chinese, 1785-1882*. Berkeley: University of California Press, 1969.

Paolino, Ernest N. *The Foundations of the American Empire: William Henry Seward and U.S. Foreign Policy*. Ithaca, N.Y.: Cornell University Press, 1973.

Perkins, Dexter. *The Monroe Doctrine, 1867-1907*. Baltimore: The Johns Hopkins Press, 1937.

Pletcher, David M. *The Awkward Years: American Foreign Relations Under Garfield and Arthur*. Columbia: University of Missouri Press, 1961.

Pletcher, David M. *The Diplomacy of Annexation: Texas, Oregon, and the Mexican War*. Columbia: University of Missouri Press, 1973.

Randall, James G. *Lincoln the President.* 4 vols. New York: Dodd,
      Mead, 1945-1955.

Schott, Joseph L. *Rails Across Panama: The Story of the Building of
      the Panama Railroad, 1849-1855.* Indianapolis, Ind.: Bobbs-Merrill,
      1967.

Smith, Goldwin. *The Treaty of Washington, 1871.* Ithaca, N.Y.: Cornell
      University Press, 1941.

Sowle, Patrick. "A Reappraisal of Seward's Memorandum of April 1, 1861,
      to Lincoln." *Journal of Southern History,* 33 (1967), 234-239.

Spencer, Donald S. *Louis Kossuth and Young America: A Study of Sec-
      tionalism and Foreign Policy, 1848-1852.* Columbia: University
      of Missouri Press, 1977.

Tate, Merze. *The United States and the Hawaiian Kingdom: A Political
      History.* New Haven, Conn.: Yale University Press, 1965.

Thomas, Benjamin P. *Russo-American Relations: 1815-1867.* Baltimore:
      Johns Hopkins Press, 1930.

Treat, Payson J. *Diplomatic Relations Between the United States and
      Japan, 1853-1895.* 2 vols. Stanford: Stanford University Press,
      1932.

Tyler, Alice F. *The Foreign Policy of James G. Blaine.* Minneapolis:
      University of Minnesota Press, 1927.

Van Deusen, Glyndon G. *William Henry Seward.* New York: Oxford Uni-
      versity Press, 1967.

Warren, Gordon H. *Fountain of Discontent: The Trent Affair and Freedom
      of the Seas.* Boston: Northeastern University Press, 1981.

Weinburg, Albert K. *Manifest Destiny.* Baltimore: Johns Hopkins Press,
      1935.

IV. FROM 1897 TO 1944

Adler, Selig. *The Uncertain Giant, 1921-1940: American Foreign Policy
      Before the War.* New York: Macmillan, 1965.

Bailey, Thomas A. *Woodrow Wilson and the Great Betrayal.* New York:
      Macmillan, 1944.

Beale, Howard K. *Theodore Roosevelt and the Rise of America to World
      Power.* Baltimore, Md.: Johns Hopkins Press, 1956.

Blount, Philip. *The American Occupation of the Philippine Islands.*
      New York: G.P. Putnam's, 1912.

Braisted, William R. *The United States Navy in the Pacific, 1897-1909*. Austin: University of Texas Press, 1958.

Browder, R.P. *The Origins of Soviet-American Diplomacy*. Princeton, N.J.: Princeton University Press, 1953.

Callcott, William H. *The Caribbean Policy of the United States, 1890-1920*. Baltimore, Md.: Johns Hopkins University Press, 1942.

Campbell, Alex E. *Great Britain and the United States, 1895-1903*. London: Longmans, 1960.

Campbell, Charles S., Jr. *Anglo-American Understanding, 1898-1903*. Baltimore, Md.: Johns Hopkins University Press, 1957.

Conn, Stetson, and Fairchild, Byron. *The Framework of Hemisphere Defense*. Washington, D.C.: Office of the Chief of Military History, Department of the Army, 1960.

Cronon, E. David. *Josephus Daniels in Mexico*. Madison: University of Wisconsin Press, 1960.

Dallek, Robert. *Franklin D. Roosevelt and American Foreign Policy, 1932-1945*. New York: Oxford University Press, 1979.

Daniels, Roger. *The Politics of Prejudice: The Anti-Japanese Movement in California and the Struggle for Japanese Exclusion*. Berkeley: University of California Press, 1962.

Denis, Alfred L.P. *Adventures in American Diplomacy, 1896-1906*. New York: Dalton, 1928.

Dennett, Tyler. *John Hay*. New York: Dodd, Mead and Company, 1933.

DeNovo, John A. "A Railroad for Turkey: The Chester Project, 1908-1913." *Business History Review*, 33 (1959), 300-329.

Divine, Robert A. *The Illusion of Neutrality*. Chicago: University of Chicago Press, 1962.

Ferrell, Robert H. *American Diplomacy in the Great Depression*. New Haven, Conn.: Yale University Press, 1957.

Foner, Philip S. *The Spanish-Cuban-American War and the Birth of American Imperialism, 1895-1902*. 2 vols. New York: Monthly Review Press, 1972.

George, Margaret. *The Warped Vision: British Foreign Policy 1933-39*. Pittsburgh: University of Pittsburgh Press, 1965.

Grenville, John A.S., and Young, George B. *Politics, Strategy and American Diplomacy: Studies in Foreign Policy, 1872-1917*. New Haven, Conn.: Yale University Press, 1966.

Healy, David. *U.S. Expansionism: The Imperialist Urge in the 1890's.* Madison: University of Wisconsin Press, 1970.

Healy, David F. *The United States in Cuba, 1898-1902.* Madison: University of Wisconsin Press, 1963.

Holt, W. Stull. *Treaties Defeated by the Senate.* Baltimore, Md.: Johns Hopkins University Press, 1933.

Kennan, George F. *Russia and the West Under Lenin and Stalin.* Boston: Little, Brown, & Co., 1960.

Kennan, George F. *Soviet-American Relations, 1917-1920.* 2 vols. Princeton, N.J.: Princeton University Press, 1956-1958.

Langer, William L., and Gleason, S.E. *The Challenge to Isolation, 1937-1940.* New York: Harper and Row, 1952.

Langer, William L., and Gleason, S.E. *The Undeclared War, 1940-1941.* New York: Harper and Row, 1953.

Link, Arthur S. *Wilson.* 5 vols. to date. Princeton: Princeton University Press, 1947.

Mayer, Arno. *Politics and Diplomacy at Peacemaking: Containment and Counterrevolution at Versailles, 1918-1919.* New York: Knopf, 1967.

McCullough, David. *The Path Between the Seas: The Creation of the Panama Canal, 1870-1914.* New York: Simon and Schuster, 1977.

Morgan, H. Wayne. *America's Road to Empire: The War with Spain and Overseas Expansion.* New York: John Wiley, 1965.

Morison, Samuel E. *The Rising Sun in the Pacific, 1931-April 1942.* Vol. III of the *History of United States Naval Operations in World War II.* Boston: Little, Brown & Co., 1948.

Moulton, Harold G., and Pasvolsky, Leo. *War Debts and World Prosperity.* Washington, D.C.: Brookings Institute, 1932.

Nevins, Allan. *Hamilton Fish: The Inner History of the Grant Administration.* New York: Dodd, Mead and Company, 1936.

Parrini, Carl B. *Heir to Empire: United States Economic Diplomacy, 1916-1923.* Pittsburgh: Pittsburgh University Press, 1969.

Perkins, Bradford. *The Great Rapprochement: England and the United States, 1895-1914.* New York: Atheneum, 1968.

Pratt, Julius W. *Cordell Hull, 1933-1944.* 2 vols. New York: Cooper Square, 1964.

Pusey, Merlo J. *Charles Evans Hughes.* 2 vols. New York: Macmillan, 1951.

Smith, Robert F. *The United States and Revolutionary Nationalism in Mexico, 1916-1932*. Chicago: University of Chicago Press, 1972.

Sprout, Margaret and Harold. *Toward a New Order of Sea Power*. Princeton, N.J.: Princeton University Press, 1940.

Stimson, Henry L., and Bundy, McGeorge. *On Active Service in Peace and War*. New York: Harper, 1949.

Tansill, Charles C. *Canadian-American Relations, 1875-1911*. New Haven, Conn.: Yale University Press, 1943.

Thomas, Hugh. *The Spanish Civil War*. New York: Harper and Row, 1961.

Varg, Paul A. *The Making of a Myth: The United States and China, 1897-1912*. East Lansing: Michigan State University Press, 1968.

Vevier, Charles. *The United States and China, 1906-1913*. New Brunswick, N.J.: Rutgers University Press, 1955.

V. FROM 1945 TO 1980

Alexander, Charles. *Holding the Line: The Eisenhower Era, 1952-1961*. Bloomington: Indiana University Press, 1975.

Aliano, Richard. *American Defense Policy from Eisenhower to Kennedy: The Politics of Changing Military Requirements, 1957-1961*. Athens: Ohio University Press, 1975.

Alperovitz, Gar. *Atomic Diplomacy: Hiroshima and Potsdam. The Use of the Atomic Bomb and the American Confrontation*. New York: Vintage Books, 1967.

Ambrose, Stephen E. *Rise to Globalism: American Foreign Policy Since 1938*. Baltimore, Md.: Penguin, 1971.

Anderson, Irvine H. *Aramco, the United States, and Saudi Arabia: A Study of the Dynamics of Foreign Oil Policy, 1933-1950*. Princeton, N.J.: Princeton University Press, 1981.

Bonsal, Philip Wilson. *Cuba, Castro and the United States*. Pittsburgh: University of Pittsburgh Press, 1971.

Divine, Robert. *Blowing in the Wind: The Nuclear Test Ban Debate, 1954-1960*. New York: Oxford University Press, 1978.

Divine, Robert A., ed. *The Cuban Missile Crisis*. Chicago: Quadrangle, 1971.

Donovan, Robert J. *Conflict and Crisis: The Presidency of Harry S. Truman, 1945-1948,* and *Tumultuous Years: The Presidency of Harry S. Truman 1949-1953*. New York: Norton, 1977 and 1982; New York: Norton, 1977.

Feis, Herbert. *Contest over Japan, 1945-1952*. New York: Norton, 1967.

Gaddis, John Lewis. *The United States and the Origins of the Cold War, 1941-1947*. New York: Columbia University Press, 1972.

Gelb, Leslie H. *The Irony of Vietnam: The System Worked*. Washington, D.C.: Brookings Institute, 1979.

Gilbert, Marlin, and Gott, Richard. *The Appeasers*. Boston: Houghton Mifflin, 1963.

Goodman, Allan. *The Lost Peace: America's Search for a Negotiated Settlement of the Vietnam War*. Stanford: Hoover Institution, 1978.

Guhin, Michael. *John Foster Dulles*. New York: Columbia University Press, 1972.

Halberstam, David. *The Best and the Brightest*. New York: Random House, 1972.

Hammer, Ellen J. *The Struggle for Indochina, 1940-1955: Vietnam and the French Experience*, rev. edition. Stanford, Calif: Stanford University Press, 1956.

Haynes, Richard. *The Awesome Power: Harry S. Truman as Commander in Chief*. Baton Rouge: Louisiana State University Press, 1973.

Herken, Gregg. *The Winning Weapon: The Atomic Bomb in the Cold War, 1945-1950*. New York: Knopf, 1980.

Herring, George C. *America's Longest War: The United States and Vietnam, 1950-1975*. New York: John Wiley, 1979.

Kalb, Marvin and Bernard. *Kissinger*. Boston: Little, Brown, 1974.

Kearns, Dorothy. *Lyndon Johnson and the American Dream*. New York: Harper and Row, 1976.

Kinnard, Douglas. *President Eisenhower and Strategy Management: A Study in Defense Politics*. Lexington: University Press of Kentucky, 1977.

Kolko, Joyce and Gabriel. *The Limits of Power: The World and United States Foreign Policy, 1945-1954*. New York: Harper and Row, 1972.

Lewy, Guenter. *America in Vietnam*. New York: Oxford University Press, 1978.

Moulton, Harland B. *From Superiority to Parity: The United States and the Strategic Arms Race, 1961-1971*. Westport, Conn.: Greenwood Press, 1973.

Porter, Gareth. *A Peace Denied: The United States, Vietnam and the Paris Agreement*. Bloomington: Indiana University Press, 1975.

Saikal, Amin. *The Rise and Fall of the Shah*. Princeton, N.J.: Princeton University Press, 1980.

Schandler, Herbert. *The Unmaking of the President: Lyndon Johnson and Vietnam*. Princeton, N.J.: Princeton University Press, 1977.

Schlesinger, Arthur M. *A Thousand Days: John F. Kennedy in the White House*. Boston: Houghton Mifflin, 1965.

Schwab, George, and Friedlander, Henry, eds. *Détente in Historical Perspective*. 2d. ed. New York: Cyrco, 1978.

Shawcross, William. *Sideshow: Kissinger, Nixon and the Destruction of Cambodia*. New York: Simon and Schuster, 1979.

Szulc, Tad. *The Illusion of Peace: Foreign Policy in the Nixon-Kissinger Years*. New York: Viking, 1978.

Ulam, Adam B. *The Rivals: America and Russia Since World War II*. New York: Viking, 1971.

U.S. Department of Defense. *The Pentagon Papers: The Defense Department History of United States Decision Making on Vietnam: The Senator Gravel Edition*. 5 vols. Boston: Beacon, 1971-1972.

Walton, Richard J. *Cold War and Counter-revolution: The Foreign Policy of John F. Kennedy*. New York: Viking, 1972.

Willrich, Mason, and Rhinelander, John B., eds. *SALT: The Moscow Agreements and Beyond*. New York: Free Press, 1974.

Wittner, Lawrence S. *Cold War America: From Hiroshima to Watergate*. New York: Praeger, 1974.

A

American Jewish Community: 1101–02

American Journal of International Law: 523–24

American Missionary Board (in Turkey): 445–46

American Peace Commission (1918): 597

American Rights Committee: 574–75

"American Trade Act" (Great Britain, 1822): 144–46, 171–72

Amhertsburg, Canada: 97

Amiens, Treaty of (1802): 79, 81–2

Amin, General Idi (Uganda): 1069, 1138

Amin, Hafizullah: 1171–72

Anaya, Pedro Maria: 232

Anchorena, Thomas Manuel de: 176

Ancón, Treaty of (Peru-Chile, 1883): 355

Ancona (ship): 528, 554

Andean Pact: 1180, 1187

Anderson, Chandler P.: 543, 548–49

Anderson, Richard C.: 157–59

Anderson, Major Robert: 288–89, 292

Andrade, José: 394–95

Andrea Doria (ship): 17

Angell, James B.: 347

Anglo-American Arbitration Treaty (1897): 402–03

Anglo-American Combined Chiefs of Staff (World War II): 797

Anglo-American Commercial Convention (1815): 127, 137

Anglo-American Convention (1818): 135–136

Anglo-American Convention (1827, on Oregon and Northeast Boundary): 162–63, 174–75

Anglo-American Convention of 1857 (not approved): 273

Anglo-American dispute (1927, on navy issue): 664

Anglo-American Naturalization Treaty (1870): 321

Anglo-American rapprochement (1895–1913): 394, 519, 739

Anglo-American Treaty of 1892: 384

Anglo-French agreements: 286, 398, 425, 472

Anglo-German agreements: 360, 395, 437, 444, 449–50

Anglo-German Naval Pact (1934): 755

Anglo-Italian Agreement (1938): 741, 636–39

Amiranian Oil Company: 647–48

Amistad incident (1839): 195–96, 198

Amman, Jordan: 1060–61, 1195

Ammen, Admiral Daniel: 333, 346

Amoy, China: 202

Amur River: 277, 444, 501–02

Anapala, Pact of: 648, 656

Anglo-Japanese Alliance (1902): 392, 453, 481, 632, 636–39

Anglo-Persian Agreement: 712

Anglo-Russian Entente (1907): 492, 508

Anglo-Russian Treaty (1942): 802

Anglo-Russian Treaty (1959): 955

Anglo-Texas Treaty (1842): 208

Angola: 831–32, 990, 1109–10, 1122, 1125, 1128–29, 1134, 1147, 1149–50, 1173–74, 1186

Ankrah, General J.A. (Ghana): 1011

An Loc, Vietnam: 1083

Annam, province: 292, 301, 356

Annapolis Convention (1786): 33–4

Annexation of Texas: 189, 209–11, 213–15, 217–18

Antafagasta, Chile: 346, 356

Antarctica: 192, 957

Anti-American Riots in
  Japan: 480
  China: 478, 484–85

Anti-Americanism in Latin America: 283, 287, 953

Anti-Ballistic Missiles (ABM): 1016–17, 1042–43, 1051–52

ABM Agreement of 1972, with U.S.S.R.: 1111

Anti-Bolshevik refugees to U.S. (1918–1919): 589–91, 602–03

Anti-British views in U.S.: 369, 450, 562–63

Anti-Comintern Pact (1936): 726–27, 751, 772–73

Anti-Communist Policy in U.S.: 856, 859

Anti-French views in U.S. (1798): 62–4

Anti-Imperialists in U.S.: 414, 426, 448, 455

Anti-Imperialists League: 426, 429–30

Anti-Masonic Party (1832): 178

Anti-Orientalism on Pacific Coast of U.S.: 347, 351, 359, 368–69

Anti-Semitism, U.S.: 747

Anti-Slavery views in U.S.: 210

Antietam, Battle of: 297–98

Antonov-Ovseenko, Vladimir: 602–03

Anzio Beachhead (World War II): 819

Anzus Tripartite Security Treaty: 899